LIBERTY, EQUALITY, POWER

A HISTORY OF THE AMERICAN PEOPLE

ENHANCED CONCISE FOURTH EDITION

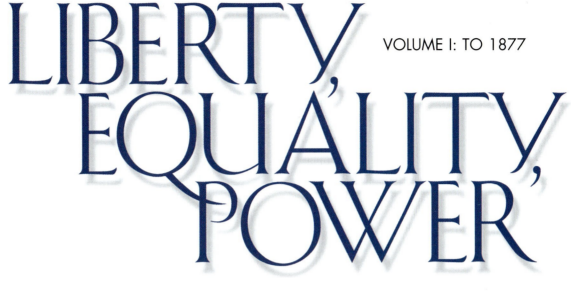

LIBERTY, EQUALITY, POWER

VOLUME I: TO 1877

A HISTORY OF THE AMERICAN PEOPLE

JOHN M. MURRIN
PRINCETON UNIVERSITY, EMERITUS

GARY GERSTLE
UNIVERSITY OF MARYLAND

PAUL E. JOHNSON
UNIVERSITY OF SOUTH CAROLINA

EMILY S. ROSENBERG
MACALESTER COLLEGE

JAMES M. McPHERSON
PRINCETON UNIVERSITY

NORMAN L. ROSENBERG
MACALESTER COLLEGE

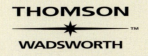

THOMSON

WADSWORTH

Australia / Canada / Mexico / Singapore / Spain / United Kingdom / United States

THOMSON

─────★─────™

WADSWORTH

Liberty, Equality, Power:
A History of the American People
Enhanced Concise Fourth Edition
Volume I: To 1877

Publisher: *Clark Baxter*
Senior Acquisitions Editor: *Ashley Dodge*
Senior Development Editor: *Margaret McAndrew Beasley*
Assistant Editor: *Ashley Spicer*
Editorial Assistant: *Heidi Kador*
Associate Development Project Manager: *Lee McCracken*
Executive Marketing Manager: *Diane Wenckebach*
Marketing Assistant: *Aimee Lewis*
Lead Marketing Communications Manager: *Tami Strang*
Senior Production Manager: *Michael Burggren*
Senior Content Project Manager: *Lauren Wheelock*
Senior Art Director: *Cate Rickard Barr*

Manufacturing Manager: *Marcia Locke*
Permissions Editor: *Roberta Broyer*
Production Service: *Lachina Publishing Services*
Text Designer: *Marsha Cohen and Dutton & Sherman Design*
Photo Researcher: *Sarah Evertson*
Cover Designer: *Dutton & Sherman Design*
Cover Image: *Wood Engraving After the Georgetown Election by Thomas Nast © CORBIS*
Cover/Text Printer: *Quebecor World - Versailles*
Compositor: *Lachina Publishing Services*

Printed in the United States of America
1 2 3 4 5 6 7 11 10 09 08

Library of Congress Control Number: 2007940026

Student Edition:
ISBN-13: 978-0-495-56634-2
ISBN-10: 0-495-56634-9

Thomson Higher Education
10 Davis Drive
Belmont, CA 94002-3098
USA

For more information about our products, contact us at:
Thomson Learning Academic Resource Center
1-800-423-0563

For permission to use material from this text or product, submit a request online at **http://www.thomsonrights.com**. Any additional questions about permissions can be submitted by e-mail to **thomsonrights@thomson.com**.

The Liberty, Equality, Power *author team (from left to right): Norman Rosenberg, Emily Rosenberg, Paul Johnson, Gary Gerstle, John Murrin, James McPherson.*

JOHN M. MURRIN PRINCETON UNIVERSITY, EMERITUS

John M. Murrin is a specialist in American colonial and revolutionary history and the early republic. He has edited one multivolume series and five books, including two co-edited collections, *Colonial America: Essays in Politics and Social Development,* Fifth Edition (2001), and *Saints and Revolutionaries: Essays in Early American History* (1984). His own essays on early American history range from ethnic tensions, the early history of trial by jury, the rise of the legal profession, and the political culture of the colonies and the new nation, to the rise of professional baseball and college football in the 19th century. Professor Murrin served as president of the Society for Historians of the Early American Republic in 1998–99.

PAUL E. JOHNSON UNIVERSITY OF SOUTH CAROLINA

A specialist in early national social and cultural history, Professor Johnson is also the author of *The Early American Republic, 1789–1829* (2006); *Sam Patch, the Famous Jumper* (2003); *A Shopkeeper's Millennium: Society and Revivals in Rochester, New York, 1815–1837,* 25th Anniversary Edition (2004); co-author (with Sean Wilentz) of

The Kingdom of Matthias: Sex and Salvation in 19th-Century America (1994); and editor of *African-American Christianity: Essays in History* (1994). He has been awarded the Merle Curti Prize of the Organization of American Historians (1980), the Richard P. McCormack Prize of the New Jersey Historical Association (1989), and fellowships from the National Endowment for the Humanities (1985–86), the John Simon Guggenheim Foundation (1995), and the Gilder Lehrman Institute (2001).

JAMES M. McPHERSON PRINCETON UNIVERSITY

James M. McPherson is a distinguished Civil War historian and was president of the American Historical Association in 2003. He won the 1989 Pulitzer Prize for his book *Battle Cry of Freedom: The Civil War Era.* His other publications include *Marching Toward Freedom: Blacks in the Civil War,* Second Edition (1991); *Ordeal by Fire: The Civil War and Reconstruction,* Third Edition (2001); *Abraham Lincoln and the Second American Revolution* (1991); *For Cause and Comrades: Why Men Fought in the Civil War* (1997), which won the Lincoln Prize in 1998; and *Crossroads of Freedom: Antietam* (2002).

GARY GERSTLE   UNIVERSITY OF MARYLAND

Gary Gerstle is a historian of the 20th-century United States. His books include *Working-Class Americanism: The Politics of Labor in a Textile City, 1914–1960* (1989), and *American Crucible: Race and Nation in the Twentieth Century* (2001), winner of the Saloutos Prize for the best work in immigration and ethnic history. He has also published three co-edited works: *The Rise and Fall of the New Deal Order, 1930–1980* (1989); *E Pluribus Unum: Immigrants, Civic Culture, and Political Incorporation* (2001); and *Ruling America: Wealth and Power in a Democracy* (2005). His articles have appeared in the *American Historical Review, Journal of American History, American Quarterly,* and other journals. He has served on the board of editors of both the *Journal of American History* and the *American Historical Review.* His honors include a National Endowment for the Humanities Fellowship and a John Simon Guggenheim Memorial Fellowship.

EMILY S. ROSENBERG   MACALESTER COLLEGE

Emily S. Rosenberg specializes in U.S. foreign relations in the 20th century and is the author of *Spreading the American Dream: American Economic and Cultural Expansion, 1890–1945* (1982); *Financial Missionaries to the World: The Politics and Culture of Dollar Diplomacy* (1999), which won the Ferrell Book Award; and *Pearl Harbor in American Memory* (2004). Her other publications include (with Norman L. Rosenberg) *In Our Times: America Since 1945,* Seventh Edition (2003), and numerous articles dealing with foreign relations in the context of international finance, American culture, and gender ideology. She has served on the board of the Organization of American Historians, on the board of editors of the *Journal of American History,* and as president of the Society for Historians of American Foreign Relations.

NORMAN L. ROSENBERG   MACALESTER COLLEGE

Norman L. Rosenberg specializes in legal history with a particular interest in legal culture and First Amendment issues. His books include *Protecting the "Best Men": An Interpretive History of the Law of Libel* (1990) and (with Emily S. Rosenberg) *In Our Times: America Since 1945,* Seventh Edition (2003). He has published articles in the *Rutgers Law Review, UCLA Law Review, Constitutional Commentary, Law & History Review,* and many other journals and law-related anthologies.

BRIEF CONTENTS

CONTENTS

3 ENGLAND DISCOVERS ITS COLONIES: EMPIRE, LIBERTY, AND EXPANSION / 67

4 PROVINCIAL AMERICA AND THE STRUGGLE FOR A CONTINENT / 95

9 THE MARKET REVOLUTION, 1815–1860 / 240

GOVERNMENT AND MARKETS / 241

10 TOWARD AN AMERICAN CULTURE / 264

THE NORTHERN MIDDLE CLASS / 265

13   MANIFEST DESTINY: AN EMPIRE FOR LIBERTY— OR SLAVERY? / 333

14   THE GATHERING TEMPEST, 1853–1860 / 357

17 RECONSTRUCTION, 1863–1877 / 440

LIST OF MAPS

LIST OF FEATURES

HISTORY THROUGH FILM

MUSICAL LINKS TO THE PAST

WHY STUDY HISTORY?

Why take a course in American history? This is a question that many college and university students ask. In many respects, students today are like the generations of Americans who have gone before them: optimistic and forward looking, far more eager to imagine where we as a nation might be going than to reflect on where we have been. If anything, this tendency has become more pronounced in recent years, as the Internet revolution has accelerated the pace and excitement of change and made even the recent past seem at best quaint, at worst uninteresting and irrelevant.

But it is precisely in these moments of change that a sense of the past can be indispensable in terms of guiding our actions in the present and future. We can find in other periods of American history moments, like our own, of dizzying technological change and economic growth, rapid alterations in the concentration of wealth and power, and basic changes in patterns of work, residence, and play. How did Americans at those times create, embrace, and resist these changes? In earlier periods of American history, the United States was home, as it is today, to a broad array of ethnic and racial groups. How did earlier generations of Americans respond to the cultural conflicts and misunderstandings that often arise from conditions of diversity? How did immigrants of the early 1900s perceive their new land? How and when did they integrate themselves into American society? To study how ordinary Americans of the past struggled with these issues is to gain perspective on the opportunities and problems that we face today.

History also provides an important guide to affairs of state. What role should America assume in world affairs? Should we participate in international bodies such as the United Nations, or insist on our ability to act autonomously and without the consent of other nations? What is the proper role of government in economic and social life? Should the government regulate the economy? To what extent should the government enforce morality regarding religion, sexual practices, drinking and drugs, movies, TV, and other forms of mass culture? And what are our responsibilities as citizens to each other and to the nation? Americans of past generations have debated these issues with verve and conviction. Learning about these debates and how they were resolved will enrich our understanding of the policy possibilities for today and tomorrow.

History, finally, is about stories—stories that we all tell about ourselves; our families; our communities; our ethnicity, race, region, and religion; and our nation. They are stories of triumph and tragedy, of engagement and flight, and of high ideals and high comedy. When telling these stories, "American history" is often the furthest thing from our minds. But, often, an implicit sense of the past informs what we say about grandparents who immigrated many years ago; the suburb in which we live; the church, synagogue, or mosque at which we worship; or the ethnic or racial group to which we belong. How well, we might ask, do we really understand these individuals, institutions, and groups? Do our stories about them capture their history and complexity? Or do our stories wittingly or unwittingly simplify or alter what these individuals and groups experienced? A study of American history helps us first to ask these questions and then to answer them. In the process, we can embark on a journey of intellectual and personal discovery and situate ourselves more firmly than we had thought possible in relation to those who came before us. We can gain a firmer self-knowledge and a greater appreciation for the richness of our nation and, indeed, of all humanity.

USING THE "DISCOVERY" SECTIONS IN THIS TEXTBOOK TO ANALYZE HISTORICAL SOURCES: DOCUMENTS, PHOTOS, AND MAPS

Astronomers investigate the universe through telescopes. Biologists study the natural world by collecting plants and animals in the field and then examining them with microscopes. Sociologists and psychologists study human behavior through observation and controlled laboratory experiments.

Historians study the past by examining historical "evidence" or "source" materials—government documents; the records of private institutions ranging from religious and charitable organizations to labor unions, corporations, and lobbying groups; letters, advertisements, paintings, music, literature, movies, and cartoons; buildings, clothing, farm implements, industrial machinery, and landscapes: anything and everything written or created by our ancestors that give clues about their lives and the times in which they lived.

Historians refer to written material as "documents." Excerpts of dozens of documents appear throughout the textbook—within the chapters and in the "Discovery" sections. Each chapter also includes many visual representations of the American past in the form of photographs of buildings, paintings, murals, individuals, cartoons, sculptures, and other kinds of historical evidence. As you read each chapter, the more you examine all this "evidence," the more you will understand the main ideas of this book and of the course you are taking. The better you become at reading evidence, the better historian you will become.

"Discovery" sections at the end of every chapter assist you in practicing these skills by taking a closer look at specific pieces of evidence—images, quotes, or maps—which will help you to connect the various threads of American history and to excel in your course.

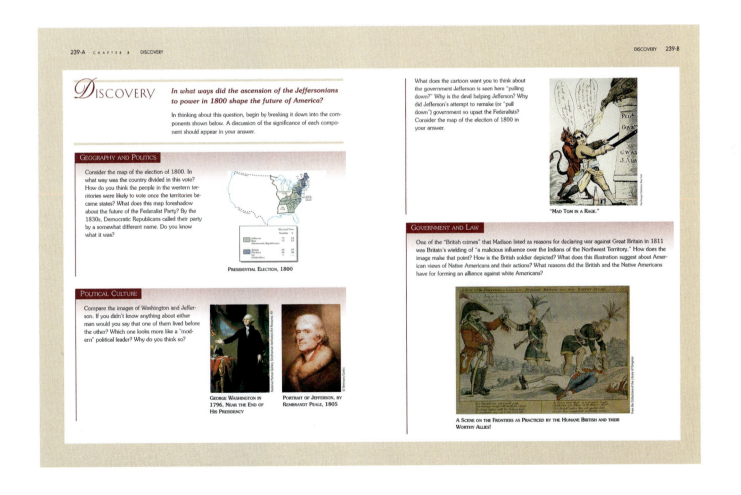

This concise version of the much admired, *Liberty, Equality, Power* is intended to make the textbook more accessible to a broad range of students and to give instructors maximum flexibility in determining how best to use it in their courses. A brief edition, for example, makes it easier for instructors both to reach out to students who might be discouraged by a longer book and to supplement a textbook with readings, web-based exercises, movies, and related materials of their own choosing.

The Concise Third Edition won praise for its successful integration of political, cultural, and social history; its thematic unity; its narrative clarity and eloquence; its extraordinary coverage of pre-Columbian America; its attention to war and conquest; its extended treatment of the Civil War; its history of economic growth and change; and its robust map and illustration programs. We have preserved and enhanced all the strengths of the third edition in the fourth.

THE *LIBERTY, EQUALITY, POWER* APPROACH

In this book we tell many small stories, and one large one: how America transformed itself, in a relatively brief era of world history, from a land inhabited by hunter-gatherer and agricultural Native American societies into the most powerful industrial nation on earth. This story has been told many times before, and those who have told it in the past have usually emphasized the political experiment in liberty and equality that took root here in the 18th century. We, too, stress the extraordinary and transformative impact that the ideals of liberty and equality exerted on American politics, society, and economics during the American Revolution and after. We show how the creation of a free economic environment— one that nourished entrepreneurship and technological innovation—underpinned American industrial might. We emphasize, too, the successful struggles for freedom that, over the course of the last 230 years, have brought—first to all white men, then to men of color and finally to women— rights and opportunities that they had not previously known. But we have also identified a third factor in this pantheon of American ideals—that of power. We examine power in many forms: the accumulation of economic fortunes that dominated the economy and politics; the dispossession of Native Americans from land that they regarded as theirs; the enslavement of millions of Africans and their African American descendants for a period of almost 250 years; the relegation of women and of racial, ethnic, and religious minorities to subordinate places in American society; and the extension of American control over foreign peoples, such as Latin Americans and Filipinos, who would have preferred to have been free and self-governing. We do not mean to suggest that American power has always been turned to these negative purposes. To the contrary: subordinate groups have themselves marshaled power to combat oppression, as in the abolitionist and civil rights crusades, the campaign for woman's suffrage, and the labor movement. In the 20th century, the federal government used its power to moderate poverty and to manage the economy in the interests of general prosperity. While one form of power sustained slavery over many generations, another, greater power abolished the institution in four years. Later, the federal government mobilized the nation's military might to defeat Nazi Germany, World War II Japan, the Cold War Soviet Union, and other enemies of freedom. The invocation of power as a variable in American history forces us to widen the lens through which we look at the past and to complicate the stories we tell. Ours has been a history of freedom and domination, of progress toward democracy and of delays and reverses, of abundance and poverty, of wars to free peoples from tyranny and battles to put foreign markets under American control.

In complicating our master narrative in this way, we think we have rendered American history more exciting and intriguing. Progress has not been automatic, but has been instead the product of ongoing struggles.

In this book we have also tried to capture the diversity of the American past, both in terms of outcomes and in terms of the variety of groups who have participated in America's making. We have not presented Native Americans simply as the victims of European aggression, but as a people diverse in their own ranks, with a variety of systems of social organization and cultural expression. We give equal treatment to the industrial titans of American history—the likes of Andrew Carnegie and John D. Rockefeller—and to those, such as small farmers and skilled workers, who resisted the corporate reorganization of economic life. We dwell on the achievements of 1863, when African Americans were freed from slavery, and of 1868, when they were made full citizens of the United States. But we also note how a majority of African Americans had to wait another 100 years, until the civil rights movement of the 1960s, to gain full access to

American freedoms. We tell similarly complex stories about women, Latinos, and groups of ethnic Americans.

Political issues, of course, are only part of America's story. Americans have always pursued individuality and happiness and, in the process, have created the world's most vibrant popular culture. They have embraced technological innovations, especially those promising to make their lives easier and more fun. In light of this history, we have devoted considerable space to a discussion of popular culture, from the founding of the first newspapers in the 18th century to the rise of movies, jazz, and the comics in the 20th century, to the cable television and Internet revolutions of recent years. We have pondered, too, how American industry has periodically altered home and personal life by making new products—such as clothing, cars, refrigerators, and computers—available to consumers. In such ways we hope to give our readers a rich portrait of how Americans spent their time, money, and leisure at various points in our history.

NEW TO THIS EDITION

In preparing for this revision, we solicited feedback from professors and scholars throughout the country, many of whom have used the Concise Third Edition of *Liberty, Equality, Power* in their classrooms. Their comments proved most helpful, and many of their suggestions have been incorporated into this edition. We have, for example, learned how much users valued the Concise Third Edition for being a third shorter than the full edition, for presenting briefer and more focused Suggested Readings at the end of chapters, and for offering the **History Through Film** series. Each of these features appears in the Concise Fourth Edition. We have also added an exciting new feature, **Musical Links to the Past**, which debuted in 2005 as part of the full Fourth Edition of *Liberty, Equality, Power.*

Musical Links to the Past represents our effort to make aspects of America's extraordinarily rich and varied musical heritage integral to the history we present to our readers. In fifteen features, we examine songs—the lyrics, the music, the performers, and the historical context—from the middle of the 18th century to the present. These pieces range from revolutionary-era odes to American liberty to 20th-century country music laments about women's domestic burdens. Represented in this textbook are pieces by artists as different as Stephen Foster and Joni Mitchell, John Philip Sousa and Bob Dylan, Duke Ellington and Grandmaster Flash. All have made important contributions to the history of American music and enriched our musical heritage.

To make this feature come alive in classrooms, we have assembled a CD containing the musical selections that we discuss. All instructors who adopt our textbook will, upon re-

quest, receive a free copy of this CD, and will, as a result, be able to play the music in their classrooms.

In preparing this feature, we turned to Dr. Harvey Cohen, a cultural historian and music expert who received his Ph.D. from the University of Maryland. Possessing an extraordinary knowledge of the history of American music, and being an accomplished musician in his own right, Harvey was the ideal scholar to guide our choice of songs. He also drafted the texts of the fifteen features, and, in the process, labored hard and imaginatively to turn his musical knowledge into history that, we think, will appeal to students. His work has been indispensable to us, and we are deeply grateful to him.

In the Concise Fourth Edition, we have also taken steps to enhance the book's design and its pedagogical program. Users of the Concise Third Edition will note that we have gone to a bigger trim size, a format that permits us to increase the size of the photographs, illustrations, and maps. We have replaced the plain Chronology boxes of the Concise Third Edition with visually engaging **Timelines** that help students understand the relationships among the events and movements of a particular era. We now open many chapter sections with **Focus Questions** that help students to grasp overarching themes and to organize the knowledge that they are acquiring. These Focus Questions reappear at the end of each chapter in **Chapter Reviews,** which are supplemented by **Critical Thinking Questions** that encourage students to range widely and imaginatively in their thinking about what they have just learned.

Two other features new to this edition, **Quick Reviews** and **Glossary Terms,** further contribute to the emphasis we have placed on pedagogy. Quick Reviews appear periodically in the margins to summarize major events, ideas, and movements discussed in the text. Glossary Terms—individuals, ideas, events, legislation, and movements that we have deemed particularly important to an understanding of the historical period in question—appear boldface in the text and then are briefly defined in the margins. We have also assembled all the glossary terms in an alphabetical appendix that appears at the end of the textbook. Taken altogether, these pedagogical changes contribute significantly to this edition. Our hope is that they will enhance the learning experience of the students who use our textbook.

Finally, we have scrutinized each page of the textbook, making sure our prose is clear, the historical issues are well presented, and the scholarship is up to date. This review, guided by the scholarly feedback we received, caused us to make numerous revisions and additions. A list of notable content changes follows.

SPECIFIC REVISIONS TO CONTENT AND COVERAGE

Chapter 1 Major addition adopts Jared Diamond's (from his best-seller, *Guns, Germs, and Steel*) geographical argument (east-west axis) for European technological superiority over Amerindians by 1492.

Chapter 2 New emphasis is placed on the importance of the Newfoundland and St. Lawrence fisheries well before 1600, as well as the role of William Byrd, William Fitzhugh, and other great planters in deliberately choosing to replace indentured servitude with hereditary slavery. The section on the rise of slavery in North America has been strengthened, and the section on South Carolina's involvement in the Indian slave trade has been expanded.

Chapter 3 The chapter now incorporates Mary Beth Norton's important book on Salem witchcraft by emphasizing witchcraft's close connection to the Indian war on the northern frontier. There is a new, brief discussion of the rise of Indian slavery in New France and a fuller account of the Yamasee War in South Carolina.

Chapter 4 There is new material on the northern colonies as modernizing societies even before independence, on women and the weaving industry, and on the conversion of slaves to Christianity in Virginia after 1720. New emphasis is placed on the random brutality of slave discipline and how the African slave trade became a major engine of Newport's economic growth in the 18th century.

Chapter 5 Coverage of colonial smuggling in relation to the Grenville Program has been expanded, as has discussion of slave unrest in South Carolina during the Stamp Act disturbances.

Chapter 6 The chapter now incorporates the major findings of David Hackett Fischer's *Washington's Crossing*, especially his arguments that a widespread rising of the militia in the Delaware Valley prompted Washington to plan his Trenton-Princeton campaign and that continued activity by the militia in what Fischer calls "the foraging war" severely wore down the strength of the British army.

ACKNOWLEDGMENTS

We recognize the contributions of reviewers who have provided feedback on the Concise Edition:

David Arnold, Columbia Basin College
Betty Brandon, University of Southern Alabama
Janet Brantley, Texarkana College
B. R. Burg, Arizona State University
Randy Finley, Georgia Perimeter College
Michael P. Gabriel, Kutztown University
Wendy Gordon, SUNY Plattsburgh
Sally Hadden, Florida State University
Kevin E. Hall, University of South Florida
Ian Harrison, University of Nevada, Las Vegas
Mary Ann Heiss, Kent State University
Terry Isaacs, South Plains College
Timothy K. Kinsella, Ursuline College
C. Douglas Kroll, College of the Desert
David F. Krugler, University of Wisconsin, Platteville
Margaret E. Newell, Ohio State University
Thomas Ott, University of North Alabama
Geoffrey Plank, University of Cincinnati
G. David Price, Santa Fe Community College (FL)
Akim D. Reinhardt, Towson University
John Paul Rossi, Penn State Erie
Steven T. Sheehan, University of Wisconsin, Fox Valley
Megan Taylor Shockley, Clemson University
Adam M. Sowards, University of Idaho
Evelyn Sterne, University of Rhode Island
Kristen L. Streater, Collin County Community College,
    Preston Ridge Campus

Sean Taylor, Minnesota State University, Moorhead
Jerry Tiarsmith, Georgia Perimeter College
Leslie V. Tischauser, Prairie State College
Stephen Webre, Louisiana Tech University
Bryan Wuthrich, Santa Fe Community College (FL)

We wish to thank the members of the Wadsworth staff who capably guided the revision and production of this concise edition: Ashley Dodge, Senior Acquisitions Editor; Lori Grebe Cook, Senior Marketing Manager; and Katy German, Production Project Manager. Thanks as well go to Mike Ederer, our Production Editor at Graphic World Publishing Services, and to Lili Weiner, who once again worked as our photo researcher. Thomas Castillo expertly assisted Gary Gerstle with the quick reviews and glossary terms for chapters 20–25, while Katarina Keane worked hard and skillfully to bring consistency to these new pedagogical features throughout the textbook's 31 chapters. Our greatest debt once again is to our longtime developmental editor, Margaret McAndrew Beasley. Margaret's editing skills, organizational expertise, good sense, and belief in this book and its authors keep us going.

John M. Murrin
Paul E. Johnson
James M. McPherson
Gary Gerstle
Emily S. Rosenberg
Norman L. Rosenberg

WHEN OLD WORLDS COLLIDE: CONTACT, CONQUEST, CATASTROPHE

When Christopher Columbus crossed the Atlantic, he did not know where he was going, and he died without ever figuring out where he had been. Yet he changed the world. In the 40 years after 1492, Europeans conquered the Americas, not just with sails, gunpowder, and steel, but also with their plants, livestock, and, most of all, their diseases. By 1600 they had created the first global economy in history and had inflicted upon the native peoples of the Americas, for the most part unintentionally, the greatest known catastrophe that human societies have ever suffered.

In the 15th century, when all of this started, the Americas were in some ways a more ancient world than Western Europe. The Portuguese, Spanish, French, and English languages were only beginning to assume their modern forms. But centuries earlier, at a time when Paris and London were insignificant, huge cities were thriving in the Andes and **Mesoamerica** (the area embracing Central America and southern and central Mexico). Which world was old and which was new is a matter of perspective. Each already had its own distinctive past.

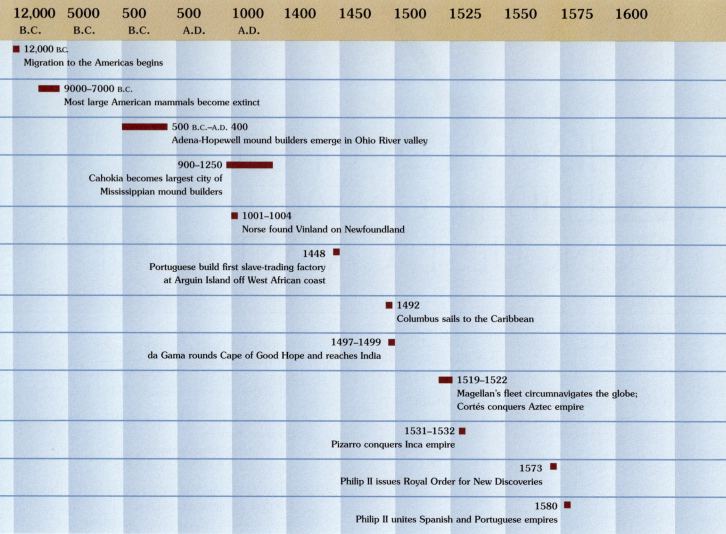

12,000 B.C.	5000 B.C.	500 B.C.	500 A.D.	1000 A.D.	1400	1450	1500	1525	1550	1575	1600

12,000 B.C.
Migration to the Americas begins

9000–7000 B.C.
Most large American mammals become extinct

500 B.C.–A.D. 400
Adena-Hopewell mound builders emerge in Ohio River valley

900–1250
Cahokia becomes largest city of
Mississippian mound builders

1001–1004
Norse found Vinland on Newfoundland

1448
Portuguese build first slave-trading factory
at Arguin Island off West African coast

1492
Columbus sails to the Caribbean

1497–1499
da Gama rounds Cape of Good Hope and reaches India

1519–1522
Magellan's fleet circumnavigates the globe;
Cortés conquers Aztec empire

1531–1532
Pizarro conquers Inca empire

1573
Philip II issues Royal Order for New Discoveries

1580
Philip II unites Spanish and Portuguese empires

*P*EOPLES IN MOTION

Long before Europeans discovered and explored the wide world around them, many different peoples had migrated thousands of miles across oceans and continents. Before **Christopher Columbus** sailed west from Spain in 1492, four distinct waves of immigrants had already swept over the Americas. Three came from Asia. The last, from northern Europe, failed to survive.

FROM BERINGIA TO THE AMERICAS

Before the most recent Ice Age ended, glaciers covered huge portions of the Americas, Europe, and Asia. The ice captured so much of the world's water that sea levels fell drastically, enough to create a land bridge 600 miles wide across the Bering Strait between Siberia and Alaska. For more than 10,000 years after 23,000 B.C., this exposed strait—now called **Beringia**—was dry land on which plants, animals, and hu-

Mesoamerica *Area encompassing Central America and southern and central Mexico.*

mans could live. People drifted in small bands from Asia to North America. No doubt many generations lived on Beringia itself, although its harsh environment on the edge of the Arctic Circle would have required unusual skills just to survive. These first immigrants to the Americas hunted animals for meat and furs and probably built small fishing vessels that could weather the Arctic storms. They made snug homes to keep themselves warm through the fierce winters.

By about 14,000 years ago, humans definitely were living in eastern Siberia, western Alaska, and Beringia. As the glaciers receded, these people spread throughout the Americas. By 8000 B.C. they had reached all the way to **Tierra del Fuego** at the southern tip of South America.

These Asians probably came in three waves. Those in the first wave, which began around 12,000 B.C., spread over most of the two continents and spoke **Amerind,** the forerunner of the vast majority of Indian languages on both continents. The Algonquian, Iroquoian, Muskogean, Siouan, Nahuatl (Aztec), Mayan, and all South American tongues derive from this source. Those in the middle wave, which came a few thousand years later, spoke what linguists call "Na-Déné," which eventually gave rise to the various Athapaskan languages of the Canadian Northwest as well as the Apache, Navajo, and related tongues in the American Southwest. The last to arrive, the ancestors of the Inuits (called Eskimos by other Indians), crossed after 7000 B.C., when Beringia was again under water. About 4,000 years ago, these people began to migrate from the Aleutian Islands and Alaska to roughly their present sites in the Americas. They migrated across the northern rim of North America and then across the North Atlantic to Greenland, where they encountered the first Europeans migrating westward—the Norsemen.

THE GREAT EXTINCTION AND THE RISE OF AGRICULTURE

As the glaciers receded and the climate warmed, the people who had wandered south and east found an attractive environment teeming with game. Imperial mammoths, huge mastodons, woolly rhinoceroses, a species of enormous bison, and giant ground sloths roamed the plains and forests, along with camels and herds of small horses. These animals had no instinctive fear of the two-legged intruders, who became ever more skillful at hunting them. A superior spear point, the **Clovis tip,** appeared in the area around present-day New Mexico and Texas some time before 9000 B.C., and within a thousand years its use had spread throughout North and South America. As it spread, the big game died off. Overhunting cannot explain the entire extinction, but it was a major factor, along with climatic change.

The hemisphere was left with a severely depleted number of animal species. The largest beasts were bears, buffalo, and moose; the biggest cat was the jaguar. The human population had multiplied and spread with ease as long as the giant species lasted. Their extinction probably led to a sharp decline in population. Some Indians raised guinea pigs, turkeys, or ducks, but apart from dogs they domesticated no large animals except for llamas (useful for hauling light loads in mountainous terrain) and alpacas (valued for their wool), both in South America.

The peoples of the Pacific Northwest, who developed complex art forms that fascinate modern collectors, sustained themselves through fishing, hunting, and the gathering of nuts, berries, and other edible plants. Men fished and hunted; women gathered. California Indians sustained some of the densest populations north of Mexico by collecting acorns and processing them into meal, which they baked into cakes. Hunter-gatherers also lived in the rain forests of Brazil, in south and central Florida, and in the cold woodlands of northern New England.

Christopher Columbus
Genoese mariner who persuaded Queen Isabella of Spain to support his voyage of discovery across the Atlantic to East Asia in 1492. Instead he discovered America.

Beringia *Land bridge during the last ice age across the Bering Strait between Siberia and Alaska, where plants, animals, and humans could live.*

Tierra del Fuego *Region at the southern tip of South America.*

Amerind *Forerunner of the vast majority of Indian languages in the Americas.*

Clovis tip *A superior spear point developed before 9000 B.C. Its use nearly everywhere in North and South America produced an improvement in hunting ability that contributed to the extinction of most large mammals.*

But most Indians could not depend indefinitely on hunting and gathering food. Some of them, probably women, began to plant and harvest crops instead of simply gathering and eating what they found. In Asia and Africa, this practice was closely linked to the domestication of animals and happened quickly enough to be called the **Neolithic** (new or late Stone Age) revolution. But in the Americas the rise of farming had little to do with animals, occurred over a period of about 3,500 years, and might better be termed the Neolithic *evolution*. Somewhere between 4000 and 1500 B.C., permanent farm villages began to dominate parts of Peru, Mexico, and the southwestern United States. The first American farmers grew amaranth (a cereal), manioc (tapioca), chili peppers, pumpkins, sweet potatoes, several varieties of beans, and, above all, maize, or Indian corn.

THE NORSEMEN

Neolithic *Period known also as the late Stone Age when agriculture developed, and stone, rather than metal, tools were used.*

Europeans also began trekking long distances. Pushed by fierce invaders from central Asia, various Germanic tribes overran the western provinces of the Roman Empire. The Norse, a Germanic people who had occupied Scandinavia, were among the most innovative of these invaders. For centuries their Viking warriors raided the coasts of the British Isles and France. Their sleek longboats, propelled by both sails and oars, enabled them to challenge the contrary currents of the North Atlantic.

Beginning in A.D. 874, the Norse occupied Iceland. In 982 and 983 Erik the Red, accused of manslaughter in Norway and then outlawed for committing more mayhem in Iceland, led his Norse followers farther west to Greenland. There they established permanent settlements.

Leif, Erik's son, sailed west from Greenland in 1001 and began to explore the coast of North America. He made three more voyages, the last in 1014, and started a colony that he called "Vinland" on the northern coast of Newfoundland at a place now named L'Anse aux Meadows. The local Indians ("Skrellings" to the Norse) resisted vigorously but were driven off. Then the Norse quarreled among themselves and destroyed the colony. They abandoned Vinland, but they continued to visit North America for perhaps another century, probably to get wood.

Several centuries later the Norse also lost Greenland. There, not long before Columbus sailed in 1492, the last Norse settler died a lonely death. In the chaos that followed the Black Death in Europe and Greenland after 1350, the colony had suffered a severe population decline and had gradually lost regular contact with the homeland. Then it slowly withered away. Despite their spectacular exploits, the Norse had no impact on the later course of American history.

EUROPE AND THE WORLD IN THE 15TH CENTURY

Nobody in the year 1400 could have foreseen the course of European expansion that was about to begin. Europe stood at the edge, not the center, of world commerce.

CHINA: THE REJECTION OF OVERSEAS EXPANSION

By just about every standard, China under the Ming dynasty was the world's most complex culture. In the 15th century the government of China, staffed by well-educated bureaucrats, ruled 100 million people. The Chinese had invented the compass, gunpowder, and early forms of printing and paper money. Foreigners coveted the silks, teas, and other fine products available in China, but they had little to offer in exchange. Most of what Europe knew about China came from *The Travels* of Marco Polo, a merchant from the Italian city-state of Venice who reached the Chinese court in 1271 and served the emperor, Kublai Khan, for the next 20 years. The Khan's capital city (today's Beijing) was the world's largest and grandest, Marco reported, and received 1,000 cartloads of silk a day. China outshone Europe and all other cultures, he insisted.

The Chinese agreed. Between 1405 and 1434 a royal eunuch, Cheng Ho, led six large fleets from China to the East Indies and the coast of East Africa, trading and exploring along the way. His ships were large enough to sail around the southern tip of Africa and "discover" Europe. Had China thrown its resources and talents into overseas expansion, the subsequent history of the world would have been vastly different. But most of what the Chinese learned about the outside world merely confirmed their belief that other cultures had little to offer their Celestial Kingdom. No one followed Cheng Ho's lead after he died. The emperor banned the construction of oceangoing ships and later forbade anyone to own a vessel with more than two masts. China, a self-contained economic and political system, did not need the rest of the world.

EUROPE VERSUS ISLAM

Western Europe was a rather backward place in 1400. Its location on the Atlantic rim of the Eurasian continent had always made access to Asian trade difficult and costly. Islam controlled overland trade with Asia and the only known seaborne route through the Persian Gulf. As of 1400, Arab mariners were the world's best. Europeans coveted East Indian spices, but because they produced little that Asians wished to buy, they had to pay for these imports with scarce silver or gold.

In fact, while Europe's sphere of influence was shrinking and while China seemed content with what it already had, Islam was well embarked on another great phase of expansion. The Ottoman Turks took Constantinople in 1453, overran the Balkans by the 1520s, and even threatened Vienna. The Safavid Empire in Iran (Persia) rose to new splendor at the same time. Other Moslems carried the Koran to Indonesia and northern India.

Yet the European economy had made impressive gains in the Middle Ages, primarily owing to agricultural advances, such as improved plows, that also fostered rapid population growth. By 1300, more than 100 million people were living in Europe. Europe's farms could not sustain further growth, however. Lean years and famines ensued, leaving people undernourished. Then in the late 1340s, the Black Death (bubonic plague) reduced the population by more than a third. Recurring bouts of plague kept the population low until about 1500. Meanwhile, overworked soil regained its fertility, and per capita income rose considerably among people who now had stronger immunities to disease.

By then European metallurgy and architecture were quite advanced. The Renaissance, which revived interest in the literature of ancient Greece and Rome, also gave a new impetus to European culture, especially after Johannes Gutenberg invented the printing press and movable type in the 1430s. This revolution in communications permitted improvements in ship design and navigational techniques to build on each other and become a self-reinforcing process. The Arabs, by contrast, had borrowed printing from China in the 10th century, only to give it up by 1400.

Unlike China, none of Europe's kingdoms was a self-contained economy. All needed to trade with one another and with the non-Christian world. No single state had a monopoly on the manufacture of firearms or on the flow of capital, a situation that proved advantageous in the long run. During the 15th century, European societies began to compete with one another in gaining access to these resources and in mastering new **maritime** and military techniques. European armies were far more formidable by 1520 than a century before, and European fleets could outsail and outfight all rivals.

THE LEGACY OF THE CRUSADES

Quite apart from the Norse explorers, Europe had a heritage of expansion that derived from the efforts of the crusaders to conquer the Holy Land from Islam. Crusaders had established their own Kingdom of Jerusalem, which survived for more than a century but was finally retaken in 1244. This overseas venture taught Europeans some important lessons. To make Palestine profitable, the crusaders had taken over sugar plantations and worked them with a combination of free and slave labor. After they were driven from the Holy Land, they retreated to the Mediterranean islands of Cyprus, Malta, Crete, and Rhodes, where they used slaves to grow sugarcane or grapes.

Long before Columbus, these planters had created the economic components of overseas expansion. They assumed that colonies should produce a **staple crop**, at least partly through slave labor, for sale in Europe. The first slaves were Moslem captives. In the 14th and 15th centuries, planters turned to pagan Slavs (hence the word "slave") from the Black Sea area and the Adriatic. Some black Africans were also acquired from Arab merchants who controlled the caravan trade across the Sahara desert, but these early plantations did not exploit their laborers with the ruthless intensity that would later characterize the Americas.

THE UNLIKELY PIONEER: PORTUGAL

It seemed improbable in 1400 that Europe was on the threshold of dramatic expansion. That Portugal would lead the way seemed even less likely. A small kingdom of fewer than a million people, Portugal had been united for less than a century. Its maritime traditions lagged well behind those of the Italian states, France, and England, and it had little capital.

Yet Portugal enjoyed internal peace and an efficient government at a time when its neighbors were beset by war and internal upheaval. Moreover, it was located at the intersection of the Mediterranean and Atlantic worlds. At first, Portuguese mariners were interested in short-term gains rather than in some all-water route to Asia. The Portuguese knew that Arab caravans crossed the Sahara to bring gold, slaves, and ivory from black Africa to Europe. The Portuguese believed that an Atlantic voyage to coastal points south of the Sahara would undercut Arab traders and bring large profits. The greatest problem they faced in this quest was Cape Bojador, with its treacherous shallows, awesome waves, and strong northerly winds.

In 1420 a member of the Portuguese royal family, Prince Henry, became head of the crusading Order of Christ and used its revenues to sponsor 15 voyages along the African coast. In 1434 one of his captains, Gil Eannes, finally sailed past the cape, explored the coastline, and then headed west into the Atlantic beyond the sight of land until he met favorable winds that carried him back to Europe. Other captains pushed farther south along the African coast. Only after they got beyond the Sahara did their efforts begin to pay off.

During the 15th century Portugal vaulted past all rivals in the ability to navigate the high seas beyond sight of land. Portuguese navigators mapped the prevailing

maritime *Of, or relating to, the sea.*

staple crop *Crops, such as tobacco and sugar, grown for commercial sale, usually produced in a colonial area and sold in Europe.*

Jon Adkins © National Geographic Society

THE CARAVEL: A SWIFT OCEANGOING VESSEL. *Shown here is a 15th-century caravel—in this case a modern reconstruction of the Niña, which crossed the Atlantic with Columbus in 1492.*

winds and currents over most of the globe. They collected geographical information. They studied the superior designs of Arab vessels, copied them, and then improved on them. They borrowed the lateen (triangular) sail from the Arabs and combined it with square rigging in the right proportion to produce a superb oceangoing vessel, the **caravel**. A caravel could make from 3 to 12 knots and could beat closer to a head wind than any other sailing ship. Portuguese captains also used the compass and adopted the Arabs' **astrolabe,** a device that permits accurate calculation of latitude, or distances north and south. They also learned how to mount heavy cannon on the decks of their ships—a formidable advantage in an age when others fought naval battles by grappling and boarding enemy vessels. Portuguese ships were able to stand farther off and literally blow their opponents out of the water.

After 1450, Portuguese mariners explored ever farther along the African coast. South of the Sahara they found the wealth they had been seeking: gold, ivory, and slaves.

AFRICA, COLONIES, AND THE SLAVE TRADE

West Africans had been supplying Europe with most of its gold for hundreds of years through indirect trade across the Sahara. West Africa's political history had seen the rise and decline of a series of large inland states. The most recent was the empire of Mali. As the Portuguese advanced past the Sahara, their commerce began to pull trade away from the desert caravans, weakening Mali and other interior states. By 1550, the empire had fallen apart.

The Portuguese also founded offshore colonies along the way. They began to settle the uninhabited Madeira Islands in 1418, took possession of the Azores between 1427 and 1450, occupied the Cape Verde group in the 1450s, and took over São Tomé in 1470. Like exploration, colonization also turned a profit. Beginning in the 1440s, Portuguese planters on the islands produced sugar or wine, increasingly with slave labor imported from nearby Africa.

At first the Portuguese acquired their slaves by landing on the African coast, attacking villages, and carrying off everyone they could catch. But these raids enraged coastal peoples and made other forms of trade more difficult. In the decades after 1450, the slave trade assumed its classic form. The Portuguese established small posts, or **factories**, along the coast or on small offshore islands, such as Arguin

caravel *New type of oceangoing vessel that could sail closer to a head wind than any other sailing ship and make speeds of 3 to 12 knots per hour.*

astrolabe *Device that permitted accurate calculation of latitude or distances north and south.*

factories *Small posts established for the early slave trade along the coast of Africa or on small offshore islands.*

Island near Cape Blanco, where they built their first African fort in 1448. Operating out of these bases, traders would buy slaves from the local rulers, who usually acquired them by waging war. During the long history of the **Atlantic slave trade**, nearly every African shipped overseas had first been enslaved by other Africans.

Slavery had long existed in Africa, but in a form less brutal than what the Europeans would impose. In Africa, slaves were not forced to toil endlessly to produce staple crops, and their descendants often became fully assimilated into the captors' society. Slaves were not isolated as a separate caste. By the time African middlemen learned about the cruel conditions of slavery under European rule, the trade had become too lucrative to stop. When the rulers of the Kongo embraced Catholicism in the 16th century, they protested against the Atlantic slave trade, only to see their own people become vulnerable to enslavement by others. The non-Christian kingdom of Benin learned the same lesson.

The Portuguese made the slave trade profitable by exploiting rivalries among the more than 200 small states of West and Central Africa. Despite many cultural similarities among these groups, West Africans had never thought of themselves as a single people. Nor did they share a universal religion that might have restrained them from selling other Africans into slavery. Moslems believed it sinful to enslave a fellow believer. Western Europeans held that enslaving fellow Christians was immoral. Enslaving pagan or Moslem Africans was another matter. Some Europeans even persuaded themselves that they were doing Africans a favor by buying them and making their souls eligible for salvation.

PORTUGAL'S ASIAN EMPIRE

Because it paid for itself through gold, ivory, and slaves, Portuguese exploration continued. In the 1480s the Portuguese government supported the quest for an all-water route to Asia. In 1487 Bartolomeu Dias reached the Cape of Good Hope at the southern tip of Africa and headed east toward the Indian Ocean, but his crew rebelled in those stormy waters, and he turned back. Ten years later Vasco da Gama led a small fleet around the Cape of Good Hope and sailed on to the Malibar Coast of southwestern India. In a voyage that lasted more than two years (1497–1499), he bargained and fought for spices that yielded a 20-to-1 profit for his investors.

To secure their Asian trade, the Portuguese established a chain of naval bases that extended from East Africa to the mouth of the Persian Gulf, then to Goa on the west coast of India, and from there to the Moluccas, or East Indies. Portuguese missionaries even penetrated Japan. The Moluccas became the Asian center of the Portuguese seaborne empire, with their spices yielding most of the wealth that Portugal extracted from its eastern holdings. Beyond assuring its continued access to spices, Portugal made little effort to govern its colonies. In all their Asian holdings, the Portuguese remained heavily outnumbered by native peoples. Only in the other hemisphere—in Brazil, discovered accidentally by Pedro Álvares Cabral in 1500 when he was blown off course while trying to round the Cape of Good Hope—had settlement become a major goal by the late 16th century.

EARLY LESSONS

As the Norse failure showed, the ability to navigate the high seas gave no guarantee of lasting success. Sustained expansion overseas required the support of a home government and ready access to what other states had learned. The experience acquired

Atlantic slave trade *A European commerce that led to the enslavement of millions of people, who were shipped from their African homelands to European colonies in the Americas.*

QUICK   REVIEW

THE BEGINNINGS OF SUSTAINED EUROPEAN EXPANSION

- Trade with China

- Renewed expansion of Islam

- Crusades left a legacy of plantation slavery in the Mediterranean

- Portugal led the European exploration of the Atlantic islands, Africa, and the all-water route to Asia

Map 1.1

AFRICA AND THE MEDITERRANEAN IN THE 15TH CENTURY. *The Mediterranean islands held by Europeans in the late Middle Ages, the Atlantic islands colonized by Portugal and Spain in the 15th century, the part of West Africa from Cape Blanco to Angola that provided the main suppliers of the Atlantic slave trade, and the Portuguese all-water route to India after 1497.*

View an animated version of this map or related maps at
http://history.wadsworth.com/murrinconcise4e.

by Italian merchants in nearby Rhodes or Cyprus could be passed on to the Portuguese and applied in the Atlantic islands of Madeira or the Azores. The lessons learned there could be relayed to distant Brazil. In launching their ventures, the Portuguese drew on Italian capital and maritime skills, as well as on Arab learning and technology. Spaniards, in turn, would learn much from the Portuguese, and the French, Dutch, and English would borrow from all of their predecessors.

The economic impulse behind colonization was thus in place long before Columbus sailed west. The desire for precious metals provided the initial stimulus, but staple crops and slavery kept that impetus alive. Before the 19th century, more than two-thirds of the people who crossed the Atlantic were slaves, not free European settlers.

Spain, Columbus, and the Americas

While the Portuguese surged east, Spaniards moved more sluggishly to the west. The Spanish kingdom of Castile sent its first settlers to the Canary Islands just after 1400. They spent the last third of the 15th century conquering the local inhabitants, the Guanches, a Berber people who had left North Africa before the rise of Islam and had been cut off from Africa and Europe for a thousand years. By the 1490s the Spanish had all but exterminated them.

Except for seizing the Canaries, the Spaniards did little exploring or colonizing. But in 1469 Prince Ferdinand of Aragon married Princess Isabella of Castile. They soon inherited their respective thrones and formed the modern kingdom of Spain. Aragon, a Mediterranean society, had made good an old claim to the Kingdom of Naples and Sicily and thus already possessed a small imperial bureaucracy with experience in administering overseas possessions. Castile, landlocked on three sides, had turned over much of its small overseas trade to merchants and mariners from Genoa in northern Italy who had settled in Seville. Castilians were more likely than the Portuguese to identify expansion with conquest rather than trade.

In January 1492 Isabella and Ferdinand completed the reconquest of Spain by taking Granada, the last outpost of Islam on the Iberian Peninsula. They gave unconverted Jews six months to become Christians or be expelled from Spain. Just over half of Spain's 80,000 Jews fled. A decade later Ferdinand and Isabella also evicted all unconverted Moors. Spain entered the 16th century as Europe's most fiercely Catholic society, and this attitude accompanied its soldiers and settlers to America.

COLUMBUS

A talented navigator from Genoa named Christopher Columbus promptly sought to benefit from the victory at Granada. He had been pleading for years with the courts of Portugal, England, France, and Spain to give him the ships and men to attempt an unprecedented feat: He believed he could reach eastern Asia by sailing west across the Atlantic. Columbus's proposed voyage was controversial, but not because he assumed the earth is round. Learned men already agreed on that point, but they disagreed about its size. Columbus put its circumference at only 16,000 miles, whereas the Portuguese calculated it, correctly, at about 26,000 miles and warned Columbus that he would perish on the vast ocean if he tried his mad scheme. Then the fall of Granada gave Columbus another chance to plead his case. Isabella, who now had men and resources to spare, put him in charge of a fleet of two caravels, the *Niña* and the *Pinta,* together with a larger, square-rigged vessel, the *Santa María,* which became his flagship.

Columbus's motives were both religious and practical. As the "Christ-bearer" (the literal meaning of his first name), Columbus was convinced that he had a role to play in bringing on the **Millennium,** the period at the end of history when Christ would return, perhaps as early as 1648, and rule with his saints for 1,000 years. But Columbus was not at all averse to acquiring wealth and glory along the way.

Embarking from the port of Palos in August 1492, Columbus headed south to the Canaries, picked up provisions, and then sailed west across the Atlantic. Despite his assurances that they had not sailed very far, the crews grew restless in early October. Columbus pushed on. Land was finally spotted, on October 12. The Spaniards splashed ashore on San Salvador, now Watling's Island in the Bahamas. Convinced that he was somewhere in the East Indies, Columbus called the local inhabitants "Indians." When the peaceful Tainos (or Arawaks) claimed that the Carib Indians on nearby islands were cannibals, Columbus interpreted their word for "Carib" to mean the great "Khan" or emperor of China, known to him through Marco Polo's *Travels.* Columbus set out to find the Caribs. For several months he poked about the Caribbean. Then, on Christmas, the *Santa María* ran onto rocks and had to be abandoned. A few weeks later Columbus sailed for Spain on the *Niña,* leaving some of the crew as a garrison on the island of Hispaniola. But the Tainos had seen enough of the European invaders. By the time Columbus returned on his second voyage in late 1493, they had killed every man that he left behind.

The voyage had immediate consequences. In 1493 Pope Alexander VI (a Spaniard) issued a bull, *Inter Caeteras,* which divided all non-Christian lands between Spain and Portugal. A year later, in the Treaty of Tordesillas, the two kingdoms adjusted the dividing line, with Spain eventually claiming most of the Western Hemisphere, plus the Philippines, and Portugal most of the Eastern Hemisphere, including the African coast, plus Brazil. As a result, Spain never acquired direct access to the African slave trade.

Columbus made three more voyages in quest of China and also served as governor of the Spanish Indies. But Castilians never really trusted him. The colonists often defied him, and in 1500, after his third voyage, they shipped him back to Spain in chains. Although later restored to royal favor, he died in 1506, a bitter, disappointed man.

SPAIN AND THE CARIBBEAN

By then overseas settlement had acquired a momentum of its own as thousands of ex-soldiers, bored **hidalgos** (minor nobles with little wealth), and assorted adventurers drifted across the Atlantic. They carried with them seeds for Europe's cereal crops and livestock, including horses, cows, sheep, goats, and pigs. On islands without fences, the animals roamed freely, eating everything in sight, and soon threatened the Tainos' food supply. Unconcerned, the Spaniards forced the increasingly malnourished Indians to work for them, mostly panning for gold. Under these pressures, even before the onset of major infectious diseases, the Indian population declined catastrophically throughout the Caribbean. A whole way of life all but vanished from the earth to be replaced by sugar, slaves, and livestock. African slaves, acquired from the Portuguese, soon arrived to replace the dead Indians as a labor force.

The Spaniards continued their explorations, however. Juan Ponce de León tramped through Florida in quest of a legendary fountain of youth. Vasco Núñez de Balboa became the first European to reach the Pacific Ocean, after crossing the Isthmus of Panama in 1513. But as late as 1519 Spain had gained little wealth from

Millennium *Period at the end of history when Christ is expected to return and rule with his saints for a thousand years.*

hidalgos *Minor nobility of Spain, often possessing little wealth and interested in improving their position through the overseas empire.*

QUICK   REVIEW

SPAIN CREATED AN ATLANTIC EMPIRE

- Columbus tried to reach Asia by sailing west across the Atlantic

- Early Spanish exploration of the Caribbean threatened peoples and ecosystems

- Cortés discovered the wealth of the Aztec empire

Hernán Cortés *Spanish conquistador who vanquished the Aztecs.*

Aztec *Last pre-Columbian high culture in the Valley of Mexico. It was conquered by the Spaniards in 1519–1521.*

Tenochtitlán *Huge Aztec capital city destroyed by Cortés.*

these new possessions. One geographer concluded that Spain had found a whole new continent, which he named "America" in honor of his informant, the explorer Amerigo Vespucci. For those who doubted, Ferdinand Magellan, a Portuguese mariner serving the king of Spain, settled the issue when his fleet sailed around the world between 1519 and 1522.

But during the same three years, **Hernán Cortés** sailed from Cuba, conquered Mexico for Spain, and found the treasure that Spaniards had been seeking. In 1519 he landed at a place he named Vera Cruz ("The True Cross") and over the next several months succeeded in tracking down the fabulous empire of the **Aztecs**, high in the Valley of Mexico. Moctezuma, the Aztec "speaker" or ruler, sent rich presents to persuade the Spaniards to leave, but the gesture had the opposite effect. The Spaniards pushed onward. When the small army of 400 men first laid eyes on the Aztec capital of **Tenochtitlán** (a metropolis of 200,000, much larger than any urban center in Western Europe), they wondered if they were dreaming. But they marched into the city.

THE EMERGENCE OF COMPLEX SOCIETIES IN THE AMERICAS

The high cultures of the Americas had been developing for thousands of years before Cortés found one of them. Their wealth fired the imagination of Europe and aroused the envy of Spain's enemies. The fabulous Aztec and **Inca** empires became the magnets that helped turn European exploration into empires of permanent settlement.

Inca *Last and most extensive pre-Columbian empire that arose in the Andes and along the Pacific coast of South America.*

sedentary *Societies that are rooted locally or are nonmigratory. Semisedentary societies are migratory for part of the year.*

slash and burn *System of agriculture in which trees were cut down, girdled, or in some way destroyed. The underbrush then was burned, and a crop was planted. The system eventually depleted the fertility of the soil, and the entire tribe would move to a new area after 10 or 20 years.*

THE RISE OF SEDENTARY CULTURES

After 4000 B.C., agriculture slowly transformed the lives of most Indians. As farming became the principal source of food in the Americas, settled villages in a few locations grew into large cities. Most of them appeared in the Valley of Mexico, Central America, or the Andes. For centuries, however, dense settlements also thrived in Chaco Canyon in present-day New Mexico and in the Mississippi River valley.

Indians became completely **sedentary** (nonmigratory) only in the most advanced cultures. Most of those living north of Mexico were migratory for part of each year. After a tribe chose a site, the men chopped down some trees, girdled others, burned away the underbrush, and often planted tobacco, a mood-altering sacred crop grown exclusively by men. Burning the underbrush fertilized the soil with ash and gave the community years of high productivity. Indian women usually erected the dwellings and planted and harvested food crops. In the fall, either the men alone or entire family groups went off hunting or fishing.

Because this **slash and burn** system of agriculture slowly depleted the soil, the whole tribe had to move to new fields after 10 or 20 years. In this semisedentary way of life, few Indians cared to acquire more personal property than the women could carry from one place to another. This limited interest in consumption would profoundly condition their response to capitalism after contact with Europeans.

Even sedentary Indians did not own land as individuals. Clans or families guarded their "use rights" to land that had been allocated to them by their chiefs. In sedentary societies both men and women worked in the fields, and families accumulated surpluses for trade. Not all sedentary peoples developed monumental architecture and elaborate state forms. But, with a few striking exceptions, such examples of cultural

Courtesy of the John Carter Brown Library at Brown University

INDIAN WOMEN AS FARMERS. *In this illustration, a French artist depicted 16th-century Indian women in southeastern North America.*

complexity emerged only among sedentary populations. In Mesoamerica and the Andes, intensive farming, cities, states, and monumental architecture came together at several different times to produce distinctive high cultures.

The spread of farming produced another population surge among both sedentary and semisedentary peoples. Estimates vary greatly, but according to the more moderate ones, at least 50 million people were living in the Western Hemisphere by 1492, and there may well have been as many as 70 million, or one-seventh of the world's population. Despite their large populations, even the most complex societies in the Americas remained Stone Age cultures. The Indians made some use of metals, although more for decorative than practical purposes. This metalworking skill originated in South America and spread to Mesoamerica a few centuries before Columbus. As far north as the Great Lakes, copper had been mined and fashioned into fishing tools and art objects since the first millennium B.C. It was traded over large areas of North America. But Indians had not learned how to make bronze (a compound of copper and tin), nor found any use for iron. Nearly all of their tools were made of stone or bone, and their sharpest weapons were made from obsidian, a hard, glassy, volcanic rock. Nor did they use the wheel or devices based on the wheel, such as pulleys or gears.

THE ANDES: CYCLES OF COMPLEX CULTURES

During the second millennium B.C., elaborate urban societies began to take shape both in the Andes and along Mexico's Gulf Coast. Ancient Andean societies devised extremely productive agricultural systems at 12,000 feet above sea level, far above the altitude at which anyone else has ever been able to raise crops. Lands using the Andean canal system never had to lie fallow. This type of irrigation took hold around Lake Titicaca about 1000 B.C. and spread throughout the region. It was abandoned around A.D. 1000, apparently in response to a drought that endured almost continuously for two centuries.

Between 3000 and 2100 B.C., monumental architecture and urbanization took hold along the Peruvian coast and in the interior. Some of the earliest temples were

COMPLEX CULTURES OF PRE-COLUMBIAN AMERICA

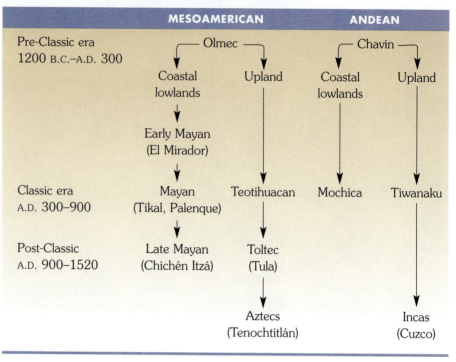

	MESOAMERICAN		ANDEAN	
Pre-Classic era 1200 B.C.–A.D. 300	── Olmec ──		── Chavin ──	
	Coastal lowlands	Upland	Coastal lowlands	Upland
	Early Mayan (El Mirador)			
Classic era A.D. 300–900	Mayan (Tikal, Palenque)	Teotihuacan	Mochica	Tiwanaku
Post-Classic A.D. 900–1520	Late Mayan (Chichén Itzá)	Toltec (Tula)		
		Aztecs (Tenochtitlán)		Incas (Cuzco)

pyramids. As more people moved into the mountains, some pyramids became immense, such as the one at Sechin Alto near Lima, more than 10 stories high, which was built between 1800 and 1500 B.C. This "Pre-Classic" Chavin culture was well established by 1000 B.C., only to collapse suddenly around 300 B.C.

Chavin culture had two offshoots, one on the coast, one in the mountains. Together they constitute the "Classic" phase of pre-Columbian history in South America. The Mochica culture, which emerged around A.D. 300 on the northwest coast of Peru, produced finely detailed pottery, much of it erotic, and built pyramids as centers of worship. At about the same time, another Classic culture arose in the mountains around the city of Tiwanaku, 12,000 feet above sea level. Terraces at various altitudes enabled the community to raise crops from different climatic zones. At the lowest levels, Tiwanakans planted cotton in the hot, humid air. Farther up the mountain, they raised maize (corn) and other crops suitable to a temperate zone. At still higher elevations, they grew potatoes and grazed their alpacas and llamas.

The Tiwanaku Empire, with its capital on the southern shores of Lake Titicaca, flourished until the horrendous drought that began at the end of the 10th century A.D. The Classic Andean cultures collapsed between the 6th and 11th centuries A.D., possibly after a conquest of the Mochica region by the Tiwanakans, who provided water to the coastal peoples until they too were overwhelmed by the drought. The disruption that followed this decline was not permanent, for complex Post-Classic cultures soon thrived both north and west of Tiwanaku.

INCA CIVILIZATION

Around A.D. 1400 the Inca (the word applies both to the ruler and to the empire's dominant nation) emerged as the new imperial power in the Andes. They built their capital at Cuzco, high in the mountains. From that upland center, the Inca

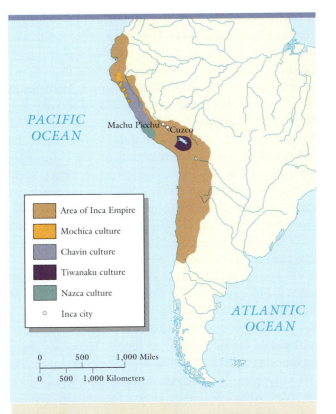

Map 1.2
INCA EMPIRE AND PRINCIPAL EARLIER CULTURES. *The Pacific coast of South America showing the location of the Mochica, Chavin, Tiwanaku, and Nazca cultures and finally the Inca empire, which covered a much larger area than its predecessors.*

controlled an empire that eventually extended more than 2,000 miles from south to north, and they bound it together with an efficient network of roads and suspension bridges. They had no written language, but high-altitude runners, who memorized the Inca's oral commands, raced along the roads to deliver their ruler's decrees over vast distances. The Incas also invented a decimal system and used it to keep accounts on a device they called a *quipu*. By 1500 the Inca Empire ruled perhaps 8 to 12 million people. No other nonliterate culture has ever matched that feat.

MESOAMERICA: CYCLES OF COMPLEX CULTURES

Mesoamerica experienced a similar cycle of change. It had its own Pre-Classic, Classic, and Post-Classic cultures comprising both upland and lowland societies.

The **Olmecs**, who appeared along the Gulf Coast around 1200 B.C., centered on three cities. The oldest, San Lorenzo, flourished from 1200 to 900 B.C., when it was conquered by invaders. Olmec influence reached its zenith during the domination of La Venta, which became an urban center around 1100 B.C., reached its peak 300 years later, and then declined. After La Venta was demolished between 500 and 400 B.C., leadership passed to the city of Tres Zapotes, which thrived for another four centuries.

Olmec *Oldest pre-Columbian high culture to appear in what is now Mexico.*

These three Olmec centers were small, with permanent populations of only about 1,000, not enough to sustain large armies. The colossal stone heads that honored their rulers were the most distinctive Olmec artifacts, but they appeared only in the homeland. Other aspects of Olmec culture became widely diffused throughout Mesoamerica. The Olmecs built the first pyramids and the first ballparks in Mesoamerica.

The Olmecs also learned how to write and developed a dual calendar system. It took 52 years for the two calendars to complete a full cycle, after which the first day of the "short" calendar would again coincide with the first day of the "long" one. Olmecs faced the closing days of each cycle with dread, lest the gods allow the sun to be destroyed—something that the Olmecs believed had already happened several times. They thought that the sacrifice of a god had been necessary to set the sun in motion once again and that only human sacrifice could placate the gods and keep the sun moving. These beliefs endured for perhaps 3,000 years and retained immense power. The arrival of Cortés created a religious as well as a political crisis, because 1519 marked the end of a 52-year cycle.

The Olmecs were succeeded by two Classic cultures. The city and empire of Teotihuacan emerged in the mountains not far from modern Mexico City. **Mayan** culture took shape mostly in the southern lowlands of Yucatán.

Teotihuacan was already a city of 40,000 by A.D. 1. Its most impressive art form was its brightly painted murals, of which only a few survive. Teotihuacan invested resources in comfortable apartment dwellings for ordinary residents, not in monuments or inscriptions to rulers. It was probably governed by something like a senate, not by a monarch. The city was able to extend its influence throughout Mesoamerica and remained a powerful force until its sudden destruction around A.D. 750, when its shrines were toppled and the city was abandoned. In all likelihood, Teotihuacan's growth had so depleted the resources of the area that the city could not have sustained itself much longer.

In the lowlands, Classic Mayan culture went through a similar cycle from expansion to ecological crisis. It was also urban but less centralized than that of Teotihuacan. For more than 1,000 years, Mayan culture rested upon a network of competing city-states. Tikal controlled commerce with Teotihuacan and housed 100,000 at its peak before A.D. 800. Twenty other cities, most about one-fourth the size of Tikal, flourished throughout the region. Mayan engineers built canals to irrigate the crops needed to support this urban network, which was well established by the first century B.C.

The earliest Mayan writings date to 50 B.C., but few survive from the next 300 years. Around A.D. 300, Mayans began to record their history in considerable detail. Since 1960 scholars have been able to decipher most Mayan inscriptions. Mayan art and writings reveal the religious beliefs of these people, including the place of human sacrifice and the role of ritual self-mutilation in their worship. Scholars have learned, for example, about the long reign of Pacal the Great, king (or "Great Sun") of the elegant city of Palenque, who was born on March 26, 603, and died on August 31, 683. Other monuments tell of the Great Suns of other cities whom Pacal vanquished and sacrificed to the gods.

Classic Mayan culture began to collapse about 50 years after the fall of Teotihuacan, which disrupted Mayan trade with the Valley of Mexico. The crisis spread rapidly. Palenque and a half-dozen other cities were abandoned between 800 and 820. The last date recorded at Tikal was in 869; the last in the southern lowlands came 40 years later. The Mayan aristocracy had grown faster than the ability of commoners to support it, until population outstripped local resources. Frequent wars hastened the decline.

After A.D. 900, the Post-Classic era saw a kind of Mayan renaissance in the northern lowlands of the Yucatán, where many refugees from the south had fled. Chichén Itzá, a city that had existed for centuries, preserved many distinctive Mayan traits but now merged them with new influences from the Valley of Mexico, where the Toltecs

Maya *Literate, highly urbanized Mesoamerican civilization that flourished for more than a thousand years before its sudden collapse in the ninth century A.D.*

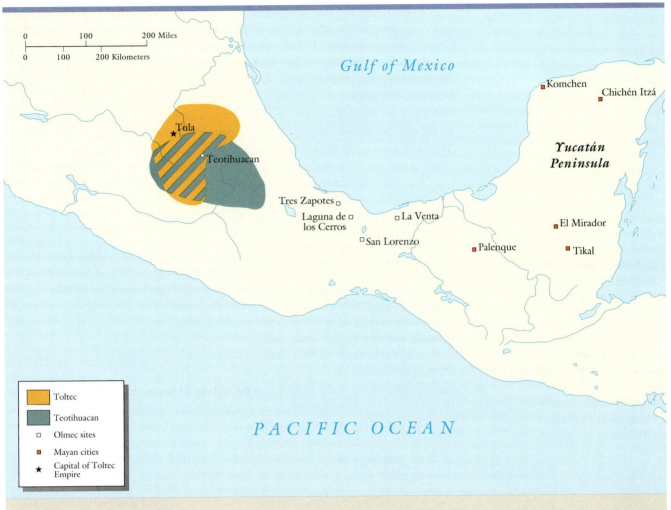

Map 1.3

ANCIENT MESOAMERICA. *The location of the three principal Olmec cities, Teotihuacan, several major Mayan cities, and the Toltec capital of Tula.*

had become dominant in the high country and may even have conquered Chichén Itzá. The Toltecs were a fierce warrior people whose capital at Tula, with 40,000 people, was one-fifth as large as Teotihuacan at its peak. They prospered from the cocoa trade with tropical lowlands but otherwise did nothing to expand the region's food supply. They controlled the Valley of Mexico for almost three centuries, until about A.D. 1200 when they too declined.

THE AZTECS AND TENOCHTITLÁN

By 1400 power in the Valley of Mexico was passing to the Aztecs, a warrior people who had migrated from the north about two centuries earlier and had settled on the shore of Lake Texcoco. They then built a great city, Tenochtitlán, out on the lake itself. Its only connection with the mainland was by several broad causeways. The Aztecs raised their agricultural productivity by creating highly productive **chinampas**, or floating gardens, right on the lake. Yet their mounting population strained the food supply. In the 1450s the threat of famine was severe.

chinampas *Highly productive gardens built on Lake Taxcoco by the Aztecs.*

As newcomers to the region, the Aztecs felt a need to prove themselves worthy heirs to the ancient culture of the Valley of Mexico. They adopted the old religion but practiced it with a terrifying intensity. They waged perpetual war to gain captives for their ceremonies. At the dedication of the Great Pyramid of the Sun in 1487, they sacrificed—if we can believe later accounts—14,000 people. Human sacrifice was an ancient ritual in Mesoamerica, familiar to everyone, but the Aztecs practiced it on a scale that had no parallel anywhere else in the world. The need for thousands of victims each year created potential enemies everywhere. After 1519, many Mesoamerican peoples would help the Spaniards topple the Aztecs. By contrast, the Spanish found few allies in the Andes, where resistance in the name of the Inca would persist for most of the 16th century.

NORTH AMERICAN MOUND BUILDERS

Cahokia *Largest city created by Mississippian mound builders. Located in Illinois near modern St. Louis, it thrived from* A.D. *900 to 1250 and then declined.*

Anasazi *Advanced pre-Columbian cliff-dwelling culture that flourished for two centuries in what are now the states of Arizona, New Mexico, Utah, and Colorado before these sites were abandoned in the late 13th century* A.D.

North of Mexico, from 3000 B.C. to about A.D. 1700, three distinct cultures of "mound builders" exerted a powerful influence over the interior of North America. These cultures arose near the Ohio and Mississippi Rivers and their tributaries. The earliest mound builders became semisedentary even before learning to grow crops. Fish, game, and the lush vegetation of the river valleys sustained them for most of the year and enabled them to erect permanent dwellings.

The oldest mound-building culture appeared among a preagricultural people in what is now northeastern Louisiana around 3400 B.C., at a site called Watson Break. Later, just 40 miles away, early mound builders flourished from 1500 B.C. to 700 B.C. at Poverty Point, a center that contained perhaps 5,000 people at its peak around 1000 B.C. The second mound-building culture, the Adena-Hopewell, emerged between 500 B.C. and A.D. 400 in the Ohio River valley. Its mounds were increasingly elaborate burial sites, indicating belief in an afterlife. Mound-building communities participated in a commerce that spanned most of the continent between the Appalachians and the Rockies, the Great Lakes and the Gulf of Mexico. Obsidian from the Yellowstone Valley in the Far West, copper from the Great Lakes basin, and shells from the Gulf of Mexico have all been found buried in the Adena-Hopewell mounds. Both the mound building and the long-distance trade largely ceased after A.D. 400, for reasons that remain unclear.

Mound building revived in a third and final Mississippian phase between A.D. 1000 and 1700. This culture dominated the Mississippi River valley from modern St. Louis to Natchez, with the largest center at Cahokia in present-day Illinois, and another important one at Moundville in Alabama. In this culture, the "Great Sun" ruled and was transported by litter from place to place. Burial mounds thus became much grander in Mississippian communities.

Cahokia, in Illinois near modern St. Louis, flourished from A.D. 900 to 1250 and may have had 30,000 residents at its peak, making it the largest city north of Mexico. Cahokia's enormous central mound, 100 feet high, is the world's largest earthen work. Similarities with Mesoamerican practices and artifacts have led many scholars to look for direct links between the two cultures. But although travel was possible between Mesoamerica and the Mississippi valley, no Mesoamerican artifacts have yet been found in the southeastern United States.

QUICK   REVIEW

PRE-COLUMBIAN AMERICA

- Cycles of Pre-Classic, Classic, and Post-Classic cultures emerged in the Andes and Mesoamerica

- Cycles of mound-building cultures developed in the North American heartland

- Complex cultures emerged in what is now the Southwestern United States

- Contact with Europeans led to cultural misunderstandings about religion, war, and gender

URBAN CULTURES OF THE SOUTHWEST

Other complex societies emerged in North America's semiarid Southwest—among them the Hohokam, the **Anasazi**, and the Pueblo. The Hohokam Indians settled in what is now central Arizona somewhere between 300 B.C. and A.D. 300. Their irri-

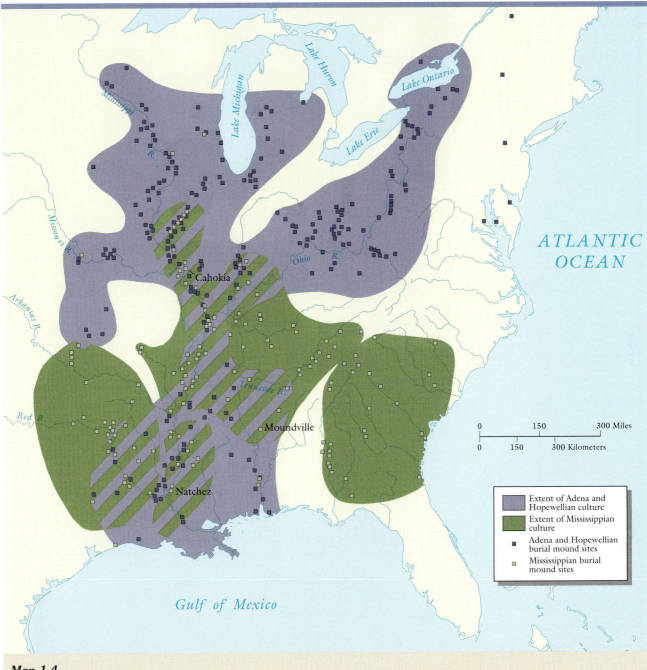

Map 1.4
MOUND-BUILDING CULTURES OF NORTH AMERICA. *Early Adena and Hopewell burial sites and later Mississippian sites and the areas that these cultures influenced.*

gation system, consisting of several hundred miles of canals, produced two harvests a year. They wove cotton cloth and made pottery with a distinctive red color. They traded with places as distant as California and Mesoamerica. Perhaps because unceasing irrigation had increased the salinity of the soil, this culture declined by 1450.

Even more tantalizing and mysterious is the brief flowering of the Anasazi, a cliff-dwelling people who have left behind some remarkable artifacts at Chaco Canyon in New Mexico, at Mesa Verde in Colorado, and at other sites. In their caves and cliffs they constructed apartment houses five stories high with as many as 500 dwellings and with ele-

MODERN RESTORATION OF AN ANASAZI
KIVA. *This* kiva, *or meeting room of the Anasazi, was located underground and was accessed by ladder through a hole in the ceiling.*

©David Muench

gant and spacious *kivas,* or meeting rooms for religious functions. The Anasazi were superb astronomers. They also built a network of roads that ran for scores of miles in several directions. They flourished for about two centuries and then, in the last quarter of the 13th century, apparently overwhelmed by a prolonged drought and by hostile invaders, they abandoned their principal sites. The Pueblo Indians claim descent from them.

CONTACT AND CULTURAL MISUNDERSTANDING

FOCUS QUESTION

Why were the native peoples of the Americas extremely vulnerable to European diseases, instead of the other way around?

After the voyage of Columbus, the peoples of Europe and America, both with ancient pasts, confronted each other. Nothing in the histories of Europeans or Indians had prepared either of them for the encounter.

RELIGIOUS DILEMMAS

Christians had trouble understanding how Indians could exist at all. The Bible never mentioned them. Were they the "lost 10 tribes" of Israel, perhaps? Some theologians, such as the Spaniard Juan Ginés de Sepúlveda, tried to resolve this dilemma by arguing that Indians were animals without souls, not human beings at all. The pope and the royal courts of Portugal and Spain listened instead to a Dominican missionary, Fray Bartolomé de Las Casas, who insisted on the Indians' humanity. But, asked Europeans, if Indians did possess immortal souls, would a compassionate God have failed to make the Gospel known to them? Some early Catholic missionaries concluded that one of the apostles must have visited America (and India) and that the natives must have rejected his message.

To Europeans, the sacrificial temples, skull racks, and snake motifs of Mesoamerica led to only one conclusion: The Aztecs worshiped Satan himself. Human sacrifice and ritual cannibalism were indeed widespread throughout the Americas. The Incas,

AZTEC SKULL RACK ALTAR. *This rack held the skulls of hundreds of sacrificial victims and shocked the invading Spaniards.*

Moctezuma's Mexico, by David Carrasco and Eduardo Mato Moctezuma, ©1992 University Press of Colorado. Photographs by Salvador Guil'liem Arroyo.

whose creation myth resembled that of Mesoamerica, offered an occasional victim to the sun or to some other god. The Indians of eastern North America frequently tortured to death their adult male captives. Christians were shocked by human sacrifice and found cannibalism revolting, but Indians regarded certain European practices with equal horror. Between 1500 and 1700, Europeans burned or hanged up to 100,000 people, usually old women, for conversing with the wrong spirits—that is, for witchcraft. The Spanish Inquisition burned thousands of heretics and blasphemers. Although Indians were exempt from its jurisdiction in the Americas, they did witness the execution of Europeans. To them these incinerations looked like human sacrifices to a vengeful god.

Even the moral message conveyed by Christians was ambiguous. Missionaries eagerly brought news of how Christ had died to save mankind from sin. Catholic worship, then as now, centered on the Mass and the Eucharist, in which a priest transforms bread and wine into the literal body and blood of Christ. Most Protestants also accepted this sacrament but interpreted it symbolically, not literally. To the Indians, Christians seemed to be a people who ate their own god but grew outraged at the lesser matter of sacrificing a human being to please an Indian god.

When Europeans tried to convert Indians to Christianity, the Indians concluded that the converts would spend the afterlife with the souls of Europeans, separated forever from their own ancestors, whose memory they revered. Neither side fully recognized these obstacles to mutual understanding. Although early Catholic missionaries converted thousands of Indians, the results were, at best, mixed. Most converts adopted some Christian practices while continuing many of their old rituals, often in secret.

WAR AS CULTURAL MISUNDERSTANDING

Such misunderstandings multiplied as Indians and Europeans came into closer contact. Both waged war, but with different objectives. Europeans tried to settle matters on the battlefield and expected to kill many enemies. Indians fought mostly to obtain captives, whether for sacrifice (as with the Aztecs) or to replace tribal losses through adoption (as with the Iroquois). To them, massive deaths on the battlefield were an appalling waste of life that could in no way appease the gods. Europeans and Indians also differed profoundly on what acts constituted atrocities. The torture and ritual sacrifice of captives horrified Europeans; the slaughter of women and children, which Europeans brought to America, appalled Indians.

GENDER AND CULTURAL MISUNDERSTANDING

Indian social organization also differed fundamentally from that of Europeans. European men owned almost all property, set the rules of inheritance, farmed the land, and performed nearly all public functions. Among many Indian peoples, descent was **matrilineal** (traced through the maternal line) and women owned nearly all movable property. European men felt incomplete unless they acquired authority over other people, especially the other members of their households. Indian men had no patriarchal ambitions. Women did the farming in semisedentary Indian cultures, and they often could demand a war or try to prevent one, although the final decision rested with men. When Europeans tried to change warriors into farmers, Indian males protested that they were being turned into women. Only over fully sedentary peoples were Europeans able to impose direct rule, because there they could build upon the social hierarchy, division of labor, and system of tribute already in place.

CONQUEST AND CATASTROPHE

FOCUS QUESTION
Why did the free-labor societies of Western Europe generate unfree labor systems all around their periphery?

Spanish **conquistadores**, or conquerors, led small armies that rarely exceeded 1,000 men. Yet they subdued two empires much larger than Spain itself and then looked around for more worlds to overrun. There, beyond the great empires, Indians had more success in resisting them.

THE CONQUEST OF MEXICO AND PERU

When Cortés entered Tenochtitlán in 1519, he seized Moctezuma, the Aztec ruler, as prisoner and hostage. Though overwhelmingly outnumbered, Cortés and his men began to destroy Aztec religious objects, replacing them with images of the Virgin Mary or other Catholic saints. In response, while Cortés was away, the Aztecs rose against the intruders, Moctezuma was killed, and the Spaniards were driven out with heavy losses. But the smallpox the Spaniards left behind was soon killing Aztecs by the thousands. Cortés found refuge with the nearby Tlaxcalans, a proudly independent people. With thousands of their warriors, he returned the next year and destroyed Tenochtitlán. With royal support from Spain, the *conquistadores* established themselves as new imperial rulers in Mesoamerica, looted all the silver and gold they could find, and built Mexico City on the ruins of Tenochtitlán.

Rumors abounded about an even richer empire far to the south, and in 1531 and 1532 Francisco Pizarro finally located the Inca Empire high in the Andes. Smallpox had preceded him and had killed the reigning Inca. In the civil war that followed, Atahualpa had defeated his brother to become the new Inca. Pizarro captured Atahualpa, held him hostage, and managed to win a few allies from among the Inca's recent enemies. Atahualpa paid a huge ransom, but Pizarro had him strangled anyway. Tens of thousands of angry Indians besieged the Spaniards for months in Cuzco, the Inca capital, but Pizarro, though vastly outnumbered, managed to hold out and

matrilineal *Society that determines inheritance and roles in life based on the female or maternal line.*

conquistadores *Spanish word for conquerors.*

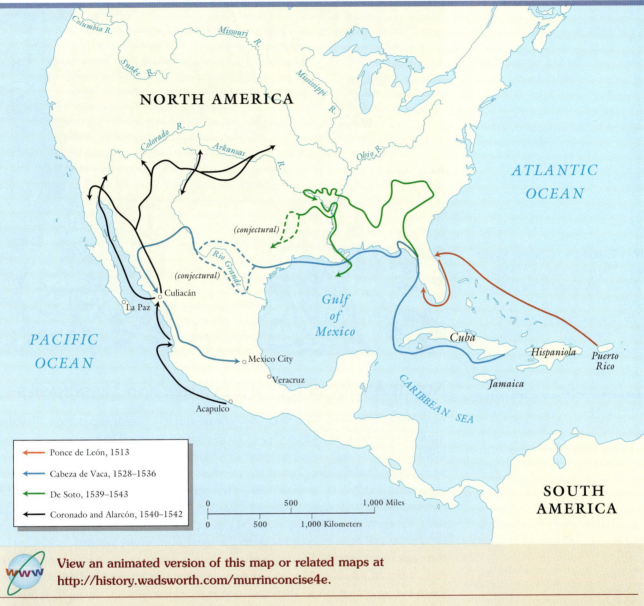

Map 1.5
PRINCIPAL SPANISH EXPLORATIONS OF NORTH AMERICA. *Four Spanish expeditions marched through much of the interior of North America between 1513 and 1543.*

View an animated version of this map or related maps at
http://history.wadsworth.com/murrinconcise4e.

finally prevailed. After subduing the insurgents, the Spanish established a new capital at Lima on the coast.

In a little more than 10 years, some hundreds of Spanish soldiers with thousands of Indian allies had conquered two enormous empires with a combined population perhaps five times greater than that of all Spain. But only in the 1540s did the Spanish finally locate the bonanza they had been seeking. The fabulous silver mines at Potosí in present-day Bolivia and other lodes in Mexico sustained Spain's military might in Europe for the next century.

New York Public Library, Astor, Lenox and Tilden Foundations, Rare Book Division

TRIBUTE LABOR (MITA) IN THE SILVER MINES. *The silver mines of Potosí, in the Andes, are about 2 miles above sea level. The work, as depicted in this 1603 engraving by Theodore de Bry, was extremely onerous and often dangerous.*

NORTH AMERICAN *CONQUISTADORES* AND MISSIONARIES

Alvar Núñez Cabeza de Vaca, a survivor of a disastrous Spanish expedition to Florida, made his way back to Mexico City in 1536 after an overland journey of eight years that took him through Texas and northern Mexico. In an account of his adventures, he mentioned Indian tales of great and populous cities to the north, and this reference soon became stories of "golden cities." Hernando de Soto landed in Florida in 1539 and roamed through much of the southeastern United States in quest of these treasures. He crossed the Mississippi in 1541, wandered through the Ozarks and eastern Oklahoma, and then marched back to the great river, where he died in 1542. His companions returned to Spanish territory. Farther west, Francisco Vasquez de Coronado marched into New Mexico and Arizona, where he encountered several Pueblo towns but no golden cities. The expedition reached the Grand Canyon, then headed east into Texas and as far north as Kansas before returning to Mexico in 1542. But the Spaniards left diseases behind that severely afflicted Indians of the interior.

After the *conquistadores* departed, Spanish priests did their best to convert thousands of North American Indians to the Catholic faith. In 1570 the Jesuits even established a mission in what is now Virginia, but the Indians soon rose and wiped it out. After this failure, the Jesuits withdrew and Franciscans took their place north of Mexico. In 1573 King Philip II issued the Royal Orders for New Discoveries, which made it illegal to enslave Indians or even attack them. Instead, unarmed priests were to bring them together in missions and convert them into peaceful Catholic subjects of Spain. The Franciscans quickly discovered that, without military support, they were more likely to win martyrdom than converts. They reluctantly accepted some military protection. Franciscans had no success among the nomadic residents of central and southern Florida. They had to build their missions within the permanent villages of northern Florida or the Pueblo communities of New Mexico. At first Indian women willingly supplied the labor needed to build and sustain these missions. By 1630 about 86,000 Pueblo, Apache, and Navajo Indians of New Mexico had accepted baptism. By mid-century there were 30 missions in Florida containing about 26,000 baptized Indians.

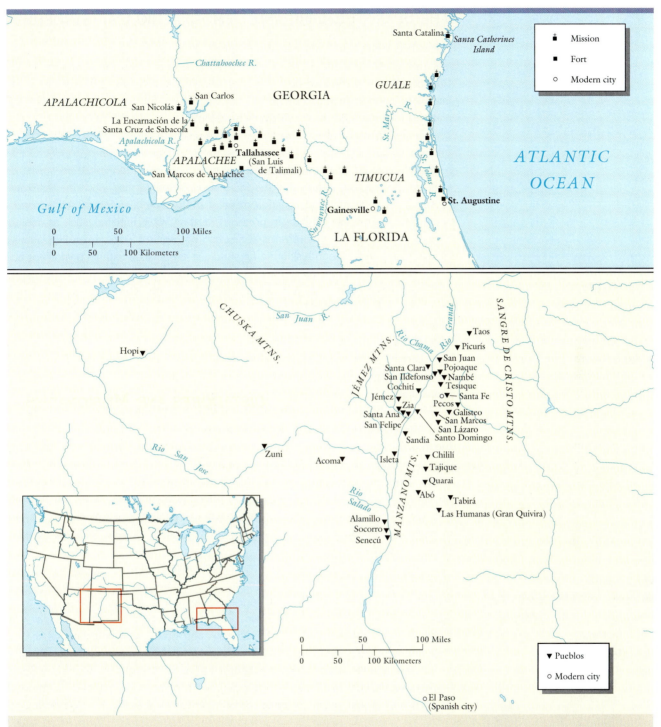

Map 1.6

Spanish Missions in Florida and New Mexico, circa 1675. *Franciscan friars established missions in Florida from the Atlantic to the Gulf of Mexico and in New Mexico along the Rio Grande Valley and, in a few cases, farther inland.*

THE SPANISH EMPIRE AND DEMOGRAPHIC CATASTROPHE

By the late 16th century, the Spanish Empire had emerged as a system of direct colonial rule in Mexico and Peru, protected by a strong defensive perimeter in the Caribbean, and surrounded by a series of frontier missions, extending in the north into Florida and New Mexico. The Spaniards also brought new systems of labor and new religious institutions to their overseas colonies.

The first Spanish rulers in Mexico and Peru relied on a form of labor tribute called **encomienda**. This system permitted the holder, or *encomendero,* to claim labor from an Indian district for a stated period of time. *Encomienda* worked because it resembled the way the Aztecs and the Incas had routinely levied labor for their own massive public buildings and irrigation projects. In time, the king intervened to correct abuses and to limit labor tribute to projects that the Crown initiated, such as mining. Spanish settlers resisted the reforms at first but then shifted from demanding labor to claiming land. In the countryside the *hacienda,* a large estate with its own crops and herds, became a familiar institution.

The Church became a massive presence during the 16th century, but America changed it, too. As missionaries acquired land and labor, they began to exhibit less zeal for Indian souls. The Franciscans—in Europe, the gentlest of Catholic religious orders—systematically tortured their Mayan converts whenever they caught them worshiping their old gods. To the Franciscans, the slightest lapse could signal a reversion to Satan worship, with human sacrifice a likely consequence.

Most important of all, the Spaniards brought deadly microbes with them. Smallpox, which could be fatal but which most Europeans survived in childhood, devastated the Indians, who had almost no immunity to it. When Cortés arrived in 1519, the Indian population of Mexico probably exceeded 15 million. In the 1620s, after waves of killing epidemics, it bottomed at 700,000. Peru's population plummeted from perhaps 10 million to 600,000. For the hemisphere as a whole, any given region probably lost 90 or 95 percent of its population within a century of sustained contact with Europeans. Lowland tropical areas usually suffered the heaviest casualties; in some of these places, all the Indians died.

The Spanish Crown eventually imposed administrative order on the unruly *conquistadores* and brought peace to its colonies. At the center of the imperial bureaucracy, in Seville, stood the Council of the Indies. It administered the three American viceroyalties of New Spain, Peru, and eventually New Granada. The Council of the Indies appointed the viceroys and other major officials, who ruled from the new cities that the Spaniards built with Indian labor at Havana, Mexico City, Lima, and elsewhere. Although centralized and autocratic in theory, the Spanish Empire allowed local officials a fair degree of initiative, if only because months or even years could elapse in trying to communicate across its immense distances.

BRAZIL

Portuguese Brazil was divided into 14 "captaincies," or provinces, and thus was far less centralized. After the colonists on the northeast coast turned to raising sugar in the late 16th century, Brazilian frontiersmen, or **bandeirantes**, foraged deep into the continent to enslave thousands of Indians. They even raided remote Spanish Andean missions, rounded up the converts, and dragged them thousands of miles to be worked to death on the sugar plantations. In the 17th century Africans gradually replaced Indians as the dominant labor force. Brazil was the major market for African slaves until the 1640s, when Caribbean demand became even greater.

---

encomienda *System of labor introduced into the Western Hemisphere by the Spanish that permitted the holder, or* encomendero, *to claim labor from Indians in a district for a stated period of time.*

bandeirantes *Brazilian frontiersmen who traveled deep into South America to enslave Indians. The slaves then were worked to death on the sugar plantations.*

QUICK   REVIEW

THE SPANISH CONQUESTS

- Hugely outnumbered, Cortés and Pizarro conquered the Aztecs and the Inca

- Conquistadores DeSoto and Coronado led the fruitless search for cities of gold

- Spanish missionaries in North America attempted to convert Indians

- Demographic catastrophe through disease, overwork, and war

- Emergence of a global economy sustained by unfree labor systems

GLOBAL COLOSSUS, GLOBAL ECONOMY

American silver made the king of Spain the most powerful monarch in Christendom. Philip II (1556–1598) commanded the largest army in Europe. In 1580, after the king of Portugal died with no direct heir, Philip claimed his throne, thus uniting under his own rule Portugal's Asian empire, Brazil, Spain's American possessions, and the Philippines. This colossus was the greatest empire the world had ever seen. It also sustained the first truly global economy, because the Portuguese used Spain's American silver to pay for the spices and silks they imported from Asia.

The Spanish colossus became part of an even broader economic pattern. **Serfdom**, which tied peasants to their lords and to the land, had been declining in Europe since the 12th century and was nearly gone by 1500. A system of free labor arose in its place, and overseas expansion strengthened that trend within Western Europe. Although free labor prevailed in the Western European homeland, unfree labor systems took root all around Europe's periphery, and the two were structurally linked. In general, free labor reigned where populations were dense and still growing. Large pools of labor kept wages low. But around the periphery of Western Europe, where land was cheap and labor expensive, coercive systems became the only efficient way for Europeans to extract from those areas the goods they desired.

FOCUS QUESTION

How important was the establishment of an oceanic system of commerce that linked East and South Asia with Europe and the Americas?

serfdom *Early medieval Europe's predominant labor system that tied peasants to their lords and the land. They were not slaves because they could not be sold from the land.*

Map 1.7

SPANISH EMPIRE AND GLOBAL LABOR SYSTEMS. *While Western European states were becoming free-labor societies, they created or encouraged the establishment of societies built on or providing laborers for various unfree labor systems in the Americas, the Caribbean, Africa, and Eastern Europe.*

The forms of unfree labor varied greatly across space and time. In New Spain, the practice of *encomienda* slowly yielded to debt peonage. Debts that could not be paid kept Indians tied to the **haciendas** of the countryside. The mining of precious metals, on the other hand, was so dangerous and unpleasant that it almost always required a coercive system of labor tribute that was called *mita* in the Andes. Similarly, any colonial region that devoted itself to the production of staple crops for sale in Europe also turned to unfree labor and eventually overt slavery. The production of sugar first reduced Indians to bondage in the Caribbean and Brazil and then, as they died off, led to the importation of African slaves by the millions. Tobacco, rice, cotton, and coffee followed similar patterns. At first these crops were considered luxuries and commanded high prices. But as they became widely available on the world market, their prices fell steeply, profit margins contracted, and planters turned overwhelmingly to coerced labor. Even in Eastern Europe, which began to specialize in producing cereal crops for sale in the more diversified West, serfdom vigorously revived.

Spain's rise had been spectacular, but its empire was vulnerable. The costs of continuous conflict, the inflation generated by a steady influx of silver, and the need to defend a much greater perimeter absorbed Spain's new resources and a great deal more. Between 1492 and 1580 Spain's population grew from 4.9 million to 8 million. But over the course of the following century, it fell by 20 percent, mostly because of the escalating costs, both financial and human, of Spain's wars.

haciendas *Large, landed estates established by the Spanish.*

EXPLANATIONS: PATTERNS OF CONQUEST, SUBMISSION, AND RESISTANCE

By the middle of the 18th century, conquest and settlement had killed millions of Indians, enslaved millions of Africans, and degraded Europeans. The benefits seemed small by comparison, even though economic gains were undeniably large. If the cruelest of the conquerors had been able to foresee the results of this process, asked the Abbé Raynal, would he have proceeded? "Is it to be imagined that there exists a being infernal enough to answer this question in the affirmative!" The success of the American Revolution, with its message of freedom and human rights, quieted such thinking for a time, but the critique has revived in recent years, especially in the developing world.

Modern historians are more interested in asking how and why these things happened. One major reason is geographical. The Eurasian land mass, the world's largest, follows an east-west axis that permits life forms and human inventions to travel immense distances without passing through forbidding changes of climate. Chinese inventions eventually reached Europe. By contrast, the Americas and sub-Saharan Africa lie along north-south axes that do impose such barriers. Another compelling explanation for European success focuses on the prolonged isolation of the Americas from the rest of the world. If two communities of equal ability are kept apart, the one with the larger and more varied population will invent more things and learn more rapidly over time. More than any other technological edge, far more than firearms or even horses, steel made military conquest possible. European armor stopped Indian spears and arrows, and European swords killed enemies swiftly without any need to reload.

The biological consequences of isolation were even more momentous than the technological. The Indians' genetic makeup was more uniform than that of Europeans, Africans, or Asians. Indians were descended from a rather small sample of the total gene pool of Eurasia. The Indians first encountered by Europeans were bigger, stronger, and—at first contact—healthier than the newcomers. But they died in appalling numbers because they had almost no resistance to European diseases.

European plants also thrived at the expense of native vegetation. For example, when British settlers first crossed the Appalachian Mountains, they marveled at the lush Kentucky bluegrass. They did not realize that they were looking at an accidental European import that had conquered the landscape even faster than they had. European animals also prevailed over potential American rivals. Horses multiplied at an astonishing rate in America, and wild herds moved north from Mexico faster than the Spaniards, transforming the way of life of the Apaches and the Sioux. But some life-forms also moved from the Americas to Europe, Asia, and Africa. Indians probably gave syphilis to the first Europeans they met. Other American exports, such as corn, potatoes, and tomatoes, were far more benign and have enriched the diet of the rest of the world.

C O N C L U S I O N

For thousands of years the Americas had been cut off from the rest of the world. The major cultures of Eurasia and Africa had existed in relative isolation, engaging in direct contact only with their immediate neighbors. Islam, which shared borders with India, the East Indies, black Africa, and Europe, had been the principal mediator among these cultures. Then suddenly, in just 40 years, daring European navigators joined the world together and challenged Islam's mediating role. Between 1492 and 1532 Europe, Africa, Asia, the Spice Islands, the Philippines, the Caribbean, Aztec Mexico, Inca Peru, and other parts of the Americas came into intense and often violent contact with one another. Spain acquired a military advantage within Europe that would last for a century. Nearly everybody else suffered, especially in the Americas and Africa.

Spain spent the rest of the 16th century trying to create an imperial system that could impose order on this turbulent reality. But Spain had many enemies. The lure of wealth and land overseas would be just as attractive to them.

QUESTIONS FOR REVIEW AND CRITICAL THINKING

Review

1. What enabled relatively backward European societies to establish dominance over the oceans of the world?
2. Why were the native peoples of the Americas extremely vulnerable to European diseases, instead of the other way around?
3. Why did the free-labor societies of Western Europe generate unfree labor systems all around their periphery?
4. How important was the establishment of an oceanic system of commerce that linked East and South Asia with Europe and the Americas?

Critical Thinking

1. European expansion inflicted enormous destruction upon the peoples of sub-Saharan Africa and the Americas. Is there any way that this vast projection of European power overseas also contributed to an eventual expansion of liberty?
2. Had Europeans been willing to treat Indian peoples as potential equals, would Christian missionaries have been in a stronger position to win converts?

Discovery

How did the differences between the societies in the Americas and the ones in Europe lead to conflict and ultimately devastation for the cultures of the Americas?

SUGGESTED READINGS

Two recent general surveys of early American history provide excellent coverage up to Independence: **Alan Taylor, American Colonies** (2001); and **Richard Middleton, Colonial America: A History, 1565–1776**, 3rd ed. (2002). For a useful collections of essays, see **Stanley N. Katz, John M. Murrin, and Douglas Greenberg, eds., Colonial America: Essays in Politics and Social Development,** 5th ed. (2001).

Brian M. Fagan, The Great Journey: The Peopling of Ancient America (1987) is a fine introduction to pre-Columbian America. For the age of explorations, see **G. V. Scammell, The First Imperial Age: European Overseas Expansion c. 1400–1715** (1989); and **Alfred W. Crosby's** classic synthesis, **The Columbian Exchange: Biological and Cultural Consequences of 1492** (1972). For the slave trade, see **John Thornton, Africa and Africans in the Making of the Modern World, 1400–1800,** 2nd ed. (1998), who insists that Africans retained control of their affairs, including the slave trade, through the 17th century; and **Patrick Manning, Slavery and African Life: Occidental, Oriental, and African Slave Trades** (1990), who emphasizes the devastating impact of the slave trade in the 18th and 19th centuries. **Ira Berlin's Many Thousands Gone: The First Two Centuries of Slavery in North America** (1998) is an effective and comprehensive synthesis of a huge subject.

James Lockhart and **Stuart B. Schwartz, Early Latin America: A History of Colonial Latin America and Brazil** (1983) is an outstanding introduction to the Iberian empires. J. H. Parry's **The Spanish Seaborne Empire** (1966) retains great value. **David J. Weber's The Spanish Frontier in North America** (1992) is easily the best introduction to its subject.

ONLINE SOURCES GUIDE

ThomsonNOW Visit ThomsonNOW to access primary sources, exercises, quizzes, and audio chapter summaries related to this chapter:

http://www.thomsonedu.com/login

DISCOVERY

How did the differences between the societies in the Americas and the ones in Europe lead to conflict and ultimately devastation for the cultures of the Americas?

In thinking about this question, begin by breaking it down into the components shown below. A discussion of the significance of each component should appear in your answer.

GEOGRAPHY

Look at the map "Mound-Building Cultures of North America." Note the expanse of territory covered by these communities—from the Appalachians to the Rockies and the Great Lakes to the Gulf of Mexico. Based on the geographic evidence, would you characterize these Native American societies as unified or separate? How did their patterns of settlement contribute to the eventual and quick conquest of these Native American societies by Europeans?

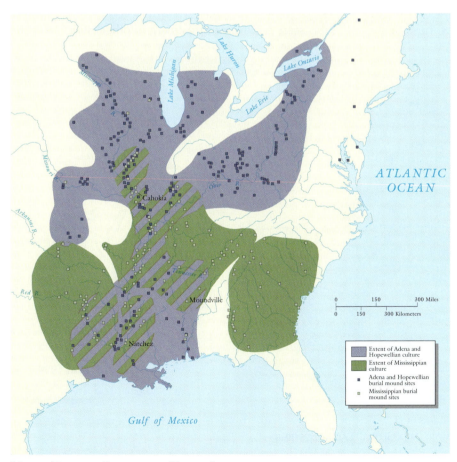

MOUND-BUILDING CULTURES OF NORTH AMERICA

RELIGION AND PHILOSOPHY

Imagine what you might think if you traveled to a distant place and discovered a sacrificial site such as the "Aztec Skull Rack Altar." Considering your own thoughts as well as the section on "Religious Dilemmas," explain how religious differences led to cultural misunderstandings and even to war. Give specific examples.

Moctezuma's Mexico, by David Carrasco and Eduardo Mato Moctezuma, ©1992 University Press of Colorado. Photographs by Salvador Guil'liem Arroyo.

AZTEC SKULL RACK ALTAR

GOVERNMENT AND LAW

Look at the map "Spanish Empire and Global Labor Systems" and the section on "Global Colossus, Global Economy." Why did the European nations that were becoming free-labor societies generate unfree labor systems all around their periphery? How did the European view of Native American civilization affect their treatment of those people? Was this seen in European treatment of other civilizations around the world?

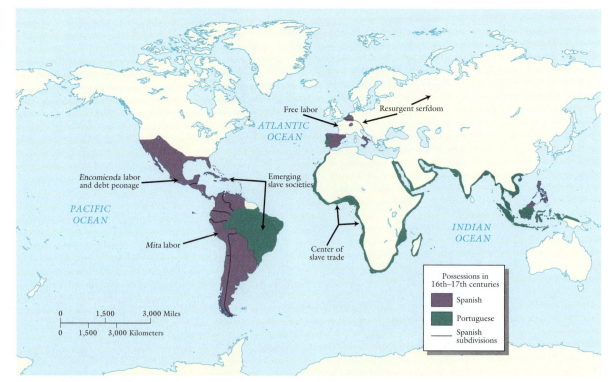

SPANISH EMPIRE AND GLOBAL LABOR SYSTEMS

2

THE CHALLENGE TO SPAIN AND THE SETTLEMENT OF NORTH AMERICA

atholic France and two Protestant countries, the Dutch Republic and England, challenged Spanish power in Europe and overseas. None of them planted a permanent settlement in North America before 1600. In the quarter century after 1600, they all did. Europeans, Indians, and Africans interacted in contrasting ways in "this strange new world." In Mexico and Peru, the Spaniards had set themselves up as a ruling class. Spain's rivals created colonies of different kinds. Some, such as Virginia and Barbados, grew staple crops with indentured servants and African slaves. New France and New Netherland developed a prosperous trade with the Indians without trying to govern them. In New England, the Puritans relied on free labor provided by hardworking family members. After 1660 the English state conquered New Netherland, and English Quakers created another free-labor society in the Delaware valley.

1500	1600	1610	1620	1630	1640	1650	1660	1670	1680	1690	1700	1710

■ **1517**
Luther begins Protestant Reformation

■ **1607**
English settlement at Jamestown begins

■ **1608**
Champlain founds Quebec

■ **1613–1614**
Rolfe grows tobacco, marries Pocohontas

■ **1619**
First Africans arrive in Virginia; House of Burgesses and headright system created

■ **1620**
Pilgrims adopt Mayflower Compact, settle at Plymouth

■ **1626**
Minuit founds New Amsterdam

■ **1630**
Puritan "great migration" to New England begins

■ **1664**
English conquer New Netherland

1670 ■
First permanent English settlements in South Carolina

■ **1681**
Penn receives charter for Pennsylvania

1683 ■
Pennsylvania and New York adopt Charters of Liberty

1705 ■
Virginia adopts comprehensive slave code

THE PROTESTANT REFORMATION AND THE CHALLENGE TO SPAIN

Protestant Reformation
Religious movement begun by Martin Luther in 1517 that led to the repudiation of the Roman Catholic Church in large parts of northern and central Europe.

Anglican *Member of the legally established Church of England, or that church itself.*

By the time Spain's enemies felt strong enough to challenge Spain overseas, the **Protestant Reformation** had shattered the religious unity of Europe. In November 1517, not long before Cortés landed at Vera Cruz, Martin Luther nailed his 95 Theses to the cathedral door at Wittenberg in the German electorate of Saxony and touched off the Reformation. Salvation comes through faith alone, he insisted, and God grants saving faith only to those who hear his Word preached to them and realize that, without God's grace, they are damned. Within a generation, the states of northern Germany and Scandinavia had embraced Lutheranism.

John Calvin, a French Protestant who took control of the Swiss city of Geneva, also embraced justification by faith. The Huguenot movement in France, the Dutch Reformed Church in the Netherlands, and the Presbyterian Kirk (or Church) of Scotland all embraced Calvin's principles. In England the **Anglican** Church adopted Calvinist doctrines but kept much Catholic liturgy, a compromise that prompted the

Puritan reform movement toward a more thoroughly Calvinist Church of England. After 1620 **Puritans** carried their religious vision across the Atlantic to New England.

Calvinists rejected the pope, all Catholic sacraments except baptism and the Lord's Supper, and the pious rituals by which Catholics strove to earn salvation. Calvin gave central importance to **predestination**. According to that doctrine, God has already decreed who will be saved and who will be damned. Christ died not for all humankind, but only for God's elect. Because salvation and damnation were beyond human power to alter, Calvinists, especially English Puritans, felt a compelling inner need to find out whether they were saved. They struggled to recognize in themselves a conversion experience, the process by which God's elect discovered that they had received divine grace.

France, the Netherlands, and England, all with powerful Protestant movements, challenged Spanish power in Europe. Until 1559 France was the main threat, with Italy as the battleground, but Spain won that phase. In the 1560s, with France embroiled in its own Wars of Religion, a new challenge came from the 17 provinces of the Netherlands, which Spain ruled. The Dutch rebelled against the heavy taxes and severe Catholic orthodoxy imposed by Philip II. As Spanish armies put down the rebellion in the 10 southern provinces (modern Belgium), merchants and Protestants fled north. Many went to Amsterdam, which replaced Spanish-controlled Antwerp as the economic center of northern Europe. The seven northern provinces gradually took shape as the Dutch Republic, or the United Provinces of the Netherlands. The conflict lasted 80 years, spread to Asia, Africa, and the Americas, and drained Spanish strength.

Puritans *English religious group that followed the teachings of John Calvin and wanted to purify the Church of England of its surviving Catholic ceremonies and vestments.*

predestination *Theory that God had decreed, even before he created the world, who would be saved and who would be damned.*

NEW FRANCE

In 1500 France had three times the population of Spain. The French made a few stabs at overseas expansion before 1600, but with little success.

EARLY FRENCH EXPLORERS

In 1524 King Francis I sent Giovanni da Verrazano, an Italian, to America in search of a northwest passage to Asia. Verrazano explored the North American coast from the Carolinas to Nova Scotia and noted Manhattan's superb potential as a harbor but found no passage to Asia. Between 1534 and 1543, Jacques Cartier made three voyages to North America. He explored the St. Lawrence Valley without finding any fabulous wealth. Severe Canadian winters made him give up. For the rest of the century, the French ignored Canada, except for some fur traders and numerous fishermen who sailed to the lower St. Lawrence valley or Newfoundland each year. By the 1580s the fisheries rivaled New Spain in the volume of shipping they employed.

After 1550 the French turned to warmer climates. **Huguenots** sacked Havana, prompting Spain to turn it into a fortified, year-round naval base, commanded by Admiral Pedro Menéndez de Avilés. Other Huguenots settled on the Atlantic coast of Florida. Menéndez attacked them in 1565, talked them into surrendering, and then executed every adult male who refused to accept the Catholic faith.

France's Wars of Religion blocked further efforts at expansion for the rest of the century. King Henry IV (1589–1610), a Protestant, converted to Catholicism and then restored peace. He granted limited toleration to Huguenots through the Edict of Nantes in 1598. Henry was a *politique*; he insisted that the survival of the state take precedence over religious differences and that survival required toleration. Another *politique* was the Catholic soldier and explorer, Samuel de Champlain.

Huguenots *French Protestants who followed the beliefs of John Calvin.*

politique *One who believed that the survival of the state took precedence over religious differences.*

HISTORY THROUGH FILM

BLACK ROBE (1991)

*Directed by Bruce Beresford; starring
Lothaire Bluteau (Father Laforgue),
Aden Young (Daniel), Jean Brusseau
(Samuel de Champlain), and
Sandrine Holt (Annuka)*

In *Black Robe* director Bruce Beresford has given us the most believable film portrayal of 17th-century North America—both the landscape and its peoples—yet produced. This Canada-Australia co-production won six Genie Awards (Canada's equivalent of the Oscar), including best picture, best director, and best cinematography.

The film is based on Brian Moore's novel of the same title, and Moore wrote the screenplay. It was filmed on location amidst the spectacular scenery in the Lac St. Jean/Saguenay region of Quebec.

In New France in the 1630s Father Laforgue (Lothaire Bluteau), a young Jesuit, and Daniel (Aden Young), his teenaged assistant and translator, leave on Laforgue's first mission assignment. Samuel de Champlain (Jean Brusseau), the governor of the colony, has persuaded the Algonquin tribe to convey the two to their mission site among the Hurons, far in the interior. Before long Daniel falls in love with An-

Black Robe, *based on Brian Moore's novel of the same title, is set in 17th-century North America.*

nuka (Sandrine Holt), the beautiful daughter of Algonquin chief Chomina (August Schellenberg). When the priest inadvertently watches the young couple making love, he knows that, according to his faith, he has committed a mortal sin. From that point his journey into the North American heartland threatens to become a descent into hell.

The Algonquins, guided by a dream quest, pursue a logic that makes no sense to the priest. Conversely, his religious message baffles them. Even so, when Chomina is wounded and Laforgue and Daniel are captured by the Iroquois, Annuka seduces their lone guard, kills him, and enables all four of them to escape. Chomina dies of his wounds, politely but firmly rejecting baptism until the end. What Indian, he asks, would want to go to the Christian heaven, populated by many black robes but none of his ancestors?

With the priest's approval, Daniel and Annuka go off by themselves. Laforgue reaches the mission, only to find many of the Indians dead or dying from some European disease. As the film closes, we learn that smallpox would devastate the mission in the following decade, and the Jesuits would abandon it in 1649.

Brian Moore's realism romanticizes nobody but treats both the Jesuits and the Algonquins with great respect. The screenplay drew criticism for its harsh depiction of the Iroquois, but it portrayed them through the eyes of the people they planned to torture. A smaller criticism is that Laforgue is the lone priest on the journey during which he commits the sin of watching Daniel and Annuka make love. Jesuits, however, traveled in pairs precisely so that they would always be accompanied by someone who could hear their confessions. Bruce Beresford, an Australian, directed *Breaker Morant* (1979), a highly acclaimed film set in the Boer War a century ago, and also *Driving Miss Daisy* (1989).

Kobal Collection/Alliance/Goldwyn

MISSIONS AND FURS

Champlain believed that Catholics and Huguenots could work together, Europeanize the Indians, convert them, and even marry them. Before his death in 1635, he made 11 voyages to Canada. During his second trip (1604–1606), he planted a predominantly Huguenot settlement in Acadia (Nova Scotia). In 1608 he sailed up the St. Lawrence River, established friendly relations with the Indians, and founded Quebec. Many Frenchmen cohabited with Indian women, but only 15 formal marriages took place between them in the 17th century. Champlain's friendly policy toward these Indians also drew him into their wars with the Iroquois Five Nations. Iroquois hostility almost destroyed New France.

Champlain failed to unite Catholics and Protestants in mutual harmony. Huguenots in France were eager to trade with Canada, but few settled there. Their ministers showed no interest in converting the Indians, whereas Catholic priests became zealous missionaries. In 1625 the French Crown declared that only the Catholic faith could be practiced in New France, thus ending Champlain's dream of a colony more tolerant than France. Acadia soon went Catholic as well.

Early New France became a tale of missionaries and furs, of attempts to convert the Indians and of efforts to trade with them. The carousing habits of the first **coureurs de bois** (roamers of the woods) did much for the fur trade but made life difficult for the missionaries.

After 1630 Jesuit missionaries made heroic efforts to bring Christ to the Indians. Uncompromising in their opposition to Protestants, Jesuits proved remarkably flexible in dealing with non-Christian peoples from China to North America. Other mis-

FOCUS QUESTION

Why did the number of Indians who chose to become Catholics far exceed the number that accepted Protestantism?

coureur de bois *French phrase interpreted as "a roamer of the woods," referring to French colonists who participated in the fur trade with the Indians and lived part of the year with them.*

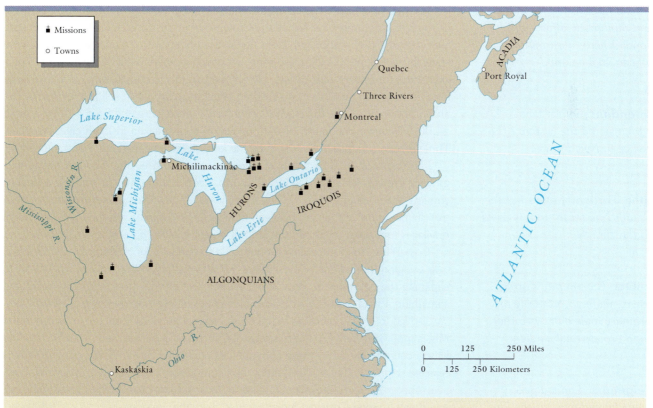

Map 2.1

NEW FRANCE AND THE JESUIT MISSIONS. *The Jesuits established Indian missions near Montreal and far into the interior of North America, most of them well beyond the range of French military aid in any emergency.*

sionaries insisted that Indians must be Europeanized before they could be converted, but the Jesuits disagreed. They saw nothing contradictory about a nation of Christians that retained many of its Indian customs.

The Jesuits converted 10,000 Indians in 40 years. They concentrated upon the five confederated Huron nations and baptized several thousand of their members. They mastered Indian languages, lived in Indian villages, and accepted most Indian customs, but their successes antagonized Indians who were still attached to their own rituals. When smallpox devastated the Hurons in the 1640s, Jesuits baptized hundreds of dying victims to ensure their salvation. Many of the Indian survivors noticed that death usually followed this mysterious rite. Suspecting witchcraft, they resisted more fiercely. In a second disaster, the Iroquois attacked, defeated, and scattered the Hurons. Despite these setbacks, the Jesuits' courage remained strong. They were the only Europeans who measured up to Indian standards of bravery, some enduring cruel deaths under torture. Even so, their efforts slowly lost ground to the fur trade, especially after the Crown assumed control of New France in 1663.

New France Under Louis XIV

Royal intervention transformed Canada after 1663 when Louis XIV and his minister, Jean-Baptiste Colbert, took charge of the colony and tried to turn it into a model absolutist society—peaceful, orderly, deferential. Government was in the hands of two appointive officials, a **governor-general** responsible for military and diplomatic affairs, and an *intendant* who administered affordable justice, partly by abolishing lawyers. The people paid few taxes, and the church **tithe** was set at half its rate in France.

The governor appointed all **militia** officers and granted promotion through merit, not by selling commissions. When the Crown sent professional soldiers to New France after 1660, the governor put them under the command of Canadian officers, who knew the woodlands. Colbert also sent 774 young women to the St. Lawrence, to provide brides for settlers and soldiers. He offered bonuses to couples who produced large families and fined fathers whose children failed to marry while still in their teens. Between 1663 and 1700, the population of New France increased from 3,000 to about 14,000. Roughly one-fourth of the population concentrated in three cities: Quebec, Three Rivers, and Montreal. Montreal, the largest, became the center of the fur trade.

Farming took hold in the St. Lawrence valley, and by the 1690s Canada was growing enough wheat to feed itself and to give its *habitants,* or settlers, a level of comfort about equal to that of New Englanders. A new class of *seigneurs*, or gentry, claimed most of the land between Quebec and Montreal, but they had few feudal privileges and never exercised the kind of power wielded by aristocrats in France.

Colbert also tried to confine the fur trade to annual fairs at Montreal and Quebec, thus bringing the Indians to the settlers, not the settlers to the Indians. This effort to eliminate the *coureurs de bois* failed, although a stint in the forests was becoming something a man did once or twice in his youth before settling down. Colbert's policy also led to a quiet rebellion in the West. Several hundred Frenchmen settled in the Mississippi valley between the missions of Cahokia and Kaskaskia in what became the Illinois country. By 1750 these communities contained 3,000 residents. The settlers rejected *seigneurs,* feudal dues, tithes, and compulsory militia service. They did, however, import African slaves from Louisiana. Most settlers prospered as wheat farmers, and many married Christian Indian women from the missions.

Like other Europeans, most of the French who crossed the Atlantic preferred the warmer climes of the Caribbean. At first the French in the West Indies joined with other enemies of Spain to prey as buccaneers upon Spanish colonies and ships.

governor-general *French official responsible for military and diplomatic affairs and for appointment of all militia officers in a colony.*

intendant *Officer who administered the system of justice in New France.*

tithe *Portion of one's income, usually one tenth, that is owed to the church.*

militia *Community's armed force, made up primarily of ordinary male citizens rather than professional soldiers.*

seigneurs *Landed gentry who claimed most of the land between Quebec and Montreal but were never as powerful as aristocrats in France.*

Then they transformed the island colonies of Saint-Domingue (modern Haiti), Guadeloupe, and Martinique into centers of sugar and coffee production, where a small planter class prospered from the labor of thousands of slaves. The sugar islands were worth far more than Canada. After 1750, Saint-Domingue became the world's richest colony.

THE DUTCH AND SWEDISH SETTLEMENTS

For most of the 17th century, the Dutch were more active overseas than the French. The Dutch republic, whose 2 million people inhabited the most densely populated part of Europe, moved ahead of all rivals in finance, shipping, and trade. In contrast to Spain, which stood for Catholic orthodoxy and the centralizing tendencies of Europe's "new monarchies," Dutch republicanism emphasized local liberties, prosperity, and, in major centers such as Amsterdam, religious toleration. Political power was decentralized to the cities, and their wealthy merchants, who favored informal toleration, tried to keep trade as free as possible and resisted the monarchical ambitions of the House of Orange. The prince of Orange usually served as *stadholder* (captain general) of Holland, the richest province, commanded its armies, and often those of several other provinces.

The Dutch Republic—with Protestant dissenters from many countries, a sizable Jewish community, and a large Catholic minority—was actually a polyglot confederation. Amsterdam's merchant republicanism competed with the Dutch Reformed Church for the allegiance of the people. Only during a military crisis could the prince of Orange mobilize the Dutch Reformed clergy and impose something like Calvinist orthodoxy, even on the cities. The **States General**, to which each province sent representatives, became a weak central government for the republic. The broader public did not vote or participate actively in public life. This tension between tolerant merchant republicanism and Calvinist orthodoxy carried over into New Netherland.

By 1620 Dutch foreign trade probably exceeded that of the rest of Europe combined. Even during the long war with Spain, the Dutch traded with Lisbon and Seville for products from the East Indies and America. This effrontery so annoyed Philip II that he twice committed a grave blunder in the 1590s, when he confiscated all the Dutch ships crowding his ports. The Dutch retaliated by sailing into the Atlantic and Indian Oceans to acquire colonial goods at the source. Spanish power finally crumbled as the cost of protecting its colonies exhausted the kingdom's resources.

THE EAST AND WEST INDIA COMPANIES

In 1602 the States General chartered the Dutch East India Company, which pressed Spain where it was weakest, in the Portuguese East Indies. Elbowing the Portuguese out of the Spice Islands and even out of Nagasaki in Japan, the Dutch set up their own capital at Batavia (now Jakarta) on the island of Java.

The Atlantic and North America also attracted the Dutch. In 1609, during a 12-year truce between Spain and the Netherlands, Henry Hudson, an Englishman in Dutch service, sailed up what the Dutch called the North River (the English later renamed it the Hudson) and claimed the whole area for the Netherlands. In 1614 some Lutheran refugees from Amsterdam built a fort near modern Albany to trade with the Mahicans and Iroquois for furs, but they did not settle permanently.

States General *Legislative assembly of the Netherlands.*

In 1621 the States General chartered the Dutch West India Company and gave it jurisdiction over the African slave trade, Brazil, the Caribbean, and North America. The company harbored strong Orangist sympathies and even Calvinist fervor, sustained by refugees fleeing from the Spanish army. It captured Portugal's slave-trading posts in West Africa and for a while even dominated Angola. It also occupied the richest sugar-producing region of Brazil until the Portuguese took it and Angola back in the 1640s.

In North America the Dutch claimed the Delaware, Hudson, and Connecticut River valleys. The company put most of its effort into the Hudson valley. The first permanent settlers arrived in 1624. Two years later, Deacon Pierre Minuit, leading 30 Walloon (French-speaking) Protestant refugee families, bought Manhattan Island from the Indians and founded the port of New Amsterdam. The Dutch established Fort Orange (modern Albany) 150 miles upriver for trade with the Iroquois. Much like New France, New Netherland depended on the goodwill of nearby Indians, and the fur trade gave the colony a similar urban flavor. But unlike New France, few Dutchmen ventured into the deep woods. There were no *coureurs de bois* and no missionaries. The Indians brought their furs to Fort Orange and exchanged them for firearms and other goods that the Dutch sold more cheaply than anyone else.

New Netherland also resembled New France in other ways. In the 1630s, before the French created *seigneuries* along the St. Lawrence, the Dutch established **patroonships,** vast estates under a single landlord, mostly along the Hudson. But the system never thrived. The one exception was Rensselaerswyck, a gigantic estate on both banks of the Hudson above and below Fort Orange, that exported wheat and flour down the river and to the Caribbean.

NEW NETHERLAND AS A PLURALISTIC SOCIETY

New Netherland became North America's first experiment in ethnic and religious pluralism. The Dutch themselves were a mixed people with a Flemish (Dutch-speaking) majority and a Walloon minority. Both came to the colony. So did Danes, Norwegians, Swedes, Finns, Germans, and Scots. The colony's government tried to use this diversity by drawing upon two conflicting precedents from the Netherlands. On the one hand, it appealed to religious refugees by emphasizing the company's Protestant role in the struggle against Spain. This policy reflected the Orangist position in the Netherlands. On the other hand, the West India Company sometimes recognized that acceptance of religious diversity might stimulate trade. The pursuit of profits through informal toleration imitated Amsterdam's role in Dutch politics. Minuit and Governor Pieter Stuyvesant embraced the religious formula for unity. They resisted toleration even for the benefit of commerce.

After Minuit returned to Europe in 1631, the emphasis shifted rapidly from piety to trade. The Dutch sold muskets to the Iroquois to expand their own access to the fur trade and exported grain to the Caribbean. In 1643, however, Willem Kieft, a stubborn and quarrelsome governor, slaughtered a tribe of Indian refugees to whom he had granted asylum from other Indians. This Pavonia Massacre, which took place across the Hudson from Manhattan, set off a war with nearby Algonquian nations that almost destroyed New Netherland. By the time Stuyvesant replaced Kieft in 1647, the colony's population had fallen to about 700 people. An autocrat, Stuyvesant made peace and then strengthened town governments and the Dutch Reformed Church. During his administration, the population rose to more than 6,000. Most newcomers arrived as members of healthy families who reproduced rapidly, enabling the population to double every 25 years.

patroonships *Vast estates along the Hudson River established by the Dutch. They had difficulty attracting peasant labor, and most were not successful.*

SWEDISH AND ENGLISH ENCROACHMENTS

Minuit, back in Europe, organized another refugee project, this one for Flemings who had been uprooted by the Spanish war. When Dutch authorities refused to back him, he turned for support to the Lutheran kingdom of Sweden. Financed by private Dutch capital, he returned to America in 1638 with Flemish and Swedish settlers to found New Sweden, with its capital at Fort Christina (modern Wilmington) near the mouth of the Delaware River, on land claimed by New Netherland. After Minuit died on his return trip to Europe, the colony became less Flemish and Calvinist and more Swedish and Lutheran, at a time when Stuyvesant was trying to make New Netherland an orthodox Calvinist society. In 1654 the Swedes seized Fort Casimir, a Dutch post that provided access to the Delaware. In response, Stuyvesant took over all of New Sweden the next year, and Amsterdam sent over settlers to guarantee Dutch control. Stuyvesant persecuted Lutherans (along with Jews and **Quakers**) in New Amsterdam but had to tolerate them in the Delaware valley settlements. Orthodoxy and harmony were not easily reconciled.

The English, already entrenched in Virginia and New England, threatened to overwhelm the Dutch as they moved from New England onto Long Island and into what is now Westchester County, New York. Kieft welcomed them in the 1640s and gave them local privileges greater than those enjoyed by the Dutch. Stuyvesant regarded these **Yankees** (a Dutch word that probably meant "land pirates") as good Calvinists, English-speaking equivalents of his Dutch Reformed settlers. They agitated for a more active role in government, but their loyalty was questionable. If England attacked the colony, would these Puritans side with their Dutch Calvinist neighbors or the Anglican invaders? Stuyvesant would learn the unpleasant answer when England attacked him in 1664.

Quakers *Term of derision used by opponents to describe members of the Society of Friends, who believed that God, in the form of the Inner Light, was present in all humans. Friends were pacifists who rejected oaths, sacraments, and all set forms of religious worship.*

Yankee *Dutch word for New Englanders that originally meant something like "land pirate."*

THE CHALLENGE FROM ELIZABETHAN ENGLAND

England's interest in America emerged slowly. In 1497 Henry VII (1485–1509) sent Giovanni Cabato (John Cabot), an Italian mariner who had moved to Bristol, to search for a northwest passage to Asia. Cabot probably reached Newfoundland, which he took to be part of Asia. He sailed again in 1498 with five ships but was lost at sea. Only one vessel returned, but Cabot's voyages gave England a vague claim to portions of the North American coast.

THE ENGLISH REFORMATION

When interest in America revived during the reign of Elizabeth I (1558–1603), England was rapidly becoming a Protestant kingdom. Elizabeth's father, Henry VIII (1509–1547), desperate for a male heir, had broken with the pope to divorce his queen. He remarried, proclaimed himself the "Only Supreme Head" of the Church of England, confiscated monastic lands, and inadvertently opened the way for committed Protestant reformers. Under Elizabeth's younger brother Edward VI (1547–1553), the government embraced Protestantism. When Edward died, Elizabeth's older sister Mary I (1553–1558) reimposed Catholicism, burned hundreds of Protestants at the stake, and drove thousands into exile, where many of them became Calvinists. Elizabeth, however, accepted Protestantism, and the exiles returned. The Church of England became Calvinist in doctrine and theology but remained largely Catholic in structure, liturgy, and ritual.

Some Protestants demanded the eradication of Catholic vestiges and the replacement of the Anglican *Book of Common Prayer* with sermons and psalms as the dominant mode of worship. These "Puritans" played a major role in England's overseas expansion. More extreme Protestants, called **Separatists**, denied that the Church of England was a true church and began to set up independent congregations of their own. Some of them would found the small colony of **Plymouth**.

HAWKINS AND DRAKE

In 1560 England was a rather backward country of 3 million people. Its chief export was woolen cloth. During the 16th century the numbers of both people and sheep grew rapidly, and they sometimes competed for the same land. When farms were enclosed for sheep pasture, laborers were set adrift, and thousands headed for London, which became the largest city in western Europe by 1700. After 1600 internal migration fueled overseas settlement. But before then, interest in America centered not in London but in the southwestern ports already involved in the Newfoundland fishery.

Taking advantage of friendly relations that still prevailed between England and Spain, John Hawkins of Plymouth made three voyages to New Spain between 1562 and 1569. On his first trip he bought slaves from the Portuguese in West Africa and sold them to the Spaniards in Hispaniola, where, by paying all legal duties, he tried to set himself up as a legitimate trader. Spanish authorities disapproved, and on his second voyage he had to trade at gunpoint. On his third trip, the Spanish viceroy sank four of his six ships. Hawkins and his young kinsman Francis Drake escaped, both vowing vengeance.

Drake even began to talk of freeing slaves from Spanish tyranny. His most dramatic exploit came between 1577 and 1580 when he rounded Cape Horn and plundered Spanish possessions along the undefended Pacific coast of Peru. Knowing that the Spaniards would be waiting for him if he returned by the same route, he sailed north, explored San Francisco Bay, and continued west around the world to England. Elizabeth rewarded him with a knighthood.

GILBERT, IRELAND, AND AMERICA

By the 1560s the idea of permanent colonization intrigued several Englishmen. England had a model close at hand in Ireland, which the English Crown had claimed for centuries. After 1560 the English tried to impose their agriculture, language, local government, legal system, aristocracy, and Protestant religion upon the Irish. The Irish responded by becoming more fiercely Catholic.

The English formed their preconceptions about American Indians largely from contact with the Irish who, claimed one Elizabethan, "live like beasts, void of law and all good order." The English tried to conquer Ulster by driving out the Catholics and replacing them with Protestants. In Munster they ejected the Catholic leaders and tried to force the remaining Catholic Irish to become tenants under Protestant landlords. Terror became an acceptable tactic, as when the English slaughtered 200 Irish at a Christmas feast in 1574.

Sir Humphrey Gilbert, a well-educated humanist, was one of the most brutal of Elizabeth's captains in the Irish wars of the 1560s. In subduing Munster in 1569,

Separatists *One of the most extreme English Protestant groups that followed the teachings of John Calvin. They began to separate from the Church of England and form their own congregations.*

Plymouth *England's first permanent colony in New England founded by Separatists in 1620.*

Gilbert killed nearly everyone in his path and destroyed all the crops, a strategy that the English later employed against Indians. Fresh from his Irish exploits, Gilbert began to think about colonizing America. He proposed that England grab control of the Newfoundland fisheries, a nursery of seamen and naval power. He urged the founding of settlements that could become bases for plundering New Spain. He obtained a royal patent in 1578 and sent out a fleet, but his ships got into a fight somewhere short of America and limped back to England. He tried again in 1583. This time his fleet sailed north to claim Newfoundland. The crews of 22 Spanish and Portuguese fishing vessels and 18 French and English ships listened in astonishment as he read his royal patent to them, divided up the land among them, assigned them rents, and established the Church of England among this mostly Catholic group. He then sailed away to explore more of the American coast. His own ship went under during a storm.

RALEGH, ROANOKE, AND WAR WITH SPAIN

Gilbert's half-brother, **Sir Walter Ralegh** (or Raleigh), obtained his own patent from the queen and tried twice to plant a colony in North America. In 1585 he sent a large expedition to Roanoke Island in Pamlico Sound, but the settlers planted no crops and exasperated the Indians with demands for food during a time of drought. In June 1586 the English killed the local chief, Wingina, whose main offense was apparently a threat to resettle his people on the mainland and leave the colonists to starve—or work. Days later, when the expected supply vessels failed to arrive on schedule, the colonists sailed back to England on the ships of Sir Francis Drake, who had just burned the Spanish city of St. Augustine with the support of Florida Indians, whom he emancipated. The supply ships reached Roanoke a little later, only to find the site abandoned. They left a small garrison there and sailed off in quest of Spanish plunder. The garrison was never heard from again.

Ralegh sent a second expedition to Roanoke in 1587, one that included some women, a sign that he envisioned a permanent colony. When Governor John White went back to England for more supplies, his return to Roanoke was delayed by the assault of the Spanish Armada on England in 1588. By the time he got back to Roanoke in 1590, the settlers had vanished, leaving a cryptic message—"CROATOAN"—carved on a tree. The colonists may have settled among the Chesapeake nation of Indians near the entrance to Chesapeake Bay. Sketchy evidence suggests that the Powhatans, the most powerful Indians in the area, wiped out the Chesapeakes, along with any English living with them, in the spring of 1607, just as the first **Jamestown** settlers were sailing into the bay.

The Spanish armada touched off a war that lasted until 1604 and strained the resources of both England and Spain. By 1600 Richard Hakluyt the elder and his cousin Richard Hakluyt the younger were publishing accounts of English exploits overseas. They celebrated the deeds of Hawkins, Drake, Gilbert, and Ralegh, who were all West Country men with large ambitions and limited financial resources. Although their plundering exploits continued to pay, they could not afford to sustain a colony like Roanoke until it could return a profit. But beginning in the 1590s, London became intensely involved in American affairs by launching privateering fleets against Spain. The city's growing involvement with Atlantic privateering marked a significant shift. The marriage of London capital and West Country experience would make permanent colonization possible.

Sir Walter Raleigh *Elizabethan courtier who, in the 1580s, tried but failed to establish an English colony on Roanoke Island in what is now North Carolina.*

Jamestown *First permanent English settlement in North America (1607) and the capital of Virginia for most of the 17th century.*

THE PATTERN OF SETTLEMENT IN THE ENGLISH COLONIES UP TO 1700

| REGION | WHO CAME (IN THOUSANDS) | | POPULATION IN 1700 (IN THOUSANDS) | |
	EUROPEANS	AFRICANS	EUROPEANS	AFRICANS
West Indies	220 (29.6%)	316 (42.5%)	33 (8.3%)	115 (28.8%)
South	135 (18.1%)	30 (4.0%)	82 (20.5%)	22 (5.5%)
Mid-Atlantic	20 (2.7%)	2 (0.3%)	51 (12.8%)	3 (0.8%)
New England	20 (2.7%)	1 (0.1%)	91 (22.8%)	2 (0.5%)
Total	395 (53.1%)	349 (46.9%)	257 (64.4%)	142 (35.6%)

THE SWARMING OF THE ENGLISH

FOCUS QUESTION

Why did the English, crossing the Atlantic at nearly the same time, create such radically different societies in the Chesapeake, the West Indies, and New England?

In the 17th century, more than 700,000 people sailed from Europe or Africa to the English colonies in North America and the Caribbean. Most of the European migrants were single young men who arrived as servants. At first even some of the Africans were regarded as servants rather than slaves.

The Europeans who settled in New England or the Hudson and Delaware valleys were the most fortunate. Because Puritans and Quakers migrated as families into healthy regions, their population expanded at a rate far beyond anything known in Europe. The descendants of this small, idealistic minority soon became a substantial part of the total population and played a role in American history far out of proportion to their original numbers. As the accompanying table shows, the New England and Middle Atlantic colonies together attracted only 5.8 percent of the immigrants, but by 1700 they contained 37 percent of all the people in the English colonies and 55 percent of the Europeans.

THE CHESAPEAKE AND WEST INDIAN COLONIES

fall line *Geographical landmark defined by the first waterfalls encountered when going up river from the sea. These waterfalls prevented oceangoing ships from sailing further inland, making the fall line a significant early barrier. Land between the falls and the ocean was called the tidewater. Land above the falls but below the mountains was called the piedmont.*

In 1606 King James I of England (1603–1625) chartered the Virginia Company with authority to colonize North America between the 34th and 45th parallels. The company had two headquarters. One, in the English city of Plymouth, received jurisdiction over the northern portion of the grant. Known as the Plymouth Company, it carried on the West Country expansionist traditions of Gilbert and Ralegh. In 1607 it planted a colony at Sagadahoc on the coast of Maine. But when the Abenaki Indians refused to trade with them, they abandoned the site in September 1608. The Plymouth Company ran out of money and gave up.

The other branch, which had its offices in London, decided to colonize the Chesapeake Bay area. In 1607 the London Company sent out three ships carrying 104 settlers. They landed at a defensible peninsula on what they called the James River, built a fort and other crude buildings, and named the place Jamestown. The investors hoped to find gold or silver, a northwest passage to Asia, a cure for syphillis, or other valuable products for sale in Europe. The settlers expected to get local Indians to work for them. If the Indians proved hostile, the settlers were told to form alliances with more distant Indians and subdue those who resisted. Company officials did not realize that a war chief named Powhatan ruled virtually all of the Indians below the **fall line**, the first waterfall on the river.

THE JAMESTOWN DISASTER

The colony was a deathtrap. Every summer the river became contaminated around Jamestown and sent out killing waves of dysentery and typhoid fever. Before long malaria also set in. Only 38 of the original 104 settlers survived the first year. Of the 325 who came before 1609, fewer than 100 remained alive in the spring of that year.

The survivors owed their good fortune to the resourcefulness of **Captain John Smith**, a soldier and adventurer who took charge. When his explorations uncovered no obvious source of wealth or any quick route across the continent to Asia, he concentrated instead on sheer survival. He tried to awe Powhatan, maintain friendly relations with him, and buy corn. Through the help of Pocahontas, Powhatan's 12-year-old daughter, he avoided war. Though Smith gave conflicting versions of the story later on, he clearly believed that Pocahontas saved his life in December 1607. But food remained scarce. The colony had too many gentlemen and specialized craftsmen who considered farming beneath their dignity. Over their protests, Smith set them to work for four hours a day raising grain.

In 1609 the London Company sent out 600 more settlers under Lieutenant Governor Thomas Gates, but his ship ran aground on Bermuda, and the crew spent a year building another vessel. About 400 new settlers reached Virginia before Gates arrived. Smith, after suffering a severe injury in an explosion, was shipped back to England, and the colony lacked firm leadership for the next year. Wearying Powhatan with their endless demands for corn at a time of severe drought, the settlers provoked the Indian war that Smith had avoided, and they nearly starved during the winter of 1610. Some escaped to the Indians, but those who were caught in that attempt were executed.

When Gates finally reached Jamestown with 175 colonists in June 1610, he found only 60 settlers alive. He packed everyone aboard ship and started down river. Virginia was going the way of Roanoke and Sagadahoc, despite its greater resources. Instead, the small fleet came abreast of the new governor, Thomas West, baron de la Warr, sailing up the James with 300 new colonists. They all went back to Jamestown, and the colony survived. De la Warr and Gates found themselves in the middle of the colony's first Indian war, which lasted from 1609 to 1614. Powhatan's warriors picked off any settlers who strayed far from Jamestown. The settlers adopted a strategy of terror, slaughtering whole villages and destroying crops. The massacre of one tribe might intimidate others. The war finally ended after the English captured Pocahontas and used her as a hostage to negotiate peace. She converted to Christianity and in 1614 married a prominent settler, John Rolfe.

Despite the Indian war, the colony's prospects improved after 1610. The governors imposed martial law on the settlers and sent some of them to healthier locations. Through Rolfe's efforts the colony began to produce a cash crop. In 1613 he imported a mild strain of tobacco from the West Indies. It brought such a good price in England that the king, who had insisted no one could build a colony "upon smoke," was proved wrong. Soon everyone was growing tobacco.

REORGANIZATION, REFORM, AND CRISIS

In 1609 a new royal charter extended Virginia's boundaries to the Pacific. A third charter in 1612 made the London Company a **joint-stock company**. It resembled a modern corporation except that each stockholder had only one vote regardless of how many shares he owned. The stockholders met quarterly in the company's General Court but entrusted everyday management to the company's treasurer, who until 1618 was Sir Thomas Smyth, a wealthy London merchant. In 1618 the stockholders replaced Smyth with Sir Edwin Sandys, a Puritan son of the archbishop of York.

Captain John Smith *Member of the Virginia Council whose strong leadership from 1607 to 1609 probably saved the colony from collapse.*

joint-stock company *Form of business organization that resembled a modern corporation in that individuals invested in the company through the purchase of shares, although each stockholder had one vote regardless of how many shares he owned. The first permanent English colonies in North America were established by joint-stock companies.*

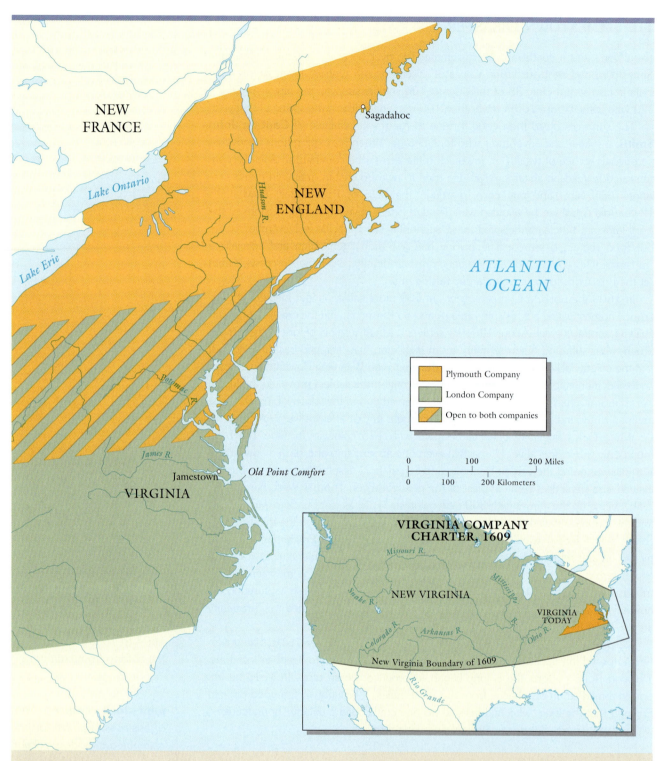

Map 2.2

VIRGINIA COMPANY CHARTER, 1606. *This charter gave the Plymouth Company jurisdiction over what would become New England and New York, and the London Company jurisdiction over most of what became Virginia and North Carolina. They shared jurisdiction over the intervening area. The insert map shows Virginia's revised sea-to-sea boundaries laid out in the 1609 charter.*

THE OPECHANCANOUGH MASSACRE OF 1622. *This famous event, as portrayed in an engraving from the workshop of Theodore de Bry, depicts the warriors as treacherous, bloodthirsty savages and the settlers as innocent victims.*

William C. Clements Library, University of Michigan, Ann Arbor

The company adopted an ambitious reform program for Virginia. It encouraged economic diversification, such as glassblowing, planting grapevines, and raising silkworms. English common law replaced martial law. The settlers were allowed to elect their own assembly, the **House of Burgesses**, to meet with the governor and his council to make local laws. Finally, settlers were permitted to own land. Under this **headright** system, a colonist received 50 acres for each person whose passage to Virginia he financed. By 1623 Sandys had shipped 4,000 settlers to Virginia, but the economic diversification program failed. Only tobacco found a market.

The flood of newcomers strained the food supply and soured relations with the Indians after Powhatan died and was succeeded by his militant brother, Opechancanough. In March 1622, the new chief launched an attack intended to wipe out the whole colony. Without a last-minute warning from a friendly Indian, Jamestown might not have survived. As it turned out, 347 settlers were killed that day, and most of the outlying settlements were destroyed. Newcomers who arrived in subsequent months had nowhere to go and, with food again scarce, hundreds died over the winter. Back in London, Smyth and his allies turned against Sandys, withdrew their capital, and asked the king to intervene. A royal commission visited the colony and found only 1,200 settlers alive out of 6,000 sent over since 1607. In 1624 the king declared the London Company bankrupt and assumed direct control of Virginia, making it the first **royal colony**, with a governor and council appointed by the Crown. The London Company invested some £200,000 in the enterprise, equal to more than £150 for every surviving settler at a time when skilled English craftsmen were lucky to earn one-third of that per year. Such extravagance guaranteed that future colonies would be organized in different ways.

House of Burgesses *Assembly of early Virginia elected by settlers that met with the governor and his council and enacted local laws. It first met in 1619.*

headright *Practice by which a colonist received 50 acres of land for every person whose passage to America he financed.*

royal colony *Colony controlled directly by the English monarch.*

TOBACCO, SERVANTS, AND SURVIVAL

Between Opechancanough's 1622 attack and the 1640s, Virginia proved that it could survive. Despite an appalling death rate, about a thousand new settlers came each year, and population grew slowly, reaching 8,100 by 1640. For 10 years the settlers warred against Opechancanough. In 1623 they poisoned 200 Indians they had invited to a peace conference. In most years they attacked the Indians just before harvest time, destroying their crops and villages. By the time both sides made peace in 1632, all Indians had been expelled from the peninsula between the James and York Rivers below Jamestown.

The export of tobacco financed the importation of **indentured servants,** even after the price of tobacco fell sharply in the 1630s. Most servants were young men who agreed to work for a term of years in exchange for the cost of passage, plus bed and board during their years of service, and modest freedom dues when their term expired. Those signing indentures in England usually had valuable skills and negotiated terms of four or five years. Those arriving without an indenture, most of whom were younger and less skilled, were sold by the ship captain to a planter. Those over age 19 served five years. Those under 19 served until age 24. The system turned servants into freemen who hoped to prosper on their own.

In 1634 Virginia was divided into counties, each with its own justices of the peace, who sat together as the county court and, by filling their own vacancies, soon became a self-perpetuating **oligarchy**. Most counties also became Anglican **parishes**, with a church and a **vestry** of prominent laymen, usually the justices. The vestry managed temporal affairs for the church, often including the choice of the minister. Though the king did not recognize the House of Burgesses until 1639, it met almost every year after 1619 and by 1640 was well established. Before long, only a justice could hope to be elected as a burgess.

Tobacco prices improved after 1640, and many former servants managed to acquire land. Some even served on the county courts and in the House of Burgesses. As tobacco prices fell after 1660, however, upward mobility became more difficult. Political offices usually went to the richest 15 percent of the settlers, those able to pay their own way across the Atlantic. They, and eventually their descendants, monopolized the posts of justice of the peace and vestryman, the pool from which burgesses and councilors were normally chosen.

MARYLAND

Maryland grew out of the social and religious vision of Sir George Calvert and his son Cecilius, both of whom looked to America as a refuge for persecuted English and Irish Catholics. Sir George, a prominent officeholder, had invested in the London Company. When he resigned his royal office after becoming a Catholic, the king made him baron Baltimore in the Irish peerage.

The Maryland charter of 1632 made Baltimore "lord proprietor" of the colony, the most sweeping delegation of power that the Crown could make. After 1630 most new colonial projects were **proprietary colonies.** Many of them embodied the distinctive social ideals of their founders.

George Calvert died as the Maryland patent was being issued, and Cecilius inherited Maryland and the peerage. Like Champlain, he believed that Catholics and Protestants could live in peace in the same colony, but he expected the servants, most of whom were Protestants, to continue to serve the Catholic gentlemen of the colony (he made them manor lords) after their indentures expired.

indentured servants *People who had their passage to America paid by a master or ship captain. They agreed to work for their master for a term of years in exchange for cost of passage, bed and board, and small freedom dues when their terms were up.*

oligarchy *Society dominated by a few persons or families.*

parish *A term used to describe an area served by one church. Gradually, the word was used to describe a political area that was the same as that served by the church, usually the Church of England.*

vestry *Group of prominent men who managed the lay affairs of the local Anglican church, often including the choice of the minister, especially in Virginia.*

proprietary colony *Colony owned by an individual(s) who had vast discretionary powers.*

Those plans were never fulfilled. The condition of English Catholics improved under Charles I (1625–1649) and his queen, Henrietta Maria, a French Catholic for whom the colony was named. Because few Catholics emigrated, most settlers were Protestants. The civil war that erupted in England in 1642 soon spread to Maryland. Protestants overthrew Lord Baltimore's regime several times between 1642 and 1660, but the English state always sided with him. During these struggles, Baltimore conceded a **bicameral legislature** to the colony, knowing that Protestants would dominate the elective assembly and that Catholics would control the appointive council. He also sponsored the Toleration Act of 1649, which granted freedom of worship to all Christians.

The manorial system did not survive these upheavals. Protestant servants, after their indentures expired, acquired their own land rather than become tenants under Catholic manor lords, most of whom died or returned to England. When Maryland's unrest ended around 1660, the colony was raising tobacco, corn, and livestock and was governed by county courts similar to those in Virginia. If anything, the proprietary family's Catholicism and its claims to special privileges made the Maryland assembly more articulate than the Virginia House of Burgesses in demanding the liberties of Englishmen. Unlike Virginia, Maryland had no **established church** and no vestries. Most Maryland Protestants had to make do without ministers until the 1690s.

CHESAPEAKE FAMILY LIFE

At first, men outnumbered women in Virginia and Maryland by 5 to 1. Among new immigrant servants as late as the 1690s, the ratio was still 5 to 2. Population became self-sustaining about 1680, when live births finally began to outnumber deaths. Among adults this transition was felt around 1700. Until then, most prominent people were immigrants. Life expectancy slowly improved as the colonists planted orchards to provide wholesome cider to drink, but it still remained much lower than in England. The Chesapeake immigrants had survived childhood diseases in Europe, but men at age 20 could expect to live only to about 45, with 70 percent dead by age 50. Women died at even younger ages, especially in areas ravaged by malaria, a dangerous disease, especially during pregnancy. England's patriarchal families found it hard to survive in the Chesapeake. About 70 percent of the men never married or, if they did, produced no children. Most men waited years after completing their service before they could marry. Because women could not marry until they had finished their indentures, most spent a good part of their childbearing years unwed. About one fifth had illegitimate children, and one third were pregnant on their wedding day.

In a typical Chesapeake marriage, the groom was in his 30s and the bride 8 or 10 years younger. This age gap meant that the husband usually died before his wife, who then quickly remarried. Native-born settlers married at a much earlier age than immigrants; women were often in their middle to late teens when they wed. Orphans were a major community problem. Stepparents were common; surviving spouses with property usually remarried. Few lived long enough to become grandparents.

Under these circumstances, family loyalties tended to focus on uncles, aunts, cousins, and older stepbrothers or stepsisters, thus contributing to the value that Virginia and Maryland placed upon hospitality. Patriarchalism remained weak. Because fathers died young, even members of the officeholding elite that took shape after 1650 had difficulty passing on their status to their sons. Only toward the end of the century were the men who held office likely to be descended from fathers of comparable distinction.

bicameral legislature *Legislature with two houses or chambers.*

established church *Church in a European state or colony that was sustained by the government and supported by public taxes.*

CRUDE HOUSING FOR SETTLERS IN NORTH AMERICA. *When the first settlers came to North America, their living quarters were anything but luxurious. The crude housing shown in this modern reconstruction of Jamestown remained typical of Virginia and Maryland through the 17th century.*

THE WEST INDIES AND THE TRANSITION TO SLAVERY

Before 1700, far more Englishmen went to the West Indies than to the Chesapeake. Between 1624 and 1640 they settled the Leeward Islands (St. Christopher, Nevis, Montserrat, and Antigua) and Barbados, tiny islands covering just over 400 square miles. In the 1650s England seized Jamaica from Spain, increasing this total by a factor of 10. At first English planters grew tobacco, using the labor of indentured servants. Then, beginning around 1645 in Barbados, sugar replaced tobacco, with dramatic social consequences. The Dutch provided some of the capital for this transition, showed the English how to raise sugar, introduced them to slave labor on a massive scale, and for a time dominated the exportation and marketing of the crop.

Sugar required a heavy investment in slaves and mills, and large planters with many slaves soon dominated the islands. Ex-servants found little employment, and most of them moved to the mainland or joined the buccaneers. Their exodus hastened the transition to slavery. In 1660 Europeans outnumbered slaves in the islands by 33,000 to 22,000. By 1700, the white population had stagnated, but the number of slaves had increased sixfold. By 1775 that number would triple again. Planters appropriated perhaps 80 percent of their slaves' labor for their own profit and often worked them to death, an unprecedented level of exploitation. Of the 316,000 Africans imported before 1700, only 115,000 remained

Map 2.3

PRINCIPAL WEST INDIAN COLONIES IN THE 17TH CENTURY. *Spain retained control of the large islands of Cuba, Hispaniola, and Puerto Rico, while its English, French, and Dutch rivals settled the smaller but fertile islands east of Puerto Rico or south of Cuba.*

alive in that year. Despite the low moral tone of the islands, they generated enormous wealth for the English empire, far more than the mainland colonies well into the 18th century,

THE RISE OF SLAVERY IN NORTH AMERICA

Africans reached Virginia in 1619 when, John Rolfe reported, a Dutch ship "sold us twenty Negars." Their status remained ambiguous for decades. In the Chesapeake some Africans were treated as servants and won their freedom after several years, including perhaps 30 percent of those on Virginia's Eastern Shore as late as the 1660s. Many of the first Africans in Virginia and Maryland had Hispanic names. They were Creoles with cross-cultural experiences that enabled them to negotiate with their masters more effectively than those who came later. But most Africans were already serving for life, a pattern that finally prevailed.

FOCUS QUESTION

In the Chesapeake colonies, why did Africans eventually become hereditary slaves serving for life instead of indentured servants bound only for several years?

QUICK   REVIEW

THE ENGLISH IN VIRGINIA, MARYLAND, AND THE CARIBBEAN

- Problems of survival due to disease, disorganization, and warfare in Virginia

- Tobacco production financed the importation of servants

- Maryland founded by Calvert family, English and Irish Catholics

- Sugar revolution in the West Indies required heavy investment in slaves and mills

- Shift to African slavery in the Chesapeake as numbers of indentured servants decreased

Because the English had no experience with slavery at home, a rigid caste system took time to crystallize. In 1680, when Katherine Watkins, a white woman, accused John Long, a mulatto, of raping her, the neighbors blamed her, not him, for engaging in grossly seductive behavior. The case of Elizabeth Key, a mulatto, a Christian, and the bastard daughter of Thomas Key, shows similar ambiguity. In 1655 when she claimed her freedom, her new owner fought to keep her enslaved. William Greensted, who had fathered two children by her, sued on her behalf, won, and then married her. He had probably fallen in love with her.

In the generation after 1680, the caste structure of the Chesapeake colonies became firmly set. Fewer indentured servants reached the Chesapeake from England, as the Delaware valley and the expanding English army and navy competed more successfully for the same young men. Slaves took their place. They cost more to buy, but they served for life. After 1680 some great planters, such as William Byrd I and William Fitzhugh, deliberately chose to replace servants with African slaves. In 1705 the Virginia legislature forbade the whipping of a white servant without a court's permission, a restriction that did not apply to the punishment of slaves. To attract more whites, Virginia also promised every ex-servant 50 acres of land. The message was obvious. Every white was now superior to any black. Racial caste was replacing opportunity as the organizing principle of Chesapeake society.

THE NEW ENGLAND COLONIES

Other Europeans founded colonies to engage in economic activities they could not pursue at home, but the New England settlers reproduced the mixed economy of old England, with some variations. Their quarrel with England was over religion, not economics. They came to America, they insisted, to worship as God commanded, not as the Church of England required.

THE PILGRIMS AND PLYMOUTH

The **Pilgrims** were Separatists who left England for the Netherlands between 1607 and 1609, convinced that the Church of England was no true daughter of the Reformation. They hoped to worship freely in Holland. After 10 years there, they realized that their children were growing up Dutch, not English. That fear prompted a minority of the congregation to move to America. After negotiating rather harsh terms with the London Company, they sailed for Virginia on the *Mayflower*. But the ship was blown off course late in 1620, landing first on Cape Cod, and then on the mainland well north of the charter boundaries of Virginia, at a place they named Plymouth. Before landing, the 100 passengers agreed to the Mayflower Compact, which bound them all to obey the decisions of the majority.

Short on supplies, the colonists suffered keenly during the first winter. Half of them died, including the governor and all but three married women. His successor was William Bradford, who would be reelected annually for all but five years until his death in 1656. The settlers fared much better when spring came. The Patuxet Indians of the area had been wiped out by disease in 1617, but their fields were ready for planting. Squanto, the only Patuxet to survive, had been kidnapped in 1614 by coastal traders and carried to England. He had just made his way home and showed up at Plymouth one day in March 1621. He taught the settlers Indian methods of fishing and growing

Pilgrims *Pious, sentimental term used by later generations to describe the Separatist settlers who sailed on the Mayflower in 1620 and founded Plymouth Colony.*

sachem *Algonquian word that meant "chief."*

corn. He also introduced them to Massasoit, the powerful Wampanoag **sachem** whose people celebrated the first thanksgiving feast with the settlers after the 1621 harvest. By 1630 the settlers numbered about 300. They had paid off their London creditors, thus gaining political autonomy and private ownership of their flourishing farms.

COVENANT THEOLOGY

A much larger Puritan exodus settled Massachusetts Bay between 1630 and 1641. To Puritans the stakes were high indeed by the late 1620s. During that early phase of Europe's Thirty Years' War (1618–1648), Catholic armies seemed about to crush the German Reformation. Charles I blundered into a brief war against both Spain and France, raised money for the war using dubious methods, and dissolved Parliament when it protested. God's wrath would descend on England, Puritans warned.

These matters were of genuine urgency to Puritans, who embraced what they called **covenant theology**. According to this system, God had made two biblical covenants with humans, the covenant of works and the covenant of grace. In the covenant of works God had promised Adam that if he kept God's law he would never die—but Adam ate of the forbidden fruit, was expelled from the Garden of Eden, and died. All of Adam's descendants remain under the same covenant, but because of his fall will never be capable of keeping the law. All humans deserve damnation. But God was merciful and answered sin with the covenant of grace. God will save his chosen people. Everyone else will be damned. Even though the covenant of works can no longer bring eternal life, it remains in force and establishes the strict moral standards that every Christian must strive to follow, before and after conversion. A Christian's inability to keep the law usually triggered the conversion experience by demonstrating that only faith, not works, could save.

At this level, covenant theology merely restated Calvinist orthodoxy, but the Puritans gave it a novel social dimension by pairing each personal covenant with a communal counterpart. The social equivalent of the covenant of grace was the church covenant. Each congregation organized itself into a church, a community of **the elect**. The founders, or "pillars," of each church, after satisfying one another of their own conversions, agreed that within their church the Gospel would be properly preached and discipline would be strictly maintained. God, in turn, promised to bestow saving grace within that church—not to everyone, of course, but presumably to most of the children of the elect. The communal counterpart of the covenant of works was the "national" covenant. It determined not who was saved or damned but the rise and fall of nations or peoples. As a people, New Englanders agreed to obey the law, and God promised them prosperity. They, in turn, covenanted with their **magistrates** to punish sinners. If magistrates enforced God's law and the people supported these efforts, God would not punish the whole community for the misdeeds of individuals. But if sinners escaped public account, God's anger would be terrible toward his chosen people of New England. In England the government had refused to assume a godly role. Puritans fleeing to America hoped to escape the divine wrath that threatened England and to create in America the kind of churches that God demanded.

MASSACHUSETTS BAY

In 1629 several English Puritans obtained a royal charter for the **Massachusetts Bay Company**, a typical joint-stock corporation except for one feature: the charter did not specify where the company was to be located. Puritan investors going to New England bought out the other stockholders. Led by Governor John Winthrop, they

covenant theology *Belief that God made two personal covenants with humans: the covenant of works and the covenant of grace.*

the elect *Those selected by God for salvation.*

magistrate *Official who enforced the law. In colonial America, this person was usually a justice of the peace or a judge in a higher court.*

Massachusetts Bay Company *Joint-stock company chartered by Charles I in 1629. It was controlled by Non-Separatists who took the charter with them to New England and, in effect, converted it into a written constitution for the colony.*

carried the charter to America, beyond the gaze of Charles I. They used it not to organize a business corporation but as the constitution for the colony. In the 1630s the General Court created by the charter became the Massachusetts legislature.

New England settlers came from the broad middle range of English society, few rich, few very poor. Most had owned property in England. When they sold it to go to America, they probably liquidated far more capital than the London Company had invested in Virginia. A godly haven was expensive to build.

An advance party that sailed in 1629 took over a fishing village on the coast and renamed it Salem. The Winthrop fleet brought 1,000 settlers in 1630. In small groups they scattered around the bay, founding Dorchester, Roxbury, Boston, Charlestown, and Cambridge. Each town formed around a minister and a magistrate. The local congregation was the first institution to take shape. From it evolved the town meeting, as the settlers began to distinguish more sharply between religious and secular affairs. Soon the colonists were raising European livestock and growing English wheat and other grains, along with corn. Perhaps 30 percent of them perished during the first winter. A few hundred others grew discouraged and returned to England. Then conditions rapidly improved, as they had at Plymouth a decade earlier. About 13,000 settlers came to New England by 1641, most as families—a unique event in Atlantic empires to that time.

Settlers did a brisk business selling grain and livestock to the newcomers arriving each year. When the flow of immigrants ceased in 1641, that trade collapsed, creating a crisis that ended only as Boston merchants opened up West Indian markets for New England grain, lumber, livestock, and fish. New Englanders possessed this flexibility because they had started to build ships in 1631. The economic success of the region depended on its ability to export food and lumber products to colonies that grew staple crops. The very existence of colonies committed to free labor was an oddity. To prosper, they had to trade with more typical colonies, the societies elsewhere in the hemisphere that raised tobacco and sugar with unfree labor.

PURITAN FAMILY LIFE

In rural areas, New Englanders soon observed a remarkable fact. After the first winter, deaths were rare. The place was undeniably healthy, and families grew rapidly as 6 or even 10 children reached maturity. The settlers had left most European diseases behind and had encountered no new ones in the bracing climate. For the founders and their children, life expectancy far exceeded the European norm. More than one fifth of the men who founded Andover lived past age 80. Infant mortality fell, and few mothers died in childbirth. Because people lived so long, New England families became intensely patriarchal. Many fathers refused to grant land titles to their sons before their own deaths. In the early years settlers often moved, looking for the richest soil, the best neighbors, and the most inspiring minister. By about 1645 most of them had found what they wanted. Migration into or out of country towns became much lower than in England, and the New England town settled into a tight community that slowly became an intricate web of cousins. Once the settlers had formed a typical farming town, they grew reluctant to admit "strangers" to their midst. They largely avoided slavery, mostly to keep outsiders from contaminating their religion.

CONVERSION, DISSENT, AND EXPANSION

The vital force behind Puritanism was the quest for conversion. Probably because of John Cotton's stirring sermons in Boston, the settlers crossed an invisible boundary in the mid-1630s. As Cotton's converts described their religious experiences, observers turned from analyzing the legitimacy of their own conversions to assessing the validity of someone else's. Churches began to test for regeneracy, or conversion, and the standards of acceptance escalated rapidly.

The conversion experience was deeply ambiguous to a Puritan. Anyone who found no inner trace of saving grace was damned. Anyone absolutely certain of salvation had to be relying on personal merit and was also damned. Conversion took months, even years to achieve. It began with the discovery that one could not keep God's law and that one *deserved* damnation, not for an occasional misdeed but for what one was at one's best—a wretched sinner. It progressed through despair to hope, which had to rest on passages of scripture that spoke to that person's condition. A "saint" at last found reason to believe that God had saved him or her. The whole process involved a painful balance between assurance and doubt. A saint was sure of salvation, but never too sure.

This quest for conversion generated dissent and new colonies. The founders of Connecticut feared that Massachusetts was too strict in certifying church members. The founders of New Haven Colony worried that the Bay Colony was too lenient. The first Rhode Islanders disagreed with all of them.

In the mid-1630s, Reverend Thomas Hooker, alarmed by Cotton's preaching, led his people west to the Connecticut River where they founded Hartford and other towns south of the charter boundary of Massachusetts. John Winthrop, Jr. built Saybrook Fort at the mouth of the river, and it soon merged with Hooker's towns into the colony of Connecticut. In 1639 an affluent group planted New Haven Colony west of Saybrook on Long Island Sound. The leading minister was John Davenport, who imposed the most severe requirements for church membership in New England. New Hampshire and Maine had independent origins under their own charters, but when England fell into civil war after 1642, Massachusetts took control of both of them for most of the 17th century.

The residents of most towns agreed on the kind of worship they preferred, but some settlers, such as Roger Williams and **Anne Hutchinson**, made greater demands. Williams was a Separatist who refused to worship with anyone who did not explicitly repudiate the Church of England. Nearly all Massachusetts Puritans were **Non-Separatists** who claimed only to be reforming the Anglican Church. In 1636, after Williams challenged the king's right as a Christian to grant Indian lands to anyone at all, the colony banished him. He fled to Narragansett Bay with a few disciples and founded Providence. He developed eloquent arguments for religious liberty and the complete separation of church and state.

Anne Hutchinson, an admirer of John Cotton, claimed that virtually all other ministers were preaching only the covenant of works, not the covenant of grace, and were leading people to hell. She won a large following in Boston. At her trial there, she claimed to have received direct messages from God (the Antinomian heresy). Banished in 1638, she and her followers also fled to Narragansett Bay, where they founded Newport and Portsmouth. These towns united with Providence to form the colony of Rhode Island. They too accepted the religious liberty and separation of church and state that Williams advocated.

Much of this territorial expansion reflected not just religious idealism but a lust for land, often to sustain their livestock that multiplied rapidly and threatened neighboring Indians. After a series of provocations on both sides, Connecticut and Massachusetts waged a war of annihilation against the Pequot Indians, who controlled the fertile Thames River valley in eastern Connecticut. In May 1637 New England soldiers debated with their chaplain which of two Pequot forts to attack, the one held by warriors or the one with few warriors but mostly women, children, and the elderly. He probably told them to remember Saul and the Amalekites because, with horrified Narragansett Indians looking on as nominal allies of the settlers, the Puritan army chose the second fort, set fire to all the wigwams, and shot everyone who tried to flee. The godly had their own uses for terrorism.

Anne Hutchinson *Religious radical who attracted a large following in Massachusetts. She warned that nearly all of the ministers were preaching a covenant of works instead of the covenant of grace. Convicted of the Antinomian heresy after claiming that she received direct messages from God, she and her most loyal followers were banished to Rhode Island in 1638.*

Non-Separatists *English Puritans who insisted that they were faithful members of the Church of England while demanding that it purge itself of its surviving Catholic rituals and vestments.*

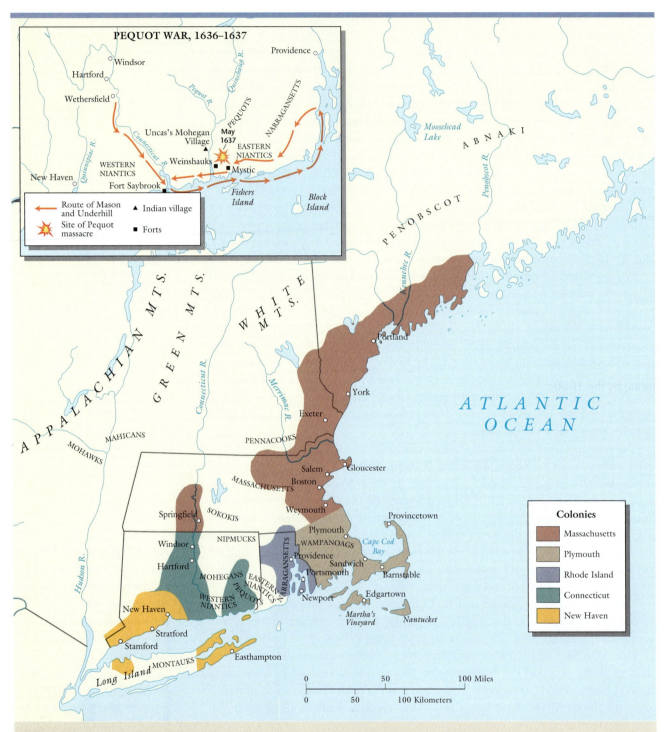

Map 2.4

NEW ENGLAND IN THE 1640S. *The five Puritan colonies spread over the Atlantic coast and nearby islands, the shores and islands of Narragansett Bay, both sides of Long Island Sound, and much of the Connecticut Valley. Although New Hampshire and Maine (not named as such on this map) were not founded by Puritans, Massachusetts extended its government over their settlers during the English civil wars. The insert map shows the principal military campaign of the Pequot War.*

CONGREGATIONS, TOWNS, AND COLONY GOVERNMENTS

These struggles helped to shape New England's basic institutions. Congregations abolished Anglican forms of worship. The sermon became the dominant rite, and each congregation chose and ordained its own minister. No singing was permitted, except of psalms. Congregations sometimes sent ministers and laymen to a synod, but its decisions were advisory, not binding. A 1648 synod issued the Cambridge Platform, which defined "Congregationalist" worship and church organization.

By then the town had become something distinct from the congregation. Some towns chose independent farms at the outset, but many adopted **open-field agriculture**, a medieval system in which farmers owned scattered strips of land within a common field, and the town decided what crops to grow. This emphasis on communal cooperation may have appealed to the founders, who were also short of oxen and plows at first and had to share them, but open fields did not survive the first generation.

Town meetings decided who got how much land. It was distributed broadly but never equally. In some villages, town meetings occurred often, made most of the decisions, and left only the details to a board of elected "selectmen." In others the selectmen did most of the governing. All adult males usually participated in local decisions, but Massachusetts and New Haven restricted the vote for colonywide offices to men who were full church members, a decision that greatly narrowed the electorate by the 1660s.

Massachusetts had a bicameral legislature by the 1640s. Voters in each town chose representatives who met as the Chamber of Deputies, or lower house. Voters also elected the governor and the magistrates, or upper house (the Council or, in its judicial capacity, the Court of Assistants). The magistrates also staffed the county courts. The Court of Assistants heard major criminal cases and appeals from the counties. Final appeals were heard by the General Court, with both houses sitting together to make judicial decisions.

Massachusetts defined its legal system in the "Body of Liberties" of 1641 (which may actually be history's first bill of rights) and in a comprehensive law code of 1648 that was widely imitated in other colonies. Massachusetts sharply reduced the number of capital offenses under English law and listed them in the order of the Ten Commandments. Unlike England, Massachusetts seldom executed anyone for a crime against property. Other distinctive features of the system included the swift punishment of crime and an explicit recognition of the liberties of women, children, servants, foreigners, and even "the Bruite Creature," or animals.

New England also transformed the traditional English jury system. New Haven abolished juries altogether because the Bible does not mention them, but the other colonies vastly expanded the role of civil (noncriminal) juries, using them even to decide appeals, something that never happened in England. Except in capital trials, however, the criminal jury—a fixture of English justice—almost disappeared in New England. The punishment of sin involved fidelity to the covenant and was too important to leave to 12 ordinary men. This system worked well because even most sinners shared its values. Most offenders appeared in court and accepted their punishments. Acquittals were rare, almost unheard of in New Haven. Yet hardly anyone ran away to avoid trial or punishment.

open-field agriculture *A medieval system of land distribution used only in the New England colonies. Farmers owned scattered strips of land within a common field, and the town as a whole decided what crops to plant.*

INFANT BAPTISM AND NEW DISSENT

Half-Way Covenant *The Puritan practice whereby parents who had been baptized but had not yet experienced conversion could bring their children before the church and have them baptized.*

Although most founders of the New England colonies became church members during the fervor of the 1630s, their children had trouble achieving conversion. They had never lived as part of a beleaguered minority in England, nor had they experienced the joy of joining with other holy refugees in founding their own church. They had to find God on their own and then persuade their elders that their conversions were authentic. Most failed. They grew up, married, and requested baptism for their children. The Cambridge Platform declared that only "saints" (the converted) and their children could be baptized. But what about the grandchildren of the saints if their own parents had not yet experienced conversion? By 1660 this problem was becoming acute.

Dissenters offered two answers, the ministers a third. In the 1640s some settlers became Baptists. Noting that scripture contains no mandate to baptize infants, they argued that only converted adults should receive that rite. Their position challenged the logic of a covenanted community by implying that New England was no different from Europe. The community was a mass of sinners from whom God would randomly choose the saints. Samuel Gorton, a Baptist expelled from Massachusetts and Plymouth, founded Warwick, Rhode Island, in the 1640s. When Massachusetts arrested him, accused him of blasphemy, and put him on trial for his life, the legislature banished him instead, but Gorton appealed to Parliament in England, and Massachusetts backed down. Baptist principles also attracted Henry Dunster, the able president of Harvard College, which had been founded in 1636 to educate ministers and magistrates for a Puritan society. When the courts began to harass Baptists, Dunster left for more tolerant Plymouth.

Even more alarming to the Puritan establishment were the Quakers (see later section in this chapter), who invaded the region from England in the 1650s. Quakers found salvation within themselves—through God, the Inner Light present in all people if they will only let it shine forth. To Puritans the Quaker answer to the conversion dilemma seemed blasphemous and Antinomian. Massachusetts hanged four Quakers who refused to stop preaching, including Mary Dyer, once a disciple of Anne Hutchinson.

The clergy's answer to the lack of conversions, worked out at a synod in 1662, became known as the **Half-Way Covenant**. Parents who had been baptized but had not yet experienced conversion could bring their children before the church, "own the covenant" (that is, subject themselves and their offspring to the doctrine and discipline of the church), and have their children baptized. In practice, women often experienced conversion before age 30, men closer to 40, but many never did. In most churches women also began to outnumber men as full members. For 15 or 20 years after 1662, most churches were still dominated by the lay members of the founding generation. Despite the urging of the clergy, aging church members resisted the Half-Way Covenant, but as the founders died off in the 1670s and 1680s, it took hold and soon led to something like universal baptism. Almost every child had an ancestor who had been a full church member.

Dissent persisted anyhow. The orthodox colonies were divided over whether to persecute or to ignore their Baptist and Quaker minorities. Ministers preached "jeremiads," shrill warnings against any backsliding from the standards of the founding generation. Many laypeople disliked the persecution of conscientious Protestants, however. By the 1670s, innovation seemed dangerous and divisive, but the past was also becoming a burden that few could shoulder.

THE ENGLISH CIVIL WARS

The 1640s were a critical decade in England and the colonies. From 1629 to 1640 Charles I governed without Parliament, but when he tried to impose the Anglican *Book of Common Prayer* on Presbyterian Scotland, his Scottish subjects rebelled and even invaded England. Needing revenue, Charles summoned two Parliaments in 1640 only to find that many of its members, especially the Puritans, sympathized with the Scots. The Church of England began to disintegrate. For two decades no new bishops were consecrated. In 1641 Irish Catholics launched a massive revolt against the Protestant colonizers of their land. King and Parliament agreed that the Irish must be crushed, but neither dared trust the other with the men and resources to do the job. Instead, they began to fight each other.

In 1642 the king and Parliament raised separate armies and went to war. Parliament gradually won the military struggle and then had to govern most of England without a king. In January 1649, after its moderate members had been purged by its own "New Model Army," Parliament beheaded Charles, abolished the House of Lords, and proclaimed England a Commonwealth (or republic). Within a few years Oliver Cromwell, Parliament's most successful general, dismissed Parliament, and the army proclaimed him "Lord Protector" of England. He convened several of his own Parliaments, but these experiments failed. The army could not win legitimacy for a government that ruled without the ancient trinity of "King, Lords, and Commons."

Cromwell died in September 1658, and his regime collapsed. Part of the army invited Charles II (1660–1685) back from exile to claim his throne. This "Restoration" government brought back the House of Lords and reestablished the Church of England under its episcopal form of government. The English state, denying any right of dissent, persecuted both Catholics and Protestant dissenters: Presbyterians, Congregationalists, Baptists, and Quakers. This persecution drove thousands of Quakers to the Delaware valley after 1675.

THE FIRST RESTORATION COLONIES

England had founded 6 of the original 13 colonies before 1640. Six others were founded or came under English rule during the **Restoration era** (1660–1688). The last, Georgia, was settled in the 1730s (see Chapter 4). All were proprietary in form. Except for Pennsylvania, the Restoration colonies were all founded by men with big ideas and small purses. The proprietors tried to attract settlers from the older colonies because importing them from Europe was expensive. The most readily available prospects were servants completing their indentures in the West Indies and being driven out by the sugar revolution. Many went to South Carolina. The most prized settlers, however, were New Englanders, who had built the most thriving colonies in North America, but few of them would go farther south than New York or New Jersey.

The Restoration colonies made it easy for settlers to acquire land, and they competed with one another by offering newcomers strong guarantees of civil and political liberties. They all promised either toleration or full religious liberty, at least for Christians. Whereas Virginia and New England (except Rhode Island)

> FOCUS QUESTION
>
> *In what ways did the Restoration colonies differ from those founded earlier in the Chesapeake and New England?*

were still homogeneous societies, the Restoration colonies all attracted a mix of religious and ethnic groups. No colony found it easy to create political stability out of this diversity.

Most of the new proprietors were **Cavaliers** who had supported Charles II and his brother James, duke of York, during their long exile. Charles owed them something, and a colonial charter cost nothing to grant. Many proprietors took part in more than one project. The eight who obtained charters for Carolina in 1663 and 1665 were also prominent in organizing the Royal African Company, which soon made England a major participant in the African slave trade. Two of the Carolina proprietors obtained a charter from the duke of York for New Jersey as well. **William Penn** became a friend of James and invested in West New Jersey before acquiring Pennsylvania.

CAROLINA, HARRINGTON, AND THE ARISTOCRATIC IDEAL

In 1663 eight courtiers obtained a charter by which they became the board of proprietors for a colony called "Carolina" in honor of the king. Most of the settlers came from two sources. Former servants from Virginia and Maryland, many in debt, claimed land around Albemarle Sound in what eventually became North Carolina. Another wave of former servants came from Barbados. They settled the area that became South Carolina, 300 miles south of Albemarle.

To the proprietors in England, these scattered settlements made up a single colony. Led by Anthony Ashley-Cooper, later the first earl of Shaftesbury and the principal organizer of England's Whig Party, the proprietors drafted the Fundamental Constitutions of Carolina in 1669, an incredibly complex plan for organizing the new colony. Philosopher John Locke, Shaftesbury's young secretary, helped write the document.

The Fundamental Constitutions drew on the work of Commonwealth England's most prominent republican thinker, James Harrington, author of *Oceana* (1656). Harrington argued that how land was distributed ought to determine whether power should be lodged in one man (monarchy), a few men (aristocracy), or many (a republic). Where ownership of land was widespread, he insisted, absolute government could not prevail. He proposed several other devices to prevent one man, or a few, from undermining a republic, such as frequent rotation of officeholders (called "term limits" today), the secret ballot, and a bicameral legislature in which the smaller house would propose laws and the larger house approve or reject them. Using Harrington's principles, Shaftesbury hoped to create an ideal aristocratic society in Carolina.

The Fundamental Constitutions proposed a government far more complex than any colony could sustain. England had three supreme courts; Carolina would have eight. A Grand Council of proprietors and councilors would exercise executive power and propose all laws. Their bills would have to pass a Parliament of nobles (called "landgraves" and "casiques") and commoners. The nobles would control 40 percent of the land. A distinct group of manor lords would also have large estates. The document guaranteed religious toleration to all who believed in God, but everyone had to join a church or lose his citizenship. The document also envisioned a class of lowly whites, "leetmen," who would live on small tracts and serve the great landlords—and it accepted slavery.

Conditions were bleak on Barbados for ex-servants, but not bleak enough to make the Fundamental Constitutions attractive to the Barbadians who settled in Carolina. Between 1670 and 1700, the proprietors tried several times, without success, to win their approval of the document. In the 1680s, weary of resistance from the predominantly Anglican Barbadians, the proprietors shipped 1,000 dissenters from England and Scotland to South Carolina. These newcomers formed the nucleus of a proprietary party in South Carolina politics and made religious diversity a social fact, but

Restoration era *Period that began in 1660 when the Stuart dynasty under Charles II was restored to the throne of England and ended with the overthrow of James II in 1688–1689.*

Cavaliers *Supporters of the Stuart family of Charles I during the civil wars.*

William Penn *A convert to the Society of Friends in the 1660s, Penn acquired a charter for Pennsylvania in 1681, and then launched a major migration of Friends to the Delaware Valley.*

their influence was never strong enough to win approval for the Fundamental Constitutions. The Barbadians remained in control.

Carolina presented its organizers with other unanticipated obstacles to these aristocratic goals. The proprietors assumed that land ownership would be the key to everything else, including wealth and status, but many settlers prospered in other ways. Some of them, especially in Albemarle, exploited the virgin forests all around them to produce masts, turpentine, tar, and pitch for sale to English shipbuilders. Other settlers raised cattle and hogs by letting them run free on open land. Some of South Carolina's early African slaves were probably America's first cowboys. The settlers also traded with the Indians, usually for deerskins at first, often acquired west of the Appalachians. As in New France and New Netherland, the Indian trade sustained a genuine city, Charleston, the first in the American South, founded in 1680 at the confluence of the Ashley and Cooper Rivers. The Indian trade also became something more dangerous than hunting or trapping animals. Carolina traders allied themselves with some Indians to attack others and drag the captives, mostly women and children, to Charleston for sale as slaves. For more than 30 years, the Indian slave trade became the largest business in the colony. South Carolina exported more enslaved Indians to other colonies than it imported Africans for its own plantations.

In the early 18th century, South Carolina and North Carolina became separate colonies, and South Carolina's economy moved in a new direction. For two decades, until the mid-1720s, a parliamentary subsidy sustained a boom in the naval stores industry, but Charleston merchants increasingly invested their capital, acquired in the Indian trade, in rice plantations. In the 1690s planters learned how to grow rice from slaves who had cultivated it in West Africa. It quickly became the staple export of South Carolina and triggered a massive growth of slavery. In 1700 more than 40 percent of the colony's population of 5,700 were African or Indian slaves. The Indian slave trade collapsed after 1715. By 1730 two thirds of the colony's 30,000 people were African slaves, most of whom toiled on rice plantations.

NEW YORK: AN EXPERIMENT IN ABSOLUTISM

In 1664 James, duke of York, obtained a charter from his royal brother for a colony between the Delaware and Connecticut Rivers. Charles II claimed that the territory of New Netherland was rightfully England's because it was included in the Virginia charter of 1606. James sent a fleet to Manhattan, and the English settlers on Long Island rose to support his claim. Stuyvesant surrendered reluctantly but without resistance. The English renamed the province New York. New Amsterdam became New York City, and Fort Orange became Albany. New York took over all of Long Island, most of which had been ruled by Connecticut, but never made good its claim to the Connecticut River as its eastern boundary on the mainland.

New York also inherited New Netherland's role as mediator between the settlers and the Iroquois Five Nations. In effect the duke of York's autocratic colony assumed most of the burdens of this relationship while unintentionally conferring most of the benefits upon the Quakers who would begin to settle the Delaware valley a decade later. The shield provided by New York and the Iroquois would make the Quaker experiment in pacifism a viable option.

Richard Nicolls, the first English governor of New York, planned to lure Yankees to the Jersey coast as a way of offsetting the preponderance of Dutch settlers in the Hudson valley. Although English soldiers abused many Dutch civilians, official policy toward the Dutch was conciliatory. Those who chose to leave could take their property with them. Those who stayed retained their property and were assured of religious toleration. Most stayed. Except in New York City and the small Dutch portion of Long Island, Dutch settlers still lived under Dutch law. England also expected to take over the colony's trade with Europe, but New York's early governors realized that a total ban on commerce with Amsterdam could ruin the colony. Under various legal subterfuges, they allowed this trade to continue.

The duke boldly tried to do in New York what he and the king did not dare attempt in England—to govern without an elective assembly. This policy upset English settlers on Long Island far more than the Dutch, who had no experience with representative government. Governor Nicolls compiled a code of laws ("the Duke's Laws") culled mostly from New England statutes. With difficulty, he secured the consent of English settlers to this code in 1665, but thereafter he taxed and governed on his own, seeking only the advice and consent of his appointed council and of a somewhat larger court of assize, also appointive, that rode circuit and dispensed justice, mostly to the English settlers.

This policy made it difficult to attract English colonists to New York, especially after New Jersey became a separate proprietary colony in 1665. The two proprietors, Sir George Carteret and John, baron Berkeley, granted settlers the right to elect an assembly, which made New Jersey far more attractive to English settlers than New York. The creation of New Jersey also slowed the flow of Dutch settlers across the Hudson and thus helped to keep New York Dutch.

The transition from a Dutch to an English colony did not go smoothly. James expected his English invaders to assimilate the conquered Dutch, but the reverse was more common for two or three decades. Most Englishmen who settled in New York after the conquest married Dutch women (few unmarried English women were available) and sent their children to the Dutch Reformed Church. In effect, the Dutch were assimilating the English. Nor did the Dutch give up their loyalty to the Netherlands. In 1673, when a Dutch fleet threatened the colony, the Dutch refused to assist the English garrison of Fort James at the southern tip of Manhattan. Eastern Long Island showed more interest in reuniting with Connecticut than in fighting the Dutch. Much like Stuyvesant nine years earlier, the English garrison gave up without resistance. New York City now became New Orange and Fort James was renamed Fort William, both in honor of young William III of Nassau, prince of Orange, the new *stadholder* (military leader) of the Dutch Republic in its struggle with France.

New Orange survived for 15 months, until the Dutch Republic again concluded that the colony was not worth what it cost and gave it back to England at the end of the war. The new governor, Major Edmund Andros, arrested seven prominent Dutch merchants and tried them as aliens after they refused to swear an oath of loyalty to England that might oblige them to fight other Dutchmen. Faced with the confiscation of their property, they gave in. Andros also helped secure bilingual ministers for Dutch Reformed pulpits. These preachers made a great show of their loyalty to the duke, a delicate matter now that James, back in England, had openly embraced the Catholic faith. Ordinary Dutch settlers looked with suspicion on the new ministers and on wealthier Dutch families who socialized with the governor or sent their sons to New England to learn English.

English merchants in New York City resented the continuing Amsterdam trade and the staying power of the Dutch elite. They believed the colony had to become more English to attract newcomers. When Andros forgot to renew the colony's basic revenue act before returning to England in 1680, the merchants refused to pay any duties not voted by an elective assembly. The court of assize, supposedly a bastion of absolutism, supported the tax strike, convicted the duke's customs collector of usurping authority, and sent him to England for punishment where, of course, James exonerated him. The justices also fined several Dutch officeholders for failing to respect English liberties. The English (but not Dutch) towns on Long Island joined in the demand for an elective assembly, an urgent matter now that William Penn's much freer colony on the Delaware threatened to drain away the small English population of New York. Several prominent merchants did move to Philadelphia.

The duke finally relented and conceded an assembly. When it met in 1683, it adopted a Charter of Liberties that proclaimed government by consent. It also imposed English law on the Dutch parts of the province. Although the drain of English settlers to Pennsylvania declined, few immigrants came to New York at a time when thousands were landing in Philadelphia. Philadelphia's thriving trade cut into New York City's profits. New York remained a Dutch society with a Yankee enclave, governed by English intruders. In 1689, when James and William fought for the English throne, their struggle would tear the colony apart.

Brotherly love: The Quakers and America

The most fascinating social experiment of the Restoration era took place in the Delaware Valley, where Quakers led another family-based, religiously motivated migration of more than 10,000 people between 1675 and 1690. Founded by George Fox during the civil wars, the Society of Friends expanded dramatically in the 1650s as it went through a heroic phase of missionaries and martyrs, including the four executed in Massachusetts. After the Restoration, Quakers faced harsh persecution in England and finally began to seek refuge in America.

Quaker Beliefs

Quakers infuriated other Christians. They insisted that God, in the form of the Inner Light, is present in all people, who can become good—even perfect—if only they will let that light shine forth. They became **pacifists**, enraging Catholics and most other Protestants, all of whom had found ways to justify war. Quakers also denounced oaths as sinful. Again, other Christians reacted with horror because their judicial systems rested on oaths.

Although orderly and peaceful, Quakers struck others as dangerous radicals whose beliefs would bring anarchy. For instance, slavery made them uncomfortable, though not yet abolitionists. Further, in what they called "the Lamb's war" against human pride, Quakers refused to doff their hats to social superiors. More than any other simple device, hats symbolized the social hierarchy of Europe. Every man knew his place so long as he understood whom to doff to, and who should doff to him. Quakers also refused to accept or to confer titles. They called everyone "thee" or "thou," familiar terms used by superiors when addressing inferiors.

The implications of Quaker beliefs appalled other Christians. The Inner Light seemed to obliterate predestination, original sin, maybe even the Trinity. Quakers had no sacraments, not even an organized clergy. They denounced Protestant ministers as "hireling priests." Other Protestants retorted that the Quakers were conspiring to return the world to "popish darkness" by abolishing a learned ministry. (The terms "papists" and "popish" were abusive labels applied to Catholics by English Protestants.) Quakers also held distinctive views about revelation. If God speaks directly to Friends, that Word must be every bit as inspired as anything in the Bible. Quakers compiled books of their "sufferings," which they thought were the equal of the "Acts of the Apostles," a claim that seemed blasphemous to others.

pacifist *Person opposed to war or violence. The religious group most committed to pacifism was the Quakers.*

Contemporaries expected the Society of Friends to fall apart as each member followed his or her own Light in some unique direction. However, after 1660 Quakers found ways to deal with discord. The heart of Quaker worship was the "weekly meeting" of the local congregation. There was no sermon or liturgy. People spoke whenever the Light inspired them. But because a few men and women spoke often and with great effect, they became recognized as **public friends**, the closest the Quakers came to having a clergy. The weekly meetings within a region sent representatives to a "monthly meeting," which resolved questions of policy and discipline. The monthly meetings sent delegates to the "yearly meeting" in London. At every level, decisions had to be unanimous because God would convey the same message to all. This insistence on unanimity provided strong safeguards against schism.

QUAKER FAMILIES

Quakers transformed the traditional family as well. Women enjoyed almost full equality, and some of them, such as Mary Dyer, became exceptional preachers, even martyrs. Women held their own formal meetings and made important decisions about discipline and betrothals. Quaker reforms also affected children, whom most Protestants saw as tiny sinners whose wills must be broken by severe discipline. But once Quakers stopped worrying about original sin, their children became innocents in whom the Light would shine if only they could be protected from worldly corruption. In America, Quakers created affectionate families and worked hard to acquire land for all their children. Earlier than other Christians, they began to limit family size to give more love to the children they did have. After the missionary impulse declined, Quakers seldom socialized with non-Quakers, and the needs of their own children became paramount. To marry an outsider meant expulsion from the Society, a fate more likely to befall poor Friends than rich ones.

Persecution in England helped to drive Quakers across the ocean, but the need to provide for their children was another powerful motive for emigration. By 1700, about half of the Quakers in England and Wales had moved to America.

WEST NEW JERSEY

In 1674 the New Jersey proprietors split their holding into two colonies. Sir George Carteret claimed what he now called East New Jersey, a province near New York City with half a dozen towns populated by Baptist, Quaker, Puritan, and Dutch Reformed settlers. Lord Berkeley claimed the western portion and promptly sold it to some Quakers, who turned it into West New Jersey and then founded Pennsylvania. In the 1680s, Quakers bought out the proprietor of East New Jersey and also gained power in Delaware (formerly New Sweden). They seemed poised to dominate the entire region between Maryland and New York. The West Jersey purchasers divided their proprietary into 100 shares. Two of the purchasers were Edward Byllinge and William Penn. They revived in West Jersey many radical ideals of the English Commonwealth era.

In 1676 Byllinge drafted the West Jersey Concessions and Agreements, which was approved by the first settlers in 1677. It lodged legislative power in a unicameral assembly, elected by secret ballot, and it empowered voters to instruct their representatives. In the court system, juries would decide both fact and law. Judges would merely preside over the court and, if asked by a juror, offer advice. West Jersey Quakers believed that godly people could live together in love—without war, lawyers, or in-

public friends *Men and women who spoke most frequently and effectively for the Society of Friends. They were as close as the Quakers came to having a clergy.*

ternal conflict. They kept government close to the people, made land easy to acquire, and promised freedom of worship to everyone. But as social and religious diversity grew, the system broke down. Non-Quakers increasingly refused to cooperate. In the 1690s the courts became impotent, and Quaker rule collapsed some years before the Crown took over the colony in 1702.

PENNSYLVANIA

By 1681 Quaker attention was already shifting to the west bank of the Delaware River. There William Penn launched a much larger, if rather more cautious, "holy experiment." The son of a Commonwealth admiral, Penn grew up surrounded by privilege. He knew well both Charles II and the duke of York, attended Oxford and the **Inns of Court** (England's law schools), and began to manage his father's Irish estates. Then something happened that enraged his father. "Mr. William Pen," reported a neighbor in December 1667, ". . . is a Quaker again, or some very melancholy thing." Penn often traveled to the continent on behalf of the Society of Friends, winning converts and recruiting settlers in the Netherlands and Germany. In England he was jailed several times for his beliefs.

Penn was no ordinary colonizer. Using his contacts at court, he converted an old debt (owed to his father by the king) into a charter for a proprietary colony that Charles named "Pennsylvania" in honor of the deceased admiral. The emerging imperial bureaucracy disliked the whole project and, after failing to block it, inserted several restrictions into the charter. Penn agreed to enforce the Navigation Acts (see Chapter 3), to let the Crown approve his choice of governor, to submit all legislation to the English Privy Council for approval, and to allow appeals from Pennsylvania courts to the Privy Council in England. Contemporaries said little about the most striking innovation attempted by the Quaker colonists. They entered America unarmed. Pennsylvanians did not even organize a militia until the 1740s. Friendly relations with Indians were essential to the project's success, and Penn was careful to deal fairly with the Lenni Lenape, or Delaware Indians.

More thought went into the planning of Pennsylvania than into the creation of any other colony. Twenty drafts survive of Penn's First Frame of Government, his 1682 constitution for the province. Under this plan, the settlers would elect a council of 72 men to staggered three-year terms. The council would draft all legislation and submit copies to the voters. In the early years the voters would meet to approve or reject these bills in person, but as the province expanded, such meetings would become impractical. Voters would then elect an assembly of 200, which would increase gradually to 500. Government would still remain close to the people. Penn gave up the power to veto bills but retained control of the distribution of land. Capital punishment for crimes other than murder was abolished. Religious liberty, trial by jury, and habeas corpus all received strong guarantees.

Settlers had been arriving in Pennsylvania for a year when Penn landed in 1682 with his First Frame of Government. The colonists persuaded Penn that the First Frame was too cumbersome for a small colony. In what became known as the Second Frame, or the Pennsylvania Charter of Liberties of 1683, the council was reduced to 18 men and the assembly to 36. The assembly's inability to initiate legislation soon became a major grievance.

In 1684, Penn returned to England to answer Lord Baltimore's complaint that Philadelphia fell within the charter boundaries of Maryland, a claim that was soon verified. This dispute troubled the Penn family until the 1760s, when the Mason-Dixon line established the modern boundary.

QUICK   REVIEW

NEW PROPRIETARY EXPERIMENTS IN THE RESTORATION COLONIES

- Carolina established with aristocratic goals, land ownership

- New Netherland (New York) conquered by England, ruled by royal absolutism

- Quaker West Jersey and Pennsylvania founded on goals of equality and religious liberty

Inns of Court *England's law schools.*

WILLIAM PENN IN ARMOR AND PENN'S CELL IN THE TOWER OF LONDON. *The son of an English admiral, William Penn was not always a pacifist. In the 1660s, an unknown artist painted him in this military pose. After his conversion to the Society of Friends, Penn paid a steep price for his religious convictions. Accused of blasphemy, he was imprisoned in this bleak cell from December 1668 to July 1669.*

In England, persecution had kept Quaker antiauthoritarianism in check, at least in relations with other Friends. In the colony these attitudes soon became conspicuous. Penn expected his settlers to defer to the leaders among them. He created the Free Society of Traders to control commerce with England and gave high offices to its members. From the start, however, wealth in Pennsylvania rested on trade, not with England, but with other colonies, especially the West Indies. That trade was dominated by Quakers from Barbados, Jamaica, New York, and Boston. These men owed little to Penn and became an opposition faction in the colony. They and others demanded more land, especially in Philadelphia. In exasperation, Penn finally appointed John Blackwell, a friend and old Cromwellian soldier, as governor in 1688, ordering him to end the quarrels but to rule "tenderly." Boys jeered Blackwell as he tried to enter Penn's Philadelphia house, and the council refused to let him use the colony's great seal. Debate in the legislature became angrier than ever. After 13 months, Blackwell resigned. Each Quaker, he complained, "prayed for the rest on the First Day [of the week], and preyed on them the other six."

In 1691, the Society of Friends suffered a brief schism in the Delaware valley. A Quaker schoolteacher, George Keith, urged all Quakers to systematize their beliefs and even wrote his own catechism, only to encounter the opposition of the public friends, who included the colony's major officeholders. When he attacked them directly, he was convicted and fined for abusing civil officers. He claimed that he was being persecuted for his religious beliefs, but the courts insisted that his only crime was his attack on public authority. In contrast to Massachusetts in the 1630s, no one was banished, and Pennsylvania remained a haven for all religions. The colony's government changed several more times before 1701, when Penn and the assembly finally agreed on the Fourth Frame, or Charter of Privileges, which gave Pennsylvania a unicameral legislature, but the colony's politics remained turbulent and unstable into the 1720s.

Despite these controversies, Pennsylvania quickly became an economic success. Quaker families prospered, and the colony's policy of religious freedom attracted thousands of outsiders. Some were German pacifists who shared the major goals of the Society of Friends. Others were Anglicans and Presbyterians who warned London that Quakers were unfit to rule—anywhere.

C O N C L U S I O N

In the 16th century, France, the Netherlands, and England all challenged Spanish power in Europe and across the ocean. After 1600 all three founded their own colonies in North America and the Caribbean. New France became a land of missionaries and fur traders. New Netherland also was founded to participate in the fur trade. Both colonies slowly acquired an agricultural base.

The English, by contrast, desired the land itself. The southern mainland and Caribbean colonies produced staple crops for sale in Europe. The Puritan and Quaker colonies became smaller versions of England's mixed economy, with an emphasis on family farms. After conquering New Netherland, England controlled the Atlantic seaboard from Maine to South Carolina, and by 1700 the population of England's mainland colonies was doubling every 25 years. England was beginning to emerge as the biggest winner in the competition for empire overseas.

QUESTIONS FOR REVIEW AND CRITICAL THINKING

Review

1. Why did the number of Indians who chose to become Catholics far exceed the number that accepted Protestantism?

2. In the Chesapeake colonies, why did Africans become hereditary slaves serving for life instead of indentured servants bound only for several years?

3. Why did Englishmen, crossing the Atlantic at roughly the same time, create such radically different societies in the Chesapeake, the West Indies, and New England?

4. In what ways did the Restoration colonies differ from those founded earlier in the Chesapeake and New England?

Critical Thinking

1. Does the splintering of New England into multiple colonies, each with a somewhat different vision of the Puritan mission, indicate that religious uniformity could be maintained only under the strong government of a single state?

2. In the 17th century, Quakers came closer than any other group to affirming equality as a positive value. Does their experience in England and America suggest how difficult it might be to persuade an entire society to embrace that value?

Discovery

What were the differences and similarities between various colonizing countries' approaches to colonial development? In particular, how did the colonies of France and England differ in their dealings with indigenous Indian populations?

SUGGESTED READINGS

W. J. Eccles, *The French in North America, 1500–1783,* rev. ed. (1998) is a concise and authoritative survey. **C.R. Boxer,** *The Dutch Seaborne Empire, 1600-1800* (1965) is still the best synthesis of Dutch activity overseas. **Joyce E. Chaplin's** *Subject Matter: Technology, the Body, and Science on the Anglo-American Frontier, 1500–1676* (2001) and **Karen O. Kupperman's** *Indians and English: Facing Off in Early America* (2000) are efforts to keep Indians and the settlers of early Virginia and New England within a common focus. **Edmund S. Morgan's** *American Slavery, American Freedom: The Ordeal of Colonial Virginia* (1975) has become a classic, but **Thad W. Tate** and **David L. Ammerman,** eds., *The Chesapeake in the Seventeenth-Century: Essays on Anglo-American Society* (1979) is also indispensable. For the West Indies, see **Richard S. Dunn,** *Sugar and Slaves: The Rise of the Planter Class in the English West Indies, 1624–1713* (1972). **Winthrop Jordan's** *White over Black: American Attitudes toward the Negro, 1550–1812* (1968) retains its freshness and acuity.

 Edmund S. Morgan's *Visible Saints: The History of a Puritan Idea* (1963) is a brief and accessible introduction to Puritan values in New England's first century. **Michael P. Winship's** *Making Heretics: Militant Protestantism and Free Grace in Massachusetts, 1636–1641* (2002) brings a challenging new perspective to the Antinomian controversy. **Carla G. Pestana's** *Quakers and Baptists in Colonial Massachusetts* (1991) deals with other dissenters from the New England Way. **Daniel Vickers,** *Farmers and Fishermen: Two Centuries of Work in Essex County, Massachusetts, 1630-1850* (1994) is the most helpful introduction to the New England economy.

 For the Restoration colonies, see especially **Robert C. Ritchie,** *The Duke's Province: A Study of New York Politics and Society, 1664–1691* (1977); **Gary B. Nash,** *Quakers and Politics: Pennsylvania Politics, 1681–1726* (1968); **Barry J. Levy,** *Quakers and the American Family: British Settlement in the Delaware Valley* (1988); **Peter H. Wood,** *Black Majority: Negroes in Colonial South Carolina from 1670 through the Stono Rebellion* (1974), and **Alan Gallay,** *The Indian Slave Trade: The Rise of the English Empire in the American South, 1670-1717* (2002).

ONLINE SOURCES GUIDE

ThomsonNOW™ Visit ThomsonNOW to access primary sources, exercises, quizzes, and audio chapter summaries related to this chapter:
http://www.thomsonedu.com/login

DISCOVERY

What were the differences and similarities between various colonizing countries' approaches to colonial development? In particular, how did the colonies of France and England differ in their dealings with indigenous Indian populations?

In thinking about this question, begin by breaking it down into the components shown below. A discussion of the significance of each component should appear in your answer.

GEOGRAPHY

Look at the maps "New France and the Jesuit Missions" and "New England in the 1640s." Where in particular did the French and English choose to colonize? Which settlements made it easier to retain close ties with their home country? What does the first map (and the map legend) suggest about France's motivation for overseas expansion? What does the second map (and the map insert) suggest about England's motivation?

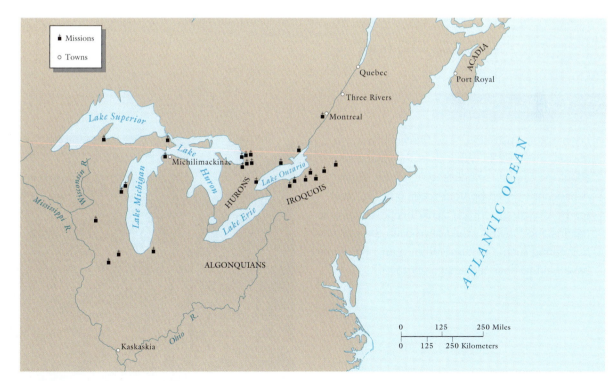

NEW FRANCE AND THE JESUIT MISSIONS

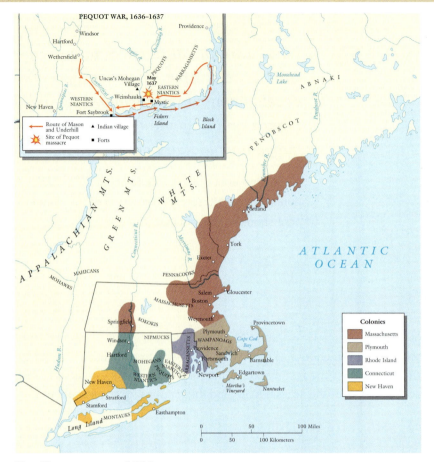

NEW ENGLAND IN THE 1640S

(Map inset) PEQUOT WAR, 1636–1637

Windsor · Hartford · Wethersfield · Providence · Uncas's Mohegan Village · PEQUOTS · May 1637 · EASTERN NIANTICS · NARRAGANSETTS · WESTERN NIANTICS · New Haven · Weinshauks · Mystic · Fort Saybrook · Fishers Island · Block Island

Route of Mason and Underhill · ▲ Indian village · ✸ Site of Pequot massacre · ■ Forts

Mooschead Lake · ABNAKI · PENOBSCOT · Portland · York · Exeter · ATLANTIC OCEAN · APPALACHIAN MTS. · GREEN MTS. · WHITE MTS. · MAHICANS · MOHAWKS · PENNACOOKS · Salem · Gloucester · Boston · MASSACHUSETTS · Weymouth · Provincetown · Springfield · SOKOKIS · Plymouth · WAMPANOAGS · Cape Cod Bay · Windsor · NIPMUCKS · Providence · Sandwich · Barnstable · Hartford · MOHEGANS · EASTERN NIANTICS · Portsmouth · Edgartown · New Haven · WESTERN NIANTICS · PEQUOTS · NARRAGANSETTS · Newport · Martha's Vineyard · Nantucket · Stratford · Stamford · MONTAUKS · Easthampton · Long Island

Colonies
- Massachusetts
- Plymouth
- Rhode Island
- Connecticut
- New Haven

0   50   100 Miles
0   50   100 Kilometers

CULTURE AND SOCIETY

Look at the illustration "The Opechancanough Massacre of 1622." What does this image say about the English colonists' view of the Native Americans? Based on your reading of the chapter, how accurate do you think this portrayal is in this instance? What would have been the motive in creating such a picture? Who, if anyone, might have paid to have this image engraved?

THE OPECHANCANOUGH MASSACRE OF 1622

William C. Clements Library, University of Michigan, Ann Arbor

ENGLAND DISCOVERS ITS COLONIES: EMPIRE, LIBERTY, AND EXPANSION

I n 1603 England was still a weak power on the fringes of Europe. By 1700 England was a global giant. It possessed 20 colonies in North America and the Caribbean, controlled much of the African slave trade, and had muscled its way into distant India. Commerce and colonies had vastly magnified England's power.

This transformation occurred during a century of political and religious upheaval at home. King and Parliament fought over their respective powers—a long struggle that led to civil war and the execution of one king in 1649 and to the overthrow of another in 1688. It produced a unique constitution that rested upon parliamentary supremacy and responsible government under the Crown.

By 1700 England and the colonies had begun to converge around the newly defined principles of English constitutionalism. All of them adopted representative government at some point during the century. All of them affirmed the values of liberty and property under the English Crown.

The sheer diversity of the colonies daunted anyone who hoped to govern them. The colonies formed not a single type, but a spectrum of settlement with contrasting economies, social relationships, and institutions. Yet by 1700 England had created a system of regulation that respected colonial liberties while asserting imperial power.

TIMELINE

| 1640 | 1650 | 1660 | 1670 | 1680 | 1690 | 1700 | 1710 | 1720 |

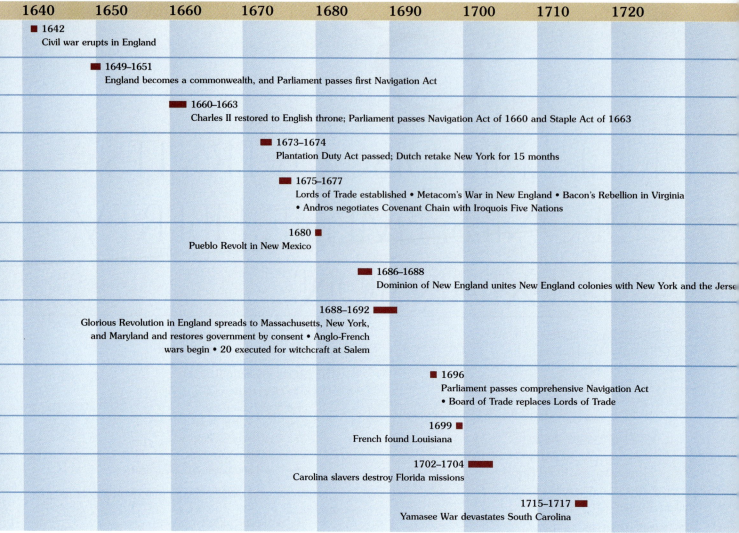

■ **1642**
Civil war erupts in England

■ **1649–1651**
England becomes a commonwealth, and Parliament passes first Navigation Act

■ **1660–1663**
Charles II restored to English throne; Parliament passes Navigation Act of 1660 and Staple Act of 1663

■ **1673–1674**
Plantation Duty Act passed; Dutch retake New York for 15 months

■ **1675–1677**
Lords of Trade established • Metacom's War in New England • Bacon's Rebellion in Virginia • Andros negotiates Covenant Chain with Iroquois Five Nations

1680 ■
Pueblo Revolt in New Mexico

■ **1686–1688**
Dominion of New England unites New England colonies with New York and the Jerse

1688–1692 ■
Glorious Revolution in England spreads to Massachusetts, New York, and Maryland and restores government by consent • Anglo-French wars begin • 20 executed for witchcraft at Salem

■ **1696**
Parliament passes comprehensive Navigation Act • Board of Trade replaces Lords of Trade

1699 ■
French found Louisiana

1702–1704 ■
Carolina slavers destroy Florida missions

1715–1717 ■
Yamasee War devastates South Carolina

THE SPECTRUM OF SETTLEMENT

Over thousands of years, the Indians of the Americas had become diversified into hundreds of distinct cultures and languages. The colonists of 17th-century North America and the Caribbean were following much the same course. America divided them. The Atlantic united them. Their connection with England gave them what unity they could sustain.

As long as its population remained small, no colony could duplicate the complexity of England. The settlers had to choose what to bring with them and what to leave behind, what they could do for themselves and what they would have to import—choices dictated both by their motives for crossing the ocean and by what the new environment would permit. The colonists sorted themselves out along a vast arc from the cold North to the subtropical Caribbean. If we imagine England as a source of white light and the Atlantic as a prism refracting that light, 17th-century America becomes a spectrum of settlement, with each color merging imperceptibly into the shade next to it. Each province had much in common with its neighbors, but shared few traits with more distant colonies.

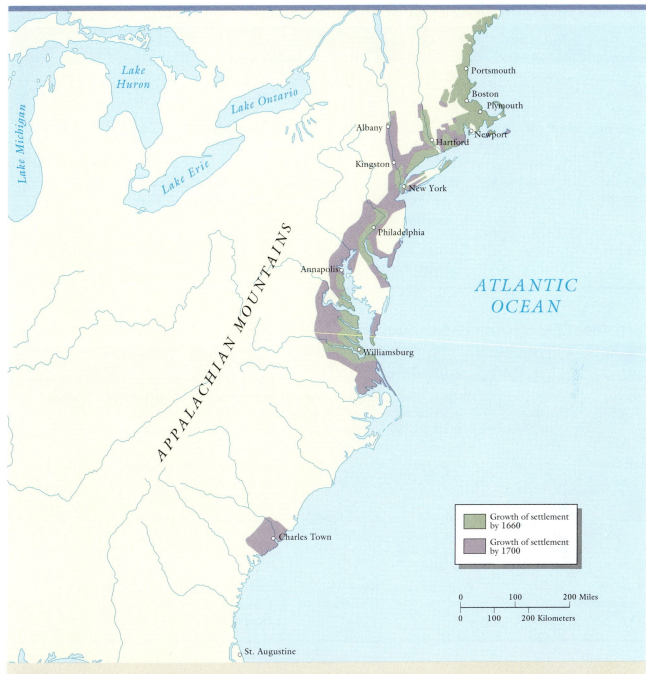

Map 3.1
AREA OF ENGLISH SETTLEMENT BY 1700. *This map differentiates the areas settled before 1660 from those settled between 1660 and 1700, or roughly the Restoration era.*

DEMOGRAPHIC DIFFERENCES

The most pronounced differences involved the sex ratio (the ratio of men to women in any society) and family structure. At one extreme were buccaneers, the all-male, multiethnic societies in the Caribbean that lived only for plunder. Because women settlers were scarce in the islands at first, the family itself seemed an endangered institution. Even when the sex ratio evened out and families began to emerge, couples had few children. In Virginia and Maryland, as natural increase replaced immigration

THE SPECTRUM OF SETTLEMENT: DEMOGRAPHY, ETHNICITY, ECONOMY, 1650–1700

CATEGORY	WEST INDIES	LOWER SOUTH	CHESAPEAKE	MID-ATLANTIC	NEW ENGLAND	NEW FRANCE
Life expectancy for men, at age 20	40	42	45	60+	Late 60s	60s
Family size	Below replacement rate	About two children	Rising after 1680	Very large	Very large	Very large
Race and ethnicity	Black majority by circa 1670s	Black majority by circa 1710	Growing black minority	Ethnic mix, N.W. Europe, English a minority	Almost all English	Almost all French
Economy	Sugar	Indian slave trade, then rice	Tobacco	Furs, farms	Farms, fishing, shipbuilding	Furs, farms

THE SPECTRUM OF SETTLEMENT: RELIGION AND GOVERNMENT, CIRCA 1675–1700

CATEGORY	WEST INDIES	LOWER SOUTH	CHESAPEAKE	MID-ATLANTIC	NEW ENGLAND	NEW FRANCE
Formal religion	Anglican church establishment	Anglican church establishment by circa 1710	Anglican church establishment (after 1692 in Md.)	Competing sects, no established church	Congregational church established	Catholic church established
Religious tone	Irreverent	Contentious	Low-church Anglican	Family-based piety, sectarian competition	Family-based piety, intensity declining	Intensely Catholic
Local government	Parish	Parish and phantom counties (i.e., no court)	County and parish	County and township	Towns and counties; parishes after 1700	Cities
Provincial government	Royal	Proprietary	Royal (Va.), proprietary (Md.)	From proprietary to royal, except in Pa.	Corporate, with Mass. and N.H. becoming royal	Royal absolutism

as the main source of white population growth after 1680, women became more numerous, married much earlier, and raised larger families.

Life expectancy varied tremendously. In the sugar colonies, men often died by age 40. In the Chesapeake colonies, for men who survived childhood diseases, life expectancy was about 45. The northern colonies were much healthier. In the Delaware valley, a man who reached adulthood could expect to live past 60. New England was one of the healthiest places in the world. Because the sex ratio rapidly approached equality and because the thriving economy permitted couples to marry perhaps two years earlier than in England, population exploded. Canada followed a similar pattern. Before 1700 the birth rate in New France caught up with New England's, and population grew at a comparable pace.

These demographic differences had major consequences. For example, the Caribbean and southern colonies were youthful societies in which men with good connections could expect to achieve high office while in their 30s. By contrast, the New England colonies gradually became dominated by grandfathers. A man was not likely to become even a selectman before his 40s. Despite the appalling death rate in the sugar and tobacco colonies, young men remained optimistic and upbeat, as they looked forward to challenging the world and making their fortunes. In New England, people grew more despondent as the century progressed, even though they lived much longer.

RACE, ETHNICITY, AND ECONOMY

The degree of racial and ethnic mixture also varied from region to region, along with economic priorities. The West Indies already had a large slave majority by 1700 when English settlers were still a clear majority in the southern mainland colonies, but African slaves became a majority in South Carolina around 1710. They would comprise 40 percent of Virginia's population by the 1730s. Africans were less numerous in the Delaware and Hudson valleys, although slavery became deeply entrenched in New York City and parts of New Jersey.

In the Middle Atlantic region, settlers from all over northwestern Europe were creating a new ethnic mosaic. English colonists were probably always a minority, outnumbered at first by the Dutch and later by Germans, Scots, and Irish. But New England was in every sense the most English of the colonies. New France was as French as New England was English. The farther south one went, the more diverse the population; the farther north, the more uniform.

Slavery and staple crops went together. The slave societies raised sugar, rice, or tobacco for sale in Europe. General farming and family labor also went together. By 1700 the Middle Atlantic was becoming the wheat belt of North America. New Englanders farmed and exported fish, livestock, and lumber to the West Indies.

RELIGION AND EDUCATION

The intensity of religious observance varied immensely across the spectrum of settlement, ranging from irreverence and indifference in the West Indies to intense piety in Pennsylvania, New England, and New France. Literacy followed a similar pattern. Colonists everywhere tried to prevent slaves from learning to read, and low literacy prevailed wherever slavery predominated. Chesapeake settlers provided almost no formal schooling for their children prior to the 1690s. By contrast, the Dutch maintained several good schools in New Netherland. Massachusetts required every town to have a writing school, and larger towns to support a Latin grammar school, in order to frustrate "ye old deluder Satan." In New France a seminary (now Laval University) was established in the 1660s, but lay literacy remained low. Along the spectrum, piety, literacy, and education usually grew stronger from south to north.

Public support for the clergy followed the same pattern. By 1710 the established church of the mother country was the legally established church in the West Indies and in the southern mainland colonies. Toleration prevailed in New York and full religious liberty in Pennsylvania. In New England, Old World dissent became the New World establishment. Public support for the clergy was much greater in the north than in the south. The sugar islands had the most wealth, but they maintained only one clergyman for every 3,000 to 9,000 people, depending on the island and the decade. In the Chesapeake the comparable ratio was about one for every 1,500 people by 1700. It was perhaps one for every 1,000 in New York, one for every 600 in New England, and still lower in New France.

LOCAL AND PROVINCIAL GOVERNMENTS

Forms of government also varied. Drawing on their English experience, settlers could choose from among parishes, boroughs (towns), and counties. The only important local institution in the sugar islands and in South Carolina was the parish, which took on many secular functions, such as poor relief. The Chesapeake colonies relied primarily on the county but also made increasing use of the parish. Few parishes were ever organized in the Middle Atlantic colonies, but the county as a form of government became a powerful institution after 1664. New England's most basic local institution was the town. Massachusetts created counties in the 1640s, followed 20 years later by Connecticut and in the 1680s by Plymouth. After 1700, towns large enough to support more than one church also created parishes.

The West Indian colonies all had royal governments by the 1660s. Before 1700 proprietary forms dominated the mainland south of New England, except for royal Virginia. Until the 1680s New England relied on corporate forms of government in which all officials, even governors, were elected. This system survived in Connecticut and Rhode Island through independence.

UNIFYING TRENDS: LANGUAGE, WAR, LAW, AND INHERITANCE

Despite this diversity, a few unifying trends developed in the 17th century. For instance, language became more uniform in America than in England. True, the New England dialect derived mostly from East Anglia, the southern accent from southern and western England, and Middle Atlantic speech from north-central England. But Londoners went to all the colonies, and London English affected every colony and softened the contrasts among the emerging regional dialects.

Another area of uniformity involved war: Colonists waged it with short-term volunteers for whom terror against Indian women and children was often the tactic of choice. Europe was moving toward limited wars; the colonists demanded quick and total victories.

Law became a simpler version of England's complex legal system. Justice was local and uncomplicated. In fact, an organized legal profession did not emerge until the 18th century. Finally, no mainland American colony rigidly followed English patterns of inheritance. Instead, some women had a chance to acquire property, usually by inheritance from a deceased husband, particularly in the Chesapeake colonies. The single women who went there as servants and stayed alive enjoyed a fantastic chance at upward mobility. Many won a respectability never available to them in England. In every colony younger sons also found their situation improved. They played a huge role in settling the colonies, and they showed little inclination to preserve institutions that had offered them no landed inheritance in England.

THE BEGINNINGS OF EMPIRE

In the chaotic 1640s, the English realized that their colonies overseas were bringing them very few benefits. England had no coherent colonial policy.

UPHEAVAL IN AMERICA: THE CRITICAL 1640S

England's civil wars rocked its emerging empire, politically and economically. As royal power collapsed in the 1640s, the West Indian colonies demanded and received elective assemblies. The Dutch took advantage of the chaos in England to finance much of the sugar revolution in Barbados and seize control of trade in and out of England's West Indian and Chesapeake colonies. By 1650 most sugar and tobacco exports were going through Amsterdam, not London.

During the civil wars, nobody in England exercised effective control over the colonies. The king had declared that their trade was to remain in English hands, but no agency existed to enforce that policy. The new elective assemblies of Barbados and the Leeward Islands preferred to trade with the Dutch, even after the English Crown took over those colonies in 1660. The mainland colonies already governed themselves. Into the 1640s, as the New England settlements expanded, the new colonies of Connecticut, Rhode Island, and New Haven did not even bother to obtain royal charters. On the mainland, only Virginia had a royal governor.

The chaos of the 1640s gave Indians a unique opportunity to resist the settlers. Some Indians began to think of driving the Europeans out altogether. In the mid-1640s, Indian wars almost destroyed New France, New Netherland, and Maryland. In Virginia in 1644 the aging warrior Opechancanough staged another massacre, killing 500 settlers without warning. This time the settlers recovered more quickly, murdered Opechancanough after he surrendered, broke up his chiefdom, and made its member tribes accept treaties of dependency.

Only New England avoided war with the Indians—just barely. Miantonomo, sachem of the Narragansetts, called for a war of extermination against the settlers, to be launched by a surprise attack in 1642. He abandoned the plan after settlers got wind of it. The colonists created their own defensive alliance in 1643, the New England Confederation, which united the four orthodox colonies of Massachusetts, Plymouth, Connecticut, and New Haven, but not Rhode Island. The confederation persuaded the Mohegans to kill Miantonomo, and tensions with the Narragansett Indians remained high. The Narragansetts controlled some of the finest land in New England. Massachusetts, Plymouth, and Connecticut all wanted that land, but the Narragansetts were still too powerful to intimidate.

What happened in the colonies seemed of little interest to the English people in the turbulent 1640s. But as the civil wars ended and the extent of Dutch commercial domination became obvious, the English turned their eyes westward once again. In a sense, England first discovered its colonies and their importance around 1650.

MERCANTILISM AS A MORAL REVOLUTION

During the 17th century, most of the European powers followed a set of policies now usually called "mercantilism." Mercantilists argued that power derived ultimately from the wealth of a country, that the increase of wealth required vigorous trade, and that colonies had become essential to economic growth. Clearly, a state had to control the commerce of its colonies. But mercantilists disagreed over the best ways to promote growth. The Dutch favored virtual free trade within Europe. England preferred some kind of state regulation of the domestic and imperial economy. Early mercantilists assumed that the world contained a fixed supply of wealth. A state, to augment its own power, would have to expropriate the wealth of a rival. Trade wars would replace religious wars.

FOCUS QUESTION

How important was England's mercantilistic system in gaining effective control over the colonies and in projecting English power against its European rivals?

©Copyright British Museum

A Pictish Man Holding a Human Head, by John White, late 16th century. *In the ancient world, the Picts were among the ancestors of the English and the Scots. John White, who painted many Indian scenes on Roanoke Island in the 1580s, believed that the English had been "savages" not all that long ago and that American Indians, like the English, could progress to "civility." America made him think of "progress."*

Nevertheless, mercantilism gradually became associated with the emerging idea of unending progress. Europeans were already familiar with two kinds of progress, one associated with Renaissance humanism, the other explicitly Christian. The opening of the Americas had already reinforced both visions. Humanists knew that the distant ancestors of Europeans had all been "barbarians" who had advanced over the centuries toward "civility." Their own encounters with the peoples of Africa, Ireland, and America underscored this dualistic view by revealing new "savages" who seemed morally and culturally inferior to the "civilized" colonists. Committed Christians shared these convictions, but they also believed that human society was progressing toward a future Millennium in which Christ would return to earth and reign with his saints for 1,000 years. The discovery of millions of **heathens** in the Americas stimulated millennial thinking. God had chosen this moment to open a new hemisphere to Christians because the Millennium was near.

But both the humanist and the Christian notions of progress were static. Humanity would advance to a certain level, and then change would cease. Mercantilism, by contrast, marked a revolution of the human imagination precisely because it could arouse visions of endless progress. Mercantilists also developed a modern concept of law, which they saw as a way to change society, not merely as a means of clarifying immemorial customs or reducing natural laws to written texts.

THE FIRST NAVIGATION ACT

English merchants began debating trade policy during a severe depression in the 1620s. They concluded that a nation's wealth depended on its **balance of trade**, that a healthy nation ought to export more than it imports, and that the difference—or balance—could be converted into military strength. They also believed that a state needed colonies to produce essential commodities unavailable at home. And they argued that a society ought to export luxuries, not import them. But for England to catch up, Parliament would have to intervene.

London merchants clamored for measures to stifle Dutch competition. In 1650 Parliament responded by banning foreign ships from English colonies. A year later, it passed its first Navigation Act. Under this law, Asian and African goods could be imported into the British Isles or the colonies only in English-owned ships, and the master and at least half of each crew had to be Englishmen. European goods could be imported into Britain or the colonies in either English ships or the ships of the producing country, but foreigners could not trade between one English port and another.

heathen *Term used by Christians to refer to people who did not worship the God of the Bible.*

balance of trade *Relationship between imports and exports. A favorable balance of trade meant that exports exceeded imports.*

This new attention from the English government angered the colonists in the West Indies and North America. Mercantilists assumed that the colonies existed only to enrich the mother country. But the young men growing sugar in Barbados or tobacco in Virginia hoped to prosper on their own. Selling their crops to the Dutch, who offered the lowest freight rates, added to their profits. Although New England produced no staple that Europeans wanted except fish, Yankee skippers cheerfully swapped their fish or forest products in the Chesapeake for tobacco, which they then carried directly to Europe, usually to Amsterdam.

Barbados greeted the Navigation Act by proclaiming virtual independence. Virginia defiantly recognized Charles II as king and continued to welcome Dutch and Yankee traders. In 1651 England dispatched a naval force to America. It compelled Barbados to submit to Parliament and then sailed to the Chesapeake, where Virginia and Maryland capitulated in 1652. But with no resident officials to enforce English policy, trade with the Dutch continued.

By 1652 England and the Netherlands were at war, the first of three Anglo-Dutch conflicts between 1652 and 1674. For two years the English navy dealt heavy blows to the Dutch. Finally, in 1654, Oliver Cromwell sent Parliament home and made peace. A militant Protestant, he preferred to fight Catholic Spain rather than the Netherlands. He sent a fleet that failed to take Hispaniola, but in 1655 it did seize Jamaica.

RESTORATION NAVIGATION ACTS

By the Restoration era, mercantilist thinking had become widespread. Although the new royalist Parliament invalidated all legislation passed during the Commonwealth period, these "Cavaliers" promptly reenacted and extended the original Navigation Act. The Navigation Act of 1660 required that all colonial trade be carried on English ships (a category that included colonial vessels but now excluded the Scots), but the master and *three-fourths* of the crew had to be English. The act also created a category of **enumerated commodities,** of which sugar and tobacco were the most important, permitting these products to be shipped from the colony of origin *only* to England or to another English colony. The colonists could still export unenumerated commodities elsewhere. New England could send fish to a French sugar island, for example, and Virginia could export wheat to Cuba, provided the French and the Spanish would let them.

In a second measure, the Staple Act of 1663, Parliament regulated goods going to the colonies. With few exceptions, products from Europe or Asia could not be delivered to the settlements unless they had first been landed in England.

A third measure, the Plantation Duty Act of 1673, required captains of colonial ships to post bond in the colonies that they would deliver all enumerated commodities to England, or else pay on the spot the duties that would be owed in England (the "plantation duty"). This measure, England hoped, would eliminate all incentives to smuggle. To make it effective, England for the first time sent customs officers to the colonies to collect the duty and prosecute all violators. Most of them won little compliance at first.

Properly enforced, the Navigation Acts would dislodge the Dutch and establish English hegemony over Atlantic trade, and that is what happened within half a century. In 1600, about 90 percent of England's exports consisted of woolen cloth. By 1700, colonial and Asian commerce accounted for 30 to 40 percent of England's overseas trade, and London had become the largest city in western Europe.

In the 1670s a war between France and the Netherlands diverted critical Dutch resources from trade to defense, thus helping England to catch up with the Dutch. In the

QUICK   REVIEW

TOWARD EMPIRE

- Upheaval in England and the colonies, Indian challenges, and Dutch competition revealed incoherent colonial policy

- Parliament passed first Navigation Act, went to war with the Netherlands

- England's Restoration government extended the Navigation Act system

enumerated commodities
Colonial staple crops, such as sugar and tobacco, that had to be shipped from the colony of origin to England or another English colony.

1690s the English navy became the most powerful fleet in the world. By 1710 or so, virtually all British colonial trade was carried on British (including colonial) ships. Sugar, tobacco, and other staple crops all passed through Britain on their way to their ultimate destinations. Nearly all imported manufactured goods consumed in the colonies were made in Britain. Most products from Europe or Asia destined for the colonies passed through Britain first, although some smuggling of these goods continued.

Few government policies have ever been as successful as England's Navigation Acts, but England achieved these results without pursuing a steady course toward increased imperial control. For example, in granting charters to Rhode Island in 1662 and to Connecticut in 1663, Charles II approved elective governors and legislatures in both colonies. (The Connecticut charter also absorbed the New Haven Colony under the Hartford government.) These elective officials could not be dismissed or punished for failure to enforce the Navigation Acts. Moreover, the Crown also chartered several new Restoration colonies (see Chapter 2), whose organizers had few incentives to obey the new laws.

INDIANS, SETTLERS, UPHEAVAL

As time passed, the commercial possibilities and limitations of North America were becoming much clearer. The French and Dutch mastered the fur trade because they controlled the two all-water routes to the interior, via the St. Lawrence system and the Hudson and Mohawk valleys. South Carolinians could go around the southern extreme of the Appalachians. They all needed Indian trading partners.

As of 1670, no sharp boundaries separated Indian lands from colonial settlements. Boston, the largest city north of Mexico, was only 15 miles from an Indian village. The outposts on the Delaware River were islands in a sea of Indians. In the event of war, nearly every European settlement was vulnerable to attack.

INDIAN STRATEGIES OF SURVIVAL

FOCUS QUESTION

Contrast the failure of New England and Virginia to preserve peaceful relations with neighboring Indians in 1675–1676 with New York's success in the same decade and later.

By the 1670s most coastal tribes had already been devastated by disease or soon would be. European diseases, by magnifying the depleted tribes' need for captives, also increased the intensity of wars among Indian peoples. The Iroquois, hard hit by smallpox and other maladies, acquired muskets from the Dutch and used them, first to attack the Hurons and other Iroquoian peoples, and then **Algonquians**. These **mourning wars** were often initiated by female relatives of a deceased loved one, who insisted that their male kin repair the loss. Her warrior relatives then launched a raid and brought back captives. Although adult male prisoners were usually tortured to death, most women and children were adopted and assimilated. Adoption worked because the captives shared the cultural values of their captors. They became Iroquois. As early as the 1660s, a majority of the Indians in the Five Nations were adoptees, not native-born Iroquois. The confederacy remained strong while its rivals declined. In the southern **piedmont**, the Sioux-speaking Catawba Indians also assimilated thousands from other tribes, as did the Creeks further south.

In some ways, America became as much a new world for the Indians as it did for the colonists. European cloth, muskets, hatchets, knives, and pots appealed to Indians and spread far into the interior, but Indians who learned to use them gradually abandoned traditional skills and became increasingly dependent on European goods.

Algonquians *Indian peoples who spoke some dialect of the Algonquian language family.*

Alcohol, an item always in demand, was also dangerous. Drunkenness became a major, if intermittent, social problem for Indians. Settlers who understood that their future depended on the fur trade tried to stay on good terms with the Indians. Pieter Stuyvesant put New Netherland on such a course, and the English governors of New York followed his lead. Edmund Andros, governor from 1674 to 1680, cultivated the friendship of the **Iroquois League**, in which the five member nations had promised not to wage war against one another. In 1677 Andros and the Five Nations agreed to make New York the easternmost link in what the English called the **Covenant Chain of Peace,** a huge defensive advantage for a lightly populated colony. Thus, while New England and Virginia fought bitter Indian wars in the 1670s, New York avoided conflict. The Covenant Chain later proved flexible enough to incorporate other Indian nations and colonies as well.

Where the Indian trade was slight, war became more likely. In 1675 it erupted in both New England and the Chesapeake. In the 1640s Virginia had imposed treaties of dependency upon the member nations of the Powhatan chiefdom. The New England colonies had, they thought, more amicable understandings with the large non-Christian nations of the region, but the Puritan governments placed even greater reliance on a growing number of Christianized Indians.

PURITAN INDIAN MISSIONS

Serious efforts to convert Indians to Protestantism began in the 1640s on the island of Martha's Vineyard under Thomas Mayhew and his son, Thomas, Jr., and in Massachusetts under John Eliot, pastor of the Roxbury church. Eliot tried to make the nearby Indian town of Natick into a model mission community.

The Mayhews were more successful than Eliot, although he received most of the publicity. They worked with local sachems and even won over some of the tribal powwows (prophets or medicine men). The Mayhews encouraged Indian men to teach the settlers of Martha's Vineyard and Nantucket how to catch whales, an activity that made them a vital part of the settlers' economy without threatening their identity as males. Eliot, by contrast, attacked the authority of both sachems and **powwows** and insisted on turning Indian men into farmers, a female role in Indian society. Yet he did translate the Bible and a few other religious works into the Massachusett language.

By the early 1670s more than 1,000 Indians, nearly all of them survivors of coastal tribes that had been decimated by disease, lived in a string of seven "praying towns," and Eliot got busy organizing five more. By 1675 about 2,300 Indians, perhaps one-quarter of all those living on the mainland of southeastern New England, were in various stages of conversion to Christianity, but only 160 of them had achieved the kind of conversion experience that Puritans required for full membership in a church. Few Indians shared the Puritan sense of sin. The more powerful nations felt threatened by this pressure to convert, and resistance to Christianity became one cause of the war that broke out in 1675. Other causes were the settlers' lust for Indian lands, the ever increasing encroachment of livestock onto Indian corn fields, the decline of the fur trade as a way to pay for European goods, and the fear of young warriors that their way of life was in danger of extinction.

METACOM'S (OR KING PHILIP'S) WAR

Metacom (whom the English called King Philip) shared these fears. He was sachem of the Wampanoags and the son of Massasoit, who had celebrated the first thanks-

Mourning War *Indian war often initiated by a widow or bereaved relative who insisted that her male relatives provide captives to compensate for her loss.*

piedmont *Land above the fall line but below the Appalachian Mountains.*

Iroquois League *Confederation of five Indian nations centered around the Mohawk Valley who were active in the fur trade.*

Covenant Chain of Peace *Agreement negotiated by Governor Edmund Andros in 1677 that linked the colony of New York to the Iroquois Five Nations and was later expanded to include other colonies and Indian peoples.*

powwow *Originally, a word used to identify tribal prophets or medicine men. Later it was also used to describe their ceremonies.*

giving feast with the Pilgrims. What came to be known as **Metacom's War** began in the frontier town of Swansea in June 1675, after settlers killed an Indian they found looting an abandoned house. When the Indians demanded satisfaction the next day, the settlers laughed in their faces. The Indians took revenge, and the violence escalated into war.

The settlers were confident of victory. But since the 1630s the Indians had acquired firearms. They had built forges to make musket balls and repair their weapons. They had even become marksmen with the flintlock musket by firing several smaller bullets, instead of a single musket ball, with each charge. The settlers were terrible shots, and many were armed with older firelocks. In the tradition of European armies, they discharged volleys without aiming. To the shock of the colonists, Metacom won several engagements against Plymouth militia, usually by ambushing the noisy intruders. He then escaped from Plymouth Colony and headed toward the upper Connecticut valley, where the local Indians, after being ordered by magistrates to disarm, joined him instead. Together they burned five Massachusetts towns in three months.

Massachusetts and Connecticut joined the fray. As winter approached, rather than attack Metacom's Wampanoags they went after the Narragansetts, who had welcomed some Wampanoag refugees but were trying hard to remain neutral. In the Great Swamp Fight of December 1675, a Puritan army attacked an unfinished Narragansett fort during a blizzard and massacred hundreds of Indians, most of them women and children, but not before the Indians had picked off a high percentage of the officers. The surviving warriors joined Metacom and showed that they too could use terror. They torched more towns. Altogether about 800 settlers were killed during the war, and two dozen towns were destroyed or badly damaged.

Frontier settlers demanded the annihilation of all nearby Indians, even Christian converts. The Massachusetts government, shocked to realize that it could not win the war without Indian allies, did what it could to protect the **praying Indians**. The magistrates evacuated them to a bleak island in Boston harbor where they spent a miserable winter of privation, but then many enlisted to fight against Metacom in the spring campaign.

The settlers finally pulled together and won the war in 1676. Governor Andros of New York persuaded the Mohawks to attack Metacom's winter camp and disperse his people, who by then were short of gunpowder. The New Englanders, working closely with Mohegan and Christian Indian allies and using Indian tactics, then hunted down Metacom's war parties, killed hundreds of Indians, including Metacom, and sold hundreds more into West Indian slavery. Some of those enslaved had not even been party to the conflict and had actually requested asylum from it. In effect the struggle had turned into a civil war among the Indian peoples of southern New England with all of the colonies supporting Metacom's Indian opponents.

VIRGINIA'S INDIAN WAR

In 1675 the Doegs, a dependent Indian nation in the Potomac valley, demanded payment of an old debt from a Virginia planter. When he refused, they ran off some of his livestock. After his overseer killed one of them, the others fled but later returned to ambush and kill the man. The county militia mustered and followed the Doegs across the Potomac into Maryland. At a fork in the trail, the militia split into two parties. Each found a group of Indians in a shack a few hundred yards up the path it was following. Both parties fired at point-blank range, killing 11 at one cabin and 14 at the other. One of the bands was Doeg; the other was not: "Susquehannock friends," blurted one Indian as he fled.

Metacom's War (King Philip's War) *War that devastated much of southern New England in 1675–76. It began as a conflict between Metacom's Wampanoags and Plymouth Colony but soon engulfed all of the New England colonies and most of the region's Indian nations.*

praying Indians *Christian Indians of New England.*

The Susquehannocks were a strong Iroquoian-speaking people with firearms who had moved south to escape Iroquois attacks. At Maryland's invitation, they had recently occupied land north of the Potomac. Virginia's governor, Sir William Berkeley, hoping to avoid war, sent John Washington with some Virginia militia to investigate the killings and, if possible, to set things right.

Washington preferred vengeance. His Virginia militia joined with a Maryland force, and together they besieged a formidable Susquehannock fort on the north bank of the Potomac. When the Indians sent out five or six sachems to negotiate, the militia murdered them and then laid siege to the fort for six weeks. The Indians, short of provisions, finally broke out one night with all their people, killing several militiamen. After hurling taunts of defiance and promises of vengeance, they disappeared into the forest. Apparently blaming Virginia more than Maryland, they killed more than 30 Virginia settlers in January 1676. The colonists began to panic.

Berkeley favored a defensive strategy against the Indians; most settlers wanted to attack. In March 1676 the governor summoned a special session of the Virginia legislature to approve the creation of a string of forts above the fall line of the major rivers, with companies of "rangers" to patrol the stretches between them. Berkeley also hoped to maintain a distinction between the clearly hostile Susquehannocks and other Indians who might still be neutral or friendly. Frontier settlers demanded war against them all. Finally, to avoid further provocation, Berkeley restricted the fur trade to a few of his close associates. To the men excluded from that circle, his actions looked like favoritism. To new settlers in frontier counties, whose access to land was blocked by the Indians and who now had to pay higher taxes, Berkeley's strategy seemed intolerable.

Colonists denounced the building of any more forts and demanded an offensive campaign waged by unpaid volunteers, who would take their rewards by plundering and enslaving Indians. In April the frontier settlers found a reckless leader in newcomer Nathaniel Bacon. Using his political connections (he was the governor's cousin by marriage), he got himself appointed to the council soon after his arrival in the colony in 1674, but was now excluded from the Indian trade under Berkeley's new rules.

BACON'S REBELLION

Ignoring Berkeley's contrary orders, Bacon marched his frontiersmen south in search of the elusive Susquehannocks. After several days his weary men reached a village of friendly Occaneechees, who offered them shelter, announced that they knew where to find a Susquehannock camp, and even offered to attack it. The Occaneechees surprised and defeated the Susquehannocks and returned with their captives to celebrate the victory with Bacon. But after they had fallen asleep, Bacon's men massacred them and seized their furs and prisoners.

By then, Berkeley had outlawed Bacon, dissolved the legislature, and called the first general election since 1661. He asked the burgesses to bring their grievances to Jamestown for redress at the June assembly. Henrico voters elected Bacon to the House of Burgesses. Berkeley had him arrested when he reached Jamestown and made him apologize on his knees for his disobedience. Berkeley then forgave him and restored him to his seat in the council. While the burgesses were passing laws to reform the county courts, the vestries, and the tax system, Bacon slipped home, summoned his followers again, and marched on Jamestown. At gunpoint, he forced Berkeley to commission him as general of volunteers and compelled the legislature to authorize another expedition against the Indians.

Bacon's Rebellion *The most serious challenge to royal authority in the English mainland colonies prior to 1775. It erupted in Virginia in 1676 after the governor and Nathaniel Bacon, the principal rebel, could not agree on how best to wage war against frontier Indians.*

UPHEAVALS OF THE 1670S

- Iroquois and Catawba strategies for survival included adoption, assimilation, merger

- Puritan missionary efforts among the Indians and encroachments onto Indian land created tensions in New England

- Metacom's (King Philip's) War devastated both settlers and Indians

- Virginia's war with the Susquehannocks led to Bacon's Rebellion

- Bacon's Rebellion revealed fissures within Virginia's governing elite and between social classes

- New York negotiated a "Covenant Chain of Peace" with the Iroquois Five Nations to avoid frontier war

Berkeley retreated downriver to Gloucester County and mustered its militia, but they refused to follow him against Bacon. They would fight only Indians. Mortified, Berkeley fled to the Eastern Shore, the only part of the colony that was still loyal to him. Bacon hastened to Jamestown, summoned a meeting of planters at the governor's Green Spring mansion, and ordered the confiscation of the estates of Berkeley's supporters. Meanwhile, Berkeley raised his own force on the Eastern Shore by promising the men an exemption from taxes for 21 years and the right to plunder the rebels. Unlike the situation in New England, few Indians killed other Indians during the upheaval. This civil war pitted settlers against each other. Royal government collapsed under the strain. During the summer of 1676, hundreds of settlers set out to make their fortunes by plundering Indians, other colonists, or both. Bacon's Rebellion was the largest upheaval in the American colonies before 1775.

Bacon never did kill a hostile Indian. While he was slaughtering and enslaving the unresisting Pamunkeys along the frontier, Berkeley assembled a small fleet and retook Jamestown in August. Bacon rushed east and laid siege to Jamestown. After suffering only a few casualties, the governor's men grew discouraged, and in early September the whole force returned to the Eastern Shore. Bacon then burned Jamestown to the ground. He also boasted of his ability to hold off an English army, unite Virginia with Maryland and Albemarle (North Carolina), and win Dutch support for setting up an independent Chesapeake republic. Instead he died of dysentery in October.

Berkeley soon regained control of Virginia. Using the ships of the London tobacco fleet, he overpowered the plantations that Bacon had fortified. Ignoring royal orders to show clemency, Berkeley executed 23 of the rebels. A new assembly repudiated the reforms of 1676, and in many counties the governor's men used their control of the courts to continue plundering the Baconians for years through confiscations and fines. Berkeley, summoned to England to defend himself, died there in 1677 before he could present his case.

CRISIS IN ENGLAND AND THE REDEFINITION OF EMPIRE

Bacon's Rebellion helped trigger a political crisis in England. Because Virginia produced little tobacco in 1676 during the uprising, English customs revenues fell sharply, and the king was obliged to ask Parliament for more money. Parliament's response was tempered by the much deeper problem of the royal succession. Charles II had fathered many bastards, but his royal marriage was childless. After the queen reached menopause in the mid-1670s, his brother James, duke of York, became his heir. By then James had become a Catholic. When Charles dissolved the Parliament that had sat from 1661 until 1678, he knew he would have to deal with a new House of Commons terrified by the prospect of a Catholic king.

THE POPISH PLOT, THE EXCLUSION CRISIS, AND THE RISE OF PARTY

In this atmosphere of distrust, a cynical adventurer, Titus Oates, fabricated the sensational story that he had uncovered a sinister "Popish Plot" to kill Charles and bring James to the throne. In the wake of these accusations, the king's ministry fell, and the parliamentary opposition won majorities in three successive elections between 1678 and 1681. Organized by Lord Shaftesbury (the Carolina proprietor), the opposition demanded that James, a Catholic, be excluded from the throne in favor of his Protestant daughters, Mary and Anne. It also called for a guarantee of frequent elections and for an independent electorate not under the influence of wealthy patrons. The king's men began castigating Shaftesbury's followers as **Whigs**, the name of an obscure sect of Scottish religious extremists who favored the assassination of both Charles and James. Whigs in turn denounced Charles's courtiers as **Tories,** a term for Irish Catholic bandits who murdered Protestant landlords. Both labels stuck. Charles ended three years of turmoil in 1681. After getting secret financial support from King Louis XIV of France, he dissolved Parliament and ruled without one for the last four years of his reign.

THE LORDS OF TRADE AND IMPERIAL REFORM

English politics of the 1670s and 1680s had a profound impact on the colonies. The duke of York emerged from the Third Anglo-Dutch War (1672–1674) as the most powerful shaper of imperial policy. At his urging, the government created a new agency in 1675, the Lords Committee of Trade and Plantations, or more simply, the Lords of Trade, a permanent committee of the Privy Council. This agency enforced the Navigation Acts and administered the colonies. The West Indies became the object of most new policies. The instruments of royal government first took shape in the islands and were then extended to the mainland.

In the 1660s the Crown took control of the governments of Barbados, Jamaica, and the Leeward Islands. The king appointed the governor and upper house of each colony; the settlers elected an assembly. The Privy Council in England reserved to itself the power to hear appeals from colonial courts and to disallow colonial legislation after the governor had approved it. The Privy Council also issued a formal commission and a lengthy set of instructions to each royal governor. In the two or three decades after 1660, these documents became standardized. From the Crown's point of view, the governor's commission *created* the constitutional structure of each colony, a claim that few settlers accepted. The colonists believed they had an inherent right to constitutional rule.

Written instructions told each royal governor how to use his broad powers. They laid out things he must do, such as command the militia, and things he must avoid, such as approve laws detrimental to English trade. Crown lawyers eventually agreed that these instructions were binding only on the governor, not on the colony as a whole. In short, royal instructions never acquired the force of law.

London also insisted that each colony pay for its own government. This requirement, ironically, strengthened colonial claims to self-rule. After a long struggle in Jamaica, the Crown imposed a compromise in 1681 that had broad significance for all the colonies. The Lords of Trade threatened to make the Jamaica assembly as weak as the Irish Parliament, which could debate and approve only those bills that had first been adopted by the English Privy Council. Under the compromise, the Jamaica assembly retained its power to initiate and amend legislation. In return it passed a long-term revenue act that later became permanent, a measure that freed the governor from financial dependence on the assembly.

Metacom's War and Bacon's Rebellion lent urgency to these reforms. The Lords of Trade ordered soldiers to Virginia along with a royal commission to investigate grievances there. In 1676 they also sent an aggressive customs officer, Edward Randolph, to Massachusetts. He recommended that the colony's charter be revoked. The Lords of Trade viewed New England and all proprietary colonies with deep suspicion.

Whigs   *Obscure sect of Scottish religious extremists who favored the assassination of Charles and James of England. The term was used to denote one of the two leading political parties of late seventeenth-century England.*

Tories   *Term for Irish Catholic peasants who murdered Protestant land-lords. It was used to describe the followers of Charles II and became one of the names of the two major political parties in England.*

quitrent *Small annual fee attached to a piece of land. It differed from other rents in that nonpayment did not lead to ejection from the land but to a suit for debt.*

QUICK REVIEW

IMPERIAL REFORMS IN AN ERA OF POLITICAL CRISIS

• Whigs and Tories emerged while Parliament debated the royal succession

• Lords of Trade enforced Navigation Acts and developed Jamaica model of royal government, which reduced power of local assemblies

• Edward Randolph recommended revocation of Massachusetts charter

• James II united the northern colonies in the autocratic Dominion of New England

They had reason for concern. As late as 1678, Virginia remained the only royal colony on the mainland. The Lords of Trade possessed no effective instruments for punishing violators of the Navigation Acts in North America. The king could demand and reprimand, but not command.

The Jamaica model assumed that each royal governor would summon an assembly on occasion, though not very often. In the 1680s the Crown imposed a similar settlement on Virginia. James conceded an assembly to New York, too. The Jamaica model was becoming the norm for the Lords of Trade. James's real preference emerged after the English Court of Chancery revoked the Massachusetts Charter in 1684. Charles II died and his brother became King James II in early 1685. The possibility of a vigorous autocracy in America suddenly reappeared.

THE DOMINION OF NEW ENGLAND

Absolutist New York now became the king's model for reorganizing New England. James disallowed the New York Charter of Liberties of 1683 (see Chapter 2) and abolished the colony's assembly but kept the permanent revenue act in force. In 1686 he sent Sir Edmund Andros, the autocratic governor of New York from 1674 to 1680, to Massachusetts to take over a new government called the Dominion of New England. James added New Hampshire, Plymouth, Rhode Island, Connecticut, New York, and both Jerseys to the Dominion. Andros governed this vast domain through an appointive council and a superior court that rode circuit dispensing justice. There was no elective assembly. Andros also imposed religious toleration on the Puritans.

At first, Andros won support from merchants who had been denied the suffrage by the Puritan requirement that they be full church members, but his rigorous enforcement of the Navigation Acts soon alienated them. When he tried to compel New England farmers to take out new land titles that included annual **quitrents,** he enraged the whole countryside. His suppression of a tax revolt in Essex County, Massachusetts, started many people thinking more highly of their rights as Englishmen than of their peculiar liberties as Puritans. By 1688, government by consent probably seemed more valuable than it ever had before.

THE GLORIOUS REVOLUTION

FOCUS QUESTION

On what common principles did English political culture begin to converge in both the mother country and the colonies after the Glorious Revolution?

Events in England and France undermined the Dominion of New England. James II proclaimed toleration for both Protestant dissenters and Catholics and, in violation of recent laws, began to name Catholics to high office. In 1685 Louis XIV revoked the 1598 Edict of Nantes that had granted toleration to Protestants and launched a vicious persecution of the Huguenots. About 160,000 fled the kingdom. Many went to England; several thousand settled in the English mainland colonies. James II tried to suppress the news of Louis's persecution, which made his own professions of toleration seem hypocritical, even though his commitment was probably genuine. Then in 1688 James II's queen gave birth to a son who would clearly be raised Catholic, thus imposing a Catholic *dynasty* on England. Several Whig and Tory leaders swallowed their mutual hatred and invited William of Orange, the *stadholder* of the Netherlands, to England. The husband of the king's older Protestant daughter Mary (by James's first marriage), William had become the most prominent Protestant soldier in Europe during a long war against Louis XIV.

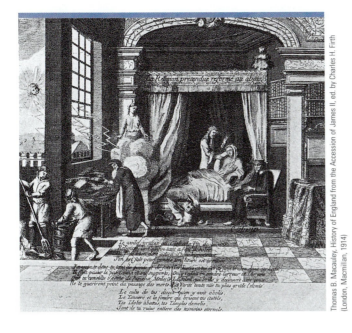

CALVINISM ON ITS DEATHBED AND LE ROY DE FRANCE. *Louis XIV's persecution of the Huguenots led his supporters to hope that France would soon be rid of all Protestants. In Le Roy de France, the Dutch Protestant response to the persecution depicts Louis, the sun king, as death.*

William landed in England in November 1688. Most of the English army sided with him, and James fled to France in late December. Parliament declared that James had abdicated the throne and named William III (1689–1702) and Mary II (1689–1694) as joint sovereigns. It also passed a Toleration Act that gave Protestant dissenters (but not Catholics) the right to worship publicly, and a Declaration of Rights that guaranteed a Protestant succession to the throne and condemned as illegal many of the acts of James II. This **Glorious Revolution** also brought England and the Netherlands into war against Louis XIV, who supported James.

THE GLORIOUS REVOLUTION IN AMERICA

The Boston militia overthrew Andros on April 18 and 19, 1689. Andros's attempt to suppress the news that William had landed in England convinced the Puritans that he was part of an Atlantic "Popish Plot" to undermine Protestant societies everywhere.

In May and June, the New York City militia took over Fort James at the southern tip of Manhattan and renamed it Fort William. Francis Nicholson, lieutenant governor in New York under Andros, refused to proclaim William and Mary as sovereigns without direct orders from England and soon sailed for home. The active rebels in New York City were nearly all Dutch who had little experience with traditional English liberties. Few had held high office. Their leader, Jacob Leisler, dreaded conquest by Catholics from New France and began to act like a Dutch *stadholder* in a nominally English colony.

Glorious Revolution
(1688) Bloodless overthrow of King James II by Whigs and Tories, who invited William of Orange to England. He and his wife Mary became King and Queen.

Military defense became Leisler's highest priority, but his demands for supplies soon alienated even his Yankee supporters on Long Island. Although he summoned an elective assembly, he made no effort to revive the Charter of Liberties of 1683 while continuing to collect duties under the permanent revenue act of that year. He showed little respect for the legal rights of his opponents, most of whom were English or were Dutch merchants who had served the Dominion of New England. Loud complaints against his administration reached the Crown in London.

In Maryland, Protestants overthrew Lord Baltimore's Catholic government in 1689. The governor of Maryland refused to proclaim William and Mary, even after all the other colonies had done so. To Lord Baltimore's dismay, the messenger he had sent from England to Maryland with orders to accept the new monarchs died en route. Had he arrived, the government probably would have survived the crisis.

THE ENGLISH RESPONSE

England responded in different ways to each of these upheavals. The Maryland rebels won the royal government they requested from England and soon established the Anglican Church in the colony. Catholics could no longer worship in public, hold office, or run their schools, but they did receive informal toleration. Most prominent Catholic families, however, remained loyal to their faith. In 1716, when the new Lord Baltimore became a Protestant, the Crown restored proprietary government.

In New York, the Leislerians suffered a deadly defeat. Leisler and his Dutch followers, who had no significant contacts at the English Court, watched helplessly as their enemies, working through the imperial bureaucracy that William inherited from James, manipulated the Dutch king of England into undermining his loyal Dutch supporters in New York. The new governor, Henry Sloughter, arrested Leisler and his son-in-law in 1691, tried both for treason, and had them hanged, drawn (disemboweled), and quartered. The assembly elected that year was controlled by Anti-Leislerians, most of whom were English. It passed a modified version of the Charter of Liberties of 1683, this time denying toleration to Catholics. Like its predecessor, it was later disallowed. Bitter struggles between Leislerians and Anti-Leislerians raged until after 1700.

Another complex struggle involved Massachusetts. In 1689 the Reverend Increase Mather, acting as the colony's agent in London, failed to get Parliament to restore the charter of 1629. Over the next two years he negotiated a new charter, which gave the Crown the power to appoint governors, justices, and militia officers and the power to veto laws and to hear judicial appeals. The 1691 charter also granted toleration to all Protestants and based voting rights on property qualifications, not church membership. In effect, liberty and property had triumphed over godliness.

While insisting on these concessions, William also accepted much of the previous history of the colony. The General Court, not the governor as in other royal colonies, retained control over the distribution of land. The council remained an elective body, although it was chosen annually by the full legislature, not directly by the voters. The governor could veto any councilor. Massachusetts also absorbed the colonies of Plymouth and Maine. New Hampshire regained its autonomy, but until 1741 it usually shared the same royal governor with Massachusetts. Rhode Island and Connecticut resumed their charter governments.

THE SALEM WITCH TRIALS

When Mather sailed into Boston harbor with the new charter in May 1692, he found the province besieged by witches. The accusations arose in Salem Village (modern Danvers) among a group of girls that included a young daughter and a niece of the local minister, Samuel Parris, and then spread to older girls, some of whom had been orphaned in the Indian wars. The girls howled, barked, and stretched themselves into frightful contortions. After enduring these torments for more than a month, they began—with adult encouragement—to accuse many neighbors of witchcraft, mostly those who did not approve of Parris. The number of accused escalated sharply in April after 14-year-old Abigail Hobbs confessed that she had made a compact with the devil in Maine in 1688 just before the outbreak of the Indian war that had since devastated most of northern New England. Altogether about 150 people were accused in Essex County and beyond. Satan, supported by Indian warriors on the frontier and witches within the colony, appeared to be destroying Massachusetts.

The trials began in June. The court, which included judges badly compromised by their willing service to the Andros regime, hanged 19 people, pressed one man to death because he refused to stand trial, and allowed several others to die in jail. Many of the victims were grandmothers, several conspicuous for their piety. One was a former minister at Salem Village who had become a Baptist. Everyone executed claimed to be innocent. Of 50 who confessed, none was hanged. The governor finally halted the trials after someone accused his wife of witchcraft. By then public support for the trials was collapsing. The **Salem witch trials** provided a bitter finale to the era of political upheaval that had afflicted Massachusetts since the loss of the colony's charter in 1684. Along with the new charter, the trials brought the Puritan era to a close.

THE COMPLETION OF EMPIRE

The Glorious Revolution killed absolutism in English America and guaranteed that royal government would be representative government in the colonies. Both Crown and colonists took it for granted that any colony settled by the English would elect an assembly to vote taxes and pass laws. Governors would be appointed by the Crown or a lord proprietor. (Governors were elected in Connecticut and Rhode Island.) But royal government soon became the norm especially after the New Jersey and Carolina proprietors surrendered their powers of government to the Crown. By the 1720s Maryland and Pennsylvania (along with Delaware, which became a separate colony under the Penn proprietorship in 1704) were the only surviving proprietary provinces on the mainland. This transition to royal government seems smoother in retrospect than it did at the time. London almost lost control of the empire in the 1690s. Overwhelmed by the pressures of the French war, the Lords of Trade could not keep pace with events in the colonies. When French privateers disrupted the tobacco trade, Scottish smugglers stepped in and began to divert it to Glasgow in defiance of the Navigation Acts. New York became a haven for pirates.

William took action in 1696. With his approval Parliament passed a new, comprehensive Navigation Act that plugged several loopholes in earlier laws and extended to America the English system of vice- admiralty courts, which dispensed quick justice without juries. When the new courts settled routine maritime disputes or condemned enemy merchant ships captured by colonial privateers, the settlers appreciated these services. But when the courts tried to assume jurisdiction over the Navigation Acts, they aroused controversy. Sometimes the common law courts intervened and took over those cases.

Salem witch trials *1692 outbreak of witchcraft accusations in a Puritan village marked by an atmosphere of fear, hysteria, and stress that led to 20 executions.*

William also replaced the Lords of Trade in 1696 with a new agency, the Board of Trade. Its powers were almost purely advisory. It corresponded with governors and other officials in the colonies, listened to lobbyists in England, and made policy recommendations to appropriate governmental bodies. The board tried to collect information on complex questions and to offer helpful advice. It was, in short, an early attempt at government by experts.

Another difficult problem was resolved in 1707 when England and Scotland agreed to merge their separate parliaments and become the single kingdom of Great Britain. At a stroke, the Act of Union placed Scotland inside the Navigation Act system, legalized Scottish participation in the tobacco trade, and opened numerous colonial offices to ambitious Scots. By the middle of the 18th century most of Scotland's growing prosperity derived from its trade with the colonies.

IMPERIAL FEDERALISM

The transformations that took place between 1689 and 1707 defined the structure of the British Empire until the American Revolution. Although Parliament claimed full power over the colonies, in practice it seldom regulated anything colonial except Atlantic commerce. Even the Woolens Act of 1699 did not prohibit the manufacture of woolen textiles in the colonies. It simply prohibited their export. The Hat Act of 1732 was similarly designed.

When Parliament regulated oceanic trade, its measures were usually enforceable. But compliance was minimal to nonexistent when Parliament tried to regulate inland affairs through statutes protecting white pines (needed as masts for the navy) or through the Iron Act of 1750, which prohibited the erection of certain types of new iron mills. To get things done within the colonies, the Crown had to win the settlers' agreement through their lawful assemblies and unsalaried local officials. In effect, the empire had stumbled into a system of de facto federalism, an arrangement that no one could quite explain or justify. Parliament exercised only limited powers, and the colonies controlled the rest. What seemed an arrangement of convenience in London soon acquired overtones of right in America, the right to consent to all taxes and local laws.

THE MIXED AND BALANCED CONSTITUTION

The Glorious Revolution transformed British politics. Britain, whose government had seemed wildly unstable for half a century, quickly became a far more powerful state than the Stuart kings had been able to sustain with their pretensions to absolute monarchy. The British constitution, which made ministers legally responsible for their public actions, proved remarkably stable. In the ancient world, free societies had degenerated into tyrannies. Liberty had always been fragile and was easily lost. Yet England had retained its liberty and grown stronger in the process. England had defied history.

The explanation, everyone agreed, lay in England's "mixed and balanced" constitution. Government by "King, Lords, and Commons" mirrored society itself—the monarchy, aristocracy, and commonality. As long as each freely consented to government measures, English liberty would be secure because each had voluntarily placed the public good ahead of its own interests. But if one of the three acquired the power to dominate or manipulate the other two, English liberty would indeed be in peril. That danger fueled an unending debate in 18th-century Britain. The underlying drama was always the struggle of power against liberty, and liberty usually meant a limitation of governmental power. Power had to be controlled, or liberty would be lost. The real danger to liberty lay, not in a military coup, but in corruption, in the

QUICK   REVIEW

REDEFINING CONSTITUTIONALISM IN ENGLAND AND THE COLONIES

- Glorious Revolution led to stronger English Parliament, Toleration Act

- Glorious Revolution led to rebellion in New York, ouster of Catholic government in Maryland, and expanded religious and civil liberties in Massachusetts

- Reforms of 1696 and the 1707 Union with Scotland completed the redefinition of empire

- Policy of imperial federalism meant regulation of Atlantic trade but little internal regulation by Parliament

- Britain's "mixed and balanced" constitution pitted Court versus County

ability of Crown ministers to use their patronage to undermine the independence of the House of Commons.

After 1689 England raised larger fleets and armies than the kingdom had ever mobilized before. To support them Parliament created for the first time a **funded national debt**, in which the state agreed to pay the interest due to its creditors ahead of all other obligations. This simple device gave Britain enormous borrowing power. In 1694 the government created the Bank of England to facilitate its own finances; the London Stock Exchange also emerged in the 1690s. To meet wartime expenses, Parliament levied a heavy land tax on the gentry and excises on ordinary people. These actions amounted to a financial revolution that enabled England to outspend France, despite having only one-fourth of France's population. And by giving public offices to members of Parliament, Crown ministers were almost assured of majority support for their measures.

Ever since the Popish Plot, public debates had pitted the "Court" against the "Country." The Court favored policies that strengthened its war-making capacity. The Country stood for liberty. Each of the parties, Whig and Tory, had Court and Country wings. But between 1680 and 1720 they reversed their polarities. Although the Tories had begun as Charles II's Court party, by 1720 most of them were a Country opposition. Whigs had defended Country positions in 1680, but by 1720 most of them were strong advocates for the Court policies of George I (1714–1727). Court spokesmen defended the military buildup, the financial revolution, and the new patronage as essential to victory over France and to sustain British strength in world politics. Their Country opponents denounced standing armies, attacked the financial revolution as an engine of corruption, favored an early peace with France, demanded more frequent elections, and tried to ban "placemen" (officeholders who sat in Parliament) from the House of Commons.

Court Whigs emerged victorious during the long ministry of Sir Robert Walpole (1721–1742), but their opponents were more eloquent and controlled more presses. By the 1720s, the opposition claimed many of the kingdom's best writers, especially the Tories Alexander Pope, Jonathan Swift, John Gay, and Henry St. John, viscount Bolingbroke. Their detestation of Walpole was shared by a smaller band of radical Whigs, including John Trenchard and Thomas Gordon, who wrote *Cato's Letters,* four volumes of collected newspaper essays. The central theme of the opposition was corruption—the insidious means by which ministers threatened the independence of Parliament and English liberty. This debate over liberty soon reached America.

funded national debt *Agreement by the state to pay the interest due to its creditors before all other obligations.*

CONTRASTING EMPIRES: SPAIN AND FRANCE IN NORTH AMERICA

After 1689, Britain's enemies were France and Spain. Until 1689 the three empires had coexisted in America without much contact among them. Europe's wars soon engulfed them all. Spain and France shared a Catholic zeal for converting Indians that exceeded anything displayed by English Protestants, but their American empires had little else in common.

THE PUEBLO REVOLT

In the late 17th century, the Spanish missions of North America entered a period of crisis. Fewer priests took the trouble to master Indian languages, insisting instead that the Indians learn Spanish. For all of their good intentions, the missionaries often

FOCUS QUESTION
What enabled sparsely settled New France to resist British expansion with great success for more than half a century, whereas Spanish Florida seemed almost helpless against a similar threat?

whipped or shackled Indians for minor infractions. Disease also took a heavy toll. A declining Indian population made labor demands by the missionaries a heavier burden, and despite strong prohibitions, some Spaniards enslaved Indians in Florida and New Mexico. After 1670 Florida also feared encroachments by English Protestants out of South Carolina, eager to enslave unarmed Indians, whether or not they had embraced Christianity, and yet Spain still refused to arm its Indians. By 1700, the European refusal to enslave other Christians protected only white people.

But the greatest challenge to Spain arose in New Mexico, where the Pueblo population had fallen from 80,000 to 17,000 since 1598. A prolonged drought, together with Apache and Navajo attacks, prompted many Pueblos to abandon the Christian God and resume their old forms of worship. Missionaries responded with whippings and even several executions in 1675. Popé, a San Juan Pueblo medicine man who had been whipped for his beliefs, moved north to Taos Pueblo, where he organized the most successful Indian revolt in American history. In 1680, in a carefully timed uprising, the Pueblos killed 400 of the 2,300 Spaniards in New Mexico and destroyed or plundered every Spanish building in the province (see map on p. 25) They desecrated every church and killed 21 of New Mexico's 33 missionaries. Spanish survivors fled from Santa Fe down the Rio Grande to El Paso.

Popé lost his influence after traditional Pueblo rites failed to end the drought or stop Apache attacks. When the Spanish returned in the 1690s, the Pueblos were badly divided. Most villages yielded without much resistance, but Santa Fe held out until December 1693. When it fell, the Spanish executed 70 men and gave 400 women and children to the returning settlers as their slaves.

In both Florida and New Mexico, missionaries had often resisted the demands of Spanish governors. By 1700 the state ruled and missionaries obeyed. Spain's attempt to create a demilitarized Christian frontier was proving a tragic failure for both Indians and missionaries.

Pueblo Revolt   *In the most successful Indian uprising in American history, the Pueblo people rose against the Spanish in 1680, killing most Spanish missionaries, devastating Spanish buildings, and forcing the surviving Spaniards to retreat down the Rio Grande.*

NEW FRANCE AND THE MIDDLE GROUND

A different story unfolded along the western borders of New France. There the Iroquois menace made possible an unusual accommodation between the colony and the Indians of the Great Lakes region. The survival of the Iroquois Five Nations depended on their ability to assimilate captives. Their raiders, armed with muskets, terrorized western Indians and carried away thousands of captives. The Iroquois wars depopu-

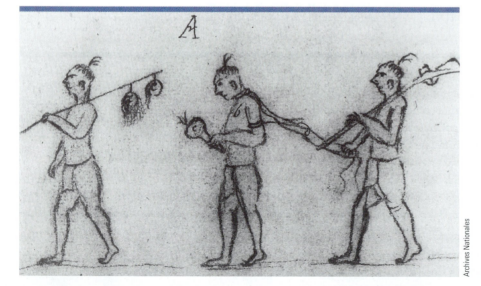

Archives Nationales

IROQUOIS WARRIORS LEADING AN INDIAN PRISONER INTO CAPTIVITY, 1660s. *Because Indian populations had been depleted by war and disease, a tribe's survival became dependent on its ability to assimilate captives. This is a French copy of an Iroquois pictograph.*

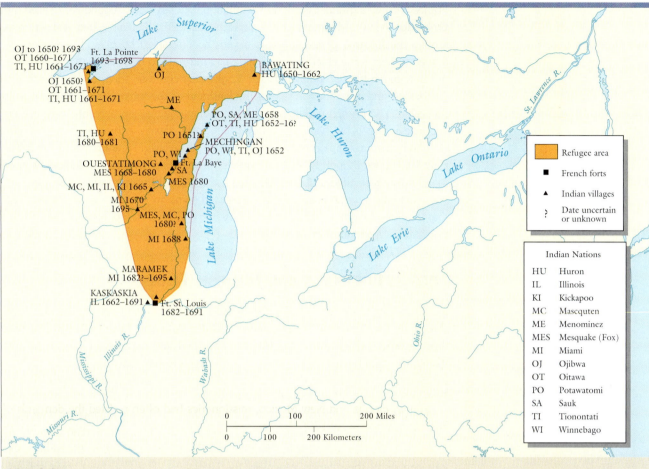

Map 3.2

FRENCH MIDDLE GROUND IN NORTH AMERICA CIRCA 1700. *French power in North America rested mostly on the arrangements French governors worked out with refugee Algonquian Indians trying to resist Iroquois raids in the Great Lakes region.*

lated nearly all of what is now the state of Ohio and much of the Ontario peninsula. The Indians around Lakes Erie and Huron either fled west or were absorbed by the Iroquois. The refugees, mostly Algonquian-speaking peoples, founded new multiethnic communities farther west. But when the refugees disagreed with one another or came into conflict with the Sioux to their west, the absence of traditional tribal structures made it difficult to resolve their differences. Over time, French soldiers, trappers, and missionaries stepped in as mediators.

The leaders of thinly populated New France were eager to erect an Algonquian shield against the Iroquois. They began by easing tensions among the Algonquians while supplying them with firearms, brandy, and other European goods. New France provided the resources that the Algonquians needed to strike back against the Iroquois. By 1701 Iroquois losses had become so heavy that the Five Nations negotiated a peace treaty with the French and the western Indians. The Iroquois agreed to remain neutral in any war between France and England. France's Indian allies, supported by a new French fort erected at Detroit in 1701, began returning to the fertile lands around Lakes Erie and Huron. That region became a **Middle Ground** over which no one could wield sovereign power, although New France exercised great influence within it.

France's success in the interior rested on intelligent negotiation, not force. Hugely outnumbered, the French knew that they could not impose their will on the Indians. But Indians respected those Frenchmen who honored their ways. The French conducted diplomacy according to Indian, not European, rules. The governor of New

Middle Ground *Area of French and Indian cooperation west of Niagara and south of the Great Lakes, over which no one exercised sovereign power.*

France became a grander version of a traditional Indian chief. Algonquians called him **Onontio** ("Great Mountain"), the supreme alliance chief who had learned that, among the Indians, persuasion was always accompanied by gifts. The respect accorded to peacetime chiefs was roughly proportionate to how much they gave away, not how much they accumulated. The English, by contrast, tried to "buy" land from the Indians and regarded the sale of the land and of the Indians' right to use it as irrevocable. The French understood that, in Indian cultures, agreements were not unalterable contracts but had to be renewed regularly, always with an exchange of gifts.

Middle Ground diplomacy came at a price. It involved New France in the Indian slave trade even though Louis XIV expressly forbade enslavement of Indians, a command finally rescinded in 1709. Because Indians fought wars mostly to acquire captives, Onontio's western allies often presented some to French traders who realized that to refuse the gift would be an insult. By the 1720s up to 5 percent of the colony's population consisted of enslaved Indians.

FRENCH LOUISIANA AND SPANISH TEXAS

In quest of a passage to Asia, Father Jacques Marquette and trader Louis Joliet paddled down the Mississippi to its juncture with the Arkansas River in 1673. But once they became convinced that the Mississippi flowed into the Gulf of Mexico and not the Pacific, they turned back. Then, in 1682, René-Robert Cavelier, *sieur* de La Salle traveled down the Mississippi to its mouth, claiming possession of the entire area for France and calling it Louisiana (for Louis XIV).

In 1699 the French returned to the Gulf of Mexico. Pierre le Moyne d'Iberville, a Canadian, landed with 80 men at Biloxi, built a fort, and began trading with the Indians. In 1702 he moved his headquarters to Mobile to get closer to the more populous nations of the interior, especially the Choctaws. The Choctaws could still field 5,000 warriors but had suffered heavy losses from slaving raids organized by South Carolinians and carried out mostly by that colony's Chickasaw and Creek allies. Using the Choctaws to anchor their trading system, the French created a weaker, southern version of the Great Lakes Middle Ground, acting as mediators while trading brandy, firearms, and other European products for furs and food. Often, during the War of the Spanish Succession (1702–1713), the French were unable to get European supplies, and they remained heavily outnumbered by the Indians. Although European diseases had been ravaging the area since the 1540s, the Indians of the lower Mississippi valley still numbered about 70,000. In 1708 the French had about 300 people, including 80 Indian slaves. They were lucky to survive.

Spain, alarmed at any challenge to its monopoly on the Gulf of Mexico, founded Pensacola in 1698 and in 1690 established several missions in eastern Texas. But the missionaries brought smallpox with them. Their explanation, that the epidemic was God's "holy will," did not mollify the Tejas Indians, who told them to get out or be killed. They fled in 1693, leaving Texas to the Indians for 20 more years.

Onontio *Algonquian word meaning "great mountain"; used by Indians of the Middle Ground to designate the governor of New France.*

AN EMPIRE OF SETTLEMENT: THE BRITISH COLONIES

By 1700, when 250,000 settlers and slaves were already living in England's mainland colonies, the population was doubling every 25 years. New France matched that pace, but with only 14,000 people in 1700, it could not close the gap. By contrast, the population of the Spanish missions continued to decline. In the struggle for empire, a growing population became Britain's greatest advantage.

THE ENGINE OF BRITISH EXPANSION: THE COLONIAL HOUSEHOLD

In England younger sons rarely owned land and were clearly not equal to the oldest son, and daughters ranked behind both. By contrast, most colonial householders tried to pass on their status to *all* their sons, and to provide dowries that would enable all their daughters to marry men of equal status. Nevertheless, colonial households were patriarchal. A mature male was expected to be the master of his household and perhaps of others. Above all, a patriarch strove to perpetuate the household itself into the next generation and to preserve his own economic "independence." Of course, complete independence was impossible. Every household owed small debts or favors to its neighbors, but these obligations seldom compromised the family's standing in the community.

Farmers tried to grow an agricultural surplus, if only as a hedge against drought, storms, and other unpredictable events. With the harvest in, farmers marketed their produce, often selling it for cash to merchants in Boston, New York, or Philadelphia. Farmers used the cash to pay taxes or their ministers' salaries and to buy British imports. Although these arrangements sometimes placed families in short-term debt to merchants, most farmers and artisans managed to avoid long-term debt. Settlers accepted temporary dependency among freemen—of sons on their parents, indentured servants on their masters, or apprentices and journeymen on master craftsmen. Sons often worked as laborers on neighboring farms, as sailors, or as journeymen craftsmen, provided that such dependence was temporary. A man who became permanently dependent on others lost the respect of his community.

THE VOLUNTARISTIC ETHIC AND PUBLIC LIFE

Householders carried their quest for independence into public life. Few freemen could be coerced into doing something of which they disapproved. They had to be persuaded or induced. Local officials serving without pay frequently ignored orders that did not serve their own interests or the interests of their community. In entering politics and waging war, the settlers' autonomy became an ethic of voluntarism. Most young men accepted military service only if it fitted in with their future plans. They would serve only under officers they knew, and then for only a single campaign. Few reenlisted. After serving, they used their bonus and their pay, and often the promise of a land grant, to speed their way to becoming masters of their own households. Military service, for those who survived, could lead to the ownership of land and an earlier marriage. For New England women, however, war reduced the supply of eligible males and raised the median age of marriage by about two years, which usually meant one fewer pregnancy per marriage.

THREE WARRING EMPIRES, 1689–1716

When the three empires went to war after 1689, the Spanish and French fought mostly to survive. The British fought to expand their holdings. None of them won a decisive advantage in the first two wars, which ended with the Treaty of Utrecht in 1713.

Smart diplomacy with the Indians protected the western flank of New France. There the French forced the Iroquois to make peace by 1701 and to promise to remain neutral in any future war between France and Britain, but the eastern parts of New France were vulnerable to English invasion. The governors of New France knew that Indian attacks against English towns would keep the English colonies disorga-

BRITISH WARS AGAINST FRANCE (AND USUALLY SPAIN), 1689–1763

EUROPEAN NAME	AMERICAN NAME	YEARS	PEACE
War of the League of Augsburg	King William's War	1689–1697	Ryswick
War of the Spanish Succession	Queen Anne's War	1702–1713	Utrecht
War of Jenkins' Ear, merging with		1739–1748	
War of the Austrian Succession	King George's War	1744–1748	Aix-la-Chapelle
Seven Years' War	French and Indian War	1754–1763*	Paris

*The French and Indian War began in America in 1754 and then merged with the Seven Years' War in Europe, which began in 1756.

nized and make them disperse their forces. Within two years of the outbreak of war between France and England in 1689, Indians had devastated most of coastal Maine and New Hampshire and had attacked the Mohawk valley town of Schenectady, killing 60 and carrying off 27.

In each of the four colonial wars between Britain and France, New Englanders called for the conquest of New France, usually through a naval expedition against Quebec, combined with an overland attack on Montreal. In King William's War (1689–1697), Sir William Phips of Massachusetts forced Acadia to surrender in 1690 (although the French soon regained it) and then sailed up the St. Lawrence. At Quebec, Phips was forced to retreat with heavy losses.

In 1704, during Queen Anne's War (1702–1713), the French and Indians destroyed Deerfield, Massachusetts, in a winter attack and marched most of its people off to captivity in Canada. Hundreds of New Englanders spent months or even years as captives. As the war dragged on, New Englanders twice failed to take Port Royal in Acadia, but a combined British and colonial force finally succeeded in 1710, renaming the colony Nova Scotia. An effort to subdue Quebec the following year met with disaster when many of the British ships ran aground in a treacherous stretch of the St. Lawrence River.

Farther south, the imperial struggle was grimmer and even more tragic. The Franciscan missions of Florida were already in decline, but mission Indians still attracted Carolina slavers, who invaded Florida between 1702 and 1704 with a large force of Indian allies, dragged off 4,000 women and children as slaves, drove 9,000 Indians from their homes, and wrecked the missions. The invaders failed to take the Spanish fortress of St. Augustine, but slaving raids spread devastation as far west as the lands of the Choctaws and far south along the Florida peninsula.

By 1715 South Carolina's greed for Indian slaves finally alienated the colony's strongest Indian allies, the Yamasees, who deeply resented the mistreatment of Indian women by the traders and their interminable quarrels with one another. Fearing that they would be the next to be enslaved, the warriors killed all the colonial traders among them and aligned with most other southeastern Indians to attack the colony. They almost destroyed it before being thrust back and nearly exterminated. Some of the Yamasees and a number of escaped African slaves fled as refugees to Spanish Florida.

The wars of 1689–1716 halted the movement of British settlers onto new lands in New England and the Carolinas. Only four Maine towns survived the wars; after half a century, South Carolina still had fewer than 6,000 settlers in 1720. But in Pennsylvania, Maryland, and Virginia—colonies that had not been deeply involved in the wars—the westward thrust continued.

C O N C L U S I O N

The variety and diversity of the colonies posed a huge challenge to the English government. After 1650 it found ways to regulate their trade, mostly for the mutual benefit of both England and the colonies. The colonies, beset by hostile Indians and internal discord, began to recognize that they needed protection that only England could provide. Once the Crown gave up its claims to absolute power, the two sides discovered much on which they could agree.

Political values in England and the colonies converged after the Glorious Revolution. Englishmen everywhere insisted that the right to property was sacred, that without it liberty could never be secure. They celebrated liberty under law, government by consent, and the toleration of all Protestants. They excluded Catholics from succession to the throne, eventually disfranchised them, and barred them from public office. In an empire dedicated to "liberty, property, and no popery," Catholics became big losers.

So did Indians and Africans. Racism directed against Indians welled up mostly from below, taking root among ordinary settlers who competed with Indians for many of the same resources, especially land. Colonial elites tried, often ineffectually, to contain the popular rage that nearly tore New England and Virginia apart in 1675–1676. By contrast, racism directed against enslaved Africans was typically imposed from above and increasingly enforced by law. Ordinary settlers and Africans knew one another by name, made love, sometimes even married, stole hogs together, ran away together, and even fought together under Nathaniel Bacon's leadership. The men who were becoming great planters used their power to criminalize most of these activities. They were terrified by the upheaval that ex-servants could create and hoped for greater stability from a labor force serving for life. They rewarded small planters and servants with white supremacy.

Nevertheless, by the 18th century, the British colonists had come to believe they were the freest people on earth. They attributed this fortune to their widespread ownership of land and to the English constitutional principles that they had incorporated into their own governments. When George I became king in 1714, they proclaimed their loyalty to the Hanoverian dynasty that guaranteed a Protestant succession to the British throne. In their minds, the British empire had become the world's last bastion of liberty. Especially since the Glorious Revolution, it had asserted this liberty while greatly magnifying its power.

QUESTIONS FOR REVIEW AND CRITICAL THINKING

Review

1. How important was England's mercantilistic system in gaining effective control over the colonies and in projecting English power against its European rivals?
2. Contrast the failure of New England and Virginia to preserve peaceful relations with neighboring Indians in 1675–1676 with New York's success in the same decade and later.
3. On what common principles did English political culture begin to converge in both the mother country and the colonies after the Glorious Revolution?
4. What enabled sparsely settled New France to resist British expansion with great success for more than half a century, whereas Spanish Florida seemed almost helpless against a similar threat?

Critical Thinking

1. From the Restoration era to the American Revolution, most Englishmen and colonists understood politics as a perpetual struggle between power and liberty, one in which victory had almost always gone to power. How then was the English empire able to increase both its power and its commitment to liberty over that period?
2. Discuss the changing forms of racism and the role they played in the English colonies between their founding and the Yamasee War.

Discovery

What difficulties did England encounter while governing its overseas empire? How did it respond to these problems? What role did cultural perspectives play in England's "problems" with the Indians?

SUGGESTED READINGS

The most comprehensive account of the Navigation Acts and England's instruments of enforcement is still **Charles M. Andrews, *The Colonial Period of American History,*** vol. 4 (1938). **Ian K. Steele's *The English Atlantic, 1675–1740: An Exploration of Communication and Community*** (1986) is original and imaginative.

Daniel K. Richter's *The Ordeal of the Longhouse: The People of the Iroquois League in the Era of European Colonization* (1992); **Richard W. Cogley's *John Eliot's Mission to the Indians before King Philip's War*** (1999); **Jill Lepore's *The Name of War: King Philip's War and the Origins of American Identity*** (1998); and **Wilcomb Washburn, *The Governor and the Rebel: A History of Bacon's Rebellion in Virginia*** (1957) are all essential to understanding the crisis of the 1670s. For Virginia's transition to slavery after Bacon's Rebellion, see **Anthony S. Parent, Jr., *Foul Means: The Formation of a Slave Society in Virginia, 1660–1740*** (2003).

For the Dominion of New England and the Glorious Revolution in the colonies, see **Richard R. Johnson, *Adjustment to Empire: The New England Colonies, 1675–1715*** (1981); **John M. Murrin,** "The Menacing Shadow of Louis XIV and the Rage of Jacob Leisler: The Constitutional Ordeal of Seventeenth-Century New York," in **Stephen L. Schechter** and **Richard B. Bernstein,** eds., ***New York and the Union: Contributions to the American Constitutional Experience*** (1990), pp. 29–71; and **Lois G. Carr** and **David W. Jordan, *Maryland's Revolution of Government, 1689–1692*** (1974). The best study of Salem witchcraft, which is also a superb introduction to the Indian wars in northern New England, is **Mary Beth Norton, *In the Devil's Snare: The Salem Witchcraft Crisis of 1692*** (2002).

For the French and Spanish colonies in these critical decades, see especially **Richard White, *The Middle Ground: Indians, Empires, and Republics in the Great Lakes Region, 1650–1815*** (1991); and **Ramón Gutiérrez, *When Jesus Came, the Corn Mothers Went Away: Marriage, Sexuality, and Power in New Mexico, 1500–1846*** (1992), particularly on the Pueblo revolt.

On the householder economy in English North America, see **Laurel Thatcher Ulrich's *Good Wives: Images and Reality in the Lives of Women in Northern New England*** (1982), and **Mary M. Schweitzer, *Custom and Contract: Household, Government, and the Economy in Colonial Pennsylvania*** (1987).

ONLINE SOURCES GUIDE

ThomsonNOW™ Visit ThomsonNOW to access primary sources, exercises, quizzes, and audio chapter summaries related to this chapter:

http://www.thomsonedu.com/login

$\mathcal{D}$ISCOVERY

What difficulties did England encounter while governing its overseas empire? How did it respond to these problems? What role did cultural perspectives play in England's "problems" with the Indians?

In thinking about this question, begin by breaking it down into the components shown below. A discussion of the significance of each component should appear in your answer.

DEMOGRAPHY, ECONOMY AND GOVERNMENT

Look at the two tables on "The Spectrum of Settlement." In the first table, why was the life expectancy of many of the English colonies so low? How would this have created political and economic problems? How did race, ethnicity, and religion influence life expectancies? Compare and contrast New France to the English colonies. Based on this comparison, in which location would you most like to have lived in this period?

In the second table, compare the various types of local and provincial governments. Which of these were most like England itself?

THE SPECTRUM OF SETTLEMENT: DEMOGRAPHY, ETHNICITY, ECONOMY, 1650–1700

CATEGORY	WEST INDIES	LOWER SOUTH	CHESAPEAKE	MID-ATLANTIC	NEW ENGLAND	NEW FRANCE
Life expectancy for men, at age 20	40	42	45	60+	Late 60s	60s
Family size	Below replacement rate	About two children	Rising after 1680	Very large	Very large	Very large
Race and ethnicity	Black majority by circa 1670s	Black majority by circa 1710	Growing black minority	Ethnic mix, N.W. Europe, English a minority	Almost all English	Almost all French
Economy	Sugar	Indian slave trade, then rice	Tobacco	Furs, farms	Farms, fishing, shipbuilding	Furs, farms

THE SPECTRUM OF SETTLEMENT: RELIGION AND GOVERNMENT, CIRCA 1675–1700

CATEGORY	WEST INDIES	LOWER SOUTH	CHESAPEAKE	MID-ATLANTIC	NEW ENGLAND	NEW FRANCE
Formal religion	Anglican church establishment	Anglican church establishment by circa 1710	Anglican church establishment (after 1692 in Md.)	Competing sects, no established church	Congregational church established	Catholic church established
Religious tone	Irreverent	Contentious	Low-church Anglican	Family-based piety, sectarian competition	Family-based piety, intensity declining	Intensely Catholic
Local government	Parish	Parish and phantom counties (i.e., no court)	County and parish	County and township	Towns and counties; parishes after 1700	Cities
Provincial government	Royal	Proprietary	Royal (Va.), proprietary (Md.)	From proprietary to royal, except in Pa.	Corporate, with Mass. and N.H. becoming royal	Royal absolutism

CULTURE AND SOCIETY

Examine the painting "A Pictish Man Holding a Human Head." Did the portrayal of Native Americans by the colonists contribute to the latter's sense of cultural superiority? If so, how? How did European attitudes toward Native Americans influence colonial policies toward Native Americans? What does an artist's depiction reveal about the artist and his or her beliefs?

A PICTISH MAN HOLDING A HUMAN HEAD

4

PROVINCIAL AMERICA AND THE STRUGGLE FOR A CONTINENT

The British colonists, who thought they were the freest people on earth, faced a growing dilemma. To maintain the opportunity that settlers had come to expect, the colonies had to expand onto new lands. But provincial society also emulated the cultural values of Great Britain—its architecture, polite learning, religion, and politics. Relentless expansion made this emulation difficult because frontier areas were not genteel. An anglicized province would become far more hierarchical than the colonies had been and might not even try to provide a rough equality of opportunity. The settlers tried to sustain both, an effort that also brought renewed conflict with the Spanish and the French after 1739. But less fortunate people among them thought differently. Slaves saw Spain, not France, as a beacon of liberty. In the eastern woodlands, most Indians identified France, not Britain, as the only ally committed to their survival and independence.

TIMELINE

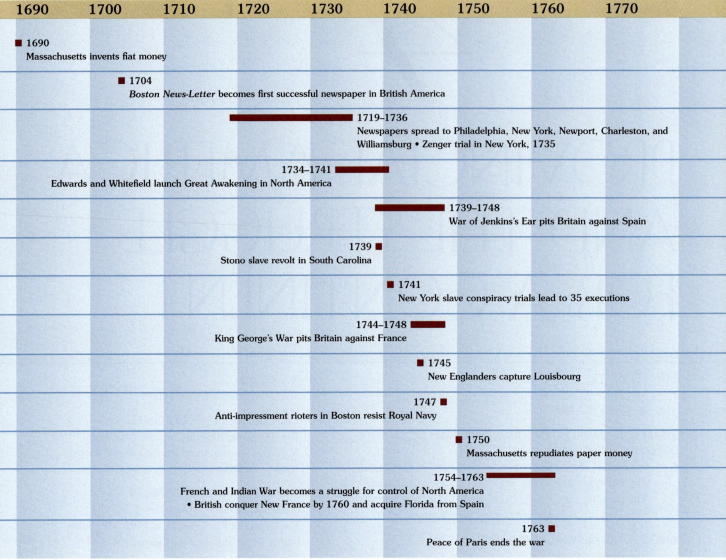

1690	1700	1710	1720	1730	1740	1750	1760	1770

■ 1690
Massachusetts invents fiat money

■ 1704
Boston News-Letter becomes first successful newspaper in British America

1719–1736
Newspapers spread to Philadelphia, New York, Newport, Charleston, and Williamsburg • Zenger trial in New York, 1735

1734–1741
Edwards and Whitefield launch Great Awakening in North America

1739–1748
War of Jenkins's Ear pits Britain against Spain

1739 ■
Stono slave revolt in South Carolina

■ 1741
New York slave conspiracy trials lead to 35 executions

1744–1748
King George's War pits Britain against France

■ 1745
New Englanders capture Louisbourg

1747 ■
Anti-impressment rioters in Boston resist Royal Navy

■ 1750
Massachusetts repudiates paper money

1754–1763
French and Indian War becomes a struggle for control of North America • British conquer New France by 1760 and acquire Florida from Spain

1763 ■
Peace of Paris ends the war

EXPANSION VERSUS ANGLICIZATION

FOCUS QUESTION

Why was it difficult to sustain both continual expansion and the anglicization of the colonies in the 18th century?

In the 18th century, as the British colonists sought to emulate their homeland, many of the things they had left behind in the 17th century began to reappear. After 1740, for example, imports of British goods grew spectacularly. The gentry and the merchants dressed in the latest London fashions and embraced that city's standards of taste and elegance. Southern planters erected "big houses" such as Mount Vernon. Newspapers and learned professions based on English models proliferated.

But the population of British North America doubled every 25 years. That meant that each generation required twice as many colleges, ministers, lawyers, physicians, craftsmen, printers, sailors, and unskilled laborers as the preceding generation. As the 18th century progressed, the colonies experienced a relentless contest between the pace of expansion and these anglicizing tendencies.

The southern colonies, which looked to England, or even Europe, to satisfy their needs for skilled talent, could no longer attract as many people as they needed. In

1700, for example, Oxford and Cambridge Universities in England had managed to fill the colonies' needs for Anglican clergymen. By 1750 the colonial demand far exceeded what stagnant Oxford and Cambridge could supply, and the colonies were also trying to attract Scottish and Irish clergymen. By contrast, northern colonies founded their own colleges and trained their own ministers, lawyers, doctors, and most skilled craftsmen. Although still colonies, they were becoming America's first modernizing societies. They learned to do for themselves what Britain had to do for the southern colonies.

Much of this change occurred during prolonged periods of warfare. By midcentury, the wars were becoming a titanic struggle for control of the North American continent. Gradually Indians realized that constant expansion for British settlers meant unending retreat for them.

THREATS TO HOUSEHOLDER AUTONOMY

As population rose, some families acquired more prestige than others. **Gentlemen** performed no manual labor, and such men began to dominate public life. Before 1700 ordinary farmers and small planters had often sat in colonial assemblies. In the 18th century the men who took part in public life above the local level came, more and more, from a higher social status. They had greater wealth, a more impressive lineage, and a better education than ordinary farmers or craftsmen.

By midcentury, despite the high value that colonists placed on householder autonomy, patterns of dependency were beginning to emerge. In tidewater Virginia by 1760, about 80 percent of the land was **entailed;** that is, the owner could not divide it but had to bequeath it intact to his heir. Younger sons had to look west for a landed inheritance. In one Maryland county, 27 percent of the householders were tenants who worked small tracts of land without slaves or were men who owned a slave or two but had no claim to land. Such families could not satisfy the ambitions of all their children. In Pennsylvania's Chester County, a new class of married farm laborers arose. Their employers would let them use a small patch of land on which they could build a cottage and raise some food. Called "inmates" ("cottagers" in England), such people made up 25 percent of the county's population.

Families that could not provide for all of their children reverted to English social norms. In Connecticut, from the 1750s to the 1770s, about 75 percent of eligible sons inherited some land, but for daughters the rate fell from 44 to 34 percent. When a father could not support all his sons, he favored the eldest over the younger sons. The younger sons took up a trade or headed for the frontier. To increase their resources and sustain household autonomy, many New England farmers added a craft or two. The goal of family independence continued to exercise great power, but it was under siege.

ANGLICIZING THE ROLE OF WOMEN

The changing role of women provides a dramatic example of the anglicizing tendencies of the 18th century. When they married, most women received a **dowry** from their father, usually in cash or goods, not land. Under the common law doctrine of **coverture,** the legal personality of the husband "covered" the wife, and he made all legally binding decisions. If he died first, his widow was entitled to **dower rights,** usually one-third of the estate. Women in many households had to work harder—at the spinning wheel, for example. New England women did virtually all of the region's

gentleman *Term used to describe a person of means who performed no manual labor.*

entail *a legal device that required a landowner to keep his estate intact and pass it on to his heir.*

dowry *The cash or goods a woman received from her father when she married.*

coverture *A common-law doctrine under which the legal personality of the husband covered the wife, and he made all legally binding decisions.*

dower rights *The right of a widow to a portion of her deceased husband's estate (usually one third of the value of the estate). It was passed to their children upon her death.*

weaving, a male occupation in Europe and the other colonies. Yet, in a sense, women were becoming more English. Until 1700 many Chesapeake widows inherited all of their husbands' property and administered their own estates. After 1700 such arrangements were rare. In New England too, women suffered losses. Before 1700, courts had routinely punished men for sexual offenses, and many men had pleaded guilty and accepted their sentence. After 1700 almost no man would plead guilty to a sexual offense, except perhaps to making love to his wife before their wedding day. However, to avoid a small fine, some husbands humiliated their wives by denying that charge, even if their wives had already pleaded guilty after giving birth to a child that had obviously been conceived before the wedding. Europe's double standard of sexual behavior, which punished women for their indiscretions while tolerating male infractions, had been in some jeopardy under the Puritan regime. It now revived.

EXPANSION, IMMIGRATION, AND REGIONAL DIFFERENTIATION

After 1715, the settled portions of North America enjoyed their longest era of peace since the arrival of Europeans. The wars had emptied the borderlands of most of their inhabitants. Until midcentury, people poured into these areas, usually without provoking the Indians of the interior, and as they expanded, the colonies evolved into distinct regions.

THE EMERGENCE OF THE OLD SOUTH

Renewed immigration drove much of the postwar expansion. After 1730 the flow became enormous. In that year, about 630,000 settlers and slaves lived in the mainland colonies. By 1775 another 248,000 Africans and 284,000 Europeans had landed, including 50,000 British convicts. Most of the 230,000 voluntary immigrants settled in the middle or southern colonies. During this period, the African slave trade to North America reached its peak. Almost 90 percent of the slaves went to the southern colonies. About 80 percent arrived from Africa on overcrowded, stinking, British-owned vessels. Most of the rest came, a few at a time, from the West Indies on New England ships. This massive influx of slaves created the Old South, a society consisting of wealthy slaveholding planters, a much larger class of small planters, and thousands of slaves.

Slaves performed most of the manual labor in the southern colonies. Their numbers transformed the social structure of the region. In 1700 most members of Virginia's House of Burgesses were small planters who raised tobacco with a few indentured servants and perhaps a slave or two. After 1730 the typical burgess was a great planter who owned at least 20 slaves. And by 1750 the rice planters of South Carolina were richer than any other group in British North America. But tobacco and rice planters had few contacts with each other and did not yet think of themselves as "southerners."

The lives of slaves in the upper South (Maryland, Virginia, and the Albemarle region of North Carolina) differed considerably from that of slaves in the lower South (from Cape Fear in North Carolina through South Carolina and eventually Georgia). The Chesapeake tobacco planters organized their slaves into gangs, supervised them closely, and kept them in the fields all day. But to make their plantations more self-sufficient, they trained perhaps 10 percent of their slaves as blacksmiths, carpenters,

A TOBACCO PLANTATION. *This illustration shows the owner and perhaps his overseer or factor supervising the completion of wooden hogsheads to hold the year's to-bacco crop. The white men are dressed as gentlemen. The African laborers wear hardly any clothing at all. Note the ships off in the distance.*

coopers, or other skilled artisans. The planters, who saw themselves as benevolent paternalists, also encouraged family life among their workers, who by the 1720s were beginning to achieve a rate of reproduction that almost equaled that of the settlers.

Paternalism soon extended to religion. In the 1720s, for the first time on any significant scale, planters began to urge their slaves to convert to Christianity. At first only adults who had a good command of the catechism, which they had to memorize because they were not allowed to become literate, were accepted into the church, but by the 1730s, growing numbers of infants were also baptized. These efforts continued to expand despite a massive slave uprising. A rumor spread that the British government had promised emancipation to any slave who converted but that the colony was suppressing the news. On a Sunday in September 1730, about 300 slaves tried to escape through the Great Dismal Swamp. The planters hired Indians to track them, crushed the rebels, and hanged 29 of them. Yet the conversion efforts continued to gain momentum, mostly, it seems, because planters hoped that Christian slaves would be more docile and dutiful.

South Carolina planters shared these paternalistic inclinations, but the rice swamps and mosquitoes defeated them. Whites who supervised slave gangs in the rice fields caught malaria, which left them vulnerable to other diseases that often killed them. Africans fared much better than whites in the marshy rice fields. Many possessed a **sickle cell** in their blood that gave them protection against malaria but could also expose their children to a deadly form of inherited anemia. As the ability of Africans to resist malaria became evident, Carolina planters seldom ventured near the rice fields. Many built their big houses on high ground and, after midcentury, chose to spend their summers in Charleston or even Rhode Island. With few exceptions, they made no effort to Christianize their slaves.

sickle cell *A crescent- or sickle-shaped red blood cell sometimes found in African Americans. It helped protect them from malaria but exposed some children to the dangerous and painful condition of sickle cell anemia.*

This situation altered work patterns. To get local manufactures, planters relied on a large class of white artisans in Charleston. To produce a crop of rice, planters devised the **task system.** Slaves had to complete certain chores each day, after which their time was their own. Slaves used this time to create an invisible economy, raising crops, hunting, or fishing. Thus, while many Chesapeake slaves were acquiring the skills of artisans, Carolina slaves were heading in the other direction. The huge profits from rice now condemned nearly all of them to monotonous, unpleasant labor in the marshes. Yet because the task system gave them more control over their own lives, they preferred it to **gang labor.** Rice culture also gave them a lower rate of reproduction than in Virginia or Maryland. Their population did not grow by natural increase until perhaps the 1770s, half a century later than in the Chesapeake.

The task system also slowed assimilation into the British world. African words and customs survived longer in South Carolina than in the Chesapeake colonies. Newly imported slaves spoke **Gullah,** a pidgin language (that is, a simple second language for everyone who spoke it). Gullah began with a few phrases common to many West African languages, gradually added English words, and became the natural language of subsequent generations, eventually evolving into modern black English.

Everywhere that slavery took hold, the system required brute force to maintain it. Slaves convicted of arson were often burned at the stake, an unthinkable punishment for a white person. Whippings were frequent, and the master or overseer determined the number of stripes. One South Carolina overseer killed five slaves in two or three years before 1712. If extreme cruelty of this sort was rare, random acts of violence were common and, from a slave's perspective, unpredictable. William Byrd II was one of Virginia's most refined settlers and owned its largest library. His diary reveals that when he and his wife Lucy disagreed, the slaves could suffer. They quarreled over whether Lucy could beat Jenny with the fire tongs. On another occasion, "My wife caused Prue to be whipped notwithstanding I desired it not," Byrd reported, "which provoked me to have Anaka whipped likewise who had deserved it much more, on which my wife flew into such a passion she hoped she would be revenged of me." House servants must have dreaded the days that Byrd spent in Williamsburg, leaving Lucy in charge of the plantation.

The southern colonies prospered in the 18th century by exchanging their staple crops for British imports. By midcentury much of this trade had been taken over by Scots. Glasgow became the leading tobacco port of the Atlantic. Profits on tobacco were precarious before 1730, but they rose in later decades, partly because a tobacco contract between Britain and France opened up a vast continental market for Chesapeake planters and because, after 1730, Virginia inspected tobacco for quality before exporting it. By 1775, over 90 percent of Chesapeake tobacco was reexported to Europe from Britain.

Other exports and new crafts also contributed to rising prosperity. South Carolina continued to export provisions to the sugar islands and deerskins to Britain. **Indigo**, used as a dye by the British textile industry, became a second staple crop around midcentury, pioneered by a woman planter, Eliza Lucas Pinckney. North Carolina sold **naval stores** (pitch, resin, turpentine) to British shipbuilders. Many Chesapeake planters turned to wheat as a second cash crop. Wheat required mills to grind it into flour, barrels in which to pack it, and ships to carry it away. The result was the growth of cities. Norfolk and Baltimore had nearly 10,000 people by 1775, and such smaller cities as Alexandria and Georgetown also thrived. Shipbuilding, closely tied to the export of wheat, became a growing Chesapeake industry.

task system *A system of slave labor under which slaves had to complete specific assignments each day. After these assignments were finished, their time was their own. It was used primarily on rice plantations. Slaves often preferred this system over gang labor because it gave them more autonomy and free time.*

gang labor *A system where planters organized their field slaves into gangs, supervised them closely, and kept them working in the fields all day. This type of labor was used on tobacco plantations.*

Gullah *A language spoken by newly imported African slaves. Originally, it was a simple second language for everyone who spoke it, but gradually evolved into modern black English.*

indigo *A blue dye obtained from plants that was used by the textile industry. The British government subsidized the commercial production of it in South Carolina.*

naval stores *Items such as pitch, resin, and turpentine that were used to manufacture ships. Most of them were obtained from pine trees.*

THE MID-ATLANTIC COLONIES: THE "BEST POOR MAN'S COUNTRY"

The Mid-Atlantic colonies had been pluralistic societies from the start. Immigration added to this ethnic and religious diversity after 1700. The region had the most prosperous family farms in America and, by 1760, the two largest cities, Philadelphia and New York. Enormous manors, granted by New York governors to political supporters, dominated the Hudson valley and discouraged immigration. As late as 1750, the small colony of New Jersey had as many settlers as New York, but fewer slaves. Pennsylvania's growth exploded, driven by both natural increase and a huge surge of immigration.

After 1720 Ireland and Germany replaced England as the source of most free immigrants. About 70 percent of Ireland's emigrants came from **Ulster**. They were Presbyterians whose forebears had come to Ireland from Scotland in the 17th century. (Historians now call them the Scots-Irish, a term seldom used at the time.) Most of them left for America to avoid an increase in rents and to enjoy greater trading privileges than the British Parliament allowed Ireland. The first Ulsterites sailed for New England in 1718. They expected a friendly reception from fellow Calvinists, but the Yankees treated them with suspicion. Some of them stayed and introduced linen manufacturing in New Hampshire, but after 1718 most immigrants from Ulster headed for the Delaware valley. About 30 percent of Irish immigrants came from southern Ireland. Most were Catholics, but perhaps one-fourth were Anglicans. They too headed for the Mid-Atlantic colonies. Perhaps 80,000 Irish reached the Delaware valley before 1776.

About 70,000 of the free immigrants were Germans. Most of them arrived as families, often as **redemptioners,** a new form of indentured service attractive to married couples because it allowed them to find and bind themselves to the same master. After redemptioners completed their service, most of them streamed into the interior of Pennsylvania. Others moved on to the southern backcountry with the Irish. The Mid-Atlantic colonies were the favored destination of free immigrants because the expanding economies of the region offered many opportunities. These colonies grew excellent wheat and built their own ships to carry it abroad. When Europe's population started to surge around 1740, the middle colonies began to ship flour across the Atlantic. By 1760 both Philadelphia and New York City had overtaken Boston's stagnant population of 15,000. Philadelphia, with 32,000 people, was the largest city in British North America by 1775.

THE BACKCOUNTRY

Many of the Scots-Irish and Germans pushed west through Pennsylvania and then south up the river valleys into the interior parts of Virginia and the Carolinas. Most of the English-speaking colonists were immigrants from Ulster, northern England, or lowland Scotland who brought their folkways with them and soon gave the region its own distinctive culture. Most farmed, but many became hunters or raised cattle. Unlike the coastal settlements, the backcountry had no newspapers, few clergymen or other professionals, and, in South Carolina's interior, almost no government. A visiting Anglican clergyman bemoaned "the abandon'd Morals and profligate Principles" of the settlers. Backcountry settlers were clannish and violent. They drank heavily and hated Indians. After 1750 tensions became acute in Pennsylvania where Quakers handled differences with Indians through peaceful negotiation. Once fighting broke out with the Indians, most backcountry residents demanded their extermination. Virginia and South Carolina faced similar tensions.

Ulster *The northern province of Ireland that provided 70 percent of the Irish immigrants in the colonial period. Nearly all of them were Presbyterians whose forebears had moved to Ireland from Scotland in the previous century. They sometimes are called Scots-Irish today.*

redemptioners *Servants with a contract of indenture that allowed them to find masters after they arrived in the colonies. Many German immigrant families were redemptioners and thus were able to stay together while they served their terms.*

NEW ENGLAND: A FALTERING ECONOMY AND PAPER MONEY

New England's relative isolation in the 17th century began to have negative social and economic effects after 1700. Life expectancy declined as Atlantic commerce brought European diseases back into the region. The first settlers had left these diseases behind, but lack of exposure in childhood made later generations vulnerable. When smallpox threatened to devastate Boston in 1721, Zabdiel Boylston, a self-taught doctor, began inoculating people with it on the theory that healthy people would survive the injection and become immune. Although the city's leading physicians opposed the experiment as too risky, it worked. But a diphtheria epidemic in the 1730s and high military losses after 1740 reduced population growth. Since the 1640s more people had been leaving the region than had been arriving.

After peace returned in 1713, New England's economy began to weaken. The region had prospered in the 17th century, mostly by exporting cod, grain, livestock, and barrel staves to the West Indies. But a blight called the **wheat blast** appeared in the 1660s and slowly spread until cultivation of wheat nearly ceased. Because Yankees preferred wheat bread to corn bread, they had to buy flour from New York and Pennsylvania and, eventually, wheat from Chesapeake Bay. Poverty became a huge social problem in Boston, where by the 1740s about one-third of all adult women were widows, mostly poor.

After grain exports declined, the once-profitable West Indian trade barely broke even. Yet its volume grew, especially after enterprising Yankees opened up new markets in the lucrative French sugar islands. Mostly, the Yankees shipped fish and forest products to the islands in exchange for molasses, which they used as a sweetener or distilled into rum. However, British West Indian planters, alarmed by the flood of cheap French molasses, urged Parliament to stamp out New England's trade with the French West Indies. Parliament passed the Molasses Act of 1733, which placed a prohibitive duty of six pence per gallon on all foreign molasses. Strictly enforced, the act could have strangled New England trade; instead it gave rise to bribery and smuggling, and the molasses continued to flow. Shipbuilding gave New England most of its leverage in the Atlantic economy. Yankees made more ships than all the other colonies combined. These ships earned enough from freight in most years to offset unfavorable trade balances, especially with England. Yankees imported many British products but produced little that anybody in Britain wanted to buy. Whale oil, used in lamps, was an exception. A prosperous whaling industry emerged on the island of Nantucket. But the grain trade with the Mid-Atlantic and Chesapeake colonies was not profitable. Chesapeake planters bought rum and a few slaves from Yankee vessels that stopped on their way back from the West Indies. Newport became deeply involved in slave trading along the African coast. Although that traffic never supplied a large percentage of North America's slaves, it became a major factor in the city's growth.

New England's experience with paper money illustrates these economic difficulties. In response to a military emergency in 1690, Massachusetts invented **fiat money**—that is, paper money the value of which was not tied to silver or gold but was backed only by the government's promise to accept it in payment of taxes. It worked well for 20 years, but then serious depreciation set in. In 1714 the declining value of money touched off a fierce debate that raged until 1750. Creditors attacked paper money as fraudulent. Only gold and silver, they claimed, had real value. Defenders retorted that, in most colonies outside New England, paper was holding its value. The problem, they insisted, lay with the New England economy,

wheat blast *A plant disease that affected wheat and first appeared in New England in the 1660s. There were no known remedies for the disease, and it gradually spread until wheat production in New England nearly ceased.*

fiat money *Paper money backed only by the promise of the government to accept it in payment of taxes. It originated in Massachusetts after a military emergency in 1690.*

which could not generate enough exports to pay for the region's imports. War disrupted shipping in the 1740s, and military expenditures sent New England currency to a new low. Then, in 1748, Parliament agreed to reimburse Massachusetts for these expenses at the 1745 exchange rate. Governor William Shirley and House Speaker Thomas Hutchinson, an opponent of paper money, barely persuaded the legislature to use the grant to retire all paper and convert to silver money. That decision was a drastic example of anglicization. Although fiat money was the colony's own invention, Massachusetts repudiated it in favor of orthodox methods of British public finance. As Hutchinson's critics had warned, however, silver gravitated to Boston and back to London to pay for imports. New England's economy entered a deep depression in the early 1750s from which it did not revive until the next French war.

MUSICAL LINK TO THE PAST

HE COULD MAKE A LASS WEEP

Composers: Francis Hopkinson (music),
Thomas Parnell (lyrics)
Title: "My Days Have Been So Wondrous Free" (1759)

Until almost the American Revolution, American music was European music, especially English music, and most of it was church music. Francis Hopkinson was America's earliest secular songwriter, and "My Days Have Been so Wondrous Free" was probably the first American secular song. Although the title and the song's rhythm suggest a jaunty mood, the song is not as upbeat as a superficial listen might indicate. Francis Hopkinson's music complimented and added depth to the lyrics written decades earlier by Thomas Parcell. A romantic and bittersweet yearning permeates the song, although whether such yearning is directed toward communing with nature or with a romantic companion is uncertain.

Hopkinson worked in an environment where no American song tradition, no American publishing companies, and no consumer demand for American secular songs existed. He was a multitalented Renaissance man in the style of his contemporaries and friends Thomas Jefferson and Benjamin Franklin, exhibiting expertise in the fields of music, painting, inventing, writing, the law, and politics (he was a delegate to the Continental Congress and signed the Declaration of Independence).

"My Days" also represented an early example of two important traditions in American songwriting. First, Hopkinson purposely crafted compositions that untrained amateurs could perform and enjoy. "The best of [my songs] is that they are so easy that any Person who can play at all may perform them without much Trouble, & I have endeavour'd to make the melodies pleasing to the untutored Ear, " he explained. Second, his songs meant to provoke emotion and emanated from "the Imagination of an Author who composes from his Heart, rather than his Head. "

Although Hopkinson's songs did not attain large popularity, they did fulfill his elevated purposes in at least one family. After Hopkinson sent Jefferson some of his songs, Jefferson replied: "Accept my thanks . . . and my daughter's . . . I will not tell you how much they have pleased us, nor how well the last of them merits praise for its pathos, but relate a fact only, which is that while my elder daughter was playing it on the harpsichord, I happened to look toward the fire, & saw the younger one in tears. I asked her if she was sick? She said 'no; but the tune was so mournful.'"

1. Why do you think the colonists took more than a hundred years to develop their own popular songs, relying instead on material imported from England and the rest of Europe?

Listen to an audio recording of this music on the *Musical Links to the Past* CD.

ANGLICIZING PROVINCIAL AMERICA

FOCUS QUESTION

How were the colonists able to embrace both the Enlightenment and evangelical religion at the same time?

What made these diverse regions more alike was what they retained or acquired from Britain. Although each exported its own distinctive products, their patterns of consumption became quite similar. In the mid-1740s, the mainland colonies and the West Indies consumed almost identical amounts of British imports. Just 10 years later the mainland provinces had forged ahead by a margin of 2 to 1. Their ability to consume ever larger quantities of British goods was making the mainland colonies more valuable to the empire than the sugar colonies.

In the 18th century, printing and newspapers, the learned professions, and the intellectual movement known as the Enlightenment all made their impact on British North America. A powerful transatlantic religious revival, the Great Awakening, swept across Britain and the colonies in the 1730s and 1740s. And colonial political systems tried to recast themselves in the image of Britain's mixed and balanced constitution.

THE WORLD OF PRINT

In 17th century America, few settlers owned books. Only Massachusetts had printing presses before the 1680s. Until independence, Boston was the printing capital of North America. By 1740 Boston had eight printers; New York and Philadelphia each had two. A few others had one.

Not surprisingly, Boston also led the way in newspaper publishing. John Campbell, the city's postmaster, established the *Boston News-Letter* in 1704. By the early 1720s two more papers had opened in Boston, and Philadelphia and New York City had each acquired one. The *South Carolina Gazette* was founded in Charleston in 1732 and the *Virginia Gazette* at Williamsburg in 1736. Benjamin Franklin took charge of the *Pennsylvania Gazette* in 1729, and **John Peter Zenger** launched the *New York Weekly Journal* in 1733. In 1735, after attacking Governor William Cosby, Zenger won a major victory for freedom of the press when a jury acquitted him of **seditious libel**, the crime of criticizing government officials. These papers were weeklies that devoted nearly all of their space to European news. At first, they merely reprinted items from the *London Gazette*. But beginning in the 1720s, the *New England Courant* also began to reprint Richard Steele's essays from *The Spectator,* Joseph Addison's pieces from *The Tatler,* and the angry and immensely popular writings, mostly aimed at religious bigotry and political and financial corruption, of "Cato," a pen name used jointly by John Trenchard and Thomas Gordon.

Benjamin Franklin personified the principles of Enlightenment that the newspapers were spreading. As a boy, although raised in Puritan Boston, he skipped church on Sundays to read Addison and Steele and to perfect his prose style. As a young printer with his brother's *New England Courant* in the 1720s, he helped to publish the writings of John Checkley, an Anglican whom the courts twice prosecuted in a vain attempt to silence him. In 1729 Franklin took over the *Pennsylvania Gazette* and made it the best-edited and most widely read paper in America.

Franklin was always looking for ways to improve society. In 1727 he and some friends founded the Junto, a debating club that later evolved into the American Philosophical Society. Franklin was a founder of North America's first Masonic lodge in 1730, the Library Company of Philadelphia a year later, the Union Fire Company in 1736, the Philadelphia Hospital in 1751, and an academy that became the College

Zenger, John Peter *Printer of the* New York Weekly *Journal who was acquitted in 1735 by a jury of the crime of seditious libel after his paper sharply criticized Governor William Cosby.*

Seditious libel *The common-law crime of openly criticizing a public official.*

of Philadelphia (now the University of Pennsylvania) in the 1750s. But his greatest fame came from his electrical experiments during the 1740s and 1750s. He invented the Franklin stove and the lightning rod. By 1760 he had become the most celebrated North American in the world.

THE ENLIGHTENMENT IN AMERICA

The English **Enlightenment,** which exalted man's capacity for knowledge and social improvement, grew out of the rational and benevolent piety favored by Low Church (latitudinarian) Anglicans in Restoration England. These Anglicans disliked rigid doctrine, scoffed at conversion experiences, attacked superstition, and rejected all "fanaticism," whether that of High Church Laudians who had provoked England's civil wars, or that of the Puritans who had executed Charles I. High Church men, a small group after 1689, stood for orthodoxy, ritual, and liturgy.

Enlightened writers greeted Sir Isaac Newton's laws of motion as one of the greatest intellectual achievements of all time and joined the philosopher John Locke in looking for ways to improve society. John Tillotson, archbishop of Canterbury before his death in 1694, embodied this "polite and Catholick {i.e., universal} spirit," preaching morality rather than dogma. He had a way of defending the doctrine of eternal damnation that left his listeners wondering how a merciful God could have ordained such a cruel punishment.

Enlightened ideas won an elite constituency in the colonies. Tillotson's sermons appeared in numerous southern libraries and made a deep impression at Harvard College, beginning with two young tutors, William Brattle and John Leverett, Jr. After Leverett became Harvard's president in 1707, Tillotson's ideas became entrenched in the curriculum. For the rest of the century most Harvard-trained ministers embraced Tillotson's latitudinarian piety. They stressed the similarities between Anglicans and Congregationalists and favored broad religious toleration. After 1800 most Harvard-educated ministers became Unitarians who no longer believed in hell or the divinity of Jesus.

In 1701, largely in reaction to this trend at Harvard, a new college was founded in Connecticut. When it finally settled in New Haven, it was named Yale College in honor of a wealthy English benefactor, Elihu Yale, who donated his library to the school. Those Anglican books did to the Yale faculty what Tillotson had done at Harvard—and more. At the commencement of 1722, the entire Yale faculty, except for a 19-year-old tutor, Jonathan Edwards, announced their conversion to the Church of England and sailed for England to be ordained by the bishop of London. Their leader, Timothy Cutler, became the principal Anglican spokesman in Boston. Samuel Johnson, another defector, became the first president of King's College (now Columbia University) in New York City in the 1750s.

LAWYERS AND DOCTORS

The rise of the legal profession helped to spread Enlightenment ideas. Most Massachusetts lawyers before 1760 were either Anglicans or young men who had rejected the ministry as a career. By the 1790s, lawyers saw themselves as the cultural vanguard of the new republic. Poet John Trumbull, playwright Royall Tyler, and novelist Hugh Henry Brackenridge all continued to practice law while writing on the side. Others turned from the law to fulltime writing, including the poet William Cullen Bryant, the writer Washington Irving, and the novelist Charles Brockden Brown.

Enlightenment *The new learning in science and philosophy that took hold, at least in England, between 1660 and the American Revolution. Nearly all of its spokesmen were religious moderates who were more interested in science than religious doctrine and who favored broad religious toleration.*

Medicine also became an enlightened profession, with Philadelphia setting the pace. William Shippen earned degrees at Princeton and prestigious Edinburgh University before returning to Philadelphia in 1762, where he became the first American to lecture on medicine, publish a treatise on chemistry, and dissect human cadavers. His student, John Morgan, became the first professor of medicine in North America when the College of Philadelphia established a medical faculty a few years later. Benjamin Rush, who also studied at Princeton and Edinburgh, brought the latest Scottish techniques to the Philadelphia Hospital. He too became an enlightened reformer. During the Revolution, many colonial physicians embraced radical politics.

GEORGIA: THE FAILURE OF AN ENLIGHTENMENT UTOPIA

In the 1730s Anglican humanitarianism and the Enlightenment belief in social improvement converged and led to the founding of Georgia, named for King George II (1727–1760). The sponsors of this project hoped to create a society that could make productive use of England's "worthy" poor. They also intended to shield South Carolina's slave society from Spanish Florida by populating Georgia with disciplined, armed freemen. They hoped to produce silk and wine, items that no other British colony had yet succeeded in making. They prohibited slavery and hard liquor. Slaves would make Georgia a simple extension of South Carolina, with all of its vulnerabilities, and the founders of Georgia were appalled by what cheap gin was doing to the sobriety and industry of England's working people.

A group of distinguished trustees set themselves up as a nonprofit corporation and announced that they would give land away, not sell it. Led by James Oglethorpe, they obtained a 20-year charter from Parliament in 1732, raised money from Anglican friends, and launched the colony. They recruited foreign Protestants, including some Germans who had just been driven out of Salzburg by its Catholic bishop, a small number of Moravian Brethren (a German pacifist sect), and French Huguenots. In England, they interviewed many prospective settlers to distinguish the worthy poor from the unworthy. They engaged silk and wine experts and recruited Scottish Highlanders as soldiers.

But the trustees refused to consult the settlers on what might be good for them or for Georgia. Under Georgia's charter, all laws had to be approved by the British Privy Council. So the trustees created no elective assembly and passed only three laws during their 20 years of rule. One laid out the land system, and the others prohibited slavery and hard liquor. The trustees governed through "regulations" instead of laws. An elective assembly, the trustees promised, would come later, after Georgia's character had been firmly established.

In 1733 the first settlers laid out Savannah, a town with spacious streets. Within 10 years, 1,800 charity cases and just over 1,000 self-supporting colonists reached Georgia. The most successful were the Salzburgers, who agreed with the prohibitions on slavery and alcohol and built a thriving settlement at Ebenezer, farther up the Savannah River. The Moravian Brethren left for North Carolina after five years rather than bear arms.

The land system never worked as planned. The trustees gave 50 acres to every male settler whose passage was paid for out of charitable funds. Those who paid their own way could claim up to 500 acres. Silk production failed. Ordinary farmers did poorly because they could not support a family on 50 acres of the sandy soil around Savannah. Because the trustees envisioned every landowner as a soldier, women could not inherit land, nor could landowners sell their plots.

The settlers clamored for rum, smuggled it into the colony when they could, and insisted that Georgia would never thrive until it had slaves. By the mid-1740s, enough people had died or left to reduce the population by more than half. Between 1750 and 1752 the trustees dropped their ban on alcohol, allowed the importation of slaves, summoned an elective assembly (but only to consult, not legislate), and finally surrendered their charter to Parliament. With the establishment of royal government in 1752, Georgia finally got an elective assembly with full powers of legislation. Thus Georgia became what it was never meant to be, a smaller version of South Carolina, producing rice and indigo with slave labor. By then, ironically, the colony had done more to spread revivalism than to vindicate Enlightenment ideals.

THE GREAT AWAKENING

Between the mid-1730s and the early 1740s, an immense religious revival, the **Great Awakening,** swept across the Protestant world. England, Scotland, Ulster, New England, the Mid-Atlantic colonies, and for a time South Carolina responded warmly to emotional calls for a spiritual rebirth.

ORIGINS OF THE REVIVALS

Some of the earliest revivals arose among the Dutch in New Jersey. Guiliam Bertholf, a farmer and cooper (barrel maker), was a lay reader who had been ordained in the Netherlands in 1694 and returned to preach in Hackensack and Passaic. His emotional piety won many adherents. After 1720 Theodorus Jacobus Frelinghuysen sparked several revivals in his congregation in New Brunswick, New Jersey. The local Presbyterian pastor, Gilbert Tennent, watched and learned.

Tennent was a younger son of William Tennent, Sr., an Anglican-turned-Presbyterian minister from Ulster who had moved to America. At Neshaminy, Pennsylvania, he set up his Log College, where he trained his sons and other young men as **evangelical** preachers. The Tennent family dominated the **Presbytery** of New Brunswick, used it to ordain ministers, and sent them off to congregations that requested them, even in other presbyteries. These intrusions angered the Philadelphia **Synod,** the governing body of the Presbyterian church in the colonies. Most of its ministers emphasized orthodoxy over a personal conversion experience. In a 1740 sermon, *The Dangers of an Unconverted Ministry,* Gilbert Tennent denounced those preachers for leading their people to hell. His attack split the church. In 1741 the outnumbered revivalists withdrew and founded their own Synod of New York.

In New England, Solomon Stoddard of Northampton presided over six revivals between the 1670s and his death in 1729. Jonathan Edwards, his grandson and successor, touched off a revival in 1734 and 1735 that rocked dozens of Connecticut valley towns. Edwards's *A Faithful Narrative of the Surprising Work of God* (1737) explained what a **revival** was—an emotional response to God's Word that brought sudden conversions to scores of people. In England, John Wesley and George Whitefield set the pace. At worldly Oxford University, Wesley and his brother Charles founded the Holy Club, a High Church society whose members sometimes fasted until they could barely walk. These methodical practices prompted scoffers to call them "Methodists." Wesley went to Georgia as a missionary in 1735, but the settlers rejected his ascetic piety. In 1737, on his return

Great Awakening *An immense religious revival that swept across the Protestant world in the 1730s and 1740s.*

evangelical *A style of Christian ministry that includes much zeal and enthusiasm. Evangelical ministers emphasized personal conversion and faith rather than religious ritual.*

Presbytery *An intermediate level of organization in the Presbyterian church, above individual congregations but below the synod. One of its primary responsibilities was the ordination and placement of ministers.*

synod *The governing body of the Presbyterian church. A synod was a meeting of Presbyterian ministers and prominent laymen to set policies for the whole church.*

revival *A series of emotional religious meetings that led to numerous public conversions.*

THE SYNOD OF PHILADELPHIA BY 1738

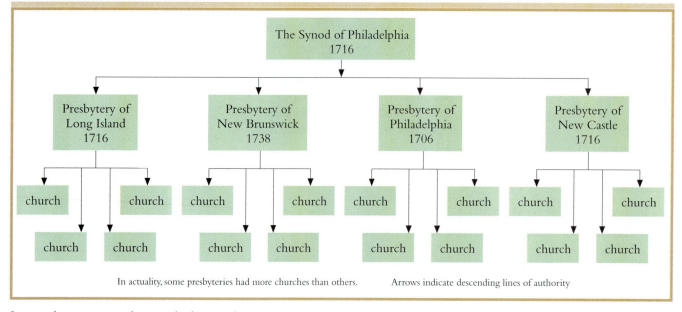

In actuality, some presbyteries had more churches than others. Arrows indicate descending lines of authority.

voyage to England, some Moravians convinced him that he had never grasped the central Protestant message, justification by faith alone. He was also deeply moved by Edwards's *Faithful Narrative.* Soon, Wesley found his life's mission, the conversion of sinners, and it launched him on an extraordinary preaching career of 50 years.

George Whitefield, who had been a talented amateur actor in his youth, joined the Holy Club at Oxford and became an Anglican minister. He followed Wesley to Georgia, founded an orphanage, then returned to England and preached all over the kingdom to raise money for it. He too began to preach the "new birth"—the necessity of a conversion experience. When many pastors banned him from their pulpits, he responded by preaching in open fields. Newspapers reported these controversies, and Whitefield's admirers began to notify the press where he would be on any given day. Colonial newspapers also followed his movements.

WHITEFIELD LAUNCHES THE TRANSATLANTIC REVIVAL

In 1739 Whitefield made his second trip to America, and thousands flocked to hear him preach. After landing in Delaware, he preached his way northward through Philadelphia, New Jersey, and New York City, and then headed south through the Chesapeake colonies and into South Carolina. In September 1740 he sailed to Newport and for two months toured New England. Using his acting skills, he imitated Christ on the cross, shedding "pious tears" for poor sinners. When he wept, his audience wept with him. When he condemned them, they fell to the ground in agony.

Although Whitefield wore the surplice of an Anglican minister, most Anglicans distrusted him. In Charleston and New York City, he was denounced by the official spokesmen for the bishop of London. But Presbyterians, Congregationalists, and Baptists embraced him, at least until some ministers decided that he was doing more harm than good. To many he embodied the old nonseparatist ideal that all English Protestants were really members of the same church.

DISRUPTIONS

After Whitefield departed, other preachers tried to assume his role, but they aroused fierce controversy. In South Carolina Hugh Bryan, a Savannah River planter, began preaching the evangelical message to his slaves. In 1742, when memories of a recent slave rebellion were still fresh, he denounced slavery as a sin. Proclaiming himself an American Moses, he attempted to part the waters of the Savannah River and lead the slaves to freedom in Georgia. Instead, he almost drowned. He confessed publicly that he had been deluded. This fiasco discredited evangelicalism among the settlers of the lower South for another generation, but African American evangelical piety, including some of the first black preachers, took root as a result of these efforts.

Whitefield's successors also disrupted New England. Gilbert Tennent preached there for months. He specialized in "Holy Laughter," the scornful peals of a triumphant God as sinners tumble into hell. He abandoned the usual garb of a minister for a robe and sandals and let his hair grow long, thereby proclaiming himself a new John the Baptist heralding the Second Coming of Christ. James Davenport, who succeeded Tennent, liked to preach by candlelight, roaring damnation at his listeners, even grabbing Satan and wrestling him back to hell. In 1743 he established the "Shepherd's Tent" in New London to train awakened preachers. This outdoor school abandoned the classical curriculum of colleges and insisted only on a valid conversion experience. He organized a book burning (in which titles by Increase Mather and other New England dignitaries went up in flames) and threw his britches on the fire, declaring them a mark of human vanity. A New England grand jury, asked to indict him, proclaimed him mad instead. Like Bryan, Davenport repented and claimed that he had been deluded. The Shepherd's Tent collapsed.

LONG-TERM CONSEQUENCES OF THE REVIVALS

As time passed, the revivals feminized evangelical churches. Amid the enthusiasm of Whitefield's tour, more men than usual had joined a church, but after another year or two, men became hard to convert. The number of women church members soared, however, and in some congregations they acquired an informal veto over the choice of the minister. Partly in reaction to the revivals, thousands of men became Freemasons, often instead of joining a church. They very nearly turned these societies into a religion of manliness, complete with secret and mysterious rituals that extolled sobriety, industry, brotherhood, benevolence, and citizenship. This movement peaked during and after the Revolution.

The revivals shattered the unity of New England's Congregational Church. Evangelicals seceded from dozens of congregations to form their own "Separate" churches, many of which went Baptist by the 1760s. In the middle colonies, the revivals strengthened denominational loyalties. In the 1730s most people in the region did not belong to a church, but the revivals prompted many of them to become **New Side** (evangelical) Presbyterians, **Old Side** (anti-revival) Presbyterians, or unevangelical Anglicans. The southern colonies were less affected, although evangelical Presbyterians made modest gains in the Virginia piedmont after 1740. Finally, in the 1760s, the Baptists began to win thousands of converts, to be followed and overtaken by the Methodists during and after the Revolution.

The revivals created new links with Britain and among colonies. Whitefield ran the most efficient publicity machine in the Atlantic world. In London, Glasgow, and Boston, periodicals called *The Christian History* carried news of revivals occurring anywhere in the empire. For years, London evangelicals held regular "Letter Days,"

New Side *Term used to describe evangelical Presbyterians.*

Old Side *Antirevival Presbyterians.*

at which they read accounts of revivals in progress. When fervor declined in New England, Edwards organized a Concert of Prayer with his Scottish allies, setting regular times for them all to beseech the Lord to pour out his grace once more. As Anglicans split into Methodists and Latitudinarians, Congregationalists into **New Lights** (pro-revival) and **Old Lights** (anti-revival), and Presbyterians into comparable New Side and Old Side synods, evangelicals discovered that they had more in common with revivalists in other denominations than with anti-revivalists in their own.

When Boston's Charles Chauncy (a clergyman committed to the Enlightenment) attacked the revivals as frauds because of their emotional excesses, Edwards replied with *A Treatise Concerning Religious Affections* (1746). Although admitting that no emotional response, however intense, was proof by itself of the presence of God in a person's soul, he insisted that intense feeling must always accompany the reception of divine grace. In effect, he countered Chauncy's emotional defense of reason with his own rational defense of emotion.

New Colleges

The Great Awakening also created several new colleges. In 1740 North America had only three: Harvard, William and Mary, and Yale. Although Yale eventually embraced the revivals, all three opposed them at first. In 1746 Middle Colony evangelicals, eager to demonstrate their respectability after the fiasco of the Shepherd's Tent, founded the College of New Jersey. It graduated its first class in 1748 and settled in Princeton in 1756. It drew students from all 13 colonies and sent its graduates throughout America, and it reshaped the Presbyterian Church. When Presbyterians healed their schism and reunited in 1758, the New Side set the terms. Outnumbered in 1741, the New Side held a large majority of ministers by 1758. Through control of Princeton, their numbers had increased rapidly. The Old Side, still dependent on the University of Glasgow in Scotland, could barely replace those who died.

New Light Baptists founded the College of Rhode Island (now Brown University) in the 1760s. Dutch Reformed revivalists established Queens College (now Rutgers University) in New Jersey. Eleazer Wheelock opened an evangelical school for Indians in Lebanon, Connecticut. After his first graduate, Samson Occum, raised £12,000 in England for the school, Wheelock moved to New Hampshire and used most of the money to found Dartmouth College instead, although Dartmouth did admit an occasional Indian student.

In the 1750s Anglicans countered with two new colleges of their own: the College of Philadelphia (now the University of Pennsylvania), which also had Old Side Presbyterian support, and King's College (now Columbia University) in New York. They graduated few students, however, and most of those rejected a ministerial career.

The Denominational Realignment

The revivals transformed American religious life. In 1700, the three strongest denominations had been the Congregationalists in New England, the Quakers in the Delaware valley, and the Anglicans in the South. By 1800, all three had lost ground to newcomers: the Methodists, the Baptists, and the Presbyterians. Methodists and Baptists did not expect their preachers to attend college, and they recruited ministers from a much broader segment of the population than their rivals could tap. Although they never organized their own Shepherd's Tent, they embraced similar principles, demanding only personal conversion, integrity, knowledge of the Bible, and a talent

---

QUICK   REVIEW

THE GROWING IMPACT OF BRITAIN ON CULTURAL, RELIGIOUS, AND POLITICAL LIFE

- Newspapers, Benjamin Franklin, the legal and medical professions, and the spread of Enlightenment values

- Georgia as an Enlightenment experiment

- Edwards, Wesley, Whitefield, and the Transatlantic revivals

- New colleges and the denominational realignment

New Lights *Term used to describe prorevival Congregationalists.*

Old Lights *Antirevival Congregationalists.*

for preaching. Anti-revivalist denominations, especially Anglicans and Quakers, lost heavily. New Light Congregationalists made only slight gains because, when their people left behind the established churches of New England and moved west, they usually joined a Presbyterian church, which provided a structure and network of support that isolated congregations in a pluralistic society could not sustain.

POLITICAL CULTURE IN THE COLONIES

In politics as in other activities, the colonies became more like Britain during the 18th century. Provincial politics began to absorb many of the values and practices that had taken hold in Britain after the Glorious Revolution. Colonists agreed that they were free because they were British, because they too had mixed constitutions that united monarchy, aristocracy, and democracy in almost perfect balance.

By the 1720s every colony (except Connecticut and Rhode Island) had an appointive governor, plus a council and an elective assembly. The governor stood for monarchy and the council for aristocracy. In Massachusetts, Rhode Island, and Connecticut the council or upper house was elected (indirectly in Massachusetts). In all other colonies except Pennsylvania, an appointive council played an active legislative role. The office of councilor was not hereditary, but many councilors served for life, and some were succeeded by their sons, especially in Virginia.

THE RISE OF THE ASSEMBLY AND THE GOVERNOR

In all 13 colonies the settlers elected the assembly. The right to vote was more widely shared than in England, where two-thirds of adult males were disfranchised. By contrast, something like three-fourths of free colonial males could vote at some point in their adult lives. The frequency of elections varied: every seven years in New York and Virginia, as well as in Britain; every three years in New Hampshire, Maryland, and South Carolina; irregular but fairly frequent in New Jersey, North Carolina, and Georgia; and every year in the other five colonies. As the century advanced, legislatures sat longer and passed more laws, and the lower house, the assembly, usually initiated major bills. The rise of the assembly was a major political trend of the century.

FOCUS QUESTION
How could both the royal governors and the colonial assemblies grow stronger at the same time?

THE SPECTRUM OF COLONIAL POLITICS

CONSTITUTIONAL TYPE	SUCCESSFUL	UNSUCCESSFUL
Northern "Court"	New York, circa 1710–1738	New York after 1738
	New Hampshire after 1741	Pennsylvania (successful in peace, ineffective in war)
	Massachusetts after 1741	
	New Jersey after 1750	
Southern "Country"	Virginia after 1720	Maryland
	South Carolina after 1730	North Carolina
	Georgia after 1752	

Connecticut and Rhode Island never really belonged to this system.

Every royal colony except New York and Georgia already had an assembly with a strong sense of its own privileges when the first royal governor arrived, but the governors also grew more powerful. Because the governor's instructions usually challenged some existing practices, the result was often a clash in which the first royal governors never got all of their demands. But they did win concessions over the years. In almost every colony the most successful governors were those who served between 1730 and 1765. Most of them had learned by then that their success depended less on their royal prerogatives than on their ability to win over the assembly through persuasion or **patronage**.

Early in the century, conflicts between the governor and an assembly majority were legalistic. Each side cited technical precedents to justify the governor's prerogatives or the assembly's privileges. Later on, when conflict spilled over into pamphlets and newspapers, it often pitted an aggrieved minority (unable to get majority support in the assembly) against the governor and assembly. These conflicts were ideological. The opposition accused the governor of corrupting the assembly, and he denounced them as a "faction." Everyone condemned factions, or political parties, as selfish and destructive.

"COUNTRY" CONSTITUTIONS: THE SOUTHERN COLONIES

In most southern colonies, the "Country" principles of the British opposition (see Chapter 3) became the common assumptions of public life, acceptable to both governor and assembly, typically after an attempt to impose the "Court" alternative had failed. When a governor, such as Virginia's Alexander Spotswood (1710–1722), used his patronage to fill the assembly with his own "placemen," the voters turned them out at the next election. Just as Spotswood learned that he could not manipulate the house through patronage, the assembly discovered that it could not coerce a governor who had a permanent salary. Accordingly, Virginia and South Carolina cultivated the **politics of harmony**. Governors found that they could get more done through persuasion than through patronage, and the assemblies responded by showing their appreciation. Factions disappeared, allowing the governor and the assembly to pursue the "common good" in an atmosphere free of rancor or corruption. Georgia adopted these practices in the 1750s.

patronage *The act of appointing people to government jobs or awarding them government contracts, often based on political favoritism rather than on abilities.*

politics of harmony *A system in which the governor and the colonial assembly worked together through persuasion rather than through patronage or bullying.*

The Saint Louis Museum Purchase 256:1948

SEA CAPTAINS CAROUSING IN SURINAM. This painting (circa 1750) by John Greenwood suggests that working men, when not kept busy, would drink themselves into oblivion.

This system worked well because the planters were doing what Britain wanted them to do: shipping staple crops to Britain. Both sides could agree on measures that would make this process more efficient, such as the Virginia Tobacco Inspection Act of 1730. In Virginia, public controversy actually ceased. Between 1720 and 1765 the governor and House of Burgesses engaged in only one public quarrel, an unparalleled record of political harmony. South Carolina's politics became almost as placid from the 1730s into the 1760s, but harmony there masked serious social problems that were beginning to emerge in the unrepresented backcountry. By contrast, the politics of harmony never took hold in Maryland, where the lord proprietor always tried to seduce assemblymen with his lavish patronage, nor in North Carolina, where tobacco and rice planters fought with each other, and the backcountry distrusted both.

"COURT" CONSTITUTIONS: THE NORTHERN COLONIES

With many economic interests and ethnic groups to satisfy, the northern colonies were more likely to give rise to political factions. Governors could win support by using patronage to reward some groups and to discipline others. William Shirley, governor of Massachusetts from 1741 to 1756, used judicial and militia appointments and war contracts to build a majority in the assembly. Like Sir Robert Walpole in Britain, he was a master of "Court" politics. In New Hampshire, Benning Wentworth created a political machine that rewarded just about every assemblyman from the 1750s to 1767. An ineffective opposition in both colonies accused the governors of corrupting the assembly, but Shirley and Wentworth each claimed that what he did was essential to his colony's needs.

The opposition, though seldom able to implement its demands at the provincial level, was important nonetheless. It kept settlers alert to any infringements on their liberties. It dominated the town of Boston from 1720 on. Boston artisans engaged in ritualized mob activities that had a sharp political edge. On Guy Fawkes's Day (November 5) every year, a North End mob and a South End mob bloodied each other for the privilege of burning effigies of the pope, the devil, and the Stuart pretender to the British throne. These men were celebrating liberty, property, and no popery—the British constitution as they understood it. The violence made many wealthy merchants nervous, and by 1765 some of them would become its targets.

New York's governors, particularly Robert Hunter (1710–1719), won great success even before 1720. Hunter's salary and perquisites became more lucrative than those attached to any other royal office in North America, and after 1716 he and his successor were so satisfied with their control of the assembly that they let 10 years pass without calling a general election. During the 25 years after 1730, later governors lost these advantages, primarily because London gave the governorship to a series of men eager to rebuild their tattered fortunes at New York's expense. This combination of greed and need gave new leverage to the assembly, which challenged many royal prerogatives during the 1740s. In the royal colonies, only the governor of New York emerged weaker by 1760 than he had been in 1720.

Pennsylvania, by contrast, kept its proprietary governor weak well into the 1750s. A unified Quaker Party won undisputed control of the assembly during the 1730s. The governor, who by this time was never a Quaker, had a lot of patronage to dispense. But it was of no use to him in controlling Quaker assemblymen, who had lost interest in becoming judges if that meant administering oaths. Nor could these pacifists be won over with military contracts, no matter how lucrative.

The colonists, both north and south, absorbed the ideology of the British opposition, which warned that those in power were usually trying to destroy liberty and that corruption was their most effective weapon. By 1776 that view would justify

QUICK REVIEW

THE IMPACT OF BRITAIN'S COURT AND COUNTRY VALUES ON COLONIAL POLITICS

- Colonial versions of Britain's mixed and balanced constitution

- Both royal governors and elected assemblies became more powerful

- "Country" constitutions: The politics of harmony in Virginia, South Carolina, and Georgia, but not in Maryland or North Carolina

- "Court" constitutions: Patronage systems took hold in Massachusetts, New Hampshire, and New York for a time, but not in Pennsylvania

independence and the repudiation of a "corrupt" king and Parliament. Before 1760, however, it served different purposes. In the south, this ideology celebrated Anglo-American harmony. In the north, it became the language of frustrated minorities unable to defeat the governor or control the assembly.

THE RENEWAL OF IMPERIAL CONFLICT

A new era of imperial war began in 1739 and continued, with only a brief interruption, until 1763. The colonies, New Spain, New France, and the Indians of the eastern woodlands all became involved.

CHALLENGES TO FRENCH POWER

In the decades of peace after 1713, the French tried to strengthen their position in North America. They erected the continent's most formidable fortress, Louisbourg, on Cape Breton Island. A naval force stationed there could guard the approaches to

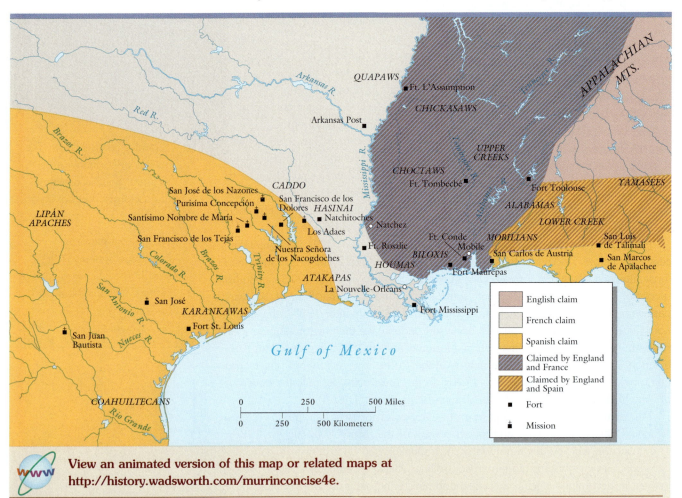

View an animated version of this map or related maps at
http://history.wadsworth.com/murrinconcise4e.

Map 4.1
FRENCH LOUISIANA AND SPANISH TEXAS, CIRCA 1730. *In this part of North America, French and Spanish settlers and missionaries were spread quite thinly over a vast area and surrounded by much larger numbers of Indian peoples.*

the St. Lawrence River. The French also built Fort St. Frédéric (the British called it Crown Point) on Lake Champlain and maintained their Great Lakes posts at Forts Frontenac, Michilimackinac, and Detroit. To bolster its weak hold on the Gulf of Mexico, France created the Company of the Indies, which shipped 7,000 settlers and 2,000 slaves to Louisiana between 1717 and 1721 but then was unable to supply them. By 1726 half of them had starved to death or fled. In 1718 the French founded New Orleans, which became the capital of Louisiana in 1722.

Despite these efforts, the French hold on the interior began to weaken. Indians returned to the Ohio Valley, mostly to trade with pacifist Pennsylvania or with Fort Oswego, a new British post on Lake Ontario. Many of the Indians founded what the French disparagingly called **republics**, villages outside the French alliance system that were eager to acquire cheaper British goods. They accepted people from all tribes—Delawares from the east, Shawnees from the south and east, Mingoes (Iroquois who had left their homeland) from the north, and other Algonquians of the Great Lakes region to the west.

Sometimes even the French system of mediation broke down. In the southwest an arrogant French officer decided to take over the lands of the Natchez Indians and ordered them to move. While pretending to comply, the Natchez planned a counterstroke and on November 28, 1729, killed every French male in the vicinity. French and Choctaw retaliation destroyed the Natchez—the last of the mound builders—as a distinct people.

In 1730 the French barely averted a massive slave uprising in New Orleans. To stir up hatred between Indians and Africans, the French turned over some of the African leaders to the Choctaws to be burned alive. Unable to afford enough gifts to hold an alliance with both the Choctaws and the Chickasaws, the French encouraged hostilities between both nations. This policy seriously damaged the French. Instead of weakening the pro-British Chickasaws, it touched off a Choctaw civil war. France lost both influence and prestige.

THE DANGER OF SLAVE REVOLTS AND WAR WITH SPAIN

To counter the French, Spain sent missionaries and soldiers into Texas between 1716 and 1720 and founded a capital at Los Adaes, a few miles from the French trading post at Natchitoches. To prevent smuggling, Spain refused to open a seaport on the Gulf Coast. As a result, its tiny outposts had to depend on French trade goods for supplies. The Texas missions won few converts and suffered frequent depredations by Indians. In 1719 the survivors of these attacks abandoned their missions in eastern Texas and fled west to San Antonio, which became the capital.

The Spanish presence proved troublesome to the British as well, especially in South Carolina. In the 16th century, Francis Drake had proclaimed himself a liberator when he attacked St. Augustine and promised freedom to Indians and Africans. By the 1730s these roles had been reversed. On several occasions after 1680, Spanish Florida had promised freedom to slaves who escaped from Carolina and were willing to accept Catholicism. In 1738 the governor established, just north of St. Augustine, a new town, Gracia Real de Santa Teresa de Mose (or Mose for short, pronounced *Moe*-shah). He put a remarkable African in charge, a man who took the name **Francisco Menéndez** at baptism. He had escaped from slavery, had fought with the Yamasees against South Carolina in 1715, and had fled to Florida, only to be enslaved again. Yet he became literate in Spanish and, while still a slave, rose to the rank of militia captain. After winning his freedom, he took charge of Mose in 1738 and made it the first community of free blacks in what is now the United States.

republics *Independent Indian villages that were willing to trade with the British and remained outside the French system of Indian alliances.*

Francisco Menéndez *An escaped South Carolina slave who fought with the Yamasee Indians against the colony, fled to Florida, was reenslaved by the Spanish, became a militia captain, was freed again, and was put in charge of the free-black town of Mose near St. Augustine in the late 1730s, the first community of its kind in what is now the United States.*

WATSON AND THE SHARK. *John Singleton Copley's 1778 painting, dramatically depicting a young man's rescue from shark attack, began the democratization of heroism. Note that a black man holds the traditional central and elevated place of honor in the painting, and that only one man on the rescue boat is a "gentleman." In this graphic work, Copley used the most refined techniques of English painting to suggest a colonial theme, that even ordinary men can become heroes.*

In 1739, the governor of Spanish Florida offered liberty to any slaves in the British colonies who could make their way to Florida. This manifesto, and rumors about Mose, touched off the Stono Rebellion in South Carolina, the most violent slave revolt in the history of the 13 colonies. On Sunday, September 9, 1739, a force of 20 slaves attacked a store at Stono (south of Charleston), killed the owner, seized weapons, and moved on to assault other houses and attract new recruits. Heading toward Florida, they killed about 25 settlers that day. When the rebels reached the Edisto River, they stopped, raised banners, and shouted "Liberty," hoping to begin a general uprising. There the militia caught them and killed about two-thirds of the growing force. In the weeks that followed, the settlers killed another 60. None of the rebels reached Florida, but, as the founders of Georgia had foreseen, South Carolina was indeed vulnerable in any dispute with Spain.

The War of Jenkins's Ear, derisively named for a ship captain who displayed his severed ear to Parliament as proof of Spanish cruelty, then broke out between Britain and Spain. Some 3,000 men from the 13 colonies, eager for plunder, joined expeditions in 1741 and 1742 against Cartegena in South America, then against Cuba and Panama. All were disasters. Most of the men died of disease; only 10 percent of the volunteers returned home. Georgia was supposed to protect South Carolina. General Oglethorpe, its governor, retaliated against the Spanish by invading Florida in 1740. He dispersed the black residents of Mose and occupied the site, but the Spaniards mauled his garrison in a surprise counterattack. Oglethorpe retreated without taking St. Augustine and brought back some disturbing reports. Spain, he said, was sending blacks into the British colonies to start slave uprisings, and Spanish priests in disguise were joining the black conspirators. This news set off panics in the rice and tobacco colonies, but it had its biggest impact in New York City.

By 1741 New York City's 2,000 slaves were the largest concentration of blacks in British North America after Charleston. When several suspicious fires broke out, the settlers grew nervous. Some of the fires probably provided cover for an interracial larceny ring that operated out of the tavern of John Hughson, a white man. When the New York Supreme Court offered freedom to Mary Burton, a 16-year-old Irish servant girl at the tavern, in exchange for her testimony, she swore that the tavern was the center of a hellish "Popish Plot" to murder the city's adult white males, free the slaves, and make Hughson king of the Africans. Several free black Spanish sailors, who had been captured and enslaved by **privateers,** also were accused, partly because they insisted they were free men. After Oglethorpe's warning reached New York in June, the number of the accused escalated, and John Ury, a High Churchman and a Latin teacher who had arrived recently, was hanged as a likely Spanish priest. The New York conspiracy trials continued from May into August 1741. Four whites and 18 slaves were hanged, 13 slaves were burned alive, and 70 were banished to the West Indies.

In 1742 King Philip V of Spain retaliated. He sent 36 ships and 2,000 soldiers from Cuba with orders to devastate Georgia and South Carolina and free the slaves. The invaders outnumbered the entire population of Georgia, but Oglethorpe raised 900 men and met the Spanish on St. Simons Island in July. He ambushed two patrols, and Spanish morale collapsed. The Spanish force departed, leaving the British colonies once again as a safe haven for liberty, property, no popery—and slavery.

Britain achieved one major success against Spain. From 1740 to 1744, Commodore George Anson rounded Cape Horn, plundered a port in Peru, crossed the Pacific, and captured the Manila galleon, the world's richest ship, loaded with silver worth over 1.3 million Spanish dollars. Alarmed for the security of its Pacific possessions, Spain would be reluctant to challenge Britain in the next war.

FRANCE VERSUS BRITAIN: KING GEORGE'S WAR

In 1744, when France joined Spain in the war against Britain, the main action shifted to the north. After the French laid siege to Annapolis Royal, the capital of Nova Scotia, Governor Shirley of Massachusetts intervened just in time to save the small garrison, and the French withdrew. Shirley then planned a rash attack on Fortress Louisbourg. With only a few lightly armed Yankee vessels at his disposal, he asked the commander of the British West Indian squadron, Sir Peter Warren, for assistance. But Shirley's expedition, which included about one-sixth of the adult males of Massachusetts, set out before Warren could respond. With no heavy artillery of his own, Shirley ordered the expedition to capture the outer batteries of the fortress and use their guns to smash its walls. Had the Yankees met a French fleet instead of the Royal Navy, which arrived in the nick of time, nearly every family in New England would have lost a close relative. The most amazing thing about this venture is that it worked. The British navy drove off the French fleet, and untrained Yankee volunteers subdued the mightiest fortress in America with its own guns. Louisbourg fell on June 16, 1745.

After that nothing went right. Plans to attack Quebec by sea in 1746 and 1747 came to nothing because no British fleet arrived. French and Indian raiders devastated the weakly defended frontier. Bristol County farmers rioted against high taxes. When the Royal Navy finally got to Boston in late 1747, its commander sent gangs of sailors ashore to compel anyone they could seize into serving with the fleet. An angry crowd descended on the sailors, took some officers hostage, and controlled the streets of Boston for three days before the commander released all the Massachusetts men he had impressed. Finally, Britain returned Louisbourg to France under the Treaty of Aix-la-Chapelle, which ended the war in 1748.

privateers *A privately owned ship that was authorized by a government to attack enemy ships during times of war. The owner and crew of the ship got to claim a portion of whatever was captured. This practice damaged any enemy country that could not dramatically increase naval protection for its merchant ships.*

King George's War *Popular term in North America for the third of the four Anglo-French wars before the American Revolution (1744–1748). It is sometimes also applied to the War of Jenkins's Ear between Spain and Britain (1739–1748).*

THE IMPENDING STORM

The war had driven back the frontiers of British settlement in North America, but the colonies had promised land grants to many volunteers. Thus peace touched off a frenzy of expansion. The British, aware that their hold on Nova Scotia was feeble, sent four regiments of redcoats and recruited 2,500 Protestants in continental Europe to populate the colony. In 1749 they founded the town of Halifax, which became the new capital of Nova Scotia.

In the 13 colonies, settlers eagerly pressed onto new lands. Yankees swarmed north into Maine and New Hampshire and west into the middle colonies. By refusing to pay rent to the manor lords of the Hudson valley, they sparked a tenant revolt in 1753 that was subdued only with difficulty. A year later, Connecticut's delegation to the Albany Congress (discussed in the next section) used bribes to acquire an Indian title to all of northern Pennsylvania, which Connecticut claimed on the basis of its sea-to-sea charter of 1663. The blatant encroachments of New York speculators and settlers on Mohawk lands so infuriated the Mohawks' Chief Hendrik that he bluntly told the governor of New York that "the Covenant Chain is broken between you and us [the Iroquois League]." New York, Pennsylvania, and Virginia competed for the trade with the new Indian "republics" between Lake Erie and the Ohio River. Virginians, whom the Indians called **long knives,** were particularly aggressive. They organized the Ohio Company of Virginia in 1747 to settle the Ohio valley and established their first outpost at the place where the Monongahela and Allegheny Rivers converge to form the Ohio River (the site of modern Pittsburgh).

The French response to these intrusions verged on panic. They rebuilt Louisbourg and erected Fort Beauséjour on the neck that connects mainland Canada to Nova Scotia. In 1755 they erected Fort Carillon (Ticonderoga to the British) on Lake Champlain to protect Crown Point.

Far more controversial was the policy the French now implemented in the area between the Great Lakes and the Ohio. The officials who had long been conducting Indian diplomacy had either died or left office by the late 1740s. Authoritarian newcomers from France replaced them and began giving orders to Indians instead of negotiating with them. Without trying to explain themselves to the Indians, they launched two expeditions into the area. In 1749 Pierre-Joseph Céloron de Blainville led several hundred men down the Allegheny to the Ohio, then up the Miami and back to Canada. Along the way Blainville buried plaques, claiming the area for France. The Indians removed them. Marquis Duquesne sent 2,000 Canadians, with almost no Indian support, to erect a line of posts from Fort Presque Isle (now Erie, Pennsylvania) to Fort Duquesne (now Pittsburgh).

The French intended to prevent British settlement west of the Alleghenies. To Duquesne, this policy was so obviously beneficial to the Indians that it needed no explanation. Yet the Mingoes warned him not to build a fort in their territory, and a delegation of Delawares and Shawnees asked the Virginians if they would be willing to expel the French from the Ohio country and then go back home. Instead Virginia sent George Washington to the Ohio country in 1753 to warn Duquesne to withdraw, and a small Virginia force began building its own fort at the forks of the Ohio. Duquesne ignored Washington, advanced toward the Ohio, expelled the Virginians, took over their fort, and finished building it. Virginia sent Washington back to the Ohio in 1754. On May 28, after discovering a French patrol nearby, Washington launched an attack. That command started a world war.

long knives *Term Indians used to describe Virginians.*

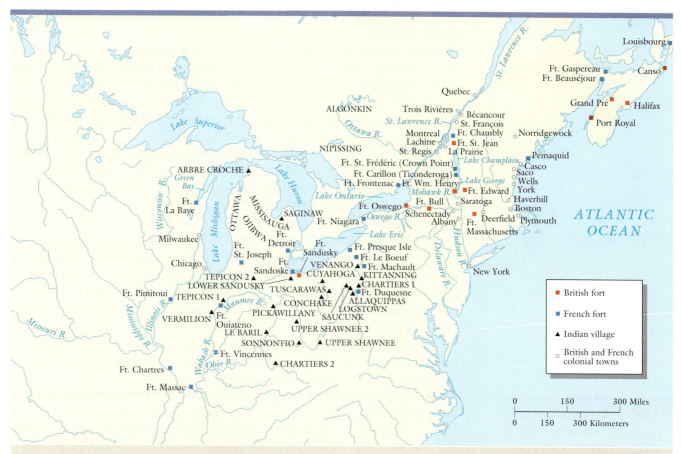

Map 4.2

FRANCE VERSUS BRITAIN IN NORTH AMERICA BY 1755. *North of the Ohio River, much of North America was becoming a series of fortresses along the frontiers separating New France from the British colonies.*

THE WAR FOR NORTH AMERICA

At first, the war with France generated fierce tensions between Britain and the colonies, but both sides gradually learned to cooperate effectively. Of the four wars fought between Britain and France from 1689 to 1763, only the last began in America. That conflict, popularly known as the **French and Indian War**, was also the biggest and produced the most sweeping results.

THE ALBANY CONGRESS AND THE ONSET OF WAR

In the spring of 1754 both New France and Virginia were expecting a clash at the forks of the Ohio. But neither anticipated the titanic struggle that confrontation would set off. Nor did the French and British governments, which hoped to limit any conflict to a few strategic posts in North America. But New Englanders saw an apocalyptic struggle erupting in North America between "Protestant freedom" and "popish slavery." The only purpose of all the new French forts, suggested Jonathan

French and Indian War *Popular name for the struggle between Britain and France for the control of North America, 1754 to 1763, in which the British conquered New France. It merged into Europe's Seven Years' War (1756–1763) that pitted Britain and Prussia against France, Austria, and Russia.*

Mayhew, a Boston preacher, must be to serve as bases for the conquest of the British colonies.

Britain ordered New York to host an intercolonial congress at Albany to meet with the Iroquois and redress their grievances. The governor invited every colony as far south as Virginia, except non-royal Connecticut and Rhode Island. Virginia and New Jersey declined to attend, but Governor Shirley of Massachusetts invited Connecticut and Rhode Island to participate, and the Massachusetts legislature instructed its delegates to work for a plan of intercolonial union.

In Philadelphia, Benjamin Franklin too was thinking about colonial union. In June 1754 he drafted his "Short Hints towards a Scheme for Uniting the Northern Colonies," which he presented to the **Albany Congress.** His plan called for a "President General" to be appointed by the Crown as commander in chief and to administer the laws of the union, and for a "Grand Council" to be elected for three-year terms by the lower houses of each colony. The union would have power to raise soldiers, build forts, levy taxes, regulate the Indian trade, purchase land from the Indians, and supervise western settlements until the Crown organized them as new colonies. To take effect, the plan would have to be approved by the Crown and by each colonial legislature and then by Parliament. The Albany Congress adopted an amended version of Franklin's proposal.

Both Shirley and Franklin were far ahead of public opinion. Newspapers did not even discuss the Albany Plan. Every colony rejected it. As Franklin later explained, the colonies feared that the President General might become too powerful. But they also distrusted one another. Despite the French threat, they did not yet see themselves as "Americans" who ought to unite in the face of a common peril. The Board of Trade responded by drafting its own plan, which resembled Franklin's, except that the Grand Council could only requisition—instead of tax—and colonial union would not require Parliament's approval. Then news arrived that Washington had surrendered his small force to the French at Great Meadows in July 1754. Britain decided that the colonies were incapable of uniting in their own defense. Even if they could, the precedent would be dangerous. So London sent redcoats to Virginia instead—two regiments commanded by General Edward Braddock. For Britain, colonial union and direct military aid were policy *alternatives.* Although military aid was more expensive to the British government than the proposed union, it seemed the safer choice.

The Congress did achieve one major objective. It urged the Crown to take charge of relations with all western Indians. London responded by creating two Indian superintendencies—one south of the Ohio, which went to Edmund Atkin, and one north of the Ohio, which went to William Johnson, an Irish immigrant with great influence among the Mohawks.

Albany Congress *An intercolonial congress that met in Albany, New York, in June 1754. The delegates urged the Crown to assume direct control of Indian relations beyond the settled boundaries of the colonies, and they drafted a plan of confederation for the continental colonies. No colony ratified it, nor did the Crown or Parliament accept it.*

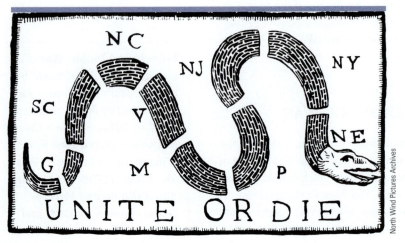

North Wind Picture Archives

BENJAMIN FRANKLIN'S SNAKE CARTOON. *The first newspaper cartoon in colonial America, this device appeared in the* Pennsylvania Gazette *in the spring of 1754. It was a call for colonial union on the eve of the Albany Congress. It drew on the folk legend that a snake, cut into pieces, could revive and live if it somehow joined its severed parts together before sundown.*

BRITAIN'S YEARS OF DEFEAT

In 1755, London hoped that a quick British victory at the forks of the Ohio would keep the war from spreading. But at a council of high officials called by Braddock at Alexandria, Virginia, Shirley persuaded him to accept New England's much broader war objectives. Instead of a single expedition aimed at one fort, the campaign of 1755 became four distinct offensives designed to crush the outer defenses of New France and leave it open to British invasion.

The redcoats were disciplined professional soldiers trained to fight other professional armies. **Irregular war** in American forests made them nervous. Provincial soldiers, by contrast, were young volunteers who usually enlisted only for a single campaign. They knew little about military drill, expected to serve under the officers who had recruited them, and sometimes flatly refused to obey orders. Provincials admired the courage of the redcoats but were shocked by the brutal discipline imposed on them. Nevertheless, several thousand colonists also enlisted in the British army.

Under the enlarged plan of 1755, the redcoats in Nova Scotia together with New England provincials would assault Fort Beauséjour. New England and New York provincials would attack Crown Point, while Shirley, who had been commissioned as a British colonel, would lead two regiments of redcoats, recruited in New England, to Niagara and cut off New France from the western Indians. Braddock, with the strongest force, would attack Fort Duquesne.

Braddock alienated the Indians. In April the western Delawares asked him whether their villages and hunting rights would be secure under British protection. "No Savage," he replied, "Should Inherit the Land." The chiefs retorted that "if they might not have Liberty To Live on the Land they would not Fight for it." Braddock then took several months to hack a road through the wilderness wide enough for his artillery. After fording the Monongahela, the British headed toward Fort Duquesne.

Fort Duquesne's commander could muster only 72 French, 146 Canadians, and 637 Indians against the 1,400 regulars under Braddock and 450 Virginia provincials, including Washington. The French ran into the British vanguard a few miles southeast of the fort. They clashed on July 9, 1755, along a narrow path with thick forest and brush on either side. The French and Indians took cover on the British flanks. Braddock's rear elements rushed toward the sound of the guns. There, massed together, they formed a gigantic red bull's eye. The Indians and the French poured round after round into them, while the British fired wild volleys at the trees. The British lost 977 killed or wounded, along with their artillery. Braddock was killed. Only 39 French and Indians were killed or wounded. The redcoats finally broke and ran. Braddock's road through the wilderness now became a highway for the enemy. For the first time in their history, Pennsylvanians faced the horrors of a frontier war.

In Nova Scotia, Fort Beauséjour fell on June 17, 1755. When the Acadians refused to take an oath that might have obliged them to bear arms against other Frenchmen, the British and Yankees rounded up between 6,000 and 7,000 of them, packed them aboard ships, and expelled them from the province, to be scattered among the 13 colonies, none of which was prepared for the influx. A second roundup in 1759 caught most of the families that had evaded the first one. The government of Nova Scotia confiscated the Acadians' land and redistributed it to Protestant settlers, mostly from New England. About 3,000 Acadian refugees, after spending miserable years as unwanted Catholic exiles in a Protestant world, made it to French Louisiana, where their descendants became known as Cajuns.

Meanwhile William Johnson led his provincials against Crown Point. The French commander, Jean-Armand, baron Dieskau, attacked a body of provincials on

irregular war *A type of war using men who were not part of a permanent or professional regular military force. It also can apply to guerilla-type warfare, usually against the civilian population.*

September 8 and drove it back in panic to the improvised Fort William Henry near Lake George. French regulars then assailed the fort but were driven off with heavy losses in a six-hour struggle. Colonial newspapers proclaimed the battle a great victory because the provincials had not only held the field but had also wounded and captured Dieskau. But Johnson failed to take Crown Point. Shirley's Niagara campaign got no farther than Oswego on Lake Ontario and then stopped for the winter, held in check by the French at Fort Frontenac on the lake's northern shore. Oswego was soon cut off by heavy snows. Malnutrition and disease ravaged the garrison.

A WORLD WAR

With the death of Braddock and the capture of Dieskau, military amateurs took over both armies: Shirley in the British colonies and Governor-General Pierre de Rigaud de Vaudreuil in New France. Vaudreuil was a Canadian who understood his colony's weakness without Indian support. The white population of the 13 colonies outnumbered that of New France by 13 to 1. Vaudreuil knew that if the British empire could concentrate its resources in a few strategic places, it had a good chance of overwhelming New France. A merciless frontier war waged by New France against ordinary settlers remained the most effective way to force the British colonies to disperse their resources.

As long as Vaudreuil was in charge, New France kept winning. Oswego fell in the summer of 1756. Vaudreuil's attacks devastated Pennsylvania's frontier settlements. Even so, the French government decided that New France needed a professional general and sent Louis-Joseph, marquis de Montcalm, in 1756. Shocked and repelled by the brutality of frontier warfare, Montcalm tried to turn the conflict into a traditional European struggle of sieges and battles in which the advantage (as Vaudreuil well understood) would pass to the British. When Fort William Henry fell the next year, Montcalm promised to let the British garrison march unmolested to Fort Edward, but his Indian allies, mostly in pursuit of plunder, killed or carried off 308 of the 2,300 prisoners, an event that colonial newspapers called the Fort William Henry Massacre. The British blamed Montcalm for the outrage; the western Indians resented his interference and never again provided him with significant support. Meanwhile, Braddock's defeat convinced the British government that the struggle with France could not be limited to a few outposts. Britain declared war on France in 1756, and the French and Indian War in the colonies merged with a general European struggle, the Seven Years' War (1756–1763).

For most of the war, Spain remained neutral, a choice that had huge implications within North America. In the previous war, Spain had touched off a slave revolt in South Carolina and had created massive unrest even in New York. At a minimum, Spanish hostilities early in the war would have forced the British to fight in another theater of conflict. Instead, Spain's neutrality permitted Britain to concentrate its resources against New France. By 1762, when Spain finally entered the war in a vain effort to prevent a total British victory, it was too late. New France had already surrendered.

IMPERIAL TENSIONS: FROM LOUDOUN TO PITT

When London suddenly realized in 1755 that Shirley, an amateur, had taken command of the British army in North America, it dispatched General John Campbell, earl of Loudoun, to replace him and began pouring in reinforcements. Loudoun had a special talent for alienating provincials. Colonial units did not care to serve under his command and sometimes bluntly rejected his orders. Provincial volunteers believed they had a contractual relationship with *their* officers; they had never agreed to serve under Loudoun's professionals. Many British officers despised the provincials, especially their officers. "The Americans are in general the dirtiest most contemptible cowardly dogs that you can conceive," snarled General James Wolfe. A few British officers held more favorable opinions. Horatio Gates, Richard Montgomery, Hugh Mercer, and Arthur St. Clair all remained in America after the war and became generals in the American army during the Revolution.

As the new commander in chief, Loudoun faced other problems: the quartering (or housing) of British soldiers, the relative rank of British and provincial officers, military discipline, revenue, and smuggling. He tried to impose authoritarian solutions on them all. When he sent redcoats into a city, he demanded that the assembly pay to quarter them or else he would take over public buildings by force. He tried to make any British major superior in rank to every provincial officer. Loudoun ordered New England troops to serve directly under British officers, an arrangement that New Englanders thought violated the terms of their enlistment. When some colonial assemblies refused to vote adequate supplies, Loudoun urged Parliament to tax the colonies directly. He sometimes imposed embargoes on colonial shipping, partly to stamp out smuggling with French colonies. Loudoun did build up his forces, but otherwise he accomplished little.

In 1757 William Pitt came to power as Britain's war minister. He understood that consent worked better than coercion in the colonies. Colonial assemblies, when asked, built barracks to house British soldiers. Pitt declared that every provincial officer would rank immediately behind the equivalent British rank but above all lesser officers, British or provincial. He then promoted every British lieutenant colonel to the rank of "colonel in America only." That decision left only about 30 British majors vulnerable to being ordered about by a provincial colonel, but few of them had independent commands anyway. Provincial units under the command of their own officers cooperated with the British army, and the officers began to impose something close to British discipline on them. Rather than levy a parliamentary tax, Pitt set aside £200,000 beginning in 1758 and told the colonies that they could claim a share of it in proportion to their contribution to the war effort. He got the colonies to compete voluntarily in support of his stupendous mobilization. The subsidies covered slightly less than half of the cost of fielding 20,000 provincials each year from 1758 to 1760 and somewhat smaller numbers in 1761 and 1762 as operations shifted to the Caribbean. Smuggling angered Pitt as much as it did anyone else, but British conquests soon reduced that problem. By 1762 Canada, Martinique, and Guadeloupe, as well as Spanish Havana, were all in British hands.

Pitt had no patience with military failure. After Loudoun called off his attack on Louisbourg in 1757, Pitt replaced him with James Abercrombie. He also put Jeffrey Amherst in charge of a new Louisbourg expedition. By 1758 the British empire had finally put together professional and provincial forces capable of overwhelming New France and had learned how to use them effectively.

THE YEARS OF BRITISH VICTORY

By 1758 the Royal Navy had cut off Canada from reinforcements and supplies. Britain had sent more than 30 regiments to North America. Combined with 20,000 provincials, thousands of **bateau** men rowing supplies into the interior, and swarms

bateau *A light, flat-bottomed boat with narrow ends that was used in Canada and the northeastern part of the colonies.*

of privateers preying on French commerce, Britain had mustered perhaps 60,000 men for the final assault. Most of them now closed in on the 75,000 people of New France. With little Indian support, Montcalm prepared to defend the approaches to Canada at Forts Duquesne, Niagara, Frontenac, Ticonderoga, Crown Point, and Louisbourg.

Spurred on by Quaker mediators, the British and colonial governments made peace with the western Indians in 1758 by promising not to seize their lands. Few settlers or officials had yet noticed a trend that was emerging during the conflict: Few

View an animated version of this map or related maps at
http://history.wadsworth.com/murrinconcise4e.

Map 4.3
CONQUEST OF CANADA, 1758–1760. *In three campaigns, the British with strong colonial support first subdued the outer defenses of New France, then took Quebec in 1759 and Montreal in 1760.*

Indians in the northeastern woodlands were willing to kill one another. In 1755, for example, some Senecas fought with New France and some Mohawks with the British, but they maneuvered carefully to avoid confronting each other.

Peace with the western Indians in 1758 permitted the British to revive the grand military plan of 1755, except that this time the overall goal was clear—the conquest of New France. Amherst and James Wolfe besieged Louisbourg for 60 days. It fell in September, thus adding Cape Breton Island to the British province of Nova Scotia. A force of 3,000 provincials under Colonel John Bradstreet took Fort Frontenac on Lake Ontario. This victory cut off the French in the Ohio Valley from their supplies. A powerful force of regulars under John Forbes and provincials under Washington marched west through Pennsylvania to attack Fort Duquesne, but the French blew up the fort and retreated north just before they arrived. The British erected Fort Pitt (now Pittsburgh) on the ruins.

The only British defeat in 1758 occurred when Abercrombie sent 6,000 regulars and 9,000 provincials against Ticonderoga (Carillon), which was defended by Montcalm and 3,500 troops. Instead of waiting for his artillery to arrive or outflanking the French, Abercrombie ordered a frontal assault against a heavily fortified position. His regulars were butchered by the withering fire, and the provincials fled. Pitt replaced Abercrombie with Amherst and ordered Wolfe to capture Quebec.

In 1759, while the provincials on Lake Ontario moved west and took Niagara, Amherst spent the summer cautiously reducing Ticonderoga and Crown Point. In June, Wolfe with 8,000 redcoats and colonial rangers laid siege to Quebec, defended by Montcalm with 16,000 regulars, Canadian militia, and Indians. Wolfe mounted howitzers across the river from Quebec and began reducing most of the city to rubble. Frustrated by the French refusal to come out and fight, he turned loose his American rangers, who ravaged and burned more than 1,400 farms. Still the French held out. By September both Wolfe and Montcalm realized that the British fleet would soon have to depart or risk being frozen in during the long winter. Wolfe made a last desperate effort. His men silently sailed up the St. Lawrence, climbed a formidable cliff above the city in darkness, and on the morning of September 13, 1759, deployed on the Plains of Abraham behind Quebec. Montcalm panicked. Instead of using his artillery to defend the walls from inside, he marched out of Quebec onto the plains. Both generals now had what they craved most, a set-piece European battle. Wolfe and Montcalm were both mortally wounded, but the British drove the French from the field and took Quebec. After the fall of Montreal in 1760, New France surrendered.

THE CHEROKEE WAR AND SPANISH INTERVENTION

In December 1759 the Cherokees, who had been allies and trading partners of South Carolina, reacted to a long string of violent incidents by attacking frontier settlers and driving them back 100 miles. South Carolina had to appeal to Amherst for help, and he sent regular soldiers who laid waste the Cherokee Lower Towns in the Appalachian foothills. When that expedition failed to bring peace, another one devastated the Middle Towns farther west. The Cherokees made peace in December 1761, but the backcountry settlers, left brutalized and lawless, became a severe political problem for South Carolina.

Only then, in January 1762, after the French and the Cherokees had been defeated, did Spain finally enter the war. British forces quickly took Havana and even Manila in the distant Philippines. France and Spain sued for peace.

Cherokee War *Between December 1759 and December 1761, the Cherokee Indians devastated the South Carolina backcountry. The British army intervened and in turn inflicted immense damage on the Cherokee.*

QUICK REVIEW

THE BRITISH DRIVE FRANCE FROM NORTH AMERICA

- The Albany Congress failed to achieve intercolonial union and Washington surrendered near the forks of the Ohio

- Braddock was defeated in 1755, but the Acadians were expelled from their homeland

- Pitt put together a victorious coalition of redcoats and provincials that defeated New France

- Spain entered the war too late to make a difference

THE PEACE OF PARIS

Peace of Paris *The 1763 treaty that ended the war between Britain on the one hand, and France and Spain on the other side. France surrendered New France to Britain. Spain ceded Florida to Britain, and France compensated its ally by ceding Louisiana to Spain.*

In 1763 the **Peace of Paris** ended the war. Britain returned Martinique and Guadeloupe to France. France surrendered to Great Britain several minor West Indian islands and all of North America east of the Mississippi, except New Orleans. In exchange for Havana, Spain ceded Florida to the British and also paid a large ransom for the return of Manila. To compensate its Spanish ally, France gave all of Louisiana west of the Mississippi, including New Orleans, to Spain.

The colonists were jubilant. Britain and the colonies could now develop their vast resources in an imperial partnership and would share unprecedented prosperity. But the western Indians angrily rejected the peace settlement. No one had conquered them, and they denied the right or the power of France to surrender their lands to Great Britain. They began to plan their own war of liberation.

CONCLUSION

Between 1713 and 1754, expansion and renewed immigration pushed the edge of North American settlement ever farther into the interior. With a population that doubled every 25 years, many householders no longer had the opportunity to give all their sons and daughters the level of economic success that they themselves enjoyed. By midcentury many farmers also had taken up a trade or moved west. As in England, many families had to favor sons over daughters and the eldest son over his younger brothers. The colonies anglicized in other ways as well. Newspapers and the learned professions spread the English Enlightenment to the colonies. English revivalists had a tremendous impact in North America, and British political values reshaped both northern and southern colonies, though in different ways.

In 1739 the imperial wars resumed. The threat of internal upheaval kept King George's War indecisive in the 1740s, but when Spain remained neutral as Britain and France went to war after 1754, the British mobilized their full resources and conquered New France.

The war left powerful memories behind. Provincials admired the courage of the redcoats and the victories they won but hated their arrogant officers. The concord and prosperity that were supposed to follow Britain's great imperial victory led instead to bitter political strife.

QUESTIONS FOR REVIEW AND CRITICAL THINKING

Review

1. Why was it difficult to sustain both continual expansion and the anglicization of the colonies at the same time?
2. How were the colonists able to embrace both the Enlightenment and evangelical religion at the same time?
3. How could both the royal governors and the colonial assemblies grow stronger at the same time?
4. What made the War for North America (1754–1763) so much more decisive than the three earlier Anglo-French conflicts?

Critical Thinking

1. "How is it that we hear the loudest yelps for liberty among the drivers of Negroes?" asked Dr. Samuel Johnson, a towering literary figure in 18th-century England, on the eve of the Revolutionary War. Thomas Jefferson, George Washington, Patrick Henry, James Madison, and many other prominent spokesmen for the American cause owned dozens, even hundreds of slaves. Is there any way that being a large slaveholder might have increased a planter's commitment to liberty as it had come to be understood in England by that time? Did Johnson have a point?

2. The duc de Choiseul, who negotiated the Treaty of Paris that ended the Seven Years' War in 1763, and the comte de Vergennes, who negotiated the Franco-American Alliance of 1778, both claimed that France's decision to cede Canada to Great Britain in 1763 was a masterstroke of French policy because, with no enemy to fear on their borders, the colonies would no longer need British protection and would soon move toward complete independence. By contrast, the leaders of colonial resistance after 1763 always insisted that Britain's postwar policies provoked both the resistance and independence. Who was right?

Discovery

What social and political changes occurred in the first half of the 1700s that would help spur the later revolutionary movement?

SUGGESTED READINGS

The best study of eighteenth-century immigration is **Bernard Bailyn, *Voyagers to the West: A Passage in the Peopling of America on the Eve of the Revolution*** (1986). **A. Roger Ekirch, *Bound for America: The Transportation of British Convicts to the Colonies*** (1987) is also important. For gentility and the Enlightenment, excellent studies include **Richard L. Bushman, *The Refinement of America: Persons, Houses, Cities*** (1992); **Ned Landsman, *From Colonials to Provincials: Thought and Culture in America, 1680–1760*** (1998); **David S. Shields, *Civil Tongues and Polite Letters in British America*** (1997); and **Charles E. Clark, *The Public Prints: The Newspaper in Anglo-American Culture, 1665–1740*** (1994). For early Georgia, see **Harold E. Davis, *The Fledgling Province: Social and Cultural Life in Colonial Georgia, 1773–1776*** (1976). **Mark A. Noll, *The Rise of Evangelicalism: The Age of Edwards, Whitefield, and the Wesleys*** (2003) provides an insightful overview of the Great Awakening. **Bernard Bailyn's *The Origins of American Politics*** (1968) has had a major impact.

For the renewal of imperial conflict after 1739, see **Jill Lepore, *New York Burning: Liberty, Slavery, and Conspiracy in Eighteenth-Century Manhattan*** (2005); **Fred Anderson, *Crucible of War: The Seven Years War and the Fate of Empire in British North America, 1754–1766*** (2000); **Timothy J. Shannon, *Indians and Colonists at the Crossroads of Empire: The Albany Congress of 1754*** (2000); **John Mack Faragher, *A Great and Noble Scheme: The Tragic Story of the Expulsion of the French Acadians from their American Homeland*** (2005); and **Ian K. Steele, *Betrayals: Fort William Henry and the "Massacre"*** (1990).

ONLINE SOURCES GUIDE

ThomsonNOW Visit ThomsonNOW to access primary sources, exercises, quizzes, and audio chapter summaries related to this chapter:
http://www.Thomsonedu.com/login

DISCOVERY

What social and political changes occurred in the first half of the 1700s that would help spur the later revolutionary movement?

In thinking about this question, begin by breaking it down into the components shown below. A discussion of the significance of each component should appear in your answer.

DIFFERENCES IN SOCIAL OUTLOOK

What hints about the differences between basic social relationships in the South and the North do you get by looking at the paintings of the tobacco plantation and the rescue at sea? Who and what kinds of people in each picture are working and not working? Who is shown making money?

TOBACCO PLANTATION

SIMILARITIES IN SOCIAL OUTLOOK

Based on what you know and have learned about social and class relations in England in the 1700s, what reasons might the English plantation owners have had to resist the control of England on their lives by 1776? Does Copley's painting have a "message" about life in the colonies? How would you describe it? Would this "message" have been well received in England? Why or why not?

WATSON AND THE SHARK

WARFARE

Look at the map "Conquest of Canada, 1758-1760." What advantages can you see that the British possessed based solely on geographic position of their settlements? Consider also what you have read in the section "The Years of British Victory." What role did the colonists and Indians play in the French and Indian War?

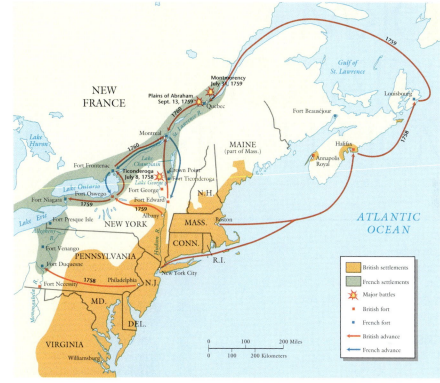

CONQUEST OF CANADA, 1758–1760

GOVERNMENT AND LAW

What do the letters G, SC, NC, and so on mean in Benjamin Franklin's snake cartoon? Based on the reading in this chapter and the cartoon, what do you think might have motivated Ben Franklin to create and print a cartoon like this for his newspaper instead of explaining his opinion in an essay? What kinds of people do you think agreed with him about the advantage of colonial unity? Who might have opposed this kind of union? Why?

BENJAMIN FRANKLIN'S SNAKE CARTOON

North Wind Picture Archives

5

REFORM, RESISTANCE, REVOLUTION

B ritain left an army in North America after 1763 and taxed the colonies to pay part of its cost. The colonists agreed that they should contribute to their own defense but insisted that taxation without representation violated their rights as Englishmen. Three successive crises shattered Britain's North American empire by 1776. In the Stamp Act crisis, the colonies first petitioned Parliament for a redress of grievances. When that effort failed, they nullified the Stamp Act and kept resisting until the tax was repealed in 1766. The settlers joyfully celebrated their victory. In the Townshend crisis of 1767–1770, Parliament imposed new taxes on certain imported goods. The colonists petitioned and resisted simul-

taneously, mostly through an intercolonial nonimportation movement. The British sent troops to Boston. After several violent confrontations, the soldiers withdrew, while Parliament modified the Townshend Revenue Act, retaining only the duty on tea. That gesture broke up the nonimportation movement. Nobody celebrated. The Tea Act of 1773 launched the third crisis, which quickly escalated. Boston destroyed British tea without petitioning first. When Parliament responded with the Coercive Acts of 1774, the colonists created the Continental Congress to organize further resistance. Neither side dared back down, and the confrontation careened toward armed violence. War broke out in April 1775. Fifteen months later the colonies declared their independence.

TIMELINE

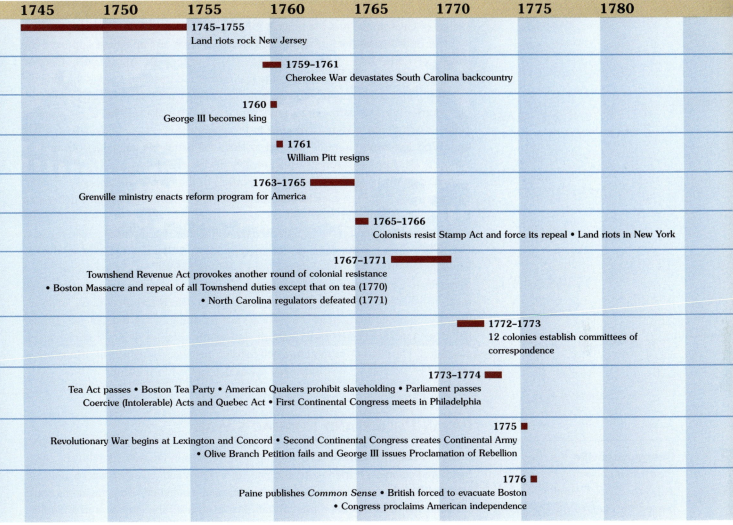

1745	1750	1755	1760	1765	1770	1775	1780

1745–1755
Land riots rock New Jersey

1759–1761
Cherokee War devastates South Carolina backcountry

1760
George III becomes king

1761
William Pitt resigns

1763–1765
Grenville ministry enacts reform program for America

1765–1766
Colonists resist Stamp Act and force its repeal • Land riots in New York

1767–1771
Townshend Revenue Act provokes another round of colonial resistance
• Boston Massacre and repeal of all Townshend duties except that on tea (1770)
• North Carolina regulators defeated (1771)

1772–1773
12 colonies establish committees of correspondence

1773–1774
Tea Act passes • Boston Tea Party • American Quakers prohibit slaveholding • Parliament passes Coercive (Intolerable) Acts and Quebec Act • First Continental Congress meets in Philadelphia

1775
Revolutionary War begins at Lexington and Concord • Second Continental Congress creates Continental Army
• Olive Branch Petition fails and George III issues Proclamation of Rebellion

1776
Paine publishes *Common Sense* • British forced to evacuate Boston
• Congress proclaims American independence

IMPERIAL REFORM

In 1760 George III (1760–1820) inherited the British throne at the age of 22. His pronouncements on behalf of religion and virtue at first won him many admirers in North America, but the political coalition leading Britain to victory over France fell apart. The king's new ministers set out to reform the empire.

FROM PITT TO GRENVILLE

The king, along with his tutor and principal adviser, John Stuart, earl of Bute, feared that the Seven Years' War would bankrupt Britain. From 1758 on, despite victory after victory, George and Bute grew more and more despondent. When **William Pitt,** the king's war minister, urged a preemptive strike on Spain before Spain could attack Britain, Bute forced him to resign in October 1761. Bute soon learned that Pitt had been right. Spain entered the war in January 1762. In May Bute replaced Thomas Pelham-Holles, duke of Newcastle, as first lord of the treasury. To economize, he reduced Britain's subsidies to Prussia, its only major ally in Europe. So eager were the

William Pitt *One of the most popular public officials in 18th-century Britain, he was best known as the minister who organized Britain's successful war effort against France in the French and Indian War.*

king and Bute to end the war that they gave back to France the wealthy West Indian islands of Guadeloupe and Martinique.

The British press harshly denounced Bute. As soon as Parliament approved the Treaty of Paris, Bute dismayed the king by resigning. In April 1763, **George Grenville** (Pitt's brother-in-law) became first lord of the treasury, though the king did not trust him and found him barely acceptable. Britain's national debt had nearly doubled during the war with France and stood at £130 million. The sheer scale of Britain's victory required more revenue just to police the conquered colonies. In 1762 and 1763 Bute and Grenville decided to leave 20 battalions (about 7,000 men) in America. Because the colonists would receive the benefit of this protection, Grenville argued, they ought to pay a reasonable portion of the cost, and eventually all of it. He never asked the colonies to contribute anything to Britain's national debt or to Britain's heavy domestic expenses.

Instead of building on the voluntaristic measures that Pitt had used to win the war, Grenville reverted to the demands for coercive reforms that had crisscrossed the Atlantic during Britain's years of defeat from 1755 to 1757. London, he believed, had to regain effective control over the colonies. To the settlers, victory over France would mean new burdens, not relief. To Grenville, the willing cooperation of the colonies after 1758 exposed the empire's weakness, not its strength. He thought that Britain had to act quickly to establish its authority before the colonies slipped completely out of control. He thus set in motion a self-fulfilling prophecy in which the British government brought about precisely what it was determined to prevent.

INDIAN POLICY AND PONTIAC'S WAR

George Grenville *As head of the British government from 1763 to 1765, Grenville passed the Sugar Act, Quartering Act, Currency Act, and the Stamp Act, provoking the imperial crisis of 1765–1766.*

Proclamation of 1763 *It was issued by the Privy Council. Among other things, it tried to prevent the colonists from encroaching upon Indian lands by prohibiting settlement west of the Appalachian watershed unless the government first purchased those lands by treaty.*

Pontiac *An Ottawa chief whose name has been attached to the great Indian uprising against the British in 1763–1764.*

Britain's **Proclamation of 1763** set up governments in Quebec, Florida, and other conquered colonies. It tried to set the pace of western settlement by establishing the so-called Proclamation Line along the Appalachian watershed. No settlements could be planted west of that line unless Britain first purchased the land by treaty. Settlers would be encouraged to move instead to Nova Scotia, northern New England, Georgia, or Florida. But General Amherst stopped distributing Indian gifts, and his contempt for Indian customs deprived Britain of most of its leverage with them at a time when their ability to unite had become stronger than ever.

In 1761 Neolin, a western Delaware, had a vision in which God commanded Indians to resume their ancestral ways. Neolin called for an end to Indian dependence on the Anglo-Americans. God was punishing Indians for accepting European ways. With a unity never seen before, the Indians struck in 1763. **Pontiac**'s War, named for an Ottawa chief, brought together Senecas, Mingos, Delawares, Shawnees, Wyandots, Miamis, Ottawas, and other nations. They attacked 13 British posts in the West. Between May 16 and June 20, all of them fell except Niagara, Fort Pitt, and Detroit. For months the Indians kept Detroit and Fort Pitt under close siege. They hoped to drive British settlers back to the eastern seaboard.

Enraged by these attacks, Amherst ordered Colonel Henry Bouquet, commander at Fort Pitt, to distribute smallpox-infested blankets among the western nations, touching off a lethal epidemic. In 1764 British and provincial forces ended resistance and restored peace. The British reluctantly accepted the role that the French had played in the Great Lakes region by distributing gifts and mediating differences.

But 10 years of conflict had brutalized the frontiersmen. Perhaps sensing the Indians' growing revulsion against warring with one another, many settlers began to assume that all Indians must be the enemies of all whites. In December 1763 the Scots-Irish of Paxton Township, Pennsylvania, murdered six unarmed Christian

View an animated version of this map or related maps at
http://history.wadsworth.com/murrinconcise4e.

Map 5.1

PONTIAC'S WAR AND THE PROCLAMATION LINE OF 1763. *Britain claimed possession of North America east of the Mississippi only to face an extraordinary challenge from the Indians of the interior, who wiped out eight garrisons but could not take Detroit, Niagara, or Fort Pitt.*

Q U I C K   R E V I E W

THE GRENVILLE PROGRAM OF IMPERIAL REFORM

- Respected Indian lands but kept an army in North America and passed a Quartering Act to maintain it

- Parliament imposed taxes on the colonies to pay part of the army's costs

- Sugar Act imposed duties on colonial trade, especially on molasses

- Stamp Act taxed legal documents, newspapers, and pamphlets

specie *Also called "hard money" as against paper money. In colonial times, it usually meant silver, but it could also include gold coins.*

virtual representation *The English concept that Members of Parliament represented the entire empire, not just a local constituency and its voters. According to this theory, settlers were represented in Parliament in the same way that nonvoting subjects in Britain were represented. The colonists accepted virtual representation for nonvoting settlers within their colonies but denied that the term could describe their relationship with Parliament.*

Indians—two old men, three women, and a child—at nearby Conestoga. Two weeks later the "Paxton Boys" slaughtered 14 more Christian Indians who had been brought to Lancaster for protection. When Governor John Penn removed 140 Moravian mission Indians to Philadelphia for safety, the Paxton Boys marched on the capital determined to kill them all.

Denouncing the Paxton Boys as "Christian white Savages," Benjamin Franklin led a delegation from the assembly that met the marchers at Germantown and persuaded them to go home after they presented a list of grievances. The Moravian Indians had been spared, but all efforts to bring the murderers to justice failed, and the frontiersmen of Pennsylvania and Virginia virtually declared an open season on Indians that continued for years. Indians had won real benefits from London's postwar policies, such as protection from land speculators, but otherwise they found little to choose between Amherst's smallpox blankets and the homicidal rage of the Paxton Boys.

THE SUGAR ACT

In a step that settlers found ominous, Grenville's Sugar Act of 1764 cracked down on smuggling and placed duties on Madeira wine, coffee, sugar, and other products, but Grenville expected to get the greatest revenue from the molasses duty of three pence per gallon. The Molasses Act of 1733 had been designed to keep French molasses out of North America by imposing a prohibitive duty of six pence per gallon. Instead, by paying a bribe of about a penny a gallon, merchants were able to get French molasses certified as British. By 1760, more than 90 percent of all molasses imported into New England came from the French islands. Planters in the British islands gave up, lost interest in New England markets, and turned their molasses into quality rum for sale in Britain and Ireland. Nobody, in short, had any interest in stopping the trade in French molasses. New England merchants said they were willing to pay a duty of one pence (what bribes were costing them), but Grenville insisted on three.

THE CURRENCY ACT AND THE QUARTERING ACT

Grenville passed several other imperial measures. The Currency Act of 1764 responded to wartime protests of London merchants against Virginia's paper money, which had lost 15 percent of its value between 1759 and 1764. The act forbade the colonies to issue any paper money as legal tender. The money question had become urgent because the Sugar Act (and, later, the Stamp Act) required that all duties be paid in **specie** (silver or gold). Supporters of those taxes argued that the new duties would keep the specie in America to pay the army, but the colonists replied that the drain of specie from some of the colonies would put impossible constraints on trade. Boston and Newport, for instance, would pay most of the molasses tax, but the specie collected there would follow the army to Quebec, New York, the Great Lakes, and Florida. Grenville saw "America" as a single region in which specie would circulate to the benefit of all. The colonists knew better. As of 1765, "America" existed only in British minds, not yet in colonial hearts.

Another reform was the Quartering Act of 1765, requested by Sir Thomas Gage, Amherst's successor as army commander. Gage asked for authority to quarter soldiers in private homes, if necessary, when on the march and away from their barracks. Parliament ordered colonial assemblies to vote specific supplies for the troops, such as beer and candles, which the assemblies were already doing. But the act also required the army to quarter its soldiers only in public buildings, such as taverns, which existed in large numbers only in cities. The Quartering Act solved no problems; it created several new ones.

THE STAMP ACT

In early 1764 when Parliament passed the Sugar Act, Grenville announced that a stamp tax on legal documents and on publications might also be needed. No one in the House of Commons, he declared, doubted that Parliament had the right to impose such a tax. Because Parliament had never levied a direct tax on the colonies, however, he also knew that he had to persuade the settlers that a stamp tax would not be a constitutional innovation. The measure, his supporters insisted, did not violate the principle of no taxation without representation. Each member of Parliament, they argued, represented the entire empire, not just a local constituency. The colonists were no different than the large majority of subjects within Great Britain who could not vote. All were **virtually represented** in Parliament. Grenville also denied that any legal difference existed between external taxes (port duties, such as that on molasses) and internal (or inland) taxes, such as the proposed stamp tax.

Grenville indicated that, if the colonies could devise a better revenue plan than a stamp tax, he would listen. His offer created confusion. All 13 colonial assemblies drafted petitions objecting to the **Stamp Act** as a form of taxation without representation. Most of them also attacked the duties imposed by the Sugar Act because they went beyond the regulation of trade. With few exceptions, they too rejected the distinction between **internal** and **external taxes.** Both kinds, they declared, violated the British constitution. While agreeing that they ought to contribute to their own defense, they urged the government to return to the traditional method of requisitions, in which the Crown asked a colony for a specific sum, and the assembly decided how (or whether) to raise it.

When the first round of these petitions reached London early in 1765, Parliament refused to receive them. To Grenville, requisitions were not a better idea. They had often been tried, had never worked efficiently, and never would. He rejected the petitions with a clear conscience. But to the colonists, he had acted in bad faith all along. He had asked their advice and had then refused even to consider it.

The Stamp Act passed in February 1765, to go into effect on November 1. All contracts, licenses, commissions, and most other legal documents would be void unless they were executed on officially stamped paper. Law courts would not recognize any document that lacked the proper stamp. A stamp duty was also put on all newspapers and pamphlets, a requirement likely to anger every printer in the colonies. Playing cards and dice were also taxed.

When the Stamp Act became law, most colonial leaders resigned themselves to a situation that seemed beyond their power to change, but ordinary settlers began to take direct action to prevent implementation of the act.

Stamp Act *Passed by the administration of George Grenville in 1765, the Stamp Act imposed duties on most legal documents in the colonies and on newspapers and other publications. Massive colonial resistance to the act created a major imperial crisis.*

internal taxes *Taxes that were imposed on land, on people, on retail items (such as excises), or on legal documents and newspapers (such as the Stamp Act). Most colonists thought that only their elective assemblies had the constitutional power to impose internal taxes.*

external taxes *Taxes based on oceanic trade, such as port duties. Some colonists thought of them more as a means of regulating trade than as taxes for revenue.*

THE STAMP ACT CRISIS

Resistance to the Stamp Act began in the spring of 1765 and continued for nearly a year until it was repealed. Patrick Henry, a newcomer to the Virginia House of Burgesses, launched the first wave by introducing five resolutions on May 30 and 31, 1765. His resolves passed by narrow margins, and one was rescinded the next day. Henry had two more in his pocket that he decided not to introduce. But over the summer the *Newport Mercury* printed six of Henry's seven resolutions, and the *Maryland Gazette* printed all of them. Neither paper reported that some had not passed.

To other colonies, Virginia's position seemed far more radical than it really was. The last resolve printed in the *Maryland Gazette* claimed that anyone defending Parliament's right to tax Virginia "shall be Deemed, an Enemy to this his Majesty's Colony."

In their fall or winter sessions, eight colonial legislatures passed new resolutions condemning the Stamp Act. Nine colonies sent delegates to the Stamp Act Congress, which met in New York in October. It passed resolutions affirming colonial loyalty to the king and "all due subordination" to Parliament but condemned the Stamp and Sugar Acts. By 1765 nearly all colonial spokesmen agreed that the Stamp Act was unconstitutional, that colonial representation in Parliament (urged by a few writers) was impractical because of the distance and the huge expense, and that therefore the Stamp Act had to be repealed. They accepted the idea of virtual representation *within* the colonies—their assemblies, they said, represented both voters and nonvoters in each colony—but the colonists ridiculed the argument when it was applied across the Atlantic. A disfranchised Englishman who acquired sufficient property could become a voter, pointed out Maryland's Daniel Dulany. But no colonist, no matter how wealthy he became, could vote for a member of Parliament. Members of Parliament paid the taxes that they levied on people within Britain, but they would never pay any tax they imposed on the colonies.

NULLIFICATION

No matter how eloquent, resolutions and pamphlets alone could not defeat the Stamp Act. Street violence might, however, and Boston showed the way, led by men calling themselves "Sons of Liberty." On August 14 the town awoke to find an effigy of Andrew Oliver, the stamp distributor, hanging on what became the town's **liberty tree** (the gallows on which enemies of the people deserved to be hanged). The sheriff admitted that he dared not remove the effigy, and after dark a crowd of men roamed the streets, shouted defiance at the governor and council, demolished a new building Oliver was erecting that "they called the Stamp Office," beheaded and burned Oliver's effigy, and invaded his home. He had already fled. Thoroughly cowed, he resigned.

On August 26 an even angrier crowd all but demolished the elegant mansion of Lt. Governor Thomas Hutchinson. Most Bostonians believed that Hutchinson had defended and even helped to draft the Stamp Act in letters to British friends. In fact, he had opposed it, although quietly. Shocked by the destruction of property, the militia finally appeared to police the streets. But when Governor Francis Bernard tried to arrest those responsible for the first riot, he got nowhere. Bostonians deplored the events of August 26 but approved those of August 14. No one was punished for either riot even though everyone knew that Ebenezer McIntosh, a poor shoemaker and a leader of the annual Pope's Day demonstrations, had organized both riots.

Everywhere except Georgia, the stamp master was forced to resign before the law took effect on November 1. With no one to distribute the stamps, the act could not be implemented. Merchants adopted **nonimportation agreements** to pressure the British into repeal. Following Boston's lead, the Sons of Liberty took control of the streets in other cities. After November 1, they agitated to open the ports and courts, which had closed down rather than operate without stamps. As winter gave way to spring, most ports and some courts resumed business. Violent resistance worked. The Stamp Act was nullified—even in Georgia, eventually. No officials had any stamps to use because nobody dared distribute them.

liberty tree *A term for the gallows on which enemies of the people deserved to be hanged. The best known was in Boston.*

nonimportation agreements *Agreements not to import goods from Great Britain. They were designed to put pressure on the British economy and force the repeal of unpopular parliamentary acts.*

REPEAL

The next move was up to Britain. For reasons that had nothing to do with the colonies, the king dismissed Grenville in the summer of 1765 and replaced his ministry with a narrow coalition organized primarily by William Augustus, duke of Cumberland, the king's uncle. An untested young nobleman, Charles Watson-Wentworth, marquess of Rockingham, took over the treasury. This "Old Whig" ministry had to deal with the riots in America, and Cumberland, the man who had sent Braddock to Virginia in the winter of 1754–1755, may have favored a similar use of force in late 1765. If so, he never had a chance to issue the order. On October 31, minutes before an emergency cabinet meeting on the American crisis, he died of a heart attack, leaving Rockingham in charge of the ministry. At first, Rockingham favored amending the Stamp Act, but by December he had decided on repeal. To win over the other ministers, the king, and Parliament, he would need great skill.

To Rockingham, the only alternative to repeal seemed to be a ruinous civil war in America, but as the king's chief minister, he could hardly tell Parliament that the world's greatest empire had to yield to unruly mobs. He needed a better reason for repeal. Even before news of the nonimportation agreements reached London, he began to mobilize the British merchants and manufacturers who traded with America. They petitioned Parliament for repeal of the Stamp Act. To them the Grenville program had been an economic disaster, and they gave Rockingham the leverage he needed.

Rockingham won the concurrence of the other ministers only by promising to support a Declaratory Act that would affirm the sovereignty of Parliament over the colonies. When William Pitt eloquently demanded repeal in the House of Commons on January 14, 1766, Rockingham gained a powerful, though temporary, ally. Parliament "may bind {the colonists'} trade, confine their manufactures, and exercise *every power whatsoever*," Pitt declared, "except that of taking their money out of their pockets without their consent." Rockingham still had to overcome resistance from the king, who hinted that he favored "modification," not repeal. George III was willing to repeal some of the stamp duties, but not all. However, only Grenville was ready to use the army to enforce even an amended Stamp Act. Rockingham, who knew the king detested Grenville, brought George III around with a threat to resign.

FOCUS QUESTION

Why, in 1766, did the colonists rejoice over the repeal of the Stamp Act and stop resisting, even though the Revenue Act of 1766 continued to tax molasses?

QUICK REVIEW

COLONIAL RESISTANCE TO THE STAMP ACT AND ITS RESULTS

- Petitions to Parliament had no effect

- Beginning in Boston, the Sons of Liberty nullified the Stamp Act by forcing stamp distributors to resign

- Merchants adopted nonimportation agreements

- Rockingham ministry coupled repeal with a Declaratory Act affirming parliamentary supremacy

- Revenue Act of 1766 amended Sugar Act by reducing the molasses duty to a penny per gallon

Courtesy of the John Carter Brown Library at Brown University

"THE REPEAL OR THE FUNERAL OF MISS AMERIC-STAMP." *This London cartoon of 1766 shows George Grenville carrying the coffin of the Stamp Act with Lord Bute behind him. Contemporaries would easily have identified the other personalities.*

Three pieces of legislation ended the crisis. One, the Declaratory Act, affirmed that Parliament had "full power and authority to make laws and statutes of sufficient force and validity to bind the colonies . . . in all cases whatsoever." Rockingham resisted pressure to insert the word "taxes" along with "laws and statutes." That omission permitted the colonists, who drew a sharp distinction between legislation (which, they conceded, Parliament had a right to pass) and taxation (which it could not), to interpret the act as an affirmation of their position, while nearly everyone in Britain read precisely the opposite meaning into the phrase "laws and statutes." The colonists saw the Declaratory Act as a face-saving gesture that made repeal of the Stamp Act possible. The second measure repealed the Stamp Act because it had been "greatly detrimental to the commercial interests" of the empire. A third statute, the Revenue Act of 1766, reduced the duty on molasses from three pence per gallon to one penny, but the duty was imposed on all molasses, British or foreign, imported into the mainland colonies. Although the act was more favorable to the molasses trade than any other law yet passed by Parliament, it was, clearly, a revenue measure, and it generated more income for the empire than any other colonial tax. Few colonists attacked it for violating the principle of no taxation without representation. In Britain it seemed that the colonists objected only to internal taxes but would accept external duties.

In the course of the struggle, both sides, British and colonial, had rejected the distinction between "internal" and "external" taxes. They could find no legal or philosophical basis for condemning the one while approving the other. Hardly anyone except Franklin noticed in 1766 that the difference was quite real and that the crisis had in fact been resolved according to that distinction. Parliament had tried to extend its authority over the internal affairs of the colonies and had failed. But it continued to collect port duties in the colonies, some to regulate trade, others for revenue. No one knew how to justify this division of authority, but in fact the external-internal cleavage marked the boundary between what Parliament could do on its own and what the Crown could do only with the consent of the colonists.

Another misunderstanding was equally grave. Only the riots had created a crisis severe enough to push Parliament into repeal, but both sides preferred to believe that economic pressure had been decisive. For the colonies, this conviction set the pattern of resistance for the next two imperial crises. But for now they celebrated repeal with great jubilation.

THE TOWNSHEND CRISIS

The reconciliation created by repeal did not last. In 1766 the king again replaced his ministry. This time he persuaded William Pitt to form a government. Pitt appealed to men of goodwill from all parties, but few responded. His ministry faced serious opposition within Parliament. Pitt compounded that problem by accepting a peerage as earl of Chatham, a decision that removed his compelling oratory from the House of Commons and eventually left Charles Townshend as his spokesman in that chamber. A witty extemporaneous speaker, Townshend had betrayed every leader he ever served. The only point of real consistency in his political career had been his attitude toward the colonies. He always took a hard line.

THE TOWNSHEND PROGRAM

New York had already created a small crisis for Chatham by objecting to the Quartering Act as a disguised form of taxation without consent. Under the old rules, the army asked for quarters and supplies, and the assembly voted them. Consent had

MUSICAL LINK TO THE PAST

AN AMERICAN HEART OF OAK

*Composers: William Boyce (music),
John Dickinson (lyrics)
Title: "Liberty Song" (1768)*

Within weeks of publication, this sprightly tune spread throughout the colonies, along with the political message embedded in its lyrics. It formed part of the attack by John Dickinson against the Townshend Revenue Act. Dickinson's pamphlet *Letters from a Farmer in Pennsylvania* argued that the Act went against traditional English philosophies of government because "no tax designed to produce revenue can be considered constitutional unless a people's elected representatives voted for it." But to reach those colonists who did not read pamphlets or newspapers, Dickinson also used popular song.

"Liberty Song" repeats Dickinson's written sentiments in a more rousing manner, and one can imagine the lyrics sung loudly by carousers in a public tavern or meeting place: "This bumper I crown for our Sov'reign's health / and this for Britannia's glory and wealth / That wealth, and that glory immortal may be / If she is but just, and if we are but free." These lines demonstrate that, like most colonists, Dickinson viewed himself as a loyal and patriotic British subject.

In his song and pamphlet, he made no arguments for independence. He claimed that if Britain treated her subjects in a "just" manner, they would continue to serve the government loyally. But this relatively new and controversial insistence on a more equal two-way relationship between Britain and its American colonies, instead of a paternalistic relationship, provoked increasing friction with the mother country, presaging more open oppositions such as the Boston Tea Party and, eventually, the Revolution.

Dickinson penned his "Liberty Song" lyrics to fit a popular 1750s British patriotic stage tune entitled "Heart of Oak" that celebrated the navy's victories in the Seven Years' War, and the song achieved quick popularity. It was also telling that "Liberty Song" was based on music from Europe. European music enjoyed a pervasive and dominating influence in the colonies. A distinctly American music would not make a significant appearance for at least another half-century.

1. Do you think that the medium of popular song is effective for spreading political messages?
2. Why do so few popular songs on today's best-selling charts feature political content?

Listen to an audio recording of this music on the *Musical Links to the Past* CD.

---

been an integral part of the process. Now one legislature (Parliament) was telling others (colonial assemblies) what they must do. New York refused. In 1767 Parliament passed the New York Restraining Act, which forbade the governor to sign any law until the assembly complied with the Quartering Act. The crisis fizzled out when the governor bent the rules and announced that the assembly had already complied with the substance of the Quartering Act before the Restraining Act went into effect.

Chatham soon learned that he could not control the House of Commons from his position in the House of Lords. During the Christmas recess of 1766–1767, he began to slip into an acute depression that lasted more than two years. After March, he refused to communicate with other ministers or even with the king. The colonists expected sympathy from his administration. Instead they got Townshend, who took charge of colonial policy in the spring of 1767.

A central aspect of Townshend's annual budget was the **Townshend Revenue Act** of 1767, which imposed new duties in colonial ports on certain imports that the colonies could legally get only from Britain: tea, paper, glass, red and white lead, and painter's colors. But Townshend also removed more duties on tea within Britain than he could offset with the new revenue collected in the colonies. Revenue, clearly, was not his object. The statute's preamble stated his real goal: to use the new revenues to

Townshend Revenue Act
Passed by Parliament in 1767, this act imposed import duties on tea, paper, glass, red and white lead, and painter's colors. It provoked the imperial crisis of 1767–1770. In 1770 Parliament repealed all of the duties except the one on tea.

pay the salaries of governors and judges in the colonies, thereby freeing them from dependence on the assemblies. This devious strategy aroused suspicions of conspiracy in the colonies. Many sober provincials began to fear that, deep in the recesses of the British government, men really were plotting to deprive them of their liberties.

Other measures gave appellate powers to the **vice-admiralty courts** in Boston, Philadelphia, and Charleston and created a separate American Board of Customs Commissioners to enforce the trade and revenue laws in the colonies. The board was placed in Boston, where resistance to the Stamp Act had been fiercest, rather than in Philadelphia, which had been rather quiet in 1765 and would have been a much more convenient location. Townshend was eager for confrontation.

The British army also began to withdraw from nearly all frontier posts and concentrate near the coast. Although the primary motive was to save money, the implications were striking. It was one thing to keep an army in America to guard the frontier and then ask the colonists to pay part of its cost. But an army far distant from the frontier presumably existed only to police the colonists themselves. Why should they pay part of its cost if its role was to enforce policies that would undermine their liberties?

Townshend ridiculed the distinction between internal and external taxes, one that he attributed to Chatham and the colonists, but declared that he would honor it anyway. Then, having won approval for his program, he died suddenly in September 1767, passing on to others the dilemmas he had created. Frederick, Lord North, replaced him as chancellor of the exchequer. Chatham resigned, and Augustus Henry Fitzroy, duke of Grafton, became prime minister.

RESISTANCE: THE POLITICS OF ESCALATION

The internal-external distinction was troublesome for the colonists. Since 1765 they had been objecting to all taxes for revenue, but in 1766 they had accepted the penny duty on molasses with few complaints. Defeating the Revenue Act of 1767 would prove tougher than nullifying the Stamp Act. Parliament had never been able to impose its will on the internal affairs of the colonies, as the Stamp Act fiasco demonstrated, but it did control the seas. Goods subject to duties might be aboard any of hundreds of ships arriving from Britain each year, but screening the cargo of every vessel threatened to impose impossible burdens on the Sons of Liberty. A policy of general nonimportation would be easier to implement, but British trade played a bigger role in the colonial economy than North American trade did in the British economy. To hurt Britain a little, the colonies would have to harm themselves a lot.

The colonists divided over strategies of resistance. The radical *Boston Gazette* called for complete nonimportation of all British goods. The merchants' paper, the *Boston Evening Post,* disagreed. In October 1767 the Boston town meeting encouraged greater use of home manufactures and authorized the voluntary nonconsumption of British goods. But there was no organized resistance to the new measures, and the Townshend duties became operative in November with little opposition. A month later, John Dickinson, a Philadelphia lawyer, tried to rouse his fellow colonists to action through 12 urgent essays that were printed in nearly every colonial newspaper. These anonymous *Letters from a Farmer in Pennsylvania* denied the distinction between internal and external taxes and insisted that all parliamentary taxes for revenue violated colonial rights.

Massachusetts again set the pace of resistance. In February 1768 its assembly petitioned the king, but not Parliament, against the new measures. Without waiting for

vice-admiralty courts *These royal courts handled the disposition of enemy ships captured in time of war, adjudicated routine maritime disputes between, for example, a ship's crew and its owner, and from time to time tried to decide cases involving parliamentary regulation of colonial commerce. This last category was the most controversial. These courts did not use juries.*

a reply, it also sent a Circular Letter to the other assemblies, urging them to pursue "constitutional measures" of resistance against the Quartering Act, the new taxes, and their use in paying the salaries of governors and judges.

Wills Hill, earl of Hillsborough and secretary of state for the American colonies (an office created in 1768), responded so sharply that he turned tepid opposition into serious resistance. He told the Massachusetts assembly to rescind the Circular Letter and ordered all governors to dissolve any assembly that dared to accept it. The Massachusetts House voted 92 to 17 in June 1768 not to rescind. Most other assemblies had shown little interest in the Townshend program, particularly in the southern colonies where governors already had fixed salaries. But the assemblies bristled when told what they could or could not debate. All of them took up the Circular Letter or began to draft their own. One by one, the governors dissolved their assemblies until government by consent really did seem in peril.

By January 1769, nonimportation at last began to take hold. Spurred on by the popular but mistaken belief that the nonimportation agreements of 1765 had forced Parliament to repeal the Stamp Act, the colonists again turned to a strategy of economic sanctions against Britain.

The next escalation again came from Boston. On March 18, 1768, the town's celebration of the anniversary of the Stamp Act's repeal grew so raucous that the governor and the new American Board of Customs Commissioners asked Hillsborough for troops. He ordered General Gage, based in New York, to send two regiments to Boston from Nova Scotia. Then on June 10, before Gage could respond, Bostonians rioted after customs collectors seized John Hancock's sloop *Liberty* for smuggling Madeira wine (taxed under the Sugar Act) on its previous voyage. By waiting until the ship had a new cargo, informers and customs officials could split larger shares when the sloop was condemned. Terrified by the fury of the popular response, the commissioners fled to Castle William in Boston harbor and again petitioned Hillsborough for troops. He sent two more regiments from Ireland.

Believing that he held the edge with the army on its way, Governor Bernard leaked this news in late August 1768. The public response stunned him. The Boston town meeting asked him to summon the legislature, which Bernard had dissolved in June after it stood by its Circular Letter. When Bernard refused, the Sons of Liberty asked the other towns to elect delegates to a "convention" in Boston. The convention had no legal standing in the colony's government. When it met, it accepted

The Granger Collection, New York

PAUL REVERE'S ENGRAVING OF THE BRITISH ARMY LANDING IN BOSTON, 1768. *The navy approached the city in battle array, a sight familiar to veterans of the French wars. To emphasize the peaceful, Christian character of Boston, Revere exaggerated the height of the church steeples.*

Boston's definition of colonial grievances but refused to sanction violence. Boston had no choice but to go along.

An Experiment in Military Coercion

The British fleet entered Boston harbor in battle array and landed 1,000 soldiers by October 2, 1768. Massachusetts had built barracks in Castle William, miles away on an island in Boston harbor, where the soldiers could hardly function as a police force. According to the Quartering Act, any attempt to quarter soldiers on private property would expose the officer responsible to being cashiered from the army. The soldiers pitched their tents on Boston Common. Eventually they took over a building that had been the Boston poorhouse. The regiments from Ireland joined them later.

While colonial newspapers reported almost every clash between soldiers and civilians in Boston, news of the Massachusetts convention of towns reached Britain. The House of Lords passed a set of resolutions calling for the deportation of colonial political offenders to England for trial. Instead of quashing dissent, this threat to colonial political autonomy infuriated the southern colonies. Virginia, Maryland, and South Carolina now adopted nonimportation agreements. In the Chesapeake, no enforcement mechanism was ever put in place, but Charleston took nonimportation seriously. Up and down the continent, the feeble resistance of mid-1768 was becoming formidable by 1769.

The Wilkes Crisis

John Wilkes, a member of Parliament and a radical opposition journalist, had fled into exile in 1763 and had been outlawed for publishing an attack on the king in his newspaper, *The North Briton* No. 45. In 1768 George III dissolved Parliament and issued writs for the usual septennial elections. Wilkes returned from France and won a seat for the county of Middlesex. He then received a sentence of one year in King's Bench Prison. Hundreds of supporters gathered to chant "Wilkes and Liberty!" On May 10, 1768, Wilkites just outside the prison clashed with soldiers who fired into the crowd, killing six and wounding 15. Wilkes denounced this confrontation as "the Massacre of St. George's Fields." The House of Commons expelled Wilkes and ordered a new election, but the voters chose him again. Two more expulsions and two more elections took place the next year, until in April 1769, after Wilkes had won again by 1,143 votes to 296, the exasperated Commons voted to seat the loser.

Wilkes had provoked a constitutional crisis. His adherents founded "the Society of Gentlemen Supporters of the Bill of Rights," which raised money to pay off his huge debts and organized a national campaign on his behalf. Wilkites called for a reduction of royal patronage and major reforms of the electoral system, and they persuaded about one-fourth of England's voters to sign petitions on their behalf. They sympathized openly with North American protests. Colonial Sons of Liberty began to identify strongly with Wilkes. In 1769 the South Carolina assembly borrowed £1,500 sterling from the colony's treasurer and donated it to Wilkes. When the assembly passed an appropriation to cover the gift, the council rejected the bill. Because neither side would back off, the assembly voted no taxes after 1769 and passed no laws after 1771. Royal government broke down over the Wilkes question.

The Townshend crisis and the Wilkite movement became an explosive combination. For the first time, many colonists began to question the decency of the British government and its commitment to liberty. That a conspiracy existed to destroy British and colonial liberty began to seem quite credible.

THE BOSTON MASSACRE

In late 1769, the Boston Sons of Liberty turned to direct confrontation with the army, and the city again faced a serious crisis. Under English **common law**, soldiers could not fire on civilians without an order from a civil magistrate, except in self-defense when their lives were in danger. By the fall of 1769 no magistrate dared to issue such a command. Clashes between soldiers and civilians grew frequent.

By 1770 the soldiers often felt under siege. Once again the Sons of Liberty felt free to intimidate merchants who violated nonimportation. They nearly lynched Ebenezer Richardson, a customs informer who fired shots from his home into a stone-throwing crowd and killed an 11-year-old boy. The lad's funeral on February 26, 1770, became an enormous display of public mourning. Richardson, although convicted of murder, was pardoned by George III.

After the funeral, tensions between soldiers and citizens reached a fatal climax. Off-duty soldiers tried to supplement their meager wages with part-time employment, a practice that angered local **artisans** who resented the competition. On Friday, March 2, 1770, three soldiers came to John Hancock's ropewalk. "Soldier, will you work?" asked Samuel Gray, a rope maker. "Yes," replied one. "Then go and clean my shit house," sneered Gray. After an ugly brawl, Gray's employer persuaded Colonel William Dalrymple to confine his men to barracks. Peace prevailed through the Puritan sabbath that ran from Saturday night to sunrise on Monday, but everyone expected trouble on Monday, March 5.

After dark on Monday, civilians and soldiers clashed at several places. A crowd hurling snowballs and rocks closed in on the lone sentinel at the hated customs house. The guard called for help. A corporal and seven soldiers rushed to his aid and loaded their weapons. Captain Thomas Preston took command and ordered the soldiers to drive the attackers slowly back with fixed bayonets. The crowd taunted the soldiers, daring them to fire. One soldier apparently slipped, discharging his musket into the air as he fell. The others then fired into the crowd, killing five and wounding six.

With the whole town turning out, the soldiers were withdrawn to Castle William. Preston and six of his men stood trial for murder and were defended, brilliantly, by two radical patriot lawyers, John Adams and Josiah Quincy Jr., who believed that every accused person ought to have a proper defense. Preston and four of the soldiers were acquitted. The other two were convicted only of manslaughter, branded on the thumb, and released. The **Boston Massacre,** as the Sons of Liberty called this encounter, became the colonial counterpart to the Massacre of St. George's Fields in England. It marked the failure of Britain's first attempt at military coercion.

PARTIAL REPEAL

The day of the massacre marked a turning point in Britain as well, for on March 5 Lord North (who had become prime minister in January 1770) asked Parliament to repeal the Townshend duties, except the one on tea. North wanted them all repealed, but the cabinet had rejected complete repeal by a 5-to-4 margin. As with the Stamp Act, Britain had three choices: enforcement, modification, or repeal. North chose the middle ground. He claimed to be retaining only a preamble without a statute, a vestige of the Townshend Revenue Act, while repealing the substance. In fact, he did the opposite. Tea provided nearly three-fourths of the revenue under the act. North kept the substance but gave up the shadow.

This news reached the colonies just after nonimportation had achieved its greatest success in 1769 (see Table 5.1). The colonies reduced imports by about one-third from what they had been in 1768, but the impact on Britain was slight. North had

common law *The heart of the English legal system was based on precedents and judicial decisions. Common-law courts offered due process through such devices as trial by jury, which usually consisted of local men.*

artisan *A skilled laborer who works with his hands. In early America, artisans often owned their own shops and produced goods either for general sale or for special order.*

Boston Massacre *The colonial term for the confrontation between colonial protestors and British soldiers in front of the customs house on March 5, 1770. Five colonists were killed and six wounded.*

TABLE 5.1

EXPORTS IN £000 STERLING FROM ENGLAND AND SCOTLAND TO THE AMERICAN COLONIES, 1766–1775

COLONY	1766	1767	1768	1769	1770	1771	1772	1773	1774	1775
New England	419	416	431	224	417	1,436*	844	543	577	85.0
New York	333	424	491	76	480	655*	349	296	460	1.5
Pennsylvania	334	383	442	205	140	747*	526	436	646	1.4
Chesapeake†	520	653	670	715	997*	1,224*	1,016	589	690	1.9
Lower South‡	376	292	357	385*	228	515*	575*	448	471	130.5
Totals	1,982	2,168	2,391	1,605	2,262	4,577*	3,310	2,312	2,844	220.3

Average total exports, 1766–1768 = £2,180
1769 = 73.6% of that average, or 67.1% of 1768 exports
1770 = 103.8% of that average, or 94.6% of 1768 exports
*These totals surpassed all previous highs
†Chesapeake = Maryland and Virginia
‡Lower South = Carolinas and Georgia

hoped that partial repeal, although it would not placate all the colonists, would at least divide them. It did. Most merchants favored renewed importation of everything but tea, while the Sons of Liberty, most of whom were artisans, still supported complete nonimportation, a policy that would increase demand for their own manufactures.

Resistance collapsed first in Newport, where smuggling had always been the preferred method of challenging British authority. It spread to New York City, where the boycott on imports had been most effective. Soon Philadelphia caved in, followed by Boston in October 1770. By contrast, nonimportation had hardly caused a ripple in the import trade of the Chesapeake colonies. North's repeal was followed everywhere by an orgy of importation of British goods, setting record highs in all the colonies.

DISAFFECTION

The Quartering Act expired quietly in 1770; some of the more objectionable features of the vice-admiralty courts were softened; and the Currency Act of 1764 was repealed in stages between 1770 and 1773, as even London began to recognize that it was harming trade. Yet North had not restored confidence in the justice and decency of the British government. To a degree hard to appreciate today, the empire ran on voluntarism, on trust, or what people at the time called "affection." Its opposite was *disaffection*, which meant something more literal and dangerous to them than it does now.

Many colonists blamed one another for failing to win complete repeal of the duties. Bostonians lamented the "immortal shame and infamy" of New Yorkers for abandoning resistance, prompting a New Yorker to call Boston "the common sewer of America into which every beast that brought with it the unclean thing has disburthened itself." These recriminations, gratifying as they must have been to British officials, masked a vast erosion of trust in the imperial government. The colonists were angry with one another for failing to appreciate how menacing British policy still was. The tea duty remained a sliver in a wound that would not heal.

That fear sometimes broke through the surface calm of the years from 1770 to 1773. In 1772 a predatory customs vessel, the *Gaspée*, ran aground in Rhode Island while pursuing some peaceful coastal ships. After dark, men with blackened faces boarded the *Gaspée*, wounded its captain, and burned the ship. Britain sent a panel

QUICK   REVIEW

THE SECOND IMPERIAL CRISIS

- Townshend Revenue Act taxed several colonial imports from Britain, especially tea

- Resistance centered in Boston beginning with the Massachusetts Circular Letter of 1768

- Britain sent army to Boston and ordered governors to dissolve assemblies that accepted the Circular Letter

- Boston Massacre led to army's withdrawal

- Repeal of Townshend duties except that on tea failed to restore colonial confidence in the British government

of dignitaries to the colony with instructions to send the perpetrators to England for trial. The inquiry failed because no one would talk.

Twelve colonial assemblies considered this threat so ominous that they created permanent **committees of correspondence** to keep in touch with one another and to *anticipate* the next assault on their liberties. Even colonial moderates now believed that the British government was conspiring to destroy liberty in America. When Governor Hutchinson announced in 1773 that Massachusetts Superior Court justices would receive their salaries from the imperial treasury, Boston created its own committee of correspondence and urged other towns to do the same. Hutchinson grew alarmed when most towns of any size followed Boston's lead. That there was a plot to destroy their liberties seemed obvious to them.

The Boston Massacre trials and the *Gaspée* affair convinced London that it was pointless to prosecute individuals for politically motivated crimes. Whole communities would have to be punished. That choice brought the government to the edge of a precipice. The use of force against entire communities could lead to outright war. The spread of committees of correspondence throughout the colonies suggested that settlers who had been unable to unite against New France at Albany in 1754 now deemed unity against Britain essential to their liberties. By 1773 several New England newspapers were calling on the colonies to create a formal union.

In effect, the Townshend crisis never ended. With the tea duty standing as a symbol of Parliament's right to tax the colonies without their consent, genuine imperial harmony was becoming impossible. North's decision to retain the tea tax in 1770 did not guarantee that armed resistance would break out five years later, but it severely narrowed the ground on which any compromise could be built.

> **committees of correspondence** *Bodies formed on both the local and colonial levels that played an important role in exchanging ideas and information. They spread primarily anti-British material and were an important step in the first tentative unity of people in different colonies.*

INTERNAL CLEAVAGES: THE CONTAGION OF LIBERTY

Any challenge to British authority carried high risks for prominent families in the colonies. They depended on the Crown for their public offices and government contracts. After the Stamp Act crisis, these families faced a dilemma. The Hutchinsons of Massachusetts kept on good terms with Britain while incurring the hatred of many of their neighbors. John Hancock championed the grievances of the community but alienated British authorities. So did the Livingstons of New York and most of the great planters in the southern colonies. The Townshend crisis was a far more accurate predictor of future behavior than response to the Stamp Act had been. Nearly everyone had denounced the Stamp Act. By contrast, the merchants and lawyers who resisted nonimportation in 1768 were likely to become loyalists by 1775. Most artisans, merchants, and lawyers who supported the boycotts became patriots.

But patriot leaders also faced challenges from within their own ranks. Artisans demanded more power, and tenant farmers in the Hudson valley protested violently against their landlords. In Boston, where the economy had been faltering since the 1740s while taxes remained high, radical artisans set the pace of resistance in every imperial crisis. In New York City, Philadelphia, and Charleston, artisans also began to play a much more assertive role in public affairs.

THE FEUDAL REVIVAL AND RURAL DISCONTENT

Tensions increased in the countryside as well as in the cities. Three interrelated processes intensified discontent in rural areas: a revival of old proprietary claims, massive foreign immigration, and the settlement of the backcountry.

> **feudal revival** *The reliance on old feudal charters for all of the profits that could be extracted from them. It took hold in several colonies in the mid-eighteenth century and caused serious problems between many landowners and tenants.*

Between about 1730 and 1750, the men who owned 17th-century proprietary charters or manorial patents began to see the prospect of huge profits by enforcing these old legal claims. The great estates of the Hudson valley had attracted few settlers before the middle of the 18th century, and those who arrived first had received generous leases. But as leases became more restrictive and as New Englanders swarmed into New York, discontent increased. In 1766 several thousand angry farmers took to the fields and the roads to protest the terms of their leases. The colony had to call in redcoats to suppress them. But when New York landlords also tried to make good their claims to the upper Connecticut valley, Yankee settlers defied them, set up their own government and, after a long struggle, became the independent state of Vermont.

The proprietors of East New Jersey claimed much of the land that was being worked by descendants of the original settlers of Newark and Elizabethtown, who thought they owned their farms. The proprietors, in firm control of the law courts, planned to sell or lease the land, either to the current occupants or to newcomers. After they expelled several farmers and replaced them with tenants, a succession of land riots rocked much of northern New Jersey for 10 years after 1745. The proprietary intruders were driven out, and the riots stopped, but tensions remained high.

In Maryland, Frederick, seventh and last Lord Baltimore, received the princely income of £30,000 sterling per year until his death in 1771. The Penns enjoyed similar gains in Pennsylvania, though more slowly. Their landed income rose to about £15,000 or £20,000 in the 1760s and then soared to £67,000 in 1773. They seemed about to turn their colony into the most lucrative piece of real estate in the Atlantic world. But their reluctance to contribute to the war effort in the 1750s had so angered Benjamin Franklin at the time that, with the assembly's support, he went to London to urge the Crown to make Pennsylvania a royal colony. This effort weakened the colony's resistance to both the Stamp Act and the Townshend Act. Meanwhile Connecticut settlers claimed all of northern Pennsylvania on the basis of Connecticut's sea-to-sea charter and touched off a small civil war there in the 1770s.

In Virginia, Thomas, sixth baron Fairfax, acquired title to the entire Northern Neck of the colony (the land between the Potomac and the Rappahannock Rivers). By 1775, the Fairfax estate's 5 million acres contained 21 counties. He received £5,000 a year from his holdings, but he muted criticism by moving to the colony and setting himself up as a great planter.

In North Carolina, John Carteret, earl of Granville–the only Carolina proprietor who had refused to sell his claim to the Crown—consolidated his lands as the Granville District after 1745. Although still living in England, he received an income of about £5,000 per year. The Granville District embraced more than half of North Carolina's land and two-thirds of its population, deprived the colony of revenue from land sales and quitrents within the district, and forced North Carolina to resort to direct taxation. For several years after Granville's death in 1763, his land office remained closed. Disgruntled settlers often rioted when they could not get title to their lands.

THE REGULATOR MOVEMENTS IN THE CAROLINAS

Massive immigration from Europe and the settlement of the backcountry created severe social tensions. Most immigrants were Scottish or Scots-Irish Presbyterians, Lutherans, or German Reformed Protestants. They were religious dissenters in the Quaker or Anglican colonies they entered. They angered Indians by squatting on their land and, quite often, by murdering some of them. In South Carolina the newcomers provoked the Cherokee War of 1759–1761, which then brutalized and demoralized the backcountry.

After the Cherokee War, great bands of outlaws, men who had been dislocated by the war, began roaming the countryside, plundering the more prosperous farmers,

Map 5.2

FEUDAL REVIVAL: GREAT ESTATES OF LATE COLONIAL AMERICA. *On the eve of the Revolution, more than half of the land between the Hudson valley and North Carolina was claimed by men who had inherited various kinds of 17th-century charters or patents.*

and often raping their wives and daughters. As the violence peaked between 1765 and 1767, the more respectable settlers organized themselves as "regulators" (a later generation would call them "vigilantes") to impose order in the absence of any organized government. Although South Carolina claimed jurisdiction over the area, the colony's law courts were in Charleston, more than 100 miles to the east. Even though most of the white settlers now lived in the backcountry, they chose only 2 of the 48 members of South Carolina's assembly. In effect, they had no local government.

After obtaining commissions from Charleston as militia officers and justices of the peace, the regulators chased the outlaws out of the colony. They then imposed order on what they called the "little people," poor settlers, many of whom made a living as hunters, who may have aided the outlaws. The discipline imposed by the regulators, typically whippings and forced labor, outraged their victims, who organized as "moderators" and got their own commissions from the governor. With both sides claiming legality, about 600 armed regulators confronted an equal force of moderators at the Saluda River in 1769. Civil war was avoided only by the timely arrival of an emissary from the governor bearing a striking message: South Carolina would finally bring government to the backcountry by providing a circuit court system for the entire colony. Violence ebbed, but tensions remained severe.

In North Carolina, the backcountry's problem was corruption, not lack of government. The settlers, mostly immigrants pushing south from Pennsylvania, found the county courts under the control of men with strong ties to powerful families in the eastern counties. Because county officials were appointed by the governor, getting ahead required gaining access to his circle. These justices, lawyers, and merchants seemed to regard county government as an engine for fleecing farmers through taxes, fees, court costs, and suits for debt. North Carolina's regulator movement arose to reform these abuses.

In 1768 the regulators refused to pay taxes in Orange County. Governor William Tryon mustered 1,300 eastern militiamen who overawed the regulators for a time. Then, in a bid for a voice in the 1769 assembly, the regulators managed to capture six seats. These new assemblymen called for the secret ballot, fixed salaries (instead of fees) for justices and other officials, and a land tax rather than **poll taxes,** but they were outvoted by the eastern majority. After losing ground in the 1770 election, they stormed into Hillsborough, closed the Orange County Court, and whipped Edmund Fanning, whose lust for fees had made him the most detested official in the backcountry. Tryon responded by marching 1,000 militiamen westward, who defeated a force of more than 2,000 poorly armed regulators in early 1771 at the battle of Alamance Creek. Seven regulators were hanged, and many fled the colony. North Carolina entered the struggle for independence as a bitterly divided society.

SLAVES AND WOMEN

In Charleston, South Carolina, in 1765, the Sons of Liberty marched through the streets chanting "Liberty and No Stamps!" To their amazement, slaves organized their own parade, shouting "Liberty! Liberty!" Merchant Henry Laurens tried to believe that they did not know the meaning of the word.

Around the middle of the 18th century, an antislavery movement arose on both sides of the Atlantic that attracted both future patriots and loyalists. In the 1740s and 1750s, Benjamin Lay, John Woolman, and Anthony Benezet urged fellow Quakers to free their slaves. In the 1750s the Quaker Yearly Meeting placed the slave trade off limits and finally, in 1774, forbade slaveholding altogether. Any Friend who did not comply by 1779 would be disowned. Britain's Methodist leader John Wesley also attacked slavery, as did several colonial disciples of Jonathan Edwards. Many evangelicals began to agree that slavery was a sin. By the 1760s, supporters of slavery

---

poll tax *A tax based on people or population rather than property. It was usually a fixed amount per adult.*

QUICK   REVIEW

DISCONTENT AND INTERNAL UPHEAVALS IN THE COLONIES

- Artisans demanded more power in the cities

- Land riots against manor lords in New York and lords proprietors in New Jersey

- The regulator movements in the Carolinas

- Slavery attracted major criticism for the first time, some of it from women

---

FOCUS   QUESTION

Ever since the ancient world, Christians had insisted that sin is a form of slavery. Why did it take them more than 1,500 years to conclude that enslaving others might be a grievous sin?

found that they had to defend the institution. Hardly anyone had bothered to do so earlier, but as equal rights became a popular topic, some began to suggest that *all* people could claim these rights, and slavery came under attack. Slavery, declared Patrick Henry, "is as repugnant to humanity as it is inconsistent with the Bible and destructive of liberty." In England, Granville Sharp, an early abolitionist, brought the Somerset case before the Court of King's Bench in 1771 and compelled a reluctant Chief Justice William Murray, baron Mansfield, to declare that slavery was incompatible with the "free air" of England. That decision gave England's 10,000 or 15,000 blacks a chance to claim their freedom.

New Englanders began to move in similar directions. Two women, Sarah Osborn and Phillis Wheatley, played leading roles in the movement. Osborn, a widow in Newport, Rhode Island, opened a school in 1744 to support her family. A friend of the revivalist George Whitefield, she also taught women and blacks and began holding evening religious meetings, which turned into a big revival. At one point in the 1760s, about one-sixth of Newport's Africans were attending her school. That made them the most literate African population in the colonies although they were living in the colonial city most deeply involved in the African slave trade. Osborn's students supported abolition of the slave trade and, later, slavery itself.

Meanwhile, in 1761 an 8-year-old girl who would become known as **Phillis Wheatley** arrived in Boston from Africa; she was purchased by wealthy John Wheatley as a servant for his wife Susannah, who treated her more like a daughter than a slave and taught her to read and write. In 1767 Phillis published her first poem in Boston, and she visited London as a celebrity in 1773 after a volume of her poetry was published there. Her poems deplored slavery but rejoiced in the Christianization of Africans. The Wheatleys emancipated her after her return to Boston.

Soon many of Boston's blacks sensed an opportunity for emancipation. On several occasions in 1773 and 1774, they petitioned the legislature or the governor for freedom, pointing out that, although they had never forfeited their natural

PHILLIS WHEATLEY. *Engraving of Phillis Wheatley opposite the title page of her collected poems, published in 1773.*

Wheatley, Phillis *Eight-year-old Phillis Wheatley arrived in Boston from Africa in 1761 and was sold as a slave to wealthy John and Susannah Wheatley. Susannah taught her to read and write, and in 1767 she published her first poem in Boston. In 1773 she visited London to celebrate the publication there of a volume of her poetry, an event that made her a transatlantic sensation. On her return to Boston, the Wheatleys emancipated her.*

rights, they were being "held in slavery in the bowels of a free and Christian Country." When the legislature passed a bill on their behalf, Governor Hutchinson vetoed it. Boston slaves made it clear to General Gage, Hutchinson's successor, that they would serve him as a loyal militia in exchange for their freedom. In short, they offered allegiance to whichever side would free them. Many patriots began to rally to their cause.

Freedom's ferment made a heady wine. After 1773, any direct challenge to British power would trigger enormous social changes within the colonies.

THE LAST IMPERIAL CRISIS

The surface calm between 1770 and 1773 ended when Lord North moved to save the East India Company from bankruptcy. The company was being undersold in southeastern England and the colonies by smuggled Dutch tea. Without solving the company's problems, North created a crisis too big for Britain to handle.

THE TEA CRISIS

FOCUS QUESTION

Why did the colonists start a revolution after the Tea Act of 1773 lowered the price of tea?

North tried to rescue the East India Company by enabling it to undersell smuggled Dutch tea. His Tea Act of 1773 repealed import duties on tea in England but retained the Townshend duty in the colonies. In both places, North estimated, legal tea would be cheaper than anyone else's. The company would be saved, and the settlers, by buying cheap legal tea, would accept Parliament's right to tax them.

Another aspect of the Tea Act antagonized most merchants in the colonies. The company had been selling tea to all comers at public auctions in London, but the Tea Act gave it a monopoly on the shipping and distribution of tea in the colonies. Only company ships could carry it, and a few consignees in each port would have the exclusive right to sell it. The combined dangers of taxation and monopoly again forged the coalition of artisans and merchants that had helped to defeat the Stamp Act in 1765 and had resisted the Townshend Act by 1769. Patriots saw the Tea Act as a Trojan horse that would destroy liberty by seducing the settlers into accepting parliamentary sovereignty. Unintentionally, North also gave a tremendous advantage to those determined to resist the Tea Act. He had devised an oceanic, or "external," measure that the colonists could actually nullify despite British control of the seas. No one would have to police the entire waterfront looking for tea importers. The patriots had only to wait for the specially chartered tea ships and then prevent them from landing their cargoes.

Direct threats of violence against shipmasters usually did the job. Most tea ships quickly departed—except in Boston. There, Governor Hutchinson decided to face down the radicals. He refused to grant clearance papers to three tea ships that, under the law, had to pay the Townshend duty within 21 days of arrival or face seizure. Hutchinson meant to force them to land the tea and pay the duty. This timetable led to urgent mass meetings for several weeks and generated a major crisis. Finally convinced that there was no other way to block the landing of the tea, the radicals, disguised as Indians, organized the **Boston Tea Party.** They threw 342 chests of tea, worth about £11,000 sterling (more than $700,000 in today's dollars), into Boston harbor on the night of December 16, 1773.

Boston Tea Party *In December 1773, Boston's Sons of Liberty, threw 342 chests of East India Company tea into Boston harbor rather than allow them to be landed and pay the hated tea duty.*

BRITAIN'S RESPONSE: THE COERCIVE ACTS

This willful destruction of private property shocked both Britain and America. Convinced that severe punishment was essential to British credibility, Parliament passed four Coercive Acts during the spring of 1774. The Boston Port Act closed the port of Boston until Bostonians paid for the tea. A new Quartering Act allowed the army to quarter soldiers among civilians if necessary. The Administration of Justice Act permitted a British soldier or official who was charged with a crime while carrying out his duties to be tried either in another colony or in England. Most controversial of all was the Massachusetts Government Act. It overturned the Massachusetts Charter of 1691, made the council appointive, and restricted town meetings. In effect, it made Massachusetts like other royal colonies. Before it passed, the king named General Gage, already the commander of the British army in North America, as the new governor of Massachusetts.

Parliament also passed a fifth law, unrelated to the Coercive Acts but significant nonetheless. The Quebec Act established French civil law and the Roman Catholic Church in the Province of Quebec, provided for trial by jury in criminal but not in civil cases, gave legislative but not taxing power to an appointive governor and council, and extended the administrative boundaries of Quebec to the area between the Great Lakes and the Ohio River. Settlers from New England to Georgia were appalled. Instead of conciliation and toleration of the French that the act hoped to achieve, they saw a deliberate revival of the power of New France and the Catholic Church on their northern border, now bolstered by Britain's naval and military might. The Quebec Act added credibility to the fear that evil ministers in London were conspiring to destroy British and colonial liberties. The settlers lumped the Quebec Act together with the **Coercive Acts** and coined their own name for all of them: the **Intolerable Acts.**

THE RADICAL EXPLOSION

The interval between the passage of the Boston Port Act in March 1774 and the Massachusetts Government Act in May permits us to compare the response that each provoked. The Port Act was quite enforceable and could not be nullified by the colonists. It led to another round of nonimportation and to the summoning of the First Continental Congress. But the Government Act *was* nullified by the colonists. It led to war. The soldiers marching to Concord on April 19, 1775, were trying to enforce it against settlers who absolutely refused to obey it.

Gage took over the governorship of Massachusetts in May 1774, before the Massachusetts Government Act was passed. In June he closed the ports of Boston and Charlestown, just north of Boston. At first, Boston split over the Port Act. Many merchants wanted to abolish the Boston Committee of Correspondence and pay for the tea to avoid an economic catastrophe. But they were badly outvoted in a huge town meeting. Boston then called for a colonial union and for immediate nonimportation and nonconsumption of British goods. By then some radicals were losing patience with nonimportation as a tactic. After all, Parliament had already shut Boston down.

Discouraging news arrived from elsewhere. A mass meeting in New York City rejected immediate nonimportation in favor of an intercolonial congress. Philadelphia followed New York's lead. In both cities, cautious merchants hoped that a congress might postpone or prevent radical forms of resistance.

Despite this momentary success, Gage soon learned that none of his major objectives was achievable. Contributions began pouring in from all the colonies to help Boston survive. When royal governors outside Massachusetts dismissed their assem-

Coercive (Intolerable) Acts
Four statutes passed by Parliament in response to the Boston Tea Party, including one that closed the port of Boston until the tea was paid for, and another that overturned the Massachusetts Charter of 1691. The colonists called them the Intolerable Acts and included the Quebec Act under that label.

blies to prevent them from joining the resistance movement, the colonists elected **provincial congresses,** or conventions, to organize resistance. As the congresses took hold, royal government began to collapse almost everywhere. Numerous calls for a continental congress made the movement irresistible. By June it was obvious that any intercolonial congress would adopt nonimportation.

Yet Gage remained optimistic well into the summer. Then news of the Massachusetts Government Act arrived on August 6. Gage's authority disintegrated when he tried to enforce the act. The **mandamus** councilors whom Gage appointed to the new upper house under the act either resigned or fled to Boston to seek the army's protection. The Superior Court could not hold its sessions because jurors refused to take an oath under the new act. At the county level (the real center of royal power in the colony), popular conventions closed the courts and took charge in August and September.

Before this explosion of radical activity, Gage had called for a new General Court to meet in Salem in October. Many towns sent representatives. But others followed the lead of the Worcester County Convention, which in August urged all towns to elect delegates to a provincial congress in Concord. Although Gage revoked his call for a General Court, about 90 representatives met at Salem anyway. When Gage refused to recognize them, they adjourned to Concord in early October and joined the 200 delegates who had already gathered there as the Massachusetts Provincial Congress. That body became the de facto government of the colony and implemented the radical demands of the Suffolk County Convention, which included the creation of a special force of armed "minutemen" and the payment of taxes to the congress in Concord, not to Gage in Boston. The Provincial Congress also collected military stores at Concord. North assumed that Gage's army would uphold the new Massachusetts government. Instead, Gage's government survived only where the army could protect it.

By October, Gage's power was limited to the Boston area, which the army held. Unable to put his 3,000 soldiers to any positive use, he wrote North on October 30 that "a small Force rather encourages Resistance than terrifys." He stunned North by asking for 20,000 redcoats, roughly as many as Britain had needed to conquer New France.

THE FIRST CONTINENTAL CONGRESS

From 1769 into 1774, colonial patriots had looked to John Wilkes in London for leadership. At the **First Continental Congress,** they began relying on themselves. Twelve colonies (all but Georgia) sent delegates. They met at Philadelphia's Carpenters' Hall in September 1774. They scarcely even debated nonimportation. The southern colonies insisted, and the New Englanders agreed, that nonimportation finally be extended to molasses. The delegates were almost unanimous in adopting nonexportation if Britain did not redress colonial grievances by September 1775. Nonexportation was a much more radical tactic than nonimportation because it contained the implicit threat of repudiating debts to British merchants, which were normally paid off with colonial exports. Joseph Galloway, a Pennsylvania loyalist, submitted a plan of imperial union that would have required all laws affecting the colonies to be passed by both Parliament and a permanent intercolonial congress, but his proposal was tabled by a vote of 6 colonies to 5. The Congress spent three weeks trying to define colonial rights. Everyone agreed that the Coercive Acts, the Quebec Act, and all surviving revenue acts had to be repealed

provincial congress *A type of convention elected by the colonists to organize resistance. They tended to be larger than the legal assemblies they displaced, and they played a major role in politicizing the countryside.*

mandamus *A legal writ ordering a person, usually a public official, to carry out a specific act. In Massachusetts in 1774, the new royal councilors were appointed by a writ of mandamus.*

First Continental Congress *This intercolonial body met in Philadelphia in September and October 1774 to organize resistance against the Coercive Acts by defining American rights, petitioning the king, and appealing to the British and American people. It created the Association, local committees in each community to enforce nonimportation.*

and that infringements on trial by jury had to be rejected. The delegates generally agreed on what would break the impasse, but they had trouble finding the precise language for their demands. They finally affirmed the new principle of no *legislation* without consent—but added a saving clause that affirmed colonial assent to acts of Parliament that regulated their trade.

Congress petitioned the king rather than Parliament, because patriots no longer recognized Parliament as a legitimate legislature for the colonies. It agreed to meet again in May 1775 if the British response was not satisfactory. And it created **the Association**—citizen committees in every community—to enforce its trade sanctions against Britain. In approving the Association, Congress was beginning to act as a central government for the United Colonies.

Association *Groups created by the First Continental Congress as local committees to enforce its trade sanctions against Britain. The creation of these groups was an important sign that Congress was beginning to act as a central government.*

TOWARD WAR

The news from Boston and Philadelphia shook North's ministry. Although Franklin kept assuring the British that Congress meant exactly what it said, both North and the opposition assumed that conciliation could be achieved on lesser terms. Lord Chatham (William Pitt) introduced a bill to prohibit Parliament from taxing the colonies, to recognize the Congress, and even to ask Congress to provide revenue for North American defense and to help reduce the national debt. His plan was voted down.

The initiative lay, of course, with North, who still hoped for a peaceful solution. But in January 1775 he took a step that made war inevitable. He ordered Gage to send troops to Concord, destroy the arms stored there, and arrest John Hancock and Samuel Adams. Only after sending this dispatch did he introduce his own Conciliatory Proposition. Parliament pledged that it would not tax any colony that met its share of the cost of imperial defense and paid proper salaries to its royal officials, but Britain would use force against delinquent colonies. To reassure hardliners that he was not turning soft, North introduced the New England Restraining Act on the same day. It barred New Englanders from the Atlantic fisheries and banned all commerce between New England and any place except Britain and the British West Indies, precisely the trade routes that Congress was blocking through nonimportation.

North's orders to Gage arrived before the Conciliatory Proposition reached America, and Gage obeyed. He hoped to surprise Concord with a predawn march, but Boston radicals knew about the expedition almost as soon as the orders were issued. They had already made careful preparations to alert the whole countryside. Their informant, in all likelihood, was Gage's wife, Margaret Kemble Gage, a New Jerseyan by birth. At 2:00 A.M. on the night of April 18–19, about 700 grenadiers and light infantry began their march toward Concord. Paul Revere, a Boston silversmith, galloped west with the news that "The redcoats are coming!" When Revere was captured past Lexington by a British patrol, Dr. Samuel Prescott managed to get the message through to Concord. As the British approached Lexington Green at dawn, they found 60 to 70 militiamen drawn up to face them. The outnumbered militia began to withdraw. Then somebody fired the first shot in what became the **Battle of Lexington.** Without orders, the British line opened fire, killing 8 and wounding 9. With fifes playing and drums beating (secrecy had become pointless), the British resumed their march to Concord. Behind and ahead of them, like angry hornets, the whole countryside swarmed toward them.

QUICK   REVIEW

THE THIRD IMPERIAL CRISIS

- Tea Act provoked Boston Tea Party

- Parliament responded with Boston Port Act, Massachusetts Government Act, and two other Coercive Acts

- Colonial reaction: Continental Congress imposed trade sanctions; Massachusetts nullified Massachusetts Government Act and collected military supplies at Concord

- War began after Governor Gage sent the army to confiscate those arms

- Second Continental Congress's failure of conciliation and the movement toward independence

Battle of Lexington *The first military engagement of the Revolutionary War. It occurred on April 19, 1775, when British soldiers fired into a much smaller body of minutemen on Lexington green.*

The Granger Collection, New York

ENGAGEMENT AT THE NORTH BRIDGE IN CONCORD, APRIL 19, 1775. *This 1775 painting by Ralph Earl is quite accurate in its details. It shows the first American military victory in the war when the militia drove the British back from Concord Bridge and eventually through Lexington and all the way to Boston.*

THE IMPROVISED WAR

In April 1775 neither side had a plan for winning a major war. Gage's soldiers were trying to enforce acts of Parliament. The militia were fighting for a political regime that Parliament was trying to change. They drove the British from Concord Bridge and pursued them all the way to Boston. Had a relief force not met the battered British survivors east of Lexington, all of them might have been lost.

Without an adequate command or supply structure, the colonists besieged Boston. After two months, Gage finally declared that all settlers bearing arms, and those who aided them, were rebels and traitors. He offered to pardon anyone who returned to his allegiance, except John Hancock and Samuel Adams. Instead of complying, the besiegers escalated the struggle two days later. They fortified the high ground on Breed's Hill (next to Bunker Hill) near Charlestown and overlooking Boston. The British sent 2,400 men, one-fifth of the garrison, to take the hills on June 17. Secure behind their defenses, the settlers shot more than 1,000 redcoats before the colonists ran out of ammunition and withdrew. The defenders suffered about 370 casualties, nearly all during the retreat.

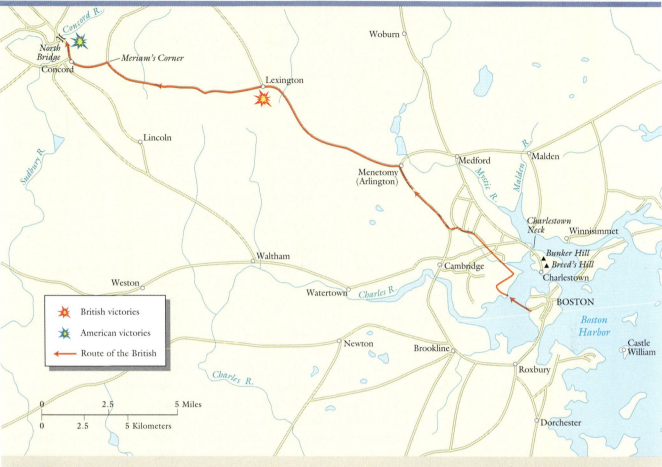

Map 5.3

Lexington, Concord, and Boston, 1775–1776. *The British march to Lexington and Concord on April 19, 1775, touched off the Revolutionary War. The colonists drove the redcoats back to Boston and then besieged the city for 11 months until the British withdrew.*

Well into 1776 both sides fought an improvised war. In May 1775 Vermont and Massachusetts militia took Ticonderoga on Lake Champlain and seized the artillery and gunpowder that would be used months later to end the siege of Boston. Crown Point also fell. With nearly all of their forces in Boston, the British were too weak to defend other positions. The collapse of royal government meant that the rebels now controlled the militia and most of the royal powder houses.

The militia became the key to political allegiance. Compulsory service with the militia politicized many waverers, who decided that they really were patriots when a redcoat shot at them or when they drove a loyalist into exile. The militia kept the countryside committed to the Revolution wherever the British army was too weak to overwhelm them.

THE SECOND CONTINENTAL CONGRESS

When the **Second Continental Congress** met in May 1775, it inherited the war. For months it pursued the conflicting strategies of armed resistance and conciliation. It voted to turn the undisciplined men besieging Boston into a "Continental Army." On June 15, at the urging of John Adams of Massachusetts, Congress made George Washing-

Second Continental Congress *The intercolonial body that met in Philadelphia in May 1775 a few weeks after the Battles of Lexington and Concord. It organized the Continental Army, appointed George Washington commander-in-chief, and simultaneously pursued policies of military resistance and conciliation. When conciliation failed, it chose independence in July 1776 and in 1777 drafted the Articles of Confederation, which finally went into force in March 1781.*

ton of Virginia commanding general. When Washington took charge of the Continental Army, he was appalled at the poor discipline among the soldiers and their casual familiarity with their officers. He insisted that officers behave with a dignity that would instill obedience, and as the months passed, most of them won his respect. But at year's end, nearly all the men went home, and Washington had to train a new army for 1776. Yet enthusiasm for the cause remained strong, and new volunteers soon filled his camp.

In June 1775, Congress, fearing that the British might recruit French Canadians to attack New York or New England, authorized an invasion of Canada. Two forces of 1,000 men each moved northward. One, under General Richard Montgomery, took Montreal in November. The other, commanded by Colonel Benedict Arnold, advanced on Quebec through the Maine forests and laid siege to the city, where Montgomery joined Arnold in December. With enlistments due to expire at year's end, they decided to assault Quebec. Their attack in a blizzard on December 31 was a disaster. Nearly half of the 900 men still with them were killed, wounded, or captured. Montgomery was killed and Arnold wounded. Both were hailed as American heroes.

The colonial objective in this fighting was still to restore government by consent under the Crown. After rejecting Lord North's Conciliatory Proposition out of hand, Congress approved an "Olive Branch Petition" to George III on July 5, 1775, in the hope of ending the bloodshed. Moderates, led by John Dickinson, strongly favored the measure. The petition affirmed the colonists' loyalty to the Crown, did not even mention "rights," and implored the king to take the initiative in devising "a happy and permanent reconciliation." Another document written mostly by Virginia's Thomas Jefferson, "The Declaration of the Causes and Necessities of Taking Up Arms," set forth the grievances of the colonies and justified their armed resistance. Like the Olive Branch Petition, the declaration assured the British people "that we mean not to dissolve that Union which has so long and so happily subsisted between us." The Olive Branch reached London along with news of Bunker Hill. George III replied with a formal proclamation of rebellion on August 23. The king's refusal to receive this moderate petition strengthened the radicals.

Congress began to function more and more like a government. With few exceptions, it assumed royal rather than parliamentary powers, which were taken over by the individual colonies instead. Congress did not tax or regulate trade, beyond encouraging nonimportation. It did not pass laws. It took command of the Continental Army, printed paper money, opened diplomatic relations with Indian nations, took over the royal post office, and decided which government was legitimate in individual colonies—all functions that had been performed by the Crown. In short, Congress thought of itself as a temporary plural executive for the continent, not as a legislature.

War and Legitimacy, 1775–1776

Throughout 1775 the British reacted with fitful displays of violence and grim threats of turning slaves and Indians against the settlers. When the weak British forces could neither restore order nor make good their threats, they conciliated no one, enraged thousands, and undermined British claims to legitimacy. The navy burned Falmouth (Portland), Maine, in October. On November 7, John Murray, earl of Dunmore and governor of Virginia, offered freedom to any slaves of rebel planters who would join his 200 redcoats. About 800 slaves mustered under his banner only to fall victim to smallpox after the Virginia militia defeated them in a single action. On January 1, Dunmore bombarded Norfolk in retaliation, setting several buildings ablaze. The patriot militia, who considered Norfolk a loyalist bastion, burned the rest of the city and then blamed Dunmore for its destruction.

British efforts suffered other disasters in Boston and the Carolinas. The greatest colonial victory came at Boston. On March 17, 1776, after Washington fortified Dorchester Heights south of the city and brought the heavy artillery from Ticonderoga to bear on it, the British pulled out and sailed for Nova Scotia. A loyalist uprising by Highland Scots in North Carolina was crushed at Moore's Creek Bridge on February 27, and a British naval expedition sent to take Charleston was repulsed with heavy losses in June. Cherokee attacks against Virginia in 1776 were defeated because they occurred after Dunmore had left and did not fit into any larger general strategy. Before spring turned to summer, patriot forces had won control of the territory of all 13 colonies.

INDEPENDENCE

George III's dismissal of the Olive Branch Petition left moderates no option but to yield or fight. In late 1775, Congress created a committee to correspond with foreign powers. By early 1776 the delegates from New England, Virginia, and Georgia already favored independence, but they knew that unless they won over all 13 colonies, the British would have the leverage to divide them. The British attack on Charleston in June nudged the Carolinas toward independence.

Resistance to independence came mostly from the mid-Atlantic colonies, from New York through Maryland. None of the five legal assemblies in the mid-Atlantic region ever repudiated the Crown. All of them had to be overthrown along with royal (or proprietary) government itself.

In the struggle for Middle Colony loyalties, Thomas Paine's pamphlet, *Common Sense,* became a huge success. First published in Philadelphia in January 1776, it sold more than 100,000 copies within a few months. Paine wasted no reverence on Britain's mixed and balanced constitution. To him, George III was "the Pharaoh of England" and "the Royal Brute of Great Britain." Paine attacked monarchy and aristocracy as decadent institutions and urged Americans to unite under a simple republican regime of their own. "There is something very absurd," he insisted, "in supposing a Continent to be perpetually governed by an island."

The British continued to alienate the colonists. The king named Lord George Germain, a hard-liner, as secretary of state for the American colonies. The British bought 17,000 soldiers from Hesse and other north German states (they were all called **Hessians** by the colonists). Disturbing (though false) rumors suggested that Britain and France were about to sign a "partition treaty" dividing the eastern half of North America between them. Many congressmen concluded that only independence could counter these dangers by engaging Britain's European enemies on America's side. As long as conciliation was the goal, France would not participate, because American success would restore the British Empire to its former might. But Louis XVI (1774–1793) might well help the colonies win their independence if that meant crippling Britain permanently.

From April to June, about 90 communities issued calls for independence. Most of them did not look further back than 1775 to justify their demand. The king had placed the colonists outside his protection, was waging war against them, and had hired foreigners to kill them. Self-defense demanded a permanent separation.

On May 15, 1776, Congress voted to suppress "every kind of authority" under the British Crown, thus giving radicals an opportunity to seize power in Pennsylvania and New Jersey. Moderates remained in control in New York, Delaware, and Maryland, but they reluctantly accepted independence as inevitable. In early June, Congress postponed a vote on independence but named a committee of five, including

FOCUS QUESTION
How and why did a resistance movement, dedicated to protecting the colonists' rights as Englishmen, end by proclaiming American independence instead?

Hessians *A term used by Americans to describe the 17,000 mercenary troops hired by Britain from various German states, especially Hesse.*

HISTORY THROUGH FILM

1776 (1972)

Directed by Peter H. Hunt; starring William Daniels (John Adams), Virginia Vestoff (Abigail), Ken Howard (Thomas Jefferson), Howard da Silva (Benjamin Franklin), and Blythe Danner (Martha)

1776 does not pretend to be a historical re-creation of actual events. It is, rather, an intelligent, offbeat, winning fantasy conceived by northeasterners at the expense, mostly, of Virginians.

1776 is a screen adaptation of a musical comedy produced on the New York stage by Stuart Ostrow. Some scenes were filmed on location at Independence Hall in Philadelphia. Sherman Edwards's lively music and lyrics carry the drama from May 1776 to the signing of the Declaration of Independence on July 4.

Director Peter Hunt made his motion picture debut with *1776*. He also directed *Give 'Em Hell, Harry* in 1975 and the 1997 Broadway version of *The Scarlet Pimpernel,* along with various films made for television.

The movie opens with John Adams (William Daniels) trying to force the Second Continental Con-

gress into a serious debate on independence. The delegates respond in a fulsome chorus, shouting: "Sit down, John! Sit down, John! For God's sake, John, sit down!" while some of them complain about the flies and the oppressive heat. Adams stalks out and then unburdens himself to his wife, Abigail (Virginia Vestoff), still at home in Massachusetts. Abigail in her reply urges him to "Tell the Congress to declare / independency. / Then sign your name, get out of there / And hurry home to me."

With Benjamin Franklin's help, Adams finally achieves his goal. The film's bite derives from its determination to move Adams to the center of the story, rather than Thomas Jefferson (Ken Howard), whom Adams and Franklin (Howard da Silva) finally maneuver into writing the first draft of the Declaration, much against his will. Adams declines to write the actual Declaration because, as he explains to Franklin and Jefferson, "If I'm the one to do it / They'll run their quill pens through it. / I'm obnoxious and disliked, / You know that, Sir."

Jefferson also declines at first because he pines for Martha (Blythe Danner), his young bride, still in Virginia. "Mr. Adams, damn you Mr. Adams! / . . . once again you stand between me and my lovely bride. / Oh, Mr. Adams you are driving me to homicide!"

This outburst prompts the other members of the drafting committee to chorus: "Homicide! Homicide! We may see murder yet!" But instead, Jefferson accepts the burden. When he is unable to write, Adams and Franklin bring Martha to Philadelphia so that, after making love to her, he can concentrate his energies on the Declaration.

Some of the delegates appear as mere caricatures, especially Richard Henry Lee of Virginia and James Wilson of Pennsylvania, two articulate delegates who, in real life, played important roles in creating the new republic. The film addresses the slavery question by showing South Carolina's fierce opposition to inclusion of an antislavery clause, a point on which Adams, Jefferson, and Franklin reluctantly yield. The film, like the play on which it is based, works well to deliver an articulate, entertaining taste of history.

1776 is a lively musical depicting events from May 1776 to the signing of the Declaration of Independence on July 4.

Jefferson, John Adams, and Franklin, to prepare a declaration that would vindicate America's decision to the whole world. Jefferson's draft justified independence on the lofty ground of "self-evident truths," including a natural right to "life, Liberty, and the pursuit of happiness." The longest section indicted George III as a tyrant.

With the necessary votes in place, Congress on July 2 passed Richard Henry Lee's resolution "that these United colonies are, and of right, ought to be, Free and Independent States; . . . and that all political connexion between them, and the state of Great Britain, is, and ought to be, totally dissolved." On the same day, the first ships of the largest armada yet sent across the Atlantic by any European state began landing British soldiers on Staten Island. Two days later, 12 colonies, with New York abstaining to await instructions, unanimously approved Jefferson's **Declaration of Independence,** as amended by Congress.

> **Declaration of Independence** *A document, drafted primarily by Thomas Jefferson of Virginia, this document justified American independence to the world by affirming "that all men are created equal" and have a natural right to "life, liberty, and the pursuit of happiness." The longest section of the Declaration condemned George III as a tyrant.*

CONCLUSION

Between 1763 and 1776 Britain and the colonies became trapped in a series of self-fulfilling prophecies. The British feared that without major reforms to guarantee Parliament's control of the empire, the colonies would drift toward independence. Colonial resistance to the new policies convinced the British that a movement for independence was indeed under way. The colonists denied that they desired independence, but they began to fear that the British government was determined to deprive them of their rights as Englishmen. Britain's policy drove them toward a closer union with one another and finally provoked armed resistance. With the onset of war, both sides felt their predictions had been vindicated.

Both sides were mistaken. The British had no systematic plan to destroy liberty in North America, and until the winter of 1775–1776 hardly any colonists favored independence. But the three imperial crises undermined mutual confidence and brought about an independent American nation. Unable to govern North America, Britain now faced the grim task of conquering it instead.

QUESTIONS FOR REVIEW AND CRITICAL THINKING

Review

1. Why, in 1766, did the colonists stop resisting and rejoice over the repeal of the Stamp Act, even though the Revenue Act of 1766 continued to tax molasses?
2. Ever since the ancient world, Christians had insisted that sin is a form of slavery. Why did it take them over 1,500 years to conclude that enslaving others might be a grievous sin?
3. Why did the colonists start a revolution after the Tea Act of 1773 *lowered* the price of tea?
4. How and why did a resistance movement, dedicated to protecting the colonists' rights as Englishmen, end by proclaiming American independence instead?

Critical Thinking

1. The colonists insisted that the right to property was essential to the preservation of liberty. Taxation without representation was unconstitutional precisely because it deprived them of their property without their consent. How then could they find it appropriate and legitimate to resist British policies by destroying the property of stamp distributors, Thomas Hutchinson, and the East India Company?
2. In 1775 Lord North promised that Parliament would not tax any colony that paid its share of the costs of imperial defense and gave adequate salaries to its civil officers, but the Second Continental Congress rejected the proposal out of hand. Had George Grenville offered something of the kind between 1763 and 1765, might Britain have averted the Revolution? Specifically, if he had praised Massachusetts men and Virginians for their vigorous cooperation with the empire during the French and Indian War while censuring Maryland and North Carolina for lack of cooperation, would Boston have rioted and Patrick Henry have urged resistance if Parliament had decided to punish those colonies for failing to meet the standards set by Massachusetts and Virginia?

Discovery

What principles were at stake during the period of the American Revolution?

SUGGESTED READINGS

The best one-volume narrative history of the coming of the Revolution remains **Merrill Jensen's The Founding of a Nation: A History of the American Revolution, 1763–1776** (1968). **Bernard Bailyn's The Ideological Origins of the American Revolution** (1967) has had an enormous impact. **Gregory Evans Dowd** provides a fresh perspective in **War Under Heaven: Pontiac, the Indian Nations, and the British Empire** (2002).

On the three imperial crises, **Edmund S. and Helen M. Morgan's The Stamp Act Crisis, Prologue to Revolution,** 3rd ed. (1953, 1995) has lost none of its saliency. **Pauline Maier's From Resistance to Revolution: Colonial Radicals and the Development of American Opposition to Britain, 1765–1776** (1972) and **Richard D. Brown's Revolutionary Politics in Massachusetts: The Boston Committee of Correspondence and the Towns** (1970) are both excellent on the process of disaffection. **David Ammerman's In the Common Cause: American Response to the Coercive Acts of 1774** (1974) is especially strong on the First Continental Congress and its aftermath. **David Hackett Fischer's Paul Revere's Ride** (1994) is a rare combination of exhaustive research and stirring prose. **Pauline Maier's American Scripture: Making the Declaration of Independence** (1997) uses 90 local declarations of independence in the spring of 1776 to give context to Jefferson's famous text.

Important studies of internal tensions include **Gary B. Nash, The Urban Crucible: Social Change, Political Consciousness, and the Origins of the American Revolution** (1979); **Woody Holton's** imaginative **Forced Founders: Indians, Debtors, Slaves, and the Making of the American Revolution in Virginia** (1999); **James P. Whittenburg's** "Planters, Merchants, and Lawyers: Social Change and the Origins of the North Carolina Regulation," **William and Mary Quarterly**, 3d ser., 34 (1977): 214–238; and **Richard M. Brown, The South Carolina Regulators** (1963) explore the internal tensions in these colonies. **David Grimsted's** "Anglo-American Racism and Phillis Wheatley's 'Sable Veil,' 'Length'ned Chain,' and 'Knitted Heart,' " in Ronald Hoffman and Peter J. Albert, eds., **Women in the Age of the American Revolution** (1989) is a superb study of the emerging antislavery movement and women's role in it.

ONLINE SOURCES GUIDE

ThomsonNOW   Visit ThomsonNOW to access primary sources, exercises, quizzes, and audio chapter summaries related to this chapter:
http://www.Thomsonedu.com/login

DISCOVERY

What principles were at stake during the period of the American Revolution?

In thinking about this question, begin by breaking it down into the components shown below. A discussion of the significance of each component should appear in your answer.

GOVERNMENT AND LAW

The section on "Independence" lists some of the "self-evident" affirmations of the Declaration of Independence such as "all men are created equal" and have a natural right to "life, liberty, and the pursuit of happiness." Did the colonists fully embrace all of the principles set forth in the Declaration of Independence? If not, which principles were not fully embraced? Why were they not?

THE DECLARATION OF INDEPENDENCE

The Unanimous Declaration of the Thirteen United States of America

When in the Course of human events it becomes necessary for one people to dissolve the political bands which have connected them with another, and to assume among the Powers of the earth, the separate and equal station to which the Laws of Nature and of Nature's God entitle them, a decent respect to the opinions of mankind requires that they should declare the causes which impel them to the separation.

We hold these truths to be self-evident, that all men are created equal, that they are endowed by their Creator with certain unalienable Rights, that among these are Life, Liberty and the pursuit of Happiness. That to secure these rights, Governments are instituted among Men, deriving their just Powers from the consent of the governed. That whenever any Form of Government becomes destructive of these ends, it is the Right of the People to alter or to abolish it, and to institute new Government, laying its foundation on such principles and organizing its Powers in such form, as to them shall seem most likely to effect their Safety and Happiness. Prudence, indeed, will dictate that Governments long established should not be changed for light and transient causes; and accordingly all experience hath shewn, that mankind are more disposed to suffer, while evils are sufferable, than to right themselves by abolishing the forms to which they are accustomed. But when a long train of abuses and usurpations, pursuing invariably the same Object evinces a design to reduce them under absolute Despotism, it is their right, it is their duty, to throw off such Government, and to provide new Guards for their future security. Such has been the patient sufferance of these Colonies; and such is now the necessity which constrains them to alter their former Systems of Government. The history of the present King of Great Britain is a history of repeated injuries and usurpations, all having in direct object the establishment of an absolute Tyranny over these States. To prove this, let Facts be submitted to a candid world.

He has refused his Assent to Laws, the most wholesome and necessary for the public good.

He has forbidden his Governors to pass Laws of immediate and pressing importance, unless suspended in their operation till his Assent should be obtained; and when so suspended, he has utterly neglected to attend to them.

He has refused to pass other Laws for the accommodation of large districts of people, unless those people would relinquish the right of Representation in the Legislature, a right inestimable to them and formidable to tyrants only.

He has called together legislative bodies at places unusual, uncomfortable, and distant from the depository of their Public Records, for the sole Purpose of fatiguing them into compliance with his measures.

He has dissolved Representative Houses repeatedly, for opposing with manly firmness his invasions on the rights of the People.

He has refused for a long time, after such dissolutions, to cause others to be elected; whereby the Legislative Powers, incapable of Annihilation, have returned to the People at large for their exercise; the State remaining in the mean time exposed to all the dangers of invasion from without, and convulsions within.

He has endeavoured to prevent the Population of these States; for that purpose obstructing the Laws for Naturalization of Foreigners; refusing to pass others to encourage their migration hither, and raising the conditions of new Appropriations of Lands.

He has obstructed the Administration of Justice, by refusing his Assent to Laws for establishing Judiciary Powers.

He has made Judges dependent on his Will alone, for the tenure of their offices, and the amount and payment of their salaries.

He has erected a multitude of New Offices, and sent hither swarms of Officers to harass our People, and eat out their substance.

He has kept among us, in times of peace, Standing Armies without the Consent of our legislatures.

He has affected to render the Military independent of and superior to the Civil Power.

He has combined with others to subject us to a jurisdiction foreign to our constitution, and unacknowledged by our laws; giving his Assent to their Acts of pretended Legislation: For Quartering large bodies of armed troops among us: For protecting them, by a mock Trial, from Punishment for any Murders which they should commit on the Inhabitants of these States: For cutting off our Trade with all parts of the world: For imposing Taxes on us without our Consent: For depriving us in many cases, of the benefits of Trial by Jury: For transporting us beyond Seas to be tried for pretended offences: For abolishing the free System of English Laws in a neighbouring Province, establishing therein an Arbitrary government, and enlarging its Boundaries so as to render it at once an example and fit instrument for introducing the same absolute rule into these Colonies: For taking away our Charters, abolishing our most valuable Laws, and altering fundamentally the Forms of our Governments: For suspending our own Legislatures, and declaring

Text is reprinted from the facsimile of the engrossed copy in the National Archives. The original spelling, capitalization, and punctuation have been retained. Paragraphing has been added.

DECLARATION OF INDEPENDENCE

CULTURE AND SOCIETY

Look at the title page of Phillis Wheatley's collected poems and note the inscription encircling the engraving of Wheatley. Why was it necessary to include such an inscription? How was her status affected by her gender or the fact that she was enslaved? Which groups were not included in the newfound ideas of independence and freedom? Why were they excluded? How did they attempt to have their voices heard?

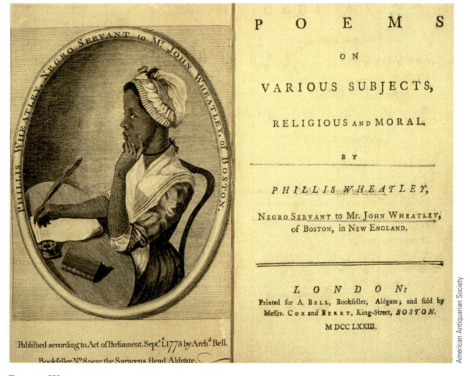

PHILLIS WHEATLEY

the king's peace. They hoped they would not have to use their huge army, but when they wrote **George Washington** to open negotiations, he refused to accept the letter because it did not address him as "General." To do so would have recognized the legitimacy of his appointment. Unable to negotiate, the Howes had to fight.

Washington had moved his army from Boston to New York City. Reluctant to abandon any large city, he divided his inferior force of 19,000 and sent half of it from Manhattan to Long Island. Most of the men dug in on Brooklyn Heights and waited for a frontal attack. The British invaded Long Island and on August 27, 1776, sent a force around the American left flank through unguarded Jamaica Pass. While Hessians feinted a frontal assault, the flanking force crushed the American left and rear.

The Howes did nothing to prevent the evacuation of the rest of the American army to Manhattan, which occurred under the cover of a fierce nor'easter storm. Instead, the British opened informal talks with several members of Congress on Staten Island on September 11. But when the Americans insisted that the British first recognize their independence, no progress was possible. Washington evacuated lower Manhattan, and the British took New York City, much of which was destroyed by fire on September 21. The Howes then offered a pardon to people willing to lay down their arms and return to British allegiance within 60 days. In southern New York State, several thousand complied.

In October, the Howes drove Washington out of Manhattan and Westchester and then turned on two garrisons he had left behind. On November 16, at a cost of 460 casualties, the British forced 3,000 men to surrender at Fort Washington on the Manhattan side of the Hudson River. General Nathanael Greene, a Quaker who had given up pacifism for soldiering, saved his men but not his supplies on the New Jersey side by abandoning Fort Lee. British success seemed to prove that no American force could stand before a properly organized British army. But to capture Washington's entire army would have been a political embarrassment, leading to massive treason trials, executions, and great bitterness. Instead, Britain's impressive victories demoralized Americans and encouraged them to go home. In September, 27,000 Americans were fit for duty in the northern theater (including the Canadian border); by December, only 6,000 remained. And most of those intended to leave when their enlistments expired on December 31.

The Howes' strategy nearly worked. In December British forces swept across New Jersey as far south as Burlington. Several thousand New Jersey residents took the king's oath. To seal off Long Island Sound from both ends, the Howes also captured Newport, Rhode Island. Many observers thought the war was all but over as sad remnants of the Continental Army crossed the Delaware River into Pennsylvania, confiscating all boats along the way so that the British could not follow them. Even Jefferson began to think about the terms on which a restoration of the monarchy might be acceptable.

THE TRENTON-PRINCETON CAMPAIGN

Washington knew he had to do something dramatic to restore morale and encourage his soldiers to reenlist. The New Jersey militia, silent for weeks, showed him how in mid-December by harassing British outposts and patrols in the Delaware valley, especially the exhausted garrison at Trenton. On the night of December 25, 1776, he crossed the ice-choked Delaware and marched south, surprising the Trenton garrison at dawn during another nor'easter. At small cost to the attackers, 1,000 Hessians surrendered. The British sent their most energetic general, Charles, earl Cornwallis, south with 8,000 men. They caught Washington at Trenton near sunset on January

George Washington *A veteran of the French and Indian War, Washington was named commander in chief of the Continental Army by the Second Continental Congress in 1775 and won notable victories at Boston, Trenton, Princeton, and Yorktown, where Lord Cornwallis's army surrendered to him in 1781. His fellow delegates chose him to preside over the deliberations of the Philadelphia Convention in 1787, and after the federal Constitution was ratified, he was unanimously chosen the first president of the United States for two terms.*

QUICK   REVIEW

UNABLE TO NEGOTIATE A RECONCILIATION, THE HOWE BROTHERS LAUNCH THEIR OFFENSIVE

- The British took Staten Island, Long Island, and Manhattan, swept across northern New Jersey

- After New Jersey militia inflicted serious losses on the British, Washington won victories at Trenton and Princeton

- After the British withdrew most of their outposts, the militia regained control

- Their foraging war cut the effective strength of the British army to less than half what it had been in August

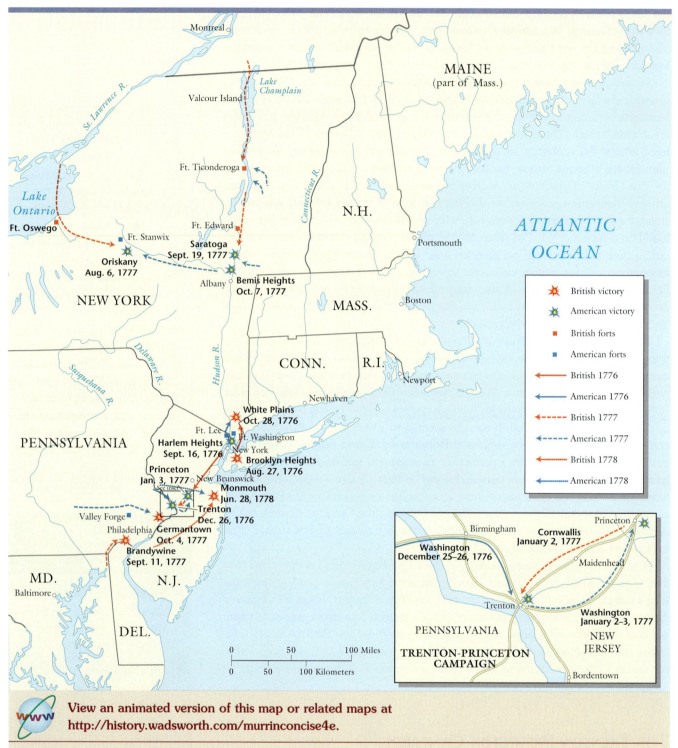

Map 6.1

REVOLUTIONARY WAR IN THE NORTHERN STATES. *This map shows the campaigns in New York and New Jersey in 1776–1777, in northern New York and around Philadelphia in 1777, and at Monmouth, New Jersey, in 1778. The inset shows Washington's Trenton and Princeton campaigns after Christmas 1776.*

2 but decided to wait until dawn before attacking. British patrols watched the Delaware to prevent another escape across the river, but Washington left his camp-fires burning, muffled the wheels of his wagons and guns, and stole around the British left flank, heading north. At dawn, he met a British regiment that was just beginning its march from Princeton to Trenton. The Battle of Princeton amounted to a series of sharp clashes in which the Americans, with a five-to-one edge, mauled yet another garrison.

Washington's two victories had an enormous impact on the war. The Howes, who until January had shown a firm grasp of revolutionary warfare, blundered in not hounding Washington's remnant of an army to its destruction after Princeton, if that was still possible. Instead, they called in their garrisons and concentrated the army along the Raritan River from New Brunswick to the sea. The Howes had encouraged **loyalists** to come forward and had then abandoned them to the king's enemies. As the British departed, the militia returned. Those who had taken the oath now grov-eled, as the price of acceptance, or fled to British lines. For the rest of the winter the militia attacked and usually defeated British patrols foraging for supplies. By spring Howe's forces were reduced to less than half the strength they had been in August. Many invaders had aroused fierce hatred by looting and raping their way across New Jersey. The British and Hessians had lost the hearts and minds of the people.

loyalists *People in the 13 colonies who remained loyal to Britain during the Revolution.*

The Campaigns of 1777 and Foreign Intervention

In 1777 General Howe again had a plan for winning the war, but it required 20,000 reinforcements that did not exist. Instead, Lord George Germain, Britain's war min-ister, ordered him to take Philadelphia. He also sent General John Burgoyne to Canada with orders to march his army south and link up with the garrison of New York City, commanded by Sir Henry Clinton. A small force under Barry St. Leger was to march down the Mohawk valley and threaten Albany from the west. When few re-inforcements reached the Howes, they decided to invade by sea rather than risk the kind of losses they had suffered over the winter. That decision allowed Washington to shift men north to oppose Burgoyne.

The British campaign made little sense. If the point of Burgoyne's march was to get his army to New York City, he should have gone by sea. If the point was to force a battle with New Englanders, it should have been larger. And if Howe's army—Britain's biggest—would not challenge Washington's, who would?

The Loss of Philadelphia

After Trenton and Princeton, Washington demanded stricter discipline and longer terms of enlistment. Congress responded by promising a cash bonus to anyone en-listing for three years and a land bounty to anyone serving for the duration. Congress never came close to raising the 75,000 men it hoped for, but these new policies did create the foundation for a more professional army.

The Continental Army acquired its own distinctive character. The men who signed up were often poor. Some recruits were British deserters. Short-term militia, by con-trast, usually held a secure place in their communities. As the 1777 recruits came in, the two northern armies, swelled by militia, grew to about 28,000 men fit for duty—17,000 in northern New York and 11,000 under Washington.

Unknown artist, Original Air Balloon, hand-colored etching, 28.5c 20.5 cm, published December 29, 1783 by G. Humphrey. Courtesy of the Lewis Walpole Library, Yale University. 783.12.29.2

CONGRESS FLEEING PHILADELPHIA BY BALLOON, 1777. *This British cartoon mocked Congress as it fled from the British army in the 1777 campaign. Hot air balloon flights were still in an experimental phase but were becoming popular in France and Britain. The first flight across the English Channel would occur in 1783.*

The Howes sailed south from New York with 13,000 men. When river pilots were unable to guarantee a safe ascent up the Delaware against American fire, the fleet went to Chesapeake Bay and landed the troops at Head of Elk, Maryland, on August 24. The British marched on Philadelphia through southeastern Pennsylvania, a region with many loyalists and neutral Quakers. Few militia turned out to help Washington, but most residents, aware of the atrocities committed in New Jersey in 1776, fled rather than greet the British army as liberators. The British burned many of their abandoned farms.

After his experience in New York, Washington was wary of being trapped in a city. Instead of trying to hold Philadelphia, he took up strong positions at Brandywine Creek along the British line of march. On September 11, Howe again outmaneuvered him, drove in his right flank, and forced the Americans to retreat. Congress fled to Lancaster, and the British occupied Philadelphia on September 26.

Washington, after failing to destroy a British outpost at Germantown, headed west to Valley Forge, where the army endured a miserable winter. There, Frederich Wilhelm, baron von Steuben, a Prussian serving with the Continental Army, devised a drill manual for Americans based on Prussian standards. Through his efforts, the Continentals became much more soldierly. Other European volunteers also helped. From France came marquis de Lafayette and Johann, baron de Kalb. The Poles sent Thaddeus Kosciuszko (a talented engineer) and Casimir, count Pulaski, both of whom were killed in American service. By war's end, perhaps one-fifth of American officers were European professionals who gave the officer corps an aristocratic tone that alarmed many civilians.

SARATOGA

In northern New York, Ticonderoga fell to Burgoyne on June 2, 1777, but little went right for the British after that. Colonel St. Leger, with 900 soldiers and an equal number of Indians, reached Fort Schuyler in the Mohawk valley in August and defeated 800 militia at Oriskany. But when Benedict Arnold approached with an additional 1,000 men, the Indians fled, and St. Leger withdrew to Oswego.

Burgoyne's army of 7,800, advancing from Ticonderoga toward Albany, was overwhelmed in the upper Hudson valley. When he detached 700 Hessians to forage in the Green Mountains, they ran into 2,600 militia raised by John Stark of New Hampshire. On August 16 at Bennington, Vermont, Stark killed or captured nearly all of them and mauled a relief force of 650 Hessians. By the time Burgoyne's surviving soldiers reached the Hudson and started toward Albany, the Americans under

Horatio Gates outnumbered them 3 to 1. The British got as far as Bemis Heights, 30 miles north of Albany, but failed to break through in two costly battles on September 19 and October 7. Burgoyne retreated 10 miles to **Saratoga**, where he surrendered his entire army on October 17.

FRENCH INTERVENTION

In May 1776, Louis XVI authorized secret aid to the American rebels. A French dramatist, Pierre-Augustin Caron de Beaumarchais, set up the firm of Roderique Hortalez et Compagnie to smuggle supplies through Britain's weak blockade of the American coast. Without this aid, the Americans could not have continued the war. In December 1776 Benjamin Franklin arrived in France as an agent of the American Congress. The 70-year-old Franklin took Parisian society by storm by wearing simple clothes, replacing his wig with a fur cap, and playing to perfection the role of innocent man of nature that French *philosophes* associated with Pennsylvania. Through Beaumarchais, he kept the supplies flowing.

The fall of Philadelphia alarmed Foreign Minister Charles Gravier, comte de Vergennes. But Burgoyne's defeat convinced Louis XVI that the Americans could win and that intervention was a good risk. Franklin and Vergennes signed two treaties in February 1778. One, a commercial agreement, granted Americans generous trading terms with France. In the other, France made a perpetual alliance with the United States, recognized American independence, agreed to fight until Britain conceded independence, and disavowed all territorial ambitions on the North American continent.

The Franco-American treaties stunned London. Lord North put together a plan of conciliation that conceded virtually everything but independence and sent a distinguished group of commissioners under Frederick Howard, earl of Carlisle, to present it to Congress and block the French alliance. In 1775 such a proposal probably would have resolved the imperial crisis, but now Congress recognized it as a sign of weakness and rejected it out of hand.

Americans now expected a quick victory, while the British regrouped. George III declared war on France, recalled the Howe brothers, and ordered General Clinton, the new commander, to abandon Philadelphia. Wary of being caught at sea by the French, Clinton marched overland to New York in June 1778. Washington's army attacked his rear at Monmouth, New Jersey, and nearly defeated the British, but the redcoats held the field and then resumed their march. Fearing a French invasion of the British Isles while most of the Royal Navy was in American waters, the British redeployed their forces on a global scale in 1778–1779.

SPANISH EXPANSION AND INTERVENTION

Like France, Spain was eager to avenge old defeats against Britain. The Spanish king, Charles III (1759–1788), had endured the loss of Florida shortly after ascending the throne but had received Louisiana from France in compensation. The province attracted 2,000 immigrants from the Canary Islands, perhaps 3,000 Acadian refugees, and other French settlers from the Illinois country, and it prospered more than it ever had before.

During this time, Spaniards also moved into California. They explored the Pacific coastline as far north as southern Alaska, set up an outpost at San Francisco Bay, and built a series of Franciscan missions under Junípero Serra. With little danger from

Saratoga *A major turning point in the Revolutionary War. American forces prevented John Burgoyne's army from reaching Albany, cut off its retreat, and forced it to surrender in October 1777. This victory helped bring France into the war.*

QUICK REVIEW

1777: YEAR OF DECISION

- Professionalism of the Continental Army grew

- British took Philadelphia after defeating Washington at Brandywine

- Burgoyne, after he took Ticonderoga, was swamped by American forces and surrendered his army at Saratoga

- Franklin negotiated an alliance with France, and a year later France brought Spain into the war

other Europeans, Spain sent relatively few soldiers to California. For the last time in the history of North America, missionaries set the tone for a whole province. As in Florida earlier, the Indians died in appalling numbers from European diseases, and many objected to the severe discipline of the missions.

Charles III never made an alliance with the United States, but in 1779 he joined France in its war against Britain, hoping to retake Gibraltar and to stabilize Spain's North American borders. Britain held Gibraltar, but Spain overran British West Florida, and at the end of the war Britain ceded East Florida as well, giving Spain for the first time in a century control of the entire coastline of the Gulf of Mexico.

THE RECONSTITUTION OF AUTHORITY

FOCUS QUESTION
How did American constitutionalism after 1776 differ from the British constitutional principles that the colonists had accepted and revered before 1776?

In 1776 the prospect of independence touched off an intense debate among Americans on constitutionalism. They agreed that every state needed a written constitution to limit the powers of government, something more explicit than the precedents and customs that made up Britain's unwritten constitution. They moved toward ever fuller expressions of popular sovereignty—the theory that all power must be derived from the people themselves. For four years, these lively debates sparked a learning process. By 1780, Americans knew what they meant when they insisted that the people must be their own governors.

JOHN ADAMS AND THE SEPARATION OF POWERS

No one learned more from this process than John Adams, who wrote *Thoughts on Government* in 1776, a tract that influenced the men drafting Virginia's constitution. In 1776 Adams was already moving away from the British notion of a "mixed and balanced" constitution, in which the government embodied the distinct social orders of British society—"King, Lords, and Commons." He was groping toward a very different notion, the **separation of powers**. Government, he affirmed, should be divided into three branches: an executive armed with veto power, a legislature, and a judiciary independent of both. The legislature, he insisted, must be bicameral, so that each house could expose the failings of the other. A free government need not embody distinct social orders to be stable. It could uphold republican values by being properly balanced within itself.

Governments exist to promote the happiness of the people, Adams declared, and happiness depends on "virtue," both public and private. **Public virtue** meant "patriotism," the willingness of independent householders to value the common good above their personal interests. The form of government that rests entirely on virtue, Adams argued, is a republic. Americans must elect legislatures that would mirror the diversity of society. Britain had put the nobility in one house and the commoners in another. But in America, everyone was a commoner. There were no "social orders." In what sense, then, could any government reflect American society?

In 1776 Adams knew only that the legislature should mirror society. **Unicameral legislatures,** such as Pennsylvania's, horrified him: "A single assembly, possessed of all the powers of government," he warned, "would make arbitrary laws for their own interest, execute all laws arbitrarily for their own interest, and adjudge all controversies in their own favor." Adams had not yet found a way to distinguish between everyday legislation and the power to create a constitution. While struggling to define what a republic ought to be, he and his admirers could not escape two assumptions on which

separation of powers *The theory that a free government, especially in a republic, should have three independent branches capable of checking or balancing one another: the executive, the legislative (usually bicameral), and the judicial.*

public virtue *Meant, to the revolutionary generation, patriotism and the willingness of a free and independent people to subordinate their interests to the common good and even to die for their country.*

European politics rested—that government itself must be sovereign, and that it alone could define the rights of the people. A few ordinary settlers had already spotted the dangers of having the two functions performed by the same body. As the citizens of Concord, Massachusetts, warned in October 1776, "A Constitution alterable by the Supreme Legislative [Power] is no Security at all to the Subject against any Encroachment of the Governing part on . . . their Rights and Privileges."

This concern would eventually prompt Americans to invent the embodiment of **popular sovereignty** in its purest form, the constitutional convention. But in 1776 most Americans still assumed that governments must be sovereign. In the early state constitutions, every state lodged **sovereign power** in its legislature and let the legislature define the rights of citizens. In 1776 the American reply to Britain's sovereign Parliament was 13 sovereign state legislatures—or 14, if Vermont is included.

THE VIRGINIA CONSTITUTION

In June 1776 Virginia became the first state to adopt a permanent, republican constitution. The legislature chose the governor, the governor's council, and all judges above the level of justice of the peace. The governor had no veto and hardly any patronage. The lower house faced annual elections, but members of the upper house served four-year terms. George Mason drafted a declaration of rights that the Virginia delegates passed before approving the constitution itself, on the theory that the people should define their rights before empowering the government. Mason's text affirmed the right to life, liberty, property, and the pursuit of happiness. The convention's amended text affirmed human equality, but not for enslaved people. The bill of rights also condemned hereditary privilege, called for rotation in office, provided strong guarantees for trial by jury and due process, and extolled religious liberty.

Other states adopted variations of the Virginia model. Because America had no aristocracy, uncertainty about the makeup of the upper house was widespread. Some states imposed higher property qualifications on "senators" than on "representatives." In three states the lower house elected the upper house. Maryland chose state senators through an electoral college, but most states created separate election districts for senators. Most states also increased the number of representatives in the lower house. Inland counties, underrepresented in most colonial assemblies, became better represented, and men of moderate wealth won a majority of seats in most states, displacing the rich who had won most colonial elections. Most states also stripped the governor of patronage and of royal prerogatives, such as the power to dissolve the legislature.

THE PENNSYLVANIA CONSTITUTION

In June 1776 Pennsylvania, radicals overthrew Crown, proprietor, and assembly, rejected the leadership of both the old Quaker and Proprietary parties, and elected artisans to office in Philadelphia and ordinary farmers in rural areas. Until 1776 most officeholders had either been Quakers or Anglicans. Now, Scots-Irish Presbyterians and German Lutherans or Calvinists replaced them and drafted a new constitution. They summoned a special convention whose only task was to write a constitution. That document established a unicameral assembly and a plural executive of 12 men, one of whom would preside and thus be called "president." All freemen who paid taxes, and their adult sons living at home, could vote. Elections were annual, voting was by secret ballot, legislative sessions were open to the public, and no representative could serve for more than four years out of any seven. All bills were to be published before passage for public discussion throughout the state. Only at the next session of the

unicameral legislature *A legislature with only one chamber or house.*

popular sovereignty *The theory that all power must be derived from the people themselves.*

sovereign power *A term used to describe supreme or final power.*

legislature could they be passed into law, except in emergencies. Pennsylvania also created a "Council of Censors" to meet every seven years to determine whether the constitution had been violated. It could also recommend amendments.

The Pennsylvania constitution, however, generated intense conflict in late 1776 as the British army drew near. In this emergency, the convention that drafted the constitution also began to pass laws, destroying any distinction between itself and the legislature it had created. Likewise, the convention and the legislatures that eventually succeeded it rarely delayed the enactment of a bill until after the voters had had time to discuss it. The war lent a sense of emergency to almost every measure. Even more alarming, many residents condemned the new constitution as illegitimate. The men driven from power in 1776 never consented to it and saw no good reason why they should accept it. The radicals, calling themselves "Constitutionalists," imposed oaths on all citizens obliging them to uphold the constitution and then disfranchised those who refused to support it, such as Quakers. These illiberal measures gave radicals a majority in the legislature into the 1780s and kept voter turnout low in most elections, although some men (mostly leaders of the old Proprietary Party) took the oaths only to form an opposition party. Called "Anticonstitutionalists" at first (that is, opponents of the 1776 constitution), they soon took the name "Republicans." In the 1780s, after the war emergency had passed, they won a majority in the assembly, secured ratification of the federal Constitution, and then, in 1790, replaced the state's radical constitution with a new one that made the legislature bicameral and added a popularly elected governor.

MASSACHUSETTS REDEFINES CONSTITUTIONALISM

Another bitter struggle occurred in Massachusetts. After four years of intense debate, Massachusetts found a way to lodge sovereignty with the people and not with government—that is, a way to distinguish a constitution from simple laws.

In response to the Massachusetts Government Act, passed by Parliament in 1774, the colonists had prevented the royal courts from sitting (see Chapter 5). The courts remained closed until the British withdrew from Boston in March 1776, and the provincial congress moved into the city and reestablished itself as the General Court under the royal charter of 1691. The legislature then reapportioned itself. The new system let towns choose representatives in proportion to population. It rewarded the older, populous eastern towns at the expense of lightly settled western towns.

When the General Court also revived royal practice by appointing its own members as county judges and justices of the peace, the western counties exploded. They attacked the reapportionment act and refused to reopen the courts in Hampshire and Berkshire counties. Berkshire's radicals insisted on contracts or compacts as the basis of authority in both church and state and continued to use county conventions in place of the courts. To these Berkshire Constitutionalists a **convention** was becoming the purest expression of the will of the people, superior to any legislature.

In the fall of 1776 the General Court asked the towns to authorize it to draft a constitution. By a 2 to 1 margin the voters agreed, a result that reflected growing *distrust* of the legislature. Six months earlier hardly anyone would have questioned such a procedure. The legislature drafted a constitution over the next year and then, in an unusual precaution, asked the towns to ratify it. The voters rejected it by the stunning margin of 5 to 1. Chastened, the General Court urged the towns to postpone the question until after the war. Hampshire County reopened its courts in April 1778, but Berkshire threatened to secede from the state unless it summoned a constitutional convention. Citing John Locke, these farmers insisted that they were now in a "state of nature," subject to no legitimate government. They might even join a neighboring

convention *In England, a meeting, usually of the houses of Parliament, to address an emergency, such as the flight of James II to France in 1688. The convention welcomed William and Mary, who then restored the traditional parliamentary system. In the United States by the 1780s, conventions had become the purest expression of the popular will, superior to the legislature, as in the convention that drafted the Massachusetts Constitution of 1780.*

state that had a proper constitution. At a time when Vermont was making good its secession from New York, this was no idle threat.

The General Court gave in, and a convention met in Boston in December 1779. John Adams drafted a constitution for it to consider, and the convention used his text as its starting point. A constitution now had to be drafted by a convention, elected for that specific purpose, and then be ratified by the people.

Like its Virginia counterpart, the Massachusetts constitution began with a bill of rights. Both houses would be elected annually. The House of Representatives would be chosen by the towns. Senators were to be elected by counties and apportioned according to property values, not population. The governor was to be popularly elected and would have a veto that two-thirds of both houses could override. Property qualifications rose as a man's civic duties increased. For purposes of ratification only, all free adult males were eligible to vote. In accepting the basic social compact, everyone (that is, all free men) would have a chance to consent.

During the spring of 1780 town meetings began the ratification process. The convention tallied the results and declared that the constitution had received the required two-thirds majority. The new constitution promptly went into effect and, though it has often been amended, is still in force today, making it the oldest functioning constitution in the world. Beginning with New Hampshire, other states soon adopted the Massachusetts model.

CONFEDERATION

Before independence, hardly anyone had given serious thought to how an American nation ought to be governed. Dozens of colonists had drafted plans for conciliation with Britain, but through 1775 only Benjamin Franklin, Connecticut's Silas Deane, and an anonymous newspaper essayist had presented plans for an American union. None of them touched off a public debate.

Congress began discussing the American union in the summer of 1776. It had been voting by state ever since the First Continental Congress in 1774. Delegates from large states favored representation according to population, but the small states insisted on being treated as equals. As long as Britain was ready to embrace any state that defected, small states had great leverage. In one early draft of the Articles of Confederation, John Dickinson rejected proportional representation in favor of state equality. He enumerated the powers of Congress, which did not include levying taxes or regulating trade. To raise money, Congress would have to print it or requisition specific amounts from the states. Congress then split over how to apportion these requisitions. Northern states wanted to count slaves in computing the ratios. Southern states wanted to apportion revenues on the basis of each state's free population. Western lands were another tough issue. States with fixed borders pressured states with boundary claims stretching into the Ohio or Mississippi valleys to surrender their claims to Congress. Congress could not resolve these issues in 1776.

Debate resumed after Washington's victories at Trenton and Princeton. Thomas Burke of North Carolina introduced a resolution that eventually became part of the "Articles of Confederation and perpetual Union": "Each state retains its sovereignty, freedom and independence, and every power, jurisdiction, and right, which is not by this confederation expressly delegated to the United States in Congress assembled." The acceptance of Burke's resolution, with only Virginia dissenting, ensured that the Articles would contain a firm commitment to state sovereignty. In the final version, Congress was given no power over western land claims, and requisitions would be based on each state's free population. In 1781 Congress tried to change the formula

QUICK REVIEW

THE EMERGENCE OF A DISTINCTLY AMERICAN FORM OF CONSTITUTIONALISM

- From the unwritten "mixed and balanced constitution" to written texts and the separation of powers

- Virginia's 1776 constitution gave nearly all power to the legislature but included a bill of rights

- Pennsylvania's radical, unicameral constitution aroused great controversy

- The Massachusetts Constitution of 1780: drafted by a popularly elected convention and ratified by the people

- Congress drafted the Articles of Confederation in 1777, but it was not ratified until 1781

so that each slave would be counted as three-fifths of a person for the purpose of apportioning requisitions, but this amendment was never ratified.

In November 1777 Congress asked the states to ratify the Articles by March 10, 1778, but only Virginia met the deadline. By midsummer 10 had ratified. The three dissenters were Delaware, New Jersey, and Maryland—all states without western land claims that feared their giant neighbors. Maryland held out for more than three years, until Virginia agreed to cede its land claims north of the Ohio River to Congress. The Articles finally went into force on March 1, 1781.

By then, the Continental Congress had lost most of its power. The congressional effort to manage everything through committees created impossible bottlenecks. In 1776 the states had looked to Congress to confer legitimacy on their new governments. But as the states adopted their own constitutions, their legitimacy became more obvious than that of Congress. Even more alarming, by the late 1770s Congress simply could not pay its bills.

THE CRISIS OF THE REVOLUTION, 1779–1783

Americans expected a quick victory under the French alliance. Instead, the struggle turned into a grim war of **attrition**. Loyalists became much more important to the British war effort. The British began to look to the Deep South as the likeliest recruiting ground for armed loyalists. The Carolinas, divided by the regulator movements and vulnerable to massive slave defections, seemed a promising source.

THE LOYALISTS

Loyalists accepted English ideas of liberty. They thought that creating a new American union was a far riskier venture than remaining part of the British empire. For many, the choice of loyalties was painful. The British, in turn, were slow to take advantage of their numbers. But as the war continued, loyalists, who stood to lose everything in an American victory, showed that they could become fierce soldiers.

About one-sixth of the white population chose the British side in the war. Unlike most patriots, loyalists served long terms because they could not go home unless they won. By 1780 the number of loyalists under arms probably exceeded the number of Continentals by 2 to 1. State governments retaliated by banishing prominent loyalists under pain of death and by confiscating their property.

attrition *A type of warfare where an effort is made to exhaust the manpower, supplies, and morale of the other side.*

LOYALIST REFUGEES, BLACK AND WHITE

FOCUS QUESTION

Why, given that the Declaration of Independence proclaimed that "all men are created equal," did most Indians and blacks, when given the chance, side with Britain?

When given the choice, most slaves south of New England sided with Britain. In New England, where they sensed that they could gain freedom by joining the rebels, many volunteered for military service. Elsewhere, although some fought for the Revolution, they saw that their best chance of emancipation lay with the British army. During the war, more than 50,000 slaves (about 10 percent) fled their owners. This decision carried risks. In South Carolina, hundreds reached the Sea Islands in an effort to join the British during Clinton's 1776 invasion, only to face their owners' wrath when the British failed to rescue them. Others approached British units only to be treated as contraband (property) and to face possible resale. But most slaves who reached British lines won their freedom. When the British left after the war, 20,000 blacks went with them, many to Jamaica, some to Nova Scotia, others to London.

HISTORY THROUGH FILM

MARY SILLIMAN'S WAR (1993)

Directed by Stephen Surjik. Starring Nancy Palk (Mary Silliman), Richard Donat (Selleck Silliman), Paul Boretski (David Holly), Joanne Miller (Amelia), Elias Williams (Peter), and Allan Royal (Thomas Jones)

Strong movies about the Revolutionary War are hard to find. *Mary Silliman's War* is the rare exception. It rests on the outstanding research of Joy Day Buel and Richard Buel, Jr., on the life of an articulate woman, Mary Fish Noyes Silliman Dickinson, a woman who was widowed three times in the course of a long life (1736–1818). She left behind numerous letters and journals that make possible the reconstruction and dramatization of her life. Steven Schechter, who co-produced the film, also wrote most of the screenplay. It picks up Mary's story in 1779 when she was living in Fairfield, Connecticut, with her second hus-

band, Gold Selleck Silliman, and their children. Selleck commanded the militia that had to respond to emergencies, and he also served as prosecuting attorney in his civilian capacity. In the northern states, the Revolutionary War had become mostly a series of destructive raids, with the British and loyalists based on Long Island and the patriots on the mainland. For good reason, both sides worried about traitors and spies in their midst.

As the film opens, Selleck is successfully prosecuting two loyalist townsmen. When they are sentenced to death, Mary objects that the war is turning neighbor against neighbor, but Selleck will not relent. In retaliation, the loyalists stage a night raid on the Silliman home, capture Selleck, and take him to New York City, which was the headquarters of the British army. The message seemed clear. If the Fairfield loyalists were to be executed, Selleck would also die. Thomas Jones, a magistrate and perhaps the most prominent loyalist living on Long Island, had known Selleck since their undergraduate days at Yale College. He acted as an intermediary. When George Washington refused to exchange a captured British officer for Selleck because he was not an officer in the Continental Army, Mary had to face an unpleasant dilemma. An American privateer, Capt. David Holly, offered to raid Long Island, capture Judge Jones, and force the British to negotiate an exchange. Mary disliked privateers and did not approve of Holly, but after the British raided Fairfield and burned most of the town, she consented. The rest of the story explores the consequences of this decision. Mary's deep religious convictions are emphasized throughout the film.

The screenplay telescopes the chronology of these events somewhat, invents a romance between Amelia (a servant in the Silliman household) and Captain Holly, and uses the slave Peter to illustrate the dilemmas that African Americans faced during the war. But the central plot line follows a drama that is well documented in the historical record and exposes a side of the Revolutionary War that few Americans are even vaguely aware of. The struggle was a long, brutal conflict that brought liberty to many and equality to smaller numbers but also turned some neighbors against others.

Fairfield Historical Society

Mary Fish Silliman at age 58, four years after the death of her second husband, Gold Selleck Silliman.

The war, in short, created an enormous stream of refugees, black and white. In addition to former slaves, some 60,000 to 70,000 colonists left the states for other parts of the British empire. About 35,000 settlers found their way to the Maritime Provinces. Another 6,000 to 10,000 fled to Quebec, settled upriver from the older French population, and in 1791 became the new province of Upper Canada (later Ontario). A generous land policy, which required an oath of allegiance to George III, attracted thousands of new immigrants to Canada from the United States in the 1780s and 1790s. By the War of 1812, four-fifths of Upper Canada's 100,000 people were American-born. Though only one-fifth of them could be traced to loyalist resettlement, the settlers supported Britain in that war. In a very real sense the American Revolution laid the foundation for two new nations—the United States and Canada—and they still competed for settlers and their loyalties long after the fighting stopped.

THE INDIAN STRUGGLE FOR UNITY AND SURVIVAL

FOCUS QUESTION

Why did racist hatred of Indians reach new levels of intensity at a time when Indians were reducing their cultural differences with the settlers, as in their increasing rejection of torture?

Indians of the eastern woodlands also began to play a more active role in the war. Most of them saw that an American victory would threaten their survival as a people on their ancestral lands. Nearly all of them sided with Britain in the hope that a British victory might stem the flood of western expansion, and they achieved a level of unity without precedent in their history.

At first, most Indians tried to remain neutral. Only the Cherokees took up arms in 1776. Short on ammunition and other British supplies, they took heavy losses before making peace and accepting neutrality. The Chickamaugas, a splinter group, continued to resist. In the Deep South, only the Catawbas fought on the American side.

Burgoyne's invasion brought the Iroquois into the war in 1777. The Mohawks in the east and the Senecas in the west sided with Britain under the leadership of Joseph Brant, a literate, educated Mohawk and a Freemason. His sister, Mary Brant, emerged as a skillful diplomat in the alliance between the Iroquois and the loyalists. A minority of Oneidas and some Tuscaroras fought with the Americans. Although the Iroquois League endured severe strains, it was not shattered until after the peace, when those who had fought for Britain migrated to Canada. A minority of Shawnees, led by Cornplanter, and of Delawares, led by White Eyes and Killbuck, also pursued friendly relations with the Americans, but they refused to fight other Indians. Christian Moravian Indians in the Ohio country took a similar stance.

Frontier racism made Indian neutrality all but impossible. Backcountry settlers from Carolina through New York refused to accept the neutrals on their own terms. Indian warriors, especially young men influenced by nativist prophets, insisted that the Great Spirit had created whites, Indians, and blacks as separate peoples who ought to remain apart. Their militancy further enraged the settlers.

The hatred of Indians grew so extreme that it threatened to undercut the American war effort. In 1777 a Continental officer had Cornplanter murdered. In 1778 American militia killed White Eyes. Four years later Americans massacred 100 unarmed Moravian mission Indians at Gnadenhutten, Ohio. Nearly all of them were women and children, who knelt in prayer as, one by one, their skulls were crushed with mallets. Until then, most Indians had refrained from the ritual torture of prisoners. After Gnadenhutten they resumed the custom—selectively. They burned alive leaders of the massacre whom they captured.

Faced with hatred, Indians united to protect their lands. They won the frontier war north of the Ohio River. The Iroquois ravaged the Wyoming valley of Pennsylvania in 1778. When an American army devastated Iroquoia in 1779, the Indians fell back on

JOSEPH BRANT, PORTRAIT BY GILBERT STUART (1786). *Brant, a Mohawk and a Freemason, was one of Britain's ablest commanders of loyalist and Indian forces. After the war he led most of the Six Nations to Canada for resettlement.*

Fenimore Art Museum, New York State Historical Association, Cooperstown, New York

the British post at Niagara and continued the struggle. In 1779 nearly all Indians from the Gulf Coast to the Great Lakes exchanged emissaries and planned to attack all along the frontier. George Rogers Clark of Virginia thwarted their offensive with a daring winter raid in which he captured Vincennes and cut off the western nations from British supplies. But the Indians regrouped and by 1782 drove Virginia's "long knives" out of the Ohio country.

ATTRITION

After 1778, George III's determination to continue the war bitterly divided his country. Political dissent increased, including widespread demands for the reduction of royal patronage and for electoral reforms. A proposal to abolish Lord George Germain's office, clearly an attack on the American war, failed in the House of Commons by only 208 votes to 201 in March 1780. A resolve condemning the influence of the Crown carried in April, 233 to 215. Desperate for men, the British army had been quietly recruiting Irish Catholics, and North supported a modest degree of toleration for English and Scottish Catholics. This leniency produced a surge of Protestant violence culminating in the Gordon riots, named for Lord George Gordon, an agitator. For a week in June 1780 crowds roared through the streets of London, smashing Catholic chapels attached to foreign embassies, liberating prisoners from city jails, and finally attacking the Bank of England. The army, supported by Lord Mayor John Wilkes, put down the rioters. The violence discredited the reformers and gave North one last chance to win the war.

Attrition also weakened the United States. Indian raids reduced harvests, and military levies kept thousands of men away from productive work. British and loyalist raids into Connecticut, New Jersey, and Virginia wore down the defenders and destroyed a great deal of property. Average household income plunged by more than 40 percent. Even some American triumphs came at a high price. Burgoyne's surrender left Americans with the burden of feeding his army for the rest of the war. Provisioning the French fleet in American waters also put an enormous strain on American resources.

These heavy demands led to the collapse of the Continental dollar in 1779–1780. Congress had been printing money to pay its bills, using the Spanish dollar as its basic monetary unit. With the French alliance bolstering American credit, this practice worked reasonably well into 1778. The money depreciated but without causing widespread dissatisfaction. But as the war ground on, the value of Continental money fell

---

QUICK REVIEW

NEW DIRECTIONS IN THE REVOLUTIONARY WAR

- Loyalists became much more important to the British war effort

- Indians fought for survival and unity, mostly on the British side

- The war of attrition weakened popular support in Britain, revived the opposition, and sparked the Gordon Riots

- The war of attrition undermined the American economy, the powers of Congress, and the army's morale

to less than a penny on the dollar in 1779. Congress agreed to stop the printing presses and to rely instead on requisitions from the states and on foreign and domestic loans, but it found that, without paper, it could not even pay the army. Congress and the army had to requisition supplies directly from farmers in exchange for certificates geared to a depreciation rate of 40 to 1, well below what it really was. Many farmers, rather than lose money on their crops, cut back production.

Continental soldiers—unpaid, ill clothed, and often poorly fed—grew mutinous. The winter of 1779–1780, the worst of the century, marked a low point in morale among the main force of Continentals snowed in with Washington at Morristown, New Jersey. Many deserted. In May 1780 two Connecticut regiments of the Continental Line, without food for three days, threatened to go home, raising the danger that the whole army might dissolve. Their officers were barely able to restore control.

THE BRITISH OFFENSIVE IN THE SOUTH

In 1780 the British attacked in the Deep South with great success. In December 1778 a small British amphibious force had taken Savannah and had held it through 1779. By early 1780 they were ready to launch a major offensive. General Clinton had finally devised a strategy for winning the war. Much of his New York army would sail to Charleston and take it. Clinton would return to New York with part of it and land on the Jersey coast with a force three times larger than Washington's at Morristown. By dividing this army into two columns, Clinton could break through both passes of the Watchung Mountains leading to Morristown. Washington would either have to hold fast and be overwhelmed, or else abandon his artillery for lack of horses and attack one of the invading columns on unfavorable terms. Either way, Clinton reasoned, the Continental Army would be destroyed. He was also negotiating secretly with an angry and disgruntled Benedict Arnold (he had received little recognition for his heroics in the Saratoga campaign) for the surrender of West Point, which would open the Hudson River to British ships. Finally, if the French landed in Newport, Clinton would then move against them with nearly his entire New York fleet and garrison. If he succeeded there too, he would have smashed every professional force in North America within a year's time. His remaining task would then be pacification, which he could pretty much leave to loyalists. But he told no one else about his New Jersey plan.

Clinton's invasion of South Carolina began with awesome successes. While the British navy sealed off Charleston from the sea, an army of 10,000 closed off the land approaches to the city, forcing its 5,000 defenders to surrender on May 12. Loyalists led by Banastre Tarleton caught the 350 remaining Continentals near the North Carolina border on May 29 and killed them all, including many prisoners.

Such calculated brutality was designed to terrorize civilians into submission. It succeeded at first. But Thomas Sumter began to fight back after loyalists burned his plantation. His mounted raiders attacked British outposts and terrorized loyalists. At Hanging Rock on August 6, Sumter's 800 men scattered 500 loyalists, killing or wounding nearly half of them.

Leaving Cornwallis in command of 8,300 men in South Carolina, Clinton sailed north with one-third of his Carolina army, only to learn that loyalists had persuaded Wilhelm, baron von Knyphausen, New York's temporary commander, to land in New Jersey with 6,000 men on the night of June 6–7, 1780. Even a force that small would pose a grave threat to Washington unless the militia came to his aid. Loyalists

SELF-PORTRAIT OF JOHN ANDRÉ. *André, a talented amateur artist, sketched this self-portrait after he had been condemned to hang for his role as General Clinton's emissary in the treason of Benedict Arnold.*

Yale University Art Gallery, Gift of Ebenezer Baldwin, B.A. 1808

hoped that the militia was so weary from the harsh winter and numerous raids that they would not turn out. To the dismay of the British, however, the militia appeared in strength on June 7.

Only then, after an inconclusive engagement, did Knyphausen learn that Clinton was on his way. The British pulled back to the coast and waited, but they had lost the element of surprise. Clinton attacked at Springfield on June 23. The battle became America's civil war in miniature. New Jersey loyalist regiments attacked the New Jersey regiments of the Continental Line, who were assisted by New Jersey militia. The defense was stout enough to persuade Clinton to withdraw to New York. Arnold's attempt to betray West Point was thwarted. Clinton's emissary was captured and hanged, but Arnold escaped to British lines and became a general in the British army. Everything now depended on the southern campaign.

Despite Sumter's harassment, Cornwallis's conquest of the Carolinas proceeded rapidly. Congress scraped together 900 tough Maryland and Delaware Continentals, put Horatio Gates in command, and sent them south against Cornwallis. Bolstered by 2,000 Virginia and North Carolina militia, Gates rashly offered battle at Camden on August 16. The militia, who lacked bayonets, fled in panic at the first British charge. The exposed Continentals fought bravely but were crushed. Gates informed Congress that he had suffered "total Defeat." Two days after Camden, Tarleton surprised Sumter's camp at Fishing Creek, killing 150 men and wounding 300. In four months the British had destroyed all the Continental forces in the Deep South and mauled Sumter's partisans. Cornwallis turned the pacification of South Carolina over to his loyalists and marched confidently on to "liberate" North Carolina.

THE PARTISAN WAR

But resistance continued. In the west, frontier riflemen, led by Daniel Morgan and enraged by Britain's support of the Indians, crossed the Blue Ridge to challenge Patrick Ferguson's loyalists at King's Mountain near the North Carolina border on October 7, 1780. Losing only 88 men, rebel marksmen picked off many defenders and finally overwhelmed the loyalists. In retaliation for Tarleton's atrocities, they shot many prisoners and hanged a dozen. Stunned, Cornwallis halted his drive into North Carolina.

In October 1780, Congress sent **Nathanael Greene** to the Carolinas with a small Continental force. When Sumter withdrew for several months to nurse a wound, Francis Marion took his place. A much abler leader, Marion operated from remote

Nathanael Greene *A general from Rhode Island whose superb strategy of irregular war reclaimed the Lower South for the American cause in 1780–1781.*

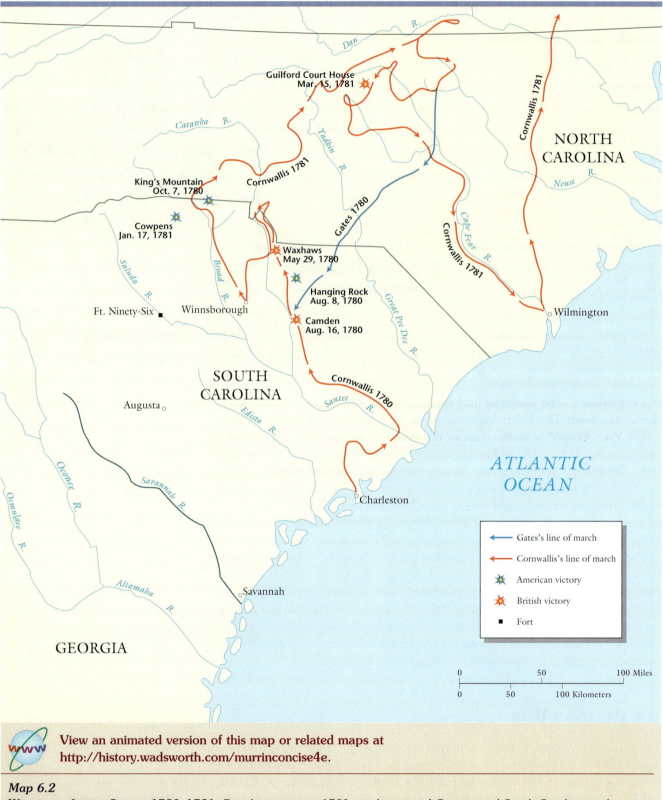

View an animated version of this map or related maps at
http://history.wadsworth.com/murrinconcise4e.

Map 6.2

WAR IN THE LOWER SOUTH, 1780–1781. *British victories in 1780 nearly restored Georgia and South Carolina to the Crown, but after Guilford Court House in March 1781, the Americans regained the advantage throughout the region.*

bases in the swampy low country. Yet Greene's prospects seemed desperate. The ugliness of the partisan war and the condition of his own soldiers appalled him.

In the face of a greatly superior enemy, Greene ignored a standard maxim of war and split up his force of 1,800 Continentals. He sent 300 men east to bolster Marion and ordered Daniel Morgan and 300 riflemen west to threaten the British outpost of Ninety-Six. Cornwallis, worried that Morgan after his King's Mountain victory might raise the entire backcountry against the British, divided his own army. He sent Tarleton with a mixed force of 1,100 British and loyalists after Morgan, who decided to stand with his back to a river at a place called Cowpens. Including militia, Morgan had 1,040 men.

Tarleton attacked on January 17, 1781. In another unorthodox move, Morgan sent his militia out front as skirmishers. He ordered them to fire two rounds and then redeploy in his rear as a reserve. As they pulled back, the British rushed forward into the Continentals, who also retreated at first, then wheeled and discharged a lethal volley. After Morgan's cavalry charged into the British left flank, the militia returned to the fray. Although Tarleton escaped, Morgan annihilated his legion.

As Morgan rejoined Greene, Cornwallis staked everything on his ability to find Greene and crush him. But Greene placed flatboats in his rear at major river crossings and then lured Cornwallis into a march of exhaustion. In a race to the Dan River, Cornwallis burned his baggage in order to travel lightly. Greene escaped on his flatboats across the Yadkin River, flooded with spring rains, just ahead of Cornwallis—who had to march 10 miles upstream, ford the river, and then march back while Greene rested. Greene repeated this stratagem all the way to the Dan until he judged that Cornwallis was so weak that the Americans could offer battle at Guilford Court House on March 15, 1781. With militia, he outnumbered Cornwallis 4,400 to 1,900. Even though the British retained possession of the battlefield, they lost one-quarter of their force. Cornwallis retreated to the coast at Wilmington to refit. He then marched north into Virginia. Instead of following him, Greene returned to South Carolina, where he and Marion took the surviving British outposts one by one. After the British evacuated Ninety-Six on July 1, 1781, they held only Savannah and Charleston in the Deep South. Against heavy odds, Greene had reclaimed the region for the Revolution.

Mutiny and Reform

After the Camden disaster, army officers and state politicians demanded reforms to strengthen Congress and win the war. State legislatures sent their ablest men to Congress. Maryland, the last state to hold out, finally completed the American union by ratifying the Articles of Confederation. But before any reforms could take effect, discontent again erupted in the army. Insisting that their three-year enlistments had expired, 1,500 men of the Pennsylvania Line got drunk on New Year's Day 1781, killed three officers, and marched out of their winter quarters at Morristown. General Clinton sent agents to promise them a pardon and their back pay if they defected to the British. But the mutineers marched south toward Princeton instead and turned Clinton's agents over to Pennsylvania authorities, who executed them. Congress, reassured, negotiated with the soldiers. More than half of them accepted discharges, and those who remained in service got furloughs and bonuses for reenlistment. Encouraged by this treatment, 200 New Jersey soldiers at Pompton also mutinied, but Washington used New England units to disarm them and executed two of the leaders.

Civilian violence also prompted Congress to change policies. Radical artisans blamed rich merchants for the inflation of 1779 and demanded price controls. The merchants blamed paper money. In October, several men were killed when the antagonists exchanged shots near the fortified Philadelphia home of James Wilson, a wealthy lawyer. Spokesmen for the radicals deplored the violence and abandoned the quest for price controls.

Congress interpreted these disturbances as a call for reform. It stopped printing money, abandoned its cumbersome committee system, and created separate executive departments of foreign affairs, finance, war, and marine. Robert Morris, a Philadelphia merchant, became the first secretary of finance, helped to organize the Bank of North America (America's first) in Philadelphia, and made certain that the Continental Army was clothed and well fed. Congress began to requisition revenue from the states. They began to impose heavy taxes but never collected enough to meet both their own and national needs. Congress tried to amend the Articles of Confederation in 1781 and asked the states for a 5 percent duty on all imports. Most states quickly ratified the "impost," but Rhode Island rejected it in 1783. Amendments to the Articles needed unanimous approval by the states, and this opposition killed the impost. A new impost proposal in 1783 was defeated by New York in 1786.

The reforms of 1781 just barely kept a smaller army in the field for the rest of the war, but the new executive departments had an unforeseen effect. Congress had been a plural executive, America's answer to the imperial Crown. But once Congress created its own departments, it looked more like a national legislature, and a feeble one at that. It began to pass, not just "orders" and "resolves," but also "ordinances," which were meant to be permanent and binding. But it could not punish anyone for noncompliance, which may be why it never passed any "laws."

FROM THE RAVAGING OF VIRGINIA TO YORKTOWN AND PEACE

Both Cornwallis and Washington believed that events in Virginia would decide the war. When a large British force raided Virginia in late 1780, Governor Thomas Jefferson called up enough militia to keep the British bottled up in Portsmouth, while he continued to ship men and supplies to Greene in the Carolinas. Thereafter, the state's ability to raise men and supplies almost collapsed.

In January 1781, Clinton sent Arnold by sea from New York with 1,600 men. They sailed up the James and gutted the new capital of Richmond. When Jefferson called out the militia, few responded. Most Virginia freemen had already done service, if only as short-term militia, many as recently as 1780. They thought it was now someone else's turn. For months, there was no one else. Cornwallis took command in April, and Arnold departed for New York. But the raids continued into summer, sweeping as far west as Charlottesville, where Tarleton scattered the Virginia legislature and almost captured Jefferson. Many of Jefferson's slaves greeted the British as liberators. Washington sent Lafayette with 1,200 New England and New Jersey Continentals to contain the damage, and Cornwallis obeyed Clinton's order to withdraw to Yorktown and fortify it.

At last, Washington saw a major opportunity. He learned that a powerful French fleet under François, comte de Grasse, would sail on August 13 with 3,000 soldiers from St. Domingue for Chesapeake Bay. He sprang his trap, cooperating closely with the French army commander, Jean Baptiste Donatien, comte de Rochambeau, who led his 5,000 soldiers from Newport to the outskirts of New York, where they joined Washington's 5,000 Continentals. After feinting an attack to freeze Clinton in place, Washington led the combined armies 400 miles south to tidewater Virginia, where they linked up with Lafayette's Americans and the other French army brought by de

Grasse. After de Grasse beat off a British relief force at the Battle of the Capes on September 5, Washington besieged Cornwallis in **Yorktown**. On October 19, 1781, Cornwallis surrendered his entire army of 8,000 men. Yorktown brought down the British government in March 1782. Lord North resigned. The British evacuated Savannah and Charleston and concentrated their remaining forces in New York City.

Contrary to the French Treaty of 1778, John Jay and John Adams opened secret peace negotiations in Paris with the British. They won British recognition of the Mississippi as the western boundary of the new republic. New Englanders retained the right to fish off Newfoundland. The treaty recognized the validity of prewar transatlantic debts, and Congress promised to urge the states to restore confiscated loyalist property. After the negotiations were far advanced, the Americans told Vergennes,

Yorktown *The last major engagement of the Revolutionary War. Washington's army, two French armies, and a French fleet trapped Lord Cornwallis at Yorktown and forced his army to surrender in October 1781.*

Map 6.3
VIRGINIA AND THE YORKTOWN CAMPAIGN. *After the British ravaged much of Virginia, Washington and a French fleet and army were able to trap Lord Cornwallis at Yorktown, force his surrender, and guarantee American independence.*

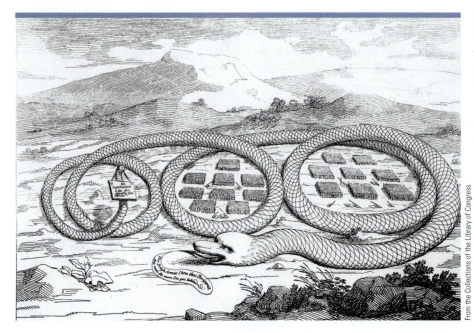

"THE AMERICAN RATTLE SNAKE." *This 1782 cartoon celebrated the victory of Yorktown, the second time in the war that an entire British army had surrendered to the United States.*

the French foreign minister, what they were doing. He feigned indignation, but the threat of a separate peace gave him the leverage he needed with Spain. Spain stopped demanding that France fight until Gibraltar surrendered. The Treaty of Paris ended the war in February 1783. Western Indians were appalled to learn that the treaty gave their lands to the United States. They knew that they had not been conquered, whatever European diplomats might say. Their war for survival continued with few breaks until 1794.

Congress still faced ominous problems. In March 1783 many Continental officers threatened a coup d'état unless Congress granted them generous pensions. Washington, confronting them at their encampment at Newburgh, New York, fumbled for his glasses and remarked, "I have grown old in the service of my country, and now find that I am growing blind." Tears filled the eyes of his comrades in arms, and the threat of a coup vanished.

In Philadelphia two months later, unpaid Pennsylvania soldiers marched on the statehouse where both Congress and the state's executive council sat. Ignoring Congress, they demanded that Pennsylvania redress their grievances. Congress felt insulted and left the city for Princeton, where it reconvened in Nassau Hall. "I confess I have great apprehensions for the union of the states," wrote Charles Thomson, secretary to Congress since 1774. Congress moved on from Princeton to Annapolis and eventually settled in New York, but the Union's survival remained uncertain.

A REVOLUTIONARY SOCIETY

FOCUS QUESTION

In what ways did the values shared by independent householders limit the reforms that the Revolution could offer to other Americans?

Independence transformed American life. The biggest winners were free householders, who gained enormous benefits from the democratization of politics and the chance to colonize the Great West. Besides the loyalists, the biggest losers were the Indians, who continued to resist settler expansion. Many slaves won their freedom, and women struggled for greater dignity. Both succeeded only when their goals proved compatible with the ambitions of white householders.

RELIGIOUS TRANSFORMATIONS

Independence left the Anglican Church vulnerable, if only because George III was its "supreme head." Although most Anglican clergymen supported the Revolution or remained neutral, an aggressive loyalist minority stirred the wrath of patriots. Religious dissenters disestablished the Anglican Church in every southern state. In 1786 Virginia passed Thomas Jefferson's eloquent Statute for Religious Freedom, which declared that efforts to use coercion in matters of religion "tend only to beget habits of hypocrisy and meanness." In Virginia, church attendance and the support of ministers became voluntary activities.

Other states moved more slowly. In New England, the Congregational churches strongly supported the Revolution and were less vulnerable to attack. Ministers' salaries continued to be paid out of public taxes. Disestablishment did not become complete until 1818 in Connecticut and 1833 in Massachusetts.

Although most states still restricted office holding to Christians or Protestants, many people were coming to regard the coercion of anyone's conscience as morally wrong. Jews and Catholics both gained from the new atmosphere of tolerance. When

MUSICAL LINK TO THE PAST

NO KING BUT GOD!

Composer: William Billings
Title: "Independence" (1778)

William Billings, America's most important musical figure during its first two decades of independence, was the first native-born composer to spend all of his time on music, a luxury both then and now. Billings was also the first person, and perhaps the only one, to compose songs inspired by the Revolution. While John Dickinson and Thomas Jefferson established political justifications for the American break with Great Britain, Billings in "Independence" offered a religious justification: "To the King they shall sing hallelujah / And all the continent shall sing: down with this earthly King / No King but God." Billings insisted that Americans were not impetuous in declaring independence because they exhibited a great respect for God and proper social institutions. In this view, Britain and King George III placed themselves in a position above God by depriving Anglo-Americans of their rights as British subjects. For a new country that already had a long history of passionate commitment to religion, this argument for American independence was probably quite convincing.

Although the idea that Americans could create art equal to or of more worth than Europeans would not become commonplace until the 20th century, Billings viewed himself as a serious American artist. Billings was also the first major American composer to lobby for a copyright law. The lack of a copyright law cost Billings a fortune when his defiant song "Chester" became the most popular song of the American Revolution, and numerous publishers bootlegged his song without permission. Under pressure from Billings and a similarly plagiarized Noah Webster (the author of America's first dictionary), Congress passed its first copyright law in 1790. Because it failed to provide any U.S. protection for foreign artists and composers, however, American publishers released and promoted floods of European works on which they did not have to pay royalties. Because Congress was unable to protect what is now known as intellectual property, William Billings, the author of "Independence," did not make a living commensurate to the musical contribution he made to his country.

1. Early American artists such as William Billings had to decide what the role of an artist in a democracy should be. Some American observers at the time and in the 19th century believed that creating art represented a frivolous and decadent occupation in the United States. Should artists in a democracy seek to create works that promote the goals and aspirations of the populace as a whole, or should they cultivate a more personal expression?

2. Do you think that today's practice of downloading music through the Internet presents a similar ethical problem to the unauthorized publishing of Billings's works that occurred during the early national period?

Listen to an audio recording of this music on the *Musical Links to the Past* CD.

John Carroll of Maryland became the first Roman Catholic bishop in the United States in 1790, hardly anyone took alarm. And in the 1780s the Church of England reorganized itself as the Protestant Episcopal Church and quietly began to consecrate its own bishops. Episcopalians and Presbyterians endorsed republican values by adopting written constitutions.

THE FIRST EMANCIPATION

The Revolution freed tens of thousands of slaves. But it also gave new vitality to slavery in the region that people were beginning to call "the South." Within a generation, slavery was abolished in the emerging "North." Race became a defining factor in both regions. In the South most blacks remained enslaved. In the North they became free but not equal. The independent householder and his voluntaristic ethic remained almost a white monopoly.

The British army enabled more than half the slaves of Georgia and perhaps one-quarter of those in South Carolina to win their freedom. A similar process was under way in Virginia in 1781, only to be cut off at Yorktown. Hundreds of New England slaves won their freedom through military service. After the Massachusetts bill of rights proclaimed that all people were "born free and equal," Elizabeth (Bett) Freeman sued her master in 1781 and won her liberty. Thereafter, most of the slaves in Massachusetts and New Hampshire simply walked away from their owners.

Elsewhere, legislative action was necessary. Pennsylvania led the way in 1780 with the modern world's first gradual **emancipation** statute. It declared that all children born to Pennsylvania slaves would become free at age 28. The slaves themselves, not their owners or the broader public, thus bore the costs of their own emancipation. This requirement left former slaves unable to compete on equal terms with free whites, who usually entered adult life with inherited property. Some masters shipped their slaves south before the moment of emancipation, and some whites kidnapped freedmen and sent them south. The Pennsylvania Abolition Society was organized largely to fight these abuses.

The Pennsylvania pattern took hold, with variations, in most other northern states. Where slaves were more than 10 percent of the population, as in southern New York and northeastern New Jersey, slaveholders' resistance delayed legislation for years. New York yielded in 1799; New Jersey in 1804.

In the upper South, Maryland and Virginia authorized the **manumission** of individual slaves. By 1810 more than one-fifth of Maryland's slaves had been freed, as had 10,000 of Virginia's 300,000 slaves, including 123 freed in Washington's will. In the South, general emancipation would have amounted to a social revolution. Planters resisted it, but they supported the Christianization of their slaves and other humane reforms.

Maryland and Virginia banned the Atlantic slave trade, as did all states outside the Deep South. But Georgia and South Carolina reopened it to offset wartime losses and to raise a new staple crop, cotton. South Carolina imported almost 60,000 more Africans before Congress prohibited that traffic in 1808.

THE CHALLENGE TO PATRIARCHY

Nothing as dramatic as emancipation altered relations between the sexes. With the men away fighting, many women were left in charge of the household. But while some women acquired new authority, nearly all of them had to work harder to keep

emancipation *Refers to release from slavery or bondage. Gradual emancipation was introduced in Pennsylvania and provided for the eventual freeing of slaves born after a certain date when they reached age 28.*

manumission of slaves *The act of freeing a slave, done at the will of the owner.*

their households functioning. The war cut them off from most European consumer goods. Household manufactures, mostly the task of women, filled the gap.

Attitudes toward marriage were also changing. The common-law rule of coverture (see Chapter 4) still denied wives any legal personality, but some of them persuaded state governments not to impoverish them by confiscating the property of their loyalist husbands. Many writers insisted that good marriages rested on mutual affection, not on property settlements. Parents were urged to respect the personalities of their children and to avoid severe discipline. Although few women demanded equal political rights during the Revolution, the New Jersey Constitution of 1776 let them vote if they headed a household (usually as a widow) and paid taxes. This right was revoked in 1807.

Philosophers, clergymen, and even popular writers began treating women as morally superior to men. In the Northeast, the first female academies opened in the 1790s, and more women learned to read and write. By 1830 nearly all native-born women in the Northeast had become literate. The ideal of the "republican wife" and the "republican mother" took hold, giving wives and mothers an expanding educational role within the family. They encouraged diligence in their husbands and patriotism in their sons. The novel became a major cultural form in the United States. Its main audience was female, as were many of the authors.

WESTERN EXPANSION, DISCONTENT, AND CONFLICT WITH INDIANS

Westward expansion continued during the Revolutionary War. With 30 axmen, **Daniel Boone** hacked out the Wilderness Road from Cumberland Gap to the Kentucky bluegrass country in early 1775. The first settlers to arrive called Kentucky "the best poor-man's country" and claimed it should belong to those who tilled its soil, not to the speculative Transylvania Company, which claimed title to the land. Although few Indians lived in Kentucky, it was the favorite hunting ground of the Shawnees and other nations. Their raids often prevented the settlers from planting crops. The settlers put up log cabins against the inside walls of large rectangular stockades, 10 feet high and built from oak logs. At each corner, a **blockhouse** with a protruding second story permitted the defenders to fire along the outside walls. Three of these "Kentucky stations" were built—at Boonesborough, St. Asaph, and Harrodsburg. Kentucky lived up to its old Indian reputation as the "dark and bloody ground." Only a few thousand settlers stuck it out until the war ended, but then they were joined by swarms of newcomers. Speculators and absentees were already trying to claim the best bluegrass lands. The Federal Census of 1790 listed 74,000 settlers and slaves in Kentucky and about half that many in Tennessee, where the Cherokees had ceded a large tract after their defeat in 1776. These settlers thrived both because few Indians lived there and because British and Spanish raiders found them hard to reach.

To the south and north, settlement was much riskier. After the war, Spain supplied arms and trade goods to Creeks, Cherokees, Choctaws, and Chickasaws willing to resist Georgia's attempt to settle its western lands. North of the Ohio River, Britain refused to withdraw its garrisons and traders from Niagara, Detroit, and a few other posts, even though, according to the Treaty of Paris, those forts now lay within the United States. To justify their refusal, the British pointed to the failure of Congress to honor American obligations to loyalists and British creditors under the treaty.

During the Revolutionary War, many states and Congress had raised soldiers by promising them land after it was over, and now they needed Indian lands to fulfill these pledges. The few Indian nations that had supported the United States suffered the most. In the 1780s, after Joseph Brant led most of the Iroquois north to Canada, New York

Boone, Daniel *A pioneer settler of Kentucky, Boone became the most famous American frontiersman of his generation.*

blockhouse *A wooden fort with an overhanging second floor. The white settlers of Kentucky used blockhouses to defend themselves against Indians.*

confiscated much of the land of the friendly Iroquois who stayed. South Carolina dispossessed the Catawbas of most of their ancestral lands. The states had a harder time seizing the land of hostile Indians, who usually had Spanish or British allies nearby.

Secessionist movements arose in the 1780s when neither Congress nor eastern state governments seemed able to solve western problems. Some Tennessee settlers seceded from North Carolina and for a time maintained a separate state called Franklin. and separatist sentiment ran strong in Kentucky. The settlers of western Pennsylvania also thought of setting up on their own after Spain closed the Mississippi to American traffic in 1784. When Congress refused to recognize Vermont's independence from New York, even the radical Green Mountain Boys sounded out Canadian officials about readmission to the British empire as a separate province.

THE NORTHWEST ORDINANCE

After Virginia ceded its land claims north of the Ohio River to Congress, other states followed suit. In the Land Ordinance of 1785, Congress authorized the survey of the Northwest Territory and its division into townships 6 miles square, each composed of 36 "sections" of 640 acres. Surveyed land would be sold at auction starting at a dollar an acre. Alternate townships would be sold in sections or as a whole, to satisfy settlers and speculators, respectively.

In July 1787, while the Constitutional Convention met in Philadelphia, Congress, sitting in New York, returned to the problem of governing the Northwest Territory. By then, Massachusetts veterans were organizing the Ohio Company under Manassah Cutler to obtain a huge land grant from Congress. Cutler joined forces with William Duer, a New York speculator who was organizing the Scioto Company. Together they pried from Congress 1.5 million acres for the Ohio Company veterans and an option on 5 million more acres, which the Ohio Company assigned to the Scioto Company. The Ohio Company agreed to pay Congress two installments of $500,000 in depreciated securities. Once again speculators, rather than settlers, seemed to be winning the West.

In the same month Congress passed the **Northwest Ordinance.** It authorized the creation of from 3 to 5 states, to be admitted to the Union as full equals of the original 13. Congress would appoint a governor and a council to rule until population reached 5,000. At that point, the settlers could elect an assembly empowered to pass laws, but the governor had an absolute veto. When population reached 60,000, the settlers could draft their own constitution and petition Congress for statehood. The ordinance protected civil liberties, provided for public education, and prohibited slavery in the territory.

Southern delegates all voted for the Northwest Ordinance despite its antislavery clause. They probably hoped that Ohio would become what Georgia had been in the 1730s, a society of armed free men able to protect a vulnerable slave state, this time Kentucky, from hostile invaders. Southern delegates also thought that most settlers would come from Maryland, Virginia, and Kentucky. Even if they could not bring slaves with them, they would have southern loyalties. New Englanders, by contrast, were counting on the Ohio Company to lure their own veterans to the region. Finally, the antislavery clause may have been part of a larger "Compromise of 1787," involving both the ordinance and the clauses on slavery in the federal Constitution. The Philadelphia Convention permitted states to count three-fifths of their slaves for purposes of representation. The antislavery concession to northerners in the ordinance was made at the same time that southern states won this concession in Philadelphia. Several congressmen were also delegates to the Constitutional Convention and traveled back and forth between the two cities while these decisions were being made. They may have struck a deal.

QUICK   REVIEW

THE REVOLUTION TRANSFORMS MANY ASPECTS OF AMERICAN SOCIETY

- Disestablishment of the Church of England and the expansion of religious freedom, even for Catholics and Jews

- Northern states emancipated their slaves, most through a gradual process

- The softening of patriarchy and the growth of female literacy

- Westward expansion, settler discontent, and the threat of separatism

- Congress responded with the Northwest Ordinance of 1787

Northwest Ordinance *This ordinance established the Northwest Territory between the Ohio River and the Great Lakes. Adopted by the Confederation Congress in 1787, it abolished slavery in the territory and provided that it be divided into 3 to 5 states that would eventually be admitted to the Union as full equals of the original 13.*

Map 6.4

WESTERN LAND CLAIMS DURING THE REVOLUTION. *One of the most difficult questions that Congress faced was the competing western land claims of several states. After Virginia ceded its claims north of the Ohio to Congress, other states followed suit, creating the national domain and what soon became the Northwest Territory.*

View an animated version of this map or related maps at
http://history.wadsworth.com/murrinconcise4e.

Congress had developed a coherent western policy, but when the first townships in Ohio were offered for sale in late 1787, there were few buyers. The Northwest Territory was too dangerous. Yet by 1789, the Ohio Company had established the town of Marietta, Kentuckians had founded a town that would soon be called Cincinnati, and tiny outposts had been set up at Columbia and Gallipolis. But without strong sup-

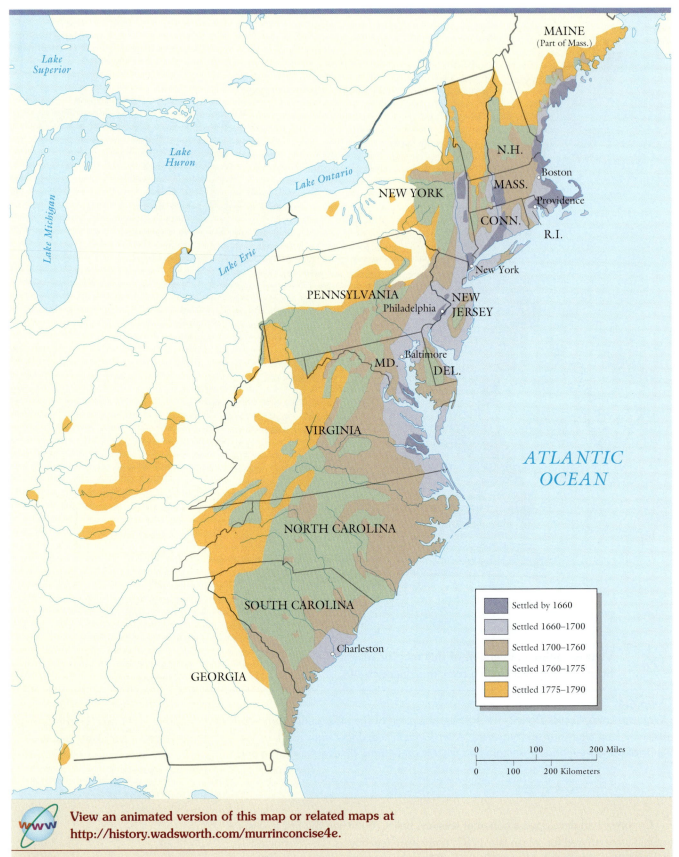

Settled by 1660
Settled 1660–1700
Settled 1700–1760
Settled 1760–1775
Settled 1775–1790

0   100   200 Miles
0   100   200 Kilometers

View an animated version of this map or related maps at
http://history.wadsworth.com/murrinconcise4e.

Map 6.5

ADVANCE OF SETTLEMENT TO 1790. *Between 1760 and 1790, America's population grew from nearly 1.6 million to almost 4 million. The area of settlement was spreading west of Pittsburgh and into much of Kentucky and parts of Tennessee.*

port from the new federal government, the settlers would have little chance of defending themselves against Indian resistance.

A MORE PERFECT UNION

The 1780s were difficult times. The economy failed to rebound, debtors fought creditors, and state politics became bitter and contentious. Out of this ferment arose the demand to amend or even replace the Articles of Confederation.

COMMERCE, DEBT, AND SHAYS'S REBELLION

In 1784 British merchants flooded American markets with exports worth £3.7 million, the greatest volume since 1771. But Americans could not pay for them. Exports to Britain that year were £750,000—less than half of the £1.9 million of 1774. When Britain invoked the Navigation Acts to close the British West Indies to American ships (but not to American goods), indirect returns through this once profitable channel also faltered. Trade with France closed some of the gap, but because the French could not offer the long-term credit that the British had provided, it remained disappointing. The American economy entered a deep depression. Private debts became a huge social problem. Merchants, dunned by British creditors, sued their customers. Farmers, faced with the loss of their farms, resisted foreclosures and looked to their state governments for relief.

About half the states issued paper money, and many passed **stay laws** to postpone the date on which a debt would come due. Massachusetts rejected both options and raised taxes to new highs. In 1786 many farmers in Hampshire County took matters into their own hands. Crowds gathered to prevent the courts from conducting business. In early 1787 the protestors, loosely organized under a Continental Army veteran, Captain Daniel Shays, threatened the federal arsenal at Springfield. Benjamin Lincoln led a volunteer army armed with artillery and scattered the Shaysites. Yet, in the May elections, Shaysites won enough seats to pass a stay law. **Shays's Rebellion** converted into nationalists many gentlemen and artisans who until then had opposed strengthening the central government.

COSMOPOLITANS VERSUS LOCALISTS

The tensions racking Massachusetts surfaced elsewhere as well. Debtors in other states closed law courts or even besieged the legislature. State politics reflected a persistent cleavage between "cosmopolitan" and "localist" coalitions. Merchants, urban artisans, most printers, commercial farmers, southern planters, and former Continental Army officers made up the cosmopolitan bloc. They favored aggressive trade policies, hard money, payment of public debts, good salaries for executive officials and judges, and leniency to returning loyalists. The "localists" were farmers, rural artisans, and militia veterans who distrusted those policies. They demanded paper money, debtor relief, and generous salaries for representatives so that ordinary men could afford to serve.

In most states, localists defeated their opponents most of the time. During and after the war, they destroyed the feudal revival (see Chapter 5) by confiscating the gigantic land claims of the Granville District, the Fairfax estate, the Calvert and Penn proprietaries, and the manorial estates of New York loyalists. Except in Ver-

stay laws *Laws that delay or postpone something. During the 1780s many states passed stay laws to delay the due date on debts because of the serious economic problems of the times.*

Shays's Rebellion *An uprising of farmers in western Massachusetts in the winter 1786–1787. They objected to high taxes and foreclosures for unpaid debts. Militia from eastern Massachusetts suppressed the rebels.*

mont, localists were much less adept at blocking the claims of land speculators. Yet cosmopolitans lost so often that many of them despaired of state politics and looked increasingly to a strengthened central government for relief. Congress also faced severe fiscal problems. Its annual income had fallen to $400,000, but interest on its debt approached $2.5 million, and the principal on the foreign debt was about to come due.

Foreign relations also took an ominous turn. In 1786 Foreign Secretary John Jay negotiated a treaty with Don Diego de Gardoqui, the Spanish minister to the United States. It offered northern merchants trading privileges with Spanish colonies in exchange for closure of the Mississippi to American traffic for 25 years. Seven northern states voted for it, but all 5 southern states in Congress rejected these terms, thus defeating the treaty, which needed 9 votes for ratification under the Articles of Confederation. Angry talk of disbanding the Union soon filled Congress. Delegates began haggling over which state would join what union if the breakup occurred.

By the mid-1780s many cosmopolitans were becoming nationalists eager to strengthen the Union. In 1785 some of them tried to see what could be done outside Congress. To resolve disputes about navigation rights on the Potomac River, Washington invited Virginia and Maryland delegates to a conference at Mount Vernon, where they drafted an agreement acceptable to both states. Prompted by James Madison, the Virginia legislature urged all the states to participate in a convention at Annapolis to explore ways to improve American trade.

Four states, including Maryland, ignored the call, and the New Englanders had not yet arrived when, in September 1786, the delegates from the 4 middle states and Virginia accepted a report drafted by Alexander Hamilton of New York. It asked all the states to send delegates to a convention at Philadelphia the next May "to devise such further provisions as shall appear to them necessary to render the constitution of the Federal Government adequate to the exigencies of the Union." Seven states responded positively before Congress endorsed the convention on February 21, 1787, and 5 accepted later. Rhode Island refused to participate.

THE PHILADELPHIA CONVENTION

The convention opened in May 1787 with a plan similar to the Virginia constitution of 1776. It proposed an almost sovereign Parliament for the United States. By September the delegates had produced a document much closer to the Massachusetts constitution of 1780, with a clear separation of powers. The delegates, in four months of secret sessions, repeated the constitutional learning process that had taken four years to unfold at the state level after 1776.

With Washington presiding, Governor Edmund Randolph proposed the Virginia, or "large state," Plan. Drafted by Madison, it proposed a bicameral legislature, with representation in both houses apportioned according to population. The legislature would choose the executive and the judiciary. It would possess all powers currently lodged in Congress and the power "to legislate in all cases to which the separate States are incompetent." It could "negative all laws passed by the several States, contravening in {its} opinion . . . the articles of Union." Remarkably, the plan did not include explicit powers to tax or regulate trade.

Within two weeks, the delegates agreed on 3-year terms for members of the lower house and 7-year terms for the upper house. The legislature would choose the executive for a single term of seven years. But in mid-June delegates from the small states struck back. William Paterson proposed the New Jersey Plan, which gave the existing Congress the power to levy import duties and a stamp tax (as in Grenville's imperial reforms of 1764 and 1765), to regulate trade, and to use force to collect delinquent requisitions from the states (as in North's Conciliatory Proposition of 1775). As under the Articles, each state would have one vote.

As another alternative, perhaps designed to terrify the small states, Hamilton suggested a government in which both the senate and the executive would serve "on good behavior"— that is, for life! To him, the British constitution still seemed the best in the world. But he never formally proposed his plan.

All the options before the convention seemed counterrevolutionary at that point. But as the summer progressed, the delegates asked themselves what the voters would or would not accept and relearned the hard lessons of popular sovereignty that the state constitutions had taught. The result was a federal Constitution that was indeed revolutionary.

Before the Constitution took its final shape, however, the debate grew as hot as the summer weather. The small states warned that their voters would never accept a constitution that let the large states swallow them. The large states insisted on proportional representation in both houses. Then the Connecticut delegates announced that they would be happy with proportional representation in one house and state equality in the other.

In July, the delegates accepted this "Connecticut Compromise" and then completed the document by September. They finally realized that they were creating a government of laws, to be enforced on individuals through federal courts, and were not propping up a system of congressional resolutions to be carried out (or ignored) by the states. Terms for representatives were reduced to two years, and terms for senators to six, with each state legislature choosing two senators. The president would serve four years, could be reelected, and would be chosen by an **Electoral College**. Each state received as many electors as it had congressmen and senators combined, and the states were free to decide how to choose their electors.

In other provisions, free and slave states agreed to count only three-fifths of the slaves in apportioning both representation and direct taxes. The enumeration of congressional powers became lengthy and explicit and included taxation, the regulation of foreign and interstate commerce, and the catchall "necessary and proper" clause. Madison's negative on state laws was replaced by the gentler "supreme law of the land" clause. Over George Mason's last-minute objection, the delegates decided not to include a bill of rights.

With little debate, the convention approved a revolutionary proposal for ratifying the Constitution. This clause called for special conventions in each state and declared that the Constitution would go into force as soon as any 9 states had accepted it, even though the Articles of Confederation required unanimous approval for all amendments. The delegates were proposing an illegal but peaceful overthrow of the existing legal order—that is, a revolution. If all the states approved, it would, they hoped, become both peaceful and legal. The Constitution would then rest on popular sovereignty in a way that the Articles never had. The **Federalists,** as supporters of the Constitution now called themselves, were willing to risk destroying the Union in order to save it.

RATIFICATION

When the Federalist delegates returned home, they made a powerful case for the Constitution in newspapers. Most "Anti-Federalists," or opponents of the Constitution, were localists with little access to the press. The first ratifying conventions met in December. Delaware ratified unanimously on December 7, Pennsylvania by a

Electoral College *The group that elects the president. Each state receives as many electors as it has congressmen and senators combined and can decide how to choose its electors. Every elector votes for two candidates, one of whom has to be from another state.*

Federalists *Supporters of the Constitution during the ratification process. Anti-Federalists resisted ratification.*

QUICK   REVIEW

ECONOMIC AND POLITICAL FERMENT IN THE 1780s LEADS TO A NEW CENTRAL GOVERNMENT

- Economic depression, private debts, and heavy taxes provoked Shays's Rebellion in Massachusetts

- Political tensions pitted cosmopolitans against localists at the state level

- Philadelphia Convention drafted federal Constitution that assumed only the people have sovereign power

- After 11 states ratified, new government was organized, and North Carolina and Rhode Island ratified by 1790

46-to-23 vote five days later, and New Jersey unanimously on December 18. Georgia ratified unanimously on January 2, and Connecticut soon approved, also by a lopsided margin.

Except in Pennsylvania, these victories were in small states. Once they had equality in the Senate, they saw many advantages in a strong central government. Under the new Constitution, import duties would go to the federal government, not to neighboring states, a clear gain for every small state but Rhode Island, which stood to lose import duties at both Providence and Newport. By contrast, Pennsylvania was the only large state with a solid majority for ratification. But Anti-Federalists there eloquently demanded a federal bill of rights and major changes in the structure of the new government. Large states could think of going it alone. Most small states could not.

The first hotly contested state was Massachusetts. Federalists won there by a slim margin (187 to 168) in February 1788. They blocked Anti-Federalist attempts to make ratification conditional on the adoption of specific amendments. Instead they won their slim majority by promising to support a bill of rights through constitutional amendment after ratification. The Rhode Island legislature refused even to summon a ratifying convention. Maryland and South Carolina ratified easily in April and May, bringing the total to 8 of the 9 states required. Then conventions met almost simultaneously in New Hampshire, Virginia, New York, and North Carolina. In each, a majority at first opposed ratification.

As resistance stiffened, the ratification controversy turned into the first great debate on what kind of a national government America ought to have. The Anti-Federalists argued that the new government would be too remote from the people to be trusted with the broad powers specified in the Constitution. They warned that in a House of Representatives divided into districts of 30,000 people (twice the size of Boston), only prominent and wealthy men would be elected and the new government would become an aristocracy or oligarchy. The absence of a bill of rights also troubled them.

During the struggle over ratification, Hamilton, Madison, and Jay wrote a series of 85 essays, published first in New York newspapers and widely reprinted elsewhere, in which they defended the Constitution almost clause by clause. Signing themselves "Publius," they later published the collected essays as *The Federalist.* In *Federalist No. Ten,* Madison challenged 2,000 years of received wisdom when he argued that a large republic would be far more stable than a small one. Small republics were inherently unstable, he insisted, because majority factions could easily gain power, trample upon the rights of minorities, and ignore the common good. But in a republic as huge and diverse as the United States, factions would seldom be able to forge a majority. "Publius" hoped that the new government would attract the talents of the wisest and best-educated citizens. To those accusing him of trying to erect an American aristocracy, he pointed out that the Constitution forbade titles and hereditary rule.

Federalists won a narrow majority (57 to 46) in New Hampshire on June 21, and Madison guided Virginia to ratification (89 to 79) five days later. New York approved, by 30 votes to 27, a month later, bringing 11 states into the Union, enough to launch the new government. North Carolina rejected the Constitution in July 1788 but finally ratified in November 1789 after the first Congress had drafted the Bill of Rights and sent it to the states. Rhode Island, after voting seven times not to call a ratifying convention, finally summoned one that ratified by a vote of only 34 to 32 in May 1790.

C O N C L U S I O N

Americans survived the most devastating war they had yet fought and won their independence, but only with massive aid from France. Most blacks and Indians sided with Britain. During the struggle white Americans affirmed liberty and equality for themselves in their new state constitutions and bills of rights, but they rarely applied these values to blacks and Indians, even though every northern state adopted either immediate or gradual emancipation. The discontent of the postwar years created the Federalist coalition, which drafted and ratified a new national Constitution to replace the Articles of Confederation. Nothing resembling the American federal system had ever been tried before. Under it, sovereignty was removed from government and bestowed on the people, who then empowered separate levels of government through their state and federal constitutions. As the Great Seal of the United States proclaimed, it was a *novus ordo seclorum,* a new order for the ages.

QUESTIONS FOR REVIEW AND CRITICAL THINKING

Review

1. How did American constitutionalism after 1776 differ from the British constitutional principles that the colonists had accepted and revered before 1776?
2. Why, given that the Declaration of Independence proclaimed that "all men are created equal," did most Indians and blacks, when given the choice, side with Britain?
3. Why did racist hatred of Indians reach new levels of intensity at a time when Indians were reducing their cultural differences with the settlers, as in their increasing rejection of torture?
4. In what ways did the values shared by independent householders limit the reforms that the Revolution could offer to other Americans?

Critical Thinking

1. The Articles of Confederation favored small states, especially in giving each state one vote in Congress. Why then did large states ratify quickly while three small states held up final ratification for years? The Constitution shifted power to large states. Why then did most small states ratify quickly while every large state except Pennsylvania came close to rejecting the new government?
2. The federal Constitution dramatically increased the power of the central government of the United States. What about liberty and equality? Did it make them more secure, or did it sacrifice part of one or both in order to empower the new government?

Discovery

Winning the War for Independence and solidifying the changes unleashed by the American Revolution were two different projects. In what ways did America change following the Revolution? What impact did this have on America's future?

SUGGESTED READINGS

Stephen Conway's The War of American Independence, 1775–1783 (1995) is a recent history that is strong and accessible. **Charles Royster's A Revolutionary People at War: The Continental Army and American Character, 1775–1783** (1979) is the best study of its kind. The essays in **John Shy's A People Numerous and Armed: Reflections on the Military Struggle for American Independence,** rev. ed. (1990) have had a tremendous influence on other historians. **David Hackett Fischer's Washington's Crossing** (2004) is the most important book on the Revolutionary War to appear in several decades. **Walter Edgar's Partisans and Redcoats: The Southern Conflict That Turned the Tide of the American Revolution** (2001) is a fresh study of the bitter partisan war in the Lower South. For the war's impact on slavery, see **Sylvia R. Frey, Water from the Rock: Black Resistance in a Revolutionary Age** (1991). **Henry Wiencek's An Imperfect God: George Washington, His Slaves, and the Creation of America** (2003) is a superb study of how and why Washington chose to emancipate his slaves. Of the numerous studies of loyalism, **Paul H. Smith's Loyalists and**

Redcoats: A Study in British Revolutionary Policy (1964) remains one of the best.

The single most important book on emerging American constitutionalism remains **Gordon S. Wood, *The Creation of the American Republic, 1776–1787*** (1969). **Jackson Turner Main's *Political Parties Before the Constitution*** (1973) carefully investigates post-war divisions within the states. **Jack N. Rakove** won a Pulitzer Prize for ***Original Meanings: Politics and Ideas in the Making of the Constitution*** (1996). **Saul Cornell** provides a thoughtful approach to ***The Other Founders: Anti-Federalism and the Dissenting Tradition in America*** (1999).

ONLINE SOURCES GUIDE

ThomsonNOW   Visit ThomsonNOW to access primary sources, exercises, quizzes, and audio chapter summaries related to this chapter:
http://www.thomsonedu.com/login

DISCOVERY

Winning the War for Independence and solidifying the changes unleashed by the American Revolution were two different projects. In what ways did America change following the Revolution? What impact did this have on America's future?

In thinking about this question, begin by breaking it down into the components shown below. A discussion of the significance of each component should appear in your answer.

GEOGRAPHY

Look at the map concerning western land claims. What problems are apparent in the new territories? How did claims to those lands impede the work of an American government? On what basis were those claims made? What areas might cause the most problems for the new government? Look at the map concerning settlement patterns. In which western territories was settlement occurring most rapidly? From where do you think those settlers were coming? In what ways do you think patterns of settlement might have affected the balance of territory and population between North and South in the first fifty years of the nineteenth century?

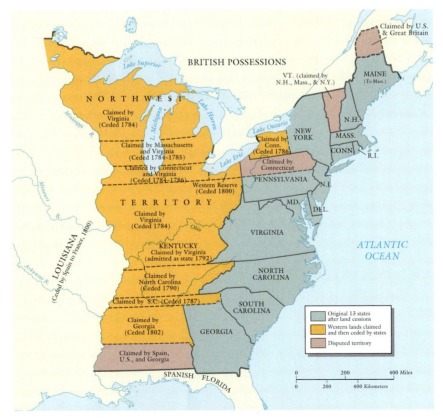

WESTERN LAND CLAIMS DURING THE REVOLUTION

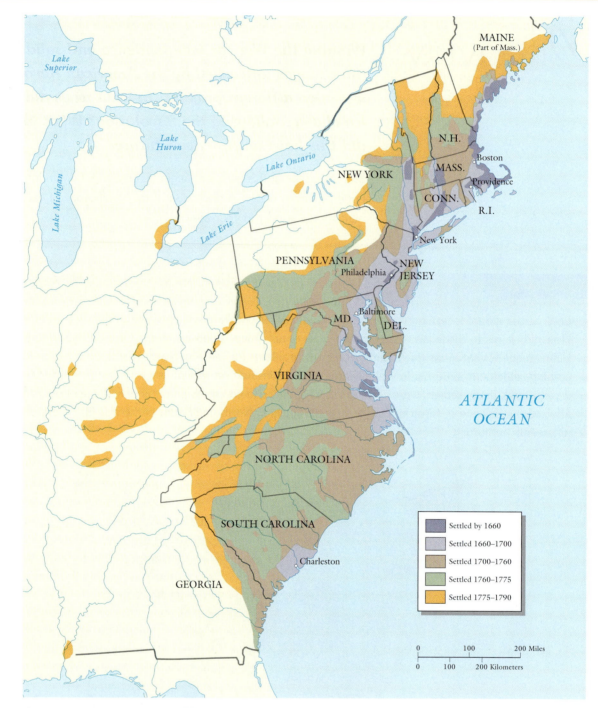

Legend:
- Settled by 1660
- Settled 1660–1700
- Settled 1700–1760
- Settled 1760–1775
- Settled 1775–1790

ADVANCE OF SETTLEMENT TO 1790

THE DEMOCRATIC REPUBLIC, 1790–1820

In 1789 Americans were an overwhelmingly rural people. Some were planters who sent crops onto world markets. Most, however, owned small farms. Whatever their level of prosperity, most American households were headed by men who owned land and who enjoyed the liberty and civil equality for which they had fought the revolution. They also wielded power—both as citizens and as governors of families that included their wives, children, slaves, and other dependents.

In the first 30 years of government under the Constitution, Americans consolidated their republic and expanded their commerce with a war-torn Europe. In these years their population shot from 4 million to 10 million people; their agrarian republic spilled across the Appalachians and reached the Mississippi River; and their seaport towns became cities. In the midst of this rapid change, increasing thousands of white men found it hard to maintain their status as propertied citizens or to pass that status on to new generations; others simply grew impatient with the responsibilities and limits of rural patriarchy. The resultant erosion of authority encouraged women, slaves, and the growing ranks of propertyless white men to imagine that the revolutionary birthrights of liberty and equality—perhaps even power—might also belong to them. By 1820 the agrarian republic, with its promise of widespread proprietorship and well-ordered paternal authority, was in deep trouble. A more individualistic, democratic, and insecure order was taking its place.

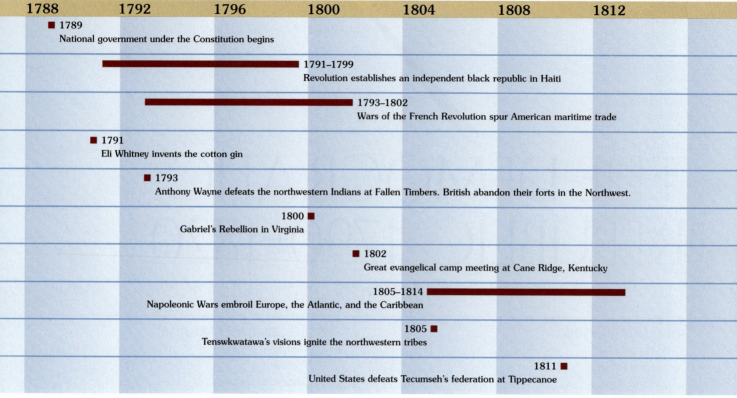

■ **1789**
National government under the Constitution begins

1791–1799
Revolution establishes an independent black republic in Haiti

1793–1802
Wars of the French Revolution spur American maritime trade

■ **1791**
Eli Whitney invents the cotton gin

■ **1793**
Anthony Wayne defeats the northwestern Indians at Fallen Timbers. British abandon their forts in the Northwest.

1800 ■
Gabriel's Rebellion in Virginia

■ **1802**
Great evangelical camp meeting at Cane Ridge, Kentucky

1805–1814
Napoleonic Wars embroil Europe, the Atlantic, and the Caribbean

1805 ■
Tenswkwatawa's visions ignite the northwestern tribes

1811 ■
United States defeats Tecumseh's federation at Tippecanoe

THE FARMER'S REPUBLIC

FOCUS QUESTION

What was the nature of the American agricultural economy and of agricultural society in the years 1790–1820?

backcountry *Term used in the 18th and early 19th centuries to refer to the western settlements and the supposed misfits who lived in them.*

competence *Understood in the early republic as the ability to live up to neighborhood economic standards while protecting the long-term independence of the household.*

In 1782 J. Hector St. John de Crèvecoeur, a French soldier who had settled in rural New York, explained American agrarianism through the words of a fictionalized farmer. First of all, he said, the American farmer owns his own land and bases his claim to dignity and citizenship on that fact: "This formerly rude soil has been converted by my father into a pleasant farm, and in return, it has established all our rights; on it is founded our rank, our freedom, our power as citizens, our importance as inhabitants of [a rural neighborhood]. . . ." Second, farm ownership endows the American farmer with the powers and responsibilities of fatherhood: "I am now doing for [my son] what my father did for me; may God enable him to live that he may perform the same operations for the same purposes when I am worn out and old!"

From New England through the mid-Atlantic and on into the southern Piedmont and **backcountry**, few farmers in 1790 thought of farming as a business. Their first concern was to provide a subsistence for their households. Their second was to achieve long-term security and the ability to pass their farm on to their sons. The goal was to create what rural folks called a **competence**: the ability to live up to neighborhood standards of material decency while protecting the long-term independence of their household—and thus the dignity and political rights of its head. Most of these farmers raised a variety of animals and plants, ate most of what they grew, traded much of the rest within their neighborhoods, and sent surpluses into outside markets.

The world's hunger for American food, however, was growing. West Indian and European markets for American meat and grain expanded dramatically between 1793 and 1815, when war disrupted farming in Europe. American farmers took advantage of these markets, but most continued to rely on family and neighbors for subsistence and risked little by sending increased surpluses overseas. Thus they profited from world markets without becoming dependent on them.

HOUSEHOLDS

Production for overseas markets did, however, alter rural households. Farm labor in postrevolutionary America was carefully divided by sex. Men worked in the fields, and production for markets both intensified that labor and made it more exclusively male. In the grain fields, for instance, the long-handled scythe was replacing the sickle as the principal harvest tool. Women could use the sickle efficiently, but the long, heavy scythe was designed to be wielded by men. At the same time, farmers completed the substitution of plows for hoes as the principal cultivating tools—not only because plows worked better but because rural Americans had developed a prejudice against women working in the fields.

At the same time, household responsibilities fell more exclusively to women. Farmwomen's labor and ingenuity helped create a more varied and nutritious rural diet in these years. Bread and salted meat were still the staples. The bread was the old mix of Indian corn and coarse wheat. A variety of other foods were now available, however. By the 1790s, improved winter feeding for cattle and better techniques for making and storing butter and cheese kept dairy products on the tables of the more prosperous farm families throughout the year. Chickens became more common, and farmwomen began to plant potatoes, turnips, cabbages, squashes, beans, and other vegetables that could be stored.

RURAL INDUSTRY

Industrial outwork provided many farmers with another means of protecting their independence. From the 1790s onward, city merchants provided country workers with raw materials and paid them for finished shoes, furniture, cloth, brooms, and other handmade goods. In Marple, Pennsylvania, a farming town near Philadelphia, fully one-third of households were engaged in weaving, furniture making, and other **household industry** in the 1790s.

Most of the outwork was taken on by large, relatively poor families, with the work organized in ways that shored up the authority of fathers. When New Hampshire women and girls fashioned hats, for example, the accounts were kept in the name of the husband or father. In general, household industry was part-time work performed only by the dependent women and children of the household. And when it was the family's principal means of support, the work was arranged in ways that supported traditional notions of fatherhood and proprietorship. In eastern Massachusetts in the 1790s, for instance, when thousands of farmers on small plots of worn-out land became household shoemakers, skilled men cut the leather and shaped the uppers, while the more menial tasks of sewing and binding were left to the women.

NEIGHBORS

Few farmers possessed the tools, the labor, and the food they would have needed to be truly independent. They regularly worked for one another, borrowed oxen and plows, and swapped surpluses of one kind of food for another. Women traded ashes,

household industry *Work such as converting raw materials into finished products done by women and children to provide additional household income.*

HISTORY THROUGH FILM

A MIDWIFE'S TALE

Directed by Richard D. Rodgers (PBS)

The historian Laurel Thatcher Ulrich's *A Midwife's Tale* won the Pulitzer Prize for history and biography in 1991. Shortly thereafter, the Public Broadcasting System turned the book into a documentary movie—a close and imaginative analysis of the diary of Martha Ballard, a Maine farmwoman and midwife of the late 18th and early 19th centuries. Events are acted out on screen, and period modes of dress, housing, gardening, washing, coffin making, spinning and weaving, and other details are reconstructed with labored accuracy. The viewer hears the sounds of footfalls, horses, handlooms, and dishes, but the only human sounds are an occasional cough, exclamation, or drinking song. The principal narrative is carried by an actress who reads passages from the diary, and Thatcher occasionally breaks in to explain her own experiences with the di-

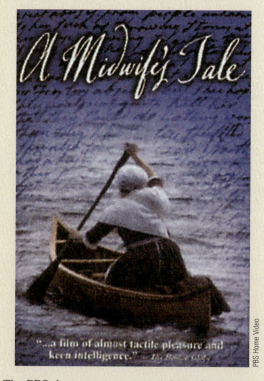

PBS Home Video

The PBS documentary movie A Midwife's Tale *is based on the Pulitzer Prize–winning book of the same name by historian Laurel Thatcher Ulrich.*

ary and its interpretation. The result is a documentary film that knows the difference between dramatizing history and making it up. It also dramatizes the ways in which a skilled and sensitive historian goes about her work. Martha Ballard was a midwife in a town on the Kennebec River. She began keeping a daily diary at the age of 50 in 1785 and continued until 1812. Most of the film is about her daily life: delivering babies, nursing the sick, helping neighbors, keeping house, raising and supervising the labor of her daughters and niece, gardening, and tending cattle and turkeys. In both the book and the film, the busyness of an ordinary woman's days—and a sense of her possibilities and limits—in the early republic comes through in exhausting detail. The dailiness of her life is interrupted only occasionally by an event: a fire at her husband's sawmill, an epidemic of scarlet fever, a parade organized to honor the death of George Washington, the rape of a minister's wife by his enemies (including the local judge, who is set free), and a neighbor's inexplicable murder of his wife and six children.

There is also the process of getting old. At the beginning, Martha Ballard is the busy wife in a well-run household. As she ages and her children leave to set up households of their own, Ballard hires local girls who—perhaps because an increasingly democratic culture has made them less subservient than Ballard would like, perhaps because Ballard is growing old and impatient, perhaps both—tend to be surly. Her husband, a surveyor who works for merchants speculating in local land, is attacked twice in the woods by squatters, and spends a year and a half in debtor's jail—not for his own debts but because, as tax collector, he failed to collect enough. While the husband is in jail and his aging wife struggles to keep the house going, their son moves his own family into the house and Martha is moved into a single room and is made to feel unwanted, a poignant and unsentimental case of the strained relations between generations that historians have discovered in the early republic.

A Midwife's Tale is a modest film that comes as close to a thorough and imaginative historian and a good filmmaker can to recreating the texture of lived experience in the northeastern countryside at the beginning of the 19th century. Students who enjoy the movie should go immediately to the book.

herbs, butter and eggs, vegetables, seedlings, baby chicks, goose feathers, and the products of their spinning wheels and looms. Some cooperative undertakings—house building, barn-raisings, and husking bees, for example—brought the whole neighborhood together, transforming a chore into a pleasant social event.

Few neighborhood transactions called for the use of money. In New England, farmers kept careful accounts of neighborhood debts. In the South and West, on the other hand, farmers used a **changing system** in which they simply remembered what they owed. Yet farmers everywhere relied more on barter than on cash. A French visitor noted that:

> [Americans] supply their needs in the countryside by direct reciprocal exchanges. The tailor and the bootmaker go and do their work at the home of the farmer . . . who most frequently provides the raw material for it and pays for the work in goods. They write down what they give and receive on both sides, and at the end of the year they settle a large variety of exchanges with a very small quantity of coin." The result was an elaborate network of neighborhood debt, which was part of a highly structured and absolutely necessary system of neighborly cooperation.

INHERITANCE

After 1790 overcrowding and the growth of markets caused the price of good farmland to rise sharply throughout the older settlements. Most young men could expect to inherit only a few acres of exhausted land or to move to wilderness land in the backcountry. Failing those, they would quit farming altogether.

In revolutionary America, fathers had been judged by their ability to support and govern their households, to serve as good neighbors, and to pass land on to their sons. After the war, fewer farm fathers were able to do that. Those in the old settlements had small farms and large families, which made it impossible for them to provide a competence for all their offspring. Sons, with no prospect of an adequate inheritance, were obliged to leave home. Most fathers tried valiantly to provide for all their heirs (generally by leaving land to their sons and personal property to their daughters). Few left all their land to one son, and many stated in their wills that the sons to whom they left the land must share barns and cider mills—even the house—on farms that could be subdivided no further.

Outside New England, farm **tenancy** was on the increase. Farmers often bought farms when they became available in the neighborhood, rented them to tenants, and then gave them to their sons when they reached adulthood. The sons of poorer farmers often rented a farm in the hope of saving enough money to buy it. Some fathers bought tracts of unimproved land in the backcountry—sometimes on speculation, more often to provide their sons with land they could make into a farm. Others paid to have their sons educated or arranged an apprenticeship to provide them with an avenue of escape from a declining countryside. As a result, more and more young men left home. The populations of the old farming communities grew older and more female, while the populations of the rising frontier settlements and seaport cities became younger and more male.

STANDARDS OF LIVING

The rise of markets in the late 18th and early 19th centuries improved living standards for some families but not for all. Most farmhouses in the older rural areas were small, one-story structures. Few farmers, especially in the South and West, bothered

QUICK   REVIEW

FARMING HOUSEHOLDS IN 1790

- Grew mixed array of plants and animals

- Used their produce to feed their families and trade with neighbors

- Organized their families along patriarchal lines

changing system *Elaborate system of neighborhood debts and bartering used primarily in the South and West where little cash money was available.*

tenancy *System under which farmers worked land that they did not own.*

THE DINING ROOM OF DR. WHIT-BRIDGE, A RHODE ISLAND COUNTRY DOCTOR, CIRCA 1815. *It is a comfortable, neatly furnished room, but there is little decoration, and the doctor must sit near the fire in layered clothing to ward off the morning chill.*

Old Dartmouth Historical Society/New Bedford Whaling Museum

to keep their surroundings clean or attractive. They repaired their fences only when they became too dilapidated to function. They rarely planted trees or shrubs, and housewives threw out garbage to feed the chickens and pigs that foraged near the house.

Inside, there were few rooms and many people. Beds stood in every room, and few family members slept alone. The hearth remained the source of heat and light in most farmhouses. One of the great disparities between wealthy families and their less affluent neighbors was that the wealthy families could light their houses at night. Another disparity was in the outward appearance of houses. The wealthier families painted their houses white as a token of pristine republicanism. But their bright houses stood apart from the weathered gray-brown clapboard siding of their neighbors in stark and unrepublican contrast.

Some improvements emerged in personal comfort. As time passed more beds had mattresses stuffed with feathers. At mealtimes, only the poorest families continued to eat with their fingers or with spoons from a common bowl. By 1800 individual place settings with knives and forks and china plates, along with chairs instead of benches, had become common in rural America. Although only the wealthiest families had upholstered furniture, ready-made chairs were widely available, and clocks appeared in the more prosperous rural households.

FROM BACKCOUNTRY TO FRONTIER

FOCUS QUESTION
What were the principal reasons why Indian peoples between the Appalachian Mountains and the Mississippi River gave way to white settlement?

The United States was a huge country in 1790, but most white Americans were still living on a thin strip of settlement along the Atlantic coast and along the few navigable rivers that emptied into the Atlantic. Some were pushing their way into the wilds of Maine and northern Vermont, and in New York they had set up communities as far west as the Mohawk valley. Pittsburgh was a struggling new settlement, and two outposts had been established on the Ohio River at Marietta and at what would become Cincinnati. Farther south, farmers had occupied the Piedmont lands up to the eastern slope of the Appalachians and were spilling through the Cumberland Gap into the new lands of Kentucky and Tennessee. But north of the Ohio River the Shawnee, Miami, Delaware, and Potawatomie nations, along with smaller tribes, controlled nearly all the land. To the south, the "Five Civilized Tribes" still occupied much of their ancestral land. Taken together, Indian peoples occupied most of the land that treaties and maps showed as the interior of the United States.

THE DESTRUCTION OF THE WOODLANDS INDIANS

Though many of the woodland tribes were still intact and still living on their ancestral lands in 1790, they were in serious trouble. The members of the old Iroquois Federation had been restricted to reservations in New York and Pennsylvania; many had fled to Canada. The once-powerful Cherokees had been severely punished for fighting on the side of the British during the revolution and by 1790 had ceded three-fourths of their territory to the Americans.

In the Old Northwest, the Shawnee, Miami, and other tribes—with the help of the British who still occupied seven forts within what was formally the United States—continued to trade furs and to impede white settlement. Skirmishes with settlers, however, brought reprisals, and the Indians faced not only hostile pioneers but the United States Army as well. In the Ohio country, expeditions led by General Josiah Harmar and General Arthur St. Clair failed in 1790 and 1791. In 1794 President Washington sent a third army, under General "Mad Anthony" Wayne, which defeated the Indians at Fallen Timbers, near present-day Toledo. The Treaty of Greenville forced the Native Americans to cede two-thirds of what now makes up Ohio and southeastern Indiana. At this point the British decided to abandon their forts in the Old Northwest. Whites filtered into what remained of Indian lands.

Relegated to smaller territory but still dependent on the European fur trade, the natives of the Northwest now fell into competition with settlers and other Indians for the diminishing supply of game. The Creeks, Choctaws, and other tribes of the Old Southwest faced the same problem: Even when they chased settlers out of their territory, the settlers managed to kill or scare off the deer and other wildlife, thus ruining the old hunting grounds. When the Shawnee sent hunting parties farther west, they were opposed by western Indians. The Choctaws also sent hunters across the Mississippi, where they found new sources of furs, along with the angry warriors of the Osage and other peoples of Louisiana and Arkansas.

Faced with shrinking territories, the disappearance of wildlife, and diminished opportunities to be traditional hunters and warriors, many Indian societies sank into despair. Epidemics of European diseases (smallpox, influenza, measles) attacked people who were increasingly sedentary and vulnerable. Murder and clan revenge plagued the tribes, and depression and suicide became more common. The use of alcohol, which had been a scourge on Indian societies for two centuries, increased.

THE FAILURE OF CULTURAL RENEWAL

Out of this cultural wreckage emerged visionary leaders who spoke of a regenerated native society and the expulsion of all whites. One of the first was Chief Alexander McGillivray, a mixed-blood Creek who had sided with the British during the revolution. Between 1783 and 1793, McGillivray tried to unite the Creeks under a national council that could override local chiefs, and to form alliances with other tribes and with Spanish Florida. McGillivray's premature death in 1793 prevented the realization of his vision.

The Cherokees north and east of the Creeks did succeed in making a unified state. Angered by the willingness of village chiefs to be bribed and flattered into selling land, a group of young chiefs staged a revolt between 1808 and 1810. Previously, being a Cherokee had meant loyalty to one's clan and kin group and adherence to the tribe's ancient customs. Now it meant remaining on the tribe's ancestral land (migration across the Mississippi was regarded as treason) and unquestioning acceptance of the laws, courts, and police controlled by the national council.

The Granger Collection, New York

TENSKWATAWA. *The Shawnee prophet Tenskwatawa ("The Open Door"), brother of Tecumseh, was painted by George Catlin in 1836—long after the defeat of his prophetic attempt to unify Native America.*

Tenskwatawa *Brother of Tecumseh, whose religious vision of 1805 called for the unification of Indians west of the Appalachians and foretold the defeat and disappearance of the whites.*

Tecumseh *Shawnee leader who assumed political and military leadership of the pan-Indian religious movement began by his brother Tenskwatawa.*

girdled trees *Trees with a line cut around them so sap would not rise in the spring.*

Among the many prophets who emerged during these years, the one who came closest to military success was **Tenskwatawa,** a fat, one-eyed, alcoholic Shawnee. When he went into a deep trance in 1805, the people thought he was dead and prepared his funeral. But he awoke and told them he had visited heaven and hell and had received a prophetic vision. First, all the Indians must stop drinking and fighting among themselves. They must also return to their traditional food, clothing, tools, and hairstyles, and must extinguish all their fires and start new ones without using European tools. All who opposed the new order (including local chiefs, medicine men, shamans, and witches) must be put down by force. When all that had been done, God (a monotheistic, punishing God borrowed from the Christians) would restore the world that Indians had known before the whites came over the mountains.

Tenskwatawa's message soon found its way to the native peoples of the Northwest. When converts flooded into the prophet's home village, he moved to Prophetstown (Tippecanoe) in what is now Indiana. There, with the help of his brother **Tecumseh,** he created an army estimated by the whites at anywhere between 650 and 3,000 warriors, and pledged to end further encroachment by whites. Tecumseh, who took control of the movement, announced that he was the sole chief of all the Indians north of the Ohio River; land cessions by anyone else would be invalid.

Tecumseh's confederacy posed a threat to the United States. A second war with England was looming, and Tecumseh was allied with the British in Canada. He was also planning to bring southern tribes into his confederacy. The prospect of unified resistance by the western tribes in league with the British jeopardized every settler west of the Appalachians. In 1811 William Henry Harrison led an army toward Prophetstown. With Tecumseh away, Tenskwatawa ordered an unwise attack on Harrison's army and was beaten at the Battle of Tippecanoe.

Tecumseh's still-formidable confederacy, joined by the traditionalist wing of the southern Creeks, fought alongside the British in the War of 1812 and lost (see Chapter 8). With that, the military power of the Indians east of the Mississippi River was destroyed. General Andrew Jackson forced the Creeks (including those who had served as his allies) to cede millions of acres of land in Georgia and Alabama. The other southern tribes, along with the members of Tecumseh's northern confederacy, watched helplessly as new settlers took over their hunting lands. Some of the Indians moved west, others tried to farm what was left of their old land. All of them had to deal with settlers and government officials who neither feared them nor took their sovereignty seriously.

THE BACKCOUNTRY, 1790–1815

To easterners, the backcountry whites who were displacing the Indians were no different from the defeated aborigines. Indeed, in accommodating themselves to a borderless forest used by both Indians and whites, many settlers had melded Indian and white ways. To clear the land, backcountry farmers simply **girdled** the trees and left them to die and fall down by themselves. Then they ploughed the land by navigating between the stumps. Like the Indians, backcountry whites depended on game for food and animal skins for trade. And like the Indians, they often spent long periods away on hunting trips, leaving the women to tend the fields.

Eastern visitors were appalled not only by the poverty, lice, and filth of frontier life but by the drunkenness and violence of the frontiersmen. Travel accounts tell of no-holds-barred fights in which frontiersmen gouged the eyes and bit off the noses and ears of their opponents. Stories arose of half-legendary heroes like Davy Crockett of Tennessee, who wrestled bears and alligators, and Mike Fink, a Pennsylvania boatman who brawled and drank his way along the rivers of the interior until he was shot and killed in a drunken episode. Samuel Holden Parsons, a New Englander serving as a judge in the Northwest Territory, called the frontiersmen "our white savages."

After 1789 the western backcountry made two demands of the new national government: protection from the Indians and a guarantee of the right to navigate the Ohio and Mississippi Rivers. The Indians were pushed back in the 1790s and finished off in the War of 1812, and in 1803 Jefferson's Louisiana Purchase (see Chapter 8) ended the European presence on the rivers. Over these years the pace of settlement quickened. In 1790 only 10,000 settlers were living west of the Appalachians—about 1 American in 40. By 1820, 2 million Americans were westerners—1 in 5.

The new settlers bought land, built frame houses surrounded by cleared fields, planted marketable crops, and settled into the struggle to make farms out of the wilderness. By 1803 four frontier states had entered the union: Vermont (1791), Kentucky (1792), Tennessee (1796), and Ohio (1803). Louisiana soon followed (1812), and with the end of the war in 1815 one frontier state after another gained admission: Indiana (1816), Mississippi (1817), Illinois (1818), Alabama (1818), Maine (1820), and Missouri (1821).

As time passed, the term *backcountry,* which easterners had used to refer to the wilderness, fell into disuse. By 1820 the term *frontier* had replaced it. The new settlements were no longer in the backwash of American civilization. They were its cutting edge.

THE PLANTATION SOUTH, 1790–1820

In 1790 the future of slavery in the Chesapeake was uncertain. The tobacco market had been precarious since before the revolution. Tobacco depleted the soil, and by the late 18th century tidewater farms and plantations were giving out. As lands west of the Appalachians were opened to settlement, white tenants, laborers, and small farmers left the Chesapeake in droves. Many of them moved to Kentucky, Tennessee, or the western reaches of Virginia. But many others found new homes in nonslave states north of the Ohio River.

> **FOCUS QUESTION**
>
> *In what geographic areas and in what ways did slavery expand between 1790 and 1820? In what areas (and, again, in what ways) was the slave system called into question?*

SLAVERY AND THE REPUBLIC

Chesapeake planters continued to switch to grain and livestock, and slaves became less necessary. Some planters divided their land into small plots and rented both the plots and their slaves to white tenant farmers. Others hired out their slaves as artisans and urban laborers. These solutions, however, could not employ the great mass of slaves or repay the planters' huge investment in slave labor.

In this situation many Chesapeake planters began to manumit their slaves. The farmers of Maryland and Delaware in particular set their slaves free. Virginia's economic and cultural commitment to the plantation was stronger, but there was a strong movement to manumit slaves there as well. George Washington manumitted his slaves by will. Robert Carter, reputedly the largest slaveholder in Virginia, also freed his slaves, as did many others.

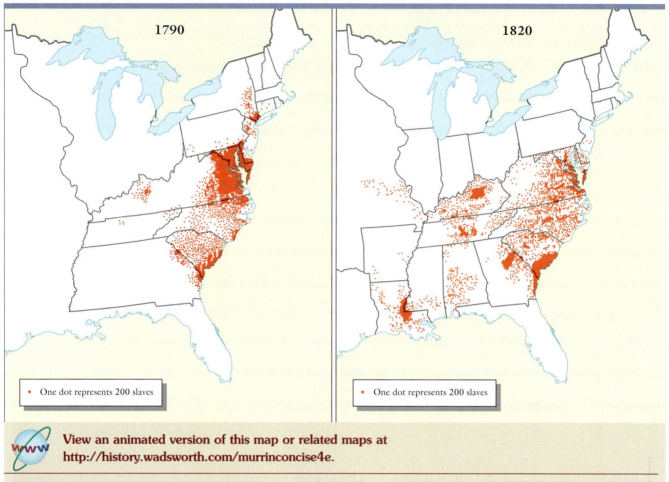

View an animated version of this map or related maps at http://history.wadsworth.com/murrinconcise4e.

Map 7.1
DISTRIBUTION OF SLAVE POPULATION, 1790–1820. *In 1790, slaves were concentrated in the Chesapeake and in the South Carolina and Georgia low country. Over the next 30 years, as a result of the decline of slave-based agriculture in Virginia and the beginnings of the cotton boom further south, Chesapeake planters were selling or freeing their slaves, whereas cotton farmers, through both the internal and international slave trade, were beginning to build a Black Belt that stretched through the interior of the Carolinas and on through the Southwest.*

There were, however, limits on the manumission of Virginia slaves. First, few planters could afford to free their slaves without compensation. Second, white Virginians feared the social consequences of black freedom. Thomas Jefferson, for instance, owned 175 slaves when he penned the phrase that "all men are created equal." He lived off their labor, sold them to pay his debts, gave them as gifts, and sometimes sold them away from their families as a punishment—all the while insisting that slavery was wrong. He could not imagine emancipation, however, without the colonization of freed slaves far from Virginia. A society of free blacks and whites, Jefferson insisted, would end in disaster.

THE RECOMMITMENT TO SLAVERY

cotton *Semitropical plant that produced white, fluffy fibers that could be made into textiles.*

Jefferson's dilemma was eased by the rise of **cotton** cultivation father south. British industrialization created a demand for cotton from the 1790s onward. But long-staple cotton, the only variety that could be profitably grown, was a delicate plant that thrived only on the Sea Islands off Georgia and South Carolina. The short-staple variety was hardier, but its sticky seeds had to be removed by hand before the cotton could be milled.

In 1793 **Eli Whitney**, a Connecticut Yankee who had come south to work as a tutor, set his mind to the problem. Within a few days he had made a model of a cotton "gin" (a southern contraction of "engine") that combed the seeds from the fiber with metal pins fitted into rollers. Working with Whitney's machine, a slave could clean 50 pounds of short-staple cotton in a day. At a stroke, cotton became the great American cash crop, and plantation agriculture was rejuvenated.

Short-staple cotton grew well in the hot, humid climate and the long growing season of the Lower South, and it grew almost anywhere. It was also a labor-intensive crop that could be grown in either small or large quantities; farmers with few or no slaves could make a decent profit, and planters with extensive land and many slaves could make enormous amounts of money. Best of all, the factories of England and, eventually, of the American Northeast had a seemingly insatiable appetite for southern cotton.

The result was the rejuvenation of plantation slavery and its rapid spread into the new cotton-growing regions of the South. Meanwhile, Chesapeake planters sold their excess slaves to planters in the cotton frontier. After 1810, most of the slaves who left Virginia were commodities in the burgeoning interstate slave trade, headed for the new plantations of Georgia, Alabama, and Mississippi.

The movement of slaves out of the Chesapeake was immense. In the 1790s about 1 in 12 Virginia and Maryland slaves was taken south and west. The figure rose to 1 in 10 between 1800 and 1810, and to 1 in 5 between 1810 and 1820. In 1790 planters in Virginia and Maryland had owned 56 percent of all American slaves; by 1860 they owned only 15 percent. The demand for slaves in the new cotton lands had thus provided many Chesapeake planters with a means of disposing of an endangered investment and with cash to pay for their transition to new crops.

The other region that had been a center of slavery during the 18th century—coastal South Carolina and Georgia—made a massive recommitment to slave labor in the years after the revolution. There the principal crop was rice, which was experiencing a sharp rise in international demand. For their secondary crop, most planters in this region were switching from indigo (a source of blue dye) to cotton, creating an increase in the demand for slaves. With slave prices rising and slave-produced crops becoming steadily more profitable, they rushed to import as many African slaves as they could before the African slave trade ended in 1808. Between 1788 and 1808, some 250,000 slaves were brought directly from Africa to the United States, nearly all of them to Charleston and Savannah.

RACE, GENDER, AND CHESAPEAKE LABOR

The transition to grain and livestock raising in the Chesapeake and the rise of the cotton belt in the Lower South imposed new kinds of labor upon the slaves. Wheat cultivation, for example, meant a switch from the hoes used for tobacco to the plow and grain cradle—both of which called for the upper-body strength of adult men. The grain economy also required carts, wagons, mills, and good roads and thus created a need for greater numbers of slave artisans, nearly all of whom were men. Many of these were hired out to urban employers. In the diversifying economy of the Chesapeake, male slaves did the plowing, mowing, sowing, ditching, and carting and performed most of the tasks requiring artisanal skills.

Slave women were left with all the lesser tasks. A few of them were assigned to such chores as cloth manufacture, sewing, candle molding, and the preparation of salt meat. But most female slaves still did farm work—hoeing, weeding, spreading manure, clean-

Eli Whitney *The Connecticut-born tutor who invented the cotton gin.*

Collection of the Maryland Historical Society, Baltimore

AN OVERSEER DOING HIS DUTY. *In 1798 the architect and engineer Benjamin Latrobe sketched a white overseer smoking a cigar and supervising slave women as they hoed newly cleared farmland near Fredricksburg, Virginia. A critic of slavery, Latrobe sarcastically entitled the sketch* An Overseer Doing His Duty.

ing stables—that was monotonous, called for little skill, and was closely supervised. This new division of labor was clearly evident during the wheat harvest. On George Washington's farm, for example, male slaves, often working alongside temporary white laborers, moved in a broad line as they mowed the grain. Following them came a gang of children and women bent over and moving along on their hands and knees as they bound wheat into shocks.

THE LOWLAND TASK SYSTEM

On the rice and cotton plantations of South Carolina and Georgia, planters faced different labor problems. Slaves made up 80 percent of the population in this region. Farms were large, and the two principal crops demanded skilled, intensive labor. The environment encouraged deadly summer diseases and kept white owners and overseers out of the fields. Planters solved these problems by organizing slaves according to the so-called "task system." Each morning the owner or overseer assigned a specific task to each slave and allowed him to work at his own pace. When the task was done, the rest of the day belonged to the slave. Slaves who did not finish their task were punished, and when too many slaves finished early, the owners assigned heavier tasks.

The task system encouraged slaves to work hard without supervision, and they turned the system to their own uses. Often several slaves would work together until all their tasks were completed. And strong young slaves would sometimes help older and weaker slaves after they had finished their own tasks. Once the day's work was done, the slaves would share their hard-earned leisure out of sight of the owner.

Slaves under the task system won the right to cultivate land as **private fields**— farms of up to five acres on which they grew produce and raised livestock for market. There was a lively trade in slave-produced goods, and by the late 1850s slaves in the low country not only produced and exchanged property but passed it on to their children. The owners tolerated such activity because slaves on the task system worked hard, required minimal supervision, and made money for their owners.

QUICK REVIEW

THE TASK SYSTEM

- Assigned a task rather than specific hours of labor

- Slaves worked without supervision until the task was completed

- Remainder of the day belonged to the slave

private fields *Farms of up to five acres on which slaves working under the task system were permitted to produce items for their own use and sale in a nearby market.*

THE SEAPORT CITIES, 1790–1815

When the first federal census takers made their rounds in 1790, they found that 94 percent of the population was living on farms and in rural villages. The remaining 6 percent lived in the 24 towns that had populations of more than 2,500. Only five communities had a population over 10,000: Boston (18,038), New York (33,131), Philadelphia (42,444), Baltimore (13,503), and Charleston (16,359). All five were seaport cities.

COMMERCE

These cities had grown steadily during the 18th century, handling imports from Europe and farm exports from America. With the outbreak of war between Britain and France in 1793, the overseas demand for American foodstuffs and for shipping to carry products from the Caribbean islands to Europe further strengthened the seaport cities. Foreign trade during these years was risky and uneven. French seizures of American shipping and the resulting undeclared war of 1798–1800, the British ban on America's reexport trade in 1805, Jefferson's importation ban of 1806 and his trade embargo of 1807, and America's entry into war in 1812 all disrupted the maritime economy. But by 1815, it was clear that wartime commerce had transformed the seaports and the institutions of American business. New York City had become the nation's largest city, with a population of 96,373 in 1810. Philadelphia's population had risen to 53,722, Boston's to 34,322, and Baltimore's to 46,555.

Seaport merchants in these years amassed huge personal fortunes. To manage those fortunes, new institutions emerged. Docking and warehousing facilities expanded dramatically. Bookkeepers were replaced by accountants familiar with the new double-entry system of accounting, and insurance and banking companies were formed to handle the risks and rewards of wartime commerce.

The bustle of prosperity was evident on the waterfronts and principal streets of the seaport cities. An Englishman who visited the New York City docks during the wartime boom left this description:

> The carters were driving in every direction; and the sailors and labourers upon the wharfs, and onboards the vessels, were moving their ponderous burdens from place to place. The merchants and their clerks were busily engaged in their counting-houses, or upon the piers. The Tontine coffee-house was filled with underwriters, brokers, merchants, traders, and politicians. . . . The steps and balcony of the coffee-house were crowded with people bidding, or listening to the several auctioneers, who had elevated themselves upon a hogshead of sugar, a puncheon of rum, or a bale of cotton. . . . Everything was in motion; all was life, bustle, and activity.

POVERTY

Away from the waterfront, the main thoroughfares and a few of the side streets were paved with cobblestones and lined with fine shops and townhouses. But in other parts of the cities, visitors learned that the boom was creating unprecedented poverty as well as wealth. A few steps off the handsome avenues were narrow streets crowded with ragged children, browsing dogs, pigs, horses, and cattle, with garbage and waste filling the open sewers. Epidemics had become more frequent and deadly. New York City, for example, experienced six severe epidemics of yellow fever between 1791 and 1822.

The slums were evidence that money created by commerce was being distributed in undemocratic ways. Per capita wealth in New York rose 60 percent between 1790 and 1825, but the wealthiest 4 percent of the population owned more than half of that wealth. The wages of skilled and unskilled labor rose in these years, but the increase in seasonal and temporary employment, together with the recurring interruptions of foreign commerce, cut deeply into the security and prosperity of ordinary women and men.

THE STATUS OF LABOR

Meanwhile, the status of artisans in the big cities was undergoing change. In 1790, independent artisans demanded and usually received the respect of their fellow citizens. Artisans constituted about half the male workforce of the seaport cities, and their respectability and usefulness, together with the role they had played in the revolution (see Chapter 6), had earned them an honorable status.

That status rested in large part on their independence. In 1790 most artisan workshops had been household operations with at most one or two apprentices and hired journeymen, who looked forward to owning their own shops one day. Most master craftsmen lived modestly (on the borderline of poverty in many cases) and aspired only to the ability to support their household in security and decency. They identified their way of life with republican virtue.

As in the countryside, however, the patriarchal base of that republicanism was being eroded. Accompanying the growth of the maritime economy was a change in the nature of construction work, shipbuilding, the clothing trades, and other specialized crafts. Artisans were being replaced by cheaper labor and were being undercut by subcontracted "slop work" performed by semiskilled outworkers. Perhaps one in five master craftsmen entered the newly emerging business class. The others took work as laborers or journeymen (the term for wage-earning craftsmen). By 1815 most young craftsmen could no longer hope to own their own shops. In the seaport cities between 1790 and 1820, the world of artisans like Paul Revere, Benjamin Franklin, and Thomas Paine was passing out of existence and was being replaced by wage labor.

The loss of independence undermined the paternal status of artisan husbands and fathers. As wage earners few could support their family unless the wife and children earned money to augment family income. Working-class women took in boarders and did laundry and found work as domestic servants or as peddlers of fruit, candy, vegetables, cakes, or hot corn. The descent into wage labor and the reliance on the earnings of women and children violated the republican, patriarchal assumptions of fathers.

The Assault on Authority

FOCUS QUESTION

How did changes within families contribute to changes in other areas of life in the years 1790–1820?

In the 50 years following the Declaration of Independence, the patriarchal republic created by the Founding Fathers became a democracy. Most Americans witnessed the initial stirrings of change as a withering of paternal authority in their own households. For some—slaves and many women in particular—the decline of patriarchy could be welcomed. For others (the fathers themselves, disinherited sons, and women who looked to the security of old ways) it was a disaster of unmeasured proportions. But whether they experienced the transformation as a personal rise or fall, Americans by the early 19th century had entered a world where received authority and the experience of the past had lost their power.

Paternal Power in Decline

From the mid-18th century onward, especially after the revolution, many young people grew up knowing that their father would be unable to help them and that they would have to make their own way in the world. The consequent decline of parental power became evident in many ways—perhaps most poignantly in changing patterns of courtship and marriage. In the countryside, young men knew that they would not inherit the family farm, and young women knew that their father would be able to provide only a small dowry. As a result, fathers had less control over marriage choices than they had had when marriage was accompanied by a significant transfer of property. Young people now courted away from parental scrutiny and made choices based

MUSICAL LINK TO THE PAST

THE MINUET IN AMERICA

Composer: Alexander Reinagle
Title: "Minuet and Gavotte" (c. 1800)

Like the quadrille, another European dance style popular at this time in the United States, the minuet and gavotte required dancers to learn highly complicated directions that took more time to master than most working people could spare. A strict formality reigned: The dances commenced with introductions and an exchange of courtesies, featured little if any contact between partners, and required balletlike technique that rendered them nearly impossible for casual, untrained dancers.

By 1800, the minuet and gavotte were becoming passé in the United States. Their stiff and formal qualities represented values of rank and privilege that reminded Americans of the monarchy they had cast aside. The newly emerging market revolution tended to reward those who worked the hardest or had the best ideas for products, not those from elite families. In the election of 1800, Americans seemed to embrace this ideal in their election of Thomas Jefferson to the presidency, over the more authoritarian and conservative "kingly" politics (according to Jefferson) espoused by the incumbent Federalist Party.

In the years surrounding the turn of the century, middle-class citizens became more involved than ever in all levels of government thanks to an increase in compensation for government positions, an explosion of voluntary political clubs, and a movement toward universal white male suffrage. The upshot of all these developments was that political, economic, and religious leadership in American society, once viewed as the province of the elite, increasingly fell to people of merit, not birthright, as it largely had been in English society. In this uniquely American atmosphere, rarefied and exclusive dance traditions such as the minuet and gavotte were rapidly losing popular favor. By the mid-19th century, these dance traditions virtually vanished in the United States.

1. Can popular dancing styles be used as evidence to document changes in American history and culture?
2. What do you think the dance crazes of today communicate about our current society?

Listen to an audio recording of this music on the Musical Links to the Past CD.

on affection and personal attraction rather than on property or parental pressure. One sign of the independence of young people (and of their lack of faith in their future) was the high number of pregnancies outside of marriage. In the second half of the 18th century and in the first decades of the 19th, the number of first births that occurred within eight months of marriage averaged between 25 and 30 percent—with the rates running much higher among poor couples.

THE ALCOHOLIC REPUBLIC

The erosion of the old family economy was paralleled by a dramatic rise in alcohol consumption. Americans had been drinking alcohol since the time of the first settlements. But drinking, like everything else that was "normal," took place within a structure of paternal authority. Americans tippled every day in the course of their ordinary activities: at family meals and around the fireside, at work, and at barn-raisings, militia musters, dances, weddings, funerals—even at the ordination of ministers. Under such circumstances, drinking, even drunkenness, seldom posed a threat to authority or to the social order.

INTERIOR OF AN AMERICAN INN, 1813. *In this democratic, neighborly scene in a country inn in the early republic, men of varying degrees of wealth, status, and inebriety are drinking and talking freely with each other. One man's wife and daughter have invaded this male domain, perhaps to question the time and money spent at the inn.*

That old pattern of communal drinking persisted into the 19th century. But during the 50 years following the revolution it gradually gave way to a new pattern. Farmers, particularly those in newly settled areas, regularly produced a surplus of grain that they turned into whiskey. Whiskey was safer than water and milk, which were often tainted, and it was cheaper than coffee or tea. It was also cheaper than imported rum. So Americans embraced whiskey as their national drink and consumed extraordinary quantities of it. By 1830 per capita consumption of distilled spirits was more than 5 gallons per year—the highest it has ever been. The United States had indeed become, as one historian has said, an "alcoholic republic."

The nation's growing thirst was driven not by conviviality or neighborliness but by a desire to get drunk. Most Americans drank regularly, though there were wide variations. Men drank far more than women, the poor and the rich drank more than the emerging middle class, city dwellers drank more than farmers, westerners drank more than easterners, and southerners drank a bit more than northerners. Throughout the nation, the heaviest drinking took place among the increasing numbers of young men who lived away from their family and outside the old social controls: soldiers and sailors, boatmen and other transport workers, lumberjacks, schoolmasters, **journeyman** craftsmen, college students. Among such men the controlled tippling of the 18th century gave way to the binge and to solitary drinking. By the 1820s social reformers branded alcohol as a threat to individual well being, to social peace, and to the republic itself.

THE DEMOCRATIZATION OF PRINT

Of course, Americans freed from the comforts and constraints of patriarchal authority did more than fornicate and drink. Many seized more constructive opportunities to think and act for themselves. That tendency was speeded by a rise in literacy and by the emergence of a print culture that catered to popular tastes. The literacy rate in the preindustrial United States was among the highest ever recorded. By 1820 all but the poorest white Americans, particularly in the North, could read and write. The rise in literacy was accompanied by an explosive growth in the amount and kinds of reading matter available to the public. At its simplest and most intimate, this took the form of personal letters. Increased mobility separated families and friends and encouraged letter writing, especially by women. Women were also the principal readers of novels. The first best-

journeyman *Wage-earning craftsman.*

selling novel in the United States was *The Power of Sympathy,* a morally ambiguous tale of seduction and betrayal that exposed hypocrisy in male authorities who punished (generally poor and vulnerable) women for their own seductions.

The most widely distributed publications, however, were newspapers. In 1790, there were 90 newspapers in the United States. In 1830 there were 370, and they had grown chattier and more informal. Still, even in New England, only 1 household in 10 or 12 subscribed to a newspaper. The papers were passed from hand to hand, read aloud in groups, and made available at taverns and public houses.

The increase in literacy and in printed matter accelerated the democratizing process. In the 18th century, when books and newspapers were scarce, most Americans had experienced the written word only as it was read aloud by fathers, ministers, or teachers. Between 1780 and 1820 private, silent reading of new kinds of texts became common—religious tracts, inexpensive Bibles, personal letters, novels, newspapers, and magazines. No longer were authority figures the sole interpreters of the world for families and neighborhoods. The new print culture encouraged Americans to read and think for themselves and to interpret information without the mediation of the old authorities.

CITIZENSHIP

The transition from republic to democracy—and the relation of that transition to the decline of rural patriarchy—took on formal, institutional shape in a redefinition of republican citizenship.

The revolutionary constitutions of most states retained the colonial freehold (property) qualifications for voting. These granted the vote to from one-half to three-quarters of adult white men. Many of the disenfranchised were dependent sons who expected to inherit citizenship along with land. Some states dropped the freehold clause and gave the vote to all adult men who paid taxes, but with little effect on the voting population. Both the freehold and taxpaying qualifications tended to grant political rights to adult men who headed households, thus reinforcing classical republican notions that granted full citizenship to independent fathers and not to their dependents.

Between 1790 and 1820 republican notions of citizenship grounded in fatherhood and proprietorship gave way to a democratic insistence on equal rights for all white men. In 1790 only Vermont granted the vote to all free men. Kentucky entered the Union in 1792 without property or taxpaying qualifications; Tennessee followed with a freehold qualification, but only for newcomers who had resided in their counties for less than six months. The federal government dropped the 50-acre freehold qualification in the territories in 1812; of the eight territories that became states between 1796 and 1821, none kept a property qualification, only three maintained a taxpaying qualification, and five explicitly granted the vote to all white men. In the same years, one eastern state after another widened the franchise. By 1840 only Rhode Island retained a propertied electorate—primarily because Yankee farmers in that state wanted to retain power in a society made up more and more of urban, immigrant wage earners.

Early 19th-century suffrage reform gave political rights to propertyless men and thus took a long step away from the Founding Fathers' republic and toward mass democracy. At the same time, however, reformers explicitly limited the democratic franchise to those who were white and male. New Jersey's revolutionary constitution, for instance, had granted the vote to "persons" who met a freehold qualification. This loophole enfranchised property-holding widows, many of whom exercised their rights. A law of 1807 abolished property restrictions and gave the vote to all white men; the same law closed the loophole that had allowed propertied women to vote.

The question of woman suffrage would not be raised again until women raised it in 1848 (see Chapter 11); it would not be settled until well into the 20th century.

New restrictions also applied to African Americans. The revolutionary constitutions of Massachusetts, New Hampshire, and Vermont granted the vote to free blacks. New York and North Carolina laws gave the vote to "all men" who met the qualifications, and propertied African Americans in many states routinely exercised the vote. Postrevolutionary laws that extended voting rights to all white men often specifically excluded or severely restricted votes for blacks. Free blacks lost the suffrage in New York, New Jersey, Pennsylvania, Connecticut, Maryland, Tennessee, and North Carolina. By 1840 fully 93 percent of blacks in the North lived in states that either banned or severely restricted their right to vote.

Thus the "universal" suffrage of which many Americans boasted was far from universal: New laws dissolved the old republican connections between political rights and property and thus saved the citizenship of thousands who were becoming propertyless tenants and wage earners; the same laws that gave the vote to all white men, however, explicitly barred other Americans from political participation. Faced with the disintegration of Jefferson's republic of proprietors, the wielders of power had chosen to blur the emerging distinctions of social class while they hardened the boundaries of sex and race.

QUICK   REVIEW

"UNIVERSAL" SUFFRAGE

• Granted to nearly all adult white men

• Taken away from the minority of women and blacks who had formerly voted

REPUBLICAN RELIGION

FOCUS QUESTION

In what specific ways was evangelical Protestantism beginning to shape American society and culture in these years?

The Founding Fathers had been largely indifferent to organized religion. Some attended church out of a sense of obligation. Many of the better educated subscribed to **deism**, the belief that God had created the universe but did not intervene in its affairs. Many simply did not bother themselves with thoughts about religion. When asked why the Constitution mentioned neither God nor religion, Alexander Hamilton is reported to have smiled and answered, "We forgot."

THE DECLINE OF THE ESTABLISHED CHURCHES

In state after state, postrevolutionary constitutions withdrew government support from religion, and the First Amendment to the U.S. Constitution clearly prescribed the separation of *organized religion from the national* state. Reduced to their own sources of support, the established churches went into decline. The Episcopal Church, which until the revolution had been the established Church of England in the southern colonies, began to lose members. In New England, the old churches fared little better. About one-third of New England's Congregational pulpits were vacant in 1780, and the situation was worse to the north and west. In 1780 there were 750 Congregational churches in the United States (nearly all of them in New England), and the total was only 1,100 in 1820—this over a period when the nation's population was rising from 4 million to 10 million. Ordinary women and men were leaving the churches that had dominated the religious life of colonial America.

THE RISE OF THE DEMOCRATIC SECTS

Deism *Belief that God created the universe but did not intervene in its affairs.*

The collapse of the established churches, the social dislocations of the postrevolutionary years, and the increasingly antiauthoritarian, democratic sensibilities of ordinary Americans provided fertile ground for the growth of new democratic sects.

These were the years of camp-meeting revivalism, years in which Methodists and Baptists grew from small, half-organized sects into the great popular denominations they have been ever since. They were also years in which fiercely independent dropouts from older churches were putting together a loosely organized movement that would become the Disciples of Christ. At the same time, ragged, half-educated preachers were spreading the Universalist and Freewill Baptist messages in up-country New England, while in western New York young Joseph Smith was receiving the visions that would lead to Mormonism (see Chapter 10).

The result was, first of all, a vast increase in the variety of choices on the American religious landscape. But within that welter of new churches was a roughly uniform democratic style shared by the fastest-growing sects. First, they renounced the need for an educated, formally authorized clergy. Religion was now a matter of the heart and not the head; **crisis conversion** (understood in most churches as personal transformation that resulted from direct experience of the Holy Spirit) was a necessary credential for preachers; a college degree was not. The new preachers substituted emotionalism and storytelling for Episcopal ritual and Congregational theological lectures; stories attracted listeners, and they were harder for the learned clergy to refute. The new churches also held up the Bible as the one source of religious knowledge, thus undercutting all theological knowledge and placing every literate Christian on a level with the best-educated minister. These tendencies often ended in **Restorationism**— the belief that all theological and institutional changes since the end of biblical times were man-made mistakes and that religious organizations must restore themselves to the purity and simplicity of the church of the Apostles. In sum, this loose democratic creed rejected learning and tradition and raised up the priesthood of all believers.

Baptists and Methodists were by far the most successful at preaching to the new populist audience. In 1820, they outnumbered Episcopalians and Congregationalists by three to one. Baptists based much of their appeal in localism and congregational democracy. Methodist success, on the other hand, was due to skillful national organization. Bishop Francis Asbury, the head of the church in its fastest-growing years, built an episcopal bureaucracy that seeded churches throughout the republic and sent **circuit-riding preachers** to places that had none. Asbury demanded much of his **itinerant preachers**, and until 1810 he strongly suggested that they remain celibate.

The Methodist preachers were common men who spoke plainly, listened carefully to others, and carried hymnbooks with simple tunes that anyone could sing. They also, particularly in the early years, shared traditional folk beliefs with their humble flocks. Some of the early circuit riders relied heavily on dreams; some could predict the future; many visited heaven and hell and returned with full descriptions. But in the end it was the hopefulness and simplicity of the Methodist message that attracted ordinary Americans. The Methodists rejected the old terrors of Calvinist determinism and

A METHODIST CAMP MEETING IN NEW ENGLAND. *The Methodists, largely through the medium of the camp meeting, made heavy inroads in the old Puritan stronghold of New England in the 19th century. In this depiction the meeting ground is well organized, the preaching is enthusiastic, and the audience is largely female.*

Old Sturbridge Village

taught that while salvation comes only through God, men and women can decide to open themselves to divine grace and thus play a decisive role in their own salvation.

THE CHRISTIANIZATION OF THE WHITE SOUTH

During these same years evangelical Protestantism became the dominant religion of the white South. That triumph constituted a powerful assault on the prerevolutionary structure of authority. The essence of southern evangelicalism was a violent conversion experience followed by a life of piety and a rejection of what evangelicals called "the world." To no small degree, "the world" was the economic, cultural, and political world controlled by the planters.

Southern Baptists, Methodists, and Presbyterians spread their democratic message in the early 19th century through the **camp meeting**. Though its origins stretched back into the 18th century, the first full-blown camp meeting took place at Cane Ridge, Kentucky, in 1801. Here the annual "Holy Feast," a three-day communion service of Scotch-Irish Presbyterians, was transformed into an outdoor, interdenominational revival at which hundreds experienced conversion. Estimates of the crowd at Cane Ridge ranged from 10,000 to 20,000 people, and by all accounts the enthusiasm was nearly unprecedented. Some converts fainted, others succumbed to uncontrolled bodily jerkings, while a few barked like dogs—all of them visibly taken by the Holy Spirit. Such exercises fell upon women and men, whites and blacks, rich and poor, momentarily erasing southern social distinctions in moments of profound and public religious ecstasy.

EVANGELICALS AND SLAVERY

Despite its critique of worldliness and its antiauthoritarian emphasis, southern evangelicalism was at bottom conservative, for it seldom questioned the need for social hierarchy. As the 19th century progressed, the Baptists, Methodists, and Presbyterians of the South, though they never stopped railing against greed and pride, learned to live comfortably within a system of fixed hierarchy and God-given social roles.

Slavery became the major case in point. For a brief period after the revolution, evangelicals included slavery on their list of worldly sins. Methodists and Baptists preached to slaves as well as to whites. In 1780 a conference of Methodist preachers ordered circuit riders to free their slaves and advised all Methodists to do the same. In 1784 the Methodists declared that they would excommunicate members who failed to free their slaves within two years. Other evangelicals shared their views. As early as 1787, southern Presbyterians prayed for "final abolition," and two years later Baptists condemned slavery as "a violent deprivation of the rights of nature and inconsistent with a republican government."

The period of greatest evangelical growth, however, came during the years in which the South was committing irrevocably to plantation slavery. As increasing numbers of both slaves and slaveowners came within the evangelical fold, the southern churches had to rethink their position on slavery. The Methodists never carried out their threat to excommunicate slaveholders. Similarly, the Baptists and Presbyterians never translated their antislavery rhetoric into action. By 1820, evangelicals were coming to terms with slavery. Instead of demanding freedom for slaves, they suggested, as the Methodist James O'Kelly put it, that slaveowners remember that slaves were "dear brethren in Christ" who should not be treated cruelly and who should be allowed to attend religious services.

QUICK   REVIEW

EVANGELICAL RELIGION

- Bible as the one source of religious knowledge

- Crisis conversion needed

- Appeal to the middle and lower classes of society

camp meeting *Outdoor revival often lasting for days; a principal means of spreading evangelical Christianity in the United States.*

THE BEGINNINGS OF AFRICAN AMERICAN CHRISTIANITY

In the South Carolina and Georgia low country there were few slave Christians before 1830. But in the slave communities of the Upper South, as well as the burgeoning free and semifree urban black populations of both the North and South, the evangelical revivals of the late 18th and early 19th centuries appealed powerfully to African Americans who sensed that the bonds of slavery were loosening. During the years from 1780 to 1820, for the first time, thousands of slaves embraced Christianity and began to turn it into a religion of their own. Slaves attended camp meetings, listened to itinerant preachers, and joined the Baptist and Methodist congregations of the southern revival.

Blacks were drawn to revival religion for many of the same reasons as whites. They found the informal, storytelling evangelical preachers more attractive than the old Anglican missionaries. The revivalists, in turn, welcomed slaves and free blacks to their meetings and sometimes recruited them as preachers. Evangelical, emotional preaching, the falling, jerking, and other camp-meeting "exercises," and the revivalists' emphasis on singing and other forms of audience participation were much more attractive than the cold, high-toned preaching of the Anglicans. So were the humility and suffering of the evangelical whites. Slaves respected Methodist missionaries who entered their cabins and talked with them on their own terms. Finally, the slaves gloried in the evangelicals' assault on the slaveholders' culture and in the antislavery sentiments of many white evangelicals. The result was a huge increase in the number of African American Christians.

Neither antislavery beliefs nor openness to black participation, however, persisted long among white evangelicals. Although there were exceptions, most "integrated" congregations in both the North and South were in fact internally segregated. Blacks began organizing independent churches. In Philadelphia, the black preachers Richard Allen and Absalom Jones rebelled against segregated seating in St. George's Methodist Church and, in 1794, founded two separate black congregations. Similar secessions resulted in new churches farther south: in Baltimore; in Wilmington, Delaware; in Richmond; in Norfolk; and in the cluster of villages that had risen to serve the Chesapeake's new mixed economy. By 1820 there were roughly 700 independent black churches in the United States; 30 years earlier there had been none at all. The creation of an independent Christian tradition among the majority of blacks who remained plantation slaves took place only after 1830 (see Chapter 10). But the democratic message of the early southern revival, the brief attempt of white and black Christians to live out the implications of that message, and the independent black churches that rose from the failure of that attempt all left a permanent stamp on southern Protestantism, black and white.

BLACK REPUBLICANISM: GABRIEL'S REBELLION

Masters who talked of liberty and natural rights sometimes worried that slaves might imagine that such language could apply to themselves. The Age of Democratic Revolution took a huge step in that direction with the French Revolution in 1789. Among the first repercussions outside of France was a revolution on the Caribbean island of Saint Dominque. That island's half-million slaves fought out a complicated political and military revolt that eventually led to the creation of the independent black republic of Haiti. Slave societies throughout the hemisphere heard tales of terror from refugee French planters and stories of hope from the slaves they brought with them.

Slaves from the 1790s onward whispered of natural rights and imagined themselves as part of the democratic revolution. This covert republic of the slaves sometimes came into the open, most ominously in Richmond in 1800, where a slave blacksmith named Gabriel hatched a well-planned conspiracy to overthrow Virginia's slave regime. Gabriel had been hired out to Richmond employers for most of his adult life; he was shaped less by plantation slavery than by the democratic, loosely interracial underworld of urban artisans. Working with his brother and other hired-out slave artisans, **Gabriel's rebellion** was planned with military precision. They recruited soldiers among slave artisans, adding plantation slaves only at the last moment. Gabriel planned to march an army of 1,000 men on Richmond in three columns. The outside columns would set diversionary fires in the warehouse district and prevent the militia from entering the town. The center would seize Capitol Square, including the treasury, the arsenal, and Governor James Monroe.

Although his army would be made up of slaves, and although his victory would end slavery in Virginia, Gabriel hoped to make a republican revolution, not a slave revolt. His chosen enemies were the Richmond "merchants" who had controlled his labor. Later, a coconspirator divulged the plan: The rebels would hold Governor Monroe hostage and split the state treasury among themselves, and "if the white people agreed to their freedom they would then hoist a white flag, and [Gabriel] would dine and drink with the merchants of the city on the day when it would be agreed to." Gabriel expected what he called "the poor white people" and "the most redoubtable republicans" to join him. He would kill anyone who opposed him, but he would spare Quakers, Methodists, and Frenchmen, for they were "friendly to liberty." Unlike those of earlier slave insurgents, Gabriel's dreams did not center on violent retribution or a return to or reconstruction of West Africa. He was an American revolutionary, and he dreamed of a truly democratic republic for Virginia. His army would march into Richmond under the banner "Death or Liberty."

Gabriel and his coconspirators recruited at least 150 soldiers who agreed to gather near Richmond on August 30, 1800. The leaders expected to be joined by 500 to 600 more rebels as they marched upon the town. But on the appointed day it rained heavily. Rebels could not reach the meeting point, and amid white terror and black betrayals Gabriel and his henchmen were hunted down, tried, and sentenced to death. In all, the state hanged 27 supposed conspirators, while others were sold and transported out of Virginia. A white Virginian marveled that the rebels on the gallows displayed a "sense of their [natural] rights, [and] a contempt of danger."

Gabriel's rebellion *Carefully planned but unsuccessful rebellion of slaves in Richmond and the surrounding area in 1800.*

C O N C L U S I O N

Between 1790 and 1820 Americans had transformed their new republic—with paradoxical results. The United States more than doubled in both size and population during these years. American trade with Britain, continental Europe, and the Caribbean skyrocketed. Some Americans amassed fortunes; others made more modest gains; others saw their positions deteriorate. Indians between the Appalachians and the Mississippi River lost everything; their hunting grounds became American farmland, much of it worked by slaves who now knew that their masters would never voluntarily free them.

The transformation stemmed both from American independence and from the expansion of agriculture and increased exports of American farm products. When Americans traded plantation staples and surplus food for European (largely British) manufactured goods and financial services, however, they deepened their colonial dependence on the old centers of the world economy—even as they insisted on their independence. It was against this cluttered backdrop of social change, economic and geographic growth, and continuing vulnerability to the whims and needs of the Old World powers that Federalists and Jeffersonian Republicans fought each other to determine the ultimate outcome of the American Revolution.

QUESTIONS FOR REVIEW AND CRITICAL THINKING

Review

1. What was the nature of the American agricultural economy and of agricultural society in the years 1790–1820?
2. What were the principal reasons why Indian peoples between the Appalachian Mountains and the Mississippi River gave way to white settlement?
3. In what geographic areas and in what ways did slavery expand between 1790 and 1820? In what areas (and, again, in what ways) was the slave system called into question?
4. How did changes within families contribute to changes in other areas of life in the years 1790–1820?
5. In what specific ways was evangelical Protestantism beginning to shape American society and culture in these years?

Critical Thinking

1. What forces drove the expansion of American slavery in the years 1790–1820? What forces were working toward emancipation? In your judgment, was the end of slavery (or the setting of a permanent course toward that end) a real possibility at any point during these years?
2. What were the sources of American economic growth in the years 1790–1820? What were the constraints upon growth, and how did those constraints help to shape economic development in these years?

Discovery

How did regional differences manifest themselves in the United States? How might these differences have shaped its history?

SUGGESTED READINGS

Douglas North, *The Economic Growth of the United States, 1790–1860* (1961) is an economic overview of these years. On rural society in the North, see **Christopher Clark,** *The Roots of Rural Capitalism: Western Massachusetts, 1780–1860* (1990), **Laurel Thatcher Ulrich,** *A Midwife's Tale: The Life of Martha Ballard, Based on Her Diary, 1785–1812* (1990), and **Jack Larkin,** *The Reshaping of Everyday Life, 1790–1840* (1988). Good accounts of Native Americans in these years include **Anthony F.C. Wallace,** *The Death and Rebirth of the Seneca* (1969) and **Gregory Evans Dowd,** *A Spirited Resistance: The North American Indian Struggle for a New World* (1992). **Stephen Aron,** *How the West Was Lost: The Transformation of Kentucky from Daniel Boone to Henry Clay* (1996), treats white settler societies. Economic change in the South is traced in **Robert William Fogel** and **Stanley L. Engerman,** *Time on the Cross: The Economics of American Negro Slavery* (1974). On urban labor, see the early chapter of **Sean Wilentz,** *Chants Democratic: New York City and the Rise of the American Working Class* (1984). The study of religion in the postrevolutionary years begins with two books: **Nathan O. Hatch,** *The Democratization of American Christianity* (1989), and **Jon Butler,** *Awash in a Sea of Faith: Christianizing the American People* (1990). The concluding section of **Gordon Wood,** *The Radicalism of the American Revolution* (1992) discusses the democratization of mind during these years.

ONLINE SOURCES GUIDE

ThomsonNOW   Visit ThomsonNOW to access primary sources, exercises, quizzes, and audio chapter summaries related to this chapter:
http://www.thomsonedu.com/login

DISCOVERY

How did regional differences manifest themselves in the United States? How might these differences have shaped its history?

In thinking about this question, begin by breaking it down into the components shown below. A discussion of the significance of each component should appear in your answer.

RELIGION AND PHILOSOPHY

Review the section on "The Rise of Democratic Sects" and look at the illustration of the Methodist camp meeting. Who is largely present at this meeting? Why do you think that is? Why might this be important in the spread of Methodism? What are some of the notable features of this camp meeting? According to the text, what accounted for the appeal of Methodism? How might this appeal have worked in the western territories as they expanded?

Old Sturbridge Village

A METHODIST CAMP MEETING IN NEW ENGLAND

CULTURE AND SOCIETY

Look at the map concerning the distribution of the slave population. Where was slavery most prevalent in 1790? Where was slavery most prevalent in 1820? Are there any differences? Did any state or region lower its number of slaves during this time? Did any state or region significantly raise its number of slaves? What accounts for the differences?

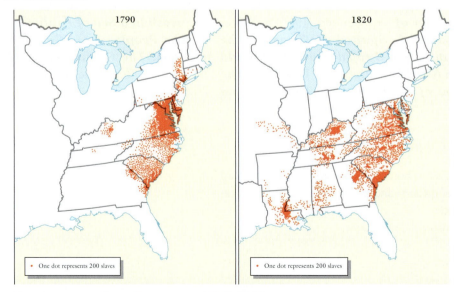

DISTRIBUTION OF SLAVE POPULATION, 1790–1820

What do you think the artist is trying to say about slavery in the illustration? Does he have a particular view of white society in the South? Does gender play a role in this illustration at all?

AN OVERSEER DOING HIS DUTY

CULTURE AND SOCIETY

What do these images tell you about society and family life in this period? Note the dining room illustration. What sense do you get from this painting? How do you think this compares to a modern dining room? What are the differences? What accounts for those differences?

DINING ROOM OF DR. WHITBRIDGE, CIRCA 1815

INTERIOR OF AN AMERICAN INN, 1813

Compare the lone figure in the dining room to the social scene in the other illustration. What kind of commentary might the artists be making? What do you think the second artist might be suggesting by including the wife and daughter in the painting of the inn? What do these images tell you about the social life of Americans in this period?

COMPLETING THE REVOLUTION, 1789–1815

Almost by acclamation, George Washington became the first president under the Constitution. Washington and his closest advisers (they would soon call themselves Federalists) believed that the balance between power and liberty had tipped toward anarchy after the revolution. They had made the Constitution to counter democratic excesses, and they came into office determined to make the national government powerful enough to command respect abroad and to impose order at home. For the most part, they succeeded. But in the process they aroused an opposition that swung the balance back toward liberty and limited government. These self-styled Democratic Republicans, led almost from the beginning by Thomas Jefferson, were as firmly tied to revolutionary ideals of limited government and the yeoman republic as the Federalists were tied to visions of an orderly commercial republic with a powerful national state. The fight between Federalists and Democratic Republicans was conducted against an ominous backdrop of international intrigue and war between France and Britain.

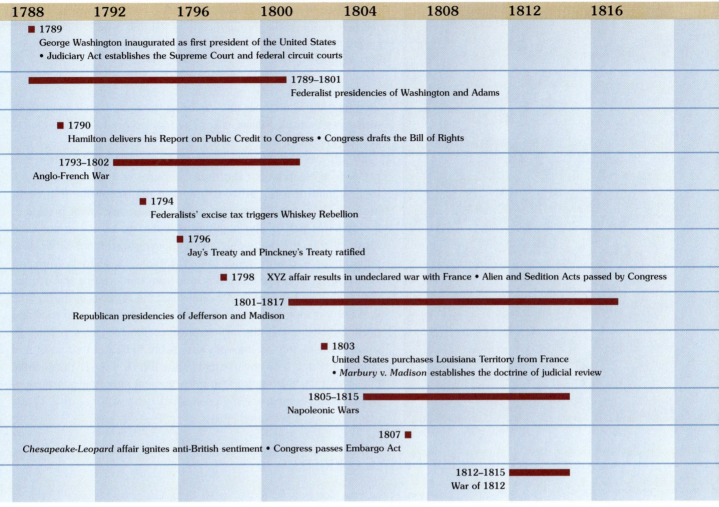

| 1788 | 1792 | 1796 | 1800 | 1804 | 1808 | 1812 | 1816 |

■ **1789**
George Washington inaugurated as first president of the United States
• Judiciary Act establishes the Supreme Court and federal circuit courts

1789–1801
Federalist presidencies of Washington and Adams

■ **1790**
Hamilton delivers his Report on Public Credit to Congress • Congress drafts the Bill of Rights

1793–1802
Anglo-French War

■ **1794**
Federalists' excise tax triggers Whiskey Rebellion

■ **1796**
Jay's Treaty and Pinckney's Treaty ratified

■ **1798**   XYZ affair results in undeclared war with France • Alien and Sedition Acts passed by Congress

1801–1817
Republican presidencies of Jefferson and Madison

■ **1803**
United States purchases Louisiana Territory from France
• *Marbury v. Madison* establishes the doctrine of judicial review

1805–1815
Napoleonic Wars

1807 ■
Chesapeake-Leopard affair ignites anti-British sentiment • Congress passes Embargo Act

1812–1815
War of 1812

ESTABLISHING THE GOVERNMENT

George Washington left Mount Vernon for the temporary capital in New York City in April 1789. Militia companies and local dignitaries escorted him from town to town, crowds cheered, church bells marked his progress, and lines of girls in white dresses waved demurely as he passed. At Newark Bay he boarded a flower-bedecked barge and crossed to New York City. He arrived on April 23 and was inaugurated seven days later.

THE "REPUBLICAN COURT"

Reporting for work, President Washington found the new government embroiled in its first controversy—an argument over the dignity that would attach to his office. Vice President John Adams had asked the Senate to create a title of honor for the president. Adams, along with many of the senators, wanted a resounding title that would reflect the power of the new executive. The titles they considered were "His Highness," "His Mightiness," "His Elective Highness," "His Most Benign Highness," "His Majesty," and "His Highness, the President of the United States, and Protector of Their Liberties." The Senate debated the question for a full month,

FOCUS QUESTION
What was the Federalist plan for organizing the national government and its finances? What were the Jeffersonian Republicans' principal objections to those plans?

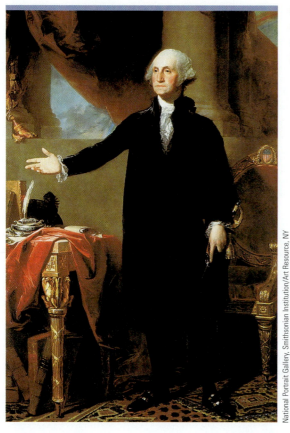

GEORGE WASHINGTON IN 1796, NEAR THE END OF HIS PRESIDENCY. *The artist here captured the formal dignity of the first president and surrounded him with gold, red velvet, a presidential throne, and other emblems of kingly office.*

then gave up when it became clear that the more democratic House of Representatives disliked titles. They settled on the austere dignity of "Mr. President."

Much was at stake in the argument over titles. The Constitution provided a blueprint for the republic, but it was George Washington's administration that would translate the blueprint into a working state. It mattered very much what citizens called their president, for that was part of the huge constellation of laws, customs, and forms of etiquette that would give the new government either a republican or a courtly tone. Many of those close to Washington wanted to protect presidential power from the localism and democracy that, they believed, had nearly killed the republic in the 1780s. Washington's inaugural tour, the endless round of formal balls and presidential dinners, the appearance of Washington's profile on some of the nation's coins—all were meant to bolster the power and grandeur of the new government. Thus the battle over presidential titles was a revealing episode in the argument over how questions of power and liberty that Americans had debated since the 1760s would finally be answered.

THE FIRST CONGRESS

Leadership of the First Congress fell to James Madison. Under his guidance Congress strengthened the new national government at every turn. First it passed a **tariff** on imports, which would be the government's chief source of income. Then it turned to amendments to the Constitution that had been demanded by the state ratifying conventions.

Madison proposed 19 constitutional amendments. The 10 that survived congressional scrutiny and ratification by the states became the **Bill of Rights**. The First Amendment guaranteed the freedoms of speech, press, and religion against federal interference. The Second and Third Amendments guaranteed the continuation of a militia of armed citizens and stated the specific conditions under which soldiers could be quartered in citizens' households. The Fourth through Eighth Amendments defined a citizen's rights in court and when under arrest. The Ninth stated that the enumeration of specific rights in the first eight amendments did not imply a denial of other rights; the Tenth stated that powers not assigned to the national government by the Constitution remained with the states and the citizenry.

Many doubters at the ratifying conventions had called for amendments that would change the government detailed in the Constitution. By sticking to the relatively innocuous area of civil liberties, Madison soothed their mistrust while preserving the government of the Constitution. The Bill of Rights was an important guarantee of individual liberties. But in the context in which it was written and ratified, it was an even more important guarantee of the power of the national government.

Congress then created the executive departments of War, State, and Treasury and guaranteed that the heads of those departments and their assistants would be appointed by the president, thus removing them from congressional control. Congress then created the federal courts that were demanded but not specified in the Constitution. The Judiciary Act of 1789 established a Supreme Court with six members,

tariff *A tax on imports.*

Bill of Rights *First ten amendments to the Constitution, which protect the rights of individuals from abuses by the federal government.*

National Portrait Gallery, Smithsonian Institution/Art Resource, NY

along with 13 district courts and three **circuit courts** of appeal. The act made it possible for certain cases to be appealed from state courts to federal circuit courts, which would be presided over by traveling Supreme Court justices.

HAMILTONIAN ECONOMICS: THE NATIONAL DEBT

Washington chose Henry Knox, an old comrade from the revolution, to be secretary of war. The State Department went to his fellow Virginian, Thomas Jefferson. He chose **Alexander Hamilton** of New York to head the Department of the Treasury.

Hamilton was a brilliant economic thinker, an admirer of the British system of centralized government and finance, and a supremely arrogant and ambitious man. More than any other cabinet member, Hamilton directed the making of a national government.

In 1789 Congress asked Secretary Hamilton to report on the public debt. The debt fell into three categories, Hamilton reported. The first was the $11 million owed to foreigners—primarily debts to France incurred during the revolution. The second and third, roughly $24 million each, were debts owed by the national and state governments to American citizens who had supplied food, arms, and other resources to the revolutionary cause. Congress agreed that both justice and the credibility of the new government dictated that the foreign debts be paid in full. But the domestic debts raised troublesome questions. Those debts consisted of notes issued during the revolution to soldiers, merchants, farmers, and others who had helped the war effort. Over the years, speculators had purchased many of these notes at a fraction of their face value; when word spread that the Constitution would create a government likely to pay its debts, speculators and their agents fanned out across the countryside buying up all the notes they could find. By 1790 the government debt was concentrated in the hands of businessmen and speculators who had bought notes at 10 to 30 percent of their original value. Full payment would bring them enormous windfall profits.

The Revolutionary War debts of the individual states were another source of contention. Nationalists wanted to assume the debts of the states as part of a national debt. The state debts had also been bought up by speculators, and they posed another problem as well: Many states had paid off most of their notes in the 1780s; the other states still had significant outstanding debts. If the federal government assumed the state debts and paid them off at face value, money would flow out of the southern, middle, and western states—which had paid most of their debts—into the Northeast.

That is precisely what Hamilton proposed in his Report on Public Credit, issued in January 1790. He urged Congress to assume the state debts and to combine them with the federal government's foreign and domestic debts into a consolidated national debt. He agreed that the foreign debt should be paid promptly, but he insisted that the domestic debt be a permanent, tax-supported fixture of government. Under his plan, the government would issue securities to its creditors and would pay an annual rate of 4 percent. A permanent debt would attract the wealthiest financiers in the country as creditors and would render them loyal and dependent on the federal government. It would bring their economic power to the government, and at the same time would require a significant enlargement of the federal civil service, national financial institutions, and increased taxes. The national debt, in short, was at the center of Alexander Hamilton's plan for a powerful national state.

HAMILTONIAN ECONOMICS: THE BANK AND THE EXCISE

As part of that plan, Hamilton asked Congress to charter a bank of the United States. The government would store its funds in the bank and would supervise its operations, but the bank would be controlled by directors representing private stockholders. The Bank of

circuit court *Court that meets at different places within a district.*

Alexander Hamilton *Secretary of the Treasury under Washington who organized the finances of the new government and led the partisan fight against the Democratic Republicans.*

the United States would print and back the national currency and would regulate other banks. Hamilton's proposal also made stock in the bank payable in government securities, thus giving the bank a powerful interest in the fiscal stability of the government.

To fund the national debt, Hamilton called for a federal **excise tax** on wines, coffee, tea, and spirits. The tax on spirits would fall most heavily on the whiskey produced on the frontier. Its purpose was not only to produce revenue but to establish the government's power to create an internal tax and to collect it in the most remote regions in the republic. The result, as we shall see, was a **Whiskey Rebellion** in the West and an overwhelming display of federal force.

THE RISE OF OPPOSITION

In 1789 nearly everyone in the national government was committed to making the new government work. In particular, Alexander Hamilton at Treasury and James Madison in the House of Representatives expected to continue their political friendship. Yet in the debate over the national debt, Madison led congressional opposition to Hamilton. In 1792 as Thomas Jefferson joined the opposition, the consensus of 1789 degenerated into an angry argument over what sort of government would finally result from the American Revolution. Hamilton presented his national debt proposal to Congress as a solution to specific problems of government finance. Madison and other southerners opposed it because they did not want northern speculators—many of whom had received information from government insiders—to reap fortunes from notes bought at rock-bottom prices from soldiers, widows, and orphans. The congressional opposition compromised: in exchange for accepting Hamilton's debt, they won his promise to locate the permanent capital of the United States at a site on the Potomac River. The compromise went to the heart of American revolutionary republicanism. Hamilton intended to tie northeastern commercial interests to the federal government. If New York or Philadelphia became the permanent capital, political and economic power might be concentrated there as it was in Paris and London. Benjamin Rush, a Philadelphian, condemned the "government which has begun so soon to ape the corruption of the British Court, conveyed to it through the impure channel of the City of New York." Madison and other agrarians considered Philadelphia just as bad, and supported Hamilton's debt only on condition that the capital be moved south. The compromise would distance the commercial power of the cities from the federal government and would put an end to the "republican court" that had formed around Washington.

JEFFERSON VERSUS HAMILTON

excise tax *Internal tax on goods or services.*

Whiskey Rebellion *Revolt in Western Pennsylvania against the federal excise tax on whiskey.*

When Hamilton proposed the Bank of the United States, republicans in Congress immediately noted its similarity to the Bank of England and voiced deep suspicion of Hamilton's economic and governmental plans. At this point Thomas Jefferson joined the opposition, arguing that Congress had no right to charter a bank. Hamilton responded with the first argument for expanded federal power under the clause in the Constitution empowering Congress "to make all laws which shall be necessary and proper" to the performance of its duties. President Washington and a majority in Congress ultimately sided with Hamilton. Jefferson argued that the federal bank was unconstitutional, that a federal excise tax was certain to arouse public opposition, and that funding the debt would reward speculators and penalize ordinary citizens. More important, Jefferson argued, Hamilton used government securities and stock in the Bank of the United States to buy the loyalty not only of merchants and speculators but also of members of Congress. "The ultimate object of all this," insisted Jefferson, "is to prepare the way for a change, from the present republican form of government, to that of a monarchy, of which the English constitution is to be the model." For their part, Hamilton and his supporters (who by now were calling themselves Federalists) insisted that the centralization of power and a strong executive were necessary to the survival of the republic. The alternative was a return to the localism and public disorder of the 1780s. The argument drew its urgency from the understanding of both Hamilton and his detractors that republics had a long history of failure. Until late 1792, however, the argument over Hamilton's centralizing schemes was limited very largely to members of the government. Hamilton and his supporters tried to mobilize the commercial elite on the side of government, while Madison and Jefferson struggled to hold off the perceived monarchical plot until the citizens could be aroused to defend their liberties. Then, as both sides began to mobilize popular support, events in Europe came to dominate the politics of the American republican experiment.

THE REPUBLIC IN A WORLD AT WAR, 1793–1800

Late in 1792 French revolutionaries rejected monarchy and proclaimed the French Republic. They beheaded Louis XVI in January 1793. Eleven days later the French declared war on conservative Britain, thus launching a war between French republicanism and British-led reaction that, with periodic outbreaks of peace, would embroil the Atlantic world until the defeat of France in 1815. The argument between Jeffersonian republicanism and Hamiltonian centralization was no longer a squabble within the United States government. National politics was now subsumed within the struggle over international republicanism.

AMERICANS AND THE FRENCH REVOLUTION

As Britain and France went to war in 1793, President Washington declared American neutrality, thereby **abrogating** obligations made in the 1778 treaties with the French. Washington and his advisers wanted to stay on good terms with Great Britain. American commerce and the financial health of the government both depended on that relationship. Moreover, Federalists genuinely sympathized with the British in the war with France. They viewed Britain as the defender of hierarchial society and ordered liberty against the homicidal anarchy of the French.

Jefferson and his friends saw things differently. They applauded the French for carrying on the republican revolution Americans had begun in 1776, and they had no affection for the "monarchical" politics of the Federalists or for Americans' continued neocolonial dependence upon British trade. The faction led by Jefferson and Madison wanted to abandon the English mercantile system and trade freely with all nations. They did not care if that course of action hurt commercial interests (most of which supported the Federalists) or impaired the government's ability to centralize power in itself. While they agreed that the United States should stay out of the war, the Jeffersonians sympathized as openly with the French as the Federalists did with the British.

CITIZEN GENÊT

In April 1793 the French sent Citizen Edmond Genêt to the United States to enlist American aid with or without the Washington administration's consent. After the president's proclamation of neutrality, Genêt openly commissioned American priva-

abrogating a treaty *Process of abolishing a treaty so that it is no longer in effect.*

teers to harass British shipping and enlisted Americans in intrigues against the Spanish outpost of New Orleans. Genêt then opened France's Caribbean colonies to American shipping, providing American shippers a choice between French free trade and British mercantilism.

The British responded to Genêt's free-trade declaration with a promise to seize any ship trading with French colonies in the Caribbean. Under these Orders in Council the British seized 250 American ships. The Royal Navy also began searching American ships for English sailors who had deserted or who had switched to safer, better paying work in the American merchant marine. Inevitably, some American sailors were kidnapped into the British navy. Meanwhile the British began promising military aid to the Indians north of the Ohio River. Thus, while the French ignored the neutrality of the United States, the English engaged in both overt and covert acts of war.

WESTERN TROUBLES

In the Northwest the situation came to a head in the summer and fall of 1794. The Shawnee and allied tribes plotted with the British and talked of driving all settlers out of their territory. At the same time, frontier whites resented a national government that could neither pacify the Indians nor guarantee their free use of the Mississippi River. President Washington heard that 2,000 Kentuckians were armed and ready to attack New Orleans—a move that would have started a war with Spain. Settlers in Georgia were making unauthorized forays against the Creeks. Worst of all, frontier settlers refused to pay the Federalists' excise tax on whiskey—a direct challenge to federal authority. In July 1794 near Pittsburgh, 500 militiamen marched on the house of General John Neville, one of the federal excise collectors. Neville, his family, and a few federal soldiers fought the militiamen, killing two and wounding six before they abandoned the house to be looted and burned. Two weeks later, 6,000 "Whiskey Rebels" met at Braddock's Field near Pittsburgh, threatening to attack the town.

Washington determined to defeat the Indians and the Whiskey Rebels by force. He sent General "Mad" Anthony Wayne against the northwestern tribes. Wayne's decisive victory at Fallen Timbers in August 1794 ended the Indian-British challenge in the Northwest for many years (see Chapter 7). In September, Washington ordered 12,000 federalized militiamen from eastern Pennsylvania, Maryland, Virginia, and New Jersey to quell the Whiskey Rebellion. As the army marched west, they met no armed resistance. Arriving at Pittsburgh, the army arrested 20 suspected rebels and marched them back to Philadelphia for trial. In the end only two "rebels," both of them feebleminded, were convicted. President Washington pardoned them, and the Whiskey Rebellion was over.

JAY'S TREATY

In 1794 President Washington sent John Jay, chief justice of the Supreme Court, to negotiate the conflicts between the United States and Britain. Armed with news of Wayne's victory, Jay extracted a promise from the British to remove their troops from American territory in the Northwest. But on every other point of dispute he agreed to British terms. Jay's Treaty re-established trade with Great Britain on a most-favored-nation basis (something that was certain to cause domestic opposition), and it made no mention of **impressment** or other violations of American maritime rights. Given the power of Great Britain, it was the best that Americans could expect. Washington passed it on to the Senate, which in June 1795 ratified it by a bare two-thirds majority.

The seaport cities and much of the Northeast reacted favorably to the treaty. It ruled out war with England and cemented an Anglo-American trade relationship that strengthened both Hamilton's national state and the established commercial interests

impressment *Removal of sailors from American ships by British naval officers.*

that supported it. Moreover, there was little enthusiasm for the French Revolution in the Northeast. The South, on the other hand, saw Jay's Treaty as a blatant sign of the designs of Britain and the Federalists to subvert republicanism in both France and the United States. The Virginia legislature branded the treaty unconstitutional, and Republican congressmen demanded to see all documents relating to Jay's negotiations. Washington responded by telling them that their request could be legitimate only if the House was planning to initiate **impeachment** proceedings, thus tying approval of the treaty to his enormous personal prestige.

Meanwhile, on March 3, 1796, Washington released the details of a treaty that Thomas Pinckney had negotiated with Spain. In this treaty, Spain recognized American neutrality and set the border between the United States and Spanish Florida on American terms. Most important, the Pinckney Treaty put an end to Spanish claims to territory in the Southwest and gave Americans the unrestricted right to navigate the Mississippi River and to transship produce at the Spanish port of New Orleans. Pinckney's Treaty helped turn the tide in favor of the unpopular Jay's Treaty. Western representatives joined the Northeast and increasing numbers of southerners to ratify Jay's Treaty.

QUICK   REVIEW

JAY'S TREATY

- British abandoned their northwestern forts
- Did not settle maritime disputes
- Established trade with Great Britain on a favored-nation basis

WASHINGTON'S FAREWELL AND THE ELECTION OF 1796

George Washington refused to run for reelection in 1796. He could be proud of his accomplishment. He had presided over the creation of a national government. He had secured American control over the western settlements by ending British, Spanish, and Indian military threats and by securing free use of the Mississippi River for western produce. Those policies, together with the federal invasion of western Pennsylvania, had made it evident that the government could and would control its most distant regions. He had also avoided war with Great Britain—though not without overlooking assaults on American sovereignty. His farewell address warned against long-term "entangling alliances" with other countries; America, he said, should stay free to operate on its own in international affairs. Washington also warned against internal political divisions. Of course, he did not regard his own Federalists as a "party"—they were simply friends of the government. But he saw the Democratic Republicans as a self-interested, irresponsible "faction." Washington's call for national unity and an end to partisanship was in fact a parting shot at the Democratic Republican opposition.

Washington's retirement opened the way to the fierce competition for public office that he had feared; in 1796 Americans experienced their first contested presidential election. The Federalists chose as their candidate John Adams, an upright conservative from Massachusetts who had served as vice president. The Democratic Republicans nominated Thomas Jefferson. According to the gentlemanly custom of the day, neither candidate campaigned in person. But the friends of the candidates, the newspaper editors who enjoyed their patronage, and even certain European governments ensured that the election would be intensely partisan.

Since it was clear that Adams would carry New England and that Jefferson would carry the South, the election would be decided in Pennsylvania and New York. Some states, most of them in the South, chose presidential electors by direct vote. But in most states, including the crucial mid-Atlantic states, state legislatures selected the presidential electors. The election of 1796 would be decided in elections to the legislatures of those states. Jefferson won in Pennsylvania, but Adams carried New York and the national election. The distribution of electoral votes revealed the bases of Federalist and Republican support: Adams received only 2 electoral votes south of the Potomac, and Jefferson received only 18 (all but 5 of them in Pennsylvania) north of the Potomac.

The voting was over, but the intriguing was not. Alexander Hamilton, who since his retirement from the Treasury in 1795 had directed Federalist affairs from his New

impeachment *Act of charging a public official with misconduct in office.*

York law office, knew that he could not manipulate Adams. So he secretly instructed South Carolina's Federalist electors to withhold their votes from Adams. That would have given the presidency to Adams's running mate, Thomas Pinckney, relegating Adams to the vice presidency. (Prior to the ratification of the Twelfth Amendment in 1804, the candidate with a majority of the electoral votes became president, and the second-place candidate became vice president.) Like some of Hamilton's other schemes, this one backfired. New England electors heard of the plan and angrily withheld their votes from Pinckney. As a result, Adams was elected president and his opponent Thomas Jefferson became vice president.

TROUBLES WITH FRANCE, 1796–1800

As Adams entered office an international crisis was already in full swing. France, regarding Jay's Treaty as an Anglo-American alliance, had broken off relations with the United States. During the crucial elections in Pennsylvania, the French had seized American ships trading with Britain, giving the Americans a taste of what would happen if they did not elect a government friendlier to France. When the election went to John Adams, the French gave up on the United States and set about denying Britain its new de facto ally. In 1797 France expelled the American minister. The French ordered that American ships carrying "so much as a handkerchief" made in England be confiscated without compensation and announced that American seamen serving in the British navy would be summarily hanged if captured.

President Adams wanted to protect American commerce, but he knew that the United States might not survive a war with France. He also knew that French grievances (including Jay's Treaty and the abrogation of the French-American treaties of 1778) were legitimate. He sent a mission to France, made up of Charles Cotesworth Pinckney of South Carolina, John Marshall of Virginia, and Elbridge Gerry of Massachusetts. But when these prestigious delegates reached Paris, they were ignored. At last three French officials (the correspondence identified them only as "X, Y, and Z"—and the incident later became known as the **XYZ affair**) discreetly hinted that France would receive them if they paid a bribe of $250,000, arranged for the United States to loan $12 million to the French government, and apologized for unpleasant remarks that John Adams had made about France. The delegates refused, saying "No, not a sixpence," and returned home. There a journalist transformed their remark into "Millions for defense, but not one cent for tribute."

President Adams asked Congress to prepare for war, and the French responded by seizing more American ships. Thus began, in April 1798, an undeclared war between France and the United States in the Caribbean. While the French navy dealt with the British in the North Atlantic, French privateers inflicted costly blows on American shipping. After nearly a year of fighting, with the British providing powder and shot for American guns, the U.S. Navy chased the French privateers out of the Caribbean.

XYZ Affair *Incident that precipitated an undeclared war with France when three French officials (identified as X, Y, and Z) demanded that American emissaries pay a bribe before negotiating disputes between the two countries.*

THE CRISIS AT HOME, 1798–1800

The troubles with France precipitated a crisis at home. The disclosure of the XYZ correspondence, together with the quasi-war in the Caribbean, produced a surge of public hostility toward the French and, to some extent, toward their Republican friends in the United States. Many Federalists, led by Alexander Hamilton, wanted to use the crisis to destroy their political opponents. Without consulting President Adams, the Federalist-dominated Congress passed a number of wartime measures. The first was a federal property tax. Congress then passed four laws known as the Alien and Sedition Acts. The first three were directed at immigrants: They extended the **natural-**

FOCUS QUESTION

What was the nature of the governmental crisis of 1798–1800, and how was it resolved?

ization period from 5 to 14 years and empowered the president to detain enemy **aliens** during wartime and to deport those he deemed dangerous to the United States. The fourth law, the Sedition Act, set jail terms and fines for persons who advocated disobedience to federal law or who wrote, printed, or spoke "false, scandalous, and malicious" statements against "the government of the United States, or the President of the United States, with intent to defame . . . or to bring them or either of them, into contempt or disrepute."

President Adams never used the powers granted under the Alien Acts. But the Sedition Act resulted in the prosecution of 14 Republicans, most of them journalists. Republicans, charging that the Alien and Sedition Acts violated the First Amendment, turned to the states for help. Southern states took the lead. Jefferson provided the Kentucky legislature with draft resolutions, and Madison did the same for the Virginia legislature. Jefferson's Kentucky Resolves reminded Congress that the Alien and Sedition Acts gave the national government powers not mentioned in the Constitution and that the Tenth Amendment reserved such powers to the states. He also argued that the Constitution was a "compact" between sovereign states and that state legislatures could "nullify" federal laws they deemed unconstitutional.

The Virginia and Kentucky Resolves had few immediate effects. Opposition to the Sedition Act ranged from popular attempts to obstruct the law to fistfights in Congress. But no other states followed the lead of Virginia and Kentucky, and talk of armed opposition to Federalist policies was limited to a few areas in the South.

THE POLITICIANS AND THE ARMY

Federalists took another ominous step by implementing President Adams's request that Congress create a military prepared for war. Adams wanted a stronger navy; Hamilton and others (who were becoming known as **High Federalists**) preferred a standing army. At the urging of Washington and against his own judgment, Adams had appointed Hamilton inspector general. As such, Hamilton would be the de facto commander of the U.S. Army. Congress authorized a 20,000-man army, and Hamilton proceeded to raise it. Congress also provided for a much larger army to be called up in the event of a declaration of war. When he appointed officers, Hamilton commissioned only his political friends. High Federalists wanted a standing army to enforce the Alien and Sedition Acts and to put down an impending rebellion in the South. Beyond that, there was little need for such a force. The Republicans, President Adams himself, and many other Federalists now became convinced that Hamilton and his High Federalists were determined to destroy their political opponents, enter into an alliance with Great Britain, and impose Hamilton's statist designs on the nation by force.

Adams was both fearful and angry. First the Hamiltonians had tried to rob him of the presidency and then had passed the Alien and Sedition Acts, the direct tax, and plans for a standing army without consulting him. None of this would have been possible had it not been for the crisis with France. Adams began looking for ways to declare peace. He opened negotiations with France and stalled the creation of Hamilton's army while the talks took place. At first the Senate refused to send an envoy to France. The senators relented when Adams threatened to resign and leave the presidency to Vice President Jefferson. In the agreement that followed, the French canceled the obligations that the United States had assumed under the treaties of 1778, but they refused to pay reparations for attacks on American shipping since 1793. Peace with France cut the ground from under the more militaristic and repressive Federalists and intensified discord among the Federalists in general.

naturalization *Process by which people born in a foreign country are granted full citizenship with all of its rights.*

alien *Person from another country who is living in the United States.*

High Federalists *A term used to describe Alexander Hamilton and some of his less-moderate supporters. They wanted the naval war with France to continue and also wanted to severely limit the rights of an opposition party.*

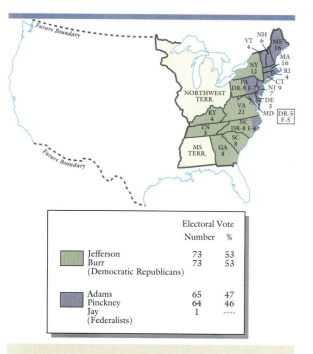

	Electoral Vote	
	Number	%
Jefferson	73	53
Burr	73	53
(Democratic Republicans)		
Adams	65	47
Pinckney	64	46
Jay	1	----
(Federalists)		

Map 8.1
PRESIDENTIAL ELECTION, 1800. *The electoral votes in 1800 split along starkly sectional lines. The South voted for Jefferson, New England voted for Adams, and the election was decided by close contests in Pennsylvania and New York.*

THE ELECTION OF 1800

Thomas Jefferson and his Democratic Republicans approached the election of 1800 better organized and more determined than they had been four years earlier. Moreover, the Alien and Sedition Acts, the direct tax of 1798, and the Federalist military buildup worked in their favor. Prosecutions under the Sedition Act revealed its partisan origins, and the Federalists showed no sign of abandoning the Alien and Sedition Acts and the new military even when peace seemed certain, giving credence to the Republicans' allegation that the Federalists were using the crisis with France to destroy their opposition and overthrow the American republic. The Federalists countered by warning that the election of Jefferson and his radical allies would release the worst horrors of the French Revolution in America.

After a heated campaign, Jefferson and his running mate, **Aaron Burr**, won with 73 electoral votes each. Adams had 65 votes, and his running mate Charles Cotesworth Pinckney had 64. Congress, which was still controlled by Federalists, would have to decide whether Jefferson or Burr was to be president of the United States. After 35 ballots, with most of the Federalists supporting Burr, a compromise was reached whereby the Federalists turned in blank ballots and thus avoided voting for the hated Jefferson.

THE JEFFERSONIANS IN POWER

FOCUS QUESTION
What were the principal reforms of the national government during Thomas Jefferson's administration? What were the implications of those reforms for the nature of republican government?

On the first Tuesday of March 1801, Thomas Jefferson left his rooms at Conrad and McMunn's boarding house in the half-built capital city of Washington and walked up Pennsylvania Avenue. There were military salutes along the way, but Jefferson forbade the pomp and ceremony that had ushered Washington into office. Accompanied by a few friends and a company of artillery from the Maryland militia, he walked up the street and into the unfinished capitol building. There he joined Vice President Burr, other members of the government, and a few foreign diplomats in the newly finished Senate chamber.

THE REPUBLICAN PROGRAM

Jefferson took the oath of office from Chief Justice John Marshall. Then he delivered his inaugural address. Referring to the political discord that had brought him into office, he began with a plea for unity, insisting that "every difference of opinion is not a difference of principle." He did not mean that he and his opponents should forget their

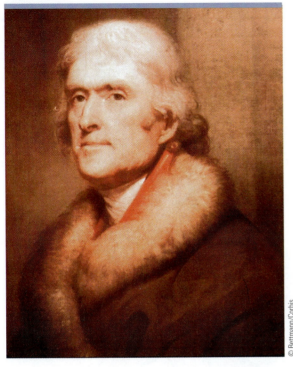

© Bettmann/Corbis

PORTRAIT OF JEFFERSON, BY REMBRANDT PEALE, 1805. *A self-consciously plain President Jefferson posed for this portrait in January 1805, near the end of his first term. He wears an unadorned fur-collared coat, is surrounded by no emblems of office, and gazes calmly and directly at the viewer.*

ideological differences. He meant only to invite moderate Federalists into a broad Republican coalition. Jefferson went on to outline the kind of government a republic should have. He declared that Americans were a free people with no need for a national state built on European models. A people blessed with isolation, bountiful resources, and liberty needed only "a wise and frugal Government, which shall restrain men from injuring one another, shall leave them otherwise free to regulate their own pursuits of industry and improvement, and shall not take from the mouth of labor the bread it has earned."

In particular, Jefferson's "wise and frugal" government would respect the powers of the individual states. It would also defend the liberties ensured by the Bill of Rights. It would be made smaller, and it would pay its debts without incurring new ones, thus ending the need for taxation. It would rely for defense on "a disciplined militia" that would fight invaders while regulars were being trained—thus getting rid of Hamilton's standing army. It would protect republican liberties from enemies at home and from the nations of Europe. The simplicity of Jefferson's inauguration set the social tone of his administration. The new president reduced the number and grandeur of formal balls, levees, and dinners. He sent his annual messages to Congress to be read by a clerk, rather than delivering them in person. He refused to ride about Washington in a carriage, preferring to carry out his errands on horseback. Abandoning the grand banquets favored by his predecessors, Jefferson entertained senators and congressmen at small dinners that were served at a roundtable without formal seating. Jefferson presided over the meals without wearing a wig and dressed in old homespun and a pair of worn bedroom slippers. The casualness did not extend to what was served, however. The food was prepared by expert chefs and accompanied by fine wines. And it was followed by brilliant conversation. The president's dinners set examples of the unpretentious excellence through which Jefferson hoped to govern the republic that he claimed to have saved from monarchists.

CLEANSING THE GOVERNMENT

Jefferson reduced the size and expense of government. He reduced the diplomatic corps and replaced officeholders who were incompetent, corrupt, or avowedly anti-republican. He made more substantial cuts in the military. Legislation passed in March 1802 reduced the army to two regiments of infantry and one of artillery—a total of 3,350 officers and men, most of whom were assigned to western posts. Similar

Aaron Burr *Vice President under Thomas Jefferson who killed Alexander Hamilton in a duel and eventually hatched schemes to detach parts of the west from the United States.*

"MAD TOM IN A RAGE." *This Federalist cartoon of 1801 portrays Jefferson, with the help of the devil and a bottle of brandy, pulling down the government that Washington and Adams had built.*

The Granger Collection, New York

cutbacks were made in the navy. The goal, Jefferson explained, was to rely mainly on the militia for national defense but to maintain a small, well-trained professional army as well. At Jefferson's urging, Congress also abolished the direct tax of 1798 and repealed the parts of the Alien and Sedition Acts that had not already expired. Jefferson personally pardoned the 10 victims of those acts who were still in jail.

Thus with a few deft strokes, Jefferson dismantled the repressive apparatus of the Federalist state. And by reducing government expenditures he reduced the government's debt. During Jefferson's administration the national debt fell from $80 million to $57 million, and the government built up a treasury surplus. Although some doubted the wisdom of such stringent economy, no one doubted Jefferson's frugality.

THE JEFFERSONIANS AND THE COURTS

Jefferson's demands for a "wise and frugal" government applied to the federal judiciary as well. The First Congress had created circuit courts presided over by the justices of the Supreme Court. Only Federalists had served on the Supreme Court under Washington and Adams, and they had extended federal authority into the hinterland. Thus Jeffersonian Republicans had ample reason to distrust the federal courts. Their distrust was intensified by the Judiciary Act of 1801, which was passed just before Jefferson's inauguration by the **lame-duck** Federalist Congress. Coupled with President Adams's appointment of the Federalist John Marshall as chief justice in January, the Judiciary Act assured long-term Federalist domination of the federal courts. First, it reduced the number of associate justices of the Supreme Court from six to five when the next vacancy occurred, thus reducing Jefferson's chances of appointing a new member to the Court. The Judiciary Act also took Supreme Court justices off circuit and created a new system of circuit courts. This allowed Adams to appoint 16 new judges, along with a full array of marshals, federal attorneys, clerks, and justices of the peace. He worked until 9 o'clock on his last night in office signing commissions for these new officers. All of them were staunch Federalists.

lame-duck administration
Period of time between an incumbent party's or officeholder's loss of an election and the succession to office of the winning party or candidate.

Jefferson and most in his party wanted the courts shielded from democratic control; at the same time, they deeply resented the uniformly Federalist **midnight judges** created by the Judiciary Act of 1801. Jefferson did replace the new federal marshals and attorneys with Republicans and dismissed some of the federal justices of the peace. But judges were appointed for life and could be removed only through impeachment. The Jeffersonians hit on a simple solution: They would get rid of the new judges by abolishing their jobs. Early in 1802 Congress repealed the Judiciary Act of 1801 and thus did away with the midnight appointees.

THE IMPEACHMENTS OF PICKERING AND CHASE

With the federal courts scaled back to their original size, Republicans in Congress went after High Federalists who were still acting as judges. As a first test of removal by impeachment they chose John Pickering, a federal attorney with the circuit court of New Hampshire. Pickering was alcoholic and insane; even Federalists considered him an embarrassment. The House drew up articles of impeachment, and Pickering was tried by the Senate, which, by a strict party vote, removed him from office.

On the same day, Congress voted to impeach Supreme Court Justice Samuel Chase. Chase was a much more prominent public figure than Pickering. He had prosecuted sedition cases with real enthusiasm. He had also delivered anti-Jeffersonian diatribes from the bench, and he had used his position and his formidable legal skills to bully young lawyers with whom he disagreed. In short, Chase was an unpleasant, overbearing, and unashamedly partisan member of the Supreme Court. But his faults did not add up to the "high crimes and misdemeanors" that are the constitutional grounds for impeachment. Moderate Republicans doubted the wisdom of the Chase impeachment, and their uneasiness grew when Virginia Congressman John Randolph, leader of a radical states rights faction, took over the prosecution. Many Republicans, including Jefferson himself, disliked Randolph as much as Chase. With Jefferson's approval, many Senate Republicans joined the Federalists in acquitting Samuel Chase.

JUSTICE MARSHALL'S COURT

Chief Justice John Marshall probably cheered the acquittal of Justice Chase, for it was clear that Marshall was next on the list. Marshall was committed to Federalist ideas of national power, as he demonstrated with his decision in the case of **Marbury v. Madison.** William Marbury was one of the justices of the peace whom Jefferson had eliminated in his first few days in office. He sued Jefferson's secretary of state, James Madison, for the nondelivery of his commission. Although Marbury never got his job, Marshall used the case to hand down a number of important rulings. The first ruling, which questioned the constitutionality of Jefferson's refusal to deliver Marbury's commission, helped to convince Republican moderates to repeal the Judiciary Act of 1801. The last ruling, delivered in February 1803, laid the basis for the Supreme Court's power of **judicial review,** which entitles the Court to rule on the constitutionality of acts of Congress. Some Republicans saw Marshall's ruling as an attempt to arrogate power to the Court. But Marshall was not a sinister man. As secretary of state under John Adams, he had helped to end the undeclared war with France, and he had expressed doubts about the Alien and Sedition Acts. Of more immediate concern, while he disliked Congress's repeal of the 1801 legislation, he did not doubt the right of Congress to make and unmake laws, and he was determined to accept the situation. While the decision in *Marbury* v. *Madison* angered many Republicans,

midnight judges *Federal judicial officials appointed under the Judiciary Act of 1801, in the last days of John Adams's presidency.*

Marbury v. Madison *1803 case involving the disputed appointment of a federal justice of the peace in which Chief Justice John Marshall expanded the Supreme Court's authority to review legislation.*

judicial review *Supreme Court's power to rule on the constitutionality of congressional acts.*

Jefferson and the moderate Republicans noted that Marshall was less interested in the power of the judiciary than in its independence. Ultimately, they decided they trusted Marshall more than they trusted the radicals in their own party. With the acquittal of Justice Chase, Jeffersonian attacks on the federal courts ceased.

LOUISIANA

It was Jefferson's good fortune that Europe remained at peace during his first term and stayed out of American affairs. Indeed the one development that posed an international threat to the United States turned into a grand triumph: the purchase of the Louisiana Territory from France in 1803.

By 1801 a half-million Americans lived west of the Appalachians. Republicans saw westward expansion as the best hope for the survival of the republic. Social inequality would almost inevitably take root in the East, but the vast lands west of the mountains would enable the republic to renew itself for many generations to come. To serve that purpose, however, the West needed ready access to markets through the river system that emptied into the Gulf of Mexico at New Orleans.

In 1801 Spain owned New Orleans and under Pinckney's Treaty allowed Americans to transship produce from the interior. The year before, however, Spain had secretly ceded the Louisiana Territory (roughly, all the land west of the Mississippi drained by the Missouri and Arkansas rivers) to France. Late in 1802, the Spanish, who had retained control of New Orleans, closed the port to American commerce, giving rise to rumors that they would soon transfer the city to France. President Jefferson sent a delegation to Paris early in 1803 with authorization to buy New Orleans for the United States.

By the time the delegates reached Paris, the slaves of Saint Dominque (present-day Haiti and the Dominican Republic) had revolted against the French and had defeated their attempts to regain control of the island (see Chapter 7). At the same time, another war between Britain and France seemed imminent. Napoleon decided to bail out of America and concentrate his resources in Europe. He astonished Jefferson's delegation by announcing that France would sell not only New Orleans but the whole Louisiana Territory for the bargain price of $15 million.

Jefferson faced a dilemma: The Constitution did not give the president the power to buy territory, but the chance to buy Louisiana was too good to refuse. It would assure Americans access to the rivers of the interior; it would eliminate a serious foreign threat on America's western border; and it would give American farmers enough land to sustain the agrarian republic for a long time to come. Swallowing his constitutional scruples, Jefferson told the American delegates to buy Louisiana. Republican senators quickly ratified the Louisiana treaty over Federalist objections, an act that met with overwhelming public approval. For his part, Jefferson was certain that the republic had gained the means of renewing itself through time.

As Jefferson stood for reelection in 1804, he could look back on an astonishingly successful first term. He had dismantled the government's power to coerce its citizens, and he had begun to wipe out the national debt. The **Louisiana Purchase** had doubled the size of the republic at remarkably little cost. Moreover, by eliminating France from North America, it had strengthened the argument for reducing the military and the debts and taxes that went with it.

The combination of international peace, territorial expansion, and inexpensive, unobtrusive government left the Federalists without an issue in the 1804 election. They went through the motions of nominating Charles Pinckney of South Carolina as their presidential candidate and then watched as Jefferson captured the electoral votes of every state but Delaware and Connecticut.

Louisiana Purchase *Land purchased from France in 1803 that doubled the size of the United States.*

THE REPUBLIC AND THE NAPOLEONIC WARS, 1804–1815

Early in 1803 Napoleon Bonaparte declared war on Great Britain. This 11-year war dominated the national politics of the United States. Most Americans wanted to remain neutral. Few Republicans supported Bonaparte, and none but the most rabid Federalists wanted to intervene on the side of Great Britain. But neither France nor Britain would permit American neutrality.

FOCUS QUESTION
What was the situation of the United States within the international politics created by the Napoleonic Wars, and how did that situation degenerate into a second war with Great Britain?

THE DILEMMAS OF NEUTRALITY

At the beginning, both Britain and France encouraged the Americans to resume their role as neutral carriers and suppliers of food. For a time, Americans made huge profits. Between 1803 and 1807 U.S. exports rose from $66.5 million to $102.2 million. Reexports—goods produced in the Caribbean, picked up by American vessels, and then reloaded in American ports onto American ships bound for Europe—rose even faster, from $13.5 million to $58.4 million.

In 1805 France and Great Britain began systematically to interfere with that trade. In 1805 the Royal Navy destroyed the French and Spanish fleets at the Battle of Trafalgar. Later that year Napoleon's armies defeated Austria and Russia at the Battle of Austerlitz. The war reached a stalemate: Napoleon's army dominated Europe, the British navy controlled the seas.

Britain decided to use its naval supremacy to blockade Europe and starve the French into submission. In the Essex Decision of 1805, Britain invoked the Rule of 1756, which stated that a European country could not use a neutral merchant marine to conduct wartime trade with its colonies if its mercantile laws forbade such use during peacetime. Translated into the realities of 1805, the Essex Decision meant that the Royal Navy could seize American ships engaged in the reexport trade with France. In the spring of 1806 Congress, angered by British seizures of American ships, passed the Non-Importation Act forbidding the importation of British goods that could be bought elsewhere or that could be manufactured in the United States. A month after that Britain blockaded long stretches of the European coast. Napoleon responded with the Berlin Decree, which outlawed all trade with the British Isles. The British answered with an Order in Council that demanded that neutral ships trading with Europe stop first for inspection and licensing in a British port. Napoleon responded with the Milan Decree, which stated that any vessel that obeyed the British decrees or allowed itself to be searched by the Royal Navy was subject to seizure by France. Beginning in 1805 and ending with the Milan Decree in December 1807, the barrage of European decrees and counterdecrees meant that virtually all American commerce with Europe had been outlawed by one or the other of the warring powers.

TROUBLE ON THE HIGH SEAS

The Royal Navy maintained a loose blockade of the North American coast, searching American ships as they left port. Hundreds of ships were seized, along with their cargoes and crews. Under British law, the Royal Navy during wartime could impress any British subject into service. The British were certain that many British subjects, including legions of deserters from the Royal Navy, were hiding in the American merchant marine. They were right. The danger, low pay, bad food, and draconian discipline on British warships encouraged many British sailors to jump ship and take jobs as American merchantmen. But the sailors the British commandeered often included Englishmen who had taken out U.S. citizenship (an act the British did not recognize) and, inevitably, native-born Americans. An estimated 6,000 American citizens were impressed into the Royal Navy between 1803 and 1812.

The kidnapping of American sailors enraged Americans and nearly started a war in the summer of 1807. In June the American naval frigate *Chesapeake,* which was outfitting in Norfolk, Virginia, signed on four English deserters from the British navy, along with some Americans who had joined the British navy and then deserted. The British warship H.M.S. *Leopard* also was docked at Norfolk, and some of the deserters spotted their old officers and taunted them on the streets. The *Leopard* left port and resumed its patrol of the American coast. Then, on June 21, its officers caught the *Chesapeake* off Hampton Roads and demanded the return of the British deserters. When the captain refused, the British fired on the *Chesapeake,* killing 3 Americans and wounding 18. The British then boarded the *Chesapeake,* seized the four deserters, and later hanged one of them.

The *Chesapeake* affair set off huge anti-British demonstrations in the seaport towns and angry cries for war throughout the country. President Jefferson responded by barring British ships from American ports and American territorial waters, and by ordering state governors to prepare to call up as many as 100,000 militiamen.

EMBARGO

Jefferson had one more card to play: He could suspend trade with Europe altogether and thus keep American ships out of harm's way. He could use trade as a means of "peaceable coercion" that would both ensure respect for American neutrality rights and keep the country out of war. "Our commerce," he wrote just before taking office, "is so valuable to them, that they will be glad to purchase it, when the only price we ask is to do us justice." Convinced that America's **yeoman** republic could survive without European luxuries more easily than Europe could survive without American food, Jefferson decided to give "peaceable coercion" a serious test. Late in 1807 he asked Congress to suspend all U.S. trade with foreign countries.

Congress passed the Embargo Act on December 22. By the following spring, however, it was clear that peaceable coercion would not work. The British found other markets and other sources of food. They encouraged the smuggling of American goods into Canada. And American merchantmen who had been at sea when the **embargo** went into effect stayed away from their home ports and functioned as part of the British merchant marine. A loophole in the Embargo Act allowed U.S. ships to leave port in order to pick up American property stranded in other countries, and an estimated 6,000 ships set sail under that excuse. Hundreds of others, plying the coastal trade, were "blown off course" and found themselves thrust into international commerce.

The embargo hurt American commerce badly. The economy slowed in every section of the country, but it ground to a halt in the cities of the Northeast. Federalists accused Jefferson of plotting an end to commerce and a reversion to rural barbarism, and they often took the lead in trying to subvert the embargo through smuggling and other means.

The Federalists gained ground in the elections of 1808. James Madison, Jefferson's old ally and chosen successor, was elected president with 122 electoral votes to 47 for his Federalist opponent, C. C. Pinckney, and Republicans retained control of both houses of Congress. But Federalists made significant gains in Congress and won control of several state legislatures. Federalist opposition to the embargo, and to the supposed southern, agrarian stranglehold on national power that stood behind it, was clearly gaining ground.

yeoman *A farmer who owned his own farm.*

embargo *Government order prohibiting the movement of merchant ships or goods in or out of its ports.*

THE ROAD TO WAR

When President Madison took office in the spring of 1809, it was clear that the embargo had failed. It had created misery in the seaport cities, choked off the imports that were the source of 90 percent of federal revenue, and revived Federalist opposition to Republican dominance. Early in 1809 Congress passed the Non-Intercourse Act, which retained the ban on trade with Britain and France but reopened trade with other nations. It also gave President Madison the power to reopen trade with either Britain or France once they had agreed to respect American rights. Neither complied, and the Non-Intercourse Act proved nearly as ineffective as the embargo.

In 1810 Congress passed Macon's Bill No. 2, which rescinded the ban on trade with France and Britain but authorized the president to reimpose it on either belligerent if the other agreed to end its restrictions on U.S. trade. In September 1810 the French foreign minister, the Duc de Cadore, promised that France would repeal the Berlin and Milan Decrees. Though the proposal was a clear attempt to lead the United States into conflict with Great Britain, Madison felt he had no choice but to go along with it. He accepted the French promise and proclaimed in November 1810 that the British had three months to follow suit.

In the end, Madison's proclamation led to war. The French repealed only those sections of the Berlin and Milan Decrees that applied to the neutral rights of the United States. The British refused to revoke their Orders in Council and told the Americans to withdraw their restrictions on British trade until the French had repealed theirs. The United States would either have to obey British orders or go to war.

THE WAR HAWK CONGRESS, 1811–1812

In 1811–1812 the Republicans controlled both houses of Congress, but they were a divided majority. The Federalist minority, which was united against Madison, was joined on many issues by northeastern Republicans who followed the Federalist line on international trade and by Republicans who wanted a more powerful military. Also opposed to Madison were the self-styled Old Republicans of the South, led by John Randolph.

In this confused situation a group of talented young congressmen took control. Nearly all of them were Republicans from the South or the West. Called the **War Hawks**, these men were ardent nationalists who were more than willing to declare war on England to protect U.S. rights. Through their organizational, oratorical, and intellectual power, they won control of Congress. Henry Clay, only 34 years old and serving his first term in Congress, was elected Speaker of the House. More vigorous than his predecessors, Clay controlled debate, packed key committees, worked tirelessly behind the scenes, and imposed order on his fellow congressmen.

War Hawks *Members of the Twelfth Congress, most of them young nationalists from southern and western areas, who promoted war with Britain.*

A SCENE ON THE FRONTIERS AS PRACTICED BY THE HUMANE BRITISH AND THEIR WORTHY ALLIES! *An overfed British officer in the Northwest pays his Indian allies for the scalps of white Americans, while the caption orders "Columbia's Sons" to take up their guns and set things right.*

In the winter and spring of 1811–1812 the War Hawks led Congress into a war. In November they voted military preparations, and in April they enacted a 90-day embargo—not to coerce the British but to get American ships safely into port before war began. On June 1, Madison sent a war message to Congress. This was to be the first war declared under the Constitution, and the president stayed out of congressional territory by not asking explicitly for a declaration of war. He did, however, present a list of British crimes that could be interpreted in no other way: the enforcement of the Orders in Council, even within the territorial waters of the United States; the impressment of American seamen; the use of spies and provocateurs within the United States; and the wielding of "a malicious influence over the Indians of the Northwest Territory." Madison concluded that war had in fact begun.

Congress declared war on June 18. The vote was far from unanimous. All 30 Federalists voted against the declaration. So did one in five Republicans, nearly all of them from the Northeast. Thus the war was declared by the Democratic Republican Party, more particularly by the Republicans of the South and the West.

WAR HAWKS AND THE WAR OF 1812

Federalists and many northeastern Republicans expected a naval war. After all, it was on the ocean that the British had committed their atrocities. Yet when Madison asked Congress to prepare for war, the War Hawks led a majority that strengthened the U.S. Army and left the navy weak. Reasoning that no U.S. naval force could challenge British control of the seas, they prepared instead for a land invasion of British Canada.

The decision to invade Canada led the Federalists, along with many of Randolph's Old Republicans, to accuse Madison and the congressional majority of planning a war of territorial aggression. Some members of Congress did indeed want to annex Canada to the United States. But most saw the invasion of Canada as a matter of strategy. Lightly garrisoned and with a population of only half a million, Canada seemed the easiest and most logical place in which to damage the British. Thus Canada was both valuable and vulnerable, and American policymakers reasoned that they could take it and hold it hostage while demanding that the British back down on other issues.

THE WAR WITH CANADA, 1812–1813

The United States opened its offensive against Canada in 1812 with disastrous results. The plan was to invade Upper Canada (Ontario) from the Northwest, thus cutting off the pro-British Indian tribes from their British support. When General William Hull, governor of Michigan Territory, took an army of militiamen and volunteers into Canada from Detroit, he found the area crawling with British troops and their Indian allies. He retreated to the garrison at Detroit. British General Isaac Brock, who knew that Hull was afraid of Indians, sent a note into the fort telling him that "the numerous body of Indians who have attached themselves to my troops, will be beyond my controul the moment the contest commences." Without consulting his officers, Hull surrendered his army of 2,000 to the smaller British force. Though Hull was later court-martialed for cowardice, the damage had been done: The British and their Indian allies occupied many of the remaining American garrisons in the Northwest and transformed the U.S. invasion of Upper Canada into a British occupation of much of the Northwest.

The invasion of Canada from the east went no better. In October a U.S. force of 6,000 faced 2,000 British and Indians across the Niagara River separating Ontario

View an animated version of this map or related maps at
http://history.wadsworth.com/murrinconcise4e.

Map 8.2

WAR OF 1812. *Early in the war, Americans chose to fight the British in Canada, with costly and inconclusive results. Later, the British determined to blockade the whole coast of the United States and, late in the war, to raid important coastal towns. The results were equally inconclusive: Both sides could inflict serious damage, but neither could conquer the other. The one clear military outcome—one that the Americans were determined to accomplish—was the destruction of Indian resistance east of the Mississippi.*

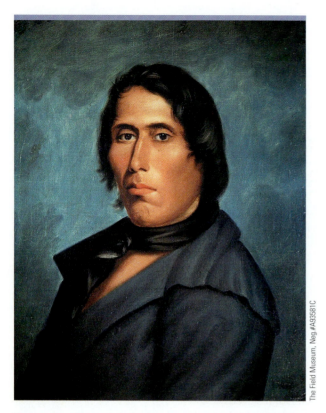

The Field Museum, Neg.#A93581C

TECUMSEH. *Tecumseh, military and political leader of the northwestern tribes that sided with the British in 1812, came closer than any other Native American leader to unifying Indian peoples against white territorial expansion.*

from western New York. The U.S. regular army crossed the river, surprised the British, and established a toehold at Queenston Heights. While the British were preparing a counterattack, New York militiamen refused to cross the river to reinforce the regular troops. The British regrouped and slaughtered the outnumbered, exhausted U.S. regulars.

As winter set in, it was clear that Canada would not fall easily. Indeed the invasion, which U.S. commanders had thought would knife through an apathetic Canadian population, had the opposite effect. The attacks by the United States turned the ragtag assortment of American loyalist émigrés, discharged British soldiers, and American-born settlers into a self-consciously British Canadian people.

TECUMSEH'S LAST STAND

Tecumseh's Indian confederacy, bruised but not broken in the Battle of Tippecanoe (see Chapter 7), allied itself with the British in 1812. On a trip to the southern tribes Tecumseh found the traditionalist wing of the Creeks—who called themselves Red Sticks—willing to join him. The augmented confederacy provided stiff resistance to the United States throughout the war. The Red Sticks chased settlers from much of Tennessee. They then attacked a group of settlers who had taken refuge in a stockade surrounding the house of an Alabama trader named George Mims. In what whites called the Massacre at Fort Mims, the Red Sticks killed at least 247 men, women, and children. In the Northwest, Tecumseh's warriors, fighting alongside the British, spread terror throughout the white settlements.

A wiser U.S. Army returned to Canada in 1813. They raided and burned the Canadian capital at York (Toronto) in April and then fought inconclusively through the summer. An autumn offensive toward Montreal failed, but the Americans had better luck on Lake Erie. In September 1813 Commodore Oliver Hazard Perry cornered the British fleet at Put-in-Bay and destroyed it. Control of Lake Erie enabled the United States to cut off supplies to the British in the Northwest, and a U.S. Army under William Henry Harrison retook the area and continued on into Canada. On October 5 Harrison caught up with a force of British and Indians at the Thames River and beat them badly. In the course of that battle Richard M. Johnson, a War Hawk congressman acting as commander of the Kentucky militia, killed Tecumseh.

The following spring General Andrew Jackson's Tennessee militia, aided by Choctaw, Creek, and Cherokee allies, attacked and slaughtered the Red Sticks who had fortified themselves at Horseshoe Bend in Alabama. The military power of the Indian peoples east of the Mississippi River was broken.

THE BRITISH OFFENSIVE, 1814

The British defeated Napoleon in April 1814, thus ending the larger war of which the War of 1812 was a part. The British decided to concentrate their resources on the American war. They had already blockaded much of the American coast.

During the summer of 1814 they began to raid the shores of Chesapeake Bay and marched on Washington, D.C., chased the army and politicians out of town, and burned down the capitol building and the president's mansion. In September the British attacked Baltimore but could not blast their way past Fort McHenry, which guarded the harbor. This was the battle that inspired Francis Scott Key to write "The Star-Spangled Banner." When a British offensive on Lake Champlain stalled during the autumn, the war reached a stalemate: Britain had prevented the invasion of Canada and had blockaded the American coast, but neither side could take and hold the other's territory.

The British now shifted their attention to the Gulf Coast. A British amphibious force landed near New Orleans. There they were opposed by an American army made up of U.S. regulars, Kentucky and Tennessee militiamen, clerks, workingmen, and free blacks from the city, and about a thousand French pirates—all under the command of Andrew Jackson of Tennessee. Throughout late December and early January, unaware that a peace treaty had been signed on December 24, the armies exchanged artillery barrages, and the British probed and attacked American lines. Then, on January 8, the British launched a frontal assault. A formation of 6,000 British soldiers marched across open ground toward 4,000 Americans concealed behind breastworks. With the first American volley, it was clear that the British had made a mistake. The charge lasted half an hour. At the end, 2,000 British soldiers lay dead or wounded. American casualties numbered only 70. Fought nearly two weeks after the peace treaty, the Battle of New Orleans had no effect on the outcome of the war or on the peace terms. But it salved the injured pride of Americans and made a national hero and a political power of Andrew Jackson.

THE HARTFORD CONVENTION

While most Americans celebrated Jackson's victory, Federalist New England was complaining. New Englanders had considered themselves the victims of Republican trade policies, and their congressmen had voted overwhelmingly against going to war. Some Federalists had openly urged resistance to the war. The British had encouraged that resistance by not extending their naval blockade to the New England coast, and throughout the first two years of the war New England merchants and farmers had traded freely with the enemy. In 1814, after the Royal Navy had extended its blockade northward and had begun to raid the towns of coastal Maine, some Federalists talked about seceding and making a separate peace with Britain.

In an attempt to undercut the secessionists, moderate Federalists called a convention at Hartford in December 1814. The Hartford Convention proposed several amendments to the Constitution. The delegates wanted the "three-fifths" clause, which led to overrepresentation of the South in Congress and the Electoral College (see Chapter 6), stricken from the Constitution. They wanted to deny naturalized citizens, who were strongly Republican, the right to hold office. They wanted to make it more difficult for new states—all of which sided with the Republicans and their southern leadership—to enter the Union. Finally, they wanted to require a two-thirds majority of both houses for a declaration of war, a requirement that would have prevented the War of 1812.

The Federalist leaders of the Hartford Convention took their proposals to Washington in mid-January. They found the capital celebrating the news of the peace treaty and Jackson's victory at New Orleans. When they aired their proposals, they were branded as unpatriotic. Although Federalists continued for a few years to wield power in southern New England, the Hartford debacle ruined any chance of a nationwide Federalist resurgence after the war.

THE TREATY OF GHENT

Britain's defeat of Napoleon spurred British and American efforts to end a war that neither wanted. In August 1814 they opened peace talks in the Belgian city of Ghent. Perhaps waiting for the results of their 1814 offensive, the British opened with proposals that the Americans were certain to reject. They demanded the right to navigate the Mississippi, territorial concessions, and the creation of the permanent, independent Indian buffer state in the Northwest that they had promised their Indian allies. The Americans ignored them and talked about impressment and maritime rights. As the war reached stalemate, both sides began to compromise. The British knew that the Americans would grant concessions in the interior only if they were thoroughly defeated, an outcome that most British commanders thought impossible. For their part, the Americans realized that the British maritime depredations were by-products of the struggle with Napoleonic France. Faced with peace in Europe and a senseless military stalemate in North America, negotiators on both sides began to withdraw their demands. The Treaty of Ghent, signed on Christmas Eve 1814, simply ended the war. The border between Canada and the United States remained where it had been in 1812; Indians south of that border—defeated and without allies—were left to the mercy of the United States; and British maritime violations were not mentioned.

C O N C L U S I O N

In 1816 Thomas Jefferson was in retirement at Monticello, satisfied that he had defended liberty against the Federalists' love of power. The High Federalists' attempt to militarize government and to jail their enemies had failed. Their direct taxes were repealed. Their debt and their national bank remained in place, but only under the watchful eyes of true republicans. And their attempt to ally the United States with the antirepublican designs of Great Britain had ended in what many called the "Second War of American Independence." Yet for all his successes, Jefferson in 1816 saw that he must sacrifice his dreams of agrarianism. Throughout his political life, Jefferson envisioned American yeomen trading farm surpluses for European manufactured goods—a relationship that would ensure rural prosperity, prevent the growth of cities and factories, and thus sustain the landed independence on which republican citizenship rested. Westward expansion, he had believed, would ensure the yeoman republic for generations to come. By 1816 that dream was ended. Arguing as Hamilton had argued in 1790, Jefferson insisted that "we must now place the manufacturer by the side of the agriculturalist." As he wrote, a Republican congress was taking steps that would help transform the yeoman republic into a market society and a boisterous capitalist democracy.

QUESTIONS FOR REVIEW AND CRITICAL THINKING

Review

1. What was the Federalist plan for organizing the national government and its finances? What were the Jeffersonian Republicans' principal objections to those plans?
2. What was the nature of the governmental crisis of 1798–1800, and how was it resolved?
3. What were the principal reforms of the national government during Thomas Jefferson's administration? What were the implications of those reforms for the nature of republican government?
4. What was the situation of the United States within the international politics created by the Napoleonic Wars, and how did that situation degenerate into a second war with Great Britain?

Critical Thinking

1. In the 1790s Federalists and Democratic Republicans argued about the nature of the new national government. On what specific issues was this argument conducted? Was there a larger argument underlying these specifics?
2. Thomas Jefferson had a vision of the American republic and of the role of the national government within it. In what ways did his presidency succeed in realizing that vision? In what ways did it fail?

Discovery

In what ways did the ascension of the Jeffersonians to power in 1800 shape the future of America?

SUGGESTED READINGS

Stanley Elkins and **Eric McKitrick,** *The Age of Federalism: The Early American Republic, 1788–1800* (1993) is definitive. An insightful essay on the Jeffersonians is **Peter S. Onuf and Leonard J. Sadosky,** *Jeffersonian America (2002).* **Thomas G. Slaughter,** *The Whiskey Rebellion: Frontier Epilogue to the American Revolution* (1986) is good on its subject. **Lance Banning,** *The Jeffersonian Persuasion: Evolution of a Party Ideology* (1980) and **Drew R. McCoy,** *The Elusive Republic: Political Economy in Jeffersonian America* (1980) are insightful studies of Jeffersonianism. On relations with other countries, see **Lawrence Kaplan,** *Entangling Alliances with None: American Foreign Policy in the Age of Jefferson* (1987) and **Donald R. Hickey,** *The War of 1812: A Forgotten Conflict* (1989). **Joseph J. Ellis,** *Founding Brothers: The Revolutionary Generation* (2000) and **Joanne B. Freeman,** *Affairs of Honor: National Politics in the New Republic* (2001) are fine studies of the political culture of the founding generation.

ONLINE SOURCES GUIDE

ThomsonNOW™ Visit ThomsonNOW to access primary sources, exercises, quizzes, and audio chapter summaries related to this chapter:
http://www.Thomsonedu.com/login

DISCOVERY

In what ways did the ascension of the Jeffersonians to power in 1800 shape the future of America?

In thinking about this question, begin by breaking it down into the components shown below. A discussion of the significance of each component should appear in your answer.

GEOGRAPHY AND POLITICS

Consider the map of the election of 1800. In what way was the country divided in this vote? How do you think the people in the western territories were likely to vote once the territories became states? What does this map foreshadow about the future of the Federalist Party? By the 1830s, Democratic Republicans called their party by a somewhat different name. Do you know what it was?

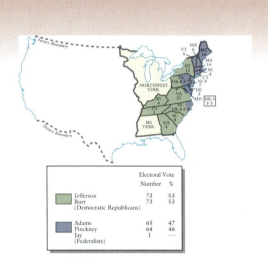

		Electoral Vote	
		Number	%
Jefferson		73	53
Burr		73	53
(Democratic Republicans)			
Adams		65	47
Pinckney		64	46
Jay		1	----
(Federalists)			

PRESIDENTIAL ELECTION, 1800

POLITICAL CULTURE

Compare the images of Washington and Jefferson. If you didn't know anything about either man would you say that one of them lived before the other? Which one looks more like a "modern" political leader? Why do you think so?

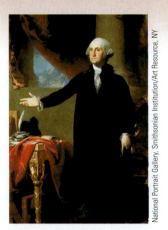

GEORGE WASHINGTON IN 1796, NEAR THE END OF HIS PRESIDENCY

PORTRAIT OF JEFFERSON, BY REMBRANDT PEALE, 1805

What does the cartoon want you to think about the government Jefferson is seen here "pulling down?" Why is the devil helping Jefferson? Why did Jefferson's attempt to remake (or "pull down") government so upset the Federalists? Consider the map of the election of 1800 in your answer.

MAD TOM IN A RAGE

GOVERNMENT AND LAW

One of the "British crimes" that Madison listed as reasons for declaring war against Great Britain in 1811 was Britain's wielding of "a malicious influence over the Indians of the Northwest Territory." How does the image make that point? How is the British soldier depicted? What does this illustration suggest about American views of Native Americans and their actions? What reasons did the British and the Native Americans have for forming an alliance against white Americans?

A SCENE ON THE FRONTIERS AS PRACTICED BY THE HUMANE BRITISH AND THEIR WORTHY ALLIES

9

THE MARKET REVOLUTION, 1815–1860

After 1815 a market revolution transformed Jefferson's republic into the market-oriented, capitalist society that it has been ever since. Improvements in transportation made that transformation possible. But it was decisions made by thousands of farmers, planters, craftsmen, and merchants that pulled farms and workshops out of old household and neighborhood arrangements and into production for distant markets. By the 1830s and 1840s the northern United States was experiencing a full-blown market revolution: New cities and towns provided financing, retailing, manu-

facturing, and markets for food; commercial farms traded food for what the cities made and sold. The South experienced a market revolution as well. The wealthiest southerners sent mountains of cotton, rice, and other plantation staples onto world markets. But the planters continued to produce for foreign markets and purchase shipping, financial services, and manufactured goods from outside the region. The planters increased their wealth and local power, the plantation regime spread into vast new lands, and the old slaveholder's republic persisted in the southern states. But now it faced an aggressive and expanding capitalist democracy in the North.

1790	1795	1800	1805	1810	1815	1820	1825	1830	1835	1840

■ **1790**
Samuel Slater builds the first American spinning mill at Pawtucket, Rhode Island

1801–1835
John Marshall's tenure as chief
justice of the Supreme Court

■ **1807**
Robert Fulton launches first steamboat

■ **1813**   Boston Associates build their first textile mill at Waltham, Massachusetts

1815–1860
International peace

■ **1816**
Congress charters Second Bank of the United States • Congress passes protective tariff • *Dartmouth College* v. *Woodward* defines a private charter as a
contract that cannot be altered by a state legislature • *McCulloch* v. *Maryland*
affirms Congress's "implied powers" under the Constitution

1818 ■
National Road completed to Ohio River at Wheeling, Virginia

■ **1822**
President Monroe vetoes National Road reparations bill

1825 ■
New York completes the Erie Canal between Buffalo and Albany

1828 ■
Baltimore and Ohio Railroad (America's first) completed

GOVERNMENT AND MARKETS

The 14th Congress met in the last days of 1815. Overwhelmingly Jeffersonian Republicans, this Congress nevertheless would reverse positions taken by Jefferson's old
party. It would charter a national bank, enact a **protective tariff**, and debate
whether or not to build a national system of roads and canals at federal expense. The
War of 1812 had demonstrated that the United States was unable to coordinate a fiscal and military effort. It had also convinced many Republicans that reliance on foreign trade rendered the United States dependent on Europe. The nation, they said,
must abandon Jefferson's export-oriented agrarianism and encourage national independence through commerce and manufacturing.

> **protective tariff** *Tariff that
> increases the price of imported
> goods that compete with Amer-
> ican products and thus protects
> American manufacturers from
> foreign competition.*

THE AMERICAN SYSTEM: THE BANK OF THE UNITED STATES

Henry Clay headed the drive for a program of protective tariffs, **internal improvements**, and a national bank. He called his program the **American System**,"
arguing that it would foster national economic growth and a salutary interdependence
between geographical sections.

In 1816 Congress chartered a Second Bank of the United States, headquartered
in Philadelphia and empowered to establish branch offices. The government agreed
to deposit its funds in the bank, to accept the bank's notes as payment for its transactions, and to buy one-fifth of the bank's stock. The fiscal horrors of the War of
1812 had convinced most representatives to move toward a national currency and
centralized control of money and credit. The alternative was to allow state banks to

> FOCUS QUESTION
> *What was the nationalizing
> dream of the American
> System, and how did
> improvements in
> transportation actually
> channel commerce within
> and between sections?*

issue unregulated and grossly inflated notes that might throw the anticipated postwar boom into chaos.

With no discussion of the constitutionality of what it was doing, Congress chartered the Bank of the United States as the sole banking institution empowered to do business throughout the country. Notes issued by the bank would be the first semblance of a national currency. Moreover, the bank could regulate the currency by demanding that state bank notes used in transactions with the federal government be redeemable in gold. In 1816 the bank set up shop in Philadelphia's Carpenter's Hall, and in 1824 moved around the corner to a Greek Revival edifice modeled after the Parthenon, a marble embodiment of the conservative republicanism that directors of the Bank of the United States adopted as their fiscal stance.

THE AMERICAN SYSTEM: TARIFFS AND INTERNAL IMPROVEMENTS

Henry Clay *Speaker of the House, senator from Kentucky, and National Republican presidential candidate who was the principal spokesman for the American System.*

internal improvements *Nineteenth-century term for transportation facilities such as roads, canals, and railroads.*

In 1816 Congress drew up the first overtly protective tariff in U.S. history. The Tariff of 1816 raised rates an average of 25 percent, extending protection to the nation's infant industries at the expense of foreign trade and American consumers. Again, wartime difficulties had paved the way: Because Americans could not depend on imported manufactures, Congress saw the encouragement of domestic manufactures as a patriotic necessity. The tariff was favored by the Northeast and the West, with enough southern support to ensure its passage by Congress.

Bills to provide federal money for roads, canals, and other "internal improvements" had a harder time winning approval. The British wartime blockade had hampered coastal shipping and had made Americans dependent on the wretched roads of the interior. Many members of the 14th Congress, after spending days of bruising travel on their way to Washington, were determined to give the United States an efficient transportation network. But consensus was hard to reach. Internal improvements were subject to local ambitions, and they were doubtful constitutionally as well. Congress agreed to complete the National Road linking the Chesapeake with the trans-Appalachian West, but President Madison and his Republican successor James Monroe both refused to support further internal improvements without a constitutional amendment.

American System *Program proposed by Henry Clay and others to foster national economic growth and interdependence among the geographical sections. It included a protective tariff, a national bank, and internal improvements.*

With a national government that was squeamish about internal improvements, state governments took up the cause. As a result, the transportation network that took shape after 1815 reflected the designs of the most ambitious states rather than the nationalizing dreams of men like Henry Clay. New York's **Erie Canal** was the most spectacular accomplishment, but the canal systems of Pennsylvania and Ohio were almost as impressive. Before 1830 most **toll roads** were built and owned by corporations chartered by state governments. Private entrepreneurs could not have built the transportation network that brought the market economy into being without the active support of state governments—through direct funding, through bond issues, and through the granting of corporate charters that gave the turnpike, canal, and railroad companies the privileges and immunities that made them attractive to private investors.

Erie Canal *Canal linking the Hudson River at Albany with the Great Lakes at Buffalo that helped to commercialize the farms of the Great Lakes watershed and to channel that commerce into New York City.*

MARKETS AND THE LAW

toll roads *Roads for which travelers were charged a fee for each use.*

The revolution replaced British courts with national and state legal systems based in English common law—systems that made legal action accessible to most white males. Thus, many of the disputes generated in the transition to a market society ended up in court. The courts tended to resolve these conflicts in ways that promoted the entrepreneurial use of private property, the sanctity of contracts, and the right to do business shielded from neighborhood restraints and the tumult of democratic politics.

John Marshall, who presided over the Supreme Court from 1801 to 1835, saw the Court as a conservative hedge against democratic legislatures. His early decisions protected the independence of the courts and their right to review legislation (see Chapter 8). From 1816 onward, his decisions encouraged business and strengthened the national government at the expense of the states. Marshall's most important decisions protected the sanctity of contracts and corporate charters against state legislatures. For example, in *Dartmouth College* v. *Woodward* (1816), Dartmouth was defending a royal charter granted in the 1760s against changes introduced by a Republican legislature that was determined to make Dartmouth a state college. Marshall ruled that Dartmouth's corporate charter could not be altered by a state legislature. Though in this case the Supreme Court was protecting Dartmouth's chartered privileges, the decision also protected turnpike and canal companies, manufacturing corporations, and other ventures that held privileges under corporate charters granted by state governments. Once the charters had been granted, the states could neither regulate the corporations nor cancel their privileges. Thus, corporate charters acquired the legal status of contracts, beyond the reach of democratic politics.

Two weeks after the *Dartmouth* decision, Marshall handed down the majority opinion in *McCulloch* v. *Maryland*. The Maryland legislature wanted to tax the Baltimore branch of the Bank of the United States, and the bank had challenged its right to do so. Marshall decided in favor of the bank. He stated, first, that the Constitution granted the federal government "implied powers" that included chartering the bank, and he denied Maryland's right to tax the bank or any other federal agency. "Americans," he said, "did not design to make their government dependent on the states." And yet there were many, particularly in Marshall's native South, who remained certain that that was precisely what the founders had intended. In *Gibbons* v. *Ogden* (1824) the Marshall Court broke a state-granted steamship monopoly in New York. The monopoly, Marshall argued, interfered with federal jurisdiction over interstate commerce. Again, this decision empowered the national government in relation to the states and encouraged private entrepreneurialism. Agreeing with congressmen who supported the American System, John Marshall's Supreme Court assumed that a natural and beneficial link existed between federal power and market society.

Meanwhile, the state courts were working equally profound transformations of American law. In the early republic, state courts had often viewed property not only as a private possession but also as part of a neighborhood. When a miller built a dam that flooded upriver farms or impaired the fishery, the courts might make him take those interests into account, often in ways that reduced the business uses of his property. By the 1830s, New England courts were routinely granting the owners of industrial mill sites unrestricted water rights, even when the exercise of those rights damaged their neighbors. As early as 1805, the New York Supreme Court in *Palmer* v. *Mulligan* had asserted that the right to develop property for business purposes was inherent in the ownership of property.

John Marshall *Chief Justice of the United States Supreme Court from 1801 to 1835. Appointed by Federalist President John Adams, Marshall's decisions tended to favor the federal government over the states and to clear legal blocks to private business.*

THE TRANSPORTATION REVOLUTION

After 1815 dramatic improvements in transportation—more and better roads, steamboats, canals, and finally railroads—tied old communities together and penetrated previously isolated neighborhoods. These improvements made the transition to a market society physically possible.

TRANSPORTATION IN 1815

In 1815 the United States was a rural nation stretching from the old settlements on the Atlantic coast to the trans-Appalachian frontier, with transportation facilities that ranged from primitive to nonexistent. West of the Appalachians, transportation was almost entirely undeveloped. Until about 1830, most westerners were southerners who settled near tributaries of the Ohio–Mississippi River system. They floated their produce downriver on jerry-built flatboats; at New Orleans it was transshipped to New York and other eastern ports. The boatmen knocked down their flatboats, sold the lumber, and then walked home to Kentucky or Ohio over the dangerous path known as the Natchez Trace.

Map 9.1

RIVERS, ROADS, AND CANALS, 1825–1860. *In the second quarter of the 19th century, transportation projects linked the North and Northwest into an integrated economic and social system. There were fewer improvements in the South: Farm produce traveled down navigable rivers from bottomland plantations to river and seaport towns, thence to New York for shipment overseas; southern legislatures and entrepreneurs saw little use for further improvements.*

Transporting goods to the western settlements was even more difficult. Keelboatmen navigated upstream using eddies and back currents, sailing when the wind was right, but usually poling their boat against the current. Skilled crews averaged only 15 miles a day. Looking for better routes, some merchants dragged finished goods across Pennsylvania and into the West at Pittsburgh, but transport costs made these goods prohibitively expensive. Consequently the trans-Appalachian settlements remained marginal to the market economy.

IMPROVEMENTS: ROADS AND RIVERS

In 1816 Congress resumed construction of the National Road (first authorized in 1802) that linked the Potomac River with the Ohio River at Wheeling, Virginia. The road reached Wheeling in 1818. At about the same time, Pennsylvania extended the Lancaster Turnpike from Philadelphia to the Ohio River at Pittsburgh. The National Road enabled settlers and a few merchants' wagons to reach the West. But the cost of moving bulky farm produce over the road remained high. Eastbound traffic on the National Road consisted largely of cattle and pigs. Farmers continued to float their corn, cotton, wheat, salt pork, and whiskey south by riverboat and thence to eastern markets.

It was the steamboat that first made commercial agriculture feasible in the West. In 1807 **Robert Fulton** launched the *Clermont* on an upriver trip from New York City to Albany. Over the next few years Americans developed flat-bottomed steamboats that could navigate rivers even at low water. The first steamboat reached Louisville from New Orleans in 1815. Two years later, with 17 steamboats already working western rivers, the *Washington* made the New Orleans–Louisville run in 25 days, a feat that convinced westerners that two-way river trade was possible. By 1820, 69 steamboats were operating on western rivers. By the eve of the Civil War 2 million tons of western produce, most of it southwestern cotton, reached the docks at New Orleans. The steamboat had transformed the interior from an isolated frontier into a busy commercial region that traded farm and plantation products for manufactured goods.

Robert Fulton *Builder of the* Clermont, *the first practical steam-driven boat.*

IMPROVEMENTS: CANALS AND RAILROADS

In 1817 Governor DeWitt Clinton talked the New York legislature into building a canal linking the Hudson River with Lake Erie, thus opening a continuous water route between the Northwest and New York City. The Erie Canal was a near-visionary feat of engineering, stretching 364 miles

THE ERIE CANAL. *The complex of locks on the Erie Canal at Lockport, New York, was among the most admired engineering feats of the 1820s and 1830s. The town itself, filled with boatmen and construction workers, had a reputation for violence.*

© Bettmann/Corbis

from Albany to Buffalo. Construction began in 1819, and the canal reached Buffalo in 1825. It was clear even before then that the canal would repay New York State's investment of $7.5 million many times over and that it would transform the territory it served.

The Erie Canal's first and most powerful effects were on western New York. By 1830 the corridor of the Erie Canal was one of the world's great grain-growing regions, dotted with market towns and new cities like Syracuse, Rochester, and Buffalo.

The Erie Canal encouraged legislators and entrepreneurs in other states to join a canal boom that lasted for 20 years. Northwestern states, Ohio in particular, built ambitious canal systems that linked isolated areas to the Great Lakes and thus to the Erie Canal. Northeastern states followed suit: A canal between Worcester and Providence linked the farms of central Massachusetts with Narragansett Bay. Another canal linked the coal mines of northeastern Pennsylvania with the Hudson River at Kingston, New York. In 1835 Pennsylvania completed a canal from Philadelphia to Pittsburgh.

The first American railroads connected burgeoning cities to rivers and canals. The Baltimore and Ohio Railroad, for example, linked Baltimore to the rivers of the West. Although the approximately 3,000 miles of railroads built between the late 1820s and 1840 helped the market positions of some cities, they did not constitute a national or even a regional rail network. A national system was created by the 5,000 miles of

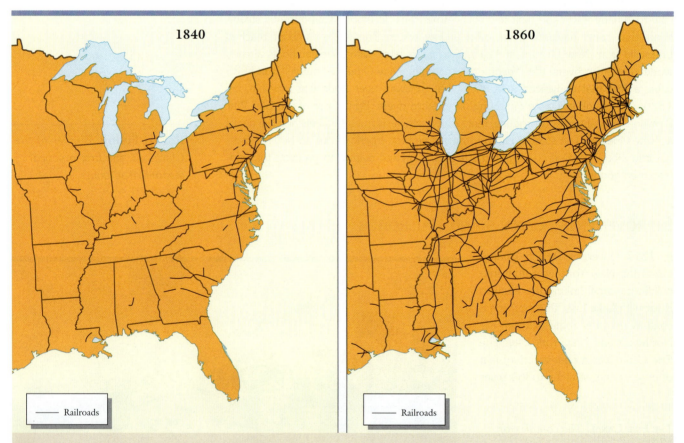

Map 9.2

RAILROADS IN THE UNITED STATES, 1840 AND 1860. *In these 20 years, both the North and South built railway systems. Northerners built rail lines that integrated the market economies of the Midwest and the East—both within sections and between them. For the most part, Southern railroads linked the plantation belt with the ocean. Revealingly, only a few lines connected the North and South.*

track laid in the 1840s and by the flurry of railroad building that gave the United States a rail network of 30,000 miles by 1860—a continuous, integrated system that created massive links between the East and the Northwest and that threatened to put canals out of business. In fact, the New York Central, which paralleled the Erie Canal, rendered that canal obsolete. Other railroads, particularly in the northwestern states, replaced canal and river transport almost completely, even though water transport remained cheaper.

TIME AND MONEY

The transportation revolution reduced the time and money it took to move heavy goods. Overall, the cost of moving goods across long distances dropped 95 percent between 1815 and 1860. Improvements in speed were nearly as dramatic. The overland route from Cincinnati to New York in 1815 (by keelboat upriver to Pittsburgh, then by wagon the rest of the way) had taken a minimum of 52 days. By the 1840s, upriver steamboats carried goods to the terminus of the Main Line Canal at Pittsburgh, which delivered them to Philadelphia, which sent them by train to New York City in a total transit time of 18 to 20 days. At about the same time, the Ohio canal system enabled Cincinnati to send goods north through Ohio, across Lake Erie, over the Erie Canal, and down the Hudson to New York City—an all-water route that reduced costs and made the trip in 18 days. Similar improvements occurred in the densely settled and increasingly urbanized Northeast. By 1840 travel time between the big northeastern cities had been reduced to from one-fourth to one-eleventh of what it had been in 1790. Such improvements in speed and economy made a national market possible.

By 1840 improved transportation had made a market revolution. Foreign trade, which had driven American economic growth up to 1815, continued to expand. Exports (now consisting more of southern cotton than of northern food crops) increased sixfold to $333.6 million by 1860; imports (mostly European manufactured goods) tripled to $353.6 million. Yet the increases in foreign trade represented vast reductions in the proportion of American market activity that involved other countries. Before 1815 Americans had exported about 15 percent of their total national product; by 1830 exports accounted for only 6 percent of total production. The reason for this shift was that after 1815 the United States developed self-sustaining domestic markets for farm produce and manufactured goods. The great engine of economic growth, particularly in the North and West, was not the old colonial relationship with Europe but a burgeoning internal market.

MARKETS AND REGIONS

Proponents of the American System dreamed of a market-driven economy that would unify the United States. But until at least 1840 the market revolution produced greater results within regions than between them. The farmers of New England traded food for finished goods from Boston, Lynn, Lowell, and other towns in what was becoming an urban, industrial region. Although the Erie Canal created a huge potential for interregional trade, until 1839 most of its eastbound tonnage originated in western New York. In the West, farmers fed such rapidly growing cities as Rochester, Cleveland, Chicago, and Cincinnati, which in turn supplied the farmers with farm tools, furniture, shoes, and other goods. Farther south, the few plantations that did not produce their own food bought surpluses from farmers in their own region. Thus until about 1840 the market revolution was more a regional than an interregional phenomenon.

In the 1840s and 1850s, however, the new transport networks turned the increasingly industrial Northeast and mid-Atlantic and the commercial farms of the Old Northwest into a unified market society. The earliest settlers in the Northwest carried on a limited trade through the river system that led to New Orleans. From the 1840s onward produce left the Northwest less often by the old Ohio River route than by canal and railroad directly to the Northeast. At the same time, canals and roads from New York, Philadelphia, and Baltimore became the favored passageways for commodities entering the West. After 1840 the Ohio–Mississippi River system carried vastly increased amounts of goods. But that increase added up to a shrinking share of the expanded total. In short, western farmers and northeastern businessmen and manufacturers were building a national market from which the South was largely excluded.

FROM YEOMAN TO BUSINESSMAN: THE RURAL NORTH AND WEST

FOCUS QUESTION

How did northern farm families experience the transition into commercial agriculture between 1815 and 1850?

In the old communities of the Northeast, the market revolution sent some young people off to cities and factory towns and others to the West. Those who remained at home engaged in new forms of agriculture on a transformed rural landscape, while their cousins in the Northwest transformed a wilderness into cash-producing farms.

SHAPING THE NORTHERN LANDSCAPE

New England grain farmers could not compete with the farmers of western New York and the Old Northwest, who possessed fertile lands and ready access to markets. At the same time, however, the factories and cities of the Northeast provided Yankee farmers with a market for meat and other perishables. Beef became the great New England cash crop. Dairy products were not far behind, and the proximity to city markets encouraged the spread of poultry and egg farms, fruit orchards, and truck gardens. The burgeoning shoe industry bought leather from the farmers, and woolen mills created a demand for wool. The rise of livestock specialization reduced the amount of land under cultivation. Early in the century New Englanders still tilled their few acres in the old three-year rotation: corn the first year, rye the second, fallow the third. By the 1820s and 1830s, as farmers raised more livestock and less grain, the land that remained in cultivation was farmed more intensively. Farmers saved manure and ashes for fertilizer, plowed more deeply and systematically, and tended their crops more carefully. These improved techniques, along with cash from the sale of their livestock and the availability of food at stores, encouraged Yankee farmers to allocate less and less land to the growing of food crops.

The transition to livestock raising transformed woodlands into open pastures. As farmers leveled the forests, they sold the wood to fuel-hungry cities. In the 1830s manufacturers began marketing cast-iron stoves that heated houses more cheaply and efficiently than open hearths, and canals brought cheap Pennsylvania anthracite to the Northeast. Farmers who needed pastureland could gain substantial onetime profits from the sale of cut wood. The result was massive deforestation. At the beginning of European settlement, 95 percent of New England had been covered by forest. By 1850 forest covered only 30 percent of Connecticut, 32 percent of Rhode Island, 40 percent of Massachusetts, 45 percent of Vermont, and 50 percent of New Hampshire.

THE TRANSFORMATION OF RURAL OUTWORK

On that denuded landscape, poor families with many children continued to supplement their income with industrial outwork (see Chapter 7). But the quickening of market activity brought new kinds of dependence. Before the 1820s outworkers had used local raw materials like wool, leather, and flax and had spent only their spare time on such work. In the 1820s the manufacture of shoes and textiles began to be concentrated in factories, and outworkers who remained were reduced to dependence. Merchants now provided them with raw materials with which to make such items as cloth-covered buttons and palm-leaf hats and set the pace of labor and the quality of the finished goods. Although outwork still helped poor families to maintain their independence, control of their labor had passed to merchants and other agents of the regional economy.

FARMERS AS CONSUMERS

With the shift to specialized market agriculture, New England farmers became customers for necessities that their forebears had produced themselves or had acquired through barter. They heated their houses with coal dug by Pennsylvania miners. They wore cotton cloth made by the factory women at Lowell. New Hampshire farm girls made straw hats for them, and the craftsmen of Lynn made their shoes. By 1830 or so, many farmers were even buying food. The Erie Canal and the western grain belt sent flour from Rochester into eastern neighborhoods where grain was no longer grown. Many farmers found it easier to produce specialized crops for market and to buy butter, cheese, eggs, and vegetables at country stores.

The turning point came in the 1820s. The storekeepers of Northampton, Massachusetts, for instance, had been increasing their stock in trade by about 7 percent per decade since the late 18th century. In the 1820s they increased it 45 percent and now carried not only local farm products and sugar, salt, and coffee, but bolts of New England cloth, sacks of western flour, a variety of necessities and little luxuries from the wholesale houses of New York City and Boston, and pattern samples from which to order silverware, dishes, wallpaper, and other household goods. Those goods were better than what could be made at home and were for the most part cheaper. The price of finished cloth, for instance, declined sixfold between 1815 and 1830; as a result, spinning wheels and handlooms disappeared from the farmhouses of New England. Coal and cast-iron stoves replaced the family hearth.

Material standards of living rose. But more and more families "felt" poor, and many more were incapable of feeding, clothing, and warming themselves in years when the market failed. By the 1820s and 1830s northeastern farmers depended on markets in ways that their fathers and grandfathers would have considered dangerous not only to family welfare but to the welfare of the republic itself.

THE NORTHWEST: SOUTHERN MIGRANTS

One reason the market revolution in the Northeast went as smoothly as it did was that young people with little hope of inheriting land in the old settlements moved away to towns and cities or to the new farmlands of the Northwest. Between 1815 and 1840 migrants from the older areas transformed the Northwest Territory into a working agricultural landscape. By 1830 there were 1,438,379 whites living in Ohio, Indiana, and Illinois. By 1860 the population of those three states, along with that of the new states of Wisconsin and Michigan, numbered 6,926,884—22 percent of the nation's

> **QUICK REVIEW**
>
> **NORTHERN FARMS**
>
> - Moved toward crop specialization
> - Moved away from household and neighborhood self-sufficiency
> - Integrated with regional markets

total population. In the Northwest until about 1830 most settlers were yeomen from Kentucky and Tennessee, usually a generation removed from Virginia, the Carolinas, and western Maryland. They moved along the Ohio and up the Muskingum, Miami, Scioto, Wabash, and Illinois Rivers to set up farms in the southern and central counties of Ohio, Indiana, and Illinois. When southerners moved north of the Ohio River into territory that banned slavery, they often did so saying that slavery blocked opportunities for poor whites. But even those who rejected slavery seldom rejected southern folkways. Like their kinfolk in Kentucky and Tennessee, the farmers of southern and central Ohio, Indiana, and Illinois remained tied to the river trade and to a mode of agriculture that favored free-ranging livestock over cultivated fields. The typical farmer fenced in a few acres of corn and left the rest of his land in woods to be roamed by southern hogs known as "razorbacks" and "land sharks." As late as 1860, southern-born farmers in the Northwest averaged 20 hogs apiece. These animals were thin and tough (they seldom grew to more than 200 pounds), and they could run long distances, leap fences, fend for themselves in the woods, and walk to distant markets. The southern-born pioneers of the Northwest, like their cousins across the Ohio River, depended more on their families and neighbors than on distant markets. Southerners insisted on repaying debts in kind and on lending tools rather than renting them, thus engaging outsiders in the elaborate network of "neighboring" through which transplanted southerners made their livings. As late as the 1840s, in the bustling town of Springfield, Illinois, barter was the preferred system of exchange.

THE NORTHWEST: NORTHERN MIGRANTS

Around 1830 a stream of northeastern migrants entered the Northwest via the Erie Canal and on Great Lakes steamboats. Most of them were New Englanders who had spent a generation in western New York. The rest came directly from New England or—from the 1840s onward—from Germany and Scandinavia. In the Northwest they duplicated the intensive, market-oriented farming they had known at home. They penned their cattle and hogs and fattened them up, making them bigger and worth more than those farther south. They planted their land in grain and transformed the region into one of the world's great wheat-producing regions. In 1820 the Northwest had exported only 12 percent of its agricultural produce. By 1840 that figure had risen to 27 percent, and it stood even higher among northern-born grain farmers. By 1860 the Northwest, intensively commercialized and tied by canals and railways to eastern markets, was exporting 70 percent of its wheat. In that year it produced 46 percent of the nation's wheat crop, nearly all of it north of the line of southern settlement.

The new settlers were notably receptive to improvements in farming techniques. They quickly adopted cast-iron plows, which cut cleanly through oak roots 4 inches thick. By the 1830s the efficient, expensive grain cradle had become the standard harvest tool in northwestern wheat fields. From the 1840s onward, even this advanced hand tool was replaced by mass-produced machinery such as the McCormick reaper. Instead of threshing their grain by driving cattle and horses over it, farmers bought new horse-powered and treadmill threshers and used hand-cranked fanning mills to speed the process of cleaning the grain.

Most agricultural improvements were tailored to grain and dairy farming and were taken up most avidly by the northern farmers. Others rejected them as expensive and "unnatural." They thought that cast-iron plows poisoned the soil and that fanning mills made a "wind contrary to nater" and thus offended God. John Chapman, an eccentric Yankee who earned the nickname "Johnny Appleseed" by planting apple tree cuttings in southern Ohio and Indiana before the settlers arrived, planted only low-yield, common trees; he regarded grafting, which farmers farther north and east were using to improve the quality of their apples, as "against nature." Southerners scoffed at the Yankee fondness for mechanical improvements, the systematic breeding of animals and plants, careful bookkeeping, and farm techniques learned from magazines and books.

Conflict between intensive agriculture and older, less market-oriented ways reached comic proportions when the Illinois legislature imposed stiff penalties on farmers who allowed their small, poorly bred bulls to run loose and impregnate cows with questionable sperm, thereby depriving the owners of high-bred bulls of their breeding fees and rendering the systematic breeding of cattle impossible. When the poorer farmers refused to pen their bulls, the law was rescinded. A local historian explained that "there was a generous feeling in the hearts of the people in favor of an equality of privileges, even among bulls."

HOUSEHOLDS

The market revolution transformed 18th-century households into 19th-century homes. For one thing, Americans began to limit the size of their families. The decline was most pronounced in the North, particularly in commercialized areas. Rural birth rates remained at 18th-century levels in the southern uplands, in the poorest and most isolated communities of the North, and on the frontier. These communities practiced the old labor-intensive agriculture and relied on the labor of large families. For farmers who used newer techniques or switched to livestock, large families made less sense. Moreover, large broods hampered the ability of future-minded parents to provide for their children and conflicted with new notions of privacy and domesticity that were taking shape among an emerging rural middle class.

The commercialization of agriculture was closely associated with the emergence of the concept of housework. Before 1815 farm wives had labored in the house, the barnyard, and the garden while their husbands and sons worked in the fields. With the market revolution came a sharper distinction between "male work" that was part of the cash economy and "female work" that was not. Even such traditional women's tasks as dairying, vegetable gardening, and poultry raising became men's work once they became cash-producing specialties.

At the same time, new kinds of women's work emerged within

A WESTERN NEW YORK FARM. *Here is a developer's rendition of a farm in western New York in the second quarter of the 19th century. The frame house (built onto the pioneer settler's log cabin) is fronted with a lawn, decorative shrubs, a shade tree, and dry walkways. Flanking the house are a vegetable garden and a well-tended orchard. Cash-crop fields stretch out behind the farmstead. A well-constructed fence marks off the home property and separates it from the road (another sign of progress) and the farm fields. The fence, the house, and a substantial barn are painted white. This was the rural comfort and respectability that northern farm families made for themselves from the 1820s onward.*

Smithsonian Institution

households. Although there were fewer children to care for, the culture began to demand forms of child rearing that were more intensive, individualized, and mother centered. Store-bought white flour, butter, and eggs and the new iron stoves eased the burdens of food preparation, but they also created demands for pies, cakes, and other fancy foods that earlier generations had only imagined. And while farmwomen no longer spun and wove their own cloth, the availability of manufactured cloth created the expectation that their families would dress more neatly and with greater variety than they had in the past—at the cost of far more time spent by women on sewing, washing, and ironing. Similar expectations demanded greater personal and domestic cleanliness, and farmwomen from the 1830s onward spent time planting flower beds, cleaning and maintaining prized furniture, mirrors, rugs, and ceramics, and scrubbing floors and children.

Housework was tied to new notions of privacy, decency, and domestic comfort. Before 1820 farmers cared little about how their houses looked, often tossing trash and garbage out the door for the pigs and chickens that foraged near the house. In the 1820s and 1830s, as farmers began to grow cash crops and adopt middle-class ways, they began to plant shade trees and kept their yards free of trash. They painted their houses and sometimes their fences and outbuildings, arranged their woodpiles into neat stacks, surrounded their houses with flowers and ornamental shrubs, and tried to hide their privies from view. Inside, prosperous farmhouses took on an air of privacy and comfort. Separate kitchens and iron stoves replaced open hearths. The availability of finished cloth permitted the regular use of tablecloths, napkins, doilies, curtains, bedspreads, and quilts. Oil lamps replaced homemade candles, and the more comfortable families began to decorate their homes with wallpaper and upholstered furniture. Farm couples moved their beds away from the hearth and (along with the children's beds that had been scattered throughout the house) put them into spaces designated as bedrooms. They took the washstands and basins, which were coming into more common use, out of the kitchen and put them into the bedroom, thus making sleeping, bathing, and sex more private than they had been in the past. At the center of this new house stood the farm wife—apart from the bustling world of commerce, but decorating and caring for the amenities that commerce bought.

NEIGHBORHOODS: THE LANDSCAPE OF PRIVACY

By the 1830s and 1840s the market revolution had transformed the rural landscape of the Northeast. The forests had been reduced, the swamps had been

A SOAP ADVERTISEMENT FROM THE 1850S. *The rigors of "Old Washing Day" lead the mother in this advertisement to abuse the children and house pets, while her husband leaves the house. With American Cream Soap, domestic bliss returns. The children and cats are happy, the husband returns, and the wife has time to sew.*

drained, and most of the streams and rivers were interrupted by mill dams. Bears, panthers, and wolves had disappeared, along with the beaver and many of the fish. Now there were extensive pastures where English cattle and sheep browsed on English grasses dotted with English wildflowers such as buttercups, daisies, and dandelions. Next to the pastures were neatly cultivated croplands that were regularly fertilized and seldom allowed to lie fallow. And at the center stood brightly painted houses and outbuildings surrounded by flowers and shrubs and vegetable gardens. Many towns, particularly in New England, had planted shade trees along the country roads, completing a rural landscape of straight lines and human cultivation, a landscape that made it easy to think of nature as a commodity to be altered and controlled.

Within that landscape, old practices and old forms of neighborliness fell into disuse. Neighbors continued to exchange goods and labor and to contract debts that might be left unpaid for years. But debts were more likely to be owed to profit-minded storekeepers and creditors, and even debts between neighbors were often paid in cash. Traditionally, storekeepers had allowed farmers to bring in produce and have it credited to a neighbor/creditor's account. In the 1830s, storekeepers began to demand cash payment or to charge lower prices to those who paid cash. Neighborly rituals like parties, husking bees, barn-raisings—with their drinking and socializing— were scorned as an inefficient and morally suspect waste of time.

Thus the efficient farmer after the 1820s concentrated on producing commodities that could be marketed outside the neighborhood and used his cash income to buy material comforts for his family and to pay debts and provide a cash inheritance for his children. Although much of the old world of household and neighborhood survived, farmers created a subsistence and maintained the independence of their households not through those spheres but through unprecedented levels of dependence on the outside world.

THE INDUSTRIAL REVOLUTION

In the 50 years following 1820, American cities grew faster than ever before or since. The fastest growth was in new cities that served commercial agriculture and in factory towns that produced for a largely rural domestic market. Even in the seaports, growth derived more from commerce with the hinterland than from international trade. Paradoxically, the market revolution in the countryside had produced the beginnings of industry and the greatest period of urban growth in U.S. history.

FACTORY TOWNS: THE RHODE ISLAND SYSTEM

Jeffersonians held that the United States must always remain rural. Americans could expand into the rich new agricultural lands of the West, trade their farm surpluses for European finished goods, and thus avoid creating cities with their dependent social classes. Federalists argued that Americans, in order to retain their independence, must produce their own manufactured goods. **Neo-Federalists** combined those arguments after the War of 1812. They argued that America's abundant water power would enable Americans to build their factories across the countryside instead of creating great industrial cities. Such a decentralized factory system would provide employment for country women and children and thus subsidize the independence of struggling farmers.

FOCUS QUESTION

What was the relationship between urban-industrial growth and the commercialization of the northern countryside?

neo-Federalists *Nationalist Republicans who favored many Federalist economic programs such as protective tariffs and a national bank.*

The first factories were textile mills. The key to the mass production of cotton and woolen textiles was a water-powered machine that spun yarn and thread. The machine had been invented and patented by the Englishman Richard Arkwright in 1769. The British government forbade the machinery or the people who operated it to leave the country. Scores of textile workers, however, defied the law and made their way to North America. One of them was Samuel Slater, who had served an apprenticeship under Jedediah Strutt, a partner of Arkwright who had improved on the original machine. Working from memory, Slater built the first Arkwright spinning mill in America at Pawtucket, Rhode Island, in 1790.

Slater's first mill was a small frame building tucked among the town's houses and craftsmen's shops. Although its capacity was limited to the spinning of cotton yarn, it provided work for children in the mill and for women who wove yarn into cloth in their homes. As his business grew and he advertised for widows with children, however, Slater was greeted by families headed by landless, impoverished men. Slater's use of children from these families prompted "respectable" farmers and craftsmen to pull their children out of Slater's growing complex of mills. More poor families arrived to take their places, and during the first years of the 19th century Pawtucket grew rapidly into a disorderly mill town.

Soon Slater and other mill owners built factory villages in the countryside. The practice became known as the Rhode Island (or "family") system. At several locations in southern New England, mill owners built whole villages surrounded by company-owned farmland that they rented to the husbands and fathers of their mill workers. The workplace was closely supervised, and drinking and other troublesome practices were forbidden in the villages. Fathers and older sons either worked on rented farms or as laborers at the mills. By the late 1820s Slater and most of the other owners were getting rid of the outworkers and were buying power looms, thus transforming the villages into disciplined, self-contained factory towns that turned raw cotton into finished cloth.

FACTORY TOWNS: THE WALTHAM SYSTEM

Touring English factory districts in 1811, a wealthy, cultivated Bostonian named **Francis Cabot Lowell** asked the plant managers questions and made secret drawings of the machines he saw. Returning home, Lowell joined with wealthy friends to form the Boston Manufacturing Company, soon known as the Boston Associates. In 1813 they built their first mill at Waltham, Massachusetts, and then expanded into Lowell, Lawrence, and other new towns near Boston during the 1820s. The company, operating under what became known as the Waltham system, built mills that differed from the early Rhode Island mills in two ways. First, they were heavily capitalized and as fully mechanized as possible; they turned raw cotton into finished cloth with little need for skilled workers. Second, the operatives who tended their machines were young, single women recruited from the farms of northern New England. The company provided carefully supervised boardinghouses for them and enforced rules of conduct both on and off the job. The young women worked steadily, never drank, seldom stayed out late, and attended church faithfully. They impressed visitors, particularly those who had seen factory workers in other places, as a dignified and self-respecting workforce.

The brick mills and prim boardinghouses set within landscaped towns and occupied by sober, well-behaved farm girls signified the Boston Associates' desire to build a profitable textile industry without creating a permanent working class. The women

Francis Cabot Lowell
Wealthy Bostonian who, with the help of the Boston Associates, built and operated integrated textile mills in eastern Massachusetts.

Samuel Slater's Mill at Pawtucket, Rhode Island. *The first mill was small, painted white, and topped with a cupola. Set among craftsmen's workshops and houses, it looked more like a Baptist meetinghouse than a first step into industrialization.*

The Granger Collection, New York

would work for a few years in a carefully controlled environment, send their wages back to their family, and return home to live as country housewives. However, these young farmwomen did not send their wages home or, as was popularly believed, use them to pay for their brothers' college education. Some saved their money to use as dowries that their fathers could not afford. More, however, spent their wages on themselves—particularly on clothes and books.

The Waltham system thus produced a self-respecting sisterhood of independent, wage-earning women. After finishing their stint in the mills, most of them married and became housewives. One in three married Lowell men and became city dwellers. Those who returned home to rural neighborhoods remained unmarried longer than their sisters who had stayed at home and then married men about their own age who worked at something other than farming. Thus through the 1840s the Boston Associates kept their promise to produce cotton cloth profitably without creating a permanent working class. But they did not succeed in shuttling young women from rural to urban paternalism and back again. Wage labor, the ultimate degradation for agrarian-republican men, opened a road out of rural patriarchy for thousands of young women.

URBAN BUSINESSMEN

The market revolution hit American cities with particular force. Here there was little concern for creating a classless industrial society: Vastly wealthy men of finance, a new middle class that bought and sold an ever-growing range of consumer goods, and the impoverished women and men who produced those goods lived together in communities that unabashedly recognized the reality of social class.

The richest men were seaport merchants who had survived and prospered during the world wars that ended in 1815. They carried on as importers and exporters, took control of banks and insurance companies, and made great fortunes in urban real estate. Below the old mercantile elite (or, in the case of the new cities of the interior, at the top of society) stood a growing middle class of wholesale and retail merchants, master craftsmen who had transformed themselves into manufacturers, and an army of lawyers, salesmen, auctioneers, clerks, bookkeepers, and accountants who took care of the paperwork for the new market society. At the head of this new middle class were the wholesale merchants of the seaports who bought hardware, crockery, and other commodities from importers and then sold them in smaller lots to storekeepers from the interior. Slightly below them were the large processors of farm products. Another step down were specialized retail merchants who dealt in books, furniture, crockery, or some other consumer goods. Alongside the merchants stood master craftsmen who had become manufacturers. With their workers busy in backrooms or in household workshops, they now called themselves shoe dealers and merchant tailors. At the bottom of this new commercial world were hordes of clerks, most of them young men who hoped to rise in the world. Both in numbers and in the nature of the work, this white-collar army formed a new class created by the market revolution.

In the 1820s and 1830s the commercial classes transformed the look and feel of American cities. As retailing and manufacturing became separate activities (even in firms that did both), the merchants, salesmen, and clerks now worked in quiet offices on downtown business streets. Both in the seaports and the new towns of the interior, impressive brick and glass storefronts appeared on the main streets. Perhaps the most striking monuments of the self-conscious new business society were the handsome retail arcades that began going up in the 1820s, providing consumers with comfortable, gracious space in which to shop.

METROPOLITAN INDUSTRIALIZATION

While businessmen were developing a new middle-class ethos, the people who made the consumer goods were growing more numerous while at the same time disappearing from view. With the exception of textiles and a few other commodities, few goods were made in mechanized factories before the 1850s. Most goods were made by hand. City merchants and master craftsmen met the growing demand by hiring more workers. The largest handicrafts—shoemaking, tailoring, and the building trades—were divided into skilled and semiskilled segments and farmed out to subcontractors who could turn a profit only by cutting labor costs. The result was the creation of an urban working class.

Take the case of tailoring. High rents and costly real estate, together with the absence of water power, made it impossible to set up large factories in cities. But the nature of the clothing trade and the availability of cheap labor gave rise to a system of subcontracting that transformed needlework into the first **sweated** trade in America. Merchants kept a few skilled male tailors to take care of the custom trade, and to cut cloth into patterned pieces for ready-made clothing. The pieces were sent out to needleworkers who sewed them together in their homes. Male tailors continued to do the finishing work on men's suits. But most of the work was done by women who worked long hours for piece rates that ranged from 75 cents to $1.50 per week. In 1860, Brooks Brothers kept 70 workers in its shops and used 2,000 to 3,000 outworkers, most of them women. Along with clothing, women in garrets and tenements manufactured the items with which the middle class decorated itself and its homes: embroidery, doilies, artificial flowers, fringe, tassels, fancy-bound books, and parasols. All provided work for ill-paid legions of female workers.

Other trades followed similar patterns. For example, shoes were made in uniform sizes in the Northeast and sent in barrels all over the country. Like tailoring, shoemaking was divided into skilled operations and time-consuming unskilled tasks. The relatively skilled and highly paid work of cutting and shaping the uppers was performed by men; the drudgery of sewing the pieces together went to low-paid women. Skilled shoemakers performed the most difficult work for taskmasters who passed the work along to subcontractors who controlled poorly paid, unskilled workers. Skilled craftsmen could earn as much as $2 a day making custom boots and shoes. Men shaping uppers in boardinghouses earned a little more than half of that; women binders could work a full week and earn as little as 50 cents. In this as in other trades,

sweated *Describes a type of worker, mostly women, who worked in their homes producing items for subcontractors, usually in the clothing industry.*

HISTORY THROUGH FILM

GANGS OF NEW YORK (2002)

Directed by Martin Scorsese. Starring Leonardo DiCaprio (Amsterdam Vallon), Daniel Day-Lewis (Bill "The Butcher" Cutting), and Cameron Diaz (Jenny Everdeane).

This is Martin Scorsese's movie about the Five Points of New York—the most dangerous neighborhood in mid-19th-century North America. It is an operatic tragedy: An Irish boy (Leonardo DiCaprio) whose father, the leader of a gang called the Dead Rabbits, is killed by a nativist chieftain (Daniel Day-Lewis) in a gang fight, spends his childhood in an orphanage, and then returns to the neighborhood to take revenge. He becomes part of the criminal entourage of his father's killer, falls in love with a beautiful and talented female thief (Cameron Diaz) who had been raised (and used) by the same gang boss, and bides his time—tortured all the while by the prospect of killing a second father figure. In the end, the Irish boy resurrects his father's gang and challenges the nativists to a battle for control of the Five Points. The battle coincides with the Draft Riots of 1863, and the film ends (as it had begun) in a horrendous bloodbath. The Irish thug kills the nativist thug, and the film ends with U2 singing about "We Who Built America."

For those who can stomach close-up fights with clubs and hatchets, it is a good enough melodrama. Unhappily, Scorsese casts his story against real history and gets most of it wrong. The film takes pains to "reconstruct" Manhattan's Five Points, but our first view of the neighborhood is taken from a painting of a Brooklyn street.

The oppressive noise and overcrowding that contemporary visitors describe are obliterated by a large public space at the center of the Points—historically nonexistent, but a fine field for the gang fights that begin and end the movie. Historically, the gangs were headquartered at saloons and firehouses, but Scorsese's operatic sensibilities move the Dead Rabbits into catacombs beneath the Old Brewery—complete with torchlight, a crude armory, and an untidy pyramid of skulls. The nativists, on the other hand, prefer an Asian motif, holding their get-togethers in an ornate Chinese theater and social house that lends an air of orientalist extravaganza to a neighborhood that knew nothing of such things. The catalog of crimes against history could go on and on: The Dead Rabbits did not follow the cross into battle (Irish street gangs were not particularly religious), Irish priests did not look like Peter the Hermit, and Leonardo DiCaprio does not have a convincing Irish accent.

The "reformers" who minister to the Five Points receive equally silly treatment. The chief of the reformers are the aristocratic Schermerhorns. In fact, most Five Points missionaries were middle-class evangelicals who had little to do with the Schermerhorns or the other old families of New York. The movie reformers hold a dance for the neighborhood; in fact, the evangelicals hated dancing and parties. The reformers also attend a public hanging, cheering as four innocent men are put to death. But New York had outlawed public executions a generation earlier; felons were now hanged within prison walls before small invited audiences. Even if public hangings had persisted, reformers would not have attended them (they had stopped going to such spectacles soon after 1815), and had they been dragged out of their parlors to witness an execution, they would not have cheered. There is also an appearance by P. T. Barnum. Barnum had made his museum the premier middle-class entertainment spot in New York by eschewing low theater, cockfights, and other raucous and violent shows. Yet the movie has Barnum sponsoring a bare-knuckle prizefight—an act that would have cost him his reputation and his livelihood. The climactic riot includes another Barnum fabrication: Barnum's museum is set on fire; his menagerie escapes, and a terrified elephant romps through the burning streets. It almost certainly did not happen, but even the most fact-bound historian must bow to Scorsese's artistic license on that one.

DANIEL DAY-LEWIS AND HIS FIVE POINTS GANG.
© *Kobal/Picture Desk.*

© Kobal/Picture Desk

wage rates and gendered tasks reflected the old family division of labor, which was based on the assumption that female workers lived with an income-earning husband or father. In fact, increasing numbers of them were young women living alone or older women who had been widowed, divorced, or abandoned—often with small children.

Members of the new middle class entertained notions of gentility based on the distinction between manual and nonmanual work. Lowly clerks and wealthy merchants prided themselves on the fact that they worked with their heads and not their hands. They fancied that their entrepreneurial and managerial skills were making the market revolution happen, while manual workers simply performed tasks thought up by the middle class. The men and women of an emerging working class struggled to create dignity and a sense of public worth in a society that hid them from view and defined them as "hands."

THE MARKET REVOLUTION IN THE SOUTH

FOCUS QUESTION

What were the nature and limits of the market revolution in the South? Why?

With the end of war in 1815, the cotton belt of the South expanded dramatically. The resumption of international trade, the revival of textile production in Britain and on the European continent, and the emergence of factory production in the northeastern United States encouraged southern planters to extend the short-staple cotton lands of South Carolina and Georgia into a belt that would stretch across the Old Southwest and beyond the Mississippi into Texas and Arkansas.

The southwestern plantation belt produced stupendous amounts of cotton. In 1810 the South produced 178,000 bales of ginned cotton, more than 59 times the 3,000 bales it had produced in 1790. By 1820 production stood at 334,000 bales. With the opening of southwestern cotton lands, production jumped to 1.35 million bales in 1840 and to 4.8 million on the eve of the Civil War. Over these years cotton

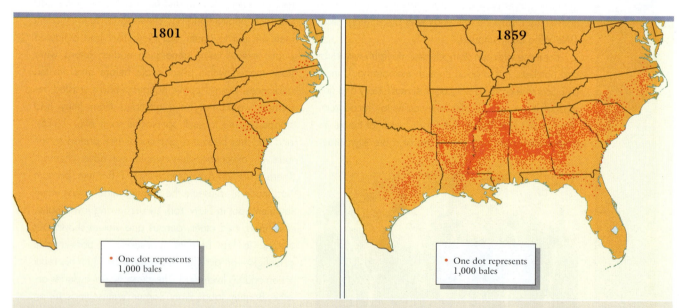

Map 9.3
COTTON PRODUCTION, 1801 AND 1859. *Short-staple cotton thrived wherever there was fertile soil, heat and humidity, low altitude, and a long growing season. As a result, a great belt of cotton and slavery took shape in the Lower South, from the midlands of South Carolina through East Texas.*

accounted for one-half to two-thirds of the value of all U.S. exports. The South produced three-fourths of the world supply of cotton—a commodity that, more than any other, was the raw material of industrialization in Britain and Europe and, increasingly, in the northeastern United States.

THE ORGANIZATION OF SLAVE LABOR

The plantations of the cotton belt were among the most intensely commercialized farms in the world. Many of them grew nothing but cotton, a practice that produced huge profits in good years but in bad years sent planters into debt. Other plantations grew supplementary cash crops and produced their own food. But nearly all of the plantation owners organized their labor in ways that maximized production and reinforced the dominance of the white men who owned the farms.

Cotton, which requires a long growing season and a lot of attention, was well suited to slave labor and to the climate of the Deep South. After the land was cleared and plowed, it was set out in individual plants. Laborers weeded the fields with hoes throughout the hot, humid growing season. In the fall, the cotton ripened unevenly. In a harvest season that lasted up to two months, pickers swept through the fields repeatedly, selecting only the ripe bolls. Plantations that grew their own food cultivated large cornfields and vegetable gardens and kept large numbers of hogs. To cope with diverse growing seasons and killing times that overlapped with the cotton cycle, planters created complex labor systems.

Although this slave force was larger than most, its organization was familiar to every southerner: Gangs of women wielded the hoes and men did the plowing, accompanied, especially during the busiest times, by strong women. The division of labor by sex was standard: Even at harvest festivals teams of men shucked the corn while women prepared the meal and the after-supper dance. And during the harvest, when every slave was in the fields, men tended to work beside men, women beside women. Most of the house slaves were women, and female slaves often worked under the direction of the plantation mistress, seeing to the dairy cattle, chickens, and geese and tending vegetable gardens and orchards. While black women routinely worked in southern fields, white women did so only on the poorest farms and only at the busiest times of the year. They took care of the poultry and cattle and the vegetable gardens—not the profit-oriented fields. As the larger farms grew into plantations, white women took on the task of supervising the household slaves instead of doing the work themselves.

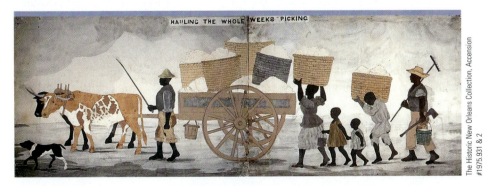

"HAULING THE WHOLE WEEK'S PICKING." *William Henry Brown made this collage of a slave harvest crew near Vicksburg, Mississippi, in 1842. The rigors of the harvest put everyone, including small children, into the fields.*

PATERNALISM

On the whole, the exploitation of slave labor after 1820 became both more systematic and more humane. Planters paid close attention to labor discipline: They supervised the work more closely than in the past, tried (often unsuccessfully) to substitute gang labor for the task system, and forcibly "corrected" slaves whose work was slow or sloppy. At the same time, however, planters clothed the new discipline within a larger attempt to make North American slavery into a system that was both paternalistic and humane. Food and clothing seem to have improved, and individual cabins for slave families became standard. State laws often forbade the more brutal forms of discipline, and they uniformly demanded that slaves not be made to work on Sunday.

The systematic paternalism on 19th-century farms and plantations was the result both of planter self-interest and a genuine attempt to exert a kindly, paternal control over slaves. Slaves endured the discipline and accepted the food, clothing, time off, and religious instruction—but used all of them to serve themselves and not the masters (see Chapter 10). But for all that, material standards rose. One rough indicator is physical height. On the eve of the Civil War, southern slaves averaged about an inch shorter than northern whites. But they were fully 3 inches taller than newly imported Africans, 2 inches taller than slaves on the Caribbean island of Trinidad, and an inch taller than British Marines. While slaves suffered greater infant mortality than whites, those who survived infancy lived out "normal" life spans. Between 1810 and 1860 the slave population of the United States increased threefold, an increase due entirely to the fact that—alone among slave populations of the Western Hemisphere—births outnumbered deaths among North American slaves.

YEOMEN AND PLANTERS

Cotton brought **economies of scale:** Planters with big farms and many slaves operated more efficiently and more profitably than farmers with fewer resources. And as the price of slaves and good land rose, fewer and fewer owners shared in the profits of the cotton economy, and wealth became more concentrated. The market revolution had commercialized southern agriculture, but a shrinking proportion of the region's white population shared in the benefits. The result was not simply an unequal distribution of wealth but the creation of a dual economy: plantations at the commercial center and a white yeomanry on the fringes.

There were, of course, small farmers in the plantation counties. They tended to be commercial farmers, growing a few bales of cotton with family labor and perhaps a slave or two. Many of them were poor relatives of prosperous plantation owners. They voted the great planters into office, used their cotton gins, and tapped into their marketing networks. Some of them worked as overseers for their wealthy neighbors, sold them food, and served on local slave patrols. Economic disparities between planters and farmers in the plantation belt continued to widen, but the farmers remained tied to the cotton economy.

Most small farmers, however, lived away from the plantations in what was called the up-country: the eastern slopes of the Appalachians from the Chesapeake through Georgia, the western slopes of the mountains in Kentucky and Tennessee, the pine-covered hill country of northern Mississippi and Alabama, parts of Texas and Louisiana, most of the Ozark Plateau in Missouri and Arkansas. All of these lands were too high, cold, isolated, and heavily wooded to support plantation crops. Here the farmers built a yeoman society that shared many of the characteristics of the 18th-century countryside (see Chapter 7). But while northern farmers commercialized,

economy of scale *Term used in both industry and agriculture to describe the economic advantages of concentrating capital, units of production, and output.*

their southern cousins continued in a household- and neighborhood-centered agriculture. Indeed many southern farmers stayed outside the market almost entirely. Farmers in large parts of the up-country South preferred to raise livestock instead of growing cotton or tobacco. They planted cornfields and let their pigs run loose in the woods and on unfenced private land. In late summer and fall they rounded up the animals and sold them to drovers who conducted cross-country drives and sold the animals to flatland merchants and planters. This way of life sustained some of the most fiercely independent neighborhoods in the country.

YEOMEN AND THE MARKET

A larger group of southern yeomen practiced mixed farming for household subsistence and neighborhood exchange, with the surplus sent to market. Most of these farmers owned their own land. These farmers practiced a "subsistence plus" agriculture. They put most of their land into subsistence crops and livestock, cultivating only a few acres of cotton. They devoted more acreage to cotton as transportation made markets more accessible, but few southern yeomen allowed themselves to become wholly dependent on the market. With the income from a few bales of cotton, they could pay their debts and taxes and buy coffee, tea, sugar, tobacco, cloth, and shoes. But they continued to enter and leave the market at will, for their own purposes. The market served the interests of southern yeomen. It seldom dominated them.

Since few farms were self-sufficient, the yeomen farmers routinely traded labor and goods with each other. In the plantation counties, such cooperation tended to reinforce the power of planters who put some of their resources at the disposal of their poorer neighbors. In the up-country, cooperation reinforced neighborliness. Debts contracted within the network of kin and neighbors were generally paid in kind or in labor, and creditors often allowed their neighbors' debts to go unpaid for years.

Among southern neighborly restraints on entrepreneurialism, none was more distinctive than the region's attitude toward fences. In the North, well-maintained fences were a sign of ambitious, hardworking farmers. The poor fences of the South, on the other hand, were interpreted as a sign of laziness. Actually, the scarcity of fences in most southern neighborhoods was the result of local custom and state law. In country neighborhoods where families fished and hunted for food and where livestock roamed freely, fences conflicted with a local economy that required neighborhood use of privately owned land. The lack of fences in the South reflected neighborhood constraints on the private use of private property and thus on individual acquisitiveness and ambition. Such constraints, however, were necessary to the subsistence of families and neighborhoods as they were organized in the upland South.

A BALANCE SHEET: THE PLANTATION AND SOUTHERN DEVELOPMENT

The owners of the South's large farms were among the richest men in the Western Hemisphere. In 1860 the 12 wealthiest counties in the United States were in the South. Southern wealth, however, was concentrated in fewer and fewer hands. The slaves whose labor created the wealth owned nothing. As many as one-third of southern white families lived in poverty, and a declining proportion of the others owned slaves. Huge disparities existed even among the slaveholding minority; in 1860 only one-fifth of the slaveholders owned 20 or more slaves, thus crossing the generally acknowledged line that separated "farmers" from "planters."

In economic terms, the concentration of wealth in the hands of a few planters had profound effects on how the market revolution affected the region. Much of the white population remained marginal to the market economy. Whereas in the North the rural demand for credit, banking facilities, farm tools, clothing, and other consumer goods fueled a revolution in commerce, finance, and industry, the South remained a poor market for manufactured goods. The slaves wore cheap cloth made in the Northeast, and the planters furnished themselves and their homes with finery from Europe. In the North the exchange of farm produce for finished goods was creating self-sustaining economic growth by the 1840s. But the South continued to export its plantation staples and to build only those factories, commercial institutions, and cities that served the plantation.

Not that the South neglected technological innovation and agricultural improvement. Southerners developed Eli Whitney's hand-operated cotton gin into equipment capable of performing complex milling operations. They also developed the cotton press, a machine with a huge wooden screw powered by horses or mules, used to compress ginned cotton into tight bales for shipping. Yet there were few such innovations, and they had to do with the processing and shipping of cotton rather than with its production. The truth is that cotton was a labor-intensive crop that discouraged innovation. Moreover, plantation slaves often resisted their enslavement by sabotaging expensive tools and draft animals, scattering manure in haphazard ways, and passively resisting innovations that would have added to their drudgery. So the cotton fields continued to be cultivated by clumsy, mule-drawn plows that barely scratched the soil, by women wielding hoes, and by gangs who harvested the crop by hand.

Southern state governments spent little on internal improvements. A Virginia canal linked the flour mills at Richmond with inland grain fields, and another connected Chesapeake Bay with the National Road. But planters in the cotton belt had ready access to the South's magnificent system of navigable rivers, while upland whites saw little need for expensive, state-supported internal improvements. Nor did the South build cities. The South used its canals and railroads mainly to move plantation staples to towns that transshipped them out of the region. Southern cities were located on the periphery of the region and served as transportation depots for plantation crops. Southern businessmen turned to New York City for credit, insurance, and coastal and export shipping. And it was from New York that they ordered finished goods for the southern market.

C O N C L U S I O N

In 1858 James H. Hammond, a slaveholding senator from South Carolina, asked: "What would happen if no cotton was furnished for three years? . . . England would topple headlong and carry the whole civilized world with her save the south. No, you dare not make war on cotton. No power on earth dares to make war on cotton. Cotton is king."

Along with other planter-politicians, Hammond argued that farmers at the fringes of the world market economy could coerce the commercial-industrial center. He was wrong. The commitment to cotton and slavery had not only isolated the South politically, but it had also deepened the South's dependence on the world's financial and industrial centers. The North and West underwent a qualitative market revolution after 1815, a revolution that enriched both and that transformed the Northeast from a part of the old colonial periphery (the suppliers of food and raw materials) into a part of the core (the suppliers of manufactured goods and financing) of the world market economy. In contrast, the South, by exporting plantation staples in exchange for imported goods, worked itself deeper and deeper into dependence.

QUESTIONS FOR REVIEW AND CRITICAL THINKING

Review

1. What was the nationalizing dream of the American System, and how did improvements in transportation actually channel commerce within and between sections?
2. How did northern farm families experience the transition into commercial agriculture between 1815 and 1850?
3. What was the relationship between urban-industrial growth and the commercialization of the northern countryside?
4. What were the nature and limits of the market revolution in the South? Why?

Critical Thinking

1. To what extent and in what ways was the transition to a market economy helped or hindered by the national and state governments?
2. "The principal differences between North and South as of 1850 stemmed from the fact that the North had experienced a thoroughgoing market revolution in the previous fifty years while the South had not." True or false?

Discovery

What changes did the transportation and market revolutions bring to the United States? How did it also reinforce the existing social fabric and regional differences?

SUGGESTED READINGS

Suggested Readings

Works on the earlier phases of questions covered in this chapter are listed in the Suggested Readings for Chapter 7. For a broad economic, cultural, and political synthesis, see **Charles G. Sellers, *The Market Revolution: Jacksonian America, 1815–1848*** (1991). **George Rogers Taylor, *The Transportation Revolution, 1815–1860*** (1951) remains the best single book on its subject. On legal and constitutional issues, see **R. Kent Newmeyer, *The Supreme Court under Marshall and Taney*** (1968) and **Morton J. Horwitz, *The Transformation of American Law, 1780–1860*** (1977). Changes in northern rural society are treated in **Christopher Clark, *The Roots of Rural Capitalism: Western Massachusetts, 1780–1860*** (1990) and **Carolyn Merchant, *Ecological Revolutions: Nature, Gender, and Science in New England*** (1989). Solid studies of industrial communities include **Thomas Dublin, *Women at Work: The Transformation of Work and Community in Lowell, Massachusetts, 1810–1860*** (1979) and **Anthony F.C. Wallace, *Rockdale: The Growth of an American Village in the Early Industrial Revolution*** (1978). On the plantation, see **Eugene D. Genovese, *The Political Economy of Slavery: Studies in the Economy and Society of the Slave South,*** 2d ed. (1989) and **R. W. Fogel, *Without Consent or Contract: The Rise and Fall of American Slavery*** (1989). On the southern yeomanry, see **Stephanie McCurry, *Masters of Small Worlds: Yeoman Households, Gender Relations, and the Political Culture of the South Carolina Lowcountry*** (1995) and **Steven Hahn, *The Roots of Southern Populism: Yeoman Farmers and the Transformation of the Georgia Upcountry, 1850–1890*** (1983).

ONLINE SOURCES GUIDE

ThomsonNOW™ Visit ThomsonNOW to access primary sources, exercises, quizzes, and audio chapter summaries related to this chapter:
http://www.Thomsonedu.com/login

$\mathcal{D}$ISCOVERY

What changes did the transportation and market revolutions bring to the United States? How did it also reinforce the existing social fabric and regional differences?

In thinking about this question, begin by breaking it down into the components shown below. A discussion of the significance of each component should appear in your answer.

TRANSPORTATION AND REGIONAL DEVELOPMENT

Based on your reading of this chapter, how did the Erie Canal and other canals transform New York and the rest of the United States? Do the images of the Erie Canal and a western New York farm offer any clues as to the impact of canal-building on development in rural areas? Look at the maps. What areas experienced the greatest expansion of canals and railroads during the first half of the nineteenth century? How do you account for the differences in the development of transportation systems in America's regions? What were the economic and demographic consequences of these differences?

RIVERS, ROADS, AND CANALS, 1825–1860

A WESTERN NEW YORK FARM

© Bettermann/Corbis

Smithsonian Institution

THE ERIE CANAL

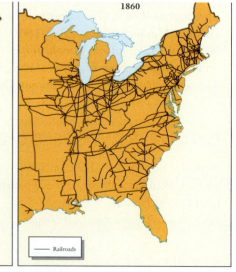

RAILROADS IN THE UNITED STATES, 1840 AND 1860

ECONOMICS AND FAMILY LIFE

Look at the maps showing cotton production. What factors combined to explain such growth in production between 1801 and 1859? Look at the illustration of hauling cotton. What are the roles of slave women and children in this harvest as depicted in this illustration? Do you think that the family labor patterns of white southerners were similar to those of slave families? Why or why not?

HAULING THE WHOLE WEEK'S PICKING

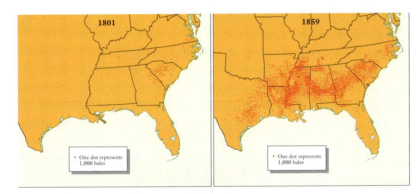

COTTON PRODUCTION, 1801 AND 1859

TRANSPORTATION AND FAMILY LIFE

Study the advertisement. Where was American Cream Soap manufactured? Identify three or more ways American Soap Company says or suggests that their soap will improve the life of a "typical" middle class family. Is this company aiming to sell their soap locally or nationally? Is there a relationship between the explosion of canals and railroads and the price and availability to American households of American Cream soap? What differences do you see between the print advertising of the 1850s and today? What similarities do you see?

A SOAP ADVERTISEMENT FROM THE 1850S

TOWARD AN AMERICAN CULTURE

Americans after 1815 experienced wave after wave of social and cultural change. Territorial expansion, the market revolution, and the spread of plantation slavery uprooted Americans and broke old social patterns. Americans in these years created distinctive forms of popular literature and art, and they found new ways of having fun. They flocked to evangelical revivals—meetings designed to produce religious conversions and led by preachers who were trained to that task—in which they revived and remade American religious life.

The emerging American culture was more or less uniformly republican, capitalist, and Protestant. But different kinds of Americans made different cultures out of the revolutionary inheritance, the market revolution, and revival religion. The result, visible from the 1830s onward, was an American national culture composed largely of subcultures based on region, class, and race.

1820	1825	1830	1835	1840	1845	1850	1855

■ **1822**
Denmark Vesey's slave conspiracy uncovered in Charleston

■ **1830**
Charles Grandison Finney leads religious revival in Rochester • Joseph Smith founds the Church of Jesus Christ of Latter-Day Saints

■ **1831**
Mount Auburn Cemetery opens near Boston • First minstrel show is presented • Nat Turner leads bloody slave revolt in Southampton County, Virginia

■ **1835**
Landscape artist Thomas Cole publishes "Essay on American Scenery"

1843 ■
William Miller's Adventists expect the world to end

1845 ■
George Lippard's lurid novel *Quaker City* becomes a best-seller

1849 ■
Astor Place theater riot in New York City leaves 20 dead

1852 ■
Harriet Beecher Stowe publishes *Uncle Tom's Cabin*

THE NORTHERN MIDDLE CLASS

"The most valuable class in any community," declared the poet-journalist Walt Whitman in 1858, "is the middle class." At that time, the term **middle class** (and the social group that it described) was no more than 30 or 40 years old. Those who claimed the title were largely the new kinds of proprietors made by the market revolution: city and country merchants, master craftsmen who had turned themselves into manufacturers, and the mass of market-oriented farmers.

A disproportionate number of them were New Englanders. New England was the first center of factory production, and southern New England farms were thoroughly commercialized by the 1830s. Yankee migrants dominated the commercial heartland of western New York and the northern regions of the Northwest. Even in the seaport cities businessmen from New England were often at the center of economic innovation. This Yankee middle class invented cultural forms that became the core of an emerging business civilization. They upheld the autonomous individual against the claims of traditional neighborhoods and traditional families. They devised an intensely private, mother-centered domestic life. Most of all, they adhered to a reformed Yankee Protestantism whose moral imperatives became the foundation of American middle-class culture.

THE EVANGELICAL BASE

In November 1830 the evangelist Charles Grandison Finney preached in Rochester, New York, to a church full of middle-class men and women. Most of them were transplanted New Englanders, the heirs of what was left of Yankee Calvinism. In their ministers' weekly sermons, in the formal articles of faith drawn up by their churches, and

FOCUS QUESTION

What were the central cultural maxims of the emerging northern middle class?

middle class *Social group that developed in the early nineteenth century comprised of urban and country merchants, master craftsmen who had turned themselves into manufacturers, and market-oriented farmers—small-scale entrepreneurs who rose within market society in the early nineteenth century.*

in the set prayers their children memorized, they reaffirmed the old Puritan beliefs in providence, predestination, and original sin. The earthly social order (the fixed relations of power and submission between men and women, rich and poor, children and parents, and so on) was necessary because humankind was innately sinful and prone to selfishness and disorder. Christians must obey the rules governing their station in life; attempts to rearrange the social order were both sinful and doomed to failure.

Yet while they reaffirmed those beliefs in church, the men and women in Finney's audience routinely ignored them in their daily lives. The benefits accruing from the market revolution were clearly the result of human effort. Just as clearly, they added up to "improvement" and "progress." And as middle-class Christians increasingly envisioned an improved material and social world, the doctrines of human inability and natural depravity, along with faith in divine providence, made less and less sense.

It was to such men and women that Charles Finney preached what became the organizing principle of northern middle-class evangelicalism: "God," he insisted, "has made man a moral free agent." Neither the social order nor the spiritual state of individuals was divinely ordained. People would make themselves and the world better by choosing right over wrong, although they would choose right only after submitting their rebellious wills to the will of God. Their new faith valued individual holiness over a permanent and sacred social order. It made the spiritual nature of individuals a matter of prayer, submission, and choice. Yankee evangelists had been moving toward Finney's formulation since the turn of the 19th century. Like Finney, they borrowed revival techniques from the Methodists (weeklong meetings, meetings in which women prayed in public, an **anxious bench** for the most likely converts), but toned them down for their own more "respectable" and affluent audience. While they used democratic methods and preached a message of individualism and free agency, however, middle-class evangelicals retained the Puritans' Old Testament sense of cosmic history: They enlisted personal holiness and spiritual democracy in a war between the forces of good and evil in this world.

DOMESTICITY

The Yankee middle class made crucial distinctions between the home and the world. Men in cities and towns now went off to work, leaving wives and children at home. The new middle-class evangelicalism encouraged this division of domestic labor. The public world of politics and economic exchange, said the preachers, was the sphere of men; women, on the other hand, exercised new kinds of moral influence within households.

The result was a feminization of domestic life. In the early republic, the fathers who owned property, headed households, and governed family labor were lawgivers and disciplinarians. Middle-class evangelicals raised new spiritual possibilities for women and children. Mothers replaced fathers as the principle child rearers, and they enlisted the doctrines of free agency and individual moral responsibility in that task. Middle-class mothers sought to develop their children's conscience and their capacity to love, to teach them to make good moral choices, and to prepare them for conversion and a lifetime of Christian service.

Middle-class mothers were able to do that because they could concentrate their efforts on household duties and because they had fewer children than their mothers or grandmothers had had. Housewives also spaced their pregnancies differently. Unlike their forebears, who gave birth to a child about once every two years throughout their childbearing years, middle-class housewives had their children at five-year intervals, which meant that they could give each child close attention. Households were quieter

anxious bench *Bench at or near the front of a religious revival meeting where the most likely converts were seated.*

Sunday schools *Schools that first appeared in the 1790s to teach working-class children to read and write but by the 1820s and 1830s were becoming moral training grounds.*

A Middle-Class New England Family at Home, 1837. *The room is carpeted and comfortably furnished. Father reads his newspaper; books rest on the table. Mother entertains their only child, and a kitten joins the family circle. This is the domestic foundation of sentimental culture on display.*

and less crowded; children learned from their mothers how to govern themselves. Thus mothers nurtured children who would be carriers of the new middle-class culture—and fathers, ministers, and other authorities recognized the importance of that job.

The new ethos of moral free agency was mirrored in the **Sunday schools.** When Sunday schools first appeared in the 1790s, their purpose was to teach working-class children to read and write by having them copy long passages from the Bible. After the revivals of the 1820s and 1830s, the emphasis shifted to preparing children's souls for conversion. Middle-class children were now included in the schools, corporal punishment was forbidden, and Sunday school teachers now tried to develop the moral sensibilities of their charges. They had the children read a few Bible verses each week and then led them in a discussion of the moral lessons of those verses. Thus Sunday schools became training grounds in free agency and moral accountability, a transformation that made sense only in a sentimental world where children could be trusted to make moral choices.

SENTIMENTALITY

Improvements in the printing, distribution, and marketing of books led to an outpouring of popular literature, much of it directed at the middle class. There were cookbooks, etiquette books, manuals on housekeeping, sermons, and sentimental novels—many of them written and most of them read by women. The works of popular religious writers such as Lydia Sigourney, Lydia Maria Child, and Timothy Shay Arthur found their way into thousands of middle-class homes. **Sarah Josepha Hale,** whose *Godey's Lady's Book* was the first mass-circulation magazine for women, was an arbiter of taste not only in furniture, clothing, and food but in sentiments and ideas. Sentimental novels written by women outsold by wide margins Nathaniel Hawthorne's *The Scarlet Letter* and *The House of Seven Gables,* Ralph Waldo Emerson's essays, Henry David Thoreau's *Walden,* Herman Melville's *Moby Dick,* and Walt Whitman's *Leaves of Grass.* Susan Warner's *The Wide, Wide World* broke all sales records when it appeared in 1850. Harriet Beecher Stowe's **Uncle Tom's Cabin** (1852) broke the records set by Warner.

These sentimental novels made sacred the middle-class home and the trials and triumphs of Christian women. The action takes place indoors, usually in the kitchen or parlor, and the central characters are women (in Stowe's book, slave Christians are included). The stories have to do with spiritual struggle and mother love. The home

QUICK REVIEW

DOMESTICITY

- Separation of home from economic and political life

- Mothers become the principal child-rearers

- Parental authority based in love not power

Sarah Josepha Hale *Editor of* Godey's Ladies Book *and an important arbiter of domesticity and taste for middle-class housewives.*

Uncle Tom's Cabin *Published by Harriet Beecher Stowe in 1852, this sentimental novel told the story of the Christian slave Uncle Tom and became a best seller and the most powerful antislavery tract of the antebellum years.*

is juxtaposed to the marketplace and the world of competition, brutality, and power. Unlike the female characters in British and European novels of the time, the women in these American novels are intelligent, generous persons who grow in strength and independence.

In sentimental **domestic fiction,** women assume the role of evangelical ministers, demonstrating Christian living by example and moral persuasion. Female moral influence is at war with the male world of politics and the marketplace—areas of power, greed, and moral compromise. The most successful sentimental novel was Harriet Beecher Stowe's *Uncle Tom's Cabin* (discussed in Chapter 13), an indictment of slavery as a system of absolute power at odds with the domestic values held dear by Stowe's audience of evangelical women. Based solidly in revival Christianity, the novel lambastes the rational calculation, greed, and power hunger of the "real world" and upholds domestic space filled with women, slaves, and children who gain spiritual power through submission to Christ. The two most telling scenes—the deaths of the Christian slave Uncle Tom and the perfect child Eva St. Claire—reenact the crucifixion of Jesus. Uncle Tom prays for his tormentors as he is beaten to death, and little Eva extracts promises of Christian behavior from her deathbed. Both are powerless, submissive characters whose deaths redeem a fallen humankind.

Uncle Tom's Cabin and other popular sentimental novels were not frivolous fairy tales into which housewives retreated from the "real" world. They were subversive depictions of a higher spiritual reality that would move the feminine ethos of the Christian home to the center of civilization. As we shall see in Chapter 11, that vision was underneath an organized public assault on irreligion, drunkenness, prostitution, slavery, and other practices and institutions that substituted passion and force for Christian love.

FINE ARTS

Educated Americans of the postrevolutionary generation associated the fine arts with the sensuality of European courts and European Catholicism. In making government buildings and monuments, building expensive homes, and painting portraits of wealthy men, American artists copied the classic simplicity of ancient Greece and Rome, republican styles that had been tested by time and that were free of any hint of sensuality or luxury. In the 1820s and 1830s, however, educated Americans began to view literature and the arts more favorably. There were a number of reasons for that change. First, American nationalists began to demand an American art that could compete with the arts of the despotic Old World. At the same time, evangelical Christianity and sentimental culture glorified a romantic cult of feeling that was, within its limits, far more receptive to aesthetic experience than Calvinism and the more spartan forms of republicanism had been. Finally, the more comfortable and educated Americans fell into a relationship with nature that called out for aesthetic expression. After 1815, with the agricultural frontier penetrating deep into the interior, educated northeasterners became certain that civilization would supplant wilderness on the North American continent. The result was a multivoiced conversation about the relations between nature and civilization, a conversation that occupied a large portion of a new American art and literature that rose between 1830 and the Civil War.

NATURE AND ART

Much of the new American art went into useful objects. Andrew Jackson Downing and other landscape designers and architects created country cottages surrounded by gardens. At the same time, cities began to build cemeteries in the surrounding coun-

domestic fiction *Sentimental literature that centered on household and domestic themes that emphasized the toil and travails of women and children who overcame adversity through religious faith and strength of character.*

tryside. In 1831 wealthy Bostonians put up the money to build Mount Auburn Cemetery. Mount Auburn was situated on rolling ground, with footpaths following the contours of the land. Much of the natural vegetation was left untouched, and wildflowers were planted to supplement it. The headstones were small and dignified. Copied in Brooklyn, Rochester, and other northern cities, the rural cemeteries embodied the faith that nature could teach moral lessons, particularly if nature was shaped and made available to humankind through art. Not surprisingly, the leading artists of this generation were landscape painters. Thomas Cole, in his "Essay on American Scenery" (1835), reminded readers that the most distinctive feature of America was its wilderness:

> In civilized Europe the primitive features of scenery have long since been destroyed or modified. . . . And to this cultivated state our western world is fast approaching; but nature is still predominant, and there are those who regret that with the improvements of cultivation the sublimity of the wilderness should pass away; for those scenes of solitude from which the hand of nature has never been lifted, affect the mind with a more deep toned emotion than aught which the hand of man has touched. Amid them the consequent associations are of God the creator—they are his undefiled works, and the mind is cast into contemplation of eternal things.

In what became a manifesto of American intellectual and aesthetic life, Cole had found God in nature, and thus endowed art that depicted nature with religious purpose. Among educated persons, art was no longer subversive of the Protestant republic; done right, it was a bulwark of good citizenship and true religion. Educated middle and upper-class northerners after 1830 defined themselves by talking about American nature—a nature that had become Christianized and benign.

That development was strongest among urban northeasterners who believed that theirs was an age of progress. Indeed some would argue that the feminization of family life, the rise of sentimentality, and the romantic cult of nature could have appeared only when American civilization had turned the tide in its age-old battle with wilderness. The most sensitive and articulate northeasterners warned that the victory might be too complete and that the United States could become as "unnatural" and "artificial" as Europe.

The Plain People of the North

From the 1830s onward, northern middle-class evangelicals proposed their religious and domestic values as a national culture for the United States. But even in their own region they were surrounded and outnumbered by Americans who rejected their cultural leadership. The plain people of the North were a varied lot: settlers in the lower Northwest who remained culturally southern; hill-country New Englanders, New Yorkers, and Pennsylvanians; refugees from the countryside who had taken up urban wage labor; and increasing thousands of Irish and German immigrants. What they shared was a cultural conservatism that rejected sentimentalism and reformist religion out of hand.

FOCUS QUESTION
Within the North, what were the alternatives to middle-class culture?

Religion and the Common Folk

The doctrines of churches favored by the northern plain folk varied as much as the people themselves. They included the most popular faiths (Baptists and Methodists came to constitute two-thirds of America's professing Protestants in both the North and the South) and such smaller sects as Hicksite Quakers, Universalists, Adventists, Moravians, and Freewill Baptists. Yet for all their diversity, most of these churches shared an evangelical emphasis on individual experience over churchly authority. Most favored democratic, local control of religious life and distrusted outside organization and religious professionalism. And they rejected middle-class optimism and reformism, reaffirming humankind's duty to accept an imperfect world.

The most pervasive strain was a belief in providence, the conviction that human history was part of God's vast and unknowable plan, and that all events were willed or allowed by God. Middle-class evangelicals spoke of providence, too, but they seemed to assume that God's plan was manifest in the progress of market society and middle-class religion. Humbler evangelicals believed that the events of everyday life were parts of a vast blueprint that existed only in the mind of God—and not in the vain aspirations of women and men.

When making plans, they added the caveat "The Lord willing," and they learned to accept misfortune with fortitude. They responded to epidemics, bad crop years, aches and pains, illness, and early death by praying for the strength to endure, asking God to "sanctify" their suffering by making it an opportunity for them to grow in faith.

In a world governed by providence, the death of a loved one was a test of faith. Plain folk considered it a privilege to witness a death in the family, for it released the sufferer from the tribulations of this world and sent him or her to a better place. The death of children in particular called for a heroic act of submission to God's will; parents mourned the loss but stopped short of displaying grief that would suggest selfishness and lack of faith. Poor families washed and dressed the dead body themselves and then buried it in a churchyard or on a hilltop plot on the family farm. While the urban middle class preferred formal funerals and carefully tended cemeteries, humbler people regarded death as a lesson in the futility of pursuing worldly goals and in the need to submit to God's will.

POPULAR MILLENNIALISM

The plain Protestants of the North seldom talked about the millennium. Middle-class evangelicals were **postmillennialists:** They believed that Christ's Second Coming would occur at the *end* of 1,000 years of social perfection that would be brought about by the missionary conversion of the world. Ordinary Baptists, Methodists, and Disciples of Christ, however, assumed that the millennium would arrive with world-destroying violence, followed by 1,000 years of Christ's rule on earth. But most did not dwell on this terrifying *premillennialism,* assuming that God would end the world in his own time. Now and then, however, the ordinary evangelicals of the North predicted the fiery end of the world. People looked for signs of the approaching millennium in thunderstorms, shooting stars, eclipses, economic panics and depressions, and—especially—in hints that God had placed in the Bible. An avid student of those hints was William Miller, a rural New York Baptist who, after years of systematic study, concluded that God would destroy the world during the year following March 1843. Miller publicized his predictions throughout the 1830s, and near the end of the decade the Millerites (as his followers were called) gathered together thousands of believers, most of them conservative Baptists, Methodists, and Disciples in hill-country New England and in poor neighborhoods in New York, Ohio, and Michigan. As the end approached, the believers read the Bible, prayed, and attended meeting after meeting. Newspapers published stories alleging that the Millerites were insane and guilty of sexual license. Some of them, the press reported, were busy sewing "ascension robes" in which they would rise straight to heaven without passing through death.

postmillennialism *Belief (held mostly by middle-class evangelists) that Christ's Second Coming would occur when missionary conversion of the world brought about a thousand years of social perfection.*

When the end of the year—March 23, 1844—came and went, most of the believers quietly returned to their churches. A committed remnant, however, kept the faith and by the 1860s founded the Seventh-Day Adventist Church. The Millerite movement was a reminder that hundreds of thousands of northern Protestants continued to believe that the God of the Old Testament governed everything from bee stings to the course of human history and that one day he would destroy the world in fire and blood.

FAMILY AND SOCIETY

Baptists, Methodists, Disciples of Christ, and the smaller popular sects evangelized primarily among people who had been bypassed or hurt by the market revolution. Often their rhetoric turned to criticism of market society, its institutions, and its centers of power. Elias Hicks, a Long Island farmer who fought the worldliness and pride of wealthy urban Quakers, listed the following among the mistakes of the early 19th century: railroads, the Erie Canal, fancy food and other luxuries, banks and the credit system, the city of Philadelphia, and the study of chemistry. The Baptist millenarian William Miller expressed his hatred of banks, insurance companies, stockjobbing, chartered monopolies, personal greed, and the city of New York. In short, what the evangelical middle-class identified as the march of progress, poorer and more conservative evangelicals often condemned as a descent into worldliness that would almost certainly provoke God's wrath.

Along with doubts about economic change and the middle-class churches that embraced it, members of the popular sects often held to the patriarchal family form in which they had been raised. For hundreds of thousands of northern Protestants, the erosion of domestic patriarchy was a profound cultural loss and not, as it was for the middle class, an avenue to personal liberation. For some, religious conversion came at a point of crisis in the traditional family. William Miller, for example, had a strict Calvinist upbringing in a family in which his father, an uncle, and his grandfather were all Baptist ministers. As a young man he rejected his family, set about making money, and became a deist—actions that deeply wounded his parents. When his father died, Miller was stricken with guilt. He moved back to his hometown, took up his family duties, became a leader of the Baptist church, and (after reading a sermon entitled "Parental Duties") began the years of Bible study that resulted in his world-ending prophecies.

THE PROPHET JOSEPH SMITH

The weakening of the patriarchal family and the attempt to shore it up were central to the life and work of one of the most unique and successful religious leaders of the period, the Mormon prophet **Joseph Smith** (see also Chapter 13). Smith's father was a landless Vermont Baptist who moved his wife and nine children to seven rented farms within 20 years. Around 1820, when young Joseph was approaching manhood, the family was struggling to make mortgage payments on a small farm outside Palmyra, New York. Despite the efforts of Joseph and his brothers, a merchant cheated the Smith family out of the farm. With that, both generations of the Smiths faced lifetimes as propertyless workers. To make matters worse, Joseph's mother and some of his siblings began to attend an evangelical Presbyterian church in Palmyra, apparently against the father's wishes.

Before the loss of the farm, Joseph had received two visions warning him away from existing churches and telling him to wait for further instructions. In 1827 the

Joseph Smith *Poor New York farm boy whose visions led him to translate the* Book of Mormon *in late 1820s. He became the founder and the prophet of the Church of Jesus Christ of Latter-day Saints (Mormons).*

Angel Moroni appeared to him and led him to golden plates that translated into *The Book of Mormon*. It told of a light-skinned people, descendants of the Hebrews, who had sailed to North America long before Columbus. They had had an epic, violent history and had been visited by Jesus following his resurrection.

Joseph Smith later declared that his discovery of *The Book of Mormon* had "brought salvation to my father's house" by unifying the family. It eventually unified thousands of others under a patriarchal faith. The good priests and secular leaders of *The Book of Mormon* are farmers who labor alongside their neighbors; the villains are self-seeking merchants, lawyers, and bad priests. Smith carried that model of brotherly cooperation and patriarchal authority into the Church of Jesus Christ of Latter-Day Saints that he founded in 1830. The new church was ruled not by professional clergy but by an elaborate lay hierarchy of adult males. On top sat the father of Joseph Smith, rescued from destitution and shame, who was appointed Patriarch of the Church. Below him were Joseph Smith and his brother Hyrum, who were called First and Second Elders. The hierarchy descended through a succession of male authorities that finally reached the fathers of households. An astute observer might have noticed the similarities between this hierarchical structure and the social order of the 18th-century North.

THE RISE OF POPULAR CULTURE

Of course, not all the northern plain folk spent their time in church. Particularly in cities and towns, they became both producers and consumers of a commercial popular culture.

BLOOD SPORTS

Urban working-class neighborhoods were particularly fertile ground for the making of popular amusements. Young working men formed a bachelor subculture that contrasted with the piety and self-restraint of the middle class. They organized volunteer fire companies and militia units that spent more time drinking and fighting rival groups than they did drilling or putting out fires. Gathering at firehouses, saloons, and street corners, they drank, joked, and boasted and nurtured notions of manliness based on physical prowess and coolness under pressure.

They also engaged in such **blood sports** as cockfighting, ratting, and dog fighting, even though many states had laws forbidding such activities. Such contests grew increasingly popular during the 1850s and were often staged by saloon keepers. One of the best known was Kit Burns of New York City, who ran Sportsman Hall, a saloon frequented by prizefighters, criminals, and their hangers-on. Behind the saloon was a space—reached through a narrow doorway that could be defended against the police—with animal pits and a small amphitheater that seated 250 but that regularly held 400 yelling spectators. Although most of the spectators were working men, a few members of the old aristocracy who rejected middle-class ways also attended these events. Frederick Van Wyck, scion of a wealthy old New York family, remembered an evening he had spent at Tommy Norris's livery stable, where he witnessed a fight between billy goats, a rat baiting, a cockfight, and a boxing match between bare-breasted women. "Certainly for a lad of 17, such as I," he recalled, "a night with Tommy Norris and his attraction was quite a night."

blood sports *Sporting activities emphasizing bloodiness that were favored by working-class men of the cities. The most popular in the early 19th century were cockfighting, ratting, dogfights, and various types of violence between animals.*

BOXING

Prizefighting emerged from the same subterranean culture that sustained cockfights and other blood sports. This sport, which was imported from Britain, called for an enclosed ring, clear rules, cornermen, a referee, and a paying audience. The early fighters were Irish or English immigrants, as were many of the promoters and spectators. Boxing's popularity rose during the 1840s and 1850s. Many of the fighters had close ties with ethnic-based saloons, militia units, fire companies, and street gangs, and many labored at occupations with a peculiarly ethnic base. Some of the best American-born fighters were New York City butchers. Butchers usually finished work by 10:00 A.M. They could then spend the rest of the day idling at a firehouse or a bar and were often prominent figures in neighborhood gangs. A prizefight between an American-born butcher and an Irish day laborer would attract a spirited audience that understood its class and ethnic meaning.

Prizefighting was a way of rewarding courage and skill and, sometimes, of settling scores through contests that were fair and limited to two combatants. Nonetheless, the fights were brutal. Boxers fought with bare knuckles, and a bout ended only when one of the fighters was unable to continue. In an infamous match in 1842, for instance, the Englishman Christopher Lilly knocked down his Irish opponent Thomas McCoy 80 times; the fight ended with round 119, when McCoy died in his corner.

Although boxing was closely associated with ethnic rivalries, the contestants often exhibited a respect for one another that crossed ethnic lines. For example, the native-born Tom Hyer, who had defeated the Irishman James "Yankee" Sullivan in one of the great early fights, later bailed Sullivan out of jail. And when in 1859 Bill Harrington, a retired native-born boxer, disappeared and left a widow and children, his Irish-born former opponent, John Morrisey, arranged a sparring match and sent the proceeds to Harrington's widow.

AN AMERICAN THEATER

In the 18th and early 19th centuries, the only theaters were in the large seaport cities. Those who attended were members of the urban elite, and nearly all the plays, managers, and actors were English. After 1815, however, improvements in transportation and communication, along with the rapid growth of cities, created a much broader audience. Theaters and theater companies sprang up not only in New York and Philadelphia but also in Cincinnati, St. Louis, San Francisco, Rochester, and dozens of other new towns west of the Appalachians, and traveling troupes carried theatrical performances to the smallest hamlets. Before 1830 the poorer theatergoers occupied the cheap balcony seats; artisans and other workingmen filled benches in the ground floor area known as "the pit"; wealthier and more genteel patrons sat in the boxes. Those sitting in the pit and balcony ate and drank, talked, and shouted encouragement and threats to the actors.

As time passed, however, rowdyism turned into violence. The less genteel members of theater audiences protested the elegant speech, gentlemanly bearing, and understated performances of the English actors, which happened to match the speech, manners, and bearing of the American urban elite. The first theater riot occurred in 1817 when the English actor Charles Incledon refused a New York audience's demand that he stop what he was doing and sing "Black-Eyed Susan." Such assaults grew more common during the 1820s. By the 1830s there were separate theaters and separate kinds of performances for rich and poor. But violence continued. It culminated in the rivalry between the American actor Edwin Forrest and the English actor William Charles Macready.

Macready was a trained Shakespearean actor, and his restrained style and attention to the subtleties of the text had won him acclaim both in Britain and in the United States. Forrest, on the other hand, played to the cheap seats. With his bombast and histrionics he transformed Shakespeare's tragedies into melodramas. Forrest and Macready carried out a well-publicized feud that led to a mob attack on Macready in 1849. Led by E. Z. C. Judson (who, under the pen name Ned Buntline, wrote scores of dime novels), the mob descended on Macready's performance at the exclusive Astor Place Opera House. The militia was waiting for them, and in the ensuing riot and gunfight 20 people lost their lives. Playhouses that catered to working-class audiences continued to feature Shakespearean tragedies, but they now shared the stage with works written in the American vernacular. The stage "Yankee," rustic but shrewd, appeared at this time and so did Mose the Bowery B'hoy, a New York volunteer fireman who performed feats of derring-do. Both frequently appeared in the company of well-dressed characters with English accents—the Yankee outsmarted them; Mose beat them up.

MINSTRELSY

The most popular form of theater was the blackface **minstrel show,** which first appeared in 1831. Although these shows conveyed blatant racism, they were the preferred entertainment of working men in northern cities from 1840 to 1880. The minstrel shows lasted an hour and a half and were presented in three sections. The first consisted of songs and dances performed in a walkaround, in which the audience was encouraged to clap and sing along. This was followed by a longer middle section in which the company sat in a row with a character named Tambo at one end and a character named Bones at the other (named for the tambourine and bones, the instruments they played), with an interlocutor in the middle. The Tambo character, often called Uncle Ned, was a simpleminded plantation slave dressed in plain clothing; the Bones character, usually called Zip Coon, was a dandified, oversexed free black dressed in top hat and tails. The interlocutor was the straight man—fashionably dressed, slightly pretentious, with an English accent. This middle portion of the show consisted of a conversation among the three, which included pointed political satire, skits ridiculing the wealthy and the educated, and sexual jokes that bordered on obscenity. The third section featured songs, dances, and jokes.

The minstrel shows introduced African American song and dance to

minstrel show *Popular form of theater among working men of the northern cities in which white men in blackface portrayed African Americans in song and dance.*

Museum of the City of New York/Corbis

AN EARLY PRINT OF "JIM CROW" RICE AT NEW YORK'S BOWERY THEATER. *The caption reads "American Theatre, Bowery, New York, Nov. 25th 1833. The 57th Night of Mr. T. D. Jim Crow Rice."*

audiences who would not have permitted black performers onto the stage. They also reinforced racial stereotypes that were near the center of American popular culture. Finally, they dealt broadly with aspects of social and political life that other performers avoided. Minstrel shows and other theatrical entertainments were among the urban products that the new transportation network carried to rural America. Actors traveled well-established circuits, calling on local amateurs for their supporting casts. Minstrel companies traveled the river system of the interior and played to enthusiastic audiences wherever the riverboats docked. Mark Twain recalled them fondly: "I remember the first Negro musical show I ever saw. It must have been in the early forties. It was a new institution. In our village of Hannibal [Missouri] . . . it burst upon us as a glad and stunning surprise." Among Americans who had been taught to distrust cities, minstrel shows and other urban entertainments gave rural folk a sense of the variety and excitement of city life.

NOVELS AND THE PENNY PRESS

Among the many commodities the market revolution made available, few were more ubiquitous than newspapers and inexpensive books. Improvements in printing and papermaking enabled entrepreneurs to sell daily newspapers for a penny. Cheap "story papers" became available in the 1830s, "yellow-back" fiction in the 1840s, and dime novels from the 1850s onward. Although these offerings were distributed throughout the North and the West, they found their first and largest audience among city workers.

Mass-audience newspapers carried political news and local advertisements, but they were heavily spiced with sensationalism. The *Philadelphia Gazette* in late summer of 1829, for instance, treated its eager readers to the following: "Female Child with Two Heads," "Bats," "Another Shark," "Horrid Murder," "Steam Boat Robbery," "Fishes Travelling on Land," "Poisoning by Milk," "Dreadful Steam Boat Disaster," "Raffling for Babies," "Combat with a Bear," "Lake Serpent," and much, much more. Henry David Thoreau commented on the "startling and monstrous events as fill the family papers," while his friend Ralph Waldo Emerson reported that Americans were "reading all day murders & railroad accidents." Such sensational stories portrayed a haunted, often demonic nature that regularly produced monstrosities and ruined the works of humankind, as well as a *human* nature that was often deceptive and depraved.

Working-class readers discovered a similarly untrustworthy world in cheap fiction. George Lippard's *Quaker City* (1845) was a fictional "exposé" of the hypocrisy, lust, and cruelty of Philadelphia's outwardly genteel and Christian elite. Lippard and other adventure writers indulged in a pornography of violence that included cannibalism, blood drinking, and murder by every imaginable means. They also dealt with sex in unprecedentedly explicit ways. The yellow-back novels of the 1840s introduced readers not only to seduction and rape but to transvestitism, child pornography, necrophilia, miscegenation, group sex, homosexuality, and—perhaps most shocking of all—women with criminal minds and insatiable sexual appetites.

Popular fictions were melodramatic contests between good and evil. Heroes met a demonic and chaotic world with courage and guile without hoping to change it. Indeed, melodramatic heroes frequently acknowledged evil in themselves while claiming moral superiority over the hypocrites and frauds who governed the world. A murderer in Ned Buntline's *G'hals of New York* (1850) remarks, "There isn't no *real* witue [virtue] and honesty nowhere, 'cept among the perfessional *dis*honest." (By contrast, in middle-class sentimental novels, the universe is benign; good can be nurtured, and evil can be defeated and transformed. Harriet Beecher Stowe's slave driver Simon Legree is evil not because of a natural disposition toward evil but because he had been deprived of a mother's love during childhood.)

FAMILY, CHURCH, AND NEIGHBORHOOD: THE WHITE SOUTH

FOCUS QUESTION

To what extent can the culture of southern whites be explained by localism?

In the South, farm and plantation labor and the routines of family life were still conducted within the household, and prospects for most whites remained rooted in inherited land and family help. While the new northern middle class nourished a cosmopolitan culture and a domestic sentimentalism that subverted traditional authority, southerners distrusted outsiders and defended rural neighborhoods grounded in the authority of fathers and the integrity of families.

SOUTHERN FAMILIES

Most southern whites regarded themselves less as individuals than as representatives of families. Southern boys often received the family names of heroes as their first names: Jefferson Davis, for example, or Thomas Jefferson (later, "Stonewall") Jackson. More often, however, they took the name of a related family—Peyton Randolph, Preston Brooks, Langdon Cheves. Children learned early on that their first duty was to their family's reputation. In the white South, reputation and the defense of family honor were everything. A boy with a reputation for cowardice, for ineptness at riding or fighting, or for failure to control his emotions or hold his liquor was an embarrassment to his family. Among southern white men, wealth generally counted for less than did maintaining one's personal and family honor and thus winning membership in the democracy of honorable males.

The code of honor, while it forged ties of equality and respect among white men, made rigid distinctions between men and women and whites and blacks. Women and girls who misbehaved damaged not only their own reputation but also the honor of the fathers, brothers, or husbands who could not control them. Such a charge could mean social death in a rural community made up of patriarchal households and watchful neighbors. In

Hunter Museum of American Art, Chattanooga, Tennessee, Gift of Mr. and Mrs. Thomas B. Whiteside

COLONEL AND MRS. WHITESIDE. *Colonel and Mrs. James Whiteside, at home in their mansion on the heights above Chattanooga, are properly comfortable and genteel. Their infant son wears the traditional small child's dress, and the slaves who serve them are rendered grotesquely small.*

1813 Bolling Hall of Alabama advised his daughter, "If you learn to restrain every thought, action, and word by virtue and religion, you will become an ornament."

The southern code of honor blunted attacks upon social hierarchy and inherited status. When sentimental northerners attacked slavery because it denied the freedom of the individual, one southerner responded in a way that was meant to end the argument: "Do you say that the slave is held to involuntary service? So is the wife, [whose] relation to her husband, in the great majority of cases, is made for her and not by her." Few white southerners would have questioned the good sense of that response. Southern life was not about freedom, individual fulfillment, or social progress; it was about honoring the obligations to which one was born.

SOUTHERN ENTERTAINMENTS

Southerners of all classes and races were leisure-loving people. But the rural character of the South threw them upon their own resources rather than on commercial entertainments. They drank, told stories, engaged in wrestling and boxing matches, and danced. For evangelicals who withdrew from such entertainments, church socials and camp meetings filled the gap, while rural southerners engaged in cornhuskings, birthday celebrations, berry-picking expeditions, and so forth. Books were not as readily available as they were in the North. Most southern families owned a Bible, and wealthier families often read histories, religious and political tracts, and English literature—with Shakespeare leading the way and Sir Walter Scott's tales of medieval chivalry not far behind. Hunting and fishing were passionate pursuits among southern men. Fox and deer hunts provided the gentry with an opportunity to display their skill with horses and guns, while the hunts of poorer whites and slaves both provided sport and enhanced their threatened roles as providers.

The commercial entertainments in the South were concentrated in the larger towns and along the major rivers. Showboats brought theatrical troupes, minstrel shows, animal acts, and other entertainment to the river towns. The gentry's love of horses and competition made New Orleans the horse-racing capital of the country. New Orleans was also the only southern city where one could watch a professional prizefight. Various violent contests appealed to New Orleans audiences. In 1819 a New Orleans impresario advertised a program that offered a bull versus six "of the strongest dogs in the country"; six bulldogs versus a Canadian bear; a "beautiful Tiger" versus a black bear; and 12 dogs versus a "strong and furious Opeloussas Bull." Although such events were outlawed in later years, they continued to be held on the sly. In 1852, a crowd of 5,000 gathered outside New Orleans to watch a bull and a grizzly bear fight to the death.

THE CAMP MEETING BECOMES RESPECTABLE

The camp-meeting revivals of the early 19th century had transformed the South into an evangelical Bible Belt (see Chapter 7). Some evangelicals had risen into the slaveholding class, and many of the old families had been converted. As a result, the Anglican gentry of the 18th century became outnumbered by earnest Baptist and Methodist planters.

Southern camp meetings continued throughout the antebellum years, but they were often limited to a single denomination—usually Methodist—and were held on permanent campgrounds maintained by the churches. Conducted with more decorum than in the past, they were routine community events: Women began baking a week ahead of time and looked forward to visiting with neighbors and relatives as much as they did to getting right with God. The goal of camp meetings was still to induce spiritual crisis and conversion, and sinners still wept and fell on their way to being saved. But such manifestations as the barking exercise and the jerks (see Chapter 7) disappeared.

The churches that grew out of southern revivals reinforced localistic neighborhoods and the patriarchal family. Some southern communities began when a whole congregation moved onto new land; others were settled by the chain migration of brothers and cousins, and subsequent revivals spread through family networks. Rural isolation limited most households to their own company during the week, but on Sundays church meetings united the neighborhood's cluster of extended families into a community of believers. In most neighborhoods, social connections seldom extended beyond that.

Religious Conservatism

Southern evangelicalism was based, like religious conservatism in the North, on the sovereignty of God, a conviction of human sinfulness, and an acceptance of disappointment and pain as part of God's grand and unknowable design. Southern church people continued to interpret misfortune as divine punishment. When yellow fever was killing 1,000 people every week in New Orleans in 1853, the Episcopal bishop Leonidas Polk asked God to "turn us from the ravages of the pestilence, wherewith for our iniquities, thou are visiting us."

The same view held at home. When the young son of a planter family died, the mother was certain that God had killed the child because the parents had loved him more than God. A grieving South Carolinian received this consolation from a relative: "Hope you are quite reconciled to the loss of your darling babe. As it was the will of God to take him, we must obey, and He will be angry at us if we go past moderate grief." It was a far cry from the middle-class North's garden cemeteries and the romantic, redemptive deaths of children in sentimental fiction.

Southern cultural conservatism was rooted in religion, in the family, and in a system of fixed social roles. Southern preachers assumed that patriarchal social relations were crucial to Christian living within an imperfect and often brutal world. Southerners revered the patriarch and slaveholder Abraham more than any other figure in the Bible. The father must, like Abraham, govern and protect his household; the mother must assist the father; and the women, children, and slaves must faithfully act out the duties of their stations. That meant a Christian must strive to be a good mother, a good father, a good slave; by the same token, a Christian never questioned his or her God-given social role.

Proslavery Christianity

In revolutionary and early national America, white southerners had been the most radical of republicans. Jeffersonian planter-politicians led the fights for equal rights and the absolute separation of church and state, and southern evangelicals were the early republic's staunchest opponents of slavery. By 1830, however, the South was an increasingly conscious minority within a democratic and capitalist nation. The northern middle classes proclaimed a link between material and moral progress, identifying both with individual autonomy and universal rights. A radical northern minority was agitating for the immediate abolition of slavery.

Southerners met this challenge with an "intellectual blockade" against outside publications and ideas and with a moral and religious defense of slavery. The Bible provided plenty of ammunition. Proslavery clergymen constantly stated that the Chosen People of the Old Testament had been patriarchs and slaveholders and that Jesus had lived in a society that sanctioned slavery and never criticized the institution. Some ministers claimed that blacks were the descendants of Ham and thus deserved enslavement. The most common religious argument, however, was that slavery had given millions of heathen Africans the priceless opportunity to become Christians and to live in a Christian society.

Like their northern counterparts, southern clergymen applauded the material improvements of the age. But they insisted that *moral* improvement occurred only when people embraced the timeless truths of the Bible. Northern notions of progress through individual liberation, equal rights, and universal Christian love were wrongheaded and dangerous. The Presbyterian John Adger asserted that relations of dominance and submission were utterly necessary to both social and individual fulfillment and that the distribution of rights and responsibilities was unequal and God-given: "The rights of the father are natural, but they belong only to the fathers. Rights of property are natural, but they belong only to those who have property"—and such natural rights were coupled with the awesome duties of fatherhood and proprietorship.

THE PRIVATE LIVES OF SLAVES

In law, in the census, and in the minds of planters, slaves were members of a plantation household over which the owner exercised absolute authority, not only as owner but also as paternal protector and lawgiver. Yet both slaveholders and slaves knew that slaves could not be treated like farm animals or little children. Wise slaveholders learned that the success of a plantation depended less on terror and draconian discipline (though whippings—and worse—were common) than on the accommodations by which slaves traded labor and obedience for some measure of privilege and autonomy within the bounds of slavery. After achieving privileges, the slaves called them their own: holidays, garden plots, friendships, and social gatherings both on and off the plantation; hunting and fishing rights; and so on. Together, these privileges provided some of the ground on which they made their own lives within slavery.

FOCUS QUESTION
Describe the cultural life that slaves made for themselves within the limits of slavery.

THE SLAVE FAMILY

The most precious privilege was the right to make and maintain families. As early as the Revolutionary War era, most Chesapeake slaves lived in units consisting of mother, father, and small children. At Thomas Jefferson's Monticello, most slave marriages were for life, and small children almost always lived with both parents. The most common exceptions to this practice were fathers who had married away from their own plantations and who visited **broad wives** and children during their off hours. Owners encouraged stable marriages because they made farms more peaceful and productive and because they flattered the owners' own religious and paternalistic sensibilities. For their part, slaves demanded families as part of the price of their labor.

Yet slave families were highly vulnerable. Many slaveholders assumed that they had the right to coerce sex from female slaves; some kept slaves as concubines, and a few even moved them into the main house. They tended, however, to keep these liaisons within bounds. A far more serious threat to slave marriages was the death, bankruptcy, or departure of the slaveholders. Between one-fifth and one-third of slave marriages were broken by such events.

"broad" wives *Wives of slave men who lived on other plantations and were visited by their husbands during off hours.*

FIVE GENERATIONS OF A SLAVE FAMILY ON A SOUTH CAROLINA SEA ISLAND PLANTATION, 1862. *Complex family ties such as those of the family shown here were among the most hard-won and vulnerable cultural accomplishments of enslaved blacks.*

Slaveholders who encouraged slave marriages knew that marriage implied a form of self-ownership that conflicted with the slaves' status as property. Some conducted ceremonies in which couples "married" by jumping over a broomstick; others had the preacher omit the phrases "let no man put asunder" and "till death do you part" from the ceremony. Slaves knew that such ceremonies had no legal force.

Slaves modified their sense of family and kinship to accommodate such uncertainties. Because separation from father or mother was common, children spread their affection among their adult relatives, treating grandparents, aunts, and uncles almost as though they were parents. In fact, slaves often referred to all their adult relatives as "parents." They also called nonrelatives "brother," "sister," "aunt," and "uncle," thus extending a sense of kinship to the slave community at large. Slaves chose as surnames for themselves the names of former owners, Anglicized versions of African names, or names that simply sounded good. They rarely chose the name of their current owner, however. Families tended to use the same given names from one generation to the next, naming boys after their father or grandfather. They seldom named girls after their mother, however. Unlike southern whites, slaves never married a first cousin. The origins and functions of some of these customs are unknown. We know only that slaves practiced them consistently, usually without the knowledge of the slaveholders.

WHITE MISSIONS

By the 1820s southern evangelicalism had long since abandoned its hostility toward slavery, and slaveholders commonly attended camp meetings and revivals. These prosperous converts faced conflicting duties. Their churches taught them that slaves had immortal souls and that planters were as responsible for the spiritual welfare of their slaves as they were for the spiritual welfare of their own children. A planter on his deathbed told his children that humane treatment and religious instruction for slaves was the duty of slave owners; if these were neglected, "we will have to answer for the loss of their souls." After Nat Turner's bloody slave revolt in 1831 (discussed shortly), missions to the slaves took on new urgency: If the churches were to help create a family-centered, Christian society in the South, that society would have to include slaves.

To this end, Charles Colcock Jones, a Presbyterian minister from Georgia, spent much of his career writing manuals on how to preach to slaves. He taught that there was no necessary connection between social position and spiritual worth—that there were good and bad slaveholders and good and bad slaves. But he also taught that slaves must accept the master's authority as God's and that obedience was their prime religious virtue. Jones warned white preachers never to become personally involved with their slave listeners. "We separate entirely their *religious* from their *civil* condition," he said, "and contend that one may be attended to without interfering with the other."

The evangelical mission to the slaves was not as completely self-serving as it may seem. For to accept one's worldly station, to be obedient and dutiful within that station, and to seek salvation outside of this world were precisely what the planters demanded of themselves and their own families. An important goal of plantation missions was, of course, to create safe and profitable plantations. Yet that goal was to be achieved by Christianizing both slaveholders and slaves.

SLAVE CHRISTIANS

The white attempt to Christianize slavery, however, depended on the acceptance of slavery by the slaves. But the biblical notion that slavery could be punishment for sin and the doctrine of divinely ordained social orders never took root among the slaves. As one maid boldly told her mistress, "God never made us to be slaves for white people."

Although the slaves ignored much of what the missionaries taught, they embraced evangelical Christianity and transformed it into an independent African American faith. Some slave owners encouraged them by building "praise houses" on their plantations and by permitting religious meetings. Others tried to resist the trend, but with little success. After 1830 most of the southern states outlawed black preachers, but the laws could not be enforced. Sometimes slaves met in a cabin—preaching, praying, and singing in a whisper. At their meetings they rehearsed a faith that was at variance with the faith of the slaveholders.

One way in which slave religion differed from what was preached to them by whites was in the practice of conjuring, folk magic, root medicine, and other occult knowledge—most of it passed down from West Africa. Such practices provided help in areas in which Christianity was useless: They could cure illnesses, make people fall in love, ensure a good day's fishing, or bring harm to one's enemies. Sometimes African magic was in competition with plantation Christianity. Just as often, however, slaves combined the two. For instance, slaves sometimes determined the guilt or innocence of a person accused of stealing by hanging a Bible by a thread, then watching the way it turned. The form was West African; the Bible was not. The slave root doctor George White boasted that he could "cure most anything," but added that "you got to talk wid God an' ask him to help out."

While Christianity could not cure sick babies or identify thieves, it gave slaves something more important: a sense of themselves as a historical people with a role to play in God's cosmic drama. In slave Christianity, Moses the liberator (and not the slaveholders' Abraham) stood beside Jesus. Indeed the slaves' appropriation of the book of Exodus denied the smug assumption of the whites that they were God's chosen people who had escaped the bondage of despotic Europe to enter the promised land of America. To the slaves, America was Egypt, they were the chosen people, and the slaveholders were Pharaoh. The slaves' religious songs, which became known as **spirituals,** told of God's people, their travails, and their ultimate deliverance. In songs and sermons the figures of Jesus and Moses were often blurred, and it was not always clear whether deliverance would take place in this world or the next. But deliverance always meant an end to slavery, with the possibility that it might bring a reversal of relations between slaves and masters.

spirituals *Term later devised to describe the religious songs of slaves.*

RELIGION AND REVOLT

In comparison with slaves in Cuba, Jamaica, Brazil, and other New World plantation societies, North American slaves seldom went into organized, armed revolt. American plantations were relatively small and dispersed, and the southern white population was large, vigilant, and very well armed. Thousands of slaves demonstrated their hatred of the system by running away. Others fought slave owners or overseers, sabotaged equipment and animals, stole from planters, and found other ways to oppose slavery. But most knew that open revolt was suicide.

Christianity convinced slaves that history was headed toward an apocalypse that would result in divine justice and their own deliverance, and thus held out the possibility of revolt. But slave preachers almost never told their congregations to become actively engaged in God's divine plan, for they knew that open resistance was hopeless. Slave Christians believed that God hated slavery and would end it, but that their role was to have faith in God, to take care of one another, to preserve their identity as a people, and to await deliverance. Only occasionally did slaves take retribution and deliverance into their own hands.

The most ambitious conspiracy was hatched by **Denmark Vesey**, a free black of Charleston, South Carolina. Vesey was a leading member of an African Methodist congregation that had seceded from the white Methodists and had been independent from 1817 to 1821. At its height, the church had 6,000 members, most of them slaves. Vesey and some of the other members talked about their delivery out of Egypt, with all white men, women, and children being cut off. They identified Charleston as Jericho and planned its destruction in 1822: A few dozen Charleston blacks would take the state armory, then arm rural slaves who would rise up to help them. They would kill the whites, take control of the city, and then commandeer ships in the harbor and make their getaway. Word of the conspiracy spread secretly into the countryside, largely through the efforts of Gullah Jack, who was both a Methodist and an African conjurer. Jack recruited African-born slaves as soldiers, provided them with charms as protection against whites, and used his spiritual powers to terrify others into keeping silent.

In the end, the Vesey plot was betrayed by slaves. As one coerced confession followed another, white authorities hanged Vesey, Gullah Jack, and 34 other accused conspirators. But frightened whites knew that most of the conspirators (estimates ranged from 600 to 9,000) remained at large and unidentified.

NAT TURNER

In August 1831, in a revolt in Southampton County, Virginia, some 60 slaves shot and hacked to death 55 white men, women, and children. Their leader was **Nat Turner,** a Baptist lay preacher. Turner was, he told his captors, an Old Testament prophet and an instrument of God's wrath. As a child, he had prayed and fasted often, and the spirit—the same spirit who had spoken to the prophets of the Bible—had spoken directly to him. When he was a young man, he had run away to escape a cruel overseer. But when God said he had not chosen Nat merely to have him run away, Nat returned. But Turner made it clear that his Master was God, not a slave owner.

Around 1830, Turner received visions of the final battle in Revelation, recast as a fight between white and black spirits. Convinced by a solar eclipse in February 1831 that the time had come, Turner began telling other slaves about his visions, recruited his force, and launched a bloody and hopeless revolt that ended in mass murder, failure, and the execution of Turner and his followers.

Denmark Vesey *Leader of a slave conspiracy in and around Charleston, South Carolina in 1822.*

Nat Turner *Baptist lay preacher whose religious visions encouraged him to lead a slave revolt in southern Virginia in 1831 in which 55 whites were killed—more than any other American slave revolt.*

The Vesey and Turner revolts, along with scores of more limited conspiracies, deeply troubled southern whites. Slaveholders were committed to a paternalism that was increasingly tied to the South's attempt to make slavery both domestic and Christian. For their part, slaves recognized that they could receive decent treatment and pockets of autonomy in return for outward docility. Vesey and Turner opened wide cracks in that mutual charade. A plantation mistress who survived Turner's revolt by hiding in a closet listened to the murders of her husband and children, then heard her house servants arguing over possession of her clothes. A Charleston grandee named Elias Horry, upon finding that his coachman was among the Vesey conspirators, asked him, "What were your intentions?" The formerly submissive slave replied that he had intended "to kill you, rip open your belly, and throw your guts in your face."

Such stories sent a chill through the white South—a suspicion that despite the appearance of peace, they were surrounded by people who would kill them in an instant. While northerners patronized plays and cheap fiction that dramatized the trickery and horror beneath placid appearances, the nightmares of slaveholding paternalists were both more savage and closer to home.

QUICK REVIEW

SLAVE RELIGION

- Incorporated Exodus as slave history
- Interpreted Revelation as deliverance, often by violence

C O N C L U S I O N

By the second quarter of the 19th century, Americans had made a patchwork of regional, class, and ethnic cultures. The new middle classes of the North and West compounded their Protestant and republican inheritance with a new entrepreneurial faith in progress. The result was a way of life grounded in the self-made and morally accountable individual and the sentimentalized domestic unit. In ways that others often found offensive, they would propose that way of life as a national culture for the United States. The middle class met resistance from poorer urban dwellers and the less prosperous farmers— a northern and western majority that remained grimly loyal to the unsentimental, male-dominated families of their fathers and grandfathers, to new and old religious sects that continued to believe in human depravity and the mysterious workings of providence, and to the suspicion that perfidy and disorder lurked behind the smiling moral order of market economics and sentimental culture. They were also people who enjoyed dark and playful popular entertainments that often mocked middle-class sentimentalism. In the South, most white farmers persisted in a neighborhood-based, intensely evangelical, and socially conservative way of life. Southern planters, while they shared in the northern elite's belief in material progress and the magic of the market, were bound by family values, a system of slave labor, and a code of honor that was strikingly at variance with middle-class faith in an orderly universe and perfectible individuals. Slaves in these years continued to make cultural forms of their own. Despite their exclusion from the white world of liberty and equality, they tied their aspirations to the family, to an evangelical Protestant God, and to the individual and collective dignity that republics promise to their citizens.

QUESTIONS FOR REVIEW AND CRITICAL THINKING

Review

1. What were the central cultural maxims of the emerging northern middle class?
2. Within the North, what were the alternatives to middle-class culture?
3. To what extent can the culture of southern whites be explained by localism?
4. Describe the cultural life that slaves made for themselves within the limits of slavery.

Critical Thinking

1. Compare and contrast the domestic lives and family values of the northern middle class and the southern planter elite.
2. The central institutions of slave culture were the family and religion. Some have argued that these institutions helped slaves accommodate to slavery, others have argued that they helped them resist it, and still others have argued that they did both. State your position on this question.

Discovery

What kind of culture emerged out of the Market Revolution that was discussed in Chapter 9? What was the impact of the religious revivals of the early nineteenth century on middle class American families?

SUGGESTED READINGS

Stuart M. Blumin, *The Emergence of the Middle Class: Social Experience in the American City, 1760–1900* (1989) is a thorough study of work and material life among the urban middle class. Studies that treat religion, family, and sentimental culture include **Paul E. Johnson, *A Shopkeeper's Millennium: Society and Revivals in Rochester New York, 1815–1837*** (1978); **Mary P. Ryan, *Cradle of the Middle Class: The Family in Oneida County, New York, 1790–1865*** (1981); and **Jane Tompkins, *Sensational Designs: The Cultural Work of American Fiction, 1790–1860*** (1985). The works of **Jon Butler** and **Nathan Hatch** listed in the Suggested Readings for Chapter 7 are the best overviews of religion in these years. Studies of popular literature and entertainments include **Elliott J. Gorn, *The Manly Art: Bare-Knuckle Prize Fighting in America*** (1986); **Eric Lott, *Love and Theft: Blackface Minstrelsy and the American Working Class*** (1993); **David S. Reynolds,**

Beneath the American Renaissance: The Subversive Imagination in the Age of Emerson and Melville (1988); and **Paul E. Johnson, *Sam Patch, the Famous Jumper*** (2003). **Peter Kolchin, *American Slavery, 1619–1877*** (1993) is a good synthesis of the literature. Now-classic treatments of slave culture are **Eugene D. Genovese, *Roll, Jordan, Roll: The World the Slaves Made*** (1974); and **Lawrence W. Levine, *Black Culture and Black Consciousness: Afro-American Folk Thought from Slavery to Freedom*** (1977). Two essential books on the culture of southern whites are **Bertram Wyatt-Brown, *Southern Honor: Ethics and Behavior in the Old South*** (1982); and **Christine Leigh Heyerman, *Southern Cross: The Beginnings of the Bible Belt*** (1997). An enlightening counterpoint between black and white understandings of the slave trade (and, by extension, of the slave South generally) is presented in **Walter Johnson, *Soul by Soul: Life Inside the Antebellum Slave Market*** (1999).

ONLINE SOURCES GUIDE

ThomsonNOW™ Visit ThomsonNOW to access primary sources, exercises, quizzes, and audio chapter summaries related to this chapter:

http://www.thomsonedu.com/login

DISCOVERY

What kind of culture emerged out of the Market Revolution that was discussed in Chapter 9? What was the impact of the religious revivals of the early nineteenth century on middle class American families?

In thinking about this question, begin by breaking it down into the components shown below. A discussion of the significance of each component should appear in your answer.

THE IMPACT OF THE MARKET ON FAMILY LIFE

Compare the images of the two families in this chapter with the picture of a doctor at home a generation earlier in Chapter 7 (page 198). All three images show educated people with a book or newspaper; what differences do you see between domestic life before canals and trains and after?

Compare these two illustrations of domestic life. What do they suggest about how middle class Americans saw their lives and their daily activities? If there were no caption to guide you, could you easily tell which family lived in the North and which lived in the South? If so, what are the clues? What did each family want to reveal about their life at home? What meaning do the terms "domesticity" and "sentimentality" have in these illustrations? What would a photograph of your family suggest to future generations about the way you lived?

A MIDDLE-CLASS NEW ENGLAND FAMILY AT HOME

Abby Aldrich Rockefeller Folk Art Center, Williamsburg, VA

COLONEL AND MRS. WHITESIDE

Hunter Museum of American Art, Chattanooga, Tennessee, Gift of Mr. and Mrs. Thomas B. Whiteside

THE IMPACT OF RELIGION ON FAMILY LIFE

Compare the image of an evening at the theater in the early nineteenth century with the illustration of a Methodist camp meeting from Chapter 7 (page 211). Which activity is seen here to attract more women? Which attracted more men? How do you account for this gender difference? Is this gender difference important?

AN EARLY PRINT OF "JIM CROW" RICE AT NEW YORK'S BOWERY THEATER

THE IMPACT OF SLAVERY ON FAMILY LIFE

Consider the photograph of the slave family. How were families formed? Were they legally recognized? Why or why not? Why would these family bonds be especially important considering the social situation of slaves? How might a slave owner exploit those bonds? Who might have taken this photograph and why?

FIVE GENERATIONS OF A SLAVE FAMILY ON A SOUTH CAROLINA SEA ISLAND PLANTATION, 1862

SOCIETY, CULTURE, AND POLITICS, 1820s–1840s

Between 1820 and 1845 Thomas Jefferson's agrarian republic became Andrew Jackson's noisy and deeply divided mass democracy. Politicians who built the Whig and Democratic Parties, which helped to bring about that change, were participants in the economic and social transformations of those years, and they were both consumers and producers of the new forms of popular culture. John Quincy Adams, Henry Clay, and their National Republican and Whig allies in the states concocted visions of smooth-running, government-sponsored transportation and monetary systems that echoed the faith in cosmic order, material progress, and moral improvement that had become cultural axioms for the more prosperous and cosmopolitan Americans. Democrats, on the other hand, defended Jefferson's republic of limited government and widespread equality and liberty. In the course of that defense, they portrayed a haunted political universe in which trickery, deceit, and special privilege lurked behind the promises and power hunger of the Whigs. Politicians constructed the Whig and Democratic coalitions largely at the neighborhood and state levels. At the same time, national debates incorporated Democratic and Whig attitudes on family, religion, race, gender, ethnicity, class, and the proper functions of government that had been shaped by state-level debates. Those local and state issues and the social and cultural constituencies that argued over them are the subjects of this chapter.

TIMELINE

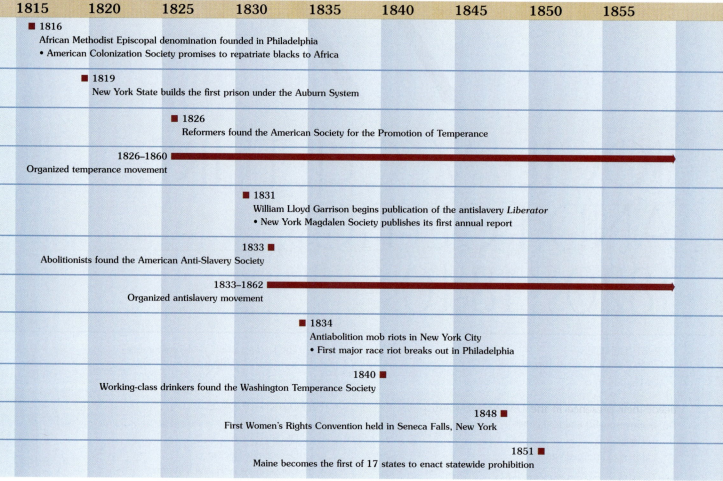

| 1815 | 1820 | 1825 | 1830 | 1835 | 1840 | 1845 | 1850 | 1855 |

1816
African Methodist Episcopal denomination founded in Philadelphia
• American Colonization Society promises to repatriate blacks to Africa

1819
New York State builds the first prison under the Auburn System

1826
Reformers found the American Society for the Promotion of Temperance

1826–1860
Organized temperance movement

1831
William Lloyd Garrison begins publication of the antislavery *Liberator*
• New York Magdalen Society publishes its first annual report

1833
Abolitionists found the American Anti-Slavery Society

1833–1862
Organized antislavery movement

1834
Antiabolition mob riots in New York City
• First major race riot breaks out in Philadelphia

1840
Working-class drinkers found the Washington Temperance Society

1848
First Women's Rights Convention held in Seneca Falls, New York

1851
Maine becomes the first of 17 states to enact statewide prohibition

CONSTITUENCIES

FOCUS QUESTION

Which Americans were likely to support the Democratic Party in the 1830s and 1840s? Which Americans were likely to support the Whigs?

The Whig and Democratic Parties were national coalitions of ill-matched regional, economic, ethnic, and religious groups. They were united by Whig and Democratic political cultures—consistent attitudes toward government and politics that were embedded in religion, family, and economic life—that reduced American diversity to two political choices. Support for the Democratic or Whig Party was a matter of personal identity as much as of political preference: A man's vote demonstrated his personal history, his cultural values, and his vision of the good society as clearly as it demonstrated his opinion on any particular political issue.

THE NORTH AND WEST

The band of Yankee commercial farms stretching across southern New England, western New York, and the Old Northwest was the northern Whig heartland. Whigs also enjoyed support in northern cities and towns. The wealthiest men in cities were Whigs. The new urban commercial classes created in the market revolution also supported the Whigs. Factory owners were solidly Whig, and native-born factory workers often joined them—in part because Whigs promised opportunities to rise in the world, in part because Whigs protected their jobs by encouraging domestic markets for what they made, and, increasingly, because Whigs pandered to their fears of immigrant labor. For similar reasons, many skilled urban artisans supported the Whigs, as did smaller numbers of dockworkers, day laborers, and others among the unskilled.

Northern Whiggery was grounded in the market revolution, but the Whig political agenda ranged far beyond economic life. Among the urban middle class and in the more market-oriented rural neighborhoods, activist evangelicals built an avowedly Christian Whig politics. Whigs called for moral legislation on such issues as Sabbath observance, temperance, and Bible-based public schools. Marching under the banner of activist government, economic development, and moral progress, Whigs set the political agenda in most northern states.

They met a determined Democratic opposition. Democrats found supporters among cultural traditionalists who had gained little from the expansion of national markets and who had no use for the moral agenda of the Whigs. The **Butternuts** (so named for the yellow vegetable dye with which they colored their homespun clothing) of the southern, river-oriented counties of the Northwest joined the Democratic Party. Farmers in the Allegheny Mountains, the Hudson River valley, and northern and western New England also supported the Democrats.

In cities and towns, Democrats made up substantial minorities among businessmen, master craftsmen, and professionals, but most urban Democrats were wage earners. Perhaps the most overwhelmingly Democratic group in the country were immigrant Irish Catholics, who were filling the lower ranks of the urban workforce. Indeed, their presence in the Democratic Party pushed increasing numbers of native Protestant workers into the Whig ranks.

When Democrats opposed evangelical legislation, Whigs labeled them the party of atheism and immorality. Democrats responded that they opposed theocracy, not religion. True, most freethinkers, atheists, and persons who simply did not care about religion supported the Democratic Party. So did immigrant Catholics, who rightfully feared the militant Protestantism of the Whigs. But Democrats won the support of hundreds of thousands of evangelical Protestants who deeply distrusted what they called "church and state" Whiggery and the mixing of politics and religion. Evangelical Democrats were joined by sectarian Christians who rejected Whig moral legislation as antirepublican and as Yankee cultural imperialism.

THE SOUTH

Throughout the 1830s and 1840s, the southern states divided their votes equally between Whigs and Democrats. But most individual southern localities were either solidly Democratic or solidly Whig. More than in the North, southern differences in party preference were tied to differences in economic life.

Democrats ran strongest in up-country communities that valued household independence and the society of neighbors and that distrusted intrusions from the outside. The more cosmopolitan southern communities tended to support the Whigs. In general, Whigs were strongest in plantation counties, where they enrolled not only wealthy planters but smaller farmers and lawyers, storekeepers, and craftsmen in county-seat towns. Upland, nonplantation neighborhoods in which Whigs ran well were places where Whigs promised state-sponsored internal improvements that would link ambitious but isolated farmers to outside markets.

Many exceptions to the link between commerce and the Whig Party were grounded in the prestige and power of local leaders. Southern statesmen who broke

Butternuts *Democrats from the southern river-oriented counties of the Northwest region whose name came from the yellow vegetable dye with which they colored their homespun clothing.*

with the Jacksonians in the 1830s—John C. Calhoun in South Carolina, Hugh Lawson White in Tennessee, and others—took personal followings with them (see Chapter 12). Politicians also had to contend with southerners such as George Reynolds of Pickens County, Alabama, who fathered 17 children and had 234 direct descendants living in his neighborhood, whom he delivered as a bloc to politicians who pleased him. But despite the vagaries of southern kinship, the core of southern Whiggery was in communities that were or wanted to be linked to commercial society.

In sharp contrast with the North and West, southern political divisions had little to do with religion. Southern Baptists, Methodists, and Presbyterians enforced morality within their own households and congregations, but they seldom asked state legislatures to pass moral legislation. Southern evangelicals who embraced the world of the market assumed, along with their northern Whig counterparts, that the new economy encouraged a Christian, civilized life. Other southern churchgoers responded to the Jacksonians' denunciations of greed and the spirit of speculation. Thus, even though many southern communities were bitterly divided over religion, the divisions seldom shaped party politics.

The social, religious, cultural, and economic bases of party divisions formed coherent Whig and Democratic political cultures. Whig voters in the North and South were persons who either were or hoped to become beneficiaries of the market revolution and who wanted government to subsidize economic development. In the North, they also demanded that government help shape market society into a prosperous, orderly, and homogeneous Christian republic. Democrats, North and South, demanded a minimal government that kept taxes low and that left citizens, their families, and their neighborhoods alone.

THE POLITICS OF ECONOMIC DEVELOPMENT

FOCUS QUESTION

What were the Whig and Democratic conceptions of the duties and limits of government?

Both the Whigs and the Democrats accepted the transition to market society, but they argued about how to direct it. Whigs wanted to use government and the market to make an economically and morally progressive—albeit hierarchical—republic. Democrats worried that both government and the institutions of the market would subvert the equal rights and rough equality of condition that were, in their view, the preconditions of republican citizenship.

GOVERNMENT AND ITS LIMITS

"The government," remarked a New York City Whig in 1848, "is not merely a machine for making wars and punishing felons, but is bound to do all that is within its power to promote the welfare of the People—its legitimate scope is not merely negative, representative, defensive, but also affirmative, creative, constructive, beneficent." The Whigs insisted that economic development, moral progress, and social harmony were linked and that government should foster them. People who developed the work habits and moral discipline required for success would be rewarded. To poor farmers and city workers who felt that the market undermined their independence, Whigs promised social mobility within a new system of interdependence—but only to deserving individuals. Whigs believed that the United States exhibited a harmony of class interests and an equality of opportunity that the virtuous would recognize and that only the resentful, mean-spirited, and unworthy would doubt.

Democrats seldom praised or condemned market society per se. Instead, they argued for the primacy of citizenship: Neither government nor the market, they said, should be allowed to subvert the civil and legal equality among independent (white) men on which the republic rested. Democrats saw government not as a tool of progress but as a dangerous, although regrettably necessary, instrument in the hands of imperfect, self-interested men. The only safe course was to limit its power. In 1837, *The United States Magazine and Democratic Review* declared: "The best government is that which governs least." Corporate charters, privileged banks, and subsidies to turnpike, canal, and railroad companies, they said, benefited insiders and turned government into an engine of inequality. George Bancroft, a Massachusetts Democrat, stated that "A republican people should be in an equality in their social and political condition; . . . pure democracy inculcates equal rights—equal laws—equal means of education—and equal means of wealth also." By contrast, the government favored by the Whigs would enrich a favored few. Bancroft and other Democrats demanded limited government that was deaf to the demands of special interests.

BANKS

Banking emerged as a central political issue in nearly every state. Whigs defended banks as agents of economic progress, arguing that they provided credit for roads and canals, loans to businessmen and commercial farmers, and the banknotes that served as the chief medium of exchange. Democrats, on the other hand, regarded banks as government-protected institutions that enabled a privileged few to make themselves rich at the public's expense.

The economic boom of the 1830s and the destruction of the national bank by the Jackson administration (see Chapter 12) created a dramatic expansion in the number of state-chartered banks. Systems varied from state to state. South Carolina, Georgia, Tennessee, Kentucky, and Arkansas had state-owned banks. Many new banks in the Old Northwest were also partially state owned. Such banks often operated as public service institutions. Georgia's Central Bank, for example, served farmers who could not qualify for private loans, as did other state-owned banks in the South.

Beginning in the 1820s many states passed uniform banking laws to replace the unique charters previously granted to individual banks. The new laws tried to stabilize currency and credit. In New York, the **Safety-Fund Law** of 1829 required banks to pool a fraction of their resources to protect both bankers and small noteholders in the case of bank failures. The result was a self-regulating and conservative community of state banks. Laws in other states required that banks maintain a high ratio of specie (precious metals) to notes in circulation. Such laws, however, were often evaded.

Hard Money Democrats (those who wanted to get rid of paper money altogether) distrusted banks and proposed that they be abolished. Banks, they claimed, with their manipulation of credit and currency, encouraged speculation, luxury, inequality, and the separation of wealth from real work. Jackson himself branded banks "a perfect humbug."

In state legislatures, Whigs defended what had become a roughly standard system of private banks chartered by state governments—banks circulated banknotes and enjoyed **limited liability** to protect directors and stockholders from debts incurred by their bank. Many Democrats proposed abolishing all banks. Others proposed reforms. They demanded a high ratio of specie reserves to banknotes as a guard against inflationary paper money. They proposed eliminating the issuance of banknotes in small denominations, thus ensuring that day-to-day business would be conducted in hard coin, protecting wage earners and small farmers from speculative ups and downs.

Safety-Fund Law *New York state law that required banks to pool a fraction of their resources to protect both bankers and small stockholders in case of bank failures.*

Hard Money Democrats *Democrats who, in the 1830s and 1840s wanted to eliminate paper money and regarded banks as centers of trickery and privilege.*

limited liability *Provisions that protected directors and stockholders of corporations from corporate debts by separating those debts from personal liabilities.*

By these and other means, Democrats in the states protected currency and credit from the government favoritism, dishonesty, and elitism that, they argued, enriched Whig insiders and impoverished honest Democrats. Whigs responded that corporate privileges and immunities and an abundant, elastic currency were keys to economic development, and they fought Democrats every step of the way.

INTERNAL IMPROVEMENTS

Democrats in Congress and the White House blocked federally funded roads and canals (see Chapter 12). In response, the states launched the transportation revolution themselves, either by taking direct action or by chartering private corporations to do the work (see Chapter 9). State legislatures everywhere debated the wisdom of direct state action, of corporate privileges, of subsidies to canals and railroads, and of the accumulation of government debt. Whigs, predictably, favored direct action by state governments. Democrats were lukewarm toward the whole idea of internal improvements, convinced that debt, favoritism, and corruption would inevitably result from government involvement in the economy.

Whigs assumed a connection between market society and moral progress—and used that relationship as a basis of their argument for internal improvements. William H. Seward, the Whig governor of New York, supported transportation projects because they broke down neighborhood isolation and hastened the emergence of a market society. In the minds of Whig legislators, a vote for internal improvements was a vote for moral progress and for individual opportunity within a prosperous and happily interdependent market society. Democratic state legislators supported at least some internal improvements. But they opposed "partial" legislation that would benefit part of their state at the expense of the rest, and they opposed projects that would lead to higher taxes and put state governments into debt. The Democrats made the same argument in every state: Beneath Whig plans for extensive improvements lay schemes to create special privilege, inequality, debt, and corruption—all at the expense of a hoodwinked people.

THE POLITICS OF SOCIAL REFORM

FOCUS QUESTION

What were the principal reform movements of these years, and how did the political parties relate to them?

In the North, the churchgoing middle class was the core of the Whig Party. Whig evangelicals believed that with God's help they could improve the world by improving the individuals within it. On a variety of issues, including prostitution, temperance, public education, and state-supported insane asylums and penitentiaries, Whigs used government to improve individual morality and discipline. Democrats, on the other hand, argued that attempts to dictate morality through legislation were both antirepublican and wrong.

PUBLIC SCHOOLS

During the second quarter of the 19th century, local and state governments built systems of tax-supported public schools, known as "common" schools. Before that time, most children learned reading, writing, and arithmetic at home, in poorly staffed town schools, in private schools, or in charity schools run by churches or other benevolent organizations. Despite the lack of any "system" of education, most children learned to read and write. That was, however, more likely among boys than among girls, among whites than among blacks, and among northeasterners than among westerners or southerners.

By the 1830s Whigs and Democrats agreed that providing **common schools** was a proper function of government. And Democrats often agreed with Whigs that schools could equalize opportunity. More radical Democrats, however, wanted public schooling that would erase snobbery. A newspaper declared in 1828 that "the children of the rich and the poor shall receive a national education, calculated to make republicans and banish aristocrats."

The reformers who created the most advanced, expensive, and centralized state school systems were Whigs: Horace Mann of Massachusetts, Henry Barnard of Connecticut, Calvin Stowe (husband of Harriet Beecher) of Ohio, and others. These reformers talked more about character building than about the three Rs, convinced that it was the schools' first duty to train youngsters to respect authority, property, hard work, and social order. They wanted schools that would downplay class divisions, but they were interested less in democratizing wealthy children than in civilizing the poor.

The schools taught a basic Whig axiom: that social questions could be reduced to questions of individual character. A textbook entitled *The Thinker, A Moral Reader* (1855) told children to "remember that all the ignorance, degradation, and misery in the world, is the result of indolence and vice." To teach that lesson, the schools had children read from the King James Bible and recite prayers acceptable to all the Protestant sects. Such texts reaffirmed a common Protestant morality while avoiding divisive doctrinal matters.

Political differences centered less on curriculum than on organization. Whigs wanted state-level centralization and proposed state superintendents and state boards of education, **normal schools** (state teachers' colleges), texts chosen at the state level, and uniform school terms. They also recruited young women as teachers. In addition to fostering Protestant morality in the schools, these women were a source of cheap labor: Salaries for female teachers in the northern states ranged from 40 to 60 percent lower than the salaries of their male coworkers.

Democrats preferred to give power to individual school districts, thus enabling local school committees to tailor the curriculum, the length of the school year, and the choice of teachers and texts to local needs. Centralization, they argued, would create a metropolitan educational culture that served the purposes of the rich but ignored the preferences of farmers and working people. It was standard Democratic social policy: inexpensive government and local control.

ETHNICITY, RELIGION, AND THE SCHOOLS

The argument between Whig centralism and Democratic localism dominated the debate over public education until the children of Irish and German Catholic immigrants entered schools by the thousands in the mid-1840s. Most immigrant families were poor and relied on their children's earned income. Consequently, the children's attendance at school was irregular at best. Moreover, most immigrants were Catholics. The Irish regarded Protestant prayers and the King James Bible as heresies. Some of the textbooks were worse. Olney's *Practical System of Modern Geography,* a standard textbook, declared that "the Irish in general are quick of apprehension, active, brave and hospitable; but passionate, ignorant, vain, and superstitious."

Many Catholic parents refused to send their children to school. Others demanded changes in textbooks, the elimination of the King James Bible, tax-supported Catholic

common schools *Tax-supported public schools built by state and local governments.*

normal schools *State colleges established for the training of teachers.*

schools, or at least tax relief for parents who sent their children to parish schools. Whigs, joined by many native-born Democrats, saw Catholic complaints as popish assaults on the Protestantism that they insisted was at the heart of American republicanism.

Many school districts, particularly in the rural areas to which many Scandinavian and German immigrants found their way, created foreign-language schools and provided bilingual instruction. In other places, state support for church-run schools persisted. But in northeastern cities, where immigrant Catholics often formed militant local majorities, demands for state support led to violence and to organized nativist (anti-immigrant) politics. In 1844 the Native American Party, with the endorsement of the Whigs, won the New York City elections. That same year in Philadelphia, riots that pitted avowedly Whig Protestants against Catholic immigrants, ostensibly over the issue of Bible reading in schools, killed 13 people.

PRISONS

From the 1820s onward, state governments built institutions to house orphans, the dependent poor, the insane, and criminals. Americans in the 18th century (and many in the 19th century as well) had assumed that poverty, crime, insanity, and other social ills were among God's ways of punishing sin and for testing the human capacity for both suffering and charity. Now reformers argued that deviance was the result of childhood deprivation.

"Normal" people, they suggested, learned discipline and respect for work, property, laws, and other people from their parents. Deviants were the products of brutal, often drunken households devoid of parental love and discipline. The cure was to place them in a controlled setting, teach them work and discipline, and turn them into useful citizens.

In state legislatures, Whigs favored institutions for rehabilitation. Democrats favored institutions that isolated the insane, warehoused the dependent poor, and punished criminals. Most state systems were a compromise between the two positions.

Pennsylvania built prisons at Pittsburgh (1826) and Philadelphia (1829) that put solitary prisoners into cells to contemplate their misdeeds and to plot a new life. This solitary confinement produced few reformations and numerous attempts at suicide. Far more common were institutions based on the model developed in New York at Auburn (1819) and Sing Sing (1825). In the **Auburn system,** prisoners slept in solitary cells and marched in military formation to meals and workshops; they were forbidden to speak to one another at any time. The rule of silence, it was believed, encouraged both discipline and contemplation.

The Auburn system was designed both to reform criminals and to reduce expenses, for the prisons sold workshop products to the outside. Between these two goals Whigs favored rehabilitation. Democrats favored profit-making workshops and thus lower operating costs and lower taxes. Robert Wiltse, named by the Democrats to run Sing Sing prison in the 1830s, used harsh punishments (including flogging and starving) and forced labor to punish criminals and make the prison pay for itself. In 1839 Whig governor William Seward fired Wiltse and appointed administrators who substituted privileges and rewards for punishment and emphasized rehabilitation over profit making. They provided religious instruction; they improved food and working conditions; and they cut back on the use of flogging. When Democrats took back the statehouse in the 1842 elections, they discovered that the Whigs' brief experiment in kindness had produced a $50,000 deficit, so they swiftly reinstated the old regime.

Auburn system *Prison system designed to reform criminals and reduce expenses through the sale of items produced in workshops. Prisoners slept in solitary cells, marched in military formation to meals and workshops, and were forbidden to speak to one another at any time.*

ASYLUMS

The leading advocate of humane treatment for the insane was **Dorothea Dix,** a Boston humanitarian. She traveled throughout the country pressuring state legislatures to build asylums committed to what reformers called "moral treatment." The asylums were to be clean and pleasant places, preferably outside the cities, and the inmates were to be treated humanely. Attendants were not to beat inmates or tie them up, although they could use cold showers as a form of discipline. Dix and other reformers wanted the asylums to be safe, nurturing environments in which people with mental illness could be made well.

By 1860 the legislatures of 28 of the 33 states had established state-run insane asylums. Whig legislators, with minimal support from Democrats, approved appropriations for the more expensive and humane moral treatment facilities. Occasionally, however, Dorothea Dix won Democratic support as well. In North Carolina, she befriended the wife of a powerful Democratic legislator as the woman lay on her deathbed; the dying woman convinced her husband to support the building of an asylum. His impassioned speech won the approval of the lower house for a state asylum to be named Dix Hill. In the North Carolina Senate, however, the proposal was supported by 91 percent of the Whigs and only 14 percent of the Democrats, a partisan division that was repeated in state after state.

THE SOUTH AND SOCIAL REFORM

On economic issues, the legislatures of the southern and northern states divided along the same lines: Whigs wanted government participation in the economy, Democrats did not. On social questions, however, southern Whigs and Democrats responded in distinctly southern ways. The South was a rural, culturally conservative region of patriarchal households in which every attempt at government intervention was seen as a threat to independence. Most southern voters, Whigs as well as Democrats, perceived attempts at "social improvement" as expensive and wrongheaded.

The southern states enacted school laws and drew up blueprints for state school systems. But because the white South was culturally homogeneous, it had little need for schools to enforce a common culture. Moreover, the South had less money and less faith in government. Consequently southern schools tended to be locally controlled, to be infused with southern evangelical culture, and to have a limited curriculum and a short school year.

By 1860 every slave state except Florida and the Carolinas operated prisons modeled on the Auburn system. Here, however, prisons stressed punishment and profits over rehabilitation. Though some southerners favored northern-style reforms, they knew that southern voters would reject them. While northern evangelicals preached that criminals could be rescued, southerners demanded Old Testament vengeance, arguing that hanging, whipping, and branding were inexpensive, more effective than mere incarceration, and sanctioned by the Bible. Other southerners, defending the code of honor, charged that victims and their relatives would be denied vengeance if criminals were tucked away in prisons. Some southern prisons leased prison labor (and sometimes whole prisons) to private entrepreneurs, while dreams of reforming southern criminals were forgotten.

The South did participate in temperance—the all-consuming reform that will be discussed in the next section. By the 1820s Baptists and Methodists had made deep inroads into southern society. Southern ministers preached against dueling, fighting, dancing, gambling, and drinking, while churchgoing women discouraged their hus-

Dorothea Dix *Boston reformer who traveled throughout the country campaigning for humane, state-supported asylums for the insane.*

THE WHIPPING POST AND PILLORY AT NEW CASTLE, DELAWARE. *Delaware was a slave state that continued to inflict public, corporal punishment on lawbreakers. Many of the witnesses to the whipping depicted here are small children, who are supposedly learning a lesson.*

Reproduced from the Collections of the Library of Congress

bands, sons, and suitors from drinking. During the 1840s the Washington Temperance Society and other voluntary temperance groups won a solid footing in southern towns. But temperance in the South was based on individual decisions to abstain. Legal prohibition, which became dominant in the North, got nowhere in the South.

At bottom, southern resistance to social reform stemmed from a conservative, Bible-based acceptance of suffering and human imperfection and a commitment to the power and independence of white men who headed families. Any proposal that sounded like social tinkering or the invasion of paternal rights was doomed to failure. To make matters worse, many reforms—public schools, Sunday schools, prohibition, humane asylums—were seen as the work of well-funded and well-organized missionaries from the Northeast who wanted to fashion society in their own self-righteous image. The southern distrust of reform was powerfully reinforced after 1830, when northern reformers began to attack slavery and call for the equality of the sexes, reforms that were unthinkable to most white southerners.

THE POLITICS OF ALCOHOL

The fight between evangelical Whigs who demanded that government regulate public (and often private) morality and Democrats who feared both big government and the Whig cultural agenda was at the center of party formation in the North. The most persistent issue within that argument was alcohol.

ARDENT SPIRITS

Drinking had been a part of social life since the beginning of English settlement. But the withering of authority and the disruptions of the market revolution led to increased consumption, increased public drunkenness, and a perceived increase in the violence and social problems caused by alcohol (see Chapter 7). Beginning in the 1790s, physicians and a few clergymen attacked not only habitual drunkenness but also alcohol itself. After 1812, Federalist politicians and Congregational clergymen formed "moral societies" in New England that discouraged strong drink. Their imperious tone, however, doomed them to failure.

The temperance crusade began in earnest in 1826, when northeastern evangelicals founded the American Society for the Promotion of Temperance (soon renamed the American Temperance Society). The movement's manifesto was Lyman Beecher's *Six Sermons on the Nature, Occasions, Signs, Evils, and Remedy of Intemperance* (1826). Addressing the churchgoing middle class, Beecher declared alcohol an addictive drug that could turn even moderate drinkers into hopeless drunkards. Temperance,

TAKING THE PLEDGE. *The drunkard slumping in the rear of this scene is pledging to abstain from alcohol. His wife and children are happy and full of hope. Repeated over and over, the argument in terms of fatherhood and family responsibility—usually accompanied by the moral urging of women and children—was at the heart of the temperance movement.*

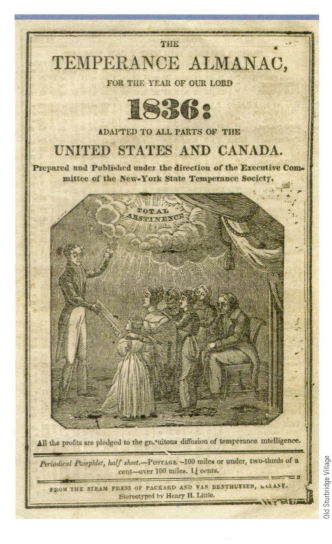

like other evangelical reforms, was a contest between self-control and slavery to one's appetites. By encouraging total abstinence, reformers hoped to halt the creation of new drunkards while the old ones died out. As middle-class evangelicals eliminated alcohol from their own lives, they would cease to offer it to their guests, buy or sell it, or provide it to their employees, and they would encourage their friends to do the same.

Charles Grandison Finney (see Chapter 10), in his revival at Rochester, made total abstinence a condition of conversion. Many other ministers and churches followed suit, and by the mid-1830s members of the middle class had largely disengaged themselves from alcohol and the people who drank it. Hundreds of evangelical businessmen refused to rent to merchants who sold liquor, sell grain to distillers, enter a store that sold alcohol, or hire employees who drank. Abstinence had become a badge of middle-class respectability.

By 1835 the American Temperance Society claimed 1.5 million members and estimated that 2 million Americans had renounced ardent spirits (whiskey, rum, and other distilled liquors). The society further estimated that 4,000 distilleries had gone out of business. Many politicians no longer bought drinks to win voters to their cause. In 1833, members of Congress formed the American Congressional Temperance Society. The U.S. Army put an end to the age-old liquor ration in 1832, and increasing numbers of militia officers stopped supplying their men with whiskey. The annual consumption of alcohol, which had reached an all-time high in the 1820s, dropped by more than half in the 1830s.

THE ORIGINS OF PROHIBITION

In the middle 1830s Whigs made temperance a political issue. Realizing that voluntary abstinence would not end drunkenness, Whig evangelicals drafted coercive, prohibitionist legislation. First, they attacked the licenses granting grocery stores and taverns the right to sell liquor by the drink and to permit it to be consumed on the premises. The licenses were important sources of revenue for local governments. They also gave local authorities the power to cancel the licenses of troublesome establishments. Militant temperance advocates, usually in association with local Whigs, demanded that the authorities use that power to outlaw all public drinking places. In communities throughout the North, the licensing issue became an issue around which local parties organized. The question first reached the state level in Massachusetts, when in 1838 a Whig legislature passed the "Fifteen-Gallon Law": merchants could sell ardent spirits only in quantities of 15 gallons or more, thus outlawing every public drinking place in the state. In 1839 Massachusetts voters sent enough Democrats to the legislature to rescind the law.

Leading Democrats agreed with Whigs that Americans drank too much. But while Whigs insisted that regulating morality was a proper function of government, Democrats warned that government intrusion into areas of private choice would violate republican liberties. In many communities, alcohol was the defining difference between Democrats and Whigs.

THE DEMOCRATIZATION OF TEMPERANCE

Democrats were ambiguous about temperance. Many of them continued to drink, while many others voluntarily abstained or cut down. Yet almost without exception, they resented the coercive tactics of the Whigs. In 1830, when Lyman Beecher's Hanover Street Church in Boston caught fire, the volunteer fire companies (which doubled as working-class drinking clubs) arrived, noted that it was the hated Beecher's church, and made no effort to put out the fire.

Democrats, despite their opposition to prohibition, often spoke out against drunkenness. Many craft unions denied membership to heavy drinkers, and hundreds of thousands of rural and urban Democrats quietly stopped drinking. Then, in the late 1830s, former antiprohibitionists launched a temperance movement of their own.

One evening in 1840 six craftsmen were drinking at Chase's Tavern in Baltimore. More or less as a joke, they sent one of their number to a nearby temperance lecture; he came back a teetotaler and converted the others. They then drew up a total abstinence pledge and promised to devote themselves to the reform of other drinkers. Within months a national movement had emerged, called the Washington Temperance Society. The Washingtonians differed from older temperance societies in several ways. First, they identified themselves as members of the laboring classes. Second, they were avowedly nonreligious. Third, the Washingtonians—at least those who called themselves "True Washingtonians"—rejected politics and legislation and concentrated on the conversion of drinkers through compassion and persuasion. Finally, they welcomed "hopeless" drunkards and hailed them as heroes when they sobered up.

TEMPERANCE SCHISMS

Whig reformers welcomed the Washingtonians at first but soon had second thoughts. The nonreligious character of the movement disturbed those who saw temperance as an arm of evangelical reform. While the temperance regulars read pamphlets and listened to lectures by clergymen, lawyers, and doctors, the Washingtonians enjoyed raucous sing-alongs, comedy routines, barnyard imitations, dramatic skits, and even full-dress minstrel shows geared to temperance themes. Meetings were organized around experience speeches offered by reformed drunkards. Speaking extemporaneously, they omitted none of the horrors of an alcoholic life: attempts at suicide, friendships betrayed, fathers and mothers desolated, wives beaten and abandoned, children dead of starvation. Though Washingtonians had given up alcohol, their melodramatic tales, street parades, songbooks, and minstrel shows owed much to popular culture. It was temperance, but it was not what Lyman Beecher and the Whigs had had in mind.

Nowhere did the Washingtonians differ more sharply from the temperance regulars than in their visions of the reformed life. Whig reformers expected men who quit drinking to withdraw from the male world in which drinking was common and retreat into the comfort of the newly feminized middle-class family. Washingtonianism, on the other hand, translated traditional male sociability into sober forms. Moreover, they called former drinkers back to the responsibilities of traditional fatherhood. Their experience stories began with the hurt drunkards had caused their wives and children and ended with their transformation into dependable providers and authoritative fathers. While the Whig temperance regulars tried to extend the ethos of individual ambition and the new middle-class domesticity into society at large, Washingtonians sought to rescue the self-respect and traditional moral authority of working-class fathers.

The Washington Temperance Society collapsed toward the end of the 1840s. Yet its legacy survived. Among former drinkers in the North, it had introduced a new sense of domestic responsibility and a healthy fear of drunkenness. Along the way, the Washingtonians and related groups created a self-consciously respectable native Protestant working class in American cities.

ETHNICITY AND ALCOHOL

It was into neighborhoods stirred by working-class revivals and temperance agitation that millions of Irish and German immigrants arrived in the 1840s and 1850s. The newcomers had their own time-honored relations to alcohol. The Germans introduced lager beer to the United States, thus providing a wholesome alternative for Americans who wished to give up spirits without joining the teetotalers. The Germans also built old-country beer halls, complete with sausage counters, oompah bands, group singing, and other family attractions. For their part, the Irish reaffirmed their love of whiskey—a love that was forged in colonial oppression and in a culture that accepted trouble with resignation, a love that legitimized levels of male drunkenness and violence that Americans, particularly the temperance forces, found appalling.

In the 1850s native resentment of Catholic immigrants drove thousands of Baptist and Methodist "respectables" out of the Democratic coalition and into nativist Whig majorities that established legal prohibition throughout New England, the middle states, and the Old Northwest. These were often the Democrats who became part of the North's Republican majority on the eve of the Civil War (see Chapter 14).

THE POLITICS OF RACE

Most whites in antebellum America believed in "natural" differences based on sex and race. God, they said, had given women and men and whites and blacks different mental, emotional, and physical capacities. And, as humankind (women and nonwhites more than others) was innately sinful and prone to disorder, God ordained a fixed social hierarchy in which white men exercised power over others. Slaves and free blacks accepted their subordinate status only as a fact of life, not as something that was natural and just. Some women also questioned patriarchy. But before 1830 hierarchy based on sex and race was seldom questioned in public, particularly by persons who were in a position to change it.

In the antebellum years, southerners and most northerners stiffened their defense of white paternalism. But northern Whig evangelicals envisioned a world based on Christian love and individual worth, not inherited status. They transformed marriage from rank domination into a sentimental partnership—unequal, but a partnership nonetheless. They also questioned the more virulent forms of racism. From among the Whig evangelicals emerged a radical minority that envisioned a world without power. While conservative Christians insisted that relations based on dominance and submission were the lot of a sinful humankind, reformers argued that such relations interposed human power, too often in the form of brute force, between God and the

FOCUS QUESTION
How did Whigs and Democrats differ on questions of race? How did they agree?

individual spirit. They called for a world that substituted spiritual freedom and Christian love for every form of worldly domination.

FREE BLACKS

Prior to the American Revolution there had been sizable pockets of slavery in the northern states. But revolutionary idealism, coupled with the growing belief that slavery was inefficient and unnecessary, led one northern state after another to abolish it. By 1804 every northern state had taken some action, usually by passing laws that called for gradual emancipation. The first of such laws, and the model for others, was passed in Pennsylvania in 1780. This law freed slaves born after 1780 when they reached their 28th birthday. Slaves born before 1780 would remain slaves, and slave children would remain slaves through their prime working years.

The rising population of northern free blacks gravitated to the cities. In many cities—Philadelphia and New York City in particular—they met a stream of free blacks and fugitive slaves from the Upper South. African Americans constituted a sizable minority in the rapidly expanding cities.

Blacks in the seaport cities tended to take stable, low-paying jobs. A few became successful entrepreneurs, while some others practiced skilled trades. Many of the others worked as waiters or porters in hotels, barbers, butlers, maids, cooks, washerwomen, and coachmen. Others were dockworkers, laborers, and sailors. Still others became dealers in used clothing, draymen with their own carts and horses, or food vendors in the streets and in basement shops.

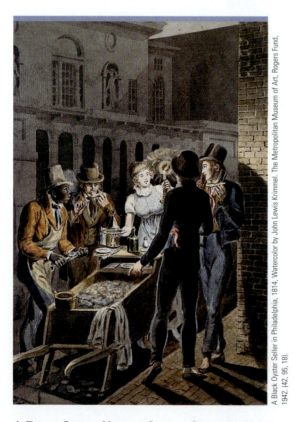

A Black Oyster Seller in Philadelphia, 1814, Watercolor by John Lewis Krimmel. The Metropolitan Museum of Art, Rogers Fund, 1942. (42, 95, 18).

A BLACK STREET VENDOR SELLING OYSTERS IN PHILADELPHIA, CIRCA 1814. *In early 19th-century New York and Philadelphia, African Americans monopolized the public sale of oysters and clams.*

DISCRIMINATION

From the 1820s onward, white wage workers began to edge blacks out of their jobs by underselling them, by pressuring employers to discriminate, and by outright violence. As a result, African Americans were almost completely eliminated from the skilled trades, and many unskilled and semiskilled blacks lost their jobs on the docks, in warehouses, and in the merchant marine. As their old jobs disappeared, blacks were systematically excluded from the new jobs that were opening up in factories. By the 1830s black workers in Philadelphia were noting "the difficulty of getting places for our sons as apprentices . . . owing to the prejudices with which we have to contend."

By accepting low wages and by rioting, intimidation, gunplay, and even murder, Irish immigrants displaced most of the remaining blacks from their toehold in the economic life of the northeastern cities. An observer of the Philadelphia docks remarked in 1849 that "when a few years ago we saw none but Blacks, we now see none but Irish."

Meanwhile, official discrimination against blacks was on the rise. Political democratization for white men was accompanied by the disfranchisement of blacks (see Chapter 7). Cities either excluded black children from public schools or set up segregated schools. In 1845, when Massachusetts passed a law declaring that all children had the right to attend neighborhood schools, the Boston School Committee blithely ruled that the law did not apply to blacks. Blacks were also excluded from white churches or sat in segregated pews.

African Americans responded by building institutions of their own. At one end were black-owned gambling houses, saloons, brothels, and dance halls—the only racially integrated institutions to be found in most cities. At the other end were black churches, schools, social clubs, and lodges. The first independent black church was the African Church of Philadelphia, founded in 1790; the African Methodist Episcopal Church, a national denomination still in existence, was founded in Philadelphia in 1816. Schools and relief societies, usually associated with churches, grew quickly, and black Masonic lodges attracted hundreds of members. It was from this matrix of black businesses and institutions that black abolitionists— David Walker in Boston, Frederick Douglass in New Bedford and Rochester, the itinerant Sojourner Truth, and many others—would emerge to demand abolition of slavery and equal rights for black citizens.

DEMOCRATIC RACISM

Neither Whigs nor Democrats encouraged the aspirations of slaves or free blacks. But it was the Democrats, from their beginnings in the 1820s, who incorporated racism into their political agenda. By the time of the Civil War, Democrats mobilized voters almost solely with threats of "Negro rule."

Democrats also contributed to the rising tide of antiblack violence. There were plenty of Whig racists, but Democrats seem to have predominated when mobs moved into black neighborhoods. Indeed many Democrats lumped together evangelical reformers, genteel Whigs, and blacks as a unified threat to the white republic. In July 1834 a New York City mob sacked the house of the abolitionist Lewis Tappan, moved on to Charles Finney's Chatham Street Chapel, where abolitionists were said to be meeting, and finished the evening by attacking a British actor at the Bowery Theater. The manager saved his theater by waving two American flags and ordering an American actor to perform popular minstrel routines for the mob.

The first major American race riot broke out in Philadelphia in 1834 between working-class whites and blacks at a street carnival. Although blacks won the first round, the whites refused to accept defeat. Over the next few nights, they wrecked a black-owned tavern; broke into black households to terrorize families and steal their property; attacked whites who lived with, socialized with, or operated businesses catering to blacks; wrecked the African Presbyterian Church; and destroyed a black church on Wharton Street by sawing through its timbers and pulling it down.

CONCEPTIONS OF RACIAL DIFFERENCE

Meanwhile, educated whites learned to think in racist terms. Among most scientists, biological determinism replaced historical and environmental explanations of racial differences; many argued that whites and blacks were separate species. Democrats welcomed that "discovery." In 1850 the *Democratic Review* confided, "Few or none now seriously adhere to the theory of the unity of the races. The whole state of the science at this moment seems to indicate that there are several distinct races of men on the earth, with entirely different capacities, physical and mental."

As whites came to perceive racial differences as God-given and immutable, they changed the nature of those differences as well. In the 18th and early 19th centuries, whites had stereotyped blacks as ignorant and prone to drunkenness and thievery, but they had also maintained a parallel stereotype of blacks as loyal and self-sacrificing servants. From the 1820s onward, racists continued to regard blacks as incompetent but now saw all blacks as treacherous, shrewd, and secretive—individuals who only pretended to feel loyalty to white families and affection for the white children they took care of, while awaiting the chance to steal from them or poison them. The writer

SKULL MEASUREMENTS. *This illustration is from* Types of Mankind: or Ethnological Researches *(1845), a "scientific" text that portrayed white men as Greek gods and black men as apes.*

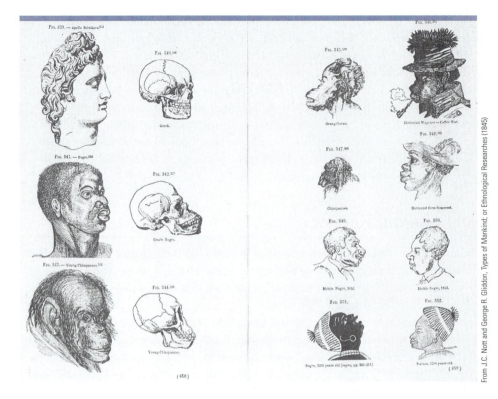

Herman Melville, a lifelong Democrat, dramatized these fears in *Benito Cereno,* a novel about slaves who commandeered a sailing ship and its captain and crew, then (with knives secretly at the throats of their captives) acted out a servile charade for unsuspecting visitors who came aboard. Above all, Democratic ideologues pronounced blacks unfit to be citizens of the white republic. Whigs often supported various forms of black suffrage; Democrats uniformly opposed it. The insistence that blacks were incapable of citizenship reinforced an equally natural white male political capacity. The exclusion of blacks (by Democrats whose own political competence was often doubted by wealthier and better-educated Whigs) protected the republic while extending citizenship to all white men. The most vicious racist assaults were often carried out beneath symbols of the revolutionary republic. Antiblack mobs in Baltimore, Cincinnati, and Toledo called themselves Minute Men and Sons of Liberty.

THE BEGINNINGS OF ANTISLAVERY

Before 1830 few whites had thought of slavery as a moral question. Washington, Jefferson, and other Chesapeake gentlemen doubted the wisdom, if not the morality, of holding slaves; New England Federalists had condemned slavery in the course of condemning Jeffersonian masters. But southerners and most northerners—when they bothered to think about it at all—tended to accept slavery as the result of human (read "black") depravity and God's unknowable plan.

American Colonization Society *Established by elite gentlemen of the middle and upper-south states in 1816, this organization encouraged voluntary emancipation of slaves, to be followed by their emigration to the West African colony of Liberia.*

Organized opposition to slavery before 1831 was largely limited to the **American Colonization Society,** founded in 1816 by wealthy, generally conservative northern churchmen and a contingent of Chesapeake gentlemen. The society proposed the voluntary, gradual, and compensated emancipation of slaves and the "repatriation" of free blacks to West Africa. Although the society transported a few thousand blacks to Liberia, it never posed a serious threat to slavery. Southerners, who owned 2 million slaves by 1830, opposed emancipation whether compensated or not, and few free blacks were interested in moving to Africa. The society's campaign to deport them so disturbed many free blacks that they substituted "Colored" for "African" in naming their institutions.

But although few white Americans actively opposed slavery before 1830, the writing was on the wall. Emancipation in the North, though it came about quietly, constituted an implicit condemnation of slavery in the South. So did events outside the United States. Toussaint L'Ouverture's successful slave revolution in Haiti in 1804 threatened slavery everywhere (see Chapter 7). The British outlawed the Atlantic slave trade in 1808. Mexico, Peru, Chile, Gran Colombia (present-day Colombia, Venezuela, Equador, and Panama), and other new republics carved out of the Spanish Empire emancipated their slaves. The most powerful blow came in 1830 when the British Parliament emancipated the slaves of Jamaica, Bermuda, and other Caribbean islands ruled by Britain.

ABOLITIONISTS

It was at this time—the late 1820s and early 1830s—that religious revivals created a reform-minded evangelical culture in the northern United States. Radical **abolitionism** dates from 1831, when William Lloyd Garrison published the first issue of *The Liberator.*

Already a veteran reformer, Garrison condemned slavery as a national sin and demanded immediate emancipation—or at least an immediate start toward emancipation.

In 1833 Garrison and like-minded abolitionists formed the **American Anti-Slavery Society.** Some of them were Unitarians who opposed slavery as an affront to both humanity and reason; others were Quakers who were happy to join the movement. But abolitionists found their greatest support in southern New England, western New York, northern Ohio, and among the new middle classes of the northeastern cities—ground that Yankee settlement, the market revolution, and Finneyite revivals had turned into the heartland of the northern Whig Party.

Opposition to slavery was a logical extension of middle-class evangelicalism, grounded in the morally accountable individual. Whig evangelicals often promised that their reforms would liberate the individual spirit from "slavery" to alcohol, lust, or ignorance—thus phrasing moral legislation as liberation, not coercion. It was not long before some discovered that slavery itself, an institution that obliterated moral choice and encouraged the worst human passions, was America's great national sin.

The American Anti-Slavery Society demanded immediate emancipation of slaves and full civil and legal rights for blacks. Assuming that God had created blacks and whites as members of one human family, abolitionists opposed the "scientific" racism spouted by Democrats and many Whigs. Moderates spoke of inherent racial characteristics but still tended to view blacks in benign (if condescending) ways. Harriet Beecher Stowe, for instance, portrayed blacks as simple, innocent, loving people who possessed a capacity for sentiment and emotionalism that most whites had lost. Radical abolitionists, however, remained committed environmentalists. Lydia Maria Child of New York City declared, "In the United States, colored persons have scarcely any chance to rise. But if colored persons are well treated, and have the same inducements to industry as others, they [will] work as well and behave as well."

AGITATION

Antislavery, unlike other reforms, was a radical attack on one of the nation's central institutions, and the movement attracted a minority even among middle-class evangelicals. Indeed, both Lyman Beecher and Charles Finney opposed the abolitionists

abolitionism *Movement begun in the north about 1830 to abolish slavery immediately and without compensation to owners.*

American Anti-Slavery Society *Organization created by northern abolitionists in 1833 that called for immediate, uncompensated emancipation of the slaves.*

"OUR *PECULIAR* DOMESTIC INSTITUTIONS."

AN ABOLITIONIST VIEW OF SLAVE SOCIETY. *This very provocative woodcut appeared in the* Anti-Slavery Almanac *for 1840 (Boston, 1839). It pictures the lynching of slaves and their abolitionist allies by a southern mob. Surrounding the hanging tree are men (there are no women in the picture) who are engaged in other activities that northern reformers insisted were a result of the brutal patriarchy of slave society. Men duel with pistols and knives, others engage in an eye-gouging wrestling match, others gamble and drink, and still others cheer for cockfights and horse races. The enemy here is not simply slavery but the debauchery and unbridled passions associated with it.*

postal campaign *Abolitionist tactic to force the nation to confront the slavery question by flooding the mails, both North and South, with anti-slavery literature. Their hope was to raise controversy within an area that was the province of the federal government.*

in the 1830s, arguing that emancipation would come about sooner or later as a result of the religious conversion of slave owners; antislavery agitation and the denunciation of slaveholders, they argued, would divide Christians, slow the revival movement, and thus actually delay emancipation.

The American Anti-Slavery Society staged a series of campaigns to force government and the public at large to confront the question of slavery. In 1835 the society launched its **postal campaign,** flooding the nation's postal system with abolitionist tracts. From 1836 onward, they petitioned Congress to abolish slavery and the slave trade in the District of Columbia and to deny the slaveholding Republic of Texas admission to the Union. These tactics forced President Andrew Jackson to permit southern postal workers to censor the mails; they also forced Democrats and southern Whigs to abridge the right of petition to avoid discussion of slavery in Congress (see Chapter 12).

In these ways, a radical minority forced politicians to demonstrate the complicity of the party system (and the Democrats in particular) in the institution of slavery, brought the slavery question to public attention, and tied it to questions of civil liberties in the North and political power in the South. They were a dangerous minority indeed.

MUSICAL LINK TO THE PAST

"THE GRAVE OF THE SLAVE"

Composers: Francis Johnson (music), Sarah Forten (lyrics) Title: "The Grave of the Slave" (1831)

"The Grave of the Slave," one of the rare abolitionist songs penned by African Americans, demonstrates the more active role blacks were beginning to take in the struggle against slavery. The lyrics of Sarah Forten, founder of the Philadelphia Anti-Slavery Society, were consistent with abolitionist arguments that, contrary to pro-slavery Southern propaganda, charged that slaves lived a miserable and unchristian existence that represented a worse fate than death: "Poor slave, shall we sorrow that Death was thy friend? / The last and the kindest that heaven could send? / The grave to the weary is welcome and blest / And death to the captive is freedom and rest."

In the early 1830s, the abolition movement reached a new political and emotional height, led by the uncompromising vision of William Lloyd Garrison (see pages 301–302). For many blacks, this represented a large improvement over the previous efforts of the white-led and largely unsuccessful American Colonization Society of the 1810s and 1820s, which advocated shipping blacks to Africa. For the first time, significant numbers of black Americans in the North joined the abolitionist movement because of Garrison's tactics.

The composer, Francis Johnson, was one of the most famous and accomplished African Americans of the antebellum period. A prolific composer and world-famous orchestra leader, Johnson and his orchestra toured across North America (avoiding the Deep South), and were probably the first American band to give concerts abroad, including a command performance before Queen Victoria, at which she presented Johnson with a silver bugle. His orchestra performed both European classical music and American popular songs (Johnson published more than 200 pieces). Although most of his music served entertainment and dancing purposes, he also composed music with political and African American themes, including "Recognition March on the Independence of Hayti [sic]" (1825) and "The Grave of the Slave." Because recording technology did not yet exist, we will never know precisely how his music sounded, but his orchestra could very well have served as a major precedent for the jazz and blues that surfaced decades later.

1. Why do you think so many of the most famous and historically significant African American figures of the 19th and 20th centuries came from the worlds of religion and entertainment?

Listen to an audio recording of this music on the Musical Links to the Past CD.

THE POLITICS OF GENDER AND SEX

Whigs valued a reformed masculinity that was lived out in the sentimentalized homes of the northern business classes or in the Christian gentility of the Whig plantation and farm. Jacksonian voters, on the other hand, often defended domestic patriarchy. Democrats often made heroes of men whose flamboyant, rakish lives directly challenged Whig domesticity. Whigs denounced Andrew Jackson for allegedly stealing his wife from her lawful husband; Democrats often admired him for the same reason. Richard M. Johnson of Kentucky, who was vice president under Martin Van Buren, openly kept a mulatto mistress and had two daughters by her; with his pistols always at hand, he accompanied her openly around Washington, D.C. "Prince" John Van

Buren, the president's son and himself a prominent New York Democrat, met a "dark-eyed, well-formed Italian lady" who became his "fancy lady," remaining with him until he lost her in a high-stakes card game. Whigs made Democratic contempt for sentimental domesticity a political issue. William Crane, a Michigan Whig, claimed that Democrats "despised no man for his sins" and went on to say that "brothel-haunters flocked to this party, because here in all political circles, and political movements, they were treated as nobility." Much of the Whig cultural agenda (and much of Democratic hatred of that agenda) was rooted in contests between Whig and Democratic masculine styles.

APPETITES

Many of the reforms urged by Whig evangelicals had to do with domestic and personal life rather than with politics. Their hopes for the perfection of the world hinged more on the character of individuals than on the role of institutions. They hoped to perfect the world by filling it with godly, self-governing individuals.

It was not an easy task, for opportunities to indulge in vanity, luxury, and sensuality were on the rise. Charles Finney, for instance, preached long and hard against vanity. Finney also worried about the effect of money, leisure time, and cheap novels on middle-class homes. He could not, he said, "believe that a person who has ever known the love of God can relish a secular novel" or open his or her home to "Byron, Scott, Shakespeare, and a host of triflers and blasphemers of God." Evangelicals also disdained luxury in home furnishings; they discouraged the use of silks and velvets and questioned the propriety of decorating the home with mahogany, mirrors, brass furnishings, and upholstered chairs and sofas.

Members of the evangelical middle class tried to define levels of material comfort that would separate them from the indulgences of those above and below them. They made similar attempts in the areas of food and sex. Sylvester Graham (now remembered for the cracker that bears his name) gave up the ministry in 1830 to become a full-time temperance lecturer. Before long, he was lecturing on the danger of excess in diet and sex. He claimed that the consumption of red meat, spiced foods, and alcohol produced bodily excitement that resulted in weakness and disease. Sex—including fornication, fantasizing, masturbation, and bestiality—affected the body in even more destructive ways, and the two appetites reinforced each other.

Acting on Graham's concerns, reformers established a system of Grahamite boardinghouses in which young men who were living away from home were provided with diets that helped them control their other appetites. Oberlin College, when it was founded by evangelicals in 1832, banned "tea and coffee, highly seasoned meats, rich pastries, and all unholsome [sic] and expensive foods." Reformers who did not actually adopt Graham's system shared his concern over the twin evils of rich food and sexual excess. John Humphrey Noyes set up a community in Oneida, New York, that indulged in plural marriage but at the same time urged sexual self-control; he also believed that in a perfect Christian world there would be no meat eating.

MORAL REFORM

Although most middle-class households did not embrace Grahamism, simple food and sexual control became badges of class status. The assumption was that men had the greatest difficulty taming their appetites. The old image of woman as seductress persisted in the more traditionalist churches and in the pulp fiction from which middle-class mothers tried to protect their sons (see Chapter 10). Whig evangelicals, on the other hand, had made the discovery that women were naturally free of desire and that only men were subject to the animal passions. The middle-class ideal combined female purity and male self-control. For the most part it was a private reform, contained within the home. Sometimes, however, evangelical domesticity produced moral crusades to impose that ethos on the world at large. Many of these crusades were led by women.

In 1828 a band of Sunday school teachers initiated an informal mission to prostitutes that grew into the New York Magdalen Society. Taking a novel approach to an age-old question, the society argued that prostitution was created by brutal fathers and husbands who abandoned their young daughters or wives, by dandies who seduced them and turned them into prostitutes, and by lustful men who bought their services. Prostitution, in other words, was not the result of the innate sinfulness of prostitutes; it was the result of the brutality and lust of men. The solution was to remove young prostitutes from their environment, pray with them, and convert them to middle-class morality.

The Magdalen Society's *First Annual Report* (1831) inveighed against male lust and printed shocking life histories of prostitutes. Some men, however, read it as pornography; others used it as a guidebook to the seamier side of New York City. The wealthy male evangelicals who had bankrolled the Magdalen Society withdrew their support, and the organization fell apart. Thereupon many of the women reformers set up the Female Moral Reform Society, with a House of Industry in which prostitutes were taught morality and household skills to prepare them for new lives as domestic servants in pious middle-class homes. This effort also failed, largely because few prostitutes were interested in domestic service or evangelical religion.

The Female Moral Reform Society was more successful with members of its own class. Its newspaper, *The Advocate of Moral Reform,* circulated throughout the evangelical North. Now, evangelical women fought prostitution by publishing the names of customers. They campaigned against pornography, obscenity, lewdness, and seduction and accepted the responsibility of rearing their sons to be pure, even when it meant dragging them out of brothels. They also publicized the names of adulterers, and they had seducers brought into court. In the process, women reformers fought the sexual double standard and assumed the power to define what was respectable and what was not.

WOMEN'S RIGHTS

From the late 1820s onward, middle-class women in the North assumed roles that would have been unthinkable to their mothers and grandmothers. Evangelical domesticity made loving mothers (and not stern fathers) the principal rearers of children. Housewives saw themselves as missionaries to their families, responsible for the choices their children and husband made between salvation or sin. It was in that role that women became arbiters of fashion, diet, and sexual behavior. That same role motivated them to join the temperance movement and moral reform societies, where they became public reformers while posing as mothers protecting their sons from rum sellers and seducers. Such experiences gave them a sense of spiritual empowerment that led some to question their own subordinate status within a system of gendered social roles.

It was through the antislavery movement that many women became advocates of women's rights. Abolitionists called for absolute human equality and rejection of impersonal institutions and prescribed social roles. It became clear to some female abolitionists that the critique of slavery applied as well to inequality based on sex.

Radical female abolitionists reached the conclusion that they were human beings first and women second. In 1837 **Sarah Grimke** announced, "The Lord Jesus de-

Sarah Grimke *Along with her sister, Angelina, this elite South Carolina woman moved north and compaigned against slavery and for temperance and women's rights.*

Seneca Falls Convention
(1848) First national convention of women's rights activists.

fines the duties of his followers in his Sermon on the Mount . . . without any reference to sex or condition . . . never even referring to the distinction now so strenuously insisted upon between masculine and feminine virtues. . . . Men and women are CREATED EQUAL!" A women's rights convention put it just as bluntly in 1851: "We deny the right of any portion of the species to decide for another portion . . . what is and what is not their 'proper sphere'; that the proper sphere for all human beings is the largest and highest to which they are able to attain."

Beginning around 1840, women lobbied state legislatures and won significant changes in the laws governing women's rights to property, to the wages of their own labor, and to custody of children in cases of divorce. Fourteen states passed such legislation, culminating in New York's Married Women's Property Act in 1860.

Women's progress in achieving political rights, however, came more slowly. The first Women's Rights Convention, held in 1848 at **Seneca Falls,** New York, began with a Declaration of Sentiments and Resolutions, based on the Declaration of Independence, that denounced "the repeated injuries and usurpations on the part of man towards woman." The central issue was the right to vote, for female participation in politics was a direct challenge to a male-ordained women's place. A distraught New York legislator warned: "It is well known that the object of these unsexed women is to overthrow the most sacred of our institutions. . . . Are we to put the stamp of truth upon the libel here set forth, that men and women, in the matrimonial relation, are to be equal?" Later, the feminist Elizabeth Cady Stanton recalled such reactions: "Political rights," she said, "involving in their last results equality everywhere, roused all the antagonism of a dominant power, against the self-assertion of a class hitherto subservient."

CONCLUSION

By the 1830s most citizens in every corner of the republic firmly identified with either the Whig or Democratic Party—so much so that party affiliation was recognized as an indicator of personal history and cultural loyalties. In the states and neighborhoods, Whigs embraced commerce and activist government, arguing that both would foster prosperity, social harmony, and moral progress; faith in progress and improvement led Northern and western Whigs to entertain the hope that liberty and equality might apply to women and blacks. Democrats, on the other hand, were generally more localistic and culturally conservative. They seldom doubted the value of commerce, but they worried that the market revolution and its organization of banking, credit, and monetary supply was creating unprecedented levels of inequality and personal dependence among the republic's white male citizenry. Democrats also looked with angry disbelief at attempts of Whigs to govern the private and public behavior of their neighbors, and sometimes even to tinker with ancient distinctions of gender and race.

In sum, Whigs reformulated the revolutionary legacy of liberty and equality, moving away from classical notions of citizenship and toward liberty of conscience and equality of opportunity within a market-driven democracy; and they often attempted to civilize that new world by using government power to encourage commerce, social interdependence, and cultural homogeneity. When Democrats argued that Whig "interdependence" in fact meant dependence and inequality, Whigs countered with promises of individual success for those who were morally worthy of it. Democrats trusted none of that. Theirs was a Jeffersonian formulation grounded in a fierce defense of the liberty and equality of white men, and in a minimal, inexpensive, decentralized government that protected the liberties of those men without threatening their independence or their power over their households and within their neighborhoods.

QUESTIONS FOR REVIEW AND CRITICAL THINKING

Review

1. Which Americans were likely to support the Democratic Party in the 1830s and 1840s? Which Americans were likely to support the Whigs?
2. What were the Whig and Democratic conceptions of the duties and limits of government?
3. What were the principal reform movements of these years, and how did the political parties relate to them?
4. How did Whigs and Democrats differ on questions of race? How did they agree?
5. How did Whigs and Democrats differ on questions of gender?

Critical Thinking

1. Choose a position either defending or attacking this statement: "Differences between Whigs and Democrats on economic policy, social reform, race, and gender boil down to differences in Whig and Democratic conceptions of white manhood."
2. What were the goals and assumptions that drove the movements for public schools, humane prisons and asylums, and temperance? Were those primarily Democratic or Whig assumptions?

Discovery

What broad social movements emerged during this period, and how did some attempt to stem these attempts at reforms?

SUGGESTED READINGS

On party ideologies, see **John Ashworth, *Agrarians & Aristocrats: Party Political Ideology in the United States, 1837–1846*** (1983), and **Daniel Walker Howe, *The Political Culture of the American Whigs*** (1979). Constituencies and state-level issues are addressed in **Lee Benson, *The Concept of Jacksonian Democracy: New York as a Test Case*** (1961), **Ronald P. Formisano, *The Transformation of Political Culture: Massachusetts Parties, 1790s–1840s*** (1983), and **Lacy K. Ford, Jr., *Origins of Southern Radicalism: The South Carolina Upcountry, 1800–1860*** (1988). **Richard J. Carwardine, *Evangelicals and Politics in Antebellum America*** (1993), is an insightful study of religion and politics in these years. On the politics of schools, see **Carl F. Kaestle, *Pillars of the Republic: Common Schools and American Society, 1780–1860*** (1983). Influential studies of prisons and asylums include **David J. Rothman, *The Discovery of the Asylum: Social Order and Disorder in the New Republic*** (1971) and **Michael Meranze, *Laboratories of Virtue: Punishment, Revolution, and Authority in Philadelphia, 1760–1835*** (1996). Drinking and temperance are the subjects of **W. J. Rorabaugh, *The Alcoholic Republic: An American Tradition*** (1979). The standard study of free blacks is **Leon F. Litwack, *North of Slavery: The Negro in the Free States, 1790–1860*** (1960), which can be supplemented with **Gary B. Nash, *Forging Freedom: The Formation of Philadelphia's Black Community, 1720–1840*** (1988). The literature on reform movements is synthesized in **Steven Mintz, *Moralists and Modernizers: Americas Pre-Civil War Reformers*** (1995). Students might also consult **Robert H. Abzug, *Cosmos Crumbling: American Reform and the Religious Imagination*** (1994), **Jean Fagan Yellin, *Women and Sisters: The Antislavery Feminists in American Culture*** (1989), and **Lori D. Ginzberg, *Women and the Work of Benevolence: Morality, Politics, and Class in the 19th-Century United States*** (1990).

ONLINE SOURCES GUIDE

ThomsonNOW Visit ThomsonNOW to access primary sources, exercises, quizzes, and audio chapter summaries related to this chapter:

http://www.thomsonedu.com/login

DISCOVERY

What broad social movements emerged during this period, and how did some attempt to stem these attempts at reform?

In thinking about this question, begin by breaking it down into the components shown below. A discussion of the significance of each component should appear in your answer.

Look at the illustration on the cover of the Temperance Almanac. What is the significance of the placement of the words "total abstinence" in the sky? Who is in attendance at this meeting? Does the man at the right—presumably the husband/father figure—look as interested or pleased as the others to be there? Why or why not? How does this illustration summarize the story and arguments of the temperance movement?

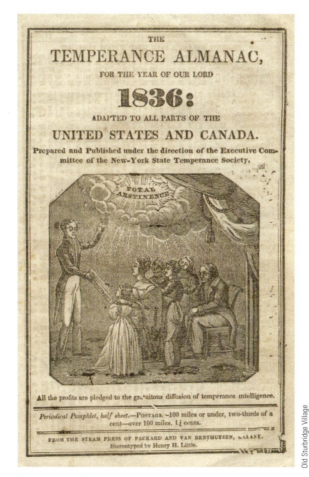

Old Sturbridge Village

TAKING THE PLEDGE

CULTURE AND SOCIETY

Look at the abolitionist depiction of slave society. Who is being lynched? In what kinds of other activities are the southerners who are attending the lynchings engaged? What does this suggest that the artist thinks about southern society and the effects of slavery on society? Is there any significance to the absence of women and children from this image?

AN ABOLITIONIST VIEW OF SLAVE SOCIETY

What do the "scientific" drawings pretend to show about differences between the races? How would images like this be used to help justify slavery in southern society?

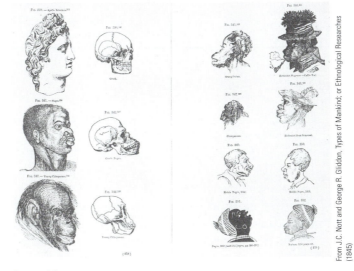

SKULL MEASUREMENTS

JACKSONIAN DEMOCRACY

National political leaders from the 1820s onward faced two persistent questions. First, the rift between slave and free states threatened the very existence of the nation. Second, explosive economic development and territorial expansion made new demands upon the political system. The Whig Party proposed the American System as the answer to both questions. Government, said the Whigs, should subsidize roads and canals, foster industry with protective tariffs, and maintain a national bank capable of exercising centralized control over credit and currency. The result would be a national market society. If the South, the West, and the Northeast were doing business with each other, the argument went, sectional jealousies would quiet down. Jacksonian Democrats, on the other hand, argued that the American System violated the rights of states and benefited wealthy insiders. Most dangerous of all, argued the Democrats, Whigs called for an activist national government that could threaten the slaveholding South. Jacksonians resurrected Jefferson's agrarian republic of states' rights and inactive, inexpensive government—all of it deeply inflected in the code of white male equality, domestic patriarchy, and racial slavery.

1815	1820	1825	1830	1835	1840

1817–1825
Presidency of James Monroe

■ **1819**
Controversy arises over Missouri's admission to the Union as a slave state
• Panic of 1819 marks the first failure of the national market economy

■ **1820**
Missouri Compromise adopted

■ **1823**
Monroe Doctrine written by Secretary of State John Quincy Adams

1824–1825
Adams appoints Henry Clay as secretary of state
• Jacksonians charge a "Corrupt Bargain" between Adams and Clay

1825–1829
Presidency of John Quincy Adams

■ **1828**
"Tariff of Abominations" passed by Congress
• John C. Calhoun's *Exposition and Protest* presents doctrine of nullification

1829–1837
Presidency of Andrew Jackson

■ **1830**
Congress passes the Indian Removal Act

1832 ■
Worcester v. Georgia exempts the Cherokee from Georgia law
• Jackson vetoes recharter of the Bank of the United States

■ **1833**
Force Bill and Tariff of 1833 end the nullification crisis

1836 ■
Congress adopts "gag rule" to table antislavery petitions

1837–1841
Presidency of Martin Van Buren • Financial panic and depression

1838 ■
U.S. Army marches the remaining Cherokee to Indian Territory

Prologue: 1819

Jacksonian democracy was rooted in two events that occurred in 1819. First, the angry debate on Missouri's admission as a slave state revealed the centrality and vulnerability of slavery within the Union. Second, a financial collapse raised the question whether the market revolution was compatible with the Jeffersonian republic. Republican politicos revived the limited-government, states'-rights coalition that had elected Thomas Jefferson. By 1828 they had formed the Democratic Party, with **Andrew Jackson** at its head.

The West, 1803–1840s

When Jefferson bought the Louisiana Territory in 1803, he knew little about the new land itself. Only a few French trappers and traders had traveled the plains between the Mississippi and the Rocky Mountains, and no white person had seen the territory

Andrew Jackson *President of the United States (1829–1837) and founder of the Democratic Party who signed the Indian Removal Act, vetoed the Second Bank, and signed the Force Bill.*

drained by the Columbia River. In 1804 Jefferson sent an expedition under Meriwether Lewis and William Clark to explore the purchase. The two kept meticulous journals of one of the epic adventures in American history.

In May 1804 **Lewis and Clark** and 41 companions boarded a keelboat and two large canoes at St. Louis. They labored 1,600 miles up the Missouri River, passing through rolling plains dotted by the farm villages of the Pawnee, Oto, Missouri, Crow, Omaha, Hidatsa, and Mandan peoples. The villages of the lower Missouri had been cut off from the western buffalo herds and reduced to dependence by mounted Sioux warriors who had begun to establish their hegemony over the northern plains.

Lewis and Clark traveled through Sioux territory and wintered at the fortified Mandan villages at the big bend of the Missouri River in Dakota country. In the spring they hired Toussaint Charbonneau, a French fur trader, to guide them to the Pacific. Although Charbonneau turned out to be useless, his wife, a teenaged Shoshone girl named Sacajawea, was an indispensable guide, interpreter, and diplomat. With her help, Lewis and Clark navigated the upper Missouri, crossed the Rockies to the Snake River, and followed that stream to the Columbia River. They reached the Pacific in November 1805. They wintered there, then retraced their steps back to St. Louis, arriving in September 1806. They brought back volumes of drawings and notes, along with assurances that the Louisiana Purchase had been had been a very good buy.

As time passed, Americans began to settle the southern portions of the Louisiana Purchase. Louisiana entered the Union in 1812, and settlers filtered into northern Louisiana and the Arkansas and Missouri territories. Farther north and west, the Sioux extended their control over the northern reaches of the land that Jefferson had bought.

The Sioux were aided by the spread of smallpox, which nearly wiped out the Mandans. The Sioux and their Cheyenne allies, who lived in small bands and were constantly on the move, fared better. Their horse-raiding parties now grew into armies of mounted invaders numbering as many as 2,000, and they extended their hunting lands south into what is now southern Nebraska and as far west as the Yellowstone River.

THE ARGUMENT OVER MISSOURI

Early in 1819 slaveholding Missouri applied to become the first new state to be carved out of the Louisiana Purchase. New York congressman James Tallmadge Jr. quickly proposed two amendments to the Missouri statehood bill. The first would bar additional slaves from being brought into Missouri. The second would emancipate Missouri slaves born after admission when they reached their 25th birthday.

The congressional debates on the Missouri question were about sectional power, not the morality of slavery. Rufus King, an old New York Federalist, insisted that he opposed the admission of a new slave state "solely in its bearing and effects upon great political interests, and upon the just and equal rights of the freemen of the nation." Northerners resented the added representation in Congress and in the Electoral College that the "three-fifths" rule granted to the slave states (see Chapter 6). The rule had, in fact, added significantly to southern power: In 1790 the South, with 40 percent of the white population, controlled 47 percent of the votes in Congress.

In 1819 the North held a majority in the House of Representatives. The South controlled a bare majority in the Senate. Voting on the Tallmadge amendments was starkly sectional: the House accepted them, but southern senators, with the help of the two Illinois senators and three northerners, defeated the amendments. Deadlocked between a Senate in favor of admitting Missouri as a slave state and a House dead set against it, Congress broke off the angry debate and went home.

Lewis and Clark *Explorers commissioned in 1804 by President Jefferson to survey the Louisiana Purchase.*

THE MISSOURI COMPROMISE

In the winter of 1819–1820 a new Congress passed the legislative package known as the **Missouri Compromise.** Massachusetts offered its northern counties as the new free state of Maine, neutralizing fears that the South would gain votes in the Senate with the admission of Missouri. Senator Jesse Thomas of Illinois then proposed the so-called Thomas Proviso: If the North would admit Missouri as a slave state, the South would agree to outlaw slavery above a line extending from the southern border of Missouri to Spanish territory. This opened Arkansas Territory to slavery and banned slavery in the remainder of the Louisiana Territory.

Congress admitted Maine with little debate. But the admission of Missouri under the terms of the Thomas Proviso met northern opposition. A joint Senate-House committee separated the two bills. With half of the southern representatives and nearly all of the northerners supporting it, the Thomas Proviso passed. Congress then took up the admission of Missouri. With the votes of a solid South and 14 compromise-minded northerners, Missouri entered the Union as a slave state.

The Missouri crisis brought the South's commitment to slavery and the North's resentment of southern political power into collision. While northerners vowed to relinquish no more territory to slavery, southerners talked openly of disunion and civil war. A Georgia politician announced that the Missouri debates had lit a fire that "seas of blood can only extinguish." Viewing the crisis from Monticello, the aging Thomas Jefferson was distraught:

> A geographical line, coinciding with a marked principle, moral and political, once conceived and held up to the angry passions of men, will never be obliterated; every new irritation will mark it deeper and deeper. . . . This momentous question, like a fire-bell in the night, awakened and filled me with terror.

THE PANIC OF 1819

Politicians debated the Missouri question against a backdrop of economic depression. The origins of the Panic of 1819 were international: European agriculture recovered from the Napoleonic wars, reducing the demand for American foodstuffs; revolution in Mexico and Peru cut off the supply of precious metals (the base of the international money supply); debt-ridden European governments hoarded the available precious metals; and American bankers and businessmen met the situation by expanding credit and issuing banknotes that were mere dreams of real money.

One of the reasons Congress had chartered the Second Bank of the United States in 1816 (see Chapter 9) was to impose order on this situation. But the Bank itself became part of the problem: The western branch offices in Cincinnati and Lexington became embroiled in the speculative boom, and insiders at the Baltimore branch hatched schemes to enrich themselves. In 1819 the bank's president was replaced by Langdon Cheves of South Carolina. Cheves curtailed credit and demanded that state banknotes received by the Bank of the United States be redeemed in specie. By doing so, Cheves rescued the bank from the paper economy created by state-chartered banks, but when the state banks were forced to redeem their notes in specie, they demanded payment from their own borrowers, and the national money and credit system collapsed.

A depression ensued. Businesses failed, and hundreds of thousands of wage workers lost their jobs. In Philadelphia, unemployment reached 75 percent; 1,800 workers in that city were imprisoned for debt. A tent city of the unemployed sprang up on the outskirts of Baltimore. Other cities and towns were hit as hard, and the situation was no better in the countryside.

Missouri Compromise *Compromise that maintained sectional balance in Congress by admitting Missouri as a slave state and Maine as a free state and by drawing a line west from the 36° 30′ parallel separating future slave and free states.*

Faced with a disaster that none could control and that few understood, many Americans directed their resentment onto the banks, particularly on the Bank of the United States. John Jacob Astor, possibly the richest man in America at that time, admitted that "there has been too much Speculation and too much assumption of Power on the Part of the Bank Directors which has caused [sic] the institution to become unpopular. . . ." William Gouge, who would become the Jacksonian Democrats' favorite economist, put it more bluntly: When the bank demanded that state banknotes be redeemed in specie, he said, "the Bank was saved and the people were ruined."

REPUBLICAN REVIVAL

FOCUS QUESTION

In terms of party development, what were the long-term results of the Missouri Controversy and the Panic of 1819?

The crises during 1819 and 1820 prompted demands for a return to Jeffersonian principles. Without opposition, Jefferson's dominant Republican Party had lost its way. The nationalist Congress of 1816 had enacted much of the Federalist program under the name of Republicanism; the result, said the old Republicans, was an aggressive government that helped bring on the Panic of 1819. At the same time, the collapse of Republican unity in Congress had allowed the Missouri question to degenerate into a sectional free-for-all. By 1820 many Republicans were calling for a Jeffersonian revival that would limit government power and guarantee southern rights within the Union.

MARTIN VAN BUREN LEADS THE WAY

Among those Republicans was Martin Van Buren of New York, who took his seat in the Senate in 1821. Van Buren had built his political career out of a commitment to Jeffersonian principles, personal charm, and party discipline. He hoped to apply his experience to the national political crisis.

Van Buren's New York believed that disciplined political parties were necessary democratic tools. Competition and party divisions were inevitable and good, he said, but they must be made to serve the republic. Working with like-minded politicians, he reconstructed the coalition of northern and southern agrarians that had elected Thomas Jefferson. The result was the Democratic Party and, ultimately, a national two-party system that persisted until the eve of the Civil War.

congressional caucus *In the early republic, the group of congressmen that traditionally chose the party's presidential candidates. By the 1820s, the American public distrusted the caucus as undemocratic since only one party contested for power. The caucus was replaced by the national nominating convention.*

THE ELECTION OF 1824

In the 1824 presidential election, Van Buren and his friends supported William H. Crawford, a staunch Georgia Republican. The Van Burenites controlled the Republican **congressional caucus,** the body that traditionally chose the party's presidential candidates. The public distrusted the caucus as undemocratic, for it represented the only party in government and thus could dictate the choice of a president. With most congressmen fearing their constituents, only a minority showed up for the caucus vote. They dutifully nominated Crawford.

With Republican Party unity broken, the list of sectional candidates grew. John Quincy Adams, New England's **favorite son,** was the son of a Federalist president, secretary of state under Monroe, and one of the converts to Republicanism who, according to people like Van Buren and Crawford, had blunted the republican thrust of

favorite son *Candidate for president supported by delegates from his home state.*

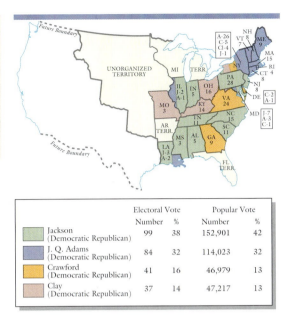

Map 12.1

PRESIDENTIAL ELECTION, 1824. *Voting in the four-cornered contest of 1824 was starkly sectional. John Quincy Adams carried his native New England, while Crawford and Clay carried only a few states in their own sections. Only Andrew Jackson enjoyed national support: He carried states in every section but New England, and he ran a strong second in many of the states that were awarded to other candidates.*

Jefferson's old party. Henry Clay of Kentucky, chief proponent of the American System of protective tariffs, centralized banking, and government-sponsored internal improvements, expected to carry the West. John C. Calhoun of South Carolina announced his candidacy, then dropped out and put himself forth as the sole candidate for vice president.

The wild card was Andrew Jackson of Tennessee, who in 1824 was known only as a military hero. He was also a frontier nabob with a reputation for violence. According to Jackson's detractors, impetuosity marked his public life as well. As commander of U.S. military forces in the South in 1818, Jackson had, without orders, invaded Spanish Florida. He occupied Spanish forts, summarily executed Seminoles whom he claimed were raiding into the United States, and hanged two British subjects. Jackson retired from public life in 1821, partly as a result of his Florida adventure. In 1824 eastern politicians knew Jackson only as a "military chieftain," "the Napoleon of the woods."

What the easterners did not take into account was Jackson's popularity. In 1824, in the 16 states that chose presidential electors by popular vote Jackson polled 152,901 votes to Adams's 114,023 and Clay's 47,217. Crawford, who suffered a crippling stroke during the campaign, won 46,979 votes. Jackson's support was large and national: he carried 84 percent of the votes of his own Southwest and won victories in Pennsylvania, New Jersey, North Carolina, Indiana, and Illinois, while running a close second in several other states.

		Electoral Vote		Popular Vote	
		Number	%	Number	%
	Jackson (Democratic Republican)	99	38	152,901	42
	J. Q. Adams (Democratic Republican)	84	32	114,023	32
	Crawford (Democratic Republican)	41	16	46,979	13
	Clay (Democratic Republican)	37	14	47,217	13

"A CORRUPT BARGAIN"

Jackson assumed that he had won: He had received 42 percent of the popular vote to his nearest rival's 32 percent, and he was clearly the nation's choice. But his 99 electoral votes were 32 shy of the plurality demanded by the Constitution. Acting under the Twelfth Amendment, the House of Representatives would select a president from among the top three candidates. As the candidate with the fewest electoral votes, Henry Clay was eliminated. But he remained Speaker of the House, and he had enough support to throw the election to either Jackson or Adams. Years later, Jackson claimed that Clay offered to support him in exchange for Clay's appointment as secretary of state—a traditional stepping stone to the presidency. Jackson turned him down, according to Jacksonian legend, and Adams accepted Clay's **corrupt bargain.** Clay's supporters, joined by several old Federalists, switched to Adams, giving him a one-vote victory. Soon after becoming president, Adams appointed Henry Clay as his secretary of state.

Reaction to the alleged "corrupt bargain" between John Quincy Adams and Henry Clay dominated the Adams administration. Before the vote took place in the House of Representatives, Andrew Jackson remarked, "Rumors say that deep

corrupt bargain *Following the election of 1824, Andrew Jackson and his supporters alleged that, in a "corrupt bargain," Henry Clay sold his support during the House vote in the disputed election of 1824 to John Quincy Adams in exchange for appointment as Secretary of State.*

intrigue is on foot" and predicted that there would be "bargain & sale" of the presidency. After the election, Jackson declared that the "gamester" Henry Clay had subverted the democratic will to his own purposes and that "the rights of the people have been bartered for promises of office." Others in Washington were equally appalled. Robert Y. Hayne of South Carolina denounced the "monstrous union between Clay & Adams," while Louis McLane of Delaware declared the coalition of Clay and Adams utterly "unnatural & preposterous."

JACKSONIAN MELODRAMA

Like hundreds of thousands of other Americans, Jackson sensed that something had gone wrong with the republic, that selfishness and intrigue had corrupted the government. In the language of revolutionary republicanism, a corrupt power once again threatened to snuff out liberty. Unlike most of his revolutionary forebears, however, Jackson believed that government should be subject to the will of popular majorities. An aroused public, he said, was the republic's best hope: "My fervent prayers are that our republican government may be perpetual, and the people alone by their virtue, and independent exercise of their free suffrage can make it perpetual."

Jackson claimed that the Panic of 1819 had been brought on by corruption in the Bank of the United States. The national debt was another source of corruption; it must be paid off and never allowed to recur. The federal government under James Monroe was filled with swindlers, and in the name of a vague nationalism they were taking power for themselves and scheming against the liberties of the people. Politicians had been bought off, said Jackson, and had attempted—through "King Caucus"—to select a president by backstairs deals. Finally, in 1825, they had stolen the presidency outright.

More completely than any of his rivals, Jackson had captured the rhetoric of the revolutionary republic. And with his fixation on secrecy, corruption, and intrigues, he transformed both that rhetoric and his own biography into popular melodrama. Finally, with a political alchemy that his rivals never understood, Jackson submerged old notions of republican citizenship into a firm faith in majoritarian democracy: Individuals might become selfish and corrupt, he believed, but a democratic majority was, by its very nature, opposed to corruption and governmental excess. Thus the republic was safe only when governed by the will of the majority.

ADAMS VERSUS JACKSON

While Jackson plotted revenge, John Quincy Adams assumed the duties of the presidency. He was well prepared. The son of a Federalist president, he had been an extraordinarily successful secretary of state under James Monroe.

NATIONALISM IN AN INTERNATIONAL ARENA

In the Rush-Bagot Treaty of 1817 and the British-American Convention of 1818 Secretary of State John Quincy Adams helped pacify the Great Lakes, restore American fishing rights off of Canada, and draw the U.S.-Canadian boundary west to the Rocky Mountains. He pacified the southern border as well. In 1819, the Adams-Onis Treaty procured Florida for the United States and defined the U.S.-Spanish border west of the Mississippi in ways that gave the Americans claims to the Pacific Coast in the Northwest.

Trickier problems had arisen when Spanish colonies in the Americas declared their independence. Spain could not prevent this, and the powers of Europe, victorious over Napoleon and determined to roll back the republican revolution, talked openly of helping the Spanish or of annexing South American territory for themselves. The Americans and the British opposed such a move, and the British proposed a joint statement outlawing the interference of any outside power (including themselves) in Latin America, but Adams wanted the United States to make its own policy. In 1823 he proposed what became known as the **Monroe Doctrine.** It declared American opposition to any European attempt at New World colonization without (as the British had wanted) denying the right of the United States to annex new territory. The British navy, and not the Monroe Doctrine, kept Europe out of the Americas. At the same time, Adams announced the American intention to become the preeminent power in the Western Hemisphere.

NATIONALISM AT HOME

As president, Adams tried to translate his fervent nationalism into domestic policy. In his first annual message to Congress, Adams outlined an ambitious program for national development under the auspices of the federal government: roads, canals, a national university, a national astronomical observatory ("lighthouses of the skies"), and other costly initiatives:

> The spirit of improvement is abroad upon the earth, . . . While foreign nations less blessed with . . . freedom . . . than ourselves are advancing with gigantic strides in the career of public improvement, were we to slumber in indolence or fold up our arms and proclaim to the world that we are palsied by the will of our constituents, would it not . . . doom ourselves to perpetual inferiority?

Congressmen could not believe their ears. Adams had received only one in three votes and had entered office accused of intrigues against the democratic will, and now he told Congress to pass an ambitious program and not to be "palsied" by the will of the electorate. Even congressmen who favored Adams's program (and there were many of them) were afraid to vote for it. Hostile politicians and journalists never tired of joking about Adams's "lighthouses to the skies." More lasting, however, was the connection they drew between federal public works projects and high taxes, intrusive government, the denial of democratic majorities, and expanded opportunities for corruption. Congress never acted on the president's proposals, and the Adams administration emerged as little more than a long prelude to the election of 1828.

THE BIRTH OF THE DEMOCRATIC PARTY

As early as 1825, it was clear that the election of 1828 would pit Adams against Andrew Jackson. To the consternation of his chief supporters, Adams did nothing to prepare for the contest. He refused to remove even his noisiest enemies from appointive office, and he built no political organization. The opposition was much more active. Van Buren and like-minded Republicans (with their candidate Crawford hopelessly incapacitated) switched their allegiance to Jackson. They wanted Jackson elected, however, not only as a popular hero but also as head of a disciplined and committed Democratic Party that would continue the states'-rights, limited-government positions of the old Jeffersonian Republicans.

Monroe Doctrine *Foreign policy doctrine proposed by Secretary of State John Quincy Adams in 1823 that denied the right of European powers to establish new colonies in the Americas while maintaining the United States' right to annex new territory.*

QUICK   REVIEW

JACKSONIANS' SOUTHERN STRATEGY

- Argued that the Union was perpetual and would be defended by force

- Believed that states should govern within their own borders

- Created a national voting coalition along party lines, rather than sectional lines

The new Democratic Party linked popular democracy with the defense of southern slavery. Van Buren began preparations for 1828 with a visit to John C. Calhoun of South Carolina. Calhoun was moving along the road from postwar nationalism to states'-rights conservatism; he also wanted to stay on as vice president and thus keep his presidential hopes alive. After convincing Calhoun to support Jackson and to endorse limited government, Van Buren wrote to Thomas Ritchie, editor of the *Richmond Enquirer* and leader of Virginia's Republicans, who could deliver Crawford's southern supporters to Jackson. In his letter, Van Buren proposed to revive the alliance of "the planters of the South and the plain Republicans of the North" that had won Jefferson the presidency. A new Democratic Party, committed to an agrarian program of states' rights and minimal government and dependent on the votes of both slaveholding and nonslaveholding states, would ensure democracy, the continuation of slavery, and the preservation of the Union.

THE ELECTION OF 1828

The presidential campaign of 1828 was an exercise in slander. Jacksonians hammered away at the "corrupt bargain" of 1825, while the Adams forces attacked Jackson's character. A newspaper circulated the rumor that Jackson was a bastard and that his mother was a prostitute, but the worst slander of the campaign centered on Andrew Jackson's marriage. In 1790 Jackson had married Rachel Donelson, who was estranged but not formally divorced from a man named Robards. Branding the marriage an "abduction," the Adams team screamed that Jackson had "torn from a husband the wife of his bosom," and had lived with her in a state of "open and notorious lewdness."

The Adams strategy backfired. Many voters agreed that Jackson's "passionate" and "lawless" nature disqualified him for the presidency. But many others criticized Adams for permitting Jackson's private life to become a public issue. Whatever the legality of their marriage, Andrew and Rachel Jackson had lived as models of marital fidelity for nearly 40 years; their neighbors had long ago forgiven whatever transgressions they may have committed. On the one hand, Jackson's supporters accused the Adams campaign of violating privacy and honor. On the other, they defended Jackson's marriage as a triumph of what was right and just over what was narrowly legal. The attempt to brand Jackson as a lawless man, in fact, enhanced his image as a melodramatic hero who battled unscrupulous, legalistic enemies by drawing on his natural nobility and force of will.

The campaign caught the public imagination. Voter turnout was double what it had been in 1824, totaling 56.3 percent. Jackson won with 56 percent of the popular vote and a margin of 178 to 83 in electoral votes. It was a clear triumph of democracy over genteel statesmanship, of limited government over expansive nationalism. Just as clearly, it was a victory of popular melodrama over old forms of cultural gentility.

A PEOPLE'S INAUGURATION

Newspapers estimated that from 15,000 to 20,000 citizens came to Washington to witness Jackson's inauguration on March 4, 1829. They were "like the inundation of the northern barbarians into Rome," remarked Senator Daniel Webster. As politicians watched uneasily, the crowd filled the open spaces and the streets near the Capitol Building, where Jackson was to deliver his inaugural address.

Jackson arrived at the Capitol in deep mourning. In December his wife Rachel read the accusations that had been made against her and fainted on the spot. Al-

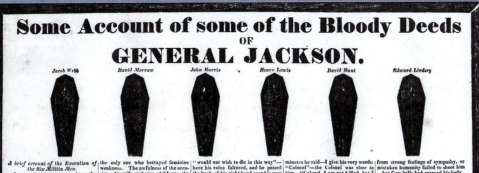

THE COFFIN HAND BILL. *During the War of 1812 General Jackson had ordered the execution of six militiamen as deserters. In the presidential campaign of 1828 Jackson's opponents distributed this handbill, accompanied by the argument that such a headstrong and vindictive man should not be president. The handbill became a symbol of the personal and violent nature of the campaign.*

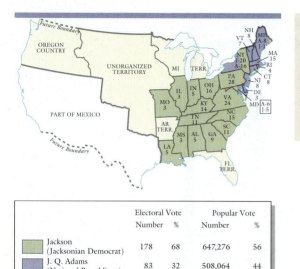

Map 12.2
PRESIDENTIAL ELECTION, 1828. *The 1828 presidential contest was a clear result of the organizing efforts that were building a national Democratic Party under the name of Andrew Jackson. Jackson picked up all of the states that had gone for Crawford or Clay in 1824, leaving only New England and small portions of the mid-Atlantic for John Quincy Adams.*

	Electoral Vote		Popular Vote	
	Number	%	Number	%
Jackson (Jacksonian Democrat)	178	68	647,276	56
J. Q. Adams (National Republican)	83	32	508,064	44

though she had been in poor health, no one would ever convince Jackson that her death in January had not been caused by his political enemies.

Jackson's inaugural address was vague. He promised "proper respect" for states' rights and a "spirit of equity, caution, and compromise" on the question of the tariff. He promised to reform the civil service, and he vowed to retire the national debt. Beyond that, he said very little, though he took every opportunity to flatter the popular majority. He had been elected "by the choice of a free people," and he pledged "the zealous dedication of my humble abilities to their service and their good." He finished by reminding Americans that a benign providence looked over them.

The new president traveled slowly from the Capitol to the White House, with the throng following and growing noisier along the way. The crowd followed him into the White House, where refreshments had been provided. Soon Jackson's well-wishers were ranging through the mansion, muddying the carpets, tipping things over, breaking dishes, and standing in dirty boots on upholstered chairs. Jackson retreated to avoid being crushed, while his staff lured the crowd outside by moving the punch bowls and liquor to the lawn.

THE SPOILS SYSTEM

Martin Van Buren, who had mobilized much of the support Jackson gained between 1824 and 1828, was the new secretary of state—positioned to succeed Jackson as president—and Jackson's most valued adviser. Other appointments were less promis-

THE PRESIDENT'S LEVEE. Robert Cruikshank drew Jackson's inaugural reception with men and women of all classes, children, dogs, and bucking horses celebrating the Old General's victory. Cruikshank subtitled his lithograph All Creation Going to the White House.

White House Collection

ing, for Jackson filled cabinet posts with old friends and political supporters who sometimes proved unfit for their jobs. The same was true in other areas of the civil service. Early in the administration, opponents complained that Jackson was replacing able, educated public servants with some dubious appointments. They soon had convincing evidence: Samuel Swarthout, whom Jackson had appointed collector of the Port of New York, stole $1.2 million and took off for Europe.

Actually, much of the furor over Jackson's **spoils system** was misdirected. All he wanted to do, Jackson claimed, was to get rid of officeholders who expected to hold lifetime appointments. Arguing that most government jobs could be performed by any honest, reasonably intelligent citizen, Jackson proposed ending the long tenures that, he said, turned the civil service into "support of the few at the expense of the many." Jackson removed about 1 in 10 executive appointees during his eight years in office, and his replacements were as wealthy and well educated as their predecessors. They were, however, *political* appointees. Acting on his own need for personal loyalty and on the advice of Van Buren, Jackson filled vacancies with Democrats who had worked for his election.

Van Buren knew the political value of patronage, and it was one of his henchmen who coined the phrase "To the victor belongs the spoils." In resorting to patronage to build the party, however, Jackson gave his opponents an important issue. Revolutionary republicans feared a government of lackeys dependent on a powerful executive, and congressional opponents argued that Jackson was using appointments to "convert the entire body of those in office into corrupt and supple instruments of power."

spoils system *System by which the victorious political party rewarded its supporters with government jobs.*

Jacksonian Democracy and the South

In 1828 Jackson ran strongly in every region but New England. The base of his support was in the South, where he won 8 of every 10 votes. Southerners were wary of an activist government controlled by a northern majority. They looked to Jackson as a Tennessee planter and republican fundamentalist. But although Jackson looked after southern interests, there was disagreement within the administration on how to protect the South. Vice President Calhoun believed that states had the right to veto federal legislation and even in extreme cases to secede from the Union. Secretary of State Van Buren insisted that the Union was inviolable and that the South's best safeguard was in a political party committed to states' rights within the Union. The differences were fought out in the contest between Calhoun and Van Buren for the right to succeed Jackson as president.

FOCUS QUESTION
At the national level, how did Jacksonian Democrats and their rivals deal with widening differences between North and South during these years?

SOUTHERNERS AND INDIANS

When Jackson entered office, a final crisis between frontier whites and the native people of the Southwest was under way. By the 1820s few Native Americans remained east of the Appalachians in the North. The Iroquois of New York were penned into tiny reservations, and the tribes of the Old Northwest were broken and scattered. But in the Old Southwest 60,000 Cherokees, Creeks, Choctaws, Chickasaws, and Seminoles remained on their ancestral lands, with tenure guaranteed by federal treaties that (at least implicitly) recognized them as sovereign peoples. Congress had appropriated funds for schools, tools, seeds, and training to help these "Civilized Tribes" make the transition to farming. Most government officials assumed that the tribes would eventually trade their old lands and use their farming skills on new land west of the Mississippi.

Southwestern whites resented federal Indian policy as an affront to white democracy and states' rights. Farmers coveted the Indians' land, and states'-rights southerners denied the federal government's authority to make treaties or to recognize sovereign peoples within their states. Resistance centered in Georgia, where Governor George Troup brought native lands under the state's jurisdiction and then turned them over to poor whites by way of lotteries. The Cherokees pressed the issue in 1827 by declaring themselves a republic with its own constitution, government, courts, and police. At the same time, a gold discovery on their land made it even more attractive to whites. The Georgia legislature promptly declared Cherokee law null and void, extended Georgia's authority into Cherokee country, and began surveying the lands for sale. Hinting at the old connection between state sovereignty and the protection of slavery, Governor Troup warned that the federal "jurisdiction claimed over one portion of our population may very soon be asserted over *another*." Alabama and Mississippi quickly followed Georgia's lead by extending state authority over Indian lands and denying federal jurisdiction.

INDIAN REMOVAL

President Jackson agreed that the federal government could not recognize native sovereignty within a state and declared that he could not protect the Civilized Tribes from state governments. Instead, he offered to remove them to federal land west of the

TRAIL OF TEARS. *In 1838 the U.S. Army marched 18,000 Cherokee men, women, and children, along with their animals and whatever they could carry, out of their home territory and into Oklahoma. At least 4,000—most of them old or very young—died on the march.*

Mississippi, where they would be under the authority of the federal government. Congress made that offer official in the **Indian Removal Act** of 1830.

The Cherokees had taken their claims of sovereignty to court in the late 1820s. In 1830 John Marshall's Supreme Court ruled in *Cherokee Nation v. Georgia* that the Indians were not sovereign peoples but "domestic dependent nations," thus dependents of the federal government and not of the states, and somehow "nations" as well. In *Worcester v. Georgia* (1832) the court banned Georgia's extension of state law into Cherokee land. President Jackson ignored the decision, however, reportedly telling a congressman, "John Marshall has made his decision: *now let him enforce it!*" Jackson did nothing as the southwestern states encroached on the Civilized Tribes. In 1838 his successor, Martin Van Buren, sent the Army to march the 18,000 remaining Cherokee to Oklahoma. Along this "Trail of Tears," 4,000 of them died of exposure, disease, starvation, and white depredation.

Indian removal had profound political consequences. It strengthened Jackson's reputation as an enemy of the rule of law and a friend of local, "democratic" solutions; it reaffirmed the link between racism and white democracy in the South; and it announced Jackson's commitment to state sovereignty and limited federal authority.

Southerners and the Tariff

In 1828 Jacksonians in Congress wrote a tariff designed to win votes for Jackson in the upcoming presidential election. Assured of support in the South, they fished for votes in the Middle Atlantic states and in the Old Northwest by including protective levies on raw wool, flax, molasses, hemp, and distilled spirits. The new tariff pleased northern and western farmers but worried the South. Protective tariffs hurt the South by diminishing exports of cotton and other staples and by raising the price of manufactured goods. Calling the new bill a "Tariff of Abominations," southern state legislatures denounced it as "unconstitutional, unwise, unjust, unequal, and oppressive."

South Carolina took the lead in opposing the Tariff of 1828. During and after the War of 1812 South Carolina had favored the economic nationalism of the American System. But the Missouri debates and the Denmark Vesey conspiracy of 1822 (see Chapter 10) spotlighted the vulnerability of slavery. So did persistent talk of gradual emancipation in other states—at a time when South Carolina's commitment to slavery was growing stronger.

Nullification

As early as 1827 Calhoun had embraced the principle that the states could nullify federal laws. In 1828 his *Exposition and Protest* argued that the Constitution was a compact between sovereign states and that the states (not the federal courts) could decide the constitutionality of federal laws. *Exposition and Protest* anticipated the secessionist arguments of 1861: the Union was a voluntary compact between sovereign states, states were the ultimate judges of the validity of federal law, and states could break the compact if they wished.

Nullification was the strongest card held by the southern extremists, and they avoided playing it. They knew that President Jackson was a states'-rights slaveholder and assumed that Vice President Calhoun would succeed to the presidency and would protect southern interests. They were wrong on both counts. Jackson favored states'

Indian Removal Act (1830) *Legislation that offered the native peoples of the lower South the option of removal to federal lands west of the Mississippi. Those who did not take the offer were removed by force in 1838.*

nullification Beginning in the late 1820s, John C. Calhoun and others argued that the Union was a voluntary compact between sovereign states, that states were the ultimate judges of the constitutionality of federal law, that states could nullify federal laws within their borders, and that they had the right to secede from the Union.

HISTORY THROUGH FILM

*A*MISTAD (1997)

*Directed by Steven Spielberg; starring
Matthew McConnaughey, Morgan Freeman,
Anthony Hopkins, Djimon Hounsou*

In 1839 an American cruiser seized the Cuban slave ship *Amistad* off the shore of Long Island. The ship carried 41 Africans who had revolted, killed the captain and crew, and commandeered the ship—along with two Spanish slave dealers who bargained for their lives by promising to sail the ship east to Africa, then steered for North America. The Africans were imprisoned at New Haven and tried for piracy and murder in federal court. The government of Spain demanded their return, and southern leaders pressured President Van Buren for a "friendly" decision. The legal case centered on whether the Africans were Cuban slaves or kidnapped Africans. (The international slave trade was by then illegal.) The New Haven court acquitted them, the federal government appealed the case, and the Supreme Court freed them again. The Africans were returned to Sierra Leone.

The Africans spend most of the movie in a dark jail or in court, and the film centers on them and their experiences with two groups of Americans: the abolition-

Amistad (1997) tells the story of 41 Africans who stage a revolt on the slave ship carrying them to Cuba and the trial that follows.

Kabal Collection/Cooper, Andrew/Dreamworks LLC

ists who are trying to free them and the political and legal officials who want to hang them, largely to keep their own political system intact. Spielberg's abolitionists are Lewis Tappan, a black activist (Morgan Freeman), an obscure young white lawyer (Matthew McConnaughey), and, in the grand finale, congressman and former president John Quincy Adams (played wonderfully by Anthony Hopkins). In the historical case, the defense was handled by veteran abolitionists or by persons who had been working with abolitionists for a long time. Spielberg shaped this group to tell his own story, beginning with reluctant and confused reformers and politicians who, along with the audience, gradually realize the moral imperatives of the case.

In one of the film's more powerful sequences the Africans' leader, Cinque (Djimon Hounsou), through a translator, tells his story to the lawyer: his village life in Sierra Leone (the one scene filmed in bright sunlight), his capture by Africans, his transportation to the slave fort of Lomboko, the horrors of the passage on the Portuguese slaver *Tecora*, the slave market in Havana, and the bloody revolt on the *Amistad*—all of it portrayed wrenchingly on the screen. The Africans' story continues in jail, as they study pictures in a Bible and try to figure out the American legal, political, and moral system. In court, they finally cut through the mumbo jumbo by standing and chanting "Give Us Free!"

In a fictive interview on the eve of the Supreme Court case, Cinque tells Adams he is optimistic, for he has called on the spirits of his ancestors to join him in court. This moment, he says, is the whole reason for their having existed at all. Adams, whose own father had helped lead the revolution, speaks for his and Cinque's ancestors before the Supreme Court. To the prosecution's argument that the Africans are pirates and murderers and to southern arguments that slavery is a natural state, he answers that America is founded on the "self-evident truth" that the one natural state is freedom. It is a fine Hollywood courtroom speech: Adams has honored his ancestors, the justices and the audience see the moral rightness of his case, and the Africans are returned to Sierra Leone. (In a subscript, Spielberg tells us that Cinque returns to a village that had been destroyed in civil war, but the final ironic note is overwhelmed by the moral triumphalism of the rest of the movie.)

rights but only within a perpetual Union. His Indian policy was simply an acknowl-edgment of state jurisdiction over institutions within state boundaries. A tariff, on the other hand, was ultimately a matter of foreign policy, clearly within the jurisdiction of the federal government. To allow a state to veto a tariff would be to deny the legal existence of the United States.

Jackson aired his views at a program celebrating Jefferson's birthday on April 13, 1830. He listened quietly as speaker after speaker defended the extreme states'-rights position, then rose to propose an after-dinner toast: "Our Federal Union," he said in measured tones, *"It must be preserved."* Dumbstruck, the southerners looked to Cal-houn, who as vice president was to propose the second toast. Obviously shaken by Jackson's unqualified defense of the Union, Calhoun offered this toast: "The Union. Next to our liberties the most dear." They were strong words, but not as strong as the President's affirmation of the Union.

Jackson rejected nullification, but he also asked Congress to reduce the tariff rates. The resulting Tariff of 1832 lowered the rates but still affirmed the principle of pro-tectionism. That, along with Boston abolitionist William Lloyd Garrison's declaration of war on slavery in 1831, followed by Nat Turner's bloody slave uprising in Virginia that same year (see Chapter 10), led the whites of South Carolina and Georgia to in-tensify their distrust of outside authority. South Carolina called a state convention that nullified the Tariffs of 1828 and 1832.

In Washington, President Jackson raged that nullification (not to mention the right of secession that followed logically from it) was illegal. Insisting that "Disunion . . . is *treason,*" he asked Congress for a Force Bill empowering him to personally lead a federal army into South Carolina. At the same time, however, he supported the rapid reduction of tariffs. When Democratic attempts at reduction bogged down, Henry Clay, now back in the Senate, took on the tricky legislative task of rescuing his beloved protective tariff while quieting southern fears. The result was the Compromise Tariff of 1833, which by lowering tariffs over the course of sev-eral years, gave southern planters the relief they demanded while maintaining mod-erate protectionism and allowing northern manufacturers time to adjust to the lower rates. Congress also passed the Force Bill. Jackson signed both into law on March 2, 1833.

With that, the nullification crisis came to a quiet end. No other southern state joined South Carolina in nullifying the tariff. The Compromise Tariff of 1833 isolated the South Carolina nullifiers. Deprived of their issue and most of their support, they declared victory and disbanded their convention—but not before nullifying the Force Bill. Jackson overlooked that last defiant gesture, and the crisis passed.

THE "PETTICOAT WARS"

The spoils system, Indian removal, nullification, and other questions of Jackson's first term were fought out against a backdrop of gossip and angry division within Jack-son's government. The talk centered on Peggy O'Neal Timberlake, a Washington tav-ern keeper's daughter who, in January 1829, had married John Henry Eaton, Jack-son's old friend and soon to be his secretary of war. Timberlake's husband had recently committed suicide; it was rumored that her affair with Eaton was the cause. Eaton was middle-aged; his bride was 29, pretty, flirtatious, and, according to Wash-ington gossip, "frivolous, wayward, [and] passionate." Knowing that his marriage might cause trouble for the new administration, Eaton had asked for and received Jackson's blessings—and, by strong implication, his protection. The marriage of John and Peggy Eaton came at a turning point in the history of both Washington society and elite sexual mores. Until the 1820s most officeholders had left their families at home. They took lodgings at taverns and boardinghouses and lived in a bachelor world of shirtsleeves, tobacco, card-playing, and occasional liaisons with local women. But in the 1820s the boardinghouse world gave way to high society. Government officials were moving into Washington houses, and their wives presided over the round of dinner parties through which much of the government's business was done. Political wives imposed new forms of gentility and politeness upon these affairs. They also drew up the guest lists. Many of them excluded Peggy Eaton.

The exclusion of Peggy Eaton split the Jackson administration in half. Jackson himself was committed to protect her. He had met his own beloved Rachel while boarding at her father's Nashville tavern, and their marriage (and the gossip that surrounded it) was a striking parallel to the affair of John and Peggy Eaton. That, coupled with Jackson's honor-bound agreement to the Eaton marriage, ensured that he would protect the Eatons. Motivated by chivalry, personal loyalty, grief, and rage over Rachel's death, and angry disbelief that political intrigue could sully the private life of a valued friend, Jackson insisted to his cabinet that Peggy Eaton was "as chaste as a virgin!" Jackson noted that the rumors were being spread not only by politicians' wives but also by prominent clergymen and blamed the "conspiracy" on "females with clergymen at their head."

In fact, Mrs. Eaton's tormentors included most of the cabinet members as well as Jackson's own White House "family." Widowed and without children, Jackson had invited his nephew and private secretary, Andrew Jackson Donelson, along with his wife and her sister, to live in the White House. Donelson's wife, serving as official hostess, shunned Peggy Eaton. Jackson assumed that schemers had invaded and subverted his own household. Before long, his suspicions centered on Vice President Calhoun, whose wife, Floride Bonneau Calhoun, a haughty and powerful Washington matron, was a leader of the assault on Peggy Eaton. Only Secretary of State Van Buren, a widower and an eminently decent man, included the Eatons in official functions. Sensing that Jackson was losing his patience with Calhoun, Van Buren's friends showed Jackson a letter revealing that while serving in Monroe's cabinet Calhoun had favored censuring Jackson for his unauthorized invasion of Florida in 1818. An open break with Calhoun became inevitable.

THE FALL OF CALHOUN

Jackson resolved the Peggy Eaton controversy, as he would resolve nullification, in ways that favored Van Buren in his contest with Calhoun. He sent Donelson, his wife, and his sister-in-law back to Tennessee and invited his friend W. B. Lewis and his daughter to take their place. But he pointedly made Peggy Eaton the official hostess at the White House. In the spring of 1831 Van Buren offered to resign his cabinet post and engineered the resignations of nearly all other members of the cabinet, thus allowing Jackson to remake his administration without firing anyone. Many of those who left were southern supporters of Calhoun. Jackson replaced them with a mixed cabinet that included political allies of Van Buren. It was also at this time that President Jackson began to consult with an informal "Kitchen Cabinet" that included journalists Amos Kendall and Francis Preston Blair, along with Van Buren and a few others.

Van Buren's victory over Calhoun came to a quick conclusion. As part of his cabinet reorganization, Jackson appointed Van Buren minister to Great Britain. Calhoun, sitting as president of the Senate, rigged the confirmation so that he cast the deciding vote against Van Buren's appointment, a petty act that turned out to be his last exercise of national power. Jackson replaced Calhoun with Van Buren as the vice presidential candidate in 1832 and let it be known that he wanted Van Buren to succeed him as president.

PETITIONS, THE GAG RULE, AND THE SOUTHERN MAILS

Democrats promised to protect slavery with a disciplined national coalition committed to states' rights within an inviolable Union. The rise of a northern antislavery movement (see Chapter 11) challenged formulation. Middle-class evangelicals, who were emerging as the reformist core of the northern Whig Party, knew that Jacksonian Democrats wanted to keep moral issues out of politics. In 1828 and 1829, when they petitioned the government to stop movement of the mail on Sundays, Jackson had turned them down. They then petitioned the government for humane treatment of the Civilized Tribes; again, the Jackson administration had refused. The evangelicals were appalled by his defense of Peggy Eaton. Most of all, they disliked the Democrats' rigid party discipline, which in each case had kept questions of morality from shaping politics.

In the early 1830s a radical minority of evangelicals formed societies committed to the immediate abolition of slavery, and they devised ways of making the national government confront the slavery question. In 1835 abolitionists launched a "postal campaign," flooding the mail with antislavery tracts that southerners and most northerners considered incendiary. From 1836 onward, they bombarded Congress with petitions—most of them for the abolition of slavery and the slave trade in the District of Columbia (where Congress had undisputed jurisdiction), others against the interstate slave trade, slavery in the federal territories, and the admission of new slave states.

Some Jacksonians, including Jackson himself, wanted to stop the postal campaign with a federal censorship law. Calhoun and other southerners, however, wanted state censorship. Amos Kendall, who had become postmaster general in the cabinet shuffle, proposed an informal solution. Without changing the law, he would simply look the other way as local postmasters removed abolitionist materials from the mail. Almost all such materials were published in New York City and mailed from there. The New York postmaster, a loyal appointee, sifted them out of the mail and thus cut off the postal campaign at its source. The few tracts that made it to the South were destroyed by local postmasters.

The Democrats dealt similarly with antislavery petitions to Congress. Southern extremists demanded that Congress disavow its power to legislate on slavery in the District of Columbia, but Van Buren reaffirmed that Congress did have that power but should never use it. In dealing with the petitions, Congress simply voted at each session from 1836 to 1844 to **table** them without reading them, thus acknowledging that they had been received but sidestepping any debate on them. This procedure, which became known as the "gag rule," was passed by southerners with the help of most northern Democrats.

Thus the Jacksonians answered the question that had arisen with the Missouri debates: how to protect the slaveholding South within the federal Union. Whereas Calhoun and other southern radicals found the answer in nullification and other forms of state sovereignty, Jackson and the Democratic coalition insisted that the Union was inviolable and that any attempt to dissolve it would be met with force. At the same time, a Democratic Party uniting northern and southern agrarians into a states'-rights, limited-government majority could guarantee southern rights within the Union. This answer to the southern question stayed in place until the breakup of the Democratic Party on the eve of the Civil War.

table a petition or bill *Act of removing a petition or bill from consideration without debate by placing it at the end of the legislative agenda.*

JACKSONIAN DEMOCRACY AND THE MARKET REVOLUTION

FOCUS QUESTION

How did Democrats and Whigs in the national government argue questions raised by economic development?

Jacksonian Democrats assumed power at the height of the market revolution, and they spent much of the 1830s and 1840s trying to reconcile the market and the ideal of the agrarian republic. They welcomed commerce as long as it served the independence and rough equality of white men on which republican citizenship rested. But paper currency and the dependence on credit that came with the market revolution posed problems. The so-called "paper economy" separated wealth from "real work" and encouraged an unrepublican spirit of luxury and greed. Worst of all, the new paper economy required government-granted privileges that the Jacksonians branded "corruption." For the same reasons, the protective tariffs and government-sponsored roads and canals of the American System were antirepublican and unacceptable. It was the goal of the Jackson presidency to curtail government involvement in the economy, to end special privilege, and thus to rescue the republic from the "Money Power."

Jacksonians were opposed by proponents of an activist central government. The opposition wished to encourage orderly economic development through the American System. Jacksonian rhetoric about the Money Power and the Old Republic, they argued, was little more than the demagoguery of self-seeking politicians.

THE SECOND BANK OF THE UNITED STATES

The argument between Jacksonians and their detractors came to focus on the Second Bank of the United States, a mixed public-private corporation chartered by Congress in 1816 (see Chapter 9). The national government deposited its revenue in the bank, thus giving it an enormous capital base. The government deposits also included state banknotes that had been used to pay customs duties or to buy public land; the Bank of the United States had the power to demand redemption of these notes in specie (gold and silver), thus discouraging state banks from issuing inflationary notes. The bank also issued notes that served as the beginnings of a national paper currency. Thus with powers granted under its federal charter, the Bank of the United States exercised central control over the nation's monetary and credit systems.

Most businessmen valued the Bank of the United States, for it promised a stable paper currency and centralized control over the banking system. But millions of Americans resented and distrusted the national bank, citing its role in the Panic of 1819. President Jackson agreed with them. He insisted that both the bank and paper money were unconstitutional, and that the only safe republican currency was gold and silver. Above all, Jackson saw the Bank of the United States as a government-sponsored concentration of power that threatened the republic.

THE BANK WAR

The charter of the Bank of the United States ran through 1836. But Senators Henry Clay and Daniel Webster encouraged Nicholas Biddle, the bank's brilliant, aristocratic president, to apply for recharter in 1832. Clay and his friends hoped to provoke the hot-tempered Jackson into a response that could be used against him in the election.

Biddle applied for a recharter of the Bank of the United States in January 1832. Congress passed the recharter bill in early July and sent it on to the president. On July 4, Van Buren visited the White House and found Jackson sick in bed; Jackson took Van Buren's hand and said, "The bank, Mr. Van Buren, is trying to kill me. *But I will kill it!*" Jackson vetoed the bill.

Jackson's Bank Veto Message was a manifesto of Jacksonian democracy. Jackson declared that the bank was "unauthorized by the Constitution, subversive of the rights of the states, and dangerous to the liberties of the people." Its charter, Jackson complained, bestowed special privilege on the bank and its stockholders. Having made most of its loans to southerners and westerners, the bank was a huge monster that sucked resources out of the agrarian South and West and poured them into the pockets of well-connected northeastern gentlemen and their English friends. The granting of special privilege to such people (or to any others) threatened the system of equal rights that was essential in a republic. Jackson concluded with a call to civic virtue and conservative, God-centered Protestantism: "Let us firmly rely on that kind Providence which I am sure watches with peculiar care over the destinies of our Republic, and on the intelligence and wisdom of our countrymen."

Henry Clay, Nicholas Biddle, and other anti-Jacksonians had expected the veto. And the Bank Veto Message was a rambling attack that, in their opinion, demonstrated Jackson's unfitness for office. "It has all the fury of a chained panther biting the bars of its cage," said Biddle. So certain were they that the public shared their views that Clay's supporters distributed Jackson's Bank Veto Message as *anti-Jackson* propaganda during the 1832 campaign. They were wrong: most voters agreed that the republic was in danger of subversion by parasites who grew rich by manipulating credit, prices, paper money, and government bestowed privileges. Jackson portrayed himself as the protector of the old republic and a melodramatic hero contending with illegitimate, aristocratic powers. With the bank and Jackson's veto as the principal issues, Jackson won by a landslide in 1832.

Jackson began his second term determined to kill the bank before Congress could reverse his veto. The bank would operate under its old charter until 1836, but Jackson hastened its death by withdrawing government deposits as they were needed and by depositing new government revenues in state banks. By law, the decision to remove the deposits had to be made by the secretary of the treasury, and Treasury Secretary Louis McLane doubted the wisdom if not the legality of withdrawing these funds. So Jackson transferred McLane to the vacant post of secretary of state and named William J. Duane as treasury secretary. Duane, too, refused to withdraw the deposits. Jackson fired him and appointed Roger B. Taney, a close adviser who had helped write the Bank Veto Message. A loyal Democrat who hated banks as much as Jackson did, Taney withdrew the deposits. In 1835, when the old Federalist John Marshall died, Jackson rewarded Taney by making him Chief Justice of the Supreme Court.

THE BEGINNINGS OF THE WHIG PARTY

It was over deposit removal and related questions of presidential power that the opposition to the Jacksonian Democrats coalesced into the Whig Party in 1834. Jackson, argued the Whigs, had transformed him-

Map 12.3
Presidential Election, 1832. *The election of 1832 was a landslide victory for Andrew Jackson. The National Republican Henry Clay carried only his native Kentucky, along with Delaware and southern New England. A defeated and resentful South Carolina ran its own candidate. Jackson, on the other hand, won in the regions in which he had been strong in 1828 and added support in New York and northern New England.*

		Electoral Vote		Popular Vote	
		Number	%	Number	%
	Jackson (Democratic)	219	76	701,780	54
	Clay (National Republican)	49	17	484,205	38
	Wirt (Anti-Masonic)	7	2.4	100,715	8
	Floyd (Independent Democrat)	11	3.8	----------	----

BORN TO COMMAND.

OF VETO MEMORY.

HAD I BEEN CONSULTED.

KING ANDREW THE FIRST.

KING ANDREW

THE FIRST,

" *Born to Command.*"

A KING who, possessing as much power as his Gracious Brother *William IV.,* makes a worse use of it.

A KING who has placed himself above the laws, as he has shown by his contempt of our judges.

A KING who would destroy our currency, and substitute *Old Rags,* payable by no one knows who, and no one knows where, instead of *good Silver Dollars.*

A KING born to command, as he has shown himself by appointing men to office contrary to the will of the People.

A KING who, while he was feeding his favourites out of the public money, denied a pittance to the *Old Soldiers* who fought and **bled** for our independence.

A KING whose *Prime Minister* and *Heir Apparent,* was thought unfit for the office of ambassador by the people:

Shall he reign over us,

Or shall the PEOPLE RULE?

KING ANDREW. *In this widely distributed opposition cartoon, "King Andrew," with a scepter in one hand and a vetoed bill in the other, tramples on internal improvements, the Bank of the United States, and the Constitution.*

self from the limited executive described in the Constitution into "King Andrew I." This had begun with the spoils system. It had become worse when Jackson began to veto congressional legislation. Jackson used the veto often—too often, said the Whigs, when the American System was at stake. In May 1830, for instance, Jackson vetoed an attempt by Congress to buy stock in a turnpike to run from the terminus of the National Road at Louisville to Maysville, Kentucky. Jackson questioned whether such federal subsidies were constitutional. More important, however, he announced that he was determined to reduce federal expenditures in order to retire the national debt—hinting strongly that he would oppose all federal public works.

The bank veto conveyed the same message, and the withdrawal of the government deposits brought the question of "executive usurpation" to a head in 1834. Nicholas Biddle, announcing that he must clean up the affairs of the Bank of the United States before closing its doors, demanded that all its loans be repaid. His demand undermined the credit system and produced a sharp financial panic. While Congress received a well-orchestrated petition campaign to restore the deposits, Henry Clay led an effort in the Senate to censure the President, which it did in March 1834. The old National Republican coalition became the new Whig Party. They were joined by southerners who resented Jackson's treatment of the South Carolina nullifiers. But it was Jackson's war on the Bank of the United States that did the most to separate the parties. His withdrawal of the deposits chased lukewarm supporters into the opposition, while Democrats who closed ranks behind him could point to an increasingly sharp division between the Money Power and the Old Republic.

A BALANCED BUDGET

One of the reasons Jackson had removed the deposits was that he anticipated a federal surplus revenue that, if handed over to the Bank of the United States, would have made it stronger than ever. The Tariffs of 1828 and 1832 produced substantial government revenue, and Jackson's frugal administration spent very little of it. The sale of public lands was adding to the surplus. Without Jackson's removal of the deposits, a growing federal treasury would have gone into the bank and would have found its way into the hated paper economy.

Early in his administration, Jackson had favored distributing surplus revenue to the states to be used for internal improvements. But he came to distrust even that minimal federal action, fearing that redistribution would encourage Congress to keep land prices and tariff rates high. Whigs, who by now despaired of ever creating a federally subsidized, coordinated transportation system, picked up the idea of redistribution. With some help from the Democrats, they passed the Deposit Act of 1836, which increased the number of banks receiving federal deposits and distributed the federal surplus to the states to be spent on roads, canals, and schools. Jackson feared that the new deposit banks would use their power to issue mountains of new banknotes. He demanded a provision limiting their right to print banknotes. With that provision, he reluctantly signed the Deposit Act.

Jackson and many members of his administration were deeply concerned about the inflationary boom that accompanied the rapid growth of commerce, credit, roads, canals, new farms, and the other manifestations of the market revolution in the 1830s. In 1836 Jackson issued a Specie Circular, which provided that speculators could buy large parcels of public land only with silver and gold coins, while settlers could continue to buy farm-sized plots with banknotes. Henceforth, speculators would have to bring wagonloads of coins from eastern banks to frontier land offices. With this provision, Jackson hoped to curtail speculation and to reverse the flow of specie out of the South and West and into the Northeast. The Specie Circular was Jackson's final assault on the paper economy.

THE SECOND AMERICAN PARTY SYSTEM

In his farewell address in 1837 Jackson warned against a revival of the Bank of the United States and against all banks, paper money, the spirit of speculation, and the "paper system." That system encouraged greed and luxury, which were at odds with republican virtue, he said. Worse, it thrived on special privilege, creating a world in which insiders could buy and sell elections. The solution, as always, was an arcadian society of small producers, a vigilant democratic electorate, and a chaste republican government that granted no special privileges.

FOCUS QUESTION
What was peculiarly "national" about the Second Party System?

"MARTIN VAN RUIN"

Sitting beside Jackson as he delivered his farewell address was his chosen successor, Martin Van Buren. In the election of 1836 the Whigs had acknowledged that Henry Clay, the leader of their party, could not win a national election. So they ran three sectional candidates—Daniel Webster in the Northeast, the old Indian fighter William Henry Harrison in the West, and Hugh Lawson White of Tennessee, a turncoat Jacksonian, in the South. Whigs hoped to deprive Van Buren of a majority and throw the election into the Whig-controlled House of Representatives.

The strategy failed. Van Buren had engineered a national Democratic Party that could avert the dangers of sectionalism, and he questioned the patriotism of the Whig sectional candidates, asserting that "true republicans can never lend their aid and influence in creating geographical parties." That, along with his association with Jackson's popular presidency, won him the election.

Van Buren had barely taken office when the inflationary boom of the mid-1830s collapsed. Economic historians ascribe the Panic of 1837 and the ensuing depression largely to events outside the country. The Bank of England, concerned over the flow of British gold to American speculators, cut off credit to firms that did business in the United States. As a result, British demand for American cotton fell sharply, and the price of cotton dropped by half. With much of the speculative boom tied to cotton, the collapse of the economy was inevitable. In May 1837 New York banks, unable to accommodate people who demanded hard coin for their notes, suspended specie payments. Other banks followed suit, and soon banks all over the country went out

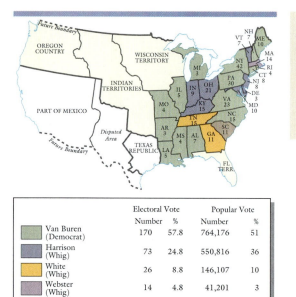

		Electoral Vote		Popular Vote	
		Number	%	Number	%
	Van Buren (Democrat)	170	57.8	764,176	51
	Harrison (Whig)	73	24.8	550,816	36
	White (Whig)	26	8.8	146,107	10
	Webster (Whig)	14	4.8	41,201	3
	Mangum (Independent Democrat)	11	3.7	----------	----

Map 12.4

PRESIDENTIAL ELECTION, 1836. *In 1836, the Whigs tried to beat the Democrats' national organization with an array of sectional candidates, hoping to throw the election into the House of Representatives. The strategy failed. Martin Van Buren, with significant support in every section of the country, defeated the three Whig candidates combined.*

of business. Although few American communities escaped the economic downturn, the commercial and export sectors of the economy suffered most. In the seaport cities, one firm after another closed its doors, and about one-third of the workforce was unemployed.

Whigs blamed the depression on Jackson's hard-money policies. With economic distress the main issue, Whigs scored huge gains in the midterm elections of 1838, castigating the president as "Martin Van Ruin." Democrats blamed the crash on speculation and Whig paper money. While Whigs demanded a new national bank, Van Buren proposed the complete divorce of government from the banking system through the "Sub-Treasury," or "Independent Treasury." Under this plan, the federal government would hold and dispense its money without depositing it in banks; it would also require that tariffs and land purchases be paid in gold and silver coins or in notes from specie-paying banks, a provision that allowed government to regulate state banknotes without resorting to a central bank. Van Buren asked Congress to set up the Independent Treasury in 1837. The Independent Treasury Bill was finally passed in 1840.

THE ELECTION OF 1840

Whigs were confident that they could blame Van Buren for the country's economic troubles and take the presidency away from him in the election of 1840. Trying to offend as few voters as possible, they passed over their best-known leaders, Senators Henry Clay and Daniel Webster, and nominated William Henry Harrison of Ohio as their presidential candidate. Harrison was the hero of the Battle of Tippecanoe (see Chapter 7) and a westerner whose Virginia origins made him palatable in the South. He was also a proven vote getter. Best of all, he was a military hero who had expressed few opinions on national issues and who had no political record to defend. As his running mate, the Whigs chose John Tyler, a states'-rights Virginian who had joined the Whigs out of hatred for Jackson. To promote this baldly pragmatic ticket, the Whigs came up with a catchy slogan: "Tippecanoe and Tyler Too."

Early in the campaign a Democratic journalist, commenting on Harrison's political inexperience and alleged unfitness for the presidency, wrote, "Give [Harrison] a barrel of hard cider, and settle a pension of two thousand a year on him, and my word for it, he will sit out the remainder of his days in his log cabin." Whigs seized on the statement and launched what was known as the "Log Cabin Campaign." The log cabin, the cider barrel, and Harrison's folksiness and heroism constituted the entire Whig campaign, while Van Buren was pictured as living in luxury at the public's expense. The Whigs conjured up an image of a nattily dressed President "Van Ruin" sitting on silk chairs and dining on gold and silver dishes while farmers and workingmen struggled to make ends meet.

Democrats howled that Whigs were peddling lies and refusing to discuss issues. But they knew they had been beaten at their own game. Harrison won only a narrow majority of the popular vote, but a landslide of 234 to 60 votes in the Electoral College.

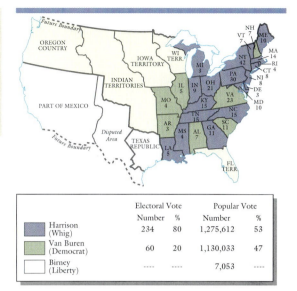

Map 12.5
PRESIDENTIAL ELECTION, 1840. *In 1840, the Whigs united under William Henry Harrison, the one Whig candidate who had won national support four years earlier. Borrowing campaign tactics from the Democrats and inventing many of their own, Whigs campaigned hard in every state. The result was a Whig victory and a truly national two-party system.*

TWO PARTIES

The election of 1840 signaled the completion of the second party system. Andrew Jackson had won in 1828 with Jefferson's old southern and western agrarian constituency; in 1832 he had carried his old voters and had won added support in the Middle Atlantic states and in northern New England. In 1836, Whigs capitalized on southern resentment of Jackson's defeat of Calhoun and nullification and on southern mistrust of the New Yorker Van Buren to break the Democratic hold on the South. The election of 1840 completed the transition: Harrison and Van Buren contested the election in nearly every state; perhaps most significantly, they received nearly equal levels of support in the slave and free states.

The election of 1840 also witnessed the high-water mark of voter turnout. Whig and Democratic organizations focused on presidential elections, and prospective voters met a quadrennial avalanche of oratory, door-to-door canvassing, torchlight parades, and party propaganda. And as the contests became national, there was no state in the Union that Democrats or Whigs could take for granted. Whigs and Democrats contested elections in nearly every neighborhood in the country, and the result was increased popular interest in politics. In 1824 about one in four adult white men had voted in the presidential election. Jackson's vengeful campaign of 1828 lifted the turnout to 56.3 percent, and it stayed at about that level in 1832 and 1836. The campaign of 1840 brought out 78 percent of the eligible voters, and the turnout remained at that high level throughout the 1840s and 1850s.

		Electoral Vote		Popular Vote	
		Number	%	Number	%
	Harrison (Whig)	234	80	1,275,612	53
	Van Buren (Democrat)	60	20	1,130,033	47
	Birney (Liberty)	----	----	7,053	----

> **QUICK REVIEW**
>
> **THE SECOND PARTY SYSTEM**
>
> - Huge voter turnouts
> - Both parties needed votes in every section
> - Both parties avoided sectional issues

C O N C L U S I O N

By 1840 American politics was conducted within a stable, national system of two parties, both of which depended on support in every section of the country. Whigs argued for the economic nationalism of the American System. Democrats argued for limited, inexpensive government. Democrats successfully fought off the American System: They dismantled the Bank of the United States, refused federal support for roads and canals, and revised the tariff in ways that mollified the export-oriented South. The result, however, was not the return to Jeffersonian agrarianism that many Democrats had wanted but an inadvertent experiment in laissez-faire capitalism. The stupendous growth of the American economy between 1830 and 1860 became a question of state and local—not national—government action. On the growing political problems surrounding slavery, the two-party system did what Van Buren had hoped it would do: Because the Whig and (especially) Democratic Parties needed both northern and southern support, they were careful to avoid discussion of sectional questions. It worked that way until the party system disintegrated on the eve of the Civil War.

QUESTIONS FOR REVIEW AND CRITICAL THINKING

Review

1. In terms of party development, what were the long-term results of the Missouri Controversy and the Panic of 1819?
2. At the national level, how did Jacksonian Democrats and their rivals deal with widening differences between North and South during these years?
3. How did Democrats and Whigs in the national government argue questions raised by economic development?
4. What was peculiarly "national" about the Second Party System?

Critical Thinking

1. Jacksonian Democrats represented themselves as a revival of Jeffersonian democracy. In what ways was that representation accurate? In what ways was it not?
2. Whigs claimed to be the party of economic progress. Yet, unlike modern "pro-growth" politicians, they demanded a powerful, interventionist national government. How did they argue that position?

Discovery

In what ways did Andrew Jackson change the presidency and politics?

SUGGESTED READINGS

Arthur M. Schlesinger, Jr., *The Age of Jackson* (1945) is a classic treatment of politics from the 1820s through the 1840s, whereas **Harry L. Watson,** *Liberty and Power: The Politics of Jacksonian America* (1990) is an excellent modern synthesis. On presidential elections, the best place to start is the essays in **Arthur M. Schlesinger, Jr., and Fred J. Israels, eds.,** *History of American Presidential Elections, 1789–1968,* 3 vols. (1971). **George Dangerfield,** *The Era of Good Feelings* (1953) and **Glover Moore,** *The Missouri Controversy, 1819–1821* (1953) are standard treatments of their subjects. On nullification, see **William W. Freehling,** *Prelude to Civil War: The Nullification Controversy in South Carolina, 1816–1836* (1965) and **Richard E. Ellis,** *The Union at Risk: Jacksonian Democracy, States' Rights and the Nullification Crisis* (1987). Two important accounts of

slavery in national politics are **William Lee Miller,** *Arguing About Slavery: The Great Battle in the United States Congress* (1996) and **Don E. Fehrenbacher,** *The Slaveholding Republic: An Account of the United States Government's Relations to Slavery* (2001). On Jackson and Indian Removal, a good introduction is **Robert V. Remini,** *Andrew Jackson and His Indian Wars* (2001). On the Bank War, see **Bray Hammond,** *Banks and Politics in America from the Revolution to the Civil War* (1957) and **Peter Temin,** *The Jacksonian Economy* (1967). The making of the party system is the subject of **Richard Hofstadter,** The Idea of a Party System: The Rise of Legitimate Opposition in the United States, 1780–1840 (1969) and **Richard P. McCormick,** *The Second American Party System: Party Formation in the Jacksonian Era* (1966).

ONLINE SOURCES GUIDE

ThomsonNOW   Visit ThomsonNOW to access primary sources, exercises, quizzes, and audio chapter summaries related to this chapter:
http://www.thomsonedu.com/login

DISCOVERY

In what ways did Andrew Jackson change the presidency and politics?

In thinking about this question, begin by breaking it down into the components shown below. A discussion of the significance of each component should appear in your answer.

POLITICS AND GEOGRAPHY

Compare the presidential election maps of 1824 and 1828. What conclusions can you draw between the victory of Andrew Jackson in 1828 and the image of Jackson's inaugural reception? Note how support for Jackson grew from one election to the next. Where was his support strongest?

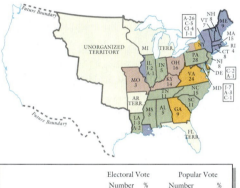

	Electoral Vote		Popular Vote	
	Number	%	Number	%
Jackson (Democratic Republican)	99	38	152,901	42
J. Q. Adams (Democratic Republican)	84	32	114,023	32
Crawford (Democratic Republican)	41	16	46,979	13
Clay (Democratic Republican)	37	14	47,217	13

PRESIDENTIAL ELECTION, 1824

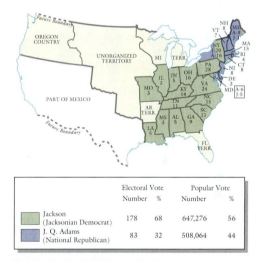

	Electoral Vote		Popular Vote	
	Number	%	Number	%
Jackson (Jacksonian Democrat)	178	68	647,276	56
J. Q. Adams (National Republican)	83	32	508,064	44

PRESIDENTIAL ELECTION, 1828

White House Collection

THE PRESIDENT'S LEVEE

GOVERNMENT AND LAW

Which groups in America disliked Jackson's policies? Look carefully at the cartoon of "King Andrew." What is the significance of the "veto" he holds on the right? Why is he shown stepping on the Constitution of the United States? Is the representation of Jackson as royalty supposed to be in support of or in opposition to him? Based on what you have read in this chapter, is this a fair portrayal? Do this cartoon and "The Coffin Hand Bill" remind you of an earlier document protesting the behavior of a king in American history?

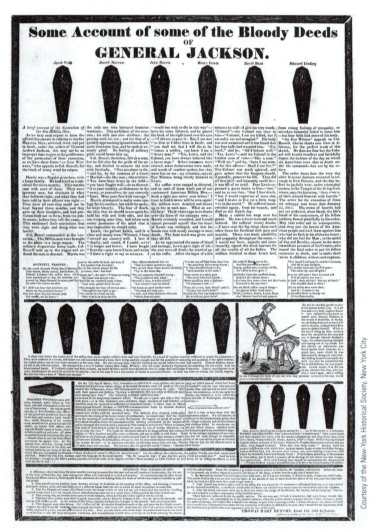

THE COFFIN HAND BILL

KING ANDREW THE FIRST.

KING ANDREW

THE FIRST,
" Born to Command."

A KING who, possessing as much power as his Gracious Brother *William IV.*, makes a worse use of it.

A KING who has placed himself above the laws, as he has shown by his contempt of our judges.

A KING who would destroy our currency, and substitute *Old Rags,* payable by no one knows who, and no one knows where, instead of *good Silver Dollars.*

A KING born to command, as he has shown himself by appointing men to office contrary to the will of the People.

A KING who, while he was feeding his favourites out of the public money, denied a pittance to the *Old Soldiers* who fought and bled for our independence.

A KING whose *Prime Minister* and *Heir Apparent,* was thought unfit for the office of ambassador by the people:

Shall he reign over us,
Or shall the PEOPLE RULE!

KING ANDREW

conquer Mexico, but it will be as the man swallows the arsenic, which brings him down in turn."

Emerson proved to be right. The poison was the reopening of the question of slavery's expansion, which had supposedly been settled by the Missouri Compromise in 1820. The admission of Texas as a huge new slave state and the possibility that more slave states might be carved out of the territory acquired from Mexico provoked northern congressmen to pass the Wilmot Proviso. Southerners bristled at this attempt to prevent the further expansion of slavery. Threats of secession and civil war poisoned the atmosphere in 1849 and 1850.

The Compromise of 1850 defused the crisis and appeared to settle the issue once again. But events would soon prove that this "compromise" had merely postponed the crisis. The fugitive slave issue and filibustering expeditions to acquire more slave territory kept sectional controversies smoldering. In 1854 the Kansas-Nebraska Act would cause them to burst into a hotter flame than ever.

QUESTIONS FOR REVIEW AND CRITICAL THINKING

Review

1. What impulses lay behind the "Manifest Destiny" of westward expansion?
2. How did westward expansion relate to the issue of slavery?
3. What were the causes and consequences of the Mexican War?
4. What issues were at stake in the congressional debates that led to the Compromise of 1850? How successfully did the Compromise resolve these issues?

Critical Thinking

1. Between 1803 and 1845 the territorial size of the United States expanded by only 5 percent (with the acquisition of Florida in 1819). Yet in the three years from 1845 to 1848 the size of the United States mushroomed by another 50 percent. How do you explain this remarkable phenomenon?
2. Why was the issue of slavery in the territories so important and controversial in the 1840s and 1850s when slavery already existed in half of the states?

Discovery

In what ways did Manifest Destiny provide opportunity but also sow the seeds of the Civil War?

SUGGESTED READINGS

For the theme of Manifest Destiny, the best introduction is **Frederick Merk**, *Manifest Destiny and Mission in American History* (1963). See also the essays in **Samuel W. Haynes and Christopher Morris, eds.,** *Manifest Destiny and Empire* (1997). Two good studies of the overland trails to California and Oregon and other points West are **John D. Unruh, Jr.,** *The Plains Across: The Overland Emigrants and the Trans-Mississippi West, 1840–1860* (1979), and **John Mack Faragher,** *Women and Men on the Overland Trail* (1978). A fine introduction to the impact of American expansion on the Indians of the West is **Philip Weeks,** *Farewell, My Nation: The American Indian and the United States 1820–1890* (rev. ed., 2000). A good study of the relationship between American expansion and the coming of war with Mexico is **David Pletcher,** *The Diplomacy of Annexation: Texas, Oregon, and the Mexican War* (1973). For the Mexican War, a good narrative is **John S. D. Eisenhower,** *So Far from God: The U.S. War with Mexico 1846–1848* (1989). Opposition to and support for the war by different elements of the public are chronicled in **John H.**

Schroeder, *Mr. Polk's War: American Opposition and Dissent, 1846–1848* (1973), and **Robert W. Johannsen,** *To the Halls of the Montezumas: The Mexican War in the American Imagination* (1985). For the conflict provoked by the issue of slavery's expansion into territory acquired from Mexico, see **David M. Potter,** *The Impending Crisis 1848–1861* (1976); **Richard H. Sewell,** *Ballots for Freedom: Antislavery Politics in the United States 1837–1860* (1976); **Michael A. Morrison,** *Slavery and the American West: The Eclipse of Manifest Destiny and the Coming of the Civil War* (1997); and **Leonard D. Richards,** *The Slave Power: The Free North and Southern Domination, 1780–1860* (2000). The best study of the Compromise of 1850 is **Holman Hamilton,** *Prologue to Conflict: The Crisis and Compromise of 1850* (1964). The passage and enforcement of the Fugitive Slave Act is the subject of **Stanley W. Campbell,** *The Slave Catchers* (1970). Still the best book on filibustering is Robert E. May, *The Southern Dream of a Caribbean Empire 1854–1861* (1971).

ONLINE SOURCES GUIDE

ThomsonNOW Visit ThomsonNOW to access primary sources, exercises, quizzes, and audio chapter summaries related to this chapter:
http://www.thomsonedu.com/login

DISCOVERY

In what ways did Manifest Destiny provide opportunity but also sow the seeds of the Civil War?

In thinking about this question, begin by breaking it down into the components shown below. A discussion of the significance of each component should appear in your answer.

GEOGRAPHY AND CULTURE

Look at the map of overland trails. Which parts of this journey do you believe would be most difficult? What kinds of problems and dangers might these groups encounter? What problems are evident in the illustration of emigrants making camp in the snow? Who is putting the camp together?

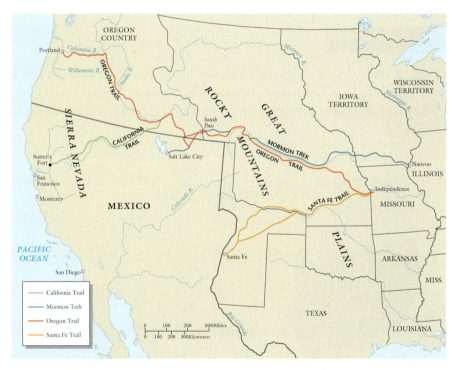

OVERLAND TRAILS, 1846

North Wind Picture Archives

EMIGRANTS MAKING CAMP IN THE SNOW

GEOGRAPHY AND POLITICS

Look at the map of free and slave states and territories. In the area acquired in the Louisiana Purchase, were there more slave states or free states? How about in the Texas Annexation and the Mexican Cession? What impact did these three large acquisitions have on the controversy over the expansion of slavery in the 1840s and 1850s?

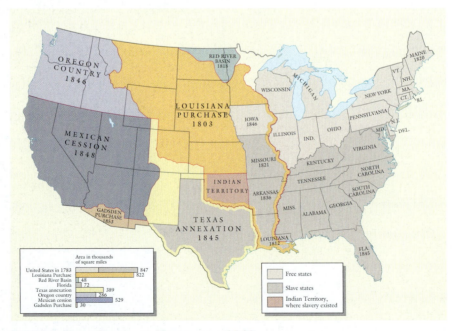

FREE AND SLAVE STATES AND TERRITORIES, 1848

Atchison raised the price once again, insisting on an explicit repeal of the Missouri Compromise. Sighing that this "will raise a hell of a storm," Douglas nevertheless agreed. He further agreed to divide the area into two territories: Kansas west of Missouri, and Nebraska west of Iowa and Minnesota. To many northerners this looked suspiciously like a scheme to mark Kansas out for slavery and Nebraska for freedom.

THE KANSAS-NEBRASKA ACT

The bill did indeed raise a hell of a storm. Douglas had failed to recognize the depth of northern opposition to the "slave power" and to the expansion of slavery. Douglas himself did not have firm moral convictions about slavery, but millions of Americans did care. They regarded the expansion of slavery as too important to be left to territorial voters. One of them was an old acquaintance of Douglas, **Abraham Lincoln**. An antislavery Whig who had served four terms in the Illinois legislature and one term in Congress, Lincoln was propelled back into politics by the shock of the Kansas-Nebraska bill. He acknowledged the constitutional right to hold slave property in the states where it already existed. But he believed slavery was "an unqualified evil to the negro, the white man, and to the state. . . . There can be no moral right in connection with one man's making a slave of another." Lincoln understood that race prejudice was a powerful obstacle to emancipation. Still, the country must face up to the problem. It must stop any further expansion of slavery as the first step on the long road to its "ultimate extinction."

Lincoln excoriated Douglas's "care not" attitude toward whether slavery was voted up or down. Lincoln branded the assertion that slavery would never be imported into Kansas anyway because of the region's unsuitable climate as a "LULLABY" argument." The climate of eastern Kansas was similar to that of the Missouri River valley in Missouri, where slaves were busily raising hemp and tobacco. Missouri slaveholders were already poised to take their slaves into the Kansas River valley.

Lincoln spoke vehemently against further expansion of slavery:

> The monstrous injustice of slavery . . . deprives our republican example of its just influence in the world—enables the enemies of free institutions, with plausibility, to taunt us as hypocrites. . . . Let us re-adopt the Declaration of Independence, and with it, the practices, and policy, which harmonize with it. . . . If we do this, we shall not only have saved the Union; but we shall have so saved it, as to make, and to keep it, forever worthy of the saving.

With this eloquent declaration, Lincoln gave voice to the feelings that fostered an uprising against the Kansas-Nebraska bill. Abolitionists, Free-Soilers, northern Whigs, and even many northern Democrats formed "anti-Nebraska" coalitions. But they could not stop passage of the bill. It cleared the Senate easily, supported by a solid South and fifteen of the twenty northern Democrats. In the House, it passed by a vote of 113 to 100.

THE DEATH OF THE WHIG PARTY

These proceedings completed the destruction of the Whigs as a national party. In 1852 the Whig Party nominated General Winfield Scott for president. Though a Virginian, Scott took a national rather than a southern view. He was the candidate of the northern Whigs in the national convention, which nominated him on the 53rd ballot after a bitter contest. A mass exodus of southern Whigs into the Democratic Party enabled Franklin Pierce to carry all but two slave states in the election. The

Kansas-Nebraska Act *Law enacted in 1854 to organize the new territories of Kansas and Nebraska that effectively repealed the provision of the 1820 Missouri Compromise by leaving the question of slavery to the territories' settlers.*

Abraham Lincoln *Illinois Whig who became the Republican Party's first successful presidential candidate in 1860 and led the Union during the Civil War.*

unanimous vote of northern Whigs in Congress against the Kansas-Nebraska bill was the final straw. The Whig Party never recovered its influence in the South.

It seemed to be on its last legs in the North as well. Antislavery Whig leaders like Seward and Lincoln hoped to channel the flood of anti-Nebraska sentiment through the Whig Party. But that was like trying to contain Niagara Falls. Free-Soilers and antislavery Democrats spurned the Whig label. Political coalitions arose under various names: Anti-Nebraska, Fusion, People's, Independent. But the name that caught on was Republican. The elections of 1854 were disastrous for northern Democrats. One-fourth of Democratic voters deserted the party. The Democrats lost control of the House of Representatives when 66 of 91 incumbent free-state Democratic congressmen went down in defeat. Combined with the increase in the number of Democratic congressmen from the South, this rout brought the party more than ever under southern domination.

But who would pick up the pieces of old parties in the North? The new Republican Party hoped to, but it suffered a shock in urban areas of the Northeast. Hostility to immigrants created a tidal wave of **nativism** that threatened to swamp the anti-Nebraska movement. Described as a "tornado," a "hurricane," and a "freak of political insanity," the anti-immigrant "**Know-Nothings**" won landslide victories in Massachusetts and Delaware, polled an estimated 40 percent of the vote in Pennsylvania, and did well elsewhere in the Northeast and border states. Who were these mysterious Know-Nothings? What did they stand for?

nativism *Hostility of native-born Americans toward immigrants.*

Know-Nothings *Adherents of nativist organizations and of the American party who wanted to restrict the political rights of immigrants.*

IMMIGRATION AND NATIVISM

FOCUS QUESTION

What were the origins of Nativism and how did this movement relate to the slavery issue?

During the early nineteenth century, immigration was less pronounced than in most other periods of U.S. history. The volume of immigration (expressed as the number of immigrants during a decade in proportion to the whole population at its beginning) was little more than 1 percent in the 1820s, increasing to 4 percent in the 1830s. Three-quarters of the newcomers were Protestants, mainly from Britain. Most of them were skilled workers, farmers, or members of white-collar occupations.

In the 1840s a combination of factors caused a sudden quadrupling in the volume of immigration and a change in its ethnic and occupational makeup. The pressure of expanding population on limited land in Germany and successive failures of the potato crop in Ireland impelled millions of German and Irish peasants to emigrate. A majority came to the United States. During the decade after 1845, 3 million immigrants entered the United States—15 percent of the total American population in 1845. Many of them, especially the Irish, joined the unskilled and semiskilled labor force in the rapidly growing eastern cities.

Most of the new arrivals were Roman Catholics. Fear of the Roman Catholic Church as autocratic and anti-republican was never far below the surface of American political culture. Several riots between Protestant and Catholic workers culminated in pitched battles and numerous deaths in Philadelphia in 1844. In several eastern cities nativist political parties sprang up in the early 1840s with the intent of curbing the political rights of immigrants.

Nativism appeared to subside with the revival of prosperity after 1844. But the decline was temporary, as the vast increase of immigration proved too much for the country to absorb. Not only were most of the new immigrants Catholics; many of them also spoke a foreign language and had alien cultural values. Older Americans perceived newer Americans as responsible for an increase of crime and poverty in the cities.

IMMIGRANTS IN POLITICS

The political power of immigrants also grew. Most of the immigrants became Democrats because that party welcomed or at least tolerated them while many Whigs did not. Foreign-born voters leaned toward the proslavery wing of the Democratic Party, even though seven-eighths of them settled in free states. Mostly working-class and poor, they supported the Democratic Party as the best means of keeping blacks in slavery and out of the North. These attitudes sparked hostility toward immigrants among many antislavery people.

The Roman Catholic hierarchy did little to allay that hostility. The leading Catholic prelate, Archbishop John Hughes of New York, attacked abolitionists, Free-Soilers, and various Protestant reform movements. In 1850, in a widely publicized address titled "The Decline of Protestantism and Its Causes," Hughes noted proudly that Catholic Church membership in the United States had grown three times faster than Protestant membership over the previous decade, and he predicted an eventual Catholic majority.

Attitudes toward immigrants had political repercussions. Two of the hottest issues in state and local politics during the early 1850s were **temperance** and schools. The temperance crusaders had grown confident and aggressive enough to go into politics. The drunkenness and rowdiness they associated with Irish immigrants became one of their particular targets. Beginning with Maine in 1851, twelve states had enacted prohibition laws by 1855. Though several of the laws were soon weakened by the courts or repealed by legislatures, they exacerbated ethnic tensions.

So did battles over public schools versus parochial schools. Catholics resented the Protestant domination of public education and the reading of the King James Bible in schools. The Church began to build **parochial schools** for the faithful, and in 1852 the first Plenary Council of American bishops decided to seek tax support for these schools or tax relief for Catholic parents who sent their children to them. This effort set off heated election contests in numerous northern cities and states. "Free school" tickets generally won by promising to defend public schools against the "bold effort" of this "despotic faith" to "uproot the tree of Liberty."

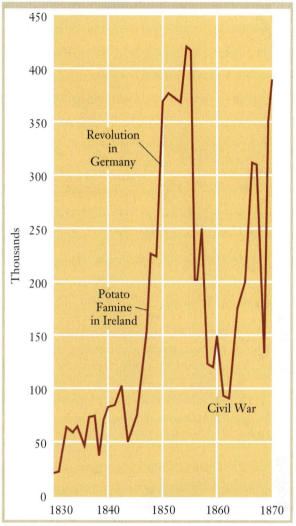

IMMIGRATION TO THE UNITED STATES

(Source: From *Division and the Stresses of Reunion 1845–1876,* by David M. Potter. Copyright © 1973 Scott, Foresman and Company. Reprinted by permission.)

THE RISE OF THE "KNOW-NOTHINGS"

It was in this context that the Know-Nothings (their formal name was the American Party) burst onto the political scene. This party was the result of the merger in 1852 of two secret fraternal societies that limited their membership to native-born Protestants: the Order of the Star-Spangled Banner and the Order of United Americans. Recruiting mainly young men in skilled blue-collar and lower white-collar occupations, the merged order had a membership of 1 million or more by 1854. The order supported temperance and opposed tax support for parochial schools. Members wanted public office restricted to native-born men and sought to lengthen the naturalization period before immigrants could become citizens. Members were pledged to secrecy about the order; if asked, they were to reply "I know nothing."

temperance *Movement that supported abstaining from alcoholic beverages.*

parochial schools *Schools associated with a church, usually Roman Catholic. The funding of these schools became a major political issue in the 1850s.*

MUSICAL LINK TO THE PAST

THE WALTZ—AN IMMORAL DANCE?

Composer: G. Jullien
Title: "Prima Donna Waltz" (c. late 1850s)

As tame and old-fashioned as the waltz may sound to modern ears, for many 19th-century observers, its arrival represented an alarming and morally dangerous development in American life. It did away with the niceties and social introductions of country dances, minuets, gavottes, and other dances championed previously in the American past. Those dances kept young people at a socially acceptable distance, constantly switching partners, never allowing a couple to concentrate on each other for an extended time. But couples who engaged in waltzing gripped each other in close embrace, intently gazed in each other's eyes at shockingly close range, and refused to share their partners or acknowledge other dancers on the floor. Worse yet, as reported by music historian Thornton Hagert, "The hypnotic effect of the unrelenting and mechanical turning, turning of the early waltz was thought to summon up uncontrollable passions that would surely lead to ridicule or even dishonor, disease and pregnancy." Despite numerous warnings of pernicious influence, waltz tempos steadily increased as the 19th century ambled forward, which presumably made dancers even

dizzier and further clouded their personal judgment and morality. In addition, waltz steps were simplified as time went on, allowing more young people to participate in the waltz fad with little training.

The torrent of controversy surrounding the waltz presaged similar outcries against future American dance crazes such as the ragtime-influenced turkey trot of the 1910s, the jazz-inflected Charleston of the 1920s, the acrobatic lindy hop of the big band era, and the anarchic mosh-pit chaos of the 1970s punk rock scene. American youth have often seized music as an outlet and excuse to exhibit and play out emotions and feelings normally excluded from public view, to the chagrin of some of their elders. Musical expression by the American youth of the mid-20th century often featured distorted and screeching electric guitars, but such contraptions and the music they accompanied were probably no more threatening to American parents of the 1950s than the graceful bugle-led strains of the "Prima Donna Waltz" were for American parents of the 1850s.

1. Why do you think popular dances became simpler and less formal as the 19th century unfolded?
2. What do you think such cultural changes said about the character of the maturing United States?

Listen to an audio recording of this music on the *Musical Links to the Past* CD.

This was the tornado that swept through the Northeast in the 1854 elections. Although the American Party drew voters from both major parties, it cut more heavily into the Whig constituency. Many northern Whigs who had not already gone over to the Republicans flocked to the Know-Nothings.

When the dust of the 1854 elections settled, it was clear that those who opposed the Democrats would control the next House of Representatives. But who would control the opposition—antislavery Republicans or nativist Americans? In truth, some northern voters and the congressmen they elected adhered to both political faiths. In New England, several Know-Nothing leaders were actually Republicans in disguise who had jumped on the nativist bandwagon with the intention of steering it in an antislavery direction.

bigotry *Intolerance based on religious beliefs or ethnic or racial differences.*

But many Republicans warned against flirting with **bigotry**. "How can any one who abhors the oppression of negroes, be in favor of degrading classes of white people?" asked Abraham Lincoln in a letter to a friend.

As a nation, we began by declaring that *"all men are created equal."* We now practically read it "all men are created equal, *except negroes.*" When the Know Nothings get control, it will read "all men are created equal, except negroes, *and foreigners, and catholics."* When it comes to this I should prefer emigrating to some country where they make no pretense of loving liberty.

Other Republicans echoed Lincoln. Since "we are against Black Slavery, because the slaves are deprived of human rights," they declared, "we are also against . . . [this] system of Northern Slavery to be created by disfranchising the Irish and Germans."

The Decline of Nativism

In 1855 Republican leaders maneuvered skillfully to divert the energies of northern Know-Nothings from their crusade against Catholicism to a crusade against the slave power. Two developments helped them. The first was turmoil in Kansas, which convinced many northerners that the slave power was a greater threat than the pope. The second was an increase in nativist sentiment in the South. The American Party won elections in Maryland, Kentucky, and Tennessee and polled at least 45 percent of the votes in five other southern states. Violence in several southern cities with large immigrant populations preceded or accompanied these elections, evidencing a significant streak of nativism in the South.

These developments had important implications at the national level. Southern Know-Nothings were proslavery, while many of their Yankee counterparts were antislavery. Just as the national Whig Party had foundered on the slavery issue, so did the American Party during 1855 and 1856. At the party's first national council in June 1855, most of the northern delegates walked out when southerners and northern conservatives joined forces to pass a resolution endorsing the Kansas-Nebraska Act. A similar scene occurred at an American Party convention in 1856. By that time, most northern members of the party had, in effect, become Republicans. At the convening of the House of Representatives in December 1855, a protracted fight for the speakership took place. The Republican candidate was Nathaniel P. Banks of Massachusetts, a former Know-Nothing who now considered himself a Republican. Banks finally won on the 133rd ballot with the support of about thirty Know-Nothings who thereby declared themselves Republicans.

By that time, nativism had faded. The volume of immigration suddenly dropped by more than half in 1855 and stayed low for the next several years. Ethnic tensions eased, and cultural issues like temperance and schools also seemed to recede. The real conflict turned out to be not the struggle between native and immigrant, or between Protestant and Catholic, but between North and South over the extension of slavery. That was the conflict that led to civil war—and the war seemed already to have begun in the territory of Kansas.

Bleeding Kansas

When it became clear that southerners had enough votes to pass the Kansas-Nebraska Act, William H. Seward told his southern colleagues: "Since there is no escaping your challenge, I accept it in behalf of the cause of freedom. We will engage in competition for the virgin soil of Kansas, and God give victory to the side which is stronger in numbers as it is in right." Senator David Atchison of Missouri wrote: "We are playing for

FREE-STATE MEN READY TO DEFEND LAWRENCE, KANSAS, IN 1856 *After proslavery forces sacked the free-state capital of Lawrence in 1856, northern settlers decided they needed more firepower to defend themselves. Somehow they got hold of a six-pound howitzer. This cannon did not fire a shot in anger during the Kansas troubles, but its existence may have deterred the "border ruffians."*

a mighty stake. If we win we carry slavery to the Pacific Ocean; if we fail we lose Missouri, Arkansas, Texas and all the territories; the game must be played boldly."

Atchison did play boldly. At first, Missouri settlers in Kansas posted the stronger numbers. But as the year 1854 progressed, settlers from the North came pouring in and the scramble for the best lands in Kansas intensified. Alarmed by the growing numbers of northern settlers, bands of Missourians, labeled **border ruffians** by the Republican press, rode into Kansas prepared to vote as many times as necessary to install a proslavery government. In the fall of 1854 they cast at least seventeen hundred illegal ballots and sent a proslavery territorial delegate to Congress. When the time came for the election of a territorial legislature the following spring, Atchison led a contingent of border ruffians to Kansas for the election. "There are eleven hundred coming over from Platte County to vote," he told his followers, "and if that ain't enough, we can send five thousand."

His count was accurate. Five thousand was about the number who came and voted illegally to elect a proslavery territorial legislature. The territorial governor pleaded with President Pierce to nullify the election. But Pierce listened to Atchison and fired the governor. Meanwhile, the new territorial legislature legalized slavery and adopted a slave code that even authorized the death penalty for helping a slave to escape.

The "free state" party, outraged by these proceedings, had no intention of obeying laws enacted by this "bogus legislature." By the fall of 1855 they constituted a majority of legitimate settlers in Kansas. So they called a convention, adopted a free-state constitution, and elected their own legislature and governor. By January 1856 two territorial governments in Kansas stood with their hands at each other's throat.

Kansas now became the leading issue in national politics. The Democratic Senate and President Pierce recognized the proslavery legislature in Lecompton, while the Republican House recognized the antislavery legislature in Lawrence. Southerners saw the struggle as crucial to their future. "The admission of Kansas into the Union

border ruffians *Term used to describe proslavery Missourians who streamed into Kansas in 1854, determined to vote as many times as necessary to install a proslavery government there.*

as a slave state is now a point of honor," wrote Congressman Preston Brooks of South Carolina. "The fate of the South is to be decided with the Kansas issue." On the other side, Charles Sumner of Massachusetts gave a well-publicized speech in the Senate on May 19 and 20. "Murderous robbers from Missouri," he charged, "from the drunken spew and vomit of an uneasy civilization" had committed the "rape of a virgin territory, compelling it to the hateful embrace of slavery." Among the southern senators Sumner singled out for special condemnation and ridicule was Andrew Butler of South Carolina, a cousin of Congressman Brooks. He accused Butler of having "chosen a mistress to whom he has made his vows . . . the harlot, Slavery."

THE CANING OF SUMNER

Sumner's speech incensed southerners, none more than Preston Brooks, who decided to avenge his cousin. Two days after the speech, Brooks walked into the Senate chamber and began beating Sumner with a heavy cane. His legs trapped beneath the desk bolted to the floor, Sumner wrenched it loose as he stood up to try to defend himself, whereupon Brooks clubbed him so ferociously that Sumner slumped forward, bloody and unconscious.

News of the incident sent a thrill of pride through the South and a rush of rage through the North. Brooks resigned from Congress after censure by the House and was unanimously reelected. From all over the South came gifts of new canes, some inscribed with such mottoes as "Hit Him Again."

But, in the North, the Republicans gained thousands of voters as a result of the affair. It seemed to prove their contentions about "the barbarism of slavery." A veteran New York politician reported that he had "never before seen anything at all like the present state of deep, determined, & desperate feelings of hatred, & hostility to the further extension of slavery, & its political power."

At about the same time, an "army" of proslavery Missourians, complete with artillery, marched on the free-state capital of Lawrence, Kansas. On May 21 they shelled and sacked the town, burning several buildings. A rival force of free-state men arrived too late to intercept them. One of the free-state "captains" was **John Brown**, an abolitionist zealot who considered himself anointed by the Lord to avenge the sins of slaveholders. When he learned of the sack of Lawrence, he declared that "Something must be done to show these barbarians that we, too, have rights." Leading four of his sons and three other men to a proslavery settlement at Pottawatomie Creek on the night of May 24–25, 1856, Brown dragged five men from their cabins and split open their heads with broadswords.

Brown's murderous act set off a veritable civil war in Kansas. Not until President Pierce sent a tough new territorial governor and thirteen hundred federal troops to Kansas in September 1856 did the violence subside—just in time to save the Democrats from possible defeat in the presidential election.

John Brown *Prominent abolitionist who fought for the antislavery cause in Kansas (1856) and led a raid to seize the Harpers Ferry arsenal in 1859.*

THE ELECTION OF 1856

By 1856 the Republicans had become the largest party in the North. They were also the first truly sectional party in American history, for they had little prospect of carrying a single county in the slave states. At their first national convention, the Republicans wrote a platform that focused mainly on slavery but also incorporated the old Whig program of federal aid to internal improvements, including a railroad to

California. For its presidential nominee, the party turned to John C. Frémont. This "Pathfinder of the West" had a dashing image as an explorer. With little political experience, he had few political enemies. The Democrats chose as their candidate James Buchanan, a veteran of thirty years in various public offices. The Democratic platform endorsed popular sovereignty and condemned the Republicans as a "sectional party" that incited "treason and armed resistance in the Territories."

This would be a three-party election, for the American Party was still in the field. It nominated ex-Whig Millard Fillmore. The three-party campaign developed into a pair

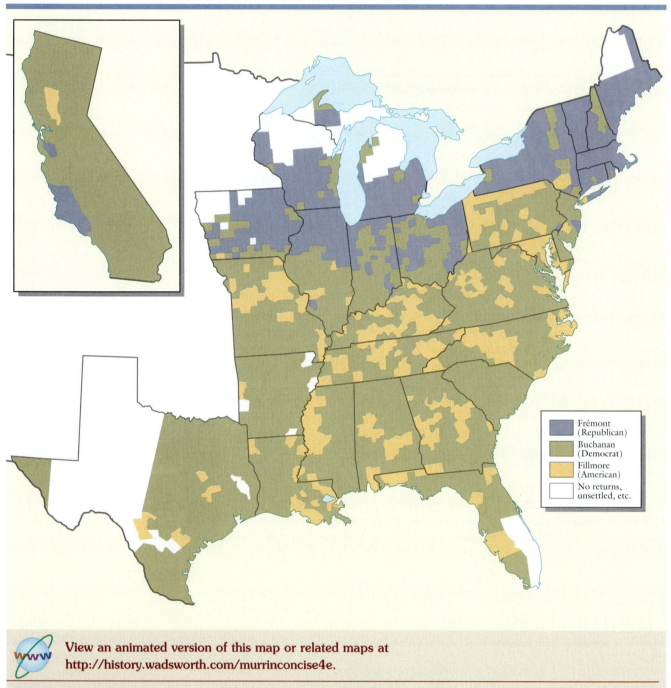

Frémont (Republican)

Buchanan (Democrat)

Fillmore (American)

No returns, unsettled, etc.

View an animated version of this map or related maps at
http://history.wadsworth.com/murrinconcise4e.

Map 14.1

COUNTIES CARRIED BY CANDIDATES IN THE 1856 PRESIDENTIAL ELECTION. *This map illustrates the sharp geographical division of the vote in 1856. The pattern of Republican counties coincided almost exactly with New England and the portions of other states settled by New England migrants during the two preceding generations.*

POPULAR AND ELECTORAL VOTES IN THE 1856 PRESIDENTIAL ELECTION

CANDIDATE	FREE STATES POPULAR	ELECTORAL	SLAVE STATES POPULAR	ELECTORAL	TOTAL POPULAR	ELECTORAL
Buchanan (Democrat)	1,227,000	62	607,000	112	1,833,000	174
Frémont (Republican)	1,338,000	114	0	0	1,338,000	114
Fillmore (American)	396,000	0	476,000	8	872,000	8

of two-party contests: Democrats versus Americans in the South, Democrats versus Republicans in the North. Fillmore, despite receiving 44 percent of the popular vote in the South, carried only Maryland. Considering Buchanan colorless but safe, the rest of the South gave him three-fourths of the electoral votes he needed for victory.

The real excitement was in the North. For many Republicans the campaign was a moral cause. Republican "Wide Awake" clubs marched in torchlight parades chanting "Free Soil, Free Speech, Free Men, Frémont!" The turnout of eligible voters in the North was a remarkable 83 percent. One awestruck journalist, anticipating a Republican victory, wrote that "the process now going on in the United States is a *Revolution.*"

Not quite. Although the Republicans swept New England and the upper parts of New York State and the Old Northwest, the contest in the lower North was close. Buchanan needed only to carry Pennsylvania and either Indiana or Illinois to win the presidency, and the campaign focused on those states. The immigrant and working-class voters of the eastern cities and the rural voters of the lower Midwest were antiblack and anti-abolitionist in sentiment. They were ripe for Democratic propaganda that accused Republicans of favoring racial equality. "**Black Republicans**," declared an Ohio Democratic newspaper, intended to "turn loose . . . millions of negroes, to elbow you in the workshops, and compete with you in fields of honest labor."

The Republicans in these areas denied that they favored racial equality. They insisted that the main reason for keeping slavery out of the territories was to enable white farmers and workers to make a living there without competition from black labor. But their denials were in vain. Support for the Republican Party by prominent black leaders, including Frederick Douglass, convinced hundreds of thousands of voters that the "Black Republicans" were racial egalitarians.

The charge that a Republican victory would destroy the Union was more effective. Buchanan set the tone in his instructions to Democratic Party leaders: "The Black Republicans must be . . . boldly assailed as disunionists, and the charge must be re-iterated again and again." It was. And southerners helped the cause by threatening to secede if Frémont won. Fears of disruption caused many conservative ex-Whigs in the North to support Buchanan. Buchanan carried Pennsylvania, New Jersey, Indiana, Illinois, and California and won the presidency.

THE DRED SCOTT CASE

The South took the offensive at the very outset of the Buchanan administration. Its instrument was the Supreme Court, which had a majority of five justices from slave states, led by Chief Justice Roger B. Taney of Maryland. Those justices saw the **Dred Scott** case as an opportunity to settle once and for all the question of slavery in the territories.

Dred Scott was a slave whose owner, an army surgeon, had kept him at military posts in Illinois and in Wisconsin Territory for several years before taking him back to

Black Republicans *Label coined by the Democratic Party to attack the Republican Party as believers in racial equality. The Democrats used this fear to convince many whites to remain loyal to them.*

Dred Scott *Missouri slave who sued for freedom on grounds of prolonged residence in a free state and free territory; in 1857, the Supreme Court found against his case, declaring the Missouri Compromise unconstitutional.*

Missouri. After the owner's death, Scott sued for his freedom on the grounds of his prolonged stay in Wisconsin Territory, where slavery had been outlawed by the Missouri Compromise. The case worked its way up from Missouri courts through a federal circuit court to the U.S. Supreme Court.

The southern Supreme Court justices decided to declare that the Missouri Compromise ban on slavery in the territories was unconstitutional. But to avoid the appearance of a purely sectional decision, they sought the concurrence of a northern Democratic justice, Robert Grier of Pennsylvania. Having obtained Justice Grier's concurrence, Chief Justice Taney issued the Court's ruling stating that Congress did not have the power to keep slavery out of a territory, because slaves were property and the Constitution protects the right of property. Five other justices wrote concurring opinions. The two non-Democratic northern justices were vigorous **dissenters**. They cited the provision of the Constitution giving Congress power to make "all needful rules and regulations" for the territories.

Republicans denounced Taney's "jesuitical decision" as based on "gross perversion" of the Constitution. Several Republican state legislatures resolved that the ruling was "not binding in law and conscience." They probably did not mean to advocate civil disobedience. But they did look forward to the election of a Republican president who could "reconstitute" the Court and secure a reversal of the decision.

THE LECOMPTON CONSTITUTION

Instead of settling the slavery controversy, the Dred Scott decision intensified it. Meanwhile, the proslavery forces, having won legalization of slavery in the territories, moved to ensure that it would remain legal when Kansas became a state. That required deft maneuvering because legitimate antislavery settlers outnumbered proslavery settlers by more than two to one. In 1857 the proslavery legislature called for a constitutional convention at Lecompton to prepare Kansas for statehood. But because the election for delegates was rigged, Free Soil voters refused to participate in it. One-fifth of the registered voters thereupon elected convention delegates, who met at Lecompton and wrote a state constitution that made slavery legal.

Then a nagging problem arose. Buchanan had promised that the Lecompton constitution would be presented to the voters in a fair **referendum**. The problem was how to get the proslavery constitution approved given the antislavery majority of voters. The convention came up with an ingenious solution. Instead of a referendum on the whole constitution, it would allow the voters to choose between a constitution "with slavery" and one "with no slavery." But there was a catch. The constitution "with no slavery" guaranteed slave owners' "inviolable" right of property in the two hundred slaves already in Kansas and their progeny.

Free-state voters branded the referendum a farce and boycotted it. One-quarter of the eligible voters went to the polls in December 1857 and approved the constitution "with slavery." Meanwhile, in a fair election policed by federal troops, the antislavery party won control of the new territorial legislature and promptly submitted both constitutions to a referendum that was boycotted by proslavery voters. This time, 70 percent of the eligible voters went to the polls and overwhelmingly rejected both constitutions.

Which referendum would the federal government recognize? That question proved even more divisive than the Kansas-Nebraska debate 4 years earlier. President Buchanan faced a dilemma. He had promised a fair referendum. But southerners, who dominated both the Democratic Party and the administration, threatened secession if Kansas was not admitted to statehood under the Lecompton constitution "with slavery." Buchanan caved in. He sent the Lecompton constitution to Congress with a message recommending statehood.

---

dissenter *Person who disagrees openly with the majority opinion.*

referendum *Procedure that allows the electorate to decide an issue through a direct vote.*

QUICK   REVIEW

REALIGNMENT OF POLITICAL PARTIES IN THE 1850S

- Kansas-Nebraska Act repealed prohibition of slavery in territories north of 36°30'

- Destruction of Whig party and sectional split in Democratic party

- Development of "Know Nothings" (American Party), centered on anti-immigrant sentiment

- Emergence of Republican party by 1856, as the American Party faded

- Split of Democratic Party by proslavery Dred Scott decision, Lecompton constitution, and a Buchanan administration dominated by Southern Democrats

What would Stephen Douglas do? If he endorsed the Lecompton constitution, he would undoubtedly be defeated in his bid for reelection to the Senate in 1858. And he regarded the Lecompton constitution as a travesty. So he broke with the administration on the issue. He could not vote to "force this constitution down the throats of the people of Kansas," he told the Senate, "in opposition to their wishes and in violation of our pledges." The fight in Congress was long and bitter. The South and the administration had the votes they needed in the Senate and won handily there. But the Democratic majority in the House was so small that the defection of even a few northern Democrats would defeat the Lecompton constitution. At one point a wild fistfight erupted between Republicans and southern Democrats. "There were some fifty middle-aged and elderly gentlemen pitching into each other like so many Tipperary savages," wrote a bemused reporter.

When the vote was finally taken, two dozen northern Democrats defected, providing enough votes to defeat Lecompton. Both sides then accepted a compromise proposal to resubmit the constitution to Kansas voters, who decisively rejected it. This meant that while Kansas would not come in as a slave state, neither would it come in as a free state for some time yet. Nevertheless, the Lecompton debate had split the Democratic Party, leaving a legacy of undying enmity between southerners and Douglas. The election of a Republican president in 1860 was now all but assured.

The Economy in the 1850s

Beginning in the mid-1840s, the American economy enjoyed a dozen years of unprecedented growth and prosperity. Railroad construction provided employment for a large number of immigrants and spurred growth in industries that produced rails, rolling stock, and other railroad equipment. Most of the railroad construction took place in the Old Northwest, linking the region more closely to the Northeast and continuing the reorientation of transportation networks from a north-south river pattern to an east-west canal and rail pattern. This reinforced the effect of slavery in creating a self-conscious "North" and "South."

Although the Old Northwest remained predominantly agricultural, the rapid expansion of railroads there laid the basis for its industrialization. During the 1850s the growth rate of industrial output in the free states west of Pennsylvania was twice as great as the rate in the Northeast and three times as great as the rate in the South. In 1847 two companies that contributed to the rapid growth of agriculture during this era built their plants in Illinois: the McCormick reaper works at Chicago and the John Deere steel-plow works at Moline.

According to almost every statistical index available from that period, the rate of economic expansion considerably outstripped even the prodigious rate of population increase. While the number of Americans grew by 44 percent during these twelve years (1844–1856), the value of both exports and imports increased by 200 percent; the tonnage of coal mined by 270 percent; the amount of banking capital, industrial capital, and industrial output by approximately 100 percent; the value of farmland by 100 percent; and the amount of cotton, wheat, and corn harvested by about 70 percent. These advances meant a significant increase of **per capita** production and income—though the distance between rich and poor was widening, a phenomenon that has characterized all capitalist economies during stages of rapid industrial growth.

By the later 1850s the United States had forged ahead of most other countries to become the second-leading industrial producer in the world, behind only Britain. But the country was still in the early stages of industrial development, with the processing

FOCUS QUESTION

How did economic developments in the 1840s and 1850s widen the breach between North and South?

per capita *Term used to measure the wealth of a nation by dividing total income by population.*

of agricultural products and raw materials still playing the dominant role. By 1860 the four leading industries, measured by value added in manufacturing, were cotton textiles, lumber products, boots and shoes, and flour milling.

"THE AMERICAN SYSTEM OF MANUFACTURES"

The United States had pioneered in one crucial feature of modern industry: the mass production of **interchangeable parts**. High wages and a shortage of the skilled craftsmen who had traditionally fashioned guns, furniture, locks, watches, and other products had compelled American entrepreneurs to seek alternative methods. The "Yankee ingenuity" that was already world famous came up with an answer: special-purpose machine tools that would cut and shape an endless number of parts that could be fitted together with other similarly produced parts to make whole guns, locks, clocks, and sewing machines in mass quantities. These products were less elegant and less durable than products made by skilled craftsmen. But they were also less expensive and thus more widely available to the "middling classes."

Such American-made products were the hit of the first World's Fair, the Crystal Palace Exhibition at London in 1851. British manufacturers were so impressed by Yankee techniques, which they dubbed "the American system of manufactures," that they sent two commissions to the United States to study them. The British firearms industry invited Samuel Colt of Connecticut, inventor of the famous six-shooting revolver, to set up a factory in England stocked with machinery from Connecticut. In testimony before a parliamentary committee in 1854, Colt summed up the American system of manufactures in a single sentence: "There is nothing that cannot be produced by machinery," thus expressing a philosophy that would enable the United States to surpass Britain as the leading industrial nation by the 1880s.

The British industrial commissions cited the American educational system as an important reason for the country's technological proficiency. By contrast, the British workman, trained by long apprenticeship "in the trade" rather than in school, lacked "the ductility of mind and the readiness of apprehension for a new thing" and was therefore "unwilling to change the methods he has been used to."

Whether this British commission was right in its belief that American schooling encouraged the "adaptative versatility" of Yankee workers, it was certainly true that public education and literacy were more widespread in the United States than in Europe. Almost 95 percent of adults in the free states were literate in 1860, compared with 65 percent in England and 55 percent in France. Nearly all children received a few years of schooling, and most completed at least six or seven years. This improvement in education coincided with the feminization of the teaching profession, which opened up new career opportunities for young women. By the 1850s nearly three-quarters of the public school teachers in New England were women (who worked for lower salaries than male teachers).

THE SOUTHERN ECONOMY

In contrast to the North, where only 6 percent of the population could not read and write, nearly 20 percent of the free population and 90 percent of the slaves in the South were illiterate. This was one of several differences between North and South that antislavery people pointed to as evidence of the backward, repressive, and pernicious nature of a slave society.

Still, the South shared in the economy's rapid growth following recovery from the depression of 1837–1843. Cotton prices and production both doubled between 1845 and 1855. Similar increases in price and output emerged in tobacco and sugar.

interchangeable parts *Industrial technique using machine tools to cut and shape a large number of similar parts that can be fitted together with other parts to make an entire item such as a gun.*

THE COUNTRY SCHOOL *This famous painting by Winslow Homer portrays the typical one-room rural schoolhouse in which millions of American children learned the three Rs in the nineteenth century. By the 1850s, elementary school teaching was a profession increasingly dominated by women, an important change from earlier generations.*

The price of slaves also doubled during this decade. Southern crops provided three-fifths of all U.S. exports, with cotton alone supplying more than half.

But a growing number of southerners deplored the fact that the **colonial economy** of the South was so dependent on the export of agricultural products and the import of manufactured goods. The ships that carried southern cotton were owned by northern or British firms; financial and commercial services were provided mostly by Yankees or Englishmen. Around 1850, many southerners began calling for economic independence from the North. How could they obtain their "rights," they asked, if they were "financially more enslaved than our negroes"?

We must "throw off this humiliating dependence," declared James D. B. De Bow, the young champion of economic diversification in the South. In 1846 De Bow had founded a periodical, *De Bow's Review.* Proclaiming on its cover that "Commerce is King," the *Review* set out to make this slogan a southern reality. De Bow took the lead in organizing annual "commercial conventions" that met in various southern cities during the 1850s. In its early years, this movement encouraged southerners to invest in shipping lines, railroads, textile mills, and other enterprises.

Economic diversification in the South did make headway during the 1850s. The slave states quadrupled their railroad mileage, increased the amount of capital invested in manufacturing by 77 percent, and boosted their output of cotton textiles by 44 percent. But like Alice in Wonderland, the faster the South ran, the farther behind it seemed to fall—for northern industry was growing even faster. In 1860 the North had five times more industrial output per capita than the South, and it had three times the railroad capital and mileage per capita and per thousand square miles. Southerners had a larger percentage of their capital invested in land and slaves in 1860 than they had had ten years earlier. By contrast, the northern economy developed a strong

colonial economy *Economy based on the export of agricultural products and the import of manufactured goods; sometimes used to describe the dependence of the South on the North.*

manufacturing and commercial sector whose combined labor force almost equaled that of agriculture by 1860.

KING COTTON

A good many southerners preferred to keep it that way. "That the North does our trading and manufacturing mostly is true," wrote an Alabama planter in 1858. "We are willing that they should. Ours is an agricultural people, and God grant that we may continue so." In the later 1850s King Cotton reasserted its primacy over King Commerce as cotton output *and* prices continued to rise, suffusing the South in a glow of prosperity. In a speech that became famous, James Hammond of South Carolina told his fellow senators in 1858 that "the slaveholding South is now the controlling power of the world. . . . No power on earth dares to make war on cotton. Cotton *is* king."

Even the commercial conventions in the South seem to have embraced this gospel. In 1854 they merged with a parallel series of planters' conventions. By the later 1850s, one of the main goals of these conventions was to reopen the African slave trade, prohibited by law since 1808. But many southerners rejected that goal, partly on moral and partly on economic grounds. Older slave states like Virginia, which profited from the sale of slaves to the booming cotton frontier of the Deep South, objected to any goal that would lower the price of their largest export.

Nowhere in the South, said defenders of slavery, did one see such "scenes of beggary, squalid poverty, and wretchedness" as one could find in any northern city. Black slaves, they insisted, enjoyed a higher standard of living than white "wage slaves" in northern factories. Black slaves never suffered from unemployment or wage cuts; they received free medical care; they were taken care of in old age.

This argument reached its fullest development in the writings of George Fitzhugh, a Virginia farmer-lawyer whose newspaper articles were gathered into two books published in 1854 and 1857, *Sociology for the South* and *Cannibals All*. Free-labor capitalism, said Fitzhugh, was a competition in which the strong exploited and starved the weak. Slavery, by contrast, was a paternal institution that guaranteed protection of the workers. "Capital exercises a more perfect compulsion over free laborers than human masters over slaves," wrote Fitzhugh, "for free laborers must at all times work or starve, and slaves are supported whether they work or not. . . . What a glorious thing is slavery, when want, misfortune, old age, debility, and sickness overtake [the slave]."

LABOR CONDITIONS IN THE NORTH

Some northern labor leaders did complain that the "slavery" of the wage system gave "bosses" control over the hours, conditions, and compensation of labor. But the use of this wage-slavery theme declined during the prosperous 1850s. And there is no evidence that a northern workingman ever offered to change places with a southern slave. Average per capita income was about 40 percent higher in the North than in the South. Although that average masked large disparities, those disparities were no greater, and probably less, in the North than in the South.

To be sure, substantial numbers of recent immigrants, day laborers, and young single women in large northern cities lived on the edge of poverty—or slipped over

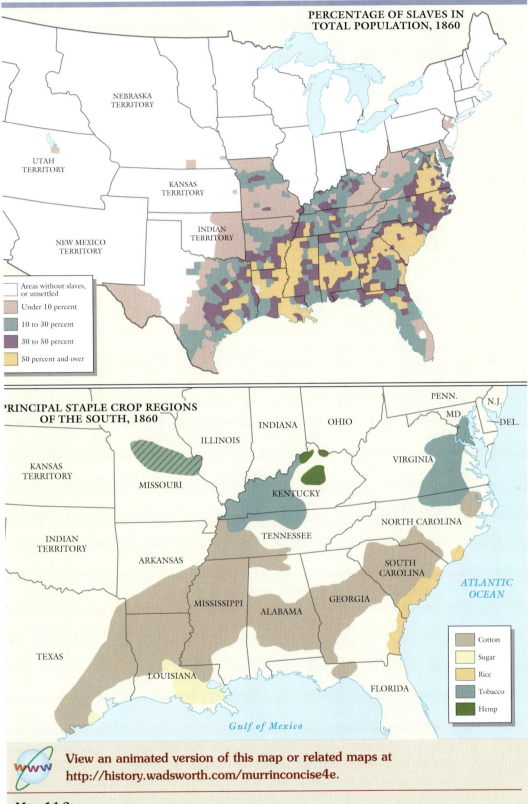

PERCENTAGE OF SLAVES IN TOTAL POPULATION, 1860

- Areas without slaves, or unsettled
- Under 10 percent
- 10 to 30 percent
- 30 to 50 percent
- 50 percent and over

PRINCIPAL STAPLE CROP REGIONS OF THE SOUTH, 1860

- Cotton
- Sugar
- Rice
- Tobacco
- Hemp

View an animated version of this map or related maps at
http://history.wadsworth.com/murrinconcise4e.

Map 14.2
SLAVERY AND STAPLE CROPS IN THE SOUTH, 1860. *Note the close correlation between the concentration of the slave population and the leading cash crops of the South. Nothing better illustrates the economic importance of slavery.*

the edge. Many women seamstresses, shoe binders, milliners, and the like, who worked sixty or seventy hours a week in the outwork system, earned less than a living wage. The widespread adoption of the newly invented sewing machine in the 1850s did nothing to make life easier for seamstresses; it only lowered their per-unit piecework wages. Many urban working-class families could not have survived on the wages of an unskilled or semiskilled father. The mother had to take in laundry, boarders, or outwork, and one or more children had to work. Much employment was seasonal or intermittent. The poverty, overcrowding, and disease in the tenement districts of large cities seemed to lend substance to proslavery claims that slaves were better off.

But they were not. Wages and opportunities for workers were greater in the North than anywhere else in the world, including the South. That was why 4 million immigrants came to the United States from 1845 to 1860 and why seven-eighths of them settled in free states. It was also why twice as many white residents of slave states migrated to free states as vice versa.

THE PANIC OF 1857

The relative prosperity of the North was interrupted by a financial panic that stemmed partly from the international economy and partly from domestic overexpansion. When the Crimean War in Europe (1854–1856) cut off Russian grain from the European market, U.S. exports mushroomed to meet the deficiency. Then they slumped in 1857 after the war ended. The sharp rise in interest rates in Britain and France, caused by the war, then spread to U.S. financial markets in 1857 and dried up sources of credit. Meanwhile, the economic boom of the preceding years had caused the American economy to overheat: Land prices had soared; railroads had built beyond the capacity of earnings to service their debts; banks had made too many risky loans.

This speculative house of cards came crashing down in September 1857. The failure of one banking house sent a wave of panic through the financial community. Banks suspended specie payments, businesses failed, railroads went bankrupt, construction halted, and factories shut down. Hundreds of thousands of workers were laid off, and others went on part-time schedules or took wage cuts. Unemployed workers in several northern cities marched in parades carrying banners demanding work or bread. On November 10 a crowd gathered in Wall Street and threatened to break into the U.S. customs house and subtreasury vaults, where $20 million was stored. Soldiers and marines had to be called out to disperse the mob.

But the country got through the winter with little violence. No one was killed in the demonstrations. Charity and public works helped tide the poor over the winter, and the panic inspired a vigorous religious revival. Spontaneous prayer meetings arose in many northern cities, bringing together bankers and seamstresses, brokers and street sweepers. Perhaps God heeded their prayers; the depression did not last long. By early 1858 banks had resumed specie payments; the stock market rebounded in the spring; factories reopened; railroad construction resumed; and by the spring of 1859 recovery was complete. The modest labor-union activities of the 1850s revived after the depression, as workers in some industries went on strike to bring wages back to pre-panic levels. In February 1860 the shoemakers of Lynn, Massachusetts, began a strike that became the largest in U.S. history up to that time, eventually involving twenty thousand workers in the New England shoe industry. Nevertheless, less than 1 percent of the labor force was unionized in 1860.

SECTIONALISM AND THE PANIC

The Panic of 1857 probably intensified sectional hostility. The South largely escaped the depression. After a brief dip, cotton and tobacco prices returned to high levels and production continued to increase: The cotton crop set new records in 1858 and 1859. Southern boasts took on added bravado. "Who can doubt, that has looked at recent events, that cotton is supreme?" asked Senator James Hammond in March 1858. "When thousands of the strongest commercial houses in the world were coming down," he told Yankees, "what brought you up? . . . We have poured in upon you one million six hundred thousand bales of cotton. . . . We have sold it for $65,000,000, and saved you."

Northerners were not grateful for their rescue. In fact, many blamed southern congressmen for blocking measures, especially higher tariffs, that would have eased the effects of the depression. They directed their arguments to workers as much as to manufacturers.

"We demand that American laborers shall be protected against the pauper labor of Europe," they declared. Tariff revision would "give employment to thousands of mechanics, artisans, laborers, who have languished for months in unwilling idleness." In each session of Congress from 1858 through 1860, however, a combination of southerners and about half of the northern Democrats blocked Republican efforts to raise tariffs.

Three other measures acquired additional significance after the Panic of 1857. Republicans supported each of them as a means to promote economic health and to aid farmers and workers. But southerners perceived all of them as aimed at helping *northern* farmers and workers and used their power to defeat them. One was a homestead act to grant 160 acres of public land to each farmer who settled and worked the land.

Southern senators defeated this bill after the House had passed it in 1859. The following year both houses passed it, but Buchanan vetoed it and southern senators blocked an effort to pass it over his veto. A similar fate befell bills for land grants to a transcontinental railroad and for building agricultural and mechanical colleges to educate farmers and workers.

> **QUICK REVIEW**
>
> **ANTEBELLUM ECONOMIC GROWTH AND DEVELOPMENT**
>
> - "American System of Manufactures" stimulated industrial growth in North
> - Dependence of Southern economy on King Cotton intensified
> - Panic of 1857 exacerbated sectional conflict
> - "Free-labor ideology" in the North emerged in the North

THE FREE-LABOR IDEOLOGY

By the later 1850s the Republican antislavery argument had become a finely honed philosophy that historians have labeled a **free-labor ideology**. It held that all work in a free society was honorable, but that slavery degraded the calling of manual labor by equating it with bondage. Slaves worked inefficiently, by compulsion; free men were stimulated to work efficiently by the desire to get ahead. Social mobility was central to the free-labor ideology. Free workers who practiced the virtues of industry, thrift, self-discipline, and sobriety could move up the ladder of success. "I am not ashamed to confess," Abraham Lincoln told a working-class audience in 1860, "that twenty-five years ago I was a hired laborer, mauling rails, at work on a flat-boat—just what might happen to any poor man's son!" But in the free states, said Lincoln, a man knows that "he can better his condition. . . . The *free* labor system opens the way for all—gives hope to all, and energy, and progress, and improvement of condition to all."

Lincoln drew too rosy a picture of northern reality, for large numbers of wage laborers in the North had little hope of advancing beyond that status. Still, he expressed a belief that was widely shared. "There is not a working boy of average ability in the New England states, at least," observed a visiting British industrialist in 1854, "who has not an idea of some mechanical invention or improvement in manufactures, by

> **FOCUS QUESTION**
> *What were the "free-labor ideology" and "herrenvolk democracy"? How did these concepts relate to the politics of the 1850s?*

> **free-labor ideology** *Belief that all work in a free society is honorable and that manual labor is degraded when it is equated with slavery or bondage.*

which, in good time, he hopes to better his condition." Americans could point to numerous examples of men who had achieved dramatic upward mobility. Belief in this "American dream" was most strongly held by Protestant farmers, skilled workers, and white-collar workers who had some real hope of getting ahead. These men tended to support the Republican Party and its goal of excluding slavery from the territories.

For slavery was the antithesis of upward mobility. Slaves could not hope to move up the ladder of success, nor could free men who lived in a society where they had to compete with slave labor. "Slavery withers and blights all it touches," insisted the Republicans. "It is a curse upon the poor, free, laboring white men." In the United States, social mobility often depended on geographic mobility. The main reason so many families moved into new territories was to get a new start, get ahead. But if slavery goes into the territories, "the free labor of all the states will not," declared a Republican editor. "If the free labor of the states goes there, the slave labor of the southern states will not, and in a few years the country will teem with an active and energetic population."

Southerners contended that free labor was prone to unrest and strikes. Of course it was, said Lincoln in a speech to a New England audience during the shoemakers' strike of 1860. *I am glad to see that a system prevails in New England under which laborers CAN strike when they want to (Cheers). . . . I like the system which lets a man quit when he wants to, and wish it might prevail everywhere (Tremendous applause)."* Strikes were one of the ways in which free workers could try to improve their prospects. "I want every man," said Lincoln, "to have the chance—and I believe a black man is entitled to it—in which he can better his condition." That was why Republicans were determined to contain the expansion of slavery, for if the South got its way in the territories "free labor that *can* strike will give way to slave labor that *cannot!*"

The Impending Crisis

From the South came a maverick voice that echoed the Republicans. Living in upcountry North Carolina, a region of small farms and few slaves, Hinton Rowan Helper had brooded for years over slavery's retarding influence on southern development. In 1857, in a book entitled *The Impending Crisis of the South,* he pictured a South mired in economic backwardness, widespread illiteracy, poverty for the masses, and great wealth for the elite. He contrasted this dismal situation with the bustling, prosperous northern economy and its near-universal literacy, neat farms, and progressive institutions. "Slavery lies at the root of all the shame, poverty, ignorance, tyranny, and imbecility of the South," he wrote. Slavery monopolized the best land, degraded all labor to the level of bond labor, denied schools to the poor, and impoverished all but "the lords of the lash." The remedy? Non-slaveholding whites must organize and use their votes to overthrow "this entire system of oligarchical despotism."

The Impending Crisis was virtually banned in the South, and few southern whites read it. But the book made a huge impact in the North. The Republican Party subsidized an abridged edition and distributed thousands of copies as campaign documents. During the late 1850s, a war of books (Helper's *Impending Crisis* versus Fitzhugh's *Cannibals All*) exacerbated sectional tensions.

Southern Non-Slaveholders

How accurate was Helper's portrayal of southern poor whites degraded by slavery and ready to revolt against it? The touchy response of many southern leaders suggested that the planters felt uneasy about that question. After all, slaveholding families constituted less than one-third of the white population in slave states, and the proportion was declining as the price of slaves continued to rise. Open hostility to the planters' domination of society and politics was evident in the mountainous and up-country regions of the South. These would become areas of Unionist sentiment during the Civil War and of Republican strength after it.

But Helper exaggerated the disaffection of most non-slaveholders in the South. Three bonds held them to the system: kinship, economic interest, and race. In the Piedmont and the low-country regions of the South, nearly half of the whites belonged to slaveholding families. Many of the rest were cousins or nephews or in-laws of slaveholders in the South's extensive and tightly knit kinship network. Moreover, many young, ambitious non-slaveholders hoped to buy slaves eventually. Some of them *rented* slaves. And because slaves could be made to do menial, unskilled labor, white workers monopolized the more skilled, higher-paying jobs.

Most important, even if they did not own slaves, white people owned the most important asset of all—a white skin. Race was a more important social distinction than class. The southern legal system, politics, and social ideology were based on the concept of **"*herrenvolk* democracy"** (the equality of all who belonged to the "master race"). Subordination was the Negro's fate, and slavery was the best means of subordination. Emancipation would loose a flood of free blacks on society and would undermine the foundations of white supremacy. Thus, many of the "poor whites" in the South and immigrant workers or poorer farmers in the North supported slavery.

The *herrenvolk* theme permeated proslavery rhetoric. "With us," said John C. Calhoun in 1848, "the two great divisions of society are not the rich and the poor, but white and black; and all the former, the poor as well as the rich, belong to the upper class, and are respected and treated as equals." True freedom as Americans understood it required equality of rights and status (though not of wealth or income). Slavery ensured that freedom for all whites. "Break down slavery," said a Virginia congressman, "and you would with the same blow destroy the great Democratic principle of equality among men."

THE LINCOLN-DOUGLAS DEBATES

Abraham Lincoln believed the opposite. For him, slavery and freedom were incompatible. This became the central theme of a memorable series of debates between Lincoln and Douglas in 1858.

The debates were arranged after Lincoln was nominated to oppose Douglas's reelection to the Senate. State legislatures elected U.S. senators at that time, so the campaign was technically for the election of the Illinois legislature. But the real issue was the senatorship, and Douglas's prominence gave the contest national significance. Lincoln launched his bid with one of his most notable speeches. "A house divided against itself cannot stand," he said. "I believe this government cannot endure, permanently half *slave* and half *free*. . . . It will become *all* one thing, or *all* the other." What, asked Lincoln, would prevent the Supreme Court from legalizing slavery in free states? (A case based on this question was then before the New York courts.) Advocates of slavery were trying to "push it forward, till it shall become lawful in *all* the States." But Republicans intended to keep slavery out of the territories, thus stopping its growth and placing it "where the public mind shall rest in the belief that it is in the course of ultimate extinction."

In response Douglas asked: Why could the country not continue to exist half slave and half free as it had for seventy years? Lincoln's talk about the "ultimate extinction"

herrenvolk **democracy** *Concept that emphasized the equality of all who belonged to the master race—not all mankind.*

Lincoln-Douglas Debates *Series of seven debates between Abraham Lincoln and Stephen Douglas in their contest for election to the U.S. Senate in 1858.*

of slavery would provoke the South to secession. Douglas professed himself no friend of slavery—but if people in the southern states or in the territories wanted it, they had the right to have it. Lincoln's policy would not only free the slaves but would grant them equality. "Are you in favor of conferring upon the negro the rights and privileges of citizenship?" Douglas asked. "Do you desire to strike out of our State Constitution that clause which keeps slaves and free negroes out of the State . . . in order that when Missouri abolishes slavery she can send one hundred thousand emancipated slaves into Illinois, to become citizens and voters on an equality with yourselves?"

Douglas thus put Lincoln on the defensive. He responded with cautious denials that he favored "social and political equality" of the races. The "ultimate extinction" of slavery might take a century and would require the voluntary cooperation of the South. But come what may, freedom must prevail. Americans must reaffirm the principles of the founding fathers. In Lincoln's words, a black person was "entitled to all the natural rights enumerated in the Declaration of Independence, the right to life, liberty and the pursuit of happiness."

Lincoln deplored Douglas's "care not" attitude toward whether slavery was voted up or down. He "*looks to no end of the institution of slavery,*" said Lincoln. Indeed, by endorsing the Dred Scott decision he looks to its "*perpetuity and nationalization.*" Douglas was thus "eradicating the light of reason and liberty in this American people." That was the real issue in the election, Lincoln insisted.

THE FREEPORT DOCTRINE

The popular vote for Republican and Democratic state legislators in Illinois was virtually even in 1858. But because apportionment favored the Democrats, they won a majority of seats and reelected Douglas. But Lincoln was the ultimate victor, for his performance in the debates lifted him from political obscurity, while Douglas further alienated southern Democrats. In the debate at Freeport, Lincoln had asked Douglas how he reconciled his support for the Dred Scott decision with his policy of popular sovereignty, which supposedly gave residents of a territory the power to vote slavery down. Douglas replied that even though the Court had legalized slavery in the territories, the enforcement of that right would depend on the people who lived there. This was a popular answer in the North. But it gave added impetus to southern demands for congressional passage of a federal slave code in territories like Kansas, where the Free Soil majority had by 1859 made slavery virtually null. In the next two sessions of Congress after the 1858 elections, southern Democrats, led by **Jefferson Davis**, tried to pass a federal slave code for all territories. Douglas and northern Democrats joined with Republicans to defeat it. Consequently, southern hostility toward Douglas mounted as the presidential election of 1860 approached.

The 1859–1860 session of Congress was particularly contentious. Once again a fight over the speakership of the House set the tone. Republicans had won a plurality of House seats, but without a majority they could not elect a speaker without the support of a few border-state representatives from the American (Know-Nothing) Party. The problem was that the Republican candidate for Speaker was John Sherman, who, along with sixty-seven other congressmen, had signed an endorsement of Hinton Rowan Helper's *The Impending Crisis of the South*. This was a red flag to southerners, who refused to vote for Sherman. Through forty-three ballots and two months, the House remained deadlocked.

As usual, southerners threatened to secede if a Black Republican became speaker. Several of them wanted a shootout on the floor of Congress. We "are willing to fight the question out," wrote one, "and to settle it right there." To avert a crisis, Sherman

Jefferson Davis *Mississippi planter and prominent leader of the Southern Democrats in the 1850s, who later served as president of the Confederacy.*

withdrew his candidacy and the House finally elected a conservative ex-Whig as speaker on the forty-fourth ballot.

JOHN BROWN AT HARPERS FERRY

Southern tempers were frayed because of what had happened at Harpers Ferry, Virginia, the October before. After his exploits in Kansas, John Brown had disappeared from public view. But he had not been idle. He had worked up a plan to capture the federal arsenal at **Harpers Ferry**, arm slaves with the muskets he seized there, and move southward along the Appalachian Mountains, attracting more slaves to his army along the way until the "whole accursed system of bondage" collapsed.

Brown recruited five black men and seventeen whites, including three of his sons, for this reckless scheme. On the night of October 16, 1859, Brown led his men across the Potomac and occupied the sleeping town of Harpers Ferry without resistance. Few slaves flocked to his banner, but the next day state militia units poured into town and drove Brown's band into the fire-engine house. At dawn on October 18 a company of U.S. marines commanded by Colonel Robert E. Lee and Lieutenant J. E. B. Stuart stormed the engine house and captured the surviving members of Brown's party. Four townsmen, one marine, and ten of Brown's men (including two of his sons) were killed; not a single slave was liberated. John Brown's raid lasted thirty-six hours; its repercussions resounded for years. Though no slaves had risen in revolt, it revived the fears of slave insurrection that were never far beneath the surface of southern consciousness. Exaggerated reports of Brown's network of abolitionist supporters confirmed southern suspicions that a widespread northern conspiracy was afoot, determined to destroy their society. Although Republican leaders denied any connection with Brown and disavowed his actions, few southerners believed them.

Kansas State Historical Society

JOHN BROWN *This modern mural of John Brown is full of symbolism. Holding an open Bible, Brown bestrides the earth like an Old Testament prophet while dead Union and Confederate soldiers lie at his feet. Other soldiers clash behind him, slaves struggle to break free, and God's wrath at a sinful nation sends a destructive tornado to earth in the background.*

Harpers Ferry *Site of John Brown's 1859 raid on a U.S. armory and arsenal for the manufacture and storage of military rifles.*

Many northerners, impressed by Brown's dignified bearing and eloquence during his trial, considered him a martyr to freedom. On the day of Brown's execution, bells tolled in hundreds of northern towns, guns fired salutes, ministers preached sermons of commemoration. "The death of no man in America has ever produced so profound a sensation," commented one northerner. Ralph Waldo Emerson declared that Brown had made "the gallows as glorious as the cross."

This outpouring of northern sympathy for Brown shocked and enraged southerners and weakened the already frayed threads of the Union. "The Harpers Ferry invasion has advanced the cause of disunion more than any event that has happened since the formation of the government," observed a Richmond newspaper. "I have always been a fervid Union man," wrote a North Carolinian, but "the endorsement of the Harpers Ferry outrage . . . has shaken my fidelity."

Something approaching a reign of terror now descended on the South. Every Yankee seemed to be another John Brown; every slave who acted suspiciously seemed to be an insurrectionist. Hundreds of northerners were run out of the South in 1860, some wearing a coat of tar and feathers. Several "incendiaries," both white and black, were lynched.

"Defend yourselves!" Senator Robert Toombs cried out to the southern people. "The enemy is at your door . . . meet him at the doorsill, and drive him from the temple of liberty, or pull down its pillars and involve him in a common ruin."

CONCLUSION

Few decades in American history witnessed a greater disjunction between economic well-being and political upheaval than the 1850s. Despite the recession following the Panic of 1857, the total output of the American economy grew by 62 percent during the decade. Railroad mileage more than tripled, value added by manufacturing nearly doubled, and gross farm product grew by 40 percent.

Yet a profound malaise gripped the country. Riots between immigrants and nativists in the mid-1850s left more than fifty people dead. Fighting in Kansas between proslavery and antislavery forces killed at least two hundred. A South Carolina congressman bludgeoned a Massachusetts senator to unconsciousness with a heavy cane. Representatives and senators came to congressional sessions armed with weapons as well as with violent words.

The nation proved capable of absorbing the large influx of immigrants. It might also have been able to absorb the huge territorial expansion of the late 1840s had it not been for the reopening of the slavery issue by the Kansas-Nebraska Act of 1854. This legislation, followed by the Dred Scott decision in 1857, seemed to authorize the unlimited expansion of slavery. But within two years of its founding in 1854, the Republican Party emerged as the largest party in the North on a platform of preventing all future expansion of slavery. By 1860 the United States had reached a fateful crossroads. As Lincoln had said, it could not endure permanently half slave and half free. The presidential election of 1860 would decide which road America would take into the future.

QUESTIONS FOR REVIEW AND CRITICAL THINKING

Review

1. Why did the Whig Party die, and why did the Republican rather than the American party emerge as the new majority party in the North?

2. What were the origins of Nativism and how did this movement relate to the slavery issue?

3. How did economic developments in the 1840s and 1850s widen the breach between North and South?

4. What were the "free-labor ideology" and "*herrenvolk democracy*"? How did these concepts relate to the politics of the 1850s?

Critical Thinking

1. Why did the northern and southern economic systems develop in such different directions? Why did the effort by some southerners to escape from their "colonial" economic relationship fail?

Discovery

How did the United States find itself on the brink of Civil War prior to the presidential election of 1860?

2. One of the main points of contention in the Lincoln-Douglas debates was the question whether the country could continue to endure half slave and half free. Why did Lincoln challenge Douglas's position that because the nation had so endured for seventy years, there was no reason why it could not continue to do so?

SUGGESTED READINGS

For a detailed and readable treatment of the mounting sectional conflict in the 1850s, see **Allan Nevins, *Ordeal of the Union,*** 2 vols. (1947), and ***The Emergence of Lincoln,*** 2 vols. (1950). The Kansas-Nebraska Act and its political consequences are treated in **Gerald W. Wolff, *The Kansas-Nebraska Bill: Party, Section, and the Coming of the Civil War*** (1977). The conflict in Kansas itself is treated in **Nicole Etcheson, *Bleeding Kansas: Contested Liberty in the Civil War Era*** (2004). For the cross-cutting issue of nativism and the Know-Nothings, see **William E. Gienapp, *The Origins of the Republican Party, 1852–1856*** (1987), and **Tyler Anbinder, *Nativism and Politics: The Know Nothing Party in the Northern United States*** (1992). Two excellent studies of the role of Abraham Lincoln in the rise of the Republican Party are **Don E. Fehrenbacher, *Prelude to Greatness: Lincoln in the 1850s*** (1962), and **Kenneth Winkle, *The Young Eagle: The Rise of Abraham Lincoln*** (2003). The southern response to the growth of antislavery political sentiment in the North is the theme of **William J. Cooper, Jr., *The South and the Politics of Slavery 1828–1856*** (1978).

The year 1857 witnessed a convergence of many crucial events; for a stimulating book that pulls together the threads of that year of crisis, see **Kenneth M. Stampp, *America in 1857: A Nation on the Brink*** (1990). For economic developments during the era, an older classic is still the best introduction: **George Rogers Taylor, *The Transportation Revolution, 1815–1860*** (1951). An important dimension of the southern economy is elucidated in **Fred Bateman and Thomas Weiss, *A Deplorable Scarcity: The Failure of Industrialization in the Slave Economy*** (1981). Still the best study of the Republican free-labor ideology is **Eric Foner, *Free Soil, Free Labor, Free Men: The Ideology of the Republican Party before the Civil War*** (2nd ed., 1995). For southern yeoman farmers, a good study is **Stephanie McCurry, *Masters of Small Worlds: Yeoman Households, Gender Relations, and the Political Culture of the Antebellum South Carolina Low Country*** (1995). The best single study of the Dred Scott case is **Don E. Fehrenbacher, *The Dred Scott Case: Its Significance in American Law and Politics*** (1978), which was published in an abridged version with the title ***Slavery, Law, and Politics: The Dred Scott Case in Historical Perspective*** (1981).

ONLINE SOURCES GUIDE

ThomsonNOW Visit ThomsonNOW to access primary sources, exercises, quizzes, and audio chapter summaries related to this chapter:
http://www.thomsonedu.com/login

DISCOVERY

How did the United States find itself on the brink of the Civil War prior to the presidential election of 1860?

In thinking about this question, begin by breaking it down into the components shown below. A discussion of the significance of each component should appear in your answer.

GEOGRAPHY AND POLITICS

Look at the map of counties in the 1856 presidential election. What regional patterns do you see in the counties that voted for each of the two major-party candidates Frémont and Buchanan? What does the distribution of votes for those two candidates suggest about the emerging sectional split in the country?

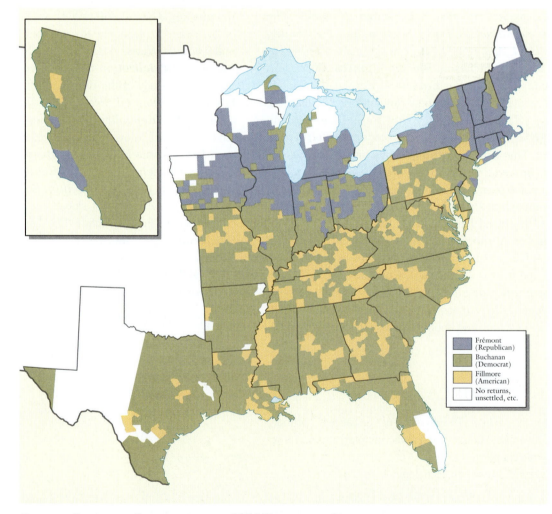

COUNTIES CARRIED BY CANDIDATES IN THE 1856 PRESIDENTIAL ELECTION

DEMOGRAPHICS AND ECONOMY

Look at the maps of slavery and staple crops. What southern states had the highest percentages of slaves? The lowest? Compare the areas of highest percentages of slaves with the principal staple crop regions of the South. Which staple crops were most dependent on slave labor?

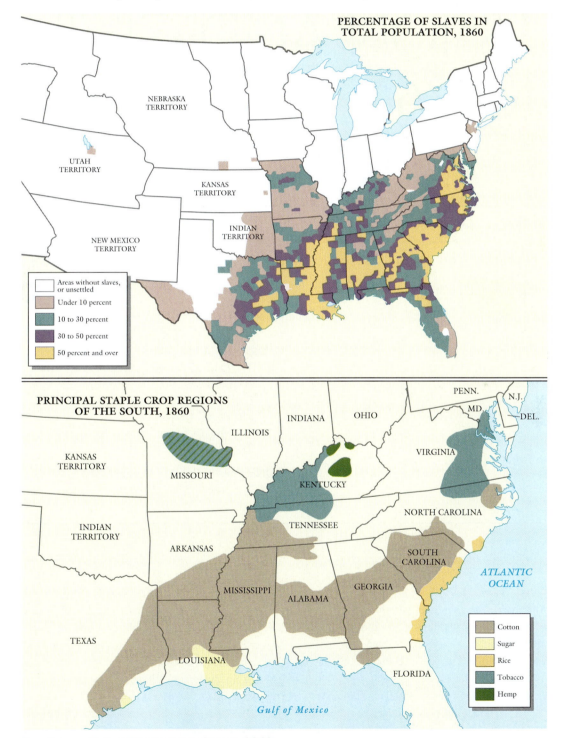

PERCENTAGE OF SLAVES IN TOTAL POPULATION, 1860

Areas without slaves, or unsettled
Under 10 percent
10 to 30 percent
30 to 50 percent
50 percent and over

PRINCIPAL STAPLE CROP REGIONS OF THE SOUTH, 1860

Cotton
Sugar
Rice
Tobacco
Hemp

SLAVERY AND STAPLE CROPS IN THE SOUTH, 1860

15

SECESSION AND CIVIL WAR, 1860–1862

As 1860 began, the Democratic Party was one of the few national institutions left in the country. The Methodists and Baptists had split into Northern and Southern churches in the 1840s over the issue of slavery; the Whig Party and the nativist American Party had been shattered by sectional antagonism in the mid-1850s. Even the Democratic Party, at its national convention in Charleston, South Carolina, in April 1860,

split into Northern and Southern camps. This virtually assured the election of a Republican president. Such a prospect aroused deep fears among whites in the South. When Abraham Lincoln was elected president, the lower-South states seceded from the Union. When Lincoln refused to remove U.S. troops from Fort Sumter, South Carolina, the new Confederate States army opened fire on the fort. Lincoln called out the militia to suppress the insurrection. Four more slave states seceded, and the country drifted into a civil war.

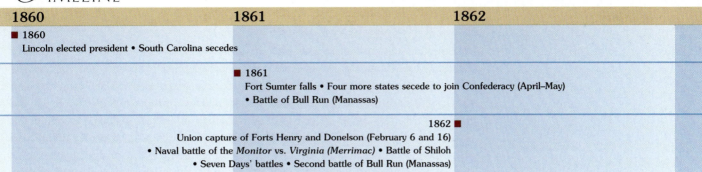

■ **1860**
Lincoln elected president • South Carolina secedes

■ **1861**
Fort Sumter falls • Four more states secede to join Confederacy (April–May)
• Battle of Bull Run (Manassas)

1862 ■
Union capture of Forts Henry and Donelson (February 6 and 16)
• Naval battle of the *Monitor* vs. *Virginia (Merrimac)* • Battle of Shiloh
• Seven Days' battles • Second battle of Bull Run (Manassas)

THE ELECTION OF 1860

A hotbed of southern-rights radicalism, Charleston turned out to be the worst possible place for the Democrats to hold their national convention. Sectional confrontations took place inside the convention hall and on the streets. Since 1836 the Democratic Party had required a two-thirds majority of delegates for a presidential nomination, a rule that in effect gave southerners veto power. Although Stephen A. Douglas had the backing of a simple majority of the delegates, southern Democrats were determined to deny him the nomination, convinced that they would be unable to control a Douglas administration.

The first test came in the debate on the platform. Southern delegates insisted on a federal slave code for the territories. Douglas could not run on a platform that contained such a plank, and if the party adopted it, Democrats were sure to lose every state in the North. By a slim majority, the convention rejected the plank and reaffirmed the 1856 platform endorsing popular sovereignty. Fifty southern delegates thereupon walked out of the convention. Even after they left, Douglas could not muster a two-thirds majority, nor could any other candidate. After 57 futile ballots, the convention adjourned to meet in Baltimore six weeks later to try again.

But the party was so badly shattered that it could not be put back together. That pleased some proslavery radicals. The election of a "Black Republican" president, they felt, would provide the shock necessary to mobilize a southern majority for **secession**. Two of the most prominent secessionists were William L. Yancey and Edmund Ruffin. In 1858, they had founded the League of United Southerners to "fire the Southern heart . . . and at the proper moment, by one organized, concerted action, we can precipitate the Cotton States into a revolution."

In Baltimore an even larger number of delegates from southern states walked out of the convention. They formed the Southern Rights Democratic Party and nominated John C. Breckinridge of Kentucky (the incumbent vice president) for president. When regular Democrats nominated Douglas, the stage was set for what would become a four-party election. A coalition of former Whigs formed the Constitutional Union Party, which nominated John Bell of Tennessee. Bell had no chance of winning; the party's purpose was to exercise a conservative influence on a campaign that threatened to polarize the country.

secession *The act of a state withdrawing from the Union. South Carolina was the first state to attempt to do this in 1860.*

THE REPUBLICANS NOMINATE LINCOLN

From the moment the Democratic Party broke apart, it became clear that 1860 could be the year when the Republican Party elected its first president. The Republicans could expect no electoral votes from the 15 slave states. But in 1856 they had won all but five northern states, and they needed only two or three of those five to win the presidency. The crucial states were Pennsylvania, Illinois, and Indiana. Douglas might carry them and throw the presidential election into the House, where anything could happen. Thus the Republicans had to carry at least two of the swing states to win.

The Republicans' leading presidential prospect was William H. Seward of New York, an experienced politician who had served as governor and senator. However, in his long career Seward had made a number of enemies. His antinativist policies had alienated some former members of the American Party, and he had a reputation for radicalism that might drive away voters in the vital swing states.

Several of the delegates, uneasy about that reputation, staged a stop-Seward movement. The candidate who then came to the fore was Abraham Lincoln. Though he too had opposed nativism, he had done so less noisily than Seward. His reputation was that of a more moderate man. He was from one of the lower-North states where the election would be close, and his rise from a poor farm boy and rail-splitter to successful lawyer and political leader perfectly reflected the free-labor theme of social mobility extolled by the Republican Party. By picking up second-choice votes from states that switched from their favorite sons, Lincoln overtook Seward and won the nomination on the third ballot.

The Republican platform appealed to many groups in the North. Its main plank pledged exclusion of slavery from the territories. Other planks called for a higher tariff (especially popular in Pennsylvania), a homestead act (popular in the Northwest), and federal aid for construction of a transcontinental railroad and for improvement of river navigation. This blend of idealism and materialism proved especially attractive to young people; a large majority of first-time voters in the North voted Republican in 1860.

SOUTHERN FEARS

Militant enthusiasm in the North was matched by fear and rage in the South. Few people there could see any difference between Lincoln and Seward. Had not Lincoln branded slavery a moral, social, and political evil? Had he not said that the Declaration of Independence applied to blacks as well as whites? Had he not expressed a

TABLE **15.1**
VOTING IN THE 1860 ELECTION

	ALL STATES		FREE STATES (18)		SLAVE STATES (15)	
	POPULAR	**ELECTORAL**	**POPULAR**	**ELECTORAL**	**POPULAR**	**ELECTORAL**
Lincoln	1,864,735	180	1,838,347	180	26,388	0
Opposition to Lincoln	2,821,157	123	1,572,637	3	1,248,520	120
"Fusion" Tickets	595,846	—	580,426	—	15,420	—
Douglas	979,425	12	815,857	3	163,568	9
Breckinridge	669,472	72	99,381	0	570,091	72
Bell	576,414	39	76,973	0	499,441	39

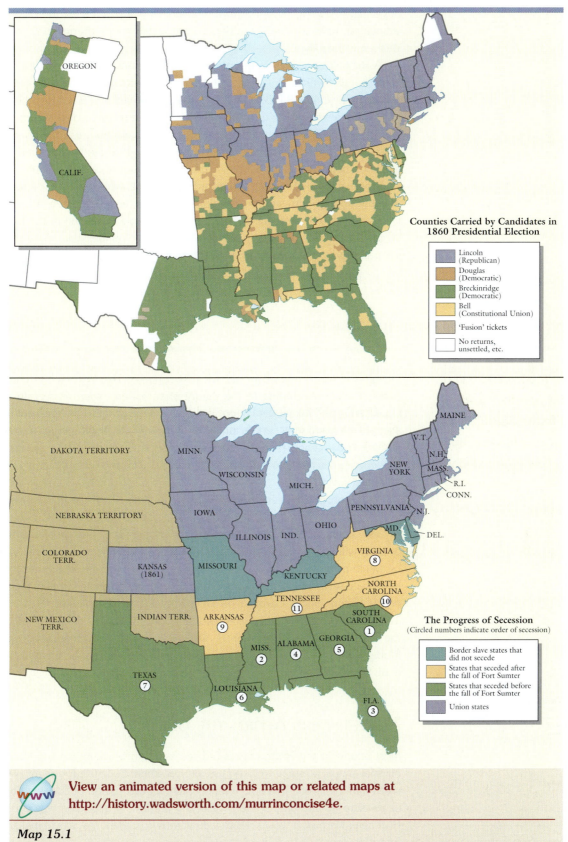

Counties Carried by Candidates in
1860 Presidential Election

- Lincoln (Republican)
- Douglas (Democratic)
- Breckinridge (Democratic)
- Bell (Constitutional Union)
- 'Fusion' tickets
- No returns, unsettled, etc.

OREGON

CALIF.

DAKOTA TERRITORY

NEBRASKA TERRITORY

COLORADO TERR.

NEW MEXICO TERR.

MINN.

WISCONSIN

IOWA

MICH.

ILLINOIS   IND.   OHIO

KANSAS (1861)

MISSOURI

KENTUCKY

INDIAN TERR.

ARKANSAS 9

TEXAS 7

LOUISIANA 6

MISS. 2   ALABAMA 4   GEORGIA 5

TENNESSEE 11

SOUTH CAROLINA 1

FLA. 3

MAINE

V.T   N.H

NEW YORK   MASS.

R.I.

CONN.

PENNSYLVANIA   N.J.

MD   DEL.

VIRGINIA 8

NORTH CAROLINA 10

The Progress of Secession
(Circled numbers indicate order of secession)

- Border slave states that did not secede
- States that seceded after the fall of Fort Sumter
- States that seceded before the fall of Fort Sumter
- Union states

View an animated version of this map or related maps at
http://history.wadsworth.com/murrinconcise4e.

Map 15.1

ELECTION OF 1860 AND SOUTHERN SECESSION. *Note the similarity of the geographical voting patterns in the upper map to the map on p. 366. Another striking pattern shows the correlation between the vote for Breckinridge (upper map) and the first seven states to secede (lower map).*

hope that excluding slavery from the territories would put it on the road to ultimate extinction? To southerners, the Republican pledge not to interfere with slavery in the states was meaningless.

A Republican victory in the presidential election would put an end to the South's control of its own destiny. Even southern moderates warned that the South could not remain in the Union if Lincoln won. "This Government and Black Republicanism cannot live together," said one. What about the three-quarters of southern whites who did not belong to slaveholding families? Lincoln's election, warned an Alabama secessionist, would show that "the North [means] to free the negroes and force amalgamation between them and the children of the poor men of the South."

Most whites in the South voted for Breckinridge, who carried 11 slave states. Bell won the upper-South states of Virginia, Kentucky, and Tennessee. Missouri went to Douglas—the only state he carried, though he came in second in the popular vote. While Lincoln received less than 40 percent of the popular vote, he won every free state and swept the presidency by a substantial margin in the electoral college.

The Lower South Secedes

FOCUS QUESTION

Why did political leaders in the lower South think that Lincoln's election made secession imperative?

Lincoln's victory provided the shock that southern **fire-eaters** had craved. Seven states seceded. According to the theory of secession, when each state ratified the Constitution and joined the Union, it authorized the national government to act as its agent in the exercise of certain functions of sovereignty, but the states had never given away their fundamental underlying sovereignty. Any state, then, by the act of its own convention, could withdraw from its "compact" with the other states and reassert its individual sovereignty.

Many conservatives and former Whigs, including Alexander H. Stephens of Georgia, shrank from the drastic step of secession. Some state convention delegates tried to delay matters with vague proposals for "cooperation" among all southern states, or even with proposals to wait until after Lincoln's inauguration to see what course he would pursue. But those minority factions were overridden by those who favored immediate secession. One after another the conventions voted to take their states out of the Union: South Carolina on December 20, 1860, Mississippi on January 9, 1861, Florida on the 10th, Alabama on the 11th, Georgia on the 19th, Louisiana on the 26th, and Texas on February 1. Delegates from the seven seceding states met in Montgomery, Alabama, in February to create a new nation to be called the Confederate States of America.

Northerners Affirm the Union

Most people in the North considered secession unconstitutional and treasonable. In his final annual message to Congress, on December 3, 1860, President Buchanan insisted that the Union was not "a mere voluntary association of States, to be dissolved at pleasure by any one of the contracting parties." If secession was consummated, Buchanan warned, it would create a disastrous precedent that would make the United States government "a rope of sand."

European monarchists and conservatives were already expressing smug satisfaction at "the great smashup." They predicted that the United States would ultimately collapse into anarchy and revolution. That was precisely what northerners and even

fire-eaters *Southerners who were eager, enthusiastic supporters of southern rights and later of secession.*

BANNER OF THE SOUTH CAROLINA SECESSION CONVENTION. *With its banner featuring a palmetto tree and a snake reminiscent of the American Revolution's "Don't Tread on Me" slogan, the South Carolina secession convention in 1860 looked forward to a grand new Southern republic composed of all 15 slave states and built on the ruins of the old Union. Note the large South Carolina keystone of the arch and the stones of free states lying cracked and broken on the ground.*

some upper-South Unionists feared. "The doctrine of secession is anarchy," declared a Cincinnati newspaper. "If any minority have the right to break up the Government at pleasure, because they have not had their way, there is an end of all government." Lincoln denied that the states had ever possessed independent sovereignty before becoming part of the United States. Rather, they had been colonies or territories that never would have become part of the United States had they not accepted unconditional sovereignty of the national government. "No State, upon its own mere motion, can lawfully get out of the Union. . . . They can only do so against law, and by revolution."

In that case, answered many southerners, we invoke the right of revolution to justify secession. After all, the United States itself was born of revolution. The secessionists maintained that they were merely following the example of their forefathers in declaring independence from a government that threatened their rights and liberties.

Northerners could scarcely deny the right of revolution. But "the right of revolution, is never a legal right," said Lincoln. "At most, it is but a moral right, when exercised for a morally justifiable cause. When exercised without such a cause revolution is no right, but simply a wicked exercise of physical power." The South, in Lincoln's view, had no morally justifiable cause. For southerners to cast themselves in the mold of 1776 was "a libel upon the whole character and conduct" of the Founding Fathers, said the antislavery poet and journalist William Cullen Bryant. They rebelled "to establish the rights of man . . . and principles of universal liberty," while southerners were rebelling to protect "a domestic despotism. . . . Their motto is not liberty, but slavery."

COMPROMISE PROPOSALS

Most people in the North agreed with Lincoln that secession was a "wicked exercise of physical power." The question was what to do about it. All kinds of compromise proposals came before Congress when it met in December 1860. To sort them out, the Senate and the House each set up a special committee. The Senate committee came up with a package of compromises sponsored by Senator John J. Crittenden of Kentucky. The Crittenden Compromise consisted of a series of proposed constitutional amendments: to guarantee slavery in the states perpetually against federal interference; to prohibit Congress from abolishing slavery in the District of Columbia or on any federal property; to deny Congress the power to interfere with the interstate slave trade; to compensate slaveholders who were prevented from recovering fugitive slaves; and, most important, to protect slavery south of latitude 36°30′ in all territories "now held *or hereafter acquired.*"

In the view of most Republicans, the latter clause might turn the United States into "a great slavebreeding and slavetrading empire." But some conservatives in the party were willing to accept it in the interest of peace and conciliation. Their votes, together with those of Democrats and upper-South Unionists whose states had not seceded, might have gotten the compromise through Congress. But President-elect Lincoln sent word to key Republican senators and congressmen to stand firm against compromise on the territorial issue. "Entertain no proposition for a compromise in regard to the *extension* of slavery," wrote Lincoln.

> Filibustering for all South of us, and making slave states would follow . . . to put us again on the high-road to a slave empire. . . . We have just carried an election on principles fairly stated to the people. Now we are told in advance, the government shall be broken up, unless we surrender to those we have beaten. . . . If we surrender, it is the end of us.

Lincoln's advice was decisive. The Republicans voted against the Crittenden Compromise. Most Republicans, though, went along with a proposal by Virginia for a "peace convention" of all the states to be held in Washington in February 1861. However, the convention came up with nothing better than a modified version of the Crittenden Compromise, which suffered the same fate as the original.

Nothing that happened in Washington would have made any difference to the seven states that had seceded. No compromise could bring them back. "We spit upon every plan to compromise," said one secessionist. No power could "stem the wild torrent of passion that is carrying everything before it," wrote former U.S. Senator Judah P. Benjamin of Louisiana. Secession "is a revolution" that "can no more be checked by human effort . . . than a prairie fire by a gardener's watering pot."

ESTABLISHMENT OF THE CONFEDERACY

While the peace convention deliberated in Washington, attention in the seceded states focused on a convention in Montgomery, Alabama, that drew up a constitution and established a government for the new Confederate States of America. The Confederate constitution contained clauses that guaranteed slavery in both the states and the territories, strengthened the principle of state sovereignty, and prohibited its Congress from granting government aid to internal improvements. It limited the president to a single six-year term. The convention delegates constituted themselves a provisional Congress until regular elections could be held in November 1861. To serve as its provisional president and vice president, the convention elected Jefferson Davis and Alexander Stephens.

Davis and Stephens were two of the ablest men in the South. Davis had commanded a regiment in the Mexican War and had been secretary of war in the Pierce administration. But perhaps the main reason they were elected was to present an image of moderation and respectability to the eight upper-South states that remained in the Union. The Confederacy needed those states—at least some of them—if it was to be a viable nation, especially if war came. Without the upper South, the Confederate states would have less than one-fifth of the population (and barely one-tenth of the free population) and only one-twentieth of the industrial capacity of the Union states.

Confederate leaders appealed to the upper South to join them because of the "common origin, pursuits, tastes, manners and customs" that "bind together in one brotherhood the . . . slaveholding states." The principal bond was slavery. In a speech at Savannah on March 21 aimed in part at the upper South, Vice President Alexander Stephens defined slavery as the "cornerstone" of the Confederacy.

Residents of the upper South were indeed concerned about preserving slavery. But the issue was less salient there. A strong heritage of Unionism competed with the commitment to slavery. Virginia had contributed more men to the pantheon of

Founding Fathers than any other state. Tennessee took pride in being the state of Andrew Jackson, famous for his stern warning: "Our Federal Union—It must be preserved." Kentucky was the home of Henry Clay, the "Great Pacificator" who had put together compromises to save the Union on three occasions. These states would not leave the Union without greater cause.

THE FORT SUMTER ISSUE

As each state seceded, it seized the forts, arsenals, and other federal property within its borders. But still in federal hands were two remote forts in the Florida Keys, another on an island off Pensacola, and Fort Moultrie in the Charleston harbor. In December 1860 the self-proclaimed republic of South Carolina demanded that the United States Army evacuate Moultrie. An obsolete fortification, Moultrie was vulnerable to attack by the South Carolina militia. On the day after Christmas 1860 its commander, Major Robert Anderson, moved his men to **Fort Sumter,** located on an artificial island in the channel leading into Charleston Bay. Sympathetic to the South but loyal to the United States, Anderson hoped that moving the garrison would ease tensions by reducing the possibility of an attack. Instead, it lit a fuse that eventually set off the war.

South Carolina sent a delegation to President Buchanan to negotiate the withdrawal of the federal troops. Buchanan surprised them by saying no. He even tried to reinforce the garrison. On January 9 the unarmed merchant ship *Star of the West,* carrying 200 soldiers for Sumter, tried to enter the bay but was driven away by South Carolina artillery. Matters then settled into an uneasy truce. The Confederate government sent General Pierre G. T. Beauregard to take command of the troops ringing Charleston Bay with their cannons pointed at Fort Sumter, and waited to see what the incoming Lincoln administration would do.

When Abraham Lincoln took the oath of office as president of the *United* States, he knew that his inaugural address would be the most important in American history. On his words would hang the issues of union or disunion, peace or war. His goal was to keep the upper South in the Union while cooling passions in the lower South. In his address, he demonstrated firmness in purpose to preserve the Union, along with forbearance in the means of doing so. He repeated his pledge not "to interfere with the institution of slavery where it exists." He assured the Confederate states that "the government will not assail *you.*" But he also said that he would "hold, occupy, and possess the property, and places belonging to the government," without defining exactly what he meant or how he would do it. Lincoln hoped to buy time with his inaugural address—time to demonstrate his peaceful intentions and to enable southern Unionists to regain the upper hand. But the day after his inauguration a dispatch from Major Anderson informed him that provisions for the soldiers at Fort Sumter would soon be exhausted. The garrison would have to be either resupplied or evacuated. Any attempt to send in supplies by force would undoubtedly provoke a response from Confederate guns at Charleston. And such an action would undoubtedly divide the North and unite the South, driving at least four more states into the Confederacy. Thus, most of the members of Lincoln's cabinet, along with the Army's general-in-chief Winfield Scott, advised Lincoln to withdraw the troops from Sumter. But having pledged to "hold, occupy, and possess" national property, could Lincoln afford to abandon that policy during his first month in office?

Lincoln finally hit upon a solution. He decided to send in unarmed ships with supplies but to hold troops and warships outside the harbor with authorization to go into action only if the Confederates used force to stop the supply ships. And he would no-

FOCUS QUESTION

Why did compromise efforts to forestall secession fail, and why did war break out at Fort Sumter?

Fort Sumter *Fort in Charleston's harbor occupied by United States troops after the secession of South Carolina.*

tify South Carolina officials in advance of his intention. This was a stroke of genius. If Confederate troops fired on the supply ships, the South would stand convicted of starting a war by attacking "a mission of humanity" bringing "food for hungry men." If Davis allowed the supplies to go in peacefully, the U.S. flag would continue to fly over Fort Sumter. The Confederacy would lose face at home and abroad, and southern Unionists would take courage. Davis did not hesitate. He ordered General Beauregard to compel Sumter's surrender before the supply ships got there. At 4:30 A.M. on April 12, 1861, Confederate guns set off the Civil War by firing on Fort Sumter. After a 33-hour bombardment, the burning fort lowered the U.S. flag in surrender.

Choosing Sides

News of the attack triggered an outburst of anger and war fever in the North. "The town is in a wild state of excitement," wrote a Philadelphia diarist. "The American flag is to be seen everywhere. . . . Men are enlisting as fast as possible." Because the tiny United States Army was inadequate to quell the "insurrection," Lincoln called on the states for 75,000 militia. The free states filled their quotas immediately. More than twice as many men volunteered as Lincoln had requested. Before the war was over, more than 2 million men would serve in the Union Army and Navy.

The eight slave states that were still in the Union rejected Lincoln's call for troops. Four of them—Virginia, Arkansas, Tennessee, and North Carolina—soon seceded and joined the Confederacy. As a former Unionist in North Carolina remarked, "The South must go with the South. . . . Blood is thicker than Water." Few found the choice harder to make than **Robert E. Lee** of Virginia. One of the most promising officers in the United States Army, Lee did not believe that southern states had a legal right to secede. However, he felt compelled to resign after the Virginia convention passed an ordinance of secession on April 17. "I must side either with or against my section," Lee told a northern friend. "I cannot raise my hand against my birthplace, my home, my children."

Most southern whites embraced war against the Yankees with more enthusiasm. When news of Sumter's surrender reached Richmond, a huge crowd poured into the

TABLE 15.2

SLAVERY AND SECESSION   The higher the proportion of slaves and slaveholders in the population of a southern state, the greater the intensity of secessionist sentiment.

ORDER OF SECESSION	PERCENTAGE OF POPULATION WHO WERE SLAVES	PERCENTAGE OF WHITE POPULATION IN SLAVEHOLDING FAMILIES
Seven states that seceded December 1860–February 1861 (South Carolina, Mississippi, Florida, Alabama, Georgia, Louisiana, Texas)	47	38
Four states that seceded after the firing on Fort Sumter (Virginia, Arkansas, Tennessee, North Carolina)	32	24
Four border slave states remaining in Union (Maryland, Delaware, Kentucky, Missouri)	14	15

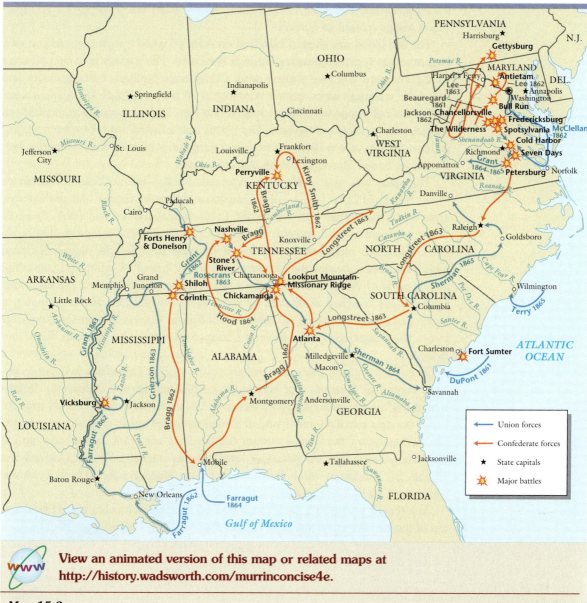

View an animated version of this map or related maps at
http://history.wadsworth.com/murrinconcise4e.

Map 15.2

PRINCIPAL MILITARY CAMPAIGNS OF THE CIVIL WAR. *This map vividly illustrates the contrast between the vast distances over which the armies fought in the western theater of the war and the concentrated campaigns of the Army of the Potomac and the Army of Northern Virginia in the East.*

state capitol square and ran up the Confederate flag. "I never in all my life witnessed such excitement," wrote a participant. The London *Times* correspondent described crowds in North Carolina with "flushed faces, wild eyes, screaming mouths." No one in those cheering crowds could know that before the war ended at least 260,000 Confederate soldiers would lose their lives.

BORDER STATES

Except for Delaware, which remained firmly in the Union, the slave states that bordered free states were sharply divided by the outbreak of war. Leaders in these states talked of "neutrality," but they were to be denied that luxury—Maryland and Missouri

Robert E. Lee *U.S. army officer until his resignation to join the Confederacy as general-in-chief.*

immediately, and Kentucky in September 1861, when first Confederate and then Union troops crossed its borders.

The first blood was shed in Maryland on April 19 when a mob attacked part of a Massachusetts regiment traveling through Baltimore. The soldiers fired back, leaving 12 Baltimoreans and four soldiers dead. Confederate partisans burned bridges and tore down telegraph wires, cutting Washington off from the North for nearly a week until additional troops from Massachusetts and New York reopened communications and seized key points in Maryland. The troops also arrested many Confederate sympathizers. To prevent Washington from becoming surrounded by enemy territory, federal forces turned Maryland into an occupied state.

The same was true of Missouri. Aggressive action by the Union commander there, Nathaniel Lyon, provoked a showdown between Unionist and pro-Confederate militia that turned into a riot in St. Louis on May 10 and 11, 1861, in which 36 people were killed. Lyon then led his troops in a summer campaign that drove the Confederate militia into Arkansas. Reinforced by Arkansas regiments, these rebel Missourians invaded their home state and on August 10 defeated Lyon in the bloody battle of Wilson's Creek in the southwest corner of Missouri. The victorious Confederates marched northward all the way to the Missouri River, capturing a Union garrison at Lexington 40 miles east of Kansas City on September 20. Union forces then regrouped and drove the ragged Missouri Confederates back into Arkansas.

From then until the war's end, military power enabled **Unionists** to maintain political control of Missouri. But continued guerrilla attacks by Confederate **"bushwhackers"** and counterinsurgency tactics by Unionist "jayhawkers" turned large areas of the state into a no-man's-land of hit-and-run raids, arson, ambush, and murder. During these years, the famous postwar outlaws Jesse and Frank James and Cole and Jim Younger rode with the notorious rebel guerrilla chieftains William Quantrill and "Bloody Bill" Anderson. More than any other state, Missouri suffered from a civil war within the Civil War, and its bitter legacy persisted for generations.

In elections held during the summer and fall of 1861, Unionists gained firm control of the Kentucky and Maryland legislatures. Kentucky Confederates, like those of Missouri, formed a state government in exile. When the Confederate Congress admitted both Kentucky and Missouri to full representation, the Confederate flag acquired its 13 stars. Nevertheless, two-thirds of the white population in the four border slave states favored the Union, though some of that support was undoubtedly induced by the presence of Union troops.

THE CREATION OF WEST VIRGINIA

The war itself produced a fifth Union border state: West Virginia. Most of the delegates from the portion of Virginia west of the Shenandoah Valley had voted against secession. A region of mountains, small farms, and few slaves, western Virginia was linked more closely to Ohio and Pennsylvania than to the South. Delegates who had opposed Virginia's secession returned home determined to secede themselves—from Virginia. Through a complicated process of conventions and referendums, carried out in the midst of raids and skirmishes, they created the new state of West Virginia, which entered the Union in 1863.

To the south and west of Missouri, civil war raged for control of the Indian Territory (present-day Oklahoma). The Native Americans, who had been resettled there in the generation before the war, chose sides and carried on bloody guerrilla warfare with each other. The more prosperous Indians of the five "civilized tribes" (Cherokees,

Unionists *Southerners who remained loyal to the Union during the Civil War.*

bushwhackers *Confederate guerrilla raiders especially active in Missouri. Jayhawkers were the Union version of the same type of people. Both groups did a tremendous amount of damage with raids, arson, ambush, and murder.*

Creeks, Seminoles, Chickasaws, and Choctaws), many of them of mixed blood and some of them slaveholders, tended to side with the Confederacy. However, aided by white and black Union regiments operating out of Kansas and Missouri, the pro-Union Indians gradually gained control of most of the Indian Territory.

In the meantime, a small army composed mostly of Texans pushed up the Rio Grande valley into New Mexico. In February 1862 they launched a deeper strike to capture Santa Fe. They hoped to push even farther westward and northward to the California and Colorado gold mines, which were helping to finance the Union war effort.

At first the Confederate drive up the Rio Grande went well. The Texans won the battle of Valverde, 100 miles south of Albuquerque, on February 21, 1862. They continued up the valley, occupied Albuquerque and Santa Fe, and pushed on toward Fort Union near Santa Fe. But Colorado miners who had organized themselves into Union regiments met the Texans in the battle of Glorieta Pass on March 26–28. The battle itself ended in a draw, but a unit of Coloradans destroyed the Confederate wagon train, forcing the Southerners into a disastrous retreat back to Texas. Of the 3,700 who had started out to win the West for the Confederacy, only 2,000 made it back.

THE BALANCE SHEET OF WAR

FOCUS QUESTION
What were Northern advantages in the Civil War? What where Southern advantages?

If one counts three-quarters of the border state population (including free blacks) as pro-Union, the total number of people in Union states in 1861 was 22.5 million, compared with 9 million in the Confederate states. The North's advantage was even greater in military manpower, since the Confederate population total included 3.7 million slaves compared with 300,000 slaves in Union areas. At first, neither side expected to recruit blacks as soldiers. Eventually, the Union did enlist black soldiers and black sailors, but the Confederacy did not do so until the war was virtually over. Altogether, about 2.1 million men fought for the Union and 850,000 for the Confederacy. That was close to half of the North's male population of military age and three-quarters of the comparable Confederate white population. Since the labor force of the South consisted mainly of slaves, the Confederacy was able to enlist a larger proportion of its white population.

In economic resources, the North's superiority was even greater. The Union states possessed nine-tenths of the country's industrial capacity and registered shipping, four-fifths of its bank capital, three-fourths of its railroad mileage and rolling stock, and three-fourths of its taxable wealth. Thus, in a long war that mobilized the total resources of both sides, the North's advantages might prove decisive. But in 1861, few anticipated how long and intense the war would be. Both sides expected a short and victorious conflict. Confederates seemed especially confident. Many Southerners really did believe that one of their own could lick three Yankees.

Although this turned out to be a grievous miscalculation, the South did have some reason to believe that its martial qualities were superior. A higher proportion of southerners than northerners had attended West Point and other military schools, had fought in the Mexican War, or had served as officers in the regular army. As a rural people, southerners were proficient in hunting, riding, and other outdoor skills useful in military operations. Moreover, the South had begun to prepare for war earlier than the North. As each state seceded, it mobilized militia and volunteer military companies. Not until the summer of 1861 would the North's greater manpower begin to make itself felt in the form of a larger army.

STRATEGY AND MORALE

Even when fully mobilized, the North's superior resources did not guarantee success. The Confederacy had come into being in firm control of 750,000 square miles. To win the war, Union forces would have to invade, conquer, and occupy much of that vast territory and destroy its armies. To "win" the war, the Confederacy did not need to invade or conquer the Union or even to destroy its armies; it needed only to hold out long enough to convince Northerners that the cost of victory was too high.

The important factor of **morale** also seemed to favor the Confederacy. To be sure, Union soldiers fought for powerful symbols: nation, flag, constitution. "We are fighting to maintain the best government on earth" was a common phrase in their letters and diaries. A Chicago newspaper declared that the South had "outraged the Constitution, set at defiance all law, and trampled under foot that flag which has been the glorious and consecrated symbol of American Liberty."

But Confederates, too, fought for nation, flag, constitution, and liberty—of whites. In addition, they fought to defend their land, homes, and families. An army fighting in defense of its homeland generally has the edge in morale. "We shall have the enormous advantage of fighting on our own territory and for our very existence," wrote a Confederate leader.

morale *The general feeling of the people toward such events as a war. Good morale greatly enhances an ability to fight or sacrifice for a cause.*

MOBILIZING FOR WAR

More than four-fifths of the soldiers on both sides were volunteers. In both North and South, patriotic rallies motivated the men of a county or town or city neighborhood to enlist in a company (100 men) organized by leading citizens in that locality. The recruits elected their own company officers (a captain and two lieutenants), who received their commissions from the state governor. A regiment consisted of 10 infantry companies, and each regiment was commanded by a colonel, with a lieutenant colonel and a major as second and third in command—all of them appointed by the governor. Cavalry regiments were organized in a similar manner. Field artillery units were known as "batteries," a grouping of four or six cannons with their limber chests and caissons (four-wheeled, horse-drawn vehicles) to carry ammunition; the full complement of a six-gun battery was 155 men and 72 horses.

Volunteer units received a state designation and number in the order of their completion—the 2nd Massachusetts Volunteer Infantry, the 5th Virginia Cavalry, and so on. In most regiments the men in each company mostly came from the same town or locality. Some Union regiments were composed of men of a particular ethnic group. By the end of the war, the Union Army had raised about 2,000 infantry and cavalry regiments and 700 batteries; the Confederates had organized just under half as many. As the war went on, the original 1,000-man complement of a regiment was

THE RICHMOND GRAYS. *This photograph depicts a typical volunteer military unit that joined the Confederate army in 1861. Note the determined and confident appearance of these young men. By 1865, one-third of them would be dead and several others maimed for life.*

Cook Collection, Valentine Museum, Richmond, Virginia

whittled down by disease, casualties, desertions, and detachments, so that the average combat strength of a regiment after several months was 500 men or less.

These were citizen soldiers, not professionals. They carried peacetime notions of democracy and discipline with them into the army. That is why the men elected their company officers and sometimes their field officers (colonel, lieutenant colonel, and major) as well. Political influence often counted for more than military training in the election and appointment of officers. These civilians in uniform were awkward and unmilitary at first, and some regiments suffered battlefield disasters because of inadequate training, discipline, and leadership. In time, however, these raw recruits became battle-hardened veterans commanded by experienced officers.

As the two sides organized their field armies, both grouped four or more regiments into brigades, and three or more brigades into divisions. By 1862, they began grouping two or more divisions into corps, and two or more corps into armies. Each of these larger units was commanded by a general appointed by the president. Some of these generals turned out to be incompetent. But as the war went on, they too either learned their trade or were weeded out.

WEAPONS AND TACTICS

In Civil War battles, the infantry rifle was the most lethal weapon. Muskets and rifles caused 80 to 90 percent of the combat casualties. From 1862 on, most of these weapons were **rifled**—that is, they had spiral grooves cut in the barrel to impart a spin to the cone-shaped lead bullet, whose base expanded upon firing to "take" the rifling of the barrel. This made it possible to load and fire a muzzle-loading rifle two or three times per minute. The rifle had greater accuracy and at least four times the effective range (400 yards or more) of the old smoothbore musket.

Civil War infantry tactics adjusted only gradually to the greater lethal range and accuracy of the new rifle, however. **Close-order assaults** against defenders equipped with rifles resulted in enormous casualties. The defensive power of the rifle became even greater when troops began digging into trenches. Massed frontal assaults became almost suicidal. Soldiers and their officers learned the hard way to adopt skirmishing tactics, taking advantage of cover and working around the enemy flank.

LOGISTICS

The Civil War is often called the world's first "modern" war because of the role played by railroads, steam-powered ships, and the telegraph. Railroads and steamboats transported supplies and soldiers with unprecedented speed and efficiency; the telegraph provided instantaneous communication between army headquarters and field commanders. Yet these modern forms of transport and communications were extremely vulnerable. Cavalry raiders and guerrillas could cut telegraph wires, burn railroad bridges, and tear up the tracks. Confederate cavalry became particularly skillful at sundering the supply lines of invading Union armies. The more deeply the Union armies penetrated into the South, the greater the number of men they had to detach to guard bridges, depots, and supply dumps. Once the campaigning armies had moved away from their railhead or wharfside supply base, they were as dependent on animal-powered transport as earlier armies had been. Union armies required one horse or mule for every two or three men. Thus a large invading Union army of 100,000 men would need about 40,000 draft animals. Confederate armies, operating mostly in friendly territory closer to their bases, needed fewer. The poorly drained

rifling *Process of cutting spiral grooves in a gun's barrel to impart a spin to the bullet. Perfected in the 1850s, it produced greater accuracy and longer range.*

close-order assault *Military tactic of attacking with little space between men. In the face of modern weapons used during the Civil War, such fighting produced a high casualty rate.*

logistics *Military activity relating to such things as the transporting, supplying, and quartering of troops and their equipment.*

dirt roads typical of much of the South turned roads into a morass of mud in wet weather.

These logistical problems did much to offset the industrial supremacy of the North, particularly during the first year of the war. By 1862, though, the North's economy had fully geared up for war. The South created war industries, especially munitions and gunpowder, but its industrial base was inadequate. Particularly troublesome for the Confederacy was its inability to replace rails and rolling stock. Although the South produced plenty of food, the railroads deteriorated to the point where they could not get that food to soldiers or civilians. As the war went into its third and fourth years, the Northern economy grew stronger and the Southern economy grew weaker.

FINANCING THE WAR

One of the greatest defects of the Confederate economy was finance. The Confederate Congress, wary of dampening patriotic ardor, was slow to raise taxes. And because most capital in the South was tied up in land and slaves, little was available for buying war bonds. Therefore, the Confederate Congress authorized a limited issue of treasury notes, to be redeemable in **specie** (gold or silver) within two years after the end of the war. The first modest issue was followed by many more because the notes declined sharply in value. By early 1863 it took eight dollars to buy what one dollar had bought two years earlier; just before the war's end the Confederate dollar was worth one U.S. cent.

In 1863 the Confederate Congress tried to stem this runaway inflation by passing a comprehensive law that taxed income, consumer purchases, and business transactions and included a "tax in kind" on agricultural products, allowing tax officials to seize 10 percent of a farmer's crops. This tax was extremely unpopular among farmers, many of whom hid their crops and livestock or refused to plant, thereby worsening the Confederacy's food shortages. The tax legislation was too little and too late to remedy the South's fiscal chaos. The Confederate government raised less than 5 percent of its revenue by taxes and less than 40 percent by loans, leaving 60 percent to be created by printing treasury notes (paper money)—a recipe for disaster.

In contrast, the Union government raised 66 percent of its revenue by selling war bonds, 21 percent by taxes, and only 13 percent by printing **treasury notes**. The Legal Tender Act authorizing these notes, the famous "greenbacks," was passed in February 1862. Instead of promising to redeem them in specie at some future date, as the South had done, Congress made them **legal tender**—that is, it required everyone to accept them as real money at face value. The North's economy suffered some inflation during the war, but it was mild compared with that experienced by the Confederacy.

The Union Congress also passed the National Banking Act of 1863. Before the war, the principal form of money had been notes issued by state-chartered banks. After Andrew Jackson's destruction of the Second Bank of the United States (Chapter 12), the number and variety of banknotes had skyrocketed until 7,000 different kinds of state banknotes were circulating in 1860. The National Banking Act of 1863 was an attempt to resurrect the centralized banking system and create a more stable banknote currency, as well as to finance the war. The act authorized the chartering of national banks, which could issue **banknotes** up to 90 percent of the value of the U.S. bonds they held. This provision created a market for the bonds and, in combination with the greenbacks, replaced the glut of state banknotes with a more uniform national currency.

specie *Metal money or coins, usually made of gold or silver.*

treasury notes *Paper money used by the Union to help finance the Civil War. One type of treasury note was known as a greenback because of its color.*

legal tender *Any type of money that the government requires everyone to accept at face value.*

banknotes *Paper money, issued by banks, that circulated as currency.*

National banknotes would be an important form of money for the next half-century. They had two defects, however. First, because the number of notes that could be issued was tied to each bank's holdings of U.S. bonds, the volume of currency available was dependent on the amount of federal debt rather than on the economic needs of the country. Second, the banknotes themselves tended to be concentrated in the Northeast, where most of the large national banks were located, leaving the South and West short. The creation of the Federal Reserve System in 1913 (Chapter 21) largely remedied these defects. But it was Civil War legislation that established the principle of a uniform national currency issued and regulated by the federal government.

Navies, the Blockade, and Foreign Relations

To sustain its war effort, the Confederacy needed to import large quantities of material from abroad, particularly from Britain. To shut off these imports, on April 19, 1861, Lincoln proclaimed a **blockade** of Confederate ports. The task was formidable; the Confederate coastline stretched for 3,500 miles, with two dozen major ports and another 150 bays and coves where cargo could be landed. The United States Navy recalled its ships from distant seas, took old sailing vessels out of mothballs, and bought or chartered merchant ships and armed them. Eventually it placed several hundred warships on blockade duty. But in 1861 the blockade was so thin that 9 of every 10 vessels slipped through it on their way to or from Confederate ports.

KING COTTON DIPLOMACY

The Confederacy, however, inadvertently contributed to the blockade's success when it adopted "King Cotton diplomacy." Cotton was vital to the British economy because textiles were at the heart of British industry, and three-fourths of Britain's supply of raw cotton came from the South. If that supply was cut off, Southerners reasoned, British factories would shut down, unemployed workers would starve, and Britain would face the prospect of revolution. Rather than risk such a consequence, people in the South believed that Britain would recognize the Confederacy's independence and then use the powerful British navy to break the blockade.

Southerners were so firmly convinced of cotton's importance to the British economy that they kept the 1861 cotton crop at home rather than try to export it through the blockade. But the strategy backfired. Bumper crops in 1859 and 1860 had piled up a surplus of raw cotton in British warehouses and delayed the anticipated "cotton famine" until 1862. In the end, the South's voluntary embargo of cotton cost them dearly. The Confederacy missed its chance to ship out its cotton and store it abroad, where it could be used to purchase war material.

Moreover, the Confederacy's King Cotton diplomacy contradicted its own foreign policy objective: to persuade the British and French governments to refuse to recognize the legality of the blockade. Under international law, a blockade must be "physically effective" to be respected by neutral nations. Confederate diplomats claimed that the Union effort was a mere "paper blockade," yet the dearth of cotton reaching European ports as a result of the South's embargo suggested to British

blockade *The closing of a country's harbors by enemy ships to prevent trade and commerce, especially to prevent traffic in military supplies.*

and French diplomats that the blockade was at least partly effective. And indeed, by 1862 it was. Although most **blockade runners** got through, by 1862 the blockade had reduced the Confederacy's seaborne commerce enough to convince the British government to recognize it as legitimate. The blockade was also squeezing the South's economy. After lifting its cotton embargo in 1862, the Confederacy found it increasingly difficult to export enough cotton through the blockade to pay for the imports it needed.

Confederate foreign policy also failed to win diplomatic recognition by other nations. That recognition would have conferred international legitimacy on the Confederacy and might even have led to treaties of alliance or of foreign aid. The French emperor Napoleon III expressed sympathy for the Confederacy, as did influential groups in the British Parliament. But Prime Minister Lord Palmerston and Foreign Minister John Russell did not want to recognize the Confederacy while it was engaged in a war it might lose, especially if recognition might jeopardize relations with the United States. The Union foreign policy team of Secretary of State Seward and Minister to England Charles Francis Adams did a superb job. Seward issued blunt warnings against recognizing the Confederacy; Adams softened them with the velvet glove of diplomacy. By 1862 it had become clear that Britain would withhold recognition until the Confederacy had virtually won its independence—but, of course, such recognition would have come too late to help the Confederacy win.

THE *TRENT* AFFAIR

If anything illustrated the frustrations of Confederate diplomacy, it was the "*Trent* Affair." In October 1861 Southern envoys James Mason and John Slidell slipped through the blockade; Mason hoped to represent the Confederacy in London and Slidell in Paris. However, on November 8, Captain Charles Wilkes of the U.S.S. *San Jacinto* stopped the British mail steamer *Trent,* with Mason and Slidell on board, near Cuba. Wilkes arrested the two Southerners and took them to Boston. When the news reached England, the government and the public were outraged by Wilkes's "highhanded" action. Britain demanded an apology and the release of Mason and Slidell. The popular press on both sides of the Atlantic stirred up war fever, but good sense soon prevailed. Britain softened its demands, and the Lincoln administration released Mason and Slidell the day after Christmas 1861, declaring that Captain Wilkes had acted "without instructions."

THE CONFEDERATE NAVY

Lacking the capacity to build a naval force at home, the Confederacy hoped to use British shipyards for the purpose. Through a loophole in the British neutrality law, two fast commerce raiders built in Liverpool made their way into Confederate hands in 1862. Named the *Florida* and the *Alabama,* they roamed the seas for the next two years, capturing or sinking Union merchant ships and whalers. The *Alabama* sank 62 merchant vessels plus a Union warship before another warship, the U.S.S. *Kearsarge,* sank it off Cherbourg, France, on June 19, 1864. Altogether, Confederate privateers and commerce raiders destroyed or captured 257 Union merchant vessels and drove at least 700 others to foreign registry. But this Confederate achievement, though spectacular, made only a tiny dent in the Union war effort.

blockade runner *A ship designed to run through a blockade.*

THE MONITOR AND MERRIMAC. The black-and-white photograph shows the crew of the Union ironclad Monitor *standing in front of its revolving two-gun turret. In action, the sun canopy above the turret would be taken down and all sailors would be at their stations inside the turret or the hull, as shown in the color painting of the famed battle, on March 9, 1862, between the* Monitor *and the Confederate* Virginia *(informally called the* Merrimac *because it had been converted from the captured U.S. frigate* Merrimack*). There is no photograph of the* Virginia*, which was blown up by its crew two months later when the Confederates retreated toward Richmond because its draft was too deep to go up the James River.*

THE MONITOR AND THE VIRGINIA

Though plagued by shortages on every hand, the Confederate Navy Department demonstrated great skill at innovation. Southern engineers developed "torpedoes" (mines) that sank or damaged 43 Union warships in southern bays and rivers. Even more innovative (though less successful) was the building of ironclad "rams" to sink the blockade ships. The most famous of these was the C.S.S. *Virginia*, commonly called the *Merrimac* because it was rebuilt from the steam frigate U.S.S. *Merrimack*. Ready for its trial-by-combat on March 8, 1862, the *Virginia* steamed out to attack the blockade squadron at Hampton Roads. It sank one frigate with its iron ram and another with its 10 guns. Union shot and shells bounced off the *Virginia*'s armor plate.

Panic seized Washington, but in the nick of time the Union's own ironclad sailed into Hampton Roads and saved the rest of the fleet. This was the U.S.S. *Monitor*, which had been completed just days earlier at the Brooklyn navy yard. Much smaller than the *Virginia*, with two 11-inch guns in a **revolving turret** (an innovation) set on a deck almost flush with the water, the *Monitor* looked like a "tin can on a shingle." It presented a small target and was capable of concentrating considerable firepower in a given direction with its revolving gun turret. The next day, the *Monitor* fought the *Virginia* in history's first battle between ironclads. It was a draw, but the *Virginia* limped home to Norfolk, never again to menace the Union fleet. Although the Confederacy built other ironclad rams, some never saw action and none achieved the initial success of the *Virginia*. By the war's end, the Union Navy had built or started 58 ships of the *Monitor* class, launching a new age in naval history.

revolving gun turret *A low structure, often round, on a ship that moved horizontally and contained mounted guns.*

Campaigns and Battles, 1861–1862

FOCUS QUESTION

How did the Union's and Confederacy's respective military advantages manifest themselves in the campaigns and battles in 1861–1862?

Wars can be won only by hard fighting. This was a truth that some leaders on both sides overlooked. One of them was Winfield Scott, general-in-chief of the United States Army. Scott, a Virginian who had remained loyal to the Union, evolved a military strategy based on his conviction that a great many Southerners were eager to be won back to the Union. The main elements of his strategy were a naval blockade and a combined Army-Navy expedition to take control of the Mississippi, thus sealing off the Confederacy on all sides. The Northern press labeled Scott's strategy as "the Anaconda Plan," after the South American snake that squeezes its prey to death.

The Battle of Bull Run

QUICK REVIEW

MOBILIZING FOR WAR

- Four upper South states seceded

- Western Virginia seceded from Virginia

- Four border slave states remained in the Union

- Northern and Southern economies and armies mobilized for war

- Confederate ports blockaded by U.S. navy

Most Northerners believed that the South could be overcome only by victory in battle. Virginia emerged as the most likely battleground, especially after the Confederate government moved its capital to Richmond in May 1861. "Forward to Richmond," clamored Northern newspapers. And forward toward Richmond moved a Union army of 35,000 men in July. They got no farther than Bull Run, a sluggish stream 25 miles southwest of Washington, where a Confederate army commanded by Beauregard had been deployed to defend a key rail junction at Manassas.

Another small Confederate army in the Shenandoah Valley under General Joseph E. Johnston had traveled to Manassas by rail to reinforce Beauregard. On July 21 the attacking Federals forded Bull Run and hit the rebels on the left flank, driving them back. By early afternoon, the Federals seemed to be on the verge of victory. But a Virginia brigade commanded by **Thomas J. Jackson** stood "like a stone wall," earning Jackson the nickname he carried ever after. By midafternoon Confederate reinforcements had grouped for a counterattack that drove the exhausted and disorganized Yankees back across Bull Run.

The Battle of Manassas (or Bull Run, as Northerners called it) made a profound impression on both sides. Of the 18,000 soldiers actually engaged on each side, Union casualties (killed, wounded, and captured) were about 2,800 and Confederate casualties 2,000. The victory exhilarated Confederates and confirmed their belief in their martial superiority. It also gave them a morale advantage in the Virginia theater that persisted for two years. And yet, Manassas also bred overconfidence. Some in the South thought the war was won. Northerners, by contrast, were jolted out of their expectations of a short war. Congress authorized the enlistment of up to a million three-year volunteers. Hundreds of thousands flocked to recruiting offices in the next few months. Lincoln called General **George B. McClellan** to Washington to organize the new troops into the Army of the Potomac.

An energetic, talented officer only 34 years old, McClellan soon won the nickname "The Young Napoleon." He organized and trained the Army of the Potomac into a large, well-disciplined, and well-equipped fighting force. He was just what the North needed after its dispiriting defeat at Bull Run. When Scott stepped down as general-in-chief on November 1, McClellan took his place.

But as winter approached and McClellan did nothing to advance against the smaller Confederate army whose outposts stood only a few miles from Washington, his failings as a commander began to show. He was afraid to take risks; he never learned the military lesson that no victory can be won without risking defeat. He con-

Thomas J. Jackson *A native of Virginia, he emerged as one of the Confederacy's best generals in 1861–1862.*

George B. McClellan *One of the most promising young officers in the U.S. army, became principal commander of Union armies in 1861–1862.*

sistently overestimated the strength of enemy forces facing him and used these faulty estimates as a reason for inaction until he could increase his own force. When criticism of McClellan began to appear in the press, he accused his critics of political motives. Having built a fine fighting machine, he was afraid to start it up for fear it might break. Lincoln removed him from command in November 1862.

NAVAL OPERATIONS

Because of McClellan, no further action occurred in the Virginia theater until the spring of 1862. Meanwhile, the Union Navy won a series of victories over Confederate coastal forts at Hatteras Inlet on the North Carolina coast, Port Royal Sound in South Carolina, and other points along the Atlantic and Gulf coasts. These successes provided new bases from which to expand and tighten the blockade, as well as take-off points for operations along the southern coast. In February and March 1862, an expeditionary force under General Ambrose Burnside occupied several crucial ports on the North Carolina sounds. Another Union force captured Fort Pulaski at the mouth of the Savannah River.

One of the Union Navy's most impressive achievements was the capture of New Orleans in April 1862. Most Confederate troops in the area had been called up the Mississippi to confront a Union invasion of Tennessee, leaving only some militia, an assortment of steamboats converted into gunboats, and two strong forts flanking the river 70 miles below the city. That was not enough to stop Union naval commander David G. Farragut, a native of Tennessee who had remained loyal to the U.S. Navy in which he had served for half a century. In a daring action on April 24, 1862, Farragut led his fleet upriver past the forts, scattering the Confederate fleet and fending off fire rafts. He lost four ships, but the rest got through and compelled the surrender of New Orleans.

FORT HENRY AND FORT DONELSON

These victories demonstrated the importance of sea power even in a civil war. Even more important were Union victories won by the combined efforts of the Army and fleets of river gunboats on the Tennessee and Cumberland Rivers, which flow through Tennessee and Kentucky and empty into the Ohio River just before it joins the Mississippi. The unlikely hero of these victories was Ulysses S. Grant, who had resigned from the military in 1854. Rejoining when war broke out, he demonstrated a quiet efficiency and a determined will that won him promotion from Illinois colonel to brigadier general. When Confederate units entered Kentucky in September, Grant moved quickly to occupy the mouths of the Cumberland and Tennessee Rivers.

Military strategists on both sides understood the importance of these navigable rivers. The Confederacy had built forts at strategic points along the rivers and had begun to convert a few steamboats into gunboats and rams to back up the forts. The Union converted steamboats into "timberclad" gunboats, so called because they were armored just enough to protect the engine and the paddle wheels. The Union also built a new class of ironclad gunboats designed for river warfare. Carrying 13 guns, these flat-bottomed, wide-beamed vessels drew only six feet of water. Their hulls and paddle wheels were protected by a sloping casemate sheathed in iron armor up to 2.5 inches thick.

When the first of these strange-looking but formidable craft were ready in February 1862, Grant struck. His objectives were Forts Henry and Donelson on the

Tennessee and Cumberland Rivers just south of the Kentucky-Tennessee border. The gunboats knocked out Fort Henry on February 6. Fort Donelson proved a tougher challenge. Its guns repulsed a gunboat attack on February 14. The next day the 17,000-man Confederate army attacked Grant's besieging army, which had been re-inforced to 27,000 men. With the calm decisiveness that became his trademark, Grant directed a counterattack that penned the defenders back up in their fort. Cut off from support by either land or river, the Confederate commander asked for sur-render terms on February 16. Grant's reply made him instantly famous when it was published in the North: "No terms except an immediate and unconditional surrender can be accepted."

The strategic consequences of these victories were far-reaching. Union gunboats now ranged all the way up the Tennessee River to northern Alabama, enabling a Union division to occupy the region, and up the Cumberland to Nashville. Confederate mili-tary units pulled out of Kentucky and most of Tennessee and reassembled at Corinth in northern Mississippi. But by the end of March 1862 the Confederate commander in the western theater, Albert Sidney Johnston (not to be confused with Joseph E. John-ston in Virginia), had built up an army of 40,000 men at Corinth. His plan was to at-tack Grant's force of 35,000, which had established a base 20 miles away at Pittsburg Landing on the Tennessee River just north of the Mississippi-Tennessee border.

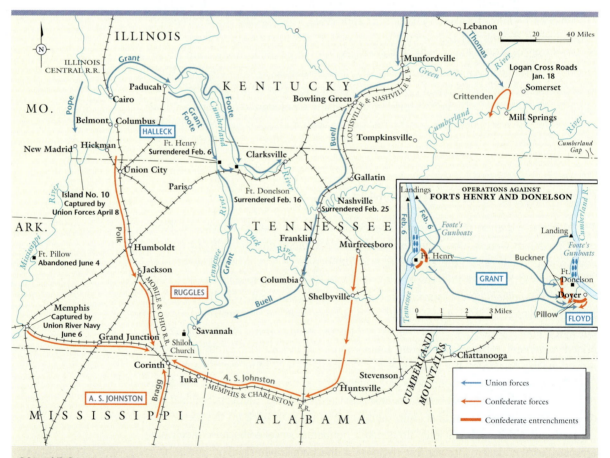

Map 15.3

KENTUCKY–TENNESSEE THEATER, WINTER–SPRING 1862. *This map illustrates the importance of rivers and rail-roads as lines of military operations and supply. Grant and Foote advanced up (southward) the Tennessee and Cumberland Rivers while Buell moved along the Louisville and Nashville Railroad. Confederate divi-sions under the overall command of General Albert Sidney Johnston used railroads to concentrate at the key junction of Corinth.*

THE BATTLE OF SHILOH

On April 6 the Confederates attacked at dawn near a church called Shiloh, which gave its name to the battle. They caught Grant by surprise and drove his army toward the river. After a day's fighting with total casualties of 15,000, Grant's men brought the Confederate onslaught to a halt at dusk. One of the Confederate casualties was Johnston, the highest-ranking general on either side to be killed in the war. Beauregard, who had been transferred from Virginia to the West, took command after Johnston's death.

Some of Grant's subordinates advised retreat, but Grant would have none of it. Reinforced by fresh troops from a Union army commanded by General Don Carlos Buell, the Union counterattacked next morning (April 7) and, after 9,000 more casualties to the two sides, drove the Confederates back to Corinth. Although Grant had achieved victory from what seemed certain defeat, his reputation suffered a decline because of the heavy casualties and the suspicion that he had been caught napping.

Union triumphs in the western theater continued. The combined armies of Grant and Buell, under the overall command of Henry W. Halleck, drove the Confederates out of Corinth at the end of May. Meanwhile, the Union gunboat fleet fought its way down the Mississippi, virtually wiping out the Confederate fleet in a spectacular battle at Memphis on June 6. At Vicksburg the Union gunboats from the north connected with part of Farragut's fleet that had come up from New Orleans, taking Baton Rouge and Natchez along the way. The heavily fortified Confederate bastion at Vicksburg, however, proved too strong for the firepower of the Union naval fleet to subdue. Nevertheless, the dramatic succession of Union triumphs convinced the North that the war was nearly won. "Every blow tells fearfully against the rebellion," boasted the *New York Tribune*. "The rebels themselves are panic-stricken, or despondent."

THE VIRGINIA THEATER

In the western theater the broad rivers had facilitated the Union's invasion of the South, but in Virginia a half-dozen small rivers flowing west to east provided the Confederates with natural lines of defense. McClellan, still in command of the Army of the Potomac, persuaded a reluctant Lincoln to approve a plan to transport his army down Chesapeake Bay to the tip of the Virginia peninsula. That would shorten the route to Richmond and give the Union Army a seaborne supply line.

This was a good plan—in theory. But a small Confederate blocking force at Yorktown held McClellan for the entire month of April as he cautiously dragged up siege guns to blast through defenses that his large army could have punched through in days on foot. McClellan then slowly followed the retreating Confederate force up the peninsula to a new defensive line only a few miles east of Richmond.

Shortly thereafter, Stonewall Jackson's month-long campaign in the Shenandoah (May 8– June 9) demonstrated what could be accomplished through deception, daring, and mobility. With only 17,000 men, Jackson moved by rapid marches, covering 350 miles in one month. During that month they won four battles against three separate Union armies, whose combined numbers surpassed Jackson's by more than two to one.

Meanwhile McClellan's army continued toward Richmond. Although it substantially outnumbered the Confederate force defending Richmond, commanded by Joseph E. Johnston, McClellan overestimated Johnston's strength at double what it actually was. Even so, by the last week of May McClellan's army was within six miles of Richmond. A botched Confederate counterattack on May 31 and June 1 (the Battle of Seven Pines) produced no result except 6,000 Confederate and 5,000 Union casualties. But one of those casualties was Joseph Johnston, who had been wounded in the shoulder. Jefferson Davis named Robert E. Lee to replace him.

THE SEVEN DAYS' BATTLES

That appointment marked a major turning point in the campaign. Lee's qualities as a commander manifested themselves when he took over what he renamed "The Army of Northern Virginia." While McClellan continued to dawdle, Lee sent his dashing cavalry commander, Jeb Stuart, to lead a reconnaissance around the Union Army to discover its weak points, brought Jackson's army in from the Shenandoah Valley, and launched a June 26 attack on McClellan's right flank in what became known as the Seven Days' Battles. Constantly attacking, Lee's army of 90,000 drove McClellan's 100,000 away from Richmond to a new fortified base on the James River. The offensive cost the Confederates 20,000 casualties (compared with 16,000 for the Union), but it reversed the momentum of the war.

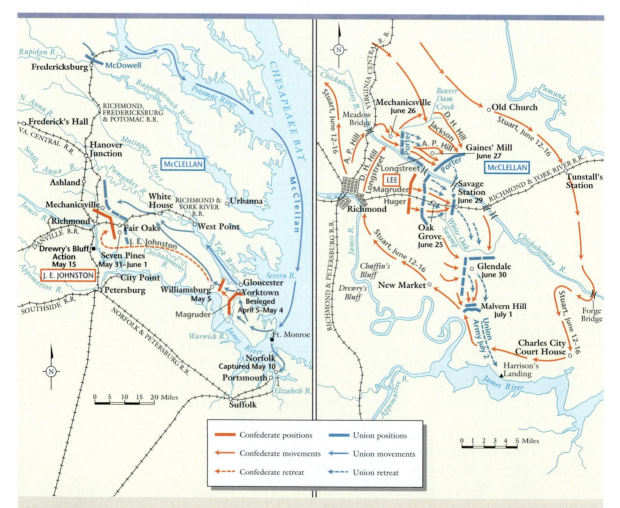

Map 15.4

PENINSULA CAMPAIGN, APRIL–MAY 1862 [AND] SEVEN DAYS' BATTLES, JUNE 25–JULY 1, 1862. *General McClellan used Union naval control of the York and James Rivers to protect his flanks in his advance up the peninsula formed by these rivers (left map). When Robert E. Lee's Army of Northern Virginia counterattacked in the Seven Days' Battles (right map), McClellan was forced back to the James River at Harrison's Landing.*

CONFEDERATE COUNTEROFFENSIVES

The tide turned in the western theater as well. Union conquests there in the spring had brought 50,000 square miles of Confederate territory under Union control. But to occupy and administer this vast area, many thousands of soldiers had to be drawn from combat forces. These depleted forces, deep in enemy territory, were vulnerable to cavalry raids. During the summer and fall of 1862 the cavalry commands of Tennesseean Nathan Bedford Forrest and Kentuckian John Hunt Morgan staged repeated raids in which they burned bridges, blew up tunnels, tore up tracks, and captured supply depots and the Union garrisons trying to defend them.

MUSICAL LINK TO THE PAST

WARTIME MUSIC AS INSPIRATION AND CATHARSIS

Composers: Stephen C. Foster (music),
James Sloan Gibbons (lyrics)
Title: "We Are Coming, Father Abraham,
300,000 More" (1862)
Composers: Stephen C. Foster (music), Cooper (lyrics)
Title: "Willie Has Gone to War" (1863)

"We Are Coming, Father Abraham, 300,000 More," with its marchlike beat and patriotic lift, probably was used to shore up sagging spirits in some northern areas. Although the song, and others with similar sentiments, sold well with its message of eager voluntarism on the part of soldiers united for the Union, it did not produce a corresponding effect on sluggish troop recruitment efforts in the North.

"Willie Has Gone To War," popular in the South as well as the North, presents the more gloomy and death-obsessed nature of Civil War music that surfaced in the second half of the conflict. For months, press dispatches reported the crushing defeats and mortal losses on both sides with violent and gory detail. The occasion of a soldier going to the front was no longer viewed as a celebratory occasion. In "Willie," the notion of oncoming tragedy and death is never stated, but it unmistakably lingers over the song, both in its bittersweet melody and in the Victorian images of nature that are cast as a poetic counterpoint to the fact of Willie going to war: "The bluebird is singing his lay, to all the sweet flowers in the dale / The wild bee is roaming at play, and soft is the sigh of the gale / I stray by the brookside alone, where oft we have wandered before / And weep for my lov'd one, my own, My Willie has gone to the war / . . . Willie has gone to the war, Willie, my loved one is gone!" The last line quoted, part of the chorus of the song, is especially haunting, as the song drops into a minor chord and features a melody that combines mournful and patriotic elements simultaneously.

Although some at the time argued that such sad music eroded morale, perhaps it would have been even more damaging to ignore the kinds of welling emotions that "Willie" and songs like it documented. The catharsis these songs provided helped Americans face the loss and sacrifice of the war, which saw over 1 million people killed and wounded. Confederate general Robert E. Lee maintained that he could not imagine fighting a war without music. George F. Root, one of the most successful songwriters and publishers of the Civil War period, insisted that, as a songwriter, he was patriotically serving his country through the medium of song and that such contributions were as important as the contributions of a general.

1. Why do you think Lee and Root attached such importance to the role of music in fighting a war?

Listen to an audio recording of this music on the Musical Links to the Past CD.

These raids paved the way for infantry counteroffensives. After recapturing some territory, Earl Van Dorn's Army of West Tennessee failed to retake Corinth on October 3 and 4. At the end of August, Braxton Bragg's Army of Tennessee launched a drive northward from Chattanooga through east Tennessee and Kentucky but was turned back at the Battle of Perryville on October 8. Even after these defeats, the Confederate forces in the western theater were in better shape than they had been four months earlier.

THE SECOND BATTLE OF BULL RUN

Most attention, though, focused on Virginia. Lincoln reorganized the Union corps near Washington into the Army of Virginia under General John Pope. In August, Lincoln ordered the withdrawal of the Army of the Potomac from the peninsula to reinforce Pope for a drive southward from Washington. To attack Pope before McClellan could reinforce him, Lee shifted most of his army to northern Virginia, sent Jackson's "foot cavalry" on a deep raid to destroy the supply base at Manassas Junction, and then brought his army back together to defeat Pope's army near Bull Run on August 29 and 30. The demoralized Union forces retreated to Washington, where Lincoln reluctantly gave McClellan command of the two armies and told him to reorganize them into one.

Lee decided to keep up the pressure by invading Maryland. On September 4, his weary troops splashed across the Potomac 40 miles upriver from Washington. Momentous possibilities accompanied this move. Another victory by Lee might influence the U.S. congressional elections in November and help Democrats gain control of Congress, which might paralyze Lincoln's war effort. The invasion of Maryland, coming on top of other Confederate successes, would have caused Britain and France to recognize the Confederacy.

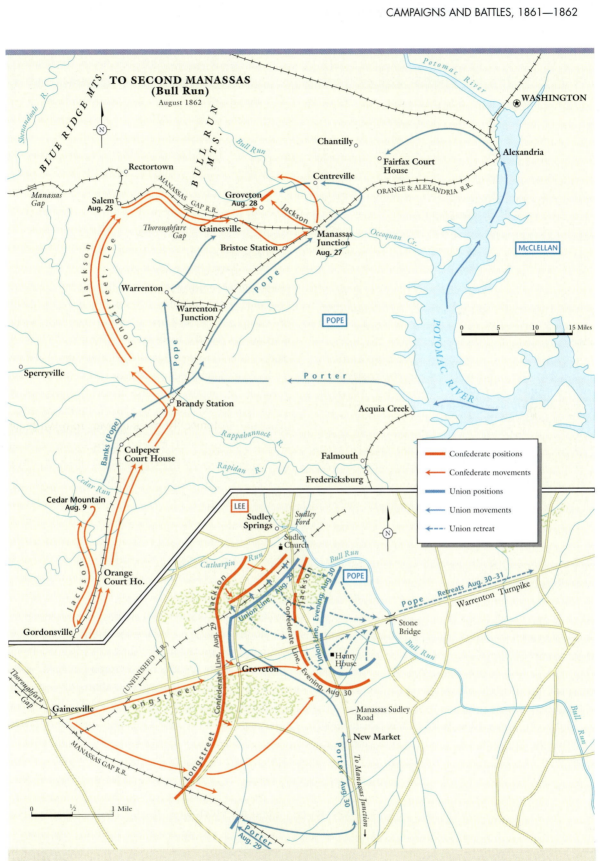

Map 15.5

SECOND BATTLE OF MANASSAS (BULL RUN), AUGUST 29–30, 1862. *Note that some of the heaviest fighting in both battles took place around the house owned by Judith Henry, which was destroyed, and the elderly widow was killed in her house in the first battle.*

C O N C L U S I O N

The election of 1860 had accomplished a national power shift of historic proportions. Southern political leaders had maintained effective control of the national government for most of the time before 1860. South Carolina's governor Francis Pickens described this leverage of power in a private letter to a fellow South Carolinian in 1857:

> We have the Executive [Buchanan] with us, and the Senate & in all probability the H[ouse of] R[epresentatives] too. Besides we have repealed the Missouri line & the Supreme Court in a decision of great power, has declared it . . . unconstitutional null and void. So, that before our enemies can reach us, they must first break down the Supreme Court—change the Senate & seize the Executive & . . . restore the Missouri line, repeal the Fugitive slave law & change the whole govern[men]t. As long as the Govt. is on our side I am for sustaining it, & using its power for our benefit.

In 1860 Pickens's worst-case scenario started to come true. With Lincoln's election as the first president of an antislavery party, the South lost control of the executive—and also probably of the House. The Senate and Supreme Court were expected to follow soon. The Republicans, Southerners feared, would launch a "revolution" to cripple slavery. The "revolutionary dogmas" of the Republicans, declared a South Carolina newspaper in 1860, were "active and bristling with terrible designs." Worst of all, the Northern "Black Republicans" would force racial equality on the South.

Thus the South seceded in order to forestall the feared revolution of liberty and equality that would be their fate if they remained in the Union. As the Confederate secretary of state put it in 1861, the southern states had formed a new nation "to preserve their old institutions" from "a revolution [that] threatened to destroy their social system."

Seldom has a preemptive counterrevolution so quickly brought on the very revolution it tried to prevent. If the Confederacy had lost the war in the spring of 1862, as appeared likely, the South might have returned to the Union with slavery still intact. But the success of Confederate counteroffensives in the summer of 1862 convinced Lincoln that the North could not win the war without striking against slavery.

QUESTIONS FOR REVIEW AND CRITICAL THINKING

Review

1. Why did political leaders in the lower South think that Lincoln's election made secession imperative?
2. Why did compromise efforts to forestall secession fail, and why did war break out at Fort Sumter?
3. What were Northern advantages in the Civil War? What where Southern advantages?
4. How did the Union's and Confederacy's respective military advantages manifest themselves in the campaigns and battles in 1861–1862?

Critical Thinking

1. Given the North's advantages in population and economic resources, how could the Confederacy have hoped to prevail in the war?
2. How did the factors of geography, terrain, and logistics shape the strategy and operations of each side in the war?

Discovery

How significant was the role of slavery in bringing about secession and the outbreak of the Civil War? Why did the fighting occur where it did?

SUGGESTED READINGS

The most comprehensive one-volume study of the Civil War years is **James M. McPherson,** *Battle Cry of Freedom: The Civil War Era* (1988). The fullest and most readable narrative of the military campaigns and battles is **Shelby Foote,** *The Civil War: A Narrative,* 3 vols. (1958–1974). For the naval war, see **Ivan Musicant,** *Divided Waters: The Naval History of the Civil War* (1995). For the perspective of the soldiers and sailors who fought the battles, see **Bell I. Wiley's** two books: *The Life of Johnny Reb* (1943) and *The Life of Billy Yank* (1952). The motives of soldiers for enlisting and fighting are treated in **James M. McPherson,** *For Cause and Comrades: Why Men Fought in the Civil War* (1997).

For the home front in North and South, see **Phillip Shaw Paludan,** *"A People's Contest": The Union and Civil War, 1861–1865* (1988), and **Emory Thomas,** *The Confederate Nation, 1861–1865* (1979). For women and children, see **Elizabeth D. Leonard,** *Yankee Women: Gender Battles in the Civil War* (1994); **George C. Rable,** *Civil Wards: Women and the Crisis of South-ern Nationalism* (1989); and **James Marten,** *The Children's Civil War* (1998).

For biographical studies of leaders on both sides, consult the following: **Phillip S. Paludan,** *The Presidency of Abraham Lincoln* (1994); **William C. Cooper,** *Jefferson Davis, American* (2000); **Brooks D. Simpson,** *Ulysses S. Grant* (2000); and **Emory M. Thomas,** *Robert E. Lee* (1995). For a study of the Fort Sumter crisis and the outbreak of the war that sets these events in their long-term context, see **Maury Klein,** *Days of Defiance: Sumter, Secession, and The Coming of the Civil War* (1997). For the guerrilla war in Missouri, the most useful of several books is **Michael Fellman,** *Inside War: The Guerrilla Conflict in Missouri during the Civil War* (1989). Of the many studies of diplomacy during the war, the most useful is **David P. Crook,** *The North, The South, and the Powers 1861–1865* (1974), an abridged version of which was published with the title *Diplomacy during the Civil War* (1975).

ONLINE SOURCES GUIDE

ThomsonNOW   Visit ThomsonNOW to access primary sources, exercises, quizzes, and audio chapter summaries related to this chapter:

http://www.thomsonedu.com/login

$\mathcal{D}$ISCOVERY

How significant was the role of slavery in bringing about secession and the outbreak of the Civil War? Why did the fighting occur where it did?

In thinking about this question, begin by breaking it down into the components shown below. A discussion of the significance of each component should appear in your answer.

POLITICS AND GEOGRAPHY

Look at the map on the progress of secession. Note which states seceded before the fall of Fort Sumter and those that seceded after. Do these two groups form coherent subregions within the South? If so, what were their characteristics? For help in answering this question, consult also Table 15.2. What is the correlation between votes for Breckinridge (upper map) and the first seven states to secede?

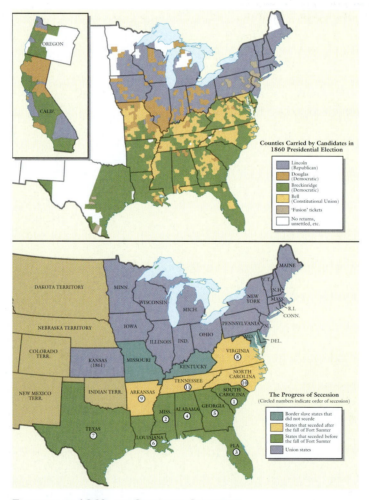

ELECTION OF 1860 AND SOUTHERN SECESSION

SLAVERY AND SECESSION   The higher the proportion of slaves and slaveholders in the population of a southern state, the greater the intensity of secessionist sentiment.

ORDER OF SECESSION	PERCENTAGE OF POPULATION WHO WERE SLAVES	PERCENTAGE OF WHITE POPULATION IN SLAVEHOLDING FAMILIES
Seven states that seceded December 1860–February 1861 (South Carolina, Mississippi, Florida, Alabama, Georgia, Louisiana, Texas)	47	38
Four states that seceded after the firing on Fort Sumter (Virginia, Arkansas, Tennessee, North Carolina)	32	24
Four border slave states remaining in Union (Maryland, Delaware, Kentucky, Missouri)	14	15

WARFARE

Look at the map of principal military campaigns. Where did most of the fighting occur? What is important or significant about the location(s) of the fighting? Why do you think the battles in the western theater were so dispersed and the ones in the East so concentrated? What different challenges do you suppose the troops in the East and West faced as a result of these varying circumstances?

PRINCIPAL MILITARY CAMPAIGNS OF THE CIVIL WAR

A NEW BIRTH OF FREEDOM, 1862–1865

One of the great issues awaiting resolution as the armies moved into Maryland in September 1862 was emancipation of the slaves. The war had moved beyond the effort to restore the old Union. It now required the mobilization or the destruction of every resource that might bring victory or inflict defeat. To abolish slavery would strike at a vital Confederate resource (slave labor). Slaves had already made clear their choice by escaping to Union lines by the tens of thousands. Lincoln had made up his mind to issue an emancipation proclamation and was waiting for a Union victory to give it credibility and potency.

This was a momentous decision that would polarize Northern public opinion and political parties. So long as the North fought simply for restoration of the Union, Northern unity had been impressive. But the events of 1862 and 1863 raised the divisive question of what kind of Union was to be restored. Would it be a Union without slavery, as abolitionists and radical Republicans hoped? Or "the Union as it was," as Democrats desired?

1861	1862	1863	1864	1865

1861–1865
Abraham Lincoln presidency

■ **1862**
Battle of Antietam • Preliminary Emancipation Proclamation
• Battle of Fredericksburg

■ **1863**
Final Emancipation Proclamation • Battle of Chancellorsville
• Battle of Gettysburg • Fall of Vicksburg

1864 ■
Battles of the Wilderness, Spotsylvania, Cold Harbor • Siege of Petersburg
• Fall of Atlanta • Reelection of Lincoln

1865 ■
Surrender of Lee at Appomattox • Ratification of 13th Amendment abolishing slavery

$\mathcal{S}$LAVERY AND THE WAR

In the North, the issue of slavery was deeply divisive. Lincoln had been elected on a pledge to contain the expansion of slavery. But that pledge had provoked most of the Southern states to quit the Union. For the administration to take action against slavery in 1861 would be to risk the breakup of the fragile coalition Lincoln had stitched together to fight the war: Republicans, Democrats, and border-state Unionists. In July 1861, with Lincoln's endorsement, Congress passed a resolution affirming that Northern war aims intended only "to defend and maintain the supremacy of the Constitution and to preserve the Union."

But many Northerners did not see things that way. They insisted that a rebellion sustained by slavery in defense of slavery could be suppressed only by striking *against* slavery. As the black leader Frederick Douglass stated, "War for the destruction of liberty must be met with war for the destruction of slavery."

Wars tend to develop a logic and momentum that go beyond their original purposes. When Northerners discovered at Bull Run in July 1861 that they were not going to win an easy victory, many of them began to take a harder look at slavery. Slaves constituted the principal labor force in the South. They raised most of the food and fiber, built most of the military fortifications, and worked on the railroads and in mines and munitions factories. Southern newspapers boasted that slavery was "a tower of strength to the Confederacy." So why not convert this Confederate asset to a Union advantage by confiscating slaves as enemy property and using them to help the Northern war effort?

THE "CONTRABANDS"

The slaves themselves entered this debate in a dramatic fashion. As Union armies penetrated the South, a growing number of slaves voted with their feet for freedom. By twos and threes, by families, eventually by scores, they escaped from their masters and came over to the Union lines.

Although some commanders returned escaped slaves to their masters or prevented them from entering Union camps, most increasingly did not. Their rationale

> FOCUS QUESTION
> *What factors led Lincoln to his decision to issue the Emancipation Proclamation?*

Eastman Johnson 1824–1906 A RIDE FOR LIBERTY—THE FUGITIVE SLAVES, circa 1862. Oil on board. The Brooklyn Museum 40.59. A Gift of Miss Gwendolyn O. L. Conkling.

A RIDE FOR LIBERTY. This splendid painting of a slave family escaping to Union lines during the Civil War dramatizes the experiences of thousands of slaves who thereby became "contrabands" and gained their freedom. Most of them came on foot, but this enterprising family stole a horse as well as themselves from their master.

was first expressed by General Benjamin Butler. In May 1861 three slaves escaped to Butler's lines near Fortress Monroe at the mouth of the James River. Butler refused to return them, on the grounds that they were **contraband of war.** For the rest of the war, slaves who came within Union lines were known as contrabands. On August 6, 1861, Congress passed an act that authorized the seizure of all property, including slaves, that was being used for Confederate military purposes. The following March, Congress forbade the return of slaves who entered Union lines.

THE BORDER STATES

On August 30, 1861, Major General John C. Frémont, who commanded Union forces in Missouri, issued an order freeing the slaves of all Confederate sympathizers in that state. This caused such a backlash among border-state Unionists that Lincoln revoked the order. In the spring of 1862, Lincoln tried persuasion instead of force. At his urging, Congress passed a resolution offering federal compensation to states that voluntarily abolished slavery. Three times Lincoln told border-state leaders that the Confederate hope that their states might join the rebellion was helping to keep the war alive. Accept the proposal for **compensated emancipation**, he pleaded, and that hope would die. The pressure for a bold antislavery policy was growing stronger, he warned them. "You cannot," he said, "be blind to the signs of the times."

But they did seem to be blind. They complained that they were being coerced, bickered about the amount of compensation, and wrung their hands over the prospects of economic ruin and race war. At a final meeting with border-state congressmen, on July 12, Lincoln, in effect, gave them an ultimatum: Accept compensated emancipation or face the consequences. "The incidents of the war cannot be avoided," he said. But again they failed to see the light and by a vote of 20 to 9, they rejected the proposal for compensated emancipation.

THE DECISION FOR EMANCIPATION

That very evening, Lincoln decided to issue an emancipation proclamation. Several factors, in addition to the recalcitrance of the border states, impelled him to this fateful decision. One was a growing demand from his own party for bolder action. Another

contraband of war *Term used to describe slaves who came within the Union lines.*

compensated emancipation *Idea that the federal government would offer compensation or money to states that voluntarily abolished slavery.*

was rising sentiment in the Army to "take off the kid gloves" when dealing with "traitors." From General Henry W. Halleck, who had been summoned to Washington as general-in-chief, went orders to General Grant in northern Mississippi instructing him on the treatment of rebel sympathizers inside Union lines: "Handle that class without gloves, and take their property for public use." Finally, Lincoln's decision reflected his sentiments about the "unqualified evil" and "monstrous injustice" of slavery.

The military situation, however, rather than his moral convictions, determined the timing and scope of Lincoln's emancipation policy. Northern hopes that the war would soon end had risen after the victories of early 1862 but had then plummeted amid the reverses of that summer. Three courses of action seemed possible. One, favored by the so-called Peace Democrats, urged an armistice and peace negotiations to patch together some kind of Union, but that would have been tantamount to conceding Confederate victory. Republicans therefore reviled the Peace Democrats as traitorous **Copperheads,** after the poisonous snake. A second alternative was to keep on fighting—in the hope that with a few more Union victories, the rebels would lay down their arms and the Union could be restored. But such a policy would leave slavery intact. The third alternative was to mobilize all the resources of the North and to destroy all the resources of the South, including slavery—a war not to restore the old Union but to build a new one.

After his meeting with the border-state representatives convinced him there could be no compromise, Lincoln made his decision. A week later he notified the cabinet of his intention to issue an emancipation proclamation. It was "a military necessity, absolutely essential to the preservation of the Union," said Lincoln. "We must free the slaves or be ourselves subdued." But Lincoln accepted the advice of Secretary of State Seward to delay the proclamation "until you can give it to the country supported by military success." Lincoln slipped his proclamation into a desk drawer and waited for a military victory.

New Calls for Troops

Meanwhile, Lincoln issued a call for 300,000 new three-year volunteers for the Army. In July, Congress passed a militia act giving the president greater powers to mobilize the state militias into federal service and to draft men into the militia if the states failed to do so. This was not yet a national draft law, but it was a step in that direction. In August, Lincoln called up 300,000 militia for nine months of service, in addition to the 300,000 three-year volunteers. The Peace Democrats railed against these measures and provoked antidraft riots in some localities. The government responded by arresting rioters and antiwar activists under the president's suspension of the writ of habeas corpus.[1]

Democrats denounced these "arbitrary arrests" and added this issue to others on which they hoped to gain control of the next House of Representatives in the fall elections. With the decline in Northern morale following the defeat at Second Bull Run, prospects for a Democratic triumph seemed bright. One more military victory by Lee's Army of Northern Virginia might crack the North's will to continue the fighting. Lee's legions began crossing the Potomac into Maryland on September 4, 1862.

---

[1] The writ of habeas corpus is an order issued by a judge to law enforcement officers requiring them to bring an arrested person before the court to be charged with a crime so that the accused can have a fair trial. The Constitution of the United States, however, permits the suspension of this writ "in cases of rebellion or invasion," so that the government can arrest enemy agents, saboteurs, or any individual who might hinder the defense of the country, and hold such individuals without trial. This issue of "arbitrary arrests" became a controversial matter in both the Union and Confederacy (where the writ was similarly suspended during part of the war).

Copperheads *Term used by some Republicans to describe Peace Democrats to imply that they were traitors to the Union.*

THE BATTLE OF ANTIETAM

The Confederate invasion ran into difficulties from the start. The people of western Maryland responded impassively to Lee's proclamation that he had come "to aid you in throwing off this foreign yoke" of Yankee rule. Lee split his army into five parts. Three of them, under the overall command of Stonewall Jackson, occupied the heights surrounding the Union garrison at Harpers Ferry, which lay athwart the Confederate supply route from the Shenandoah Valley. The other two remained on watch in the South Mountain passes west of Frederick. But on September 13, in a field near Frederick, two Union soldiers found a copy of Lee's orders for these deployments, apparently dropped by a careless officer. With this new information, Union commander George B. McClellan planned to pounce on the separated segments of Lee's army before they could reunite.

Union troops overwhelmed the Confederate defenders of the South Mountain passes on September 14. But they advanced too slowly to save the garrison at Harpers Ferry, which surrendered 12,000 men to Jackson on September 15. Lee then managed to reunite most of his army near the village of Sharpsburg by Sep-

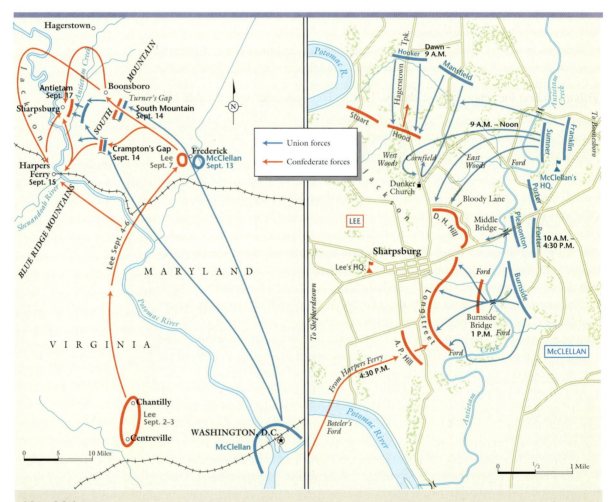

Map 16.1

LEE'S INVASION OF MARYLAND, 1862 [AND] BATTLE OF ANTIETAM, SEPTEMBER 17, 1862. *Both the advantages and disadvantages of Lee's defensive position in this battle are illustrated by the righthand map. The Confederate flanks were protected by water barriers (the Potomac River on the left and Antietam Creek on the right), but the Confederates fought with their back to the Potomac and only Boteler's Ford as the single line of retreat across the river. If Burnside's attack on the Confederate right had succeeded before A. P. Hill's division arrived, Lee's forces could have been trapped north of the river.*

tember 17, when McClellan finally crossed Antietam Creek to attack. The battle of Antietam (called Sharpsburg by the Confederates) proved to be the single bloodiest day in American history, with more than 23,000 casualties (killed, wounded, and captured) in the two armies.

Attacking from right to left on a four-mile front, McClellan's Army of the Potomac achieved potential breakthroughs at a sunken road northeast of Sharpsburg and in the rolling fields southeast of town. But fearing counterattacks, McClellan held back 20,000 of his troops and failed to follow through. Thus the battle ended in a draw. The battered Confederates still clung to their precarious line, with the Potomac at their back, at the end of a day in which more than 6,000 men on both sides were killed or mortally wounded. Even though he received reinforcements the next day and Lee received none, McClellan did not renew the attack.

The Emancipation Proclamation

Lincoln was not happy with this equivocal Union victory. But it was a victory with important consequences. Britain and France decided to withhold diplomatic recognition of the Confederacy. Northern Democrats failed to gain control of the House in the fall elections. And most significant of all, on September 22, Lincoln seized the occasion to issue his preliminary emancipation proclamation. It did not come as a total surprise. A month earlier, after Horace Greeley had written a strong editorial in the *New York Tribune* calling for action against slavery, Lincoln had responded with a public letter to Greeley. "My paramount object in this struggle," wrote Lincoln, "*is to save the Union. . . . If I could save the Union without freeing *any* slave I would do it, and if I could save it by freeing *all* the slaves I would do it; and if I could save it by freeing some and leaving others alone I would also do that." Lincoln had crafted these phrases carefully to maximize public support for his proclamation. He portrayed emancipation not as an end in itself but as a *means* toward the end of saving the Union.

Lincoln's proclamation did not go into effect immediately. Rather, it stipulated that if any state, or part of a state, was still in rebellion on January 1, 1863, the president would proclaim the slaves therein "forever free." Confederate leaders scorned this warning, and by January 1 no Southern state had returned to the Union. On New Year's Day Lincoln signed the final proclamation.

The Emancipation Proclamation exempted the border states, plus Tennessee and those portions of Louisiana and Virginia that were already under Union occupation, since these areas were deemed not to be in rebellion, and Lincoln's constitutional authority for the proclamation derived from his power as commander in chief to confiscate enemy property. The proclamation made the Northern soldiers an army of liberation. The North was now fighting for freedom as well as for Union.

A Winter of Discontent

Although Lee's retreat from Maryland and Braxton Bragg's retreat from Kentucky suggested that the Confederate tide might be ebbing, the tide soon turned. The Union could never win the war simply by turning back Confederate invasions. Northern armies would have to invade the South, defeat its armies, and destroy its ability to fight.

Displeased by McClellan's "slows" after Antietam, Lincoln replaced him on November 7, 1862, with General Ambrose E. Burnside. Burnside proposed to cross the Rappahannock River at Fredericksburg for a move on Richmond before bad weather

FOCUS QUESTION
What were the sources of internal dissent and dissension in the Confederacy? In the Union?

forced both sides into winter quarters. Although Lee put his men into a strong defensive position on the heights behind Fredericksburg, Burnside nevertheless attacked on December 13. He was repulsed with heavy casualties that shook the morale of both the Army and the public.

News from the western theater did little to dispel the gloom in Washington. The Confederates had fortified Vicksburg on bluffs commanding the Mississippi River. This preserved transportation links between the states to the east and west. To sever those links was the goal of Grant, who in November 1862 launched a two-pronged drive against Vicksburg. With 40,000 men, he marched 50 miles southward from Memphis by land, while his principal subordinate, William T. Sherman, came down the river with 32,000 men accompanied by a gunboat fleet. But raids by Confederate cavalry destroyed the railroads and supply depots in Grant's rear, forcing him to retreat to Memphis. Meanwhile, Sherman attacked the Confederates at Chickasaw Bluffs on December 29, with no more success than Burnside had enjoyed at Fredericksburg.

The only bit of cheer for the North came in central Tennessee. There, Lincoln had removed General Don Carlos Buell from command of the Army of the Cumberland and replaced him with William S. Rosecrans. On the Confederate side, Davis stuck with Braxton Bragg as commander of the Army of Tennessee.

On the day after Christmas Rosecrans moved from his base at Nashville to attack Bragg's force 30 miles to the south at Murfreesboro. The ensuing three-day battle (called Stones River by the Union and Murfreesboro by the Confederacy) resulted in Confederate success on the first day (December 31) but defeat on the last. Both armies suffered devastating casualties. The Confederate retreat to a new base 40 miles farther south enabled the North to call Stones River a victory.

Elsewhere, however, things went from bad to worse. Renewing the campaign against Vicksburg, Grant was bogged down in the swamps and rivers that protected that Confederate bastion on three sides. Only on the east, away from the river, was there high ground suitable for an assault on Vicksburg's defenses. Grant's problem was to get his army across the Mississippi to that high ground, along with supplies and transportation to support an assault. For three months, he floundered in the Mississippi-Yazoo bottomlands, while disease and exposure took a fearful toll of his troops.

THE RISE OF THE COPPERHEADS

During the winter of 1863, the Copperhead faction of the Democratic Party found a ready audience for its message that the war was a failure and should be abandoned. Having won control of the Illinois and Indiana legislatures the preceding fall, Democrats there called for an armistice and a peace conference. They also demanded retraction of the "wicked, inhuman, and unholy" Emancipation Proclamation.

In Ohio the foremost Peace Democrat, Congressman Clement L. Vallandigham, was planning to run for governor. What had this wicked war accomplished, Vallandigham asked Northern audiences. "Let the dead at Fredericksburg and Vicksburg answer." The Confederacy could never be conquered; the only trophies of the war were "debt, defeat, sepulchres." The solution was to "stop the fighting. Make an armistice. Withdraw your army from the seceded states." Above all, give up the unconstitutional effort to abolish slavery.

Vallandigham and other Copperhead spokesmen had a powerful effect on Northern morale. Alarmed by a wave of desertions, the army commander in Ohio had Vallandigham arrested in May 1863. A military court convicted him of treason for aiding and abetting the enemy. The court's action raised serious questions of civil liberties. Was the conviction a violation of Vallandigham's First Amendment right of free speech? Could a military court try a civilian under **martial law** in a state like Ohio where civil courts were functioning?

Lincoln was embarrassed by the swift arrest and trial of Vallandigham, which he learned about from the newspapers. To keep Vallandigham from becoming a martyr, Lincoln commuted his sentence from imprisonment to banishment. On May 15, Union cavalry escorted Vallandigham under a flag of truce to Confederate lines in Tennessee. He soon escaped to Canada on a blockade runner. There, from exile, Vallandigham conducted his campaign for governor of Ohio—an election he lost in October 1863.

> **martial law** *Government by military force rather than by citizens.*

ECONOMIC PROBLEMS IN THE SOUTH

Southerners were buoyed by their military success but were suffering from economic problems caused by the Union blockade, the weaknesses and imbalances of the Confederate economy, the escape of slaves to Union lines, and enemy occupation of some of the South's prime agricultural areas. Despite the conversion of hundreds of thousands of acres from cotton to food production, the deterioration of Southern railroads and the priority given to army shipments made food scarce in some areas. Prices rose much faster than wages. The price of salt—necessary to preserve meat in that prerefrigeration age—shot out of sight. Even the middle class suffered, especially in Richmond, whose population had more than doubled since 1861. One man wrote that the rats in his kitchen were so hungry that they nibbled bread crumbs from his daughter's hand "as tame as kittens. Perhaps we shall have to eat them!"

Things were even worse for the poor, especially for the wives and children of non-slaveholders who were away in the army. By the spring of 1863, food supplies were virtually gone. "I have 6 little children and my husband in the armey and what am I to do?" wrote a North Carolina farmwoman.

Some women took matters into their own hands. Denouncing "speculators" who allegedly hoarded goods to drive up prices, they marched to stores, denounced "extortion," and took what they wanted without paying. On April 2, 1863, a mob of more than 1,000 women and boys looted several shops in Richmond before the militia forced them to disperse. The Confederate government subsequently released some emergency food stocks to civilians, and state and county governments aided the families of soldiers. Better crops in 1863 helped to alleviate the worst shortages, but serious problems persisted.

THE WARTIME DRAFT AND CLASS TENSIONS

In both South and North, the draft intensified social unrest and turned it in the direction of class conflict. In April 1862 the Confederacy enacted a draft that made all white men aged 18 to 35 liable to conscription. A drafted man could hire a substitute, but the price of substitutes soon rose beyond the means of the

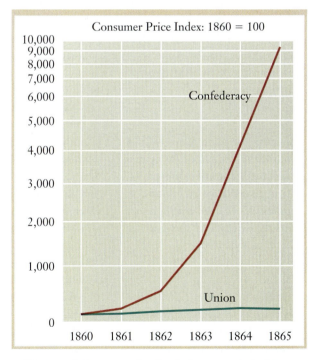

Wartime Inflation in the Confederacy and the Union

average Southern farmer or worker, giving rise to the bitter cry that it was "a rich man's war and a poor man's fight."

The cry grew louder in October 1862 when the Confederate Congress raised the draft age to 45 and added a clause exempting one white man from the draft on every plantation with 20 or more slaves. The purpose of this "overseer exemption" was to keep up production and prevent slave uprisings. But the so-called **Twenty Negro Law** was regarded as blatant discrimination against non-slaveholding farm families. The law provoked widespread draft dodging and desertions.

Similar discontent greeted the enactment of a conscription law in the North. In the summer of 1863, some 30,000 Union soldiers would be leaving military service, along with 80,000 of the nine-month militia called into service the preceding autumn. To meet the shortfall, Congress decreed in March that all male citizens aged 20 to 45 must enroll for the draft. Not all of them would necessarily be called, but all would be liable.

The law was intended more to encourage volunteers to come forward than it was to draft men directly. The War Department set a quota for every congressional district and gave it 50 days to meet its quota with volunteers before resorting to a draft lottery. Some districts avoided having to draft anyone by offering large bounties to volunteers. The bounty system produced glaring abuses, including **bounty jumpers** who enlisted and then deserted as soon as they got their money—often to enlist again under another name somewhere else.

The drafting process itself was also open to abuse. Like the Confederate law, the Union law permitted the hiring of substitutes. The Union law also allowed a drafted man the alternative of paying a **commutation fee** of $300 that exempted him from the current draft call (but not necessarily from the next one). That provision raised the cry of "rich man's war, poor man's fight" in the North as well. This sense of class resentment was nurtured by the Democratic Party. Democrats in Congress opposed conscription. Democratic newspapers told white workers that the draft would force them to fight a war to free the slaves, who would then come north to take their jobs. This volatile issue sparked widespread violence when the Northern draft got under way in the summer of 1863. The worst riot occurred in New York City on July 13–16, where huge mobs consisting mostly of Irish Americans demolished draft offices, lynched several blacks, and destroyed huge areas of the city in four days of looting and burning.

A POOR MAN'S FIGHT?

But the grievance that it was a rich man's war and a poor man's fight was more apparent than real. The principal forms of taxation to sustain the war were property, excise, and income taxes that bore proportionately more heavily on the wealthy than on the poor. In the South, the property of the rich suffered greater damage and confiscation than did the property of non-slaveholders. The war liberated 4 million slaves, the poorest class in America. Both the Union and Confederate armies were made up of men from all strata of society in proportion to their percentage of the population. If anything, among those who volunteered in 1861 and·1862, the planter class was overrepresented in the Confederate army and the middle class in the Union forces. Those volunteers, especially the officers, suffered the highest percentage of combat casualties.

Nor did conscription itself fall much more heavily on the poor than on the rich. Those who escaped the draft by decamping to the woods, the territories, or Canada came mostly from the poor. The Confederacy abolished substitution in December

Twenty Negro Law *Confederate conscription law that exempted from the draft one white man on every plantation owning 20 or more slaves. The law's purpose was to exempt overseers or owners who would ensure discipline over the slaves and keep up production but was regarded as discrimination by non-slaveholding families.*

bounty jumpers *Men who enlisted in the Union army to collect the bounties offered by some districts to fill military quotas; these men would enlist and then desert as soon as they got their money.*

commutation fee *$300 fee that could be paid by a man drafted into the Union army to exempt him from the current draft call.*

1863 and made men who had previously sent substitutes liable to the draft. In the North, several city councils, political machines, and businesses contributed funds to pay the commutation fees of drafted men who were too poor to pay out of their own pockets. In the end, it was neither a rich man's war nor a poor man's fight. It was an all-American war.

BLUEPRINT FOR MODERN AMERICA

The 37th Congress (1861–1863)—the Congress that enacted conscription, passed measures for confiscation and emancipation, and created the greenbacks and the national banking system (see Chapter 15)—also enacted three laws that provided what one historian has called "a blueprint for modern America": the Homestead Act, the Morrill Land-Grant College Act, and the Pacific Railroad Act. The Homestead Act granted a farmer 160 acres of land virtually free after he had lived on the land for five years and had made improvements on it. The Morrill Land-Grant College Act gave each state thousands of acres to fund the establishment of colleges for the teaching of "agricultural and mechanical arts." The Pacific Railroad Act granted land and loans to railroad companies to spur the building of a transcontinental railroad from Omaha to Sacramento. These laws helped farmers settle some of the most fertile land in the world, studded the land with state colleges, and spanned it with steel rails in a manner that altered the landscape of the western half of the country.

WOMEN AND THE WAR

The war advanced many other social changes, particularly with respect to women. In factories and on farms women took the place of the men who had gone off to war. The war accelerated the entry of women into the teaching profession, a trend that had already begun in the Northeast and now spread to other parts of the country. It also brought significant numbers of women into the civil service. The huge expansion of government bureaucracies after 1861 and the departure of male clerks to the army provided openings that were filled partly by women.

But women's most visible impact was in the field of medicine. The outbreak of war prompted the organization of soldiers' aid societies, hospital societies, and other voluntary associations, with women playing a leading role. Their most important function was to help the armies' medical branches provide more efficient, humane care for sick and wounded soldiers. Dr. Elizabeth Blackwell, the first American woman to earn an M.D. (1849), organized a meeting of 3,000 women in New York City on April 29, 1861. They put together the Women's Central Association for Relief, which became the nucleus for the most powerful voluntary association of the war, the United States Sanitary Commission. The Sanitary Commission was an essential adjunct of the Union Army's medical bureau. Most of its local volunteers were women. So were most of the nurses it provided to army hospitals. Nursing was not a new profession for women, but it had not been a respectable wartime profession. The fame won by Florence Nightingale of Britain during the Crimean War a half-dozen years earlier had begun to change that perception. And the flocking of thousands of middle- and even upper-class women volunteers to army hospitals did a great deal to transform nursing from a menial occupation to a respected profession. The nurses had to overcome the deep-grained suspicions of army surgeons and the opposition of husbands and fathers

QUICK   REVIEW

THE HOME FRONTS

- Peace Democrats ("Copperheads") opposed war

- Crippling inflation in the South

- Conscription and antidraft riots created tensions in North

- Women provided crucial contributions to the war effort

Reproduced from the Collections of the Library of Congress

Courtesy of the Illinois State Historical Library

FEMALE SPIES AND SOLDIERS. *In addition to working in war industries and serving as army nurses, some women pursued traditionally male wartime careers as spies and soldiers. One of the most famous Confederate spies was Rose O'Neal Greenhow, a Washington widow and socialite who fed information to officials in Richmond. Federal officers arrested her in August 1861 and deported her to Richmond in the spring of 1862. She was photographed with her daughter in the Old Capitol prison in Washington, D.C., while awaiting trial. In October 1864 she drowned in a lifeboat off Wilmington, North Carolina, after a blockade runner carrying her back from a European mission was run aground by a Union warship.*

The second photograph shows a Union soldier who enlisted in the 95th Illinois Infantry under the name of Albert Cashier and fought through the war. Not until a farm accident in 1911 revealed Albert Cashier to be a woman, whose real name was Jennie Hodgers, was her secret disclosed. Most of the other estimated 400 women who evaded the superficial physical exams and passed as men to enlist in the Union and Confederate armies were more quickly discovered and discharged—six of them after they had babies while in the army. A few, however, served long enough to be killed in action.

who shared the cultural sentiment that the shocking, embarrassingly physical atmosphere of an army hospital was no place for a respectable woman. But many thousands of women did it, winning grudging and then enthusiastic admiration.

The war also bolstered the fledgling women's rights movement. It was no coincidence that Elizabeth Cady Stanton and Susan B. Anthony founded the National Woman Suffrage Association in 1869, only four years after the war. Although it did not win final victory for half a century, this movement could not have achieved the momentum that made it a force in American life without the work of women in the Civil War.

THE CONFEDERATE TIDE CRESTS AND RECEDES

The Army of Northern Virginia and the Army of the Potomac spent the winter of 1862–1863 on opposite banks of the Rappahannock River. With the coming of spring, Union commander Joe Hooker resumed the offensive. On April 30, Hooker crossed with his men several miles upriver and came in on Lee's rear. But Lee quickly faced most of his troops about and confronted the enemy in dense woods near the crossroads hostelry of Chancellorsville. Nonplussed, Hooker lost the initiative.

THE BATTLE OF CHANCELLORSVILLE

Even though the Union forces outnumbered the Confederates by almost two to one, Lee boldly went over to the offensive. On May 2, Stonewall Jackson led 28,000 men on a stealthy march through the woods to attack the Union right flank late in the afternoon. The surprise was complete, and Jackson's assault crumpled the Union flank. Lee resumed the attack the next day. In three more days of fighting that brought 12,800 Confederate and 16,800 Union casualties (the largest number for a single battle in the war so far), Lee drove the Union troops back across the Rappahannock.

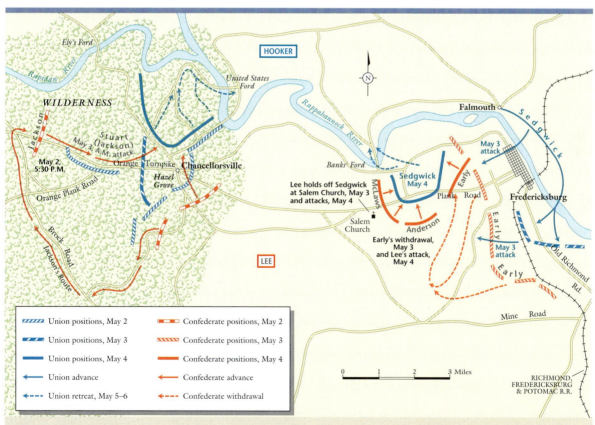

Map 16.2

BATTLE OF CHANCELLORSVILLE, MAY 2–6, 1863. *This map demonstrates the advantage of holding "interior lines," which enabled General Lee to shift troops back and forth to and from the Chancellorsville and Fredericksburg fronts over the course of three days while the two parts of the Union Army remained separated.*

"My God!" exclaimed Lincoln when he heard the news of Chancellorsville. "What will the country say?" Copperhead opposition intensified. Southern sympathizers in Britain renewed efforts for diplomatic recognition of the Confederacy. Lee decided to parlay his tactical victory at Chancellorsville into a strategic offensive by again invading the North. A victory on Union soil would convince Northerners and foreigners alike that the Confederacy was invincible. As his army moved north in June 1863, Lee was confident of success.

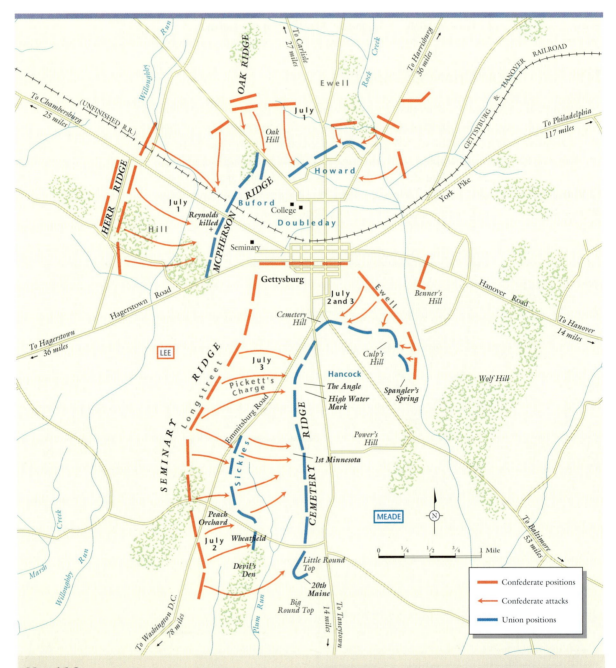

Map 16.3
BATTLE OF GETTYSBURG, JULY 1–3, 1863. *On July 2 and 3, the Union Army had the advantage of interior lines at Gettysburg, which enabled General Meade to shift reinforcements from his right on Culp's Hill to his left near Little Round Top over a much shorter distance than Confederate reinforcements from one flank to the other would have to travel.*

THE GETTYSBURG CAMPAIGN

At first, all went well. The Confederates brushed aside or captured Union forces in the northern Shenandoah Valley and in Pennsylvania. Stuart's cavalry threw a scare into Washington by raiding behind Union lines into Maryland and Pennsylvania. But that very success led to trouble. With Stuart's cavalry separated from the rest of the army, Lee was deprived of vital intelligence. By June 28 several detachments of Lee's forces were scattered about Pennsylvania, far from their base and vulnerable to being cut off.

At this point, Lee learned that the Army of the Potomac was moving toward him, now under the command of George Gordon Meade. Lee immediately ordered his own army to reassemble in the vicinity of Gettysburg. There, on the morning of July 1, the vanguard of the two armies met in a clash that grew into the greatest battle in American history.

As the fighting spread west and north of town, reinforcements were summoned to both sides. The Confederates got more men into the battle and broke the Union lines late that afternoon, driving the survivors to a defensive position on Cemetery Hill south of town. Judging this position too strong to take with his own troops, General Richard Ewell chose not to press the attack as the sun went down on what he presumed would be another Confederate victory. But when the sun rose next morning, the reinforced Union Army was holding a superb defensive position from Culp's Hill and Cemetery Hill south to Little Round Top. Lee's principal subordinate, First Corps commander James Longstreet, advised against attack, but Lee believed his army invincible. Pointing to the Union lines, he said: "The enemy is there, and I am going to attack him there."

Longstreet reluctantly led the attack on the Union left. His men fought with fury, but the Union troops fought back with equal fury. By the end of the day, Confederate forces had made small gains at great cost, but the main Union line had held firm.

Lee was not yet ready to yield the offensive. Having attacked both Union flanks, he thought the center might be weak, so on July 3 he ordered a frontal attack on Cemetery Ridge, led by a fresh division under George Pickett. After a two-hour artillery barrage, Pickett's troops moved forward. "Pickett's Charge" was shot to pieces; scarcely half of the men returned unwounded to their own lines. It was the final act in an awesome three-day drama that left some 50,000 men killed, wounded, or captured.

Lee limped back to Virginia pursued by the Union troops. Lincoln was unhappy with Meade for not cutting off the Confederate retreat. Nevertheless, Gettysburg was a great Northern victory. And it came at the same time as other important Union successes in Mississippi, Louisiana, and Tennessee.

THE VICKSBURG CAMPAIGN

In mid-April, Grant had begun a move that would put Vicksburg in a vise. The Union ironclad fleet ran downriver past the big guns at Vicksburg with little damage. Grant's troops marched down the Mississippi's west bank and were ferried across the river 40 miles south of Vicksburg. There they kept the Confederate defenders off balance by striking east toward Jackson instead of marching north to Vicksburg. Grant's purpose was to scatter the Confederate forces in central Mississippi and to destroy the rail network so that his rear would be secure when he turned toward Vicksburg. It was a brilliant strategy, flawlessly executed. Grant's troops trapped 32,000 Confederate troops and 3,000 civilians in Vicksburg.

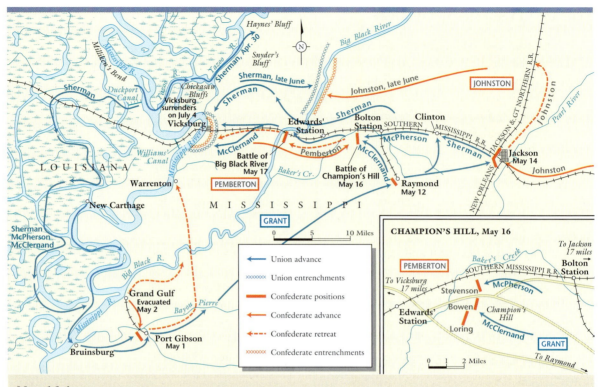

Map 16.4

VICKSBURG CAMPAIGN, APRIL–JULY 1863. *This map illustrates Grant's brilliant orchestration of the campaign that involved Sherman's feint at Haynes' Bluff (top of map) on April 30 while the rest of the Union forces crossed at Bruinsburg (bottom of map) and then cleared Confederate resistance out of the way eastward to Jackson before turning west to invest Vicksburg.*

The Confederate army threw back Union assaults against the Vicksburg trenches on May 19 and 22. Grant then settled down for a siege. Running out of supplies, the Vicksburg garrison surrendered on July 4. On July 9, the Confederate garrison at Port Hudson, 200 river miles south of Vicksburg, surrendered to a besieging Union Army. Northern forces now controlled the entire length of the Mississippi River. The Confederacy had been torn in two.

CHICKAMAUGA AND CHATTANOOGA

QUICK REVIEW

THE PENDULUM OF WAR

- Confederate victory at Chancellorsville

- Union victories at Gettysburg and Vicksburg

- Confederate success at Chickamauga

- Union success at Chattanooga

Northerners had scarcely finished celebrating the twin victories of Gettysburg and Vicksburg when they learned of an important—and almost bloodless—triumph. On June 24, Union commander Rosecrans assaulted the Confederate defenses in the Cumberland foothills of east-central Tennessee. He used his cavalry and a mounted infantry brigade armed with new repeating rifles to get around the Confederate flanks while his infantry threatened the Confederate front. In the first week of July, the Confederates retreated all the way to Chattanooga.

After a pause for resupply, Rosecrans's army advanced again in August, this time in tandem with a smaller Union Army in eastern Tennessee commanded by Burnside. Again the outnumbered Confederates fell back, evacuating Knoxville on September 2 and Chattanooga on September 9. This action severed the South's only direct east-west rail link. Union forces now stood poised for a campaign into Georgia. For the Confederacy it was a stunning reversal of the situation only four months earlier, when the Union cause had appeared hopeless.

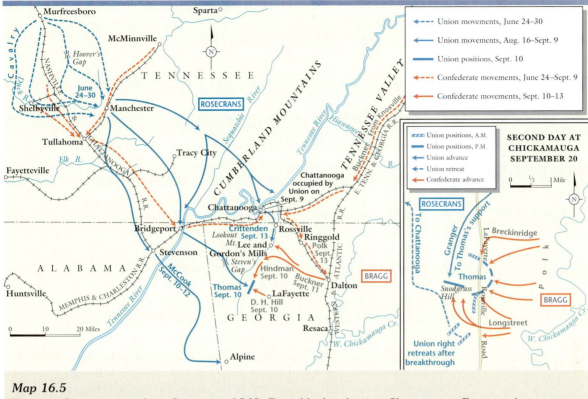

Map 16.5

ROAD TO CHICKAMAUGA, JUNE–SEPTEMBER 1863. *From Murfreesboro to Chattanooga, Rosecrans' campaign of maneuver on multiple fronts, as shown on this map, forced Bragg's Army of Tennessee all the way south into Georgia in a campaign with minimal casualties before Bragg counterattacked at Chickamauga.*

But Confederate General Braxton Bragg sent fake deserters into Union lines with tales of a Confederate retreat toward Atlanta. He then laid a trap for Rosecrans's troops as they advanced through the mountain passes south of Chattanooga. To help him spring it, Davis approved the detachment of Longstreet with two divisions from Lee's army to reinforce Bragg. On September 19, the Confederates turned and counterattacked Rosecrans's army in the valley of Chickamauga Creek.

Over the next two days, in ferocious fighting that produced more casualties (36,000) than any other single battle save Gettysburg, the Confederates finally scored a victory. On September 20 Longstreet's men broke through the Union line, sending part of the Union Army reeling back to Chattanooga. Only a firm stand by corps commander George H. Thomas prevented a rout. Lincoln subsequently appointed Thomas commander of the Army of the Cumberland to replace Rosecrans.

Lincoln also sent two army corps from Virginia under Hooker and two from Vicksburg under Sherman to reinforce Thomas, whose troops in Chattanooga were under virtual siege by Bragg's forces, which held most of the surrounding heights. More important, Lincoln put Grant in overall command of the beefed-up Union forces there. When Grant arrived in late October, he welded the various Northern units into a new army and opened a new supply line into Chattanooga. On November 24, Hooker's troops drove Confederate besiegers off massive Lookout Mountain. Next day, an assault on Bragg's main line at Missionary Ridge east of Chattanooga drove the Confederates off the ridge and 20 miles south into Georgia.

These battles climaxed a string of Union victories in the second half of 1863. The Southern diarist Mary Boykin Chesnut described "gloom and unspoken despondency hang[ing] like a pall everywhere." Jefferson Davis replaced Bragg with Joseph E.

Johnston. Lincoln summoned Grant to Washington and appointed him general-in-chief of all Union armies. The stage was set for a fight to the finish.

BLACK MEN IN BLUE

FOCUS QUESTION
What contributions did women and African Americans make to the war efforts in both North and South?

The events of the second half of 1863 also confirmed emancipation as a Union war aim. Northerners had not greeted the Emancipation Proclamation with great enthusiasm. Democrats and border-state Unionists continued to denounce it, and many Union soldiers resented the idea that they would now be risking their lives for black freedom. The Democratic Party had hoped to capitalize on this opposition, and on Union military failures, to win important off-year elections. Northern military victories knocked one prop out from under the Democratic platform, and the performance of black soldiers fighting for the Union knocked out another.

The enlistment of black soldiers was a logical corollary of emancipation. Proposals to recruit black soldiers, Democrats said, were part of a Republican plot to establish "the equality of the black and white races." In a way, that charge was correct. One consequence of black men fighting for the Union would be to advance the black race a long way toward equal rights. "Once let the black man get upon his person the brass letters, U.S.," said Frederick Douglass, "and a musket on his shoulder and bullets in his pocket, and there is no power on earth which can deny that he has earned the right to citizenship."

But it was pragmatism more than principle that pushed the North toward black recruitment. One purpose of emancipation was to deprive the Confederacy of black laborers and to use them for the Union. Some Union commanders in occupied portions of Louisiana, South Carolina, and Missouri began to organize black regiments in 1862. The Emancipation Proclamation legitimized this policy with its proposal to enroll able-bodied male contrabands in new black regiments. However, under this policy black soldiers would not serve as combat troops. They would be paid less than white soldiers, and their officers would be white.

PART OF COMPANY E, 4TH U.S. COLORED INFANTRY. *Organized in July 1863, most of the men were former slaves from North Carolina. The 4th fought in several actions on the Petersburg and Richmond fronts in 1864, helping to capture part of the Petersburg defenses on June 15. Of the 166 black regiments in the Union Army, the 4th suffered the fourth-largest number of combat deaths.*

BLACK SOLDIERS IN COMBAT

Continuing pressure from abolitionists, as well as military necessity, eroded discrimination somewhat. Congress enacted equal pay in 1864. The regiments themselves lobbied for the right to fight as combat soldiers. In May and June 1863, black regiments in Louisiana fought well at Port Hudson and Milliken's Bend, near Vicksburg. "The bravery of the blacks in the battle of Milliken's Bend completely revolutionized the sentiment of the army with regard to the employment of negro troops," wrote the assistant secretary of war.

Even more significant was the action of the 54th Massachusetts Infantry, the first black regiment raised in the North. Its officers, headed by Colonel Robert Gould Shaw, came from prominent New England antislavery families. Shaw worked hard to win the right for the regiment to fight, and on July 18, 1863, he succeeded: The 54th was assigned to lead an assault on Fort Wagner, part of the network of Confederate defenses protecting Charleston. Though the attack failed, the 54th fought courageously, suffering 50 percent casualties, including Colonel Shaw, who was killed.

The battle took place just after the occurrence of draft riots in New York, where white mobs had lynched blacks. Abolitionist and Republican commentators drew the moral: Black men who fought for the Union deserved more respect than white men who rioted against it. Lincoln made this point eloquently in a widely published letter to a political meeting in August 1863. When final victory was achieved, he wrote, "there will be some black men who can remember that, with silent tongue, and clenched teeth, and steady eye, and well-poised bayonet, they have helped mankind on to this great consummation; while, I fear, there will be some white ones, unable to forget that, with malignant heart, and deceitful speech, they have strove to hinder it."

EMANCIPATION CONFIRMED

Lincoln's letter set the tone for Republican campaigns in state elections that fall. The party swept them all. In effect, the elections were a powerful endorsement of the administration's emancipation policy. On November 19 Lincoln alluded indirectly to this achievement in his address to the crowd assembled at Gettysburg to dedicate the cemetery for the Union soldiers who had died in the battle there. From those honored dead, said Lincoln, let us take "increased devotion to that cause for which they gave the last full measure of devotion," that the nation "shall not perish from the earth" but "shall have a new birth of freedom."

But emancipation would not be assured of survival until it had been christened by the Constitution. On April 8, 1864, the Senate passed the Thirteenth Amendment to abolish slavery, but Democrats in the House blocked the required two-thirds majority there. Not until after Lincoln's reelection in 1864 would the House pass the amendment, which became part of the Constitution on December 6, 1865. In the end, though, the fate of slavery depended on the outcome of the war. And some of the heaviest fighting lay ahead.

THE YEAR OF DECISION

Many Southerners succumbed to defeatism in the winter of 1863–1864. Desertions from Confederate armies increased. Inflation galloped out of control. According to a Richmond diarist, a merchant told a poor woman in October 1863 that the price of

HISTORY THROUGH FILM

GLORY (1989)

Directed by Edward Zwick; starring Matthew Broderick (Robert Gould Shaw), Denzel Washington (Trip), Morgan Freeman (Rawlins)

Glory was the first feature film to treat the role of black soldiers in the Civil War. It tells the story of the 54th Massachusetts Volunteer Infantry from its organization in early 1863 through its climactic assault on Fort Wagner six months later. When the 54th moved out at dusk on July 18 to lead the attack, the idea of black combat troops still seemed a risky experiment. The *New York Tribune,* a strong supporter of black enlistment, had nevertheless observed in May 1863 that many Northern whites "have no faith" that black soldiers would stand and fight Southern whites who considered themselves a master race. The unflinching behavior of the regiment in the face of an overwhelming hail of lead and iron and its casualties of some 50 percent settled the matter. "Who now asks in doubt and derision 'Will the Negro fight?'" commented one abolitionist. "The answer comes to us from those graves beneath Fort Wagner's walls, which the American people will surely never forget."

Many did forget, but *Glory* revived their collective memory. Its combat scenes, climaxed by the assault on Fort Wagner, are among the most realistic and effective in any war movie. Morgan Freeman and Denzel Washington give memorable perfor-

mances as a fatherly sergeant and a rebellious private who nevertheless picks up the flag when the color-bearer falls and carries it to the ramparts of Fort Wagner where he too is killed. Matthew Broderick's portrayal of Colonel Robert Gould Shaw is less memorable, for the real Shaw was more assertive and mature than Broderick's Shaw.

Except for Shaw, the principal characters in the film are fictional. There were no real Major Cabot Forbes; no tough Irish Sergeant Mulcahy; no black Sergeant John Rawlins; no brash, hardened Private Trip. Indeed, a larger fiction is involved here. The movie gives the impression that most of the 54th's soldiers were former slaves. In fact, this atypical black regiment was recruited mainly in the North, so most of the men had always been free. The story that screenwriter Kevin Jarre and director Edward Zwick chose to tell is not simply about the 54th Massachusetts but about black soldiers in the Civil War. Most of the 179,000 African Americans in the Union army (and at least 10,000 in the navy) were slaves until a few months, even days, before they joined up. Fighting for the Union bestowed upon former slaves a new dignity, self-respect, and militancy, which helped them achieve equal citizenship and political rights—for a time—after the war.

Many of the events dramatized in *Glory* are also fictional: the incident of the racist quartermaster who initially refuses to distribute shoes to Shaw's men; the whipping Trip receives as punishment for going AWOL; Shaw's threat to expose his superior officer's corruption as a way of securing a combat assignment for the 54th; and the religious meeting the night before the assault on Fort Wagner. All of these scenes point toward a larger truth, however, most vividly portrayed symbolically in a surreal, and at first glance, irrelevant scene. During a training exercise, Shaw gallops his horse along a path flanked by stakes, each holding aloft a watermelon. Shaw slashes right and left with his sword, slicing and smashing every melon. The point becomes clear when we recall the identification of watermelons with the "darky" stereotype. The image of smashed melons drives home the essential message of *Glory.*

A scene from Glory showing black soldiers of the 54th Massachusetts ready to fire at the enemy.

a barrel of flour was $70: "'My God!' exclaimed she, 'how can I pay such prices? I have seven children; what shall I do?' 'I don't know, madam,' said he, coolly, 'unless you eat your children.'" The Davis administration, like the Lincoln administration a year earlier, had to face congressional elections during a time of public discontent, for the Confederate constitution mandated such elections in odd-numbered years. Political parties had ceased to exist in the Confederacy after Democrats and former Whigs had tacitly declared a truce in 1861. By 1863, however, significant hostility to Davis had emerged.

Some anti-administration candidates ran on a quasi-peace platform (analogous to that of the Copperheads in the North) that called for an armistice and peace negotiations. Left unresolved were the terms of such negotiations—reunion or independence. But any peace overture from a position of weakness was tantamount to conceding defeat. Still, anti-administration candidates made significant gains in the 1863 Confederate elections, though they fell about 15 seats short of a majority in the House and two seats short in the Senate.

Out of the Wilderness

Shortages, inflation, political discontent, military defeat, high casualties, and the loss of thousands of slaves did not break the Southern spirit. The Confederate armies were no longer powerful enough to invade the North or to try to win the war with a knockout blow, but they were still strong enough to fight a war of attrition. If they could hold out long enough and inflict enough casualties on the Union armies, they might weaken the Northern will to continue fighting.

Northerners were vulnerable to this strategy. Military success in 1863 had created a mood of confidence, and people expected a quick, decisive victory in 1864. When Grant decided to remain in Virginia with the Army of the Potomac and to leave Sherman in command of the Union forces in northern Georgia, Northerners expected these two heavyweights to floor the Confederacy with a one-two punch. Lincoln was alarmed by this euphoria, fearing that disappointment might trigger despair.

And that is what almost happened. Grant's strategic plan was elegant in its simplicity. While smaller Union armies in peripheral theaters carried out auxiliary campaigns, the two principal armies in Virginia and Georgia would attack the main Confederate forces under Lee and Johnston. Grant ordered simultaneous offensives on all fronts, to prevent the Confederates from shifting reinforcements from one theater to another.

Grant's offensives began in the first week of May. The heaviest fighting occurred in Virginia. When the Army of the Potomac crossed the Rapidan River, Lee attacked it in the flank while it was still in the Wilderness, a thick scrub forest where Union superiority in numbers and artillery would count for little. Lee's action brought on two days (May 5–6) of the most confused, frenzied fighting the war had yet seen. The battle surged back and forth, with the Confederates inflicting 18,000 casualties and suffering 12,000 themselves. Having apparently halted Grant's offensive, they claimed a victory.

Spotsylvania and Cold Harbor

But Grant did not retreat. Instead, he moved toward Spotsylvania Courthouse, a key crossroads 10 miles closer to Richmond. Skillfully, Lee pulled back to cover the road junction. Repeated Union assaults during the next 12 days (May 8–19) left another 18,000 Northerners and 12,000 Southerners killed, wounded, or captured. The

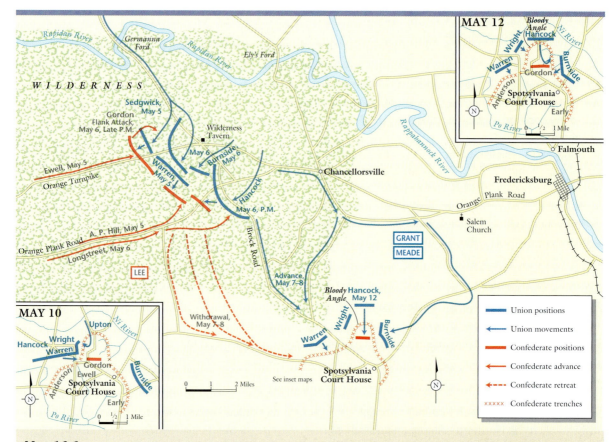

Map 16.6

BATTLE OF THE WILDERNESS AND SPOTSYLVANIA, MAY 5–12, 1864. *Four major battles with a total of more than 100,000 casualties to both sides were fought within a few miles of Fredericksburg between December 1862 and May 1864. Compare this map with the Chancellorsville map on p. 421. The first battle of Fredericksburg on December 13, 1862 (described pp. 415–416) was fought in the same vicinity as the Fredericksburg fighting on May 3, 1863, shown on the Chancellorsville map.*

Confederates fought from an elaborate network of trenches and log breastworks they had constructed virtually overnight.

Having achieved no better than stalemate around Spotsylvania, Grant moved south around Lee's right flank in an effort to force the outnumbered Confederates into an open fight. But Lee, anticipating Grant's moves, confronted him from behind formidable defenses at the North Anna River, Totopotomoy Creek, and near the crossroads inn of Cold Harbor, only 10 miles northeast of Richmond. Believing the Confederates must be exhausted and demoralized by their repeated retreats, Grant decided to attack at Cold Harbor on June 3—a costly mistake. Lee's troops were ragged and hungry but far from demoralized. Their withering fire inflicted 7,000 casualties in less than an hour.

STALEMATE IN VIRGINIA

Now Grant moved all the way across the James River to strike at Petersburg, an industrial city and rail center 20 miles south of Richmond. If Petersburg fell, the Confederates could not hold Richmond. But once more Lee's troops raced southward and blocked Grant's troops. Four days of Union assaults (June 15–18) produced another 11,000 Northern casualties but no breakthrough.

Union losses in just six weeks had been so high that the Army of the Potomac had lost its offensive power. Grant reluctantly settled down for a siege along the Petersburg-Richmond front that would last more than nine grueling months.

Meanwhile, other Union operations in Virginia had achieved little success. Benjamin Butler bungled an attack up the James River against Richmond and was stopped by a scraped-together army under Beauregard. A Union thrust up the Shenandoah Valley was blocked at Lynchburg in June by Jubal Early. Early then led a raid all the way to the outskirts of Washington on July 11 and 12 before being driven back to Virginia. Union cavalry under Philip Sheridan inflicted considerable damage on Confederate resources in Virginia, but they did not strike a crippling blow. In the North, frustration set in.

THE ATLANTA CAMPAIGN

In Georgia, Sherman forced Johnston south toward Atlanta by constantly flanking him to the Union right, generally without bloody battles. By the end of June, Sherman had advanced 80 miles at the cost of 17,000 casualties to Johnston's 14,000—only one-third of the combined losses of Grant and Lee.

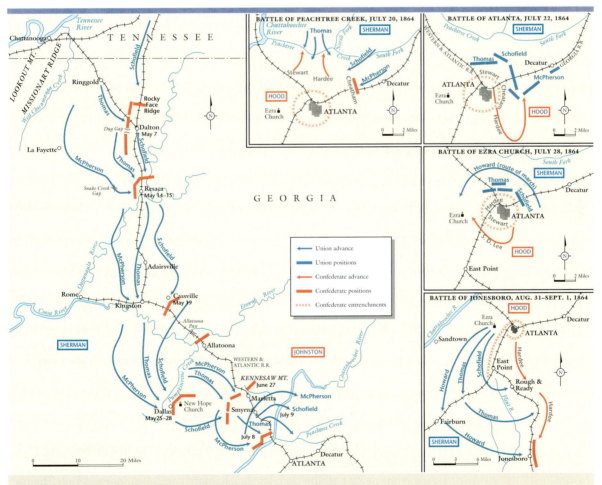

Map 16.7
CAMPAIGN FOR ATLANTA, MAY–SEPTEMBER 1864. *The main map illustrates Sherman's campaign of maneuver that forced Johnston back to Atlanta with relatively few battles. The first three inset maps show the Confederate counterattacks launched by Hood and the fourth shows how the Union Army got astride the last two railroads entering Atlanta from the south and forced Hood to evacuate the city.*

Davis grew alarmed by Johnston's apparent willingness to yield territory without a fight. Sherman again flanked the Confederate defenses at Kennesaw Mountain in early July. He crossed the Chattahoochee River and drove Johnston back to Peachtree Creek less than five miles from Atlanta. Fearing that Johnston would abandon the city, Davis replaced him with John Bell Hood.

Hood immediately prepared to counterattack against the Yankees. He did so three times, in late July. Each time, the Confederates reeled back in defeat, suffering a total of 15,000 casualties to Sherman's 6,000. At last, Hood retreated into the formidable earthworks ringing Atlanta and launched no more attacks. But his army did manage to keep Sherman's cavalry and infantry from taking the two railroads leading into Atlanta from the south. Like Grant at Petersburg, Sherman seemed to settle down for a siege.

Peace Overtures

By August, the Confederate strategy of attrition seemed to be working. Union casualties on all fronts during the preceding three months totaled a staggering 110,000. "Who shall revive the withered hopes that bloomed at the opening of Grant's campaign?" asked the leading Democratic newspaper, the New York World. "STOP THE WAR!" shouted Democratic headlines. "All are tired of this damnable tragedy."

Even Republicans joined the chorus of despair. "Our bleeding, bankrupt, almost dying country longs for peace," wrote Horace Greeley of the New York Tribune. Greeley became involved in abortive "peace negotiations" spawned by Confederate agents in Canada. Those agents convinced Greeley that they carried peace overtures from Davis, but Lincoln was skeptical. Still, given the mood of the North in midsummer 1864, Lincoln could not reject any opportunity to stop the bloodshed. He deputized Greeley to meet with the Confederate agents in Niagara Falls on the Canadian side of the border. At almost the same time (mid-July), two other Northerners met under a flag of truce with Davis in Richmond. Lincoln had carefully instructed them—and Greeley—that his conditions for peace were "restoration of the Union and abandonment of slavery."

Of course, Davis would no more accept those terms than Lincoln would accept his. Although neither of the peace contacts came to anything, the Confederates gained a propaganda victory by claiming that Lincoln's terms had been the only obstacle to peace. Northern Democrats ignored the Southern refusal to accept reunion and focused on the slavery issue as the sole stumbling block. "Tens of thousands of white men must yet bite the dust to allay the negro mania of the President," ran a typical Democratic editorial. By August, even staunch Republicans were convinced that Lincoln's reelection was an impossibility. Lincoln thought so too. "I am going to be beaten," he told a friend, "and unless some great change takes place, *badly* beaten."

Lincoln faced enormous pressure to drop emancipation as a condition of peace, but he refused to yield. He would rather lose the election than go back on the promise he had made in the Emancipation Proclamation. Some 130,000 black soldiers and sailors were fighting for the Union. They would not do so if they thought the North intended to forsake them.

At the end of August, the Democrats nominated McClellan for president. The platform on which he ran declared that "after four years of failure to restore the Union by the experiment of war . . . [we] demand that immediate efforts be made for a cessation of hostilities." Southerners were jubilant. Democratic victory on that platform, said the Charleston Mercury, "must lead to peace and our independence" if "for the next two months we *hold our own and prevent military success by our foes.*"

THE PRISONER-EXCHANGE CONTROVERSY

The Democratic platform also raised another contentious matter. By midsummer 1864 the plight of Union and Confederate captives had become one of the most bitter issues of the war. Because of the upcoming presidential election, and also because conditions were generally worse in Southern prisons, it was a political issue mainly in the North.

In 1862 the Union and Confederate armed forces had signed a cartel for the exchange of prisoners captured in battle. The arrangement had worked reasonably well for a year, making large prison camps unnecessary. But when the Union Army began to organize regiments of former slaves, the Confederate government announced that if they were captured, they and their white officers would be put to death. However, Lincoln threatened retaliation on Confederate prisoners of war if it did so. Nevertheless, Confederate troops sometimes murdered black soldiers and their officers as they tried to surrender.

In most cases, though, Confederate officers returned captured black soldiers to slavery or put them to hard labor on Southern fortifications. Expressing outrage at this treatment, in 1863 the Lincoln administration suspended the exchange of prisoners until the Confederacy agreed to treat white and black prisoners alike. The Confederacy refused.

There matters stood as the heavy fighting of 1864 poured scores of thousands of captured soldiers into hastily contrived prison compounds that quickly became death camps. Prisoners were subjected to overcrowding, poor sanitation, contaminated water, scanty rations, inadequate medical facilities, and the exposure of Union prisoners to the heat of a deep-South summer and Confederate prisoners to the cold of a Northern winter. The suffering of Northern prisoners was especially acute because of the deterioration of the Southern economy. Nearly 16 percent of all Union soldiers held in Southern prison camps died. Andersonville was the most notorious hellhole. A stockade camp of 26 acres with neither huts nor tents, designed to accommodate 15,000 prisoners, it held 33,000 in August 1864. They died at the rate of more than 100 a day. Altogether, 13,000 Union soldiers died at Andersonville.

The Lincoln administration came under pressure to renew exchanges, but the Confederates would not budge on the question of exchanging black soldiers. After a series of battles on the Richmond-Petersburg front in September 1864, Lee proposed an informal exchange of prisoners. Grant agreed, on condition that black soldiers captured in the fighting be included "the same as white soldiers." Lee replied that "negroes belonging to our citizens are not considered subjects of exchange and were not included in my proposition." No exchange, then, responded Grant. Lincoln backed this policy. He would not sacrifice the principle of equal treatment of black prisoners, even though local Republican leaders warned that many in the North "will work and vote against the President."

THE ISSUE OF BLACK SOLDIERS IN THE CONFEDERATE ARMY

During the winter of 1864–1865 the Confederate government quietly abandoned its refusal to exchange black prisoners, and exchanges resumed. One reason for this reversal was a Confederate decision to recruit slaves to fight for the South. Two years earlier, Davis had denounced the North's arming of freed slaves. But by February 1865, Southern armies were desperate for manpower, and slaves constituted the only remaining reserve. Davis pressed the Confederate Congress to enact a bill for recruitment of black soldiers. The assumption that any slaves who fought for the South would have to be granted freedom generated bitter opposition. "What did we go to war for, if not to protect our property?" asked a Virginia senator. By three votes in the House and one in the Senate, the Confederate Congress finally passed the bill on March 13, 1865. Before any Southern black regiments could be organized, however, the war ended.

LINCOLN'S REELECTION AND THE END OF THE CONFEDERACY

FOCUS QUESTION

Why did Lincoln expect in August 1864 to be defeated for reelection? What changed to enable him to win reelection by a substantial margin?

Despite Republicans' fears, events on the battlefield, rather than political controversies, had the strongest impact on U.S. voters in 1864. In effect, the election became a referendum on whether to continue fighting for unconditional victory. And suddenly the military situation changed dramatically.

THE CAPTURE OF ATLANTA

This change was foreshadowed by a Union naval success on August 5, 1864, when Admiral David G. Farragut led a fleet past the forts guarding the entrance to Mobile Bay and cut that important blockade-running port off from the sea. Even more important was the fall of Atlanta.

After a month of apparent stalemate on the Atlanta front, Sherman's army again made a large movement by the right flank to attack the last rail link into Atlanta from the south. At the battle of Jonesboro on August 31 and September 1, Sherman's men captured the railroad. Hood abandoned Atlanta to save his army. On September 2, jubilant Union troops marched into the city.

This news had an enormous impact on the election. A New York Republican wrote that the capture of Atlanta, "coming at this political crisis, is the greatest event of the war." The *Richmond Examiner* glumly concurred. The fall of Atlanta, it declared, "came in the very nick of time" to "save the party of Lincoln from irretrievable ruin."

THE SHENANDOAH VALLEY

If Atlanta was not enough to brighten the prospects for Lincoln's reelection, events in Virginia's Shenandoah Valley were. After Early's raid through the valley in July, Grant put Philip Sheridan in charge of a reinforced Army of the Shenandoah, telling him to "go after Early and follow him to the death." Sheridan infused the same spirit into the Army of the Shenandoah that he had previously imbued in his cavalry. On September 19 they attacked Early's force near Winchester and after a daylong battle sent the Confederates flying to the south. Sheridan pursued them, attacking again on September 22 at Fisher's Hill 20 miles south of Winchester. Early's line collapsed, and his routed army fled 60 more miles southward.

But Jubal Early was not yet willing to give up. Reinforced by a division from Lee, on October 19 he launched a dawn attack across Cedar Creek, 12 miles south of Winchester. He caught the Yankees by surprise and drove them back in disorder. At the time of the attack, Sheridan was returning to his army from Washington, where he had gone to confer on strategy. He jumped onto his horse and sped to the battlefield. By sundown, Sheridan's charisma and tactical leadership had turned the battle from a Union defeat into another Confederate rout.

The victories won by Sherman and Sheridan ensured Lincoln's reelection on November 8 by a majority of 212 to 21 in the Electoral College. Soldiers played a notable role in the balloting. Every Northern state except three whose legislatures were controlled by Democrats had passed laws allowing absentee voting by soldiers. Seventy-eight percent of the military vote went to Lincoln, compared with 54 percent of the civilian vote. The men who were doing the fighting had sent a clear message that they meant to finish the job.

FROM ATLANTA TO THE SEA

Many Southerners got the message. But not Davis. The Confederacy remained "as erect and defiant as ever," he told his Congress in November 1864. It was this last-ditch resistance that Sherman set out to break in his famous march from Atlanta to the sea.

Sherman had concluded that defeat of the Confederate armies was not enough to win the war; the railroads, factories, and farms that supported those armies must also be destroyed. The will of the civilians who sustained the war must be crushed. Sherman expressed more bluntly than anyone else the meaning of this strategy. "We cannot change the hearts of those people of the South," he said, "but we can make war so terrible and make them so sick of war that generations would pass away before they would again appeal to it."

Sherman urged Grant to let him march through the heart of Georgia, living off the land and destroying all resources not needed by his army. Grant and Lincoln were reluctant to authorize such a risky move, especially with Hood's army of 40,000 men still intact in northern Alabama. But Sherman assured them that he would send George Thomas to take command of a force of 60,000 men in Tennessee who would be more than a match for Hood. With another 60,000, Sherman could "move through Georgia, smashing things to the sea."

Lincoln and Grant finally consented. On November 16, Sherman's avengers marched out of Atlanta after burning a third of the city, including some nonmilitary property. Southward they marched 280 miles to Savannah, wrecking everything in their path that could by any stretch of the imagination be considered of military value and much that could not.

THE BATTLES OF FRANKLIN AND NASHVILLE

They encountered little resistance. Instead of chasing Sherman, Hood invaded Tennessee with the hope of recovering that state for the Confederacy. But this campaign turned into a disaster that virtually destroyed his army. On November 30, the Confederates attacked part of the Union force at Franklin, 20 miles south of Nashville. It was a slaughter. But instead of retreating, Hood moved on to Nashville, where on December 15 and 16 Thomas launched an attack that almost wiped out the Army of Tennessee. Its remnants retreated to Mississippi, where Hood resigned in January 1865.

FORT FISHER AND SHERMAN'S MARCH THROUGH THE CAROLINAS

News of Hood's defeat produced, in the words of a Southern diarist, "the darkest and most dismal day" of the Confederacy's short history. But worse was yet to come. Lee's army in Virginia drew its dwindling supplies overland from the Carolinas and through the port of Wilmington, North Carolina, the only city still accessible to blockade runners. The mouth of the Cape Fear River below Wilmington was guarded by massive Fort Fisher, whose big guns kept blockade ships at bay and protected the runners. In January 1865 the largest armada of the war—58 ships with 627 guns—pounded Fort Fisher for two days, disabling most of its big guns. Army troops and marines landed and stormed the fort, capturing it on January 15. That ended the blockade running, and Sherman soon put an end to supplies from the Carolinas as well.

At the end of January, Sherman's soldiers headed north from Savannah, eager to take revenge on South Carolina, which to their mind had started the war. Here, they made even less distinction between civilian and military property than they had in Georgia and left even less of Columbia standing than they had of Atlanta. Seemingly invincible, Sherman's army pushed into North Carolina and brushed aside the force that Joseph E. Johnston had assembled to stop them.

THE ROAD TO APPOMATTOX

The Army of Northern Virginia was the only entity that now kept the Confederacy alive, but it was on the verge of disintegration. Scores of its soldiers were deserting every day. On April 1, Sheridan's cavalry and an infantry corps smashed the right flank of Lee's line at Five Forks and cut off the last railroad into Petersburg. The next day, Grant attacked all along the line and forced Lee to abandon both Petersburg and Richmond. As the Confederate government fled its capital, its army set fire to all the military stores it could not carry. The fires spread and destroyed more of Richmond than the Northern troops had destroyed of Atlanta or Columbia.

Lee's starving men limped westward, hoping to turn south and join the remnants of Johnston's army in North Carolina. But Sheridan's cavalry raced ahead and cut them off at Appomattox, 90 miles from Petersburg, on April 8. When the weary Confederates tried a breakout attack the next morning, their first probe revealed solid ranks of Union infantry arrayed behind the cavalry. It was the end. "There is nothing left for me to do," said Lee, "but to go and see General Grant." Lee met with Grant at the house of Wilmer McLean. There, Grant dictated the terms of surrender.

The terms were generous. Thirty thousand captured Confederates were allowed to go home on condition that they promise never again to take up arms against the

QUICK   REVIEW

BATTLE FRONTS AND HOME FRONTS 1864–1865

- Stalemate in Virginia despite heavy fighting

- Failure of peace overtures in 1864

- Capture of Atlanta by Sherman and victories in the Shenandoah Valley broke stalemate

- Reelection of Lincoln meant war to final victory at Appomattox

TABLE 16.1

CASUALTIES IN CIVIL WAR ARMIES AND NAVIES   Confederate records are incomplete; the Confederate data listed here are therefore estimates. The actual Confederate totals were probably higher.

	KILLED AND MORTALLY WOUNDED IN COMBAT	DIED OF DISEASE	DIED IN PRISON	MISCELLANEOUS DEATHS*	TOTAL DEATHS	WOUNDED, NOT MORTALLY	TOTAL CASUALTIES
Union	111,904	197,388	30,192	24,881	364,345	277,401	641,766
Confederate (estimated)	94,000	140,000	26,000	No Estimates	260,000	195,000	455,000
Both armies (estimated)	205,904	337,388	56,192	24, 881	624,345	472,401	1,096,766

*Accidents, drownings, causes not stated, etc.

ABRAHAM LINCOLN IN 1865. *This is the last photograph of Lincoln, taken on April 10, 1865, four days before his assassination. Four years of war had left their mark on the 56-year-old president; note the lines of strain, fatigue, and sadness in his face.*

United States. After completing the surrender formalities on April 9, Grant introduced Lee to his staff, which included Colonel Ely Parker, a Seneca Indian. As Lee shook hands with Parker, he stared for a moment at Parker's dark features and said: "I am glad to see one real American here." Parker replied solemnly: "We are all Americans."

THE ASSASSINATION OF LINCOLN

Wild celebrations broke out in the North at the news of the fall of Richmond, followed soon by news of Appomattox. But almost overnight, the celebrations turned to mourning. On the evening of April 14, the careworn Abraham Lincoln sought to relax by attending a comedy at Ford's Theatre. In the middle of the play, John Wilkes Booth broke into Lincoln's box and shot the president fatally in the head. An aspiring actor, Booth was a native of Maryland and a frustrated, unstable egotist who hated Lincoln for what he had done to Booth's beloved South. As he jumped from Lincoln's box to the stage and escaped out a back door, he shouted Virginia's state motto at the stunned audience: "Sic semper tyrannis" ("Thus always to tyrants").

Lincoln's death in the early morning of April 15 produced an outpouring of grief throughout the North and among newly freed slaves in the South. The martyred president did not live to see the culmination of his great achievement in leading the nation to a victory that preserved its existence and abolished slavery. Within 10 weeks after Lincoln's death, his assassin was trapped and killed in a burning barn in Virginia (April 26), the remaining Confederate armies surrendered one after another (April 26, May 4, May 26, June 23), and Union cavalry captured the fleeing Jefferson Davis in Georgia (May 10). The trauma of the Civil War was over, but the problems of peace and reconstruction had just begun.

C O N C L U S I O N

Northern victory in the Civil War resolved two fundamental questions that had been left unresolved by the revolution of 1776 and the Constitution of 1789: whether this fragile experiment in federalism called the United States would survive as one nation, and whether that nation, founded on a charter of liberty, would continue to exist as the largest slaveholding country in the world. Before 1861 the question of whether a state could secede from the Union had remained open. Eleven states did secede, but their defeat in a war that cost 625,000 lives resolved the issue. Since 1865 no state has seriously threatened secession. And in 1865 the adoption of the Thirteenth Amendment to the Constitution confirmed the supreme power of the national government to abolish slavery and ensure the liberty of all Americans.

At the same time the Civil War accomplished a regional transfer of power from South to North. From 1800 to 1860 the slave states had used their leverage in the Jeffersonian Republican and Jacksonian Democratic parties to control national politics. A southern slaveholder was president of the United States during two-thirds of the years from 1789 to 1861. Most congressional leaders and Supreme Court justices during that period were southerners. But for half a century after 1861 no native of a southern state was elected president, only one served as Speaker of the House and none as president pro tem of the Senate, and only 5 of the 26 Supreme Court justices appointed during that half-century were from the South. In 1860 the South's share of the national wealth was 30 percent; in 1870 it was 12 percent. The institutions and ideology of a plantation society and a caste system that had dominated half of the country before 1861 went down with a great crash in 1865—to be replaced by the institutions and ideology of free-labor capitalism. Once feared as the gravest threat to liberty, the power of the national government sustained by a large army had achieved the greatest triumph of liberty in American history. With victory and peace in 1865, the reunited nation turned its attention to the issue of equality.

QUESTIONS FOR REVIEW AND CRITICAL THINKING

Review

1. What factors led Lincoln to his decision to issue the Emancipation Proclamation?
2. What were the sources of internal dissent and dissension in the Confederacy? In the Union?
3. What contributions did women and African Americans make to the war efforts in both North and South?
4. Why did Lincoln expect in August 1864 to be defeated for reelection? What changed to enable him to win reelection by a substantial margin?

Discovery

What kinds of broad social changes did the Civil War bring?

Critical Thinking

1. How did a war that began, on the part of the North, with the goal of restoring a Union in which slavery existed in half of the country, become transformed into a war to give the nation a new birth of freedom?
2. In the winter of 1862–1863 Northern morale was at rock bottom and the prospects for Confederate success appeared bright. Yet two years later the Confederacy lay in ruins and its dream of independent nationhood was doomed. How and why did this happen?

SUGGESTED READINGS

Several studies offer important information and insights about questions of strategy and command in military operations: **Joseph G. Glatthaar, *Partners in Command: The Relationships between Leaders in the Civil War*** (1993); **Richard M. McMurry, *Two Great Rebel Armies*** (1989); **Michael C. Adams, *Our Masters the Rebels: A Speculation on Union Military Defeat in the East, 1861–1865*** (1978), reissued under the title ***Fighting for Defeat*** (1992); **Mark Grimsley, *The Hard Hand of War: Union Military Policy toward Southern Civilians, 1861–1865*** (1995); and **Gary W. Gallagher, *The Confederate War*** (1997). Of the many books about black soldiers in the Union Army, the most useful is **Joseph T. Glatthaar, *Forged in Battle: The Civil War Alliance of Black Soldiers and White Officers*** (1990). The Confederate debate about enlisting and freeing slave soldiers is chronicled in **Robert Durden, *The Gray and the Black: The Confederate Debate on Emancipation*** (1972). Conscription in the Confederacy and Union is treated in **Albert B. Moore, *Conscription and Conflict in the Confederacy*** (1924), and **James W. Geary, *We Need Men: The Union Draft in the Civil War*** (1991).

For the draft riots in New York, see **Adrian Cook, *The Armies of the Streets: The New York Draft Riots of 1863*** (1974). The best study of the civil liberties issue in the North is **Mark E. Neely, Jr., *The Fate of Liberty: Abraham Lincoln and Civil Liberties*** (1990), and the same author has covered the same issue in the Confederacy in **Southern Rights: Political Prisoners and the Myth of Confederate Constitutionalism** (1999). For Civil War medicine, **Alfred Jay Bollet, *Civil War Medicine: Challenges and Triumphs*** (2002) is indispensable. A succinct account of the emancipation issue is **Ira Berlin, et al., *Slaves No More: Three Essays on Emancipation and the Civil War*** (1992).

The activities of women in the U.S. Sanitary Commission, as spies, and even as soldiers, are covered in **Jeanie Attie, *Patriotic Toil: Northern Women and the Civil War*** (1998); **Elizabeth D. Leonard, *All the Daring of a Soldier: Women of the Civil War Armies*** (1999); and **Deanne Blanton and Lauren M. Cook, *They Fought Like Demons: Women Soldiers in the American Civil War*** (2002).

ONLINE SOURCES GUIDE

ThomsonNOW™   Visit ThomsonNOW to access primary sources, exercises, quizzes, and audio chapter summaries related to this chapter:
http://www.thomsonedu.com/login

DISCOVERY

What kinds of broad social changes did the Civil War bring?

In thinking about this question, begin by breaking it down into the components shown below. A discussion of the significance of each component should appear in your answer.

WARFARE

Look at the photograph of the African American soldiers and think about the reading in this chapter. Why was it more dangerous to be an African American soldier than a white soldier for the Union? What were the potential consequences? What effect(s) did the employment of African American soldiers have on the movement toward equal rights?

PART OF COMPANY E, 4TH U.S. COLORED INFANTRY

CULTURE AND SOCIETY

Consider the photograph of a female soldier, Jennie Hodgers, who posed as a man in order to enlist. What roles did women play in the war? What reasons might a woman have for secretly serving in a combat role? Both militaries seem to have discharged any woman discovered serving in the ranks. Why would the military not want women in the army?

Courtesy of the Illinois State Historical Library

FEMALE SOLDIER

17

RECONSTRUCTION, 1863–1877

From the beginning of the Civil War, the North fought to "reconstruct" the Union. At first Lincoln's purpose was to restore the Union as it had existed before 1861. But once the abolition of slavery became a Northern war aim, the Union could never be reconstructed on its old foundations. Instead, it must experience a "new birth of freedom," as Lincoln had said at the dedication of the military cemetery at Gettysburg.

But precisely what did "a new birth of freedom" mean? At the very least it meant the end of slavery. The slave states would be reconstructed on a free-labor basis. But what would be the dimensions of liberty for the 4 million freed slaves? Would they become citizens equal to their former masters in the eyes of the law? And on what terms should the Confederate states return to the Union? What would be the powers of the states and of the national government in a reconstructed Union?

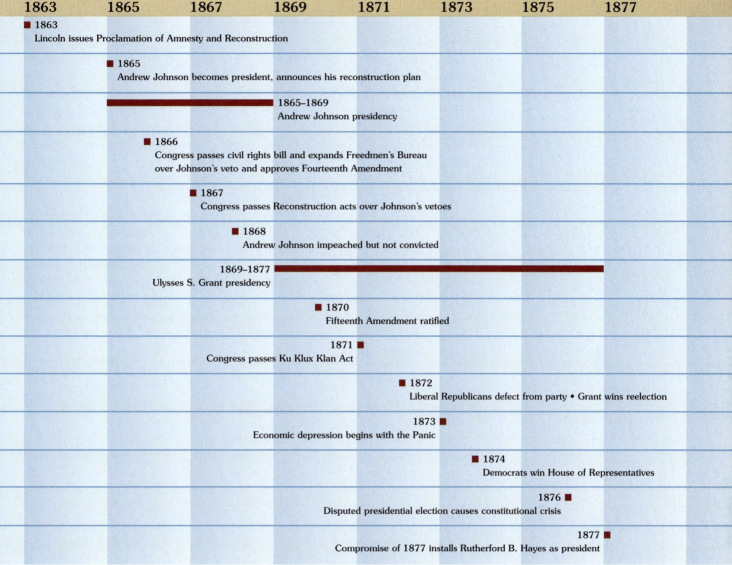

1863	1865	1867	1869	1871	1873	1875	1877

1863
Lincoln issues Proclamation of Amnesty and Reconstruction

1865
Andrew Johnson becomes president, announces his reconstruction plan

1865–1869
Andrew Johnson presidency

1866
Congress passes civil rights bill and expands Freedmen's Bureau over Johnson's veto and approves Fourteenth Amendment

1867
Congress passes Reconstruction acts over Johnson's vetoes

1868
Andrew Johnson impeached but not convicted

1869–1877
Ulysses S. Grant presidency

1870
Fifteenth Amendment ratified

1871
Congress passes Ku Klux Klan Act

1872
Liberal Republicans defect from party • Grant wins reelection

1873
Economic depression begins with the Panic

1874
Democrats win House of Representatives

1876
Disputed presidential election causes constitutional crisis

1877
Compromise of 1877 installs Rutherford B. Hayes as president

WARTIME RECONSTRUCTION

Lincoln pondered these questions long and hard. At first he feared that whites in the South would never extend equal rights to the freed slaves. In 1862 and 1863, Lincoln encouraged freedpeople to emigrate to all-black countries like Haiti. But black leaders, abolitionists, and many Republicans objected to that policy. Black people were Americans. Why should they not have the rights of American citizens instead of being urged to leave the country?

Lincoln eventually was converted to the logic and justice of that view. But in beginning the process of reconstruction, Lincoln first reached out to southern *whites* whose allegiance to the Confederacy was lukewarm. On December 8, 1863, Lincoln issued his Proclamation of **Amnesty** and Reconstruction, which offered presidential pardon to southern whites who took an oath of allegiance to the United States and accepted the abolition of slavery. In any state where the number of white males aged

amnesty *General pardon granted to a large group of people.*

21 or older who took this oath equaled 10 percent of the number of voters in 1860, that nucleus could reestablish a state government to which Lincoln promised presidential recognition.

Because the war was still raging, this policy could be carried out only where Union troops controlled substantial portions of a Confederate state: Louisiana, Arkansas, and Tennessee in early 1864. Nevertheless, Lincoln hoped that once the process had begun in those areas, it might snowball as Union military victories convinced more and more Confederates that their cause was hopeless. As matters turned out, those military victories were long delayed, and reconstruction in most parts of the South did not begin until 1865. Another problem that slowed the process was growing opposition within Lincoln's own party. Many Republicans believed that white men who had fought *against* the Union should not be rewarded with restoration of their political rights while black men who had fought *for* the Union were denied those rights. The Proclamation of Reconstruction stated that "any provision which may be adopted by [a reconstructed] State government in relation to the freed people of such State, which shall recognize and declare their permanent freedom, provide for their education, and which may yet be consistent, as a temporary arrangement, with their present condition as a laboring, landless, and homeless class, will not be objected to by the national Executive." This seemed to mean that white landowners and former slaveholders could adopt labor regulations and other measures to control former slaves, so long as they recognized their freedom.

RADICAL REPUBLICANS AND RECONSTRUCTION

These were radical advances over slavery, but for many Republicans they were not radical enough. If the freedpeople were landless, they said, provide them with land by confiscating the plantations of leading Confederates as punishment for treason. Radical Republicans also distrusted oaths of allegiance sworn by ex-Confederates. Rather than simply restoring the old ruling class to power, they asked, why not give freed slaves the vote, to provide a genuinely loyal nucleus of supporters in the South?

These radical positions did not command a majority of Congress in 1864. Yet the experience of Louisiana, the first state to reorganize under Lincoln's more moderate policy, convinced even nonradical Republicans to block that policy. Enough white men in the occupied portion of the state took the oath of allegiance to satisfy Lincoln's conditions. They adopted a new state constitution and formed a government that abolished slavery and provided a school system for blacks. But the new government did not grant blacks the right to vote. It also authorized planters to enforce restrictive labor policies on black plantation workers. Louisiana's actions alienated a majority of congressional Republicans, who refused to admit representatives and senators from the "reconstructed" state.

At the same time, though, Congress failed to enact a reconstruction policy of its own. This was not for lack of trying. In fact, both houses passed the Wade-Davis reconstruction bill (named for Senator Benjamin Wade of Ohio and Representative Henry Winter Davis of Maryland) in July 1864. That bill did not enfranchise blacks, but it did impose such stringent loyalty requirements on southern whites that few of them could take the required oath. Lincoln therefore vetoed it.

Lincoln's action infuriated many Republicans. Wade and Davis published a blistering "manifesto" denouncing the president. This bitter squabble threatened for a time to destroy Lincoln's chances of being reelected. But Union military success in the fall of 1864 reunited the Republicans behind Lincoln. The collapse of Confederate military resistance the following spring set the stage for compromise on a policy for the postwar South. Two days after Appomattox, Lincoln promised that he would soon announce such a policy. But three days later he was assassinated.

Andrew Johnson and Reconstruction

FOCUS QUESTION

What were the positions of Presidents Abraham Lincoln and Andrew Johnson and of moderate and radical Republicans in Congress on the issues of restoring the South to the Union and protecting the rights of freed slaves?

In 1864 Republicans had adopted the name "Union Party" to attract the votes of War Democrats and border-state Unionists who could not bring themselves to vote Republican. For the same reason, they also nominated Andrew Johnson of Tennessee as Lincoln's running mate.

Of "poor white" heritage, Johnson had clawed his way up in the rough-and-tumble politics of east Tennessee. This was a region of small farms and few slaves, where there was little love for the planters who controlled the state. Johnson denounced the planters as "stuck-up aristocrats" who had no empathy with the **southern yeomen** for whom Johnson became a self-appointed spokesman. Johnson was the only senator from a seceding state who refused to support the Confederacy. For this, the Republicans rewarded him with the vice presidential nomination, hoping to attract the votes of prowar Democrats and upper-South Unionists.

Booth's bullet therefore elevated to the presidency a man who still thought of himself as primarily a Democrat and a southerner. The trouble this might cause in a party that was mostly Republican and northern was not immediately apparent, however. In fact, Johnson's enmity toward the "stuck-up aristocrats" whom he blamed for leading the South into secession prompted him to utter dire threats against "traitors." "Traitors must be impoverished," he said. "They must not only be punished, but their social power must be destroyed."

Radical Republicans liked the sound of this. It seemed to promise the type of reconstruction they favored—one that would deny political power to ex-Confederates and enfranchise blacks. They envisioned a coalition between these new black voters and the small minority of southern whites who had never supported the Confederacy. These men could be expected to vote Republican. Republican governments in southern states would guarantee freedom and would pass laws to provide civil rights and economic opportunity for freed slaves.

JOHNSON'S POLICY

From a combination of pragmatic, partisan, and idealistic motives, therefore, radical Republicans prepared to implement a progressive reconstruction policy. But Johnson unexpectedly refused to cooperate. Instead of calling Congress into special session, he moved ahead on his own. On May 29, Johnson issued two proclamations. The first provided for a blanket amnesty for all but the highest-ranking Confederate officials and military officers and those ex-Confederates with taxable property worth $20,000 or more. The second named a provisional governor for North Carolina and directed him to call an election of delegates to frame a new state constitution. Only white men who had received amnesty and taken an oath of allegiance could vote. Similar proclamations soon followed for other former Confederate states. Johnson's policy was clear. He would exclude both blacks and upper-class whites from the reconstruction process.

Many Republicans supported Johnson's policy at first. But the radicals feared that restricting the vote to whites would open the door to the restoration of the old power

southern yeoman *Farmer who owned relatively little land and few or no slaves.*

structure in the South. They began to sense that Johnson was as dedicated to white supremacy as any Confederate. "White men alone must govern the South," he told a Democratic senator. After a tense confrontation with a group of black men led by Frederick Douglass, Johnson told his private secretary: "I know that damned Douglass; he's just like any nigger, and he would sooner cut a white man's throat than not."

Moderate Republicans believed that black men should participate to some degree in the reconstruction process, but in 1865 they were not yet prepared to break with the president. They regarded his policy as an "experiment" that would be modified as time went on. "Loyal negroes must not be put down, while disloyal white men are put up," wrote a moderate Republican. "But I am quite willing to see what will come of Mr. Johnson's experiment."

SOUTHERN DEFIANCE

As it happened, none of the state conventions enfranchised a single black. Some of them even balked at ratifying the Thirteenth Amendment (which abolished slavery). Reports from Unionists and army officers in the South told of neo-Confederate violence against blacks and their white sympathizers. Johnson seemed to encourage such activities by allowing the organization of white militia units in the South. "What can be hatched from such an egg," asked a Republican newspaper, "but another rebellion?"

Then there was the matter of presidential pardons. After talking fiercely about punishing traitors, and after excluding several classes of them from his amnesty proclamation, Johnson began to issue special pardons to many ex-Confederates, restoring to them all property and political rights. Moreover, under the new state constitutions southern voters were electing hundreds of ex-Confederates to state offices. Even more alarming to northerners, who thought they had won the war, was the election to Congress of no fewer than nine ex-Confederate congressmen, seven ex-Confederate state officials, four generals, four colonels, and even the former Confederate vice president, Alexander H. Stephens.

Somehow the aristocrats and traitors Johnson had denounced in April had taken over the reconstruction process. What had happened? Flattery was part of the answer. In applying for pardons, thousands of prominent ex-Confederates or their tearful female relatives had confessed the error of their ways and had appealed for presidential mercy. Reveling in his power, Johnson waxed eloquent on his "love, respect, and confidence" toward southern whites, for whom he now felt "forbearing and forgiving."

More important, perhaps, was the praise and support Johnson received from leading northern Democrats. Though the Republicans had placed him on their presidential ticket in 1864, Johnson was after all a Democrat. That party's leaders enticed Johnson with visions of reelection as a Democrat in 1868 if he could manage to reconstruct the South in a manner that would preserve a Democratic majority there.

THE BLACK CODES

That was just what the Republicans feared. Their concern was confirmed in the fall of 1865 when some state governments enacted **Black Codes.**

One of the first tasks of the legislatures of the reconstructed states was to define the rights of 4 million former slaves who were now free. The option of treating them exactly like white citizens was scarcely considered. Instead, the states excluded black people from juries and the ballot box, did not permit them to testify against whites in court, banned interracial marriage, and punished them more severely than whites for

Black Codes *Laws passed by southern states that restricted the rights and liberties of former slaves.*

certain crimes. Some states defined any unemployed black person as a vagrant and hired him out to a planter, forbade blacks to lease land, and provided for the apprenticing to whites of black youths who did not have adequate parental support.

These Black Codes aroused anger among northern Republicans, who saw them as a brazen attempt to reinstate a **quasi-slavery.** "We tell the white men of Mississippi," declared the *Chicago Tribune,* "that the men of the North will convert the State of Mississippi into a frog pond before they will allow such laws to disgrace one foot of the soil in which the bones of our soldiers sleep and over which the flag of freedom waves." And, in fact, the Union Army's occupation forces did suspend the implementation of Black Codes that discriminated on racial grounds.

LAND AND LABOR IN THE POSTWAR SOUTH

The Black Codes, though discriminatory, were designed to address a genuine problem. The end of the war had left black-white relations in the South in a state of limbo. The South's economy was in a shambles. Burned-out plantations, fields growing up in weeds, and railroads without tracks, bridges, or **rolling stock** marked the trail of war. Most tangible assets except the land itself had been destroyed. Law and order broke down in many areas. The war had ended early enough in the spring to allow the planting of at least some food crops. But who would plant and cultivate them? One-quarter of the South's white farmers had been killed in the war; the slaves were slaves no more. "We have nothing left to begin anew with," lamented a South Carolina planter. "I never did a day's work in my life, and I don't know how to begin."

But despite all, life went on. Slaveless planters and their wives, soldiers' widows and their children, plowed and planted. Confederate veterans drifted home and went to work. Former slave owners asked their former slaves to work the land for wages or shares of the crop, and many did so. But others refused, because for them to leave the old place was an essential part of freedom. "You ain't, none o' you, gwinter feel rale free," said a black preacher to his congregation, "till you shakes de dus' ob de Ole Plantashun offen yore feet" (dialect in original source).

Thus in the summer of 1865 the roads were alive with freedpeople on the move. Many of them signed on to work at farms just a few miles from their old homes. Others moved into town. Some looked for relatives who had been sold away during slavery or from whom they had been separated during the war. Some wandered aimlessly. Crime increased, and whites organized vigilante groups to discipline blacks and force them to work.

THE FREEDMEN'S BUREAU

Into this vacuum stepped the United States Army and the **Freedmen's Bureau.** Tens of thousands of troops remained in the South until civil government could be restored. The Freedmen's Bureau (its official title was Bureau of Refugees, Freedmen, and Abandoned Lands), created by Congress in March 1865, became the principal agency for overseeing relations between former slaves and owners. Staffed by army officers, the bureau established posts throughout the South to supervise free-labor wage contracts between landowners and freedpeople. The Freedmen's Bureau also issued food rations to 150,000 people daily during 1865, one-third of them to whites.

The Freedmen's Bureau was viewed with hostility by southern whites. But without it, the postwar chaos and devastation in the South would have been much greater.

quasi-slavery *Position that resembled slavery, such as that created by the Black Codes.*

rolling stock *Locomotives, freight cars, and other types of wheeled equipment owned by railroads.*

Freedmen's Bureau *Federal agency created in 1865 to supervise newly freed people. It oversaw relations between whites and blacks in the South, issued food rations, and supervised labor contracts.*

share wages *Payment of workers' wages with a share of the crop rather than with cash.*

sharecropping *Working land in return for a share of the crops produced instead of paying cash rent.*

40 acres and a mule *Largely unfulfilled hope of many former slaves that they would receive free land from the confiscated property of ex-Confederates.*

Bureau agents used their influence with black people to encourage them to sign free-labor contracts and return to work.

In negotiating labor contracts, the bureau tried to establish minimum wages. Because there was so little money in the South, however, many contracts called for **share wages**—that is, paying workers with shares of the crop. At first, landowners worked their laborers in large groups called gangs. But many black workers resented this system. Thus, a new system evolved, called **sharecropping,** whereby a black family worked a specific piece of land in return for a share of the crop produced on it. This system represented an uneasy and imperfect compromise between landowners who wanted to control their workers and freedpeople who wanted greater independence.

LAND FOR THE LANDLESS

Freedpeople, of course, would have preferred to farm their own land. "What's de use of being free if you don't own land enough to be buried in?" asked one black sharecropper (dialect in original). Some black farmers did manage to save up enough money to buy small plots of land. Demobilized black soldiers purchased land with their bounty payments, sometimes pooling their money to buy an entire plantation, on which several black families settled. Northern philanthropists helped some freedmen buy land. But for most ex-slaves the purchase of land was impossible. Few of them had money, and even if they did, whites often refused to sell.

Several northern radicals proposed legislation to confiscate ex-Confederate land and redistribute it to freedpeople. But those proposals got nowhere. And the most promising effort to put thousands of slaves on land of their own also failed. In January 1865, after his march through Georgia, General William T. Sherman had issued a military order setting aside thousands of acres of abandoned plantation land in the Georgia and South Carolina low country for settlement by freed slaves. The army even turned over some of its surplus mules to black farmers. The expectation of **40 acres and a mule** excited freedpeople in 1865. But President Johnson's Amnesty Proclamation and his wholesale issuance of pardons restored most of this property to pardoned ex-Confederates. The same thing happened to white-owned land elsewhere in the South. Placed under the temporary care of the Freedmen's Bureau for subsequent possible distribution to freedpeople, by 1866 nearly all of this land had been restored to its former owners by order of President Johnson.

©Bettmann/Corbis

SHARECROPPERS WORKING IN THE FIELDS. *After the war, former planters tried to employ their former slaves in gang labor to grow cotton and tobacco, with the only difference from slavery being the grudging payment of wages. Freedpeople resisted this system as being too reminiscent of slavery. They compelled landowners to rent them plots of land on which these black families struggled to raise corn and cotton or tobacco, paying a share of the crop as rent—hence "sharecropping." This posed photograph was intended to depict the family labor of sharecroppers; in reality, most black farmers had a mule to pull their plow.*

A BLACK SCHOOL DURING RECONSTRUCTION. *In the antebellum South, teaching slaves to read and write was forbidden. Thus, about 90 percent of the freedpeople were illiterate in 1865. One of their top priorities was education. At first, most of the teachers in the freedmen's schools established by northern missionary societies were northern white women. But as black teachers were trained, they took over the elementary schools, such as this one photographed in the 1870s.*

EDUCATION

Abolitionists were more successful in helping freedpeople get an education. During the war, freedmen's aid societies and missionary societies founded by abolitionists had sent teachers to Union-occupied areas of the South to set up schools for freed slaves. After the war, this effort was expanded with the aid of the Freedmen's Bureau. Two thousand northern teachers fanned out into every part of the South to train black teachers. After 1870 missionary societies concentrated on making higher education available to African Americans. They founded many of the black colleges in the South. These efforts reduced the southern black illiteracy rate to 70 percent by 1880 and to 48 percent by 1900.

THE ADVENT OF CONGRESSIONAL RECONSTRUCTION

The civil and political rights of freedpeople would be shaped by the terms of reconstruction. By the time Congress met in December 1865, the Republican majority was determined to take control of the process by which former Confederate states would be restored to full representation. Congress refused to admit the representatives and senators elected by the former Confederate states under Johnson's reconstruction policy, and set up a special committee to formulate new terms. The committee held hearings at which southern Unionists, freedpeople, and U.S. Army officers testified to abuse and terrorism in the South. Their testimony convinced Republicans of the need for stronger federal intervention to define and protect the civil rights of freedpeople. However, because racism was still strong in the North, the special committee decided to draft a constitutional amendment that would encourage southern states to enfranchise blacks but would not require them to do so.

SCHISM BETWEEN PRESIDENT AND CONGRESS

Meanwhile, Congress passed two laws to protect the economic and civil rights of freedpeople. The first extended the life of the Freedmen's Bureau and expanded its powers. The second defined freedpeople as citizens with equal legal rights and gave federal courts appellate jurisdiction to enforce those rights. But to the dismay of moderates who were trying to heal the widening breach between the president and Congress, Johnson vetoed both measures. He followed this action with a speech to Democratic supporters in which he denounced Republican leaders as traitors who did not want to restore the Union except on terms that would degrade white southerners. Democratic newspapers applauded the president for vetoing bills that would "compound our race with niggers, gypsies, and baboons."

THE FOURTEENTH AMENDMENT

Johnson had thrown down the gauntlet to congressional Republicans. But with better than a two-thirds majority in both houses, they passed the Freedmen's Bureau and Civil Rights bills over the president's vetoes. Then on April 30, the special committee submitted to Congress its proposed Fourteenth Amendment to the Constitution. After lengthy debate, the amendment received the required two-thirds majority in Congress on June 13 and went to the states for ratification. Section 1 defined all native-born or naturalized persons, including blacks, as American citizens and prohibited the states from abridging the "privileges and immunities" of citizens, from depriving "any person of life, liberty, or property without due process of law," and from denying to any person "the equal protection of the laws." Section 2 gave states the option of either enfranchising black males or losing a proportionate number of congressional seats and electoral votes. Section 3 disqualified a significant number of ex-Confederates from holding federal or state office. Section 4 guaranteed the national debt and repudiated the Confederate debt. Section 5 empowered Congress to enforce the Fourteenth Amendment by "appropriate legislation."

The Fourteenth Amendment had far-reaching consequences. Section 1 has become the most important provision in the Constitution for defining and enforcing civil rights. It vastly expanded federal powers to prevent state violations of civil rights. It also greatly enlarged the rights of blacks.

THE 1866 ELECTIONS

During the campaign for the 1866 congressional elections Republicans made clear that any ex-Confederate state that ratified the Fourteenth Amendment would be declared "reconstructed" and that its representatives and senators would be seated in Congress. Tennessee ratified the amendment, but Johnson counseled other southern

made its first appearance during the elections. Nevertheless, voters in seven states ratified their constitutions and elected new legislatures that ratified the Fourteenth Amendment in the spring of 1868. That amendment became part of the United States Constitution the following summer, and the newly elected representatives and senators from those seven states, nearly all of them Republicans, took their seats in the House and Senate.

THE FIFTEENTH AMENDMENT

The remaining three southern states completed the Reconstruction process in 1869 and 1870. Congress required them to ratify the Fifteenth as well as the Fourteenth Amendment. The Fifteenth Amendment prohibited states from denying the right to vote on grounds of race, color, or previous condition of servitude. Its purpose was not only to prevent any future revocation of black suffrage by the reconstructed states but also to extend equal suffrage to the border states and to the North. But the challenge of enforcement lay ahead.

THE ELECTION OF 1868

Just as the presidential election of 1864 was a referendum on Lincoln's war policies, so the election of 1868 was a referendum on the Reconstruction policy of the Republicans. The Republican nominee was General **Ulysses S. Grant.** Though he had no political experience, Grant commanded greater authority and prestige than anyone else in the country. Grant agreed to run for the presidency in order to preserve in peace the victory for Union and liberty he had won in war.

The Democrats turned away from Andrew Johnson and nominated Horatio Seymour, the wartime governor of New York. They adopted a militant platform denouncing the Reconstruction acts as "a flagrant usurpation of power . . . unconstitutional, revolutionary, and void." The platform also demanded "the abolition of the Freedmen's Bureau, and all political instrumentalities designed to secure negro supremacy."

The vice presidential candidate, Frank Blair of Missouri, became the point man for the Democrats. In a public letter he proclaimed, "There is but one way to restore the Government and the Constitution, and that is for the President-elect to declare these [Reconstruction] acts null and void, compel the army to undo its usurpations at the South, disperse the carpet-bag State Governments, [and] allow the white people to reorganize their own governments."

The only way to achieve this bold counterrevolutionary goal was to suppress Republican voters in the South. This the Ku Klux Klan tried its best to do. Federal troops had only limited success in preventing the violence. In Louisiana, Georgia, Arkansas, and Tennessee, the Klan or Klan-like groups committed dozens of murders and intimidated thousands of black voters. The violence helped the Democratic cause in the South but probably hurt it in the North, where many voters perceived the Klan as an organization of neo-Confederate paramilitary guerrillas.

Seymour did well in the South, carrying five former slave states and coming close in others despite the solid Republican vote of the newly enfranchised blacks. But Grant swept the electoral vote 214 to 80. Seymour actually won a slight majority of the white voters nationally, so without black enfranchisement, Grant would have had a minority of the popular vote.

QUICK   REVIEW

GOALS OF RECONSTRUCTION

- To bring ex-Confederate states back into the Union

- To define and protect the rights of ex-slaves

- Johnson's Plan: rapid restoration of states to Union but minimal rights and economic opportunities for freedpeople

- Radical Republicans' plan: equal civil and political rights for freedpeople plus land and education

Ulysses S. Grant *General-in-chief of Union armies who led those armies to victory in the Civil War.*

THE GRANT ADMINISTRATION

FOCUS QUESTION

What were the achievements of Reconstruction? What were its failures?

Grant is usually branded a failure as president. His two administrations (1869–1877) were plagued by scandals. His private secretary allegedly became involved in the infamous **whiskey ring,** a network of distillers and revenue agents that deprived the government of millions of tax dollars; his secretary of war was impeached for selling appointments to army posts and Indian reservations; and his attorney general and secretary of the interior resigned under suspicion of malfeasance in 1875.

Honest himself, Grant was too trusting of subordinates. But not all of the scandals were Grant's fault. This was an era notorious for corruption at all levels of government. The Tammany Hall "Ring" of "Boss" William Marcy Tweed in New York City may have stolen more money from taxpayers than all the federal agencies combined. In Washington, one of the most widely publicized scandals, the Credit Mobilier affair, concerned Congress rather than the Grant administration. Several congressmen had accepted stock in the **Credit Mobilier,** a construction company for the Union Pacific Railroad, which received loans and land grants from the government in return for ensuring lax congressional supervision, thereby permitting financial manipulations by the company.

What accounted for this explosion of corruption in the postwar decade? The expansion of government contracts and the bureaucracy during the war had created new opportunities for the unscrupulous. Then came a relaxation of tensions and standards following the intense sacrifices of the war years. Rapid postwar economic growth, led by an extraordinary rush of railroad construction, encouraged greed and get-rich-quick schemes of the kind satirized by Mark Twain and Charles Dudley Warner in their 1873 novel *The Gilded Age,* which gave its name to the era.

CIVIL SERVICE REFORM

But some of the increase in corruption during the Gilded Age was more apparent than real. Reformers focused on the dark corners of corruption hitherto unilluminated because of the nation's preoccupation with war and reconstruction. Thus, the actual extent of corruption may have been exaggerated by the publicity that reformers gave it. In reality, during the Grant administration several government agencies made real progress in eliminating abuses that had flourished in earlier administrations.

One area of progress was civil service reform. Its chief target was the **spoils system.** With the slogan "To the victor belong the spoils," the victorious party in an election rewarded party workers with appointments as postmasters, customs collectors, and the like. The hope of getting appointed to a government post was the glue that kept the faithful together when a party was out of power. The spoils system politicized the bureaucracy and staffed it with unqualified personnel who spent more time working for their party than for the government.

Civil service reformers wanted to separate the bureaucracy from politics by requiring competitive examinations for the appointment of civil servants. This movement gathered steam during the 1870s and finally achieved success in 1883 with the passage of the Pendleton Act, which established the modern structure of the civil service. When Grant took office, he seemed to share the sentiments of civil service reformers. Grant named a civil service commission headed by George William Curtis, a leading reformer and editor of *Harper's Weekly.* But many congressmen, senators, and other politicians resisted civil service reform because **patronage** was the grease of the political machines that kept them in office. They managed to subvert reform,

whiskey ring *Network of distillers and revenue agents that cheated the government out of millions of tax dollars.*

Credit Mobilier *Construction company for the Union Pacific Railroad that gave shares of stock to some congressmen in return for favors.*

spoils system *System by which the victorious political party rewarded its supporters with government jobs.*

patronage *Government jobs given out by political figures to their supporters, regardless of ability.*

sometimes using Grant as an unwitting ally and thus turning many reformers against the president.

FOREIGN POLICY ISSUES

A foreign policy fiasco added to Grant's woes. The irregular procedures by which his private secretary had negotiated a treaty to annex Santo Domingo (now the Dominican Republic) alienated leading Republican senators, who defeated ratification of the treaty. Grant's political inexperience led him to act like a general who needed only to give orders rather than as a president who must cultivate supporters. The fallout from the Santo Domingo affair widened the fissure in the Republican Party.

But the Grant administration had some solid foreign policy achievements to its credit. Hamilton Fish, the able secretary of state, negotiated the Treaty of Washington in 1871 to settle the vexing "Alabama Claims." These were damage claims against Britain for the destruction of American shipping by the C.S.S. *Alabama* and other Confederate commerce raiders built in British shipyards. The treaty established an international tribunal to arbitrate the U.S. claims, resulting in the award of $15.5 million in damages to U.S. ship owners and a British expression of regret.

The events leading to the Treaty of Washington also resolved another long-festering issue between Britain and the United States: the status of Canada. The seven separate British North American colonies were especially vulnerable to U.S. desires for annexation. In 1867 Parliament passed the British North America Act, which united most of the Canadian colonies into a new and largely self-governing Dominion of Canada.

The successful conclusion of the treaty cooled Canadian-American tensions. It also led to the resolution of disputes over American commercial fishing in Canadian waters. American demands for annexation of Canada faded away. These events gave birth to the modern nation of Canada, whose 3,500-mile border with the United States remains the longest unfortified frontier in the world.

RECONSTRUCTION IN THE SOUTH

During Grant's two administrations, the "Southern Question" was the most intractable issue. A phrase in Grant's acceptance of the presidential nomination in 1868 had struck a responsive chord in the North: "Let us have peace." With the ratification of the Fifteenth Amendment, many people breathed a sigh of relief at this apparent resolution of "the last great point that remained to be settled of the issues of the war." It was time to deal with other matters that had been long neglected.

But there was no peace. State governments elected by black and white voters were in place in the South, but Democratic violence protesting Reconstruction and the instability of the Republican coalition that sustained it portended trouble.

BLACKS IN OFFICE

In the North, the Republican Party represented the most prosperous, educated, and influential elements of the population; but in the South, most of its adherents were poor, illiterate, and propertyless. About 80 percent of southern Republican voters were black. Although most black leaders were educated and many had been free before the war, the mass of black voters were illiterate ex-slaves. Neither the leaders nor their constituents, however, were as ignorant as stereotypes have portrayed them. Of

14 black representatives and two black senators elected in the South between 1868 and 1876, all but three had attended secondary school and four had attended college. Several of the blacks elected to state offices were among the best-educated men of their day. For example, Jonathan Gibbs, secretary of state in Florida from 1868 to 1872 and state superintendent of education from 1872 to 1874, was a graduate of Dartmouth College and Princeton Theological Seminary. It is true that some lower-level black officeholders, as well as their constituents, could not read or write. But illiteracy did not preclude an understanding of political issues for them any more than it did for Irish American voters in the North, many of whom also were illiterate. Southern blacks thirsted for education. Participation in the Union League and the experience of voting were themselves a form of education. Black churches and fraternal organizations proliferated during Reconstruction and tutored African Americans in their rights and responsibilities.

Linked to the myth of black incompetence was the legend of the "Africanization" of southern governments during Reconstruction. The theme of "Negro rule" was a staple of Democratic propaganda. It was enshrined in folk memory and textbooks. In fact, blacks held only 15 to 20 percent of public offices, even at the height of Reconstruction in the early 1870s. There were no black governors and only one black state supreme court justice. Nowhere except in South Carolina did blacks hold office in numbers anywhere near their proportion of the population.

"CARPETBAGGERS"

Next to "Negro rule," carpetbagger corruption and scalawag rascality have been the prevailing myths of Reconstruction. "Carpetbaggers" did hold a disproportionate number of high political offices in southern state governments during Reconstruction. A few did resemble the proverbial adventurer who came south with nothing but a carpetbag in which to stow the loot plundered from a helpless people. But most were Union Army officers who stayed on after the war as Freedmen's Bureau agents, teachers in black schools, or business investors.

Those who settled in the postwar South hoped to rebuild its society in the image of the free-labor North. Many were college graduates. Most brought not empty carpetbags but considerable capital, which they invested in what they hoped would become a new South. They also invested human capital—themselves—in a drive to modernize the region's social structure and democratize its politics. But they underestimated the hostility of southern whites, most of whom regarded them as agents of an alien culture.

"SCALAWAGS"

Most of the native-born whites who joined the southern Republican Party came from the up-country Unionist areas of western North Carolina and Virginia and eastern Tennessee. Others were former Whigs. Republicans, said a North Carolina scalawag, were the "party of progress, of education, of development."

But Democrats were aware that the southern Republican Party they abhorred was a fragile coalition of blacks and whites, Yankees and southerners, hill-country yeomen and low-country entrepreneurs, illiterates and college graduates. The party was weakest along the seams where these disparate elements joined, especially the racial seam. Democrats attacked that weakness with every weapon at their command, including violence.

HISTORY THROUGH FILM

BIRTH OF A NATION (1915)

*Directed by D. W. Griffith; starring
Lillian Gish (Elsie Stoneman),
Henry B. Walthall (Ben Cameron),
Ralph Lewis (Austin Stoneman),
George Siegmann (Silas Lynch)*

Few if any films have had such a pernicious impact on historical understanding and race relations as *Birth of a Nation*. This movie popularized a version of Reconstruction that portrayed predatory carpetbaggers and stupid, brutish blacks plundering a prostrate South and lusting after white women. It perpetuated vicious stereotypes of rapacious black males. It glorified the Ku Klux Klan of the Reconstruction era, inspiring the founding of the "second Klan" in 1915 that became a powerful force in the 1920s (see Chapter 24). The first half of the film offers a conventional Victorian romance of the Civil War. The two sons and daughter of Austin Stoneman (a malevolent radical Republican who is a thinly disguised Thaddeus Stevens) become friends with the three sons and two daughters of the Cameron family of "Piedmont," South Carolina, through the friendship of Ben Cameron and Phil Stoneman at college. The Civil War tragically separates the families. The Stoneman and Cameron boys enlist in the Union and Confederate armies and—predictably—face each other on the battlefield. Two Camerons and one Stoneman are killed in the war, and Ben Cameron is badly wounded and captured, to be nursed back to health by—you guessed it—Elsie Stoneman.

After the war the younger Camerons and Stonemans renew their friendship. During the Stonemans' visit to South Carolina, Ben Cameron and Elsie Stoneman, and Phil Stoneman and Flora Cameron, fall in love. If the story had stopped there, *Birth of a Nation* would have been just another Hollywood romance. But Austin Stoneman brings south with him Silas Lynch, an ambitious, leering mulatto demagogue who stirs up the animal passions of the ignorant black majority to demand "Equal Rights, Equal Politics, Equal Marriage." A "renegade Negro," Gus, stalks the youngest Cameron daughter, who saves herself from rape by jumping from a cliff to her death. Silas Lynch tries to force Elsie to marry him. "I will build a Black Empire," he tells the beautiful, virginal Elsie (Lillian Gish was the Hollywood beauty queen of silent films), "and you as my queen shall rule by my side."

Finally provoked beyond endurance, white South Carolinians led by Ben Cameron organize the Ku Klux Klan to save "the Aryan race." Riding to the rescue of embattled whites in stirring scenes that anticipated the heroic actions of the cavalry against Indians in later Hollywood westerns, the Klan executes Gus, saves Elsie, disperses black soldiers and mobs, and carries the next election for white rule by intimidating black voters. The film ends with a double marriage that unites the Camerons and Stonemans in a symbolic rebirth of a nation that joins whites of the North and South in a new union rightfully based on the supremacy of "the Aryan race."

The son of a Confederate lieutenant colonel, David Wark (D. W.) Griffith was the foremost director of the silent movie era. *Birth of a Nation* was the first real full-length feature film, technically and artistically superior to anything before it. Apart from its place in the history of cinema, though, why should anyone today watch a movie that perpetuates such wrongheaded history and noxious racist stereotypes? Precisely *because* it reflects and amplifies an interpretation of Reconstruction that prevailed from the 1890s to the 1950s, and thereby shaped not only historical understanding but also contemporary behavior (as in its inspiration for the Klan of the 1920s).

©Bettmann/Corbis

Colonel Ben Cameron (Henry B. Walthall) kissing the hand of Elsie Stoneman (Lillian Gish) in Birth of a Nation.

THE KU KLUX KLAN

habeas corpus *Right of an individual to have the legality of his arrest and detention decided by a court.*

The generic name for the secret groups that terrorized the southern countryside was the Ku Klux Klan. But some went by other names (the Knights of the White Camelia in Louisiana, for example). Part of the Klan's purpose was social control of the black population. Sharecroppers who tried to extract better terms from landowners, or black people who were considered too "uppity," were likely to receive a midnight whipping—or worse—from white-sheeted Klansmen. Scores of black schools, perceived as a particular threat to white supremacy, went up in flames.

But the Klan's main purpose was political: to destroy the Republican Party by terrorizing its voters and, if necessary, murdering its leaders. No one knows the number of politically motivated killings that took place, but it was certainly in the hundreds, probably in the thousands. Nearly all the victims were Republicans; most of them were black. In one notorious incident, the "Colfax Massacre" in Louisiana (April 18, 1873), a clash between black militia and armed whites left three whites and nearly 100 blacks dead.

In some places, notably Tennessee and Arkansas, militias formed by Republicans suppressed and disarmed many Klansmen. But in most areas the militias were outgunned and outmaneuvered by ex-Confederate veterans who had joined the Klan. Some Republican governors were reluctant to use black militia against white guerrillas for fear of sparking a racial bloodbath, as happened at Colfax.

The answer seemed to be federal troops. In 1870 and 1871 Congress enacted three laws intended to enforce the Fourteenth and Fifteenth Amendments. Interference with voting rights became a federal offense, and any attempt to deprive another person of civil or political rights became a felony. The third law, passed on April 20, 1871, and popularly called the Ku Klux Klan Act, gave the president power to suspend the writ of **habeas corpus** and send in federal troops to suppress armed resistance to federal law.

Armed with these laws, the Grant administration moved against the Klan. But Grant did so with restraint. He suspended the writ of habeas corpus only in nine South Carolina counties. Nevertheless, there and elsewhere federal marshals backed by troops arrested thousands of suspected Klansmen. Federal grand juries indicted more than 3,000, and several hundred defendants pleaded guilty in return for suspended sentences; the Justice Department dropped charges against nearly 2,000 others. About 600 Klansmen were convicted. Most of them received fines or light jail sentences, but 65 went to a federal penitentiary for terms of up to five years.

THE ELECTION OF 1872

These measures broke the back of the Klan in time for the 1872 presidential election. A group of dissident Republicans had emerged to challenge Grant's reelection. They believed that con-

TWO MEMBERS OF THE KU KLUX KLAN. *Founded in Pulaski, Tennessee, in 1866 as a social organization similar to a college fraternity, the Klan evolved into a terrorist group whose purpose was intimidation of southern Republicans. The Klan, in which former Confederate soldiers played a prominent part, was responsible for the beating and murder of hundreds of blacks and whites alike from 1868 to 1871.*

ciliation of southern whites rather than continued military intervention was the only way to achieve peace in the South. Calling themselves Liberal Republicans, these dissidents nominated Horace Greeley, the famous editor of the *New York Tribune.* Under the slogan "Anything to beat Grant," the Democratic Party also endorsed Greeley's nomination. On a platform denouncing "bayonet rule" in the South, Greeley urged his fellow northerners to put the issues of the Civil War behind them.

Most voters in the North were still not prepared to trust Democrats or southern whites, however. Anti-Greeley cartoons by Thomas Nast showed Greeley shaking the hand of a Klansman dripping with the blood of a murdered black Republican. On Election Day Grant swamped Greeley. Republicans carried every northern state and 10 of the 16 southern and border states. But this apparent triumph of Republicanism and Reconstruction would soon unravel.

THE PANIC OF 1873

The U.S. economy had grown at an unprecedented pace since 1867. The first **transcontinental railroad** had been completed on May 10, 1869, when a golden spike was driven at Promontory Point, Utah Territory, linking the Union Pacific and the Central Pacific. But it was the building of a second transcontinental line, the Northern Pacific, that precipitated a Wall Street panic in 1873 and plunged the economy into a five-year depression.

Jay Cooke's banking firm, fresh from its triumphant marketing of Union war bonds, took over the Northern Pacific in 1869. Cooke pyramided every conceivable kind of equity and loan financing to raise the money to begin laying rails west from Duluth, Minnesota. Other investment firms did the same as a fever of speculative financing gripped the country. In September 1873 the pyramid of paper collapsed. Cooke's firm was the first to go bankrupt. Like dominoes, hundreds of banks and businesses also collapsed. Unemployment rose to 14 percent and hard times set in.

transcontinental railroad
Railroad line that connected with other lines to provide continuous rail transportation from coast to coast.

THE RETREAT FROM RECONSTRUCTION

Democrats made large gains in the congressional elections of 1874, winning a majority in the House for the first time in 18 years. Public opinion also began to turn against Republican policies in the South. Intra-party battles among Republicans in southern states enabled Democrats to regain control of several state governments. Well-publicized corruption scandals also discredited Republican leaders. Although corruption was probably no worse in southern states than in many parts of the North, the postwar poverty of the South made waste and extravagance seem worse. White Democrats scored propaganda points by claiming that corruption proved the incompetence of "Negro-carpetbag" regimes. Northerners grew increasingly weary of what seemed the endless turmoil of southern politics. Most of them had never had a very strong commitment to racial equality, and they were growing more and more willing to let white supremacy regain sway in the South. "The truth is," confessed a northern Republican, "our people are tired out with this worn out cry of 'Southern outrages'!!!"

By 1875 only four southern states remained under Republican control: South Carolina, Florida, Mississippi, and Louisiana. In those states, white Democrats had revived paramilitary organizations under various names: White Leagues (Louisiana);

FOCUS QUESTION
Why did a majority of the northern people and their political leaders turn against continued federal involvement in southern Reconstruction in the 1870s?

Rifle Clubs (Mississippi); and Red Shirts (South Carolina). Unlike the Klan, these groups operated openly. In Louisiana, they fought pitched battles with Republican militias in which scores were killed. When the Grant administration sent large numbers of federal troops to Louisiana, people in both North and South cried out against military rule. The protests grew even louder when soldiers marched onto the floor of the Louisiana legislature in January 1875 and expelled several Democratic legislators after a contested election.

THE MISSISSIPPI ELECTION OF 1875

The backlash against the Grant administration affected the Mississippi state election of 1875. Democrats there devised a strategy called the Mississippi Plan. The first step was to "persuade" the 10 to 15 percent of white voters still calling themselves Republicans to switch to the Democrats. Only a handful of carpetbaggers could resist the economic pressures, social ostracism, and threats that made it "too damned hot for [us] to stay out," wrote one white Republican who changed parties.

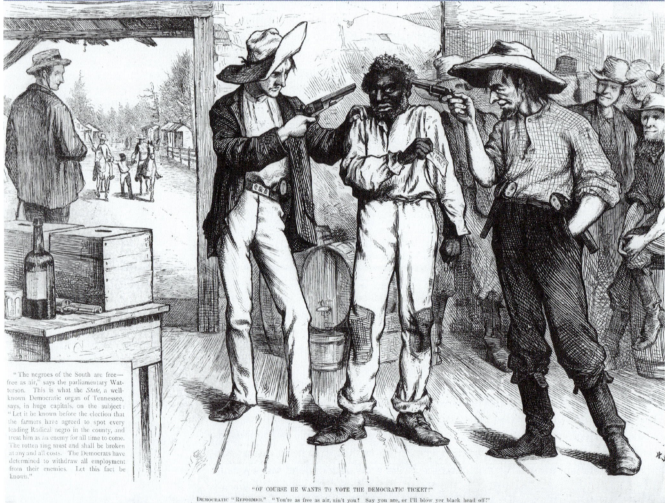

"The negroes of the South are free— free as air," says the parliamentary Watterson. This is what the *State,* a well-known Democratic organ of Tennessee, says, in huge capitals, on the subject: "Let it be known before the election that the farmers have agreed to spot every leading Radical negro in the county, and treat him as an enemy for all time to come. The rotten ring must and shall be broken at any and all costs. The Democrats have determined to withdraw all employment from their enemies. Let this fact be known."

"OF COURSE HE WANTS TO VOTE THE DEMOCRATIC TICKET!"

DEMOCRATIC "REFORMER." "You're as free as air, ain't you? Say you are, or I'll blow yer black head off!"

HOW THE MISSISSIPPI PLAN WORKED. *This cartoon shows how black counties could report large Democratic majorities in the Mississippi state election of 1875. The black voter holds a Democratic ticket while one of the men, described in the caption as a "Democratic reformer," holds a revolver to his head and says: "You're as free as air, ain't you? Say you are, or I'll blow your black head off!"*

The second step in the Mississippi Plan was to intimidate black voters, for even with all whites voting Democratic, the party could still be defeated by the 55 percent black majority. Economic coercion against black sharecroppers and workers kept some of them away from the polls. But violence was the most effective method. Democratic "rifle clubs" showed up at Republican rallies, provoked riots, and shot down dozens of blacks in the ensuing melees. Governor Adelbert Ames called for federal troops to control the violence. Grant intended to comply, but Ohio Republicans warned him that if he sent troops to Mississippi, the Democrats would exploit the issue of bayonet rule to carry Ohio in that year's state elections. Grant yielded—in effect giving up Mississippi for Ohio.

Governor Ames did try to organize a loyal state militia. But that proved difficult—and in any case, he was reluctant to use a black militia for fear of provoking a race war. "No matter if they are going to carry the State," said Ames with weary resignation, "let them carry it, and let us be at peace and have no more killing." The Mississippi Plan worked like a charm. What had been a Republican majority of 30,000 in 1874 became a Democratic majority of 30,000 in 1875.

THE SUPREME COURT AND RECONSTRUCTION

Even if Grant had been willing to continue intervening in southern state elections, Congress and the courts would have constricted such efforts. The new Democratic majority in the House threatened to cut any appropriations intended for use in the South. And in 1876 the Supreme Court handed down two decisions that declared parts of the 1870 and 1871 laws for enforcement of the Fourteenth and Fifteenth Amendments unconstitutional. In *U.S.* v. *Cruikshank* and *U.S.* v. *Reese,* the Court ruled that the Fourteenth and Fifteenth Amendments apply to actions by *states:* "No State shall . . . deprive any person of life, liberty, or property . . . nor deny to any person . . . equal protection of the laws"; the right to vote "shall not be denied . . . by any State." Therefore, the portions of these laws that empowered the federal government to prosecute *individuals* were unconstitutional. The Court did not say what could be done when states were controlled by white-supremacy Democrats who had no intention of enforcing equal rights.

Meanwhile, in the *Civil Rights Cases* (1883), the Court declared unconstitutional a civil rights law passed by Congress in 1875. That law banned racial discrimination in all forms of public transportation and public accommodations. If enforced, it would have effected a sweeping transformation of race relations—in the North as well as in the South. But even some of the congressmen who voted for the bill doubted its constitutionality, and the Justice Department had made little effort to enforce it. Several cases made their way to the Supreme Court, which in 1883 ruled the law unconstitutional, again on grounds that the Fourteenth Amendment applied only to states, not to individuals. Several states, all in the North, passed their own civil rights laws in the 1870s and 1880s, but less than 10 percent of the black population resided in those states. The mass of African Americans lived a segregated existence.

THE ELECTION OF 1876

In 1876 the Republican state governments that still survived in the South fell victim to the passion for "reform." The mounting revelations of corruption at all levels of government ensured that reform would be the leading issue in the presidential election. Both major parties gave their presidential nominations to governors who had earned reform reputations in their states: Democrat Samuel J. Tilden of New York and Republican Rutherford B. Hayes of Ohio.

Democrats entered the campaign as favorites for the first time in two decades. It seemed likely that they would be able to put together an electoral majority from a "solid South" plus New York and two or three other northern states. To ensure a solid South, they looked to the lessons of the Mississippi Plan. In 1876 a new word came into use to describe Democratic techniques of intimidation: **bulldozing.** To bulldoze black voters meant to trample them down or keep them away from the polls. In South Carolina and Louisiana, the Red Shirts and the White Leagues mobilized for an all-out bulldozing effort.

The most notorious incident, the "Hamburg Massacre," occurred in the village of Hamburg, South Carolina, where a battle between a black militia unit and 200 Red Shirts resulted in the capture of several militiamen, five of whom were shot "while attempting to escape." This time Grant did send in federal troops. He pronounced the Hamburg Massacre "cruel, blood-thirsty, wanton, unprovoked . . . a repetition of the course that has been pursued in other Southern States."

The federal government also put several thousand deputy marshals and election supervisors on duty in the South. Though they kept an uneasy peace at the polls, they could do little to prevent assaults, threats, and economic coercion in backcountry districts, which reduced the potential Republican tally in the former Confederate states by at least 250,000 votes.

DISPUTED RESULTS

When the results were in, Tilden had carried four northern states, including New York with its 35 electoral votes, and all the former slave states except—apparently—Louisiana, South Carolina, and Florida. From those three states came disputed returns. Since Tilden needed only one of them to win the presidency, while Hayes needed all three, and since Tilden seemed to have carried Louisiana and Florida, it appeared initially that he had won the presidency. But fraud and irregularities reported from several bulldozed districts in the three states clouded the issue. The official returns ultimately sent to Washington gave all three states—and therefore the presidency—to Hayes. But the Democrats refused to recognize the results, and they controlled the House.

The country now faced a serious constitutional crisis. Many people feared another civil war. The Constitution offered no clear guidance on how to deal with the matter. It required the concurrence of both houses of Congress in order to count the electoral votes of the states, but with a Democratic House and a Republican Senate such concurrence was not forthcoming. To break the deadlock, Congress created a special electoral commission consisting of five representatives, five senators, and five Supreme Court justices split evenly between the two parties, with one member, a Supreme Court justice, supposedly an independent—but in fact a Republican.

Tilden had won a national majority of 252,000 popular votes, and the raw returns gave him a majority in the three disputed states. But an estimated 250,000 southern Republicans had been bulldozed away from the polls. In a genuinely fair and free election, the Republicans might have carried Mississippi and North Carolina as well as the three disputed states. While the commission agonized, Democrats and Republicans in Louisiana and South Carolina each inaugurated their own separate governors and legislatures. Only federal troops in the capitals at New Orleans and Columbia protected the Republican governments in those states.

bulldozing *Using force to keep African Americans from voting.*

THE COMPROMISE OF 1877

In February 1877, three months after voters had gone to the polls, the electoral commission issued its ruling. By a partisan vote of 8 to 7—with the "independent" justice voting with the Republicans—it awarded all the disputed states to Hayes. The Democrats cried foul and began a **filibuster** in the House to delay the final electoral count beyond the inauguration date of March 4. But, behind the scenes, a compromise began to take shape. Hayes promised his support as president for federal appropriations to rebuild war-destroyed **levees** on the lower Mississippi and federal aid for a southern transcontinental railroad. Hayes's lieutenants also hinted at the appointment of a southerner as postmaster general, who would have a considerable amount of patronage at his disposal. Hayes also signaled his intention to end "bayonet rule." He believed that the goodwill and influence of southern moderates would offer better protection for black rights than federal troops could provide. In return for his commitment to withdraw the troops, Hayes asked for—and received—promises of fair treatment of freedpeople and respect for their constitutional rights.

filibuster *Congressional delaying tactic involving lengthy speeches that prevent legislation from being enacted.*

levee *Earthen dike or mound, usually along the banks of rivers, used to prevent flooding.*

THE END OF RECONSTRUCTION

Such promises were easier to make than to keep, as future years would reveal. In any case, the Democratic filibuster collapsed and Hayes was inaugurated on March 4. He soon fulfilled his part of the Compromise of 1877: ex-Confederate Democrat David Key of Tennessee became postmaster general; the South received more federal money in 1878 for internal improvements than ever before; and federal troops left the capitals of Louisiana and South Carolina. The last two Republican state governments collapsed. Any remaining voices of protest could scarcely be heard above the sighs of relief that the crisis was over.

QUICK REVIEW

END OF RECONSTRUCTION

- Growing Northern weariness with the Southern Question
- Renewal of Southern white resistance
- Supreme Court limited federal government's enforcement powers
- Federal troops removed from South after disputed election of 1876

CONCLUSION

Before the Civil War, most Americans had viewed a powerful government as a threat to individual liberties. That is why the first 10 amendments to the Constitution (the Bill of Rights) imposed strict limits on the powers of the federal government. But during the Civil War and especially during Reconstruction, it became clear that the national government would have to exert an unprecedented amount of power to free the slaves and guarantee their equal rights as free citizens. That is why the Thirteenth, Fourteenth, and Fifteenth Amendments to the Constitution contained clauses stating that "Congress shall have power" to enforce these provisions for liberty and equal rights.

During the post–Civil War decade, Congress passed civil rights laws and enforcement legislation to accomplish this purpose. Federal marshals and troops patrolled the polls to protect black voters, arrested thousands of Klansmen and other violators of black civil rights, and even occupied state capitals to prevent Democratic paramilitary groups from overthrowing legitimately elected Republican state governments. But by 1875 many northerners had grown tired of or alarmed by this continued use of military power to intervene in the internal affairs of states. The Supreme Court stripped the federal government of much of its authority to enforce certain provisions of the Fourteenth and Fifteenth Amendments.

The withdrawal of federal troops from the South in 1877 constituted both a symbolic and a substantive end of the 12-year postwar era known as Reconstruction. Reconstruction had achieved the two great objectives inherited from the Civil War: to reincorporate the former Confederate states into the Union, and to accomplish a transition from slavery to freedom in the South. But that transition was marred by the economic inequity of sharecropping and the social injustice of white supremacy. And a third goal of Reconstruction, enforcement of the equal civil and political rights promised in the Fourteenth and Fifteenth Amendments, was betrayed by the Compromise of 1877. In subsequent decades the freed slaves and their descendants suffered repression into segregated second-class citizenship.

QUESTIONS FOR REVIEW AND CRITICAL THINKING

Review

1. What were the positions of Presidents Abraham Lincoln and Andrew Johnson and of moderate and radical Republicans in Congress on the issues of restoring the South to the Union and protecting the rights of freed slaves?
2. Why was Andrew Johnson impeached? Why was he acquitted?
3. What were the achievements of Reconstruction? What were its failures?
4. Why did a majority of the Northern people and their political leaders turn against continued federal involvement in Southern Reconstruction in the 1870s?

Critical Thinking

1. The two main goals of Reconstruction were to bring the former Confederate states back into the Union and to ensure the equal citizenship and rights of the former slaves. Why was the first goal more successfully achieved than the second?
2. Why have "carpetbaggers" and "scalawags" had such a bad historical image? Did they deserve it?

Discovery

Evaluate the success with which African Americans were integrated into American society during Reconstruction.

SUGGESTED READINGS

The most comprehensive and incisive history of Reconstruction is **Eric Foner, *Reconstruction: America's Unfinished Revolution 1863–1872*** (1988). For a skillful abridgement of this book, see **Foner, *A Short History of Reconstruction*** (1990). Also valuable is **Kenneth M. Stampp, *The Era of Reconstruction, 1865–1877*** (1965). Important for their insights on Lincoln and the Reconstruction question are **Peyton McCrary, *Abraham Lincoln and Reconstruction: The Louisiana Experiment*** (1978) and **LaWanda Cox, *Lincoln and Black Freedom: A Study in Presidential Leadership*** (1981). A superb study of the South Carolina Sea Islands as a laboratory of Reconstruction is **Willie Lee Rose, *Rehearsal for Reconstruction: The Port Royal Experiment*** (1964).

Three important studies of Andrew Johnson and his conflict with Congress over Reconstruction are **Eric L. McKitrick, *Andrew Johnson and Reconstruction*** (1960); **Hans L. Trefousse, *The Radical Republicans: Lincoln's Vanguard for Racial Justice*** (1969); **and Michael Les Benedict, *The Impeachment and Trial of Andrew Johnson*** (1973). Two books by **Michael Perman** connect events in the South and in Washington during Reconstruction: ***Reunion without Compromise: The South and Reconstruction, 1865–1868*** (1973) and ***The Road to Redemption: Southern Politics 1868–1879*** (1984). For counter-Reconstruction violence in the South, see **George C. Rable, *But There Was No Peace: The Role of Violence in the Politics of Reconstruction*** (1984). The evolution of sharecropping and other aspects of the transition from slavery to freedom are treated in **Roger L. Ransom and Richard Sutch, *One Kind of Freedom: The Economic Consequences of Emancipation*** (1977).

Of the many books on African Americans in Reconstruction, the following are perhaps the most valuable: **Thomas Holt, *Black over White: Negro Political Leadership in South Carolina during Reconstruction*** (1977) and **Laura F. Edwards, *Gendered Strife and Confusion: The Political Culture of Reconstruction*** (1997). An excellent collection of essays on the Freedmen's Bureau is **Paul A. Cimbala and Randall Miller, eds., *The Freedmen's Bureau and Reconstruction*** (1999). Both black and white churches are the subject of **Daniel Stowell, *Rebuilding Zion: The Religious Reconstruction of the South, 1863–1877*** (1998).

ONLINE SOURCES GUIDE

ThomsonNOW™   Visit ThomsonNOW to access primary sources, exercises, quizzes, and audio chapter summaries related to this chapter:

http://www.thomsonedu.com/login

$\mathcal{D}$ISCOVERY

Evaluate the success with which African Americans were integrated into American society during Reconstruction.

In thinking about this question, begin by breaking it down into the components shown below. A discussion of the significance of each component should appear in your answer.

CULTURE AND SOCIETY

From your reading in this chapter and your examination of these two illustrations, what observations can you make about the role of violence and/or intimidation in suppressing Republican votes across the South in the 1870s? In the cartoon on the Mississippi Plan, how are the two gun-toting southern whites portrayed? Does this scene appear to represent a spontaneous, isolated incident or a systematic effort to influence votes? What is common between the two images?

From the Collections of the Library of Congress

TWO MEMBERS OF THE KU KLUX KLAN

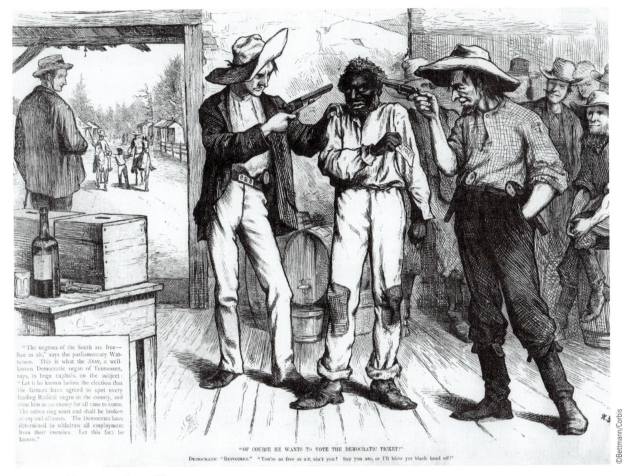

How the Mississippi Plan Worked

THE DECLARATION OF INDEPENDENCE

The Unanimous Declaration of the Thirteen United States of America

When in the Course of human events it becomes necessary for one people to dissolve the political bands which have connected them with another, and to assume among the Powers of the earth, the separate and equal station to which the Laws of Nature and of Nature's God entitle them, a decent respect to the opinions of mankind requires that they should declare the causes which impel them to the separation.

We hold these truths to be self-evident, that all men are created equal, that they are endowed by their Creator with certain unalienable Rights, that among these are Life, Liberty and the pursuit of Happiness. That to secure these rights, Governments are instituted among Men, deriving their just Powers from the consent of the governed. That whenever any Form of Government becomes destructive of these ends, it is the Right of the People to alter or to abolish it, and to institute new Government, laying its foundation on such principles and organizing its Powers in such form, as to them shall seem most likely to effect their Safety and Happiness. Prudence, indeed, will dictate that Governments long established should not be changed for light and transient causes; and accordingly all experience hath shewn, that mankind are more disposed to suffer, while evils are sufferable, than to right themselves by abolishing the forms to which they are accustomed. But when a long train of abuses and usurpations, pursuing invariably the same Object evinces a design to reduce them under absolute Despotism, it is their right, it is their duty, to throw off such Government, and to provide new Guards for their future security. Such has been the patient sufferance of these Colonies; and such is now the necessity which constrains them to alter their former Systems of Government. The history of the present King of Great Britain is a history of repeated injuries and usurpations, all having in direct object the establishment of an absolute Tyranny over these States. To prove this, let Facts be submitted to a candid world.

He has refused his Assent to Laws, the most wholesome and necessary for the public good.

He has forbidden his Governors to pass Laws of immediate and pressing importance, unless suspended in their operation till his Assent should be obtained; and when so suspended, he has utterly neglected to attend to them.

He has refused to pass other Laws for the accommodation of large districts of people, unless those people would relinquish the right of Representation in the Legislature, a right inestimable to them and formidable to tyrants only.

He has called together legislative bodies at places unusual, uncomfortable, and distant from the depository of their Public Records, for the sole Purpose of fatiguing them into compliance with his measures.

He has dissolved Representative Houses repeatedly, for opposing with manly firmness his invasions on the rights of the People.

He has refused for a long time, after such dissolutions, to cause others to be elected; whereby the Legislative Powers, incapable of Annihilation, have returned to the People at large for their exercise; the State remaining in the mean time exposed to all the dangers of invasion from without, and convulsions within.

He has endeavoured to prevent the Population of these States; for that purpose obstructing the Laws for Naturalization of Foreigners; refusing to pass others to encourage their migrations hither, and raising the conditions of new Appropriations of Lands.

He has obstructed the Administration of Justice, by refusing his Assent to Laws for establishing Judiciary Powers.

He has made Judges dependent on his Will alone, for the tenure of their offices, and the amount and payment of their salaries.

He has erected a multitude of New Offices, and sent hither swarms of Officers to harass our People, and eat out their substance.

He has kept among us, in times of peace, Standing Armies without the Consent of our legislatures.

He has affected to render the Military independent of and superior to the Civil Power.

He has combined with others to subject us to a jurisdiction foreign to our constitution, and unacknowledged by our laws; giving his Assent to their Acts of pretended Legislation: For Quartering large bodies of armed troops among us: For protecting them, by a mock Trial, from Punishment for any Murders which they should commit on the Inhabitants of these States: For cutting off our Trade with all parts of the world: For imposing Taxes on us without our Consent: For depriving us in many cases, of the benefits of Trial by Jury: For transporting us beyond Seas to be tried for pretended offences: For abolishing the free System of English Laws in a neighbouring Province, establishing therein an Arbitrary government, and enlarging its Boundaries so as to render it at once an example and fit instrument for introducing the same absolute rule into these Colonies: For taking away our Charters, abolishing our most valuable Laws, and altering fundamentally the Forms of our Governments: For suspending our own Legislatures, and declaring

Text is reprinted from the facsimile of the engrossed copy in the National Archives. The original spelling, capitalization, and punctuation have been retained. Paragraphing has been added.

themselves invested with Power to legislate for us in all cases whatsoever.

He has abdicated Government here, by declaring us out of his Protection, and waging War against us.

He has plundered our seas, ravaged our Coasts, burnt our towns, and destroyed the lives of our people.

He is at this time transporting large Armies of foreign Mercenaries to compleat the works of death, desolation and tyranny, already begun with circumstances of Cruelty and perfidy scarcely paralleled in the most barbarous ages, and totally unworthy the Head of a civilized nation.

He has constrained our fellow Citizens taken Captive on the high Seas to bear Arms against their Country, to become the executioners of their friends and Brethren, or to fall themselves by their Hands.

He has excited domestic insurrections amongst us, and has endeavoured to bring on the inhabitants of our frontiers, the merciless Indian Savages, whose known rule of warfare, is an undistinguished destruction of all ages, sexes and conditions.

In every stage of these Oppressions We have Petitioned for Redress in the most humble terms: Our repeated Petitions have been answered only by repeated injury. A Prince, whose character is thus marked by every act which may define a Tyrant, is unfit to be the ruler of a free People.

Nor have We been wanting in attentions to our British brethren. We have warned them from time to time of attempts by their legislature to extend an unwarrantable jurisdiction over us. We have reminded them of the circumstances of our emigration and settlement here. We have appealed to their native justice and magnanimity, and we have conjured them by the ties of our common kindred to disavow these usurpations, which, would inevitably interrupt our connections and correspondence. They too have been deaf to the voice of justice and of consanguinity. We must, therefore, acquiesce in the necessity, which denounces our Separation, and hold them, as we hold the rest of mankind, Enemies in War, in Peace Friends.

We, therefore, the Representatives of the United States of America, in General Congress, Assembled, appealing to the Supreme Judge of the world for the rectitude of our intentions, do, in the Name, and by Authority of the good People of these Colonies, solemnly publish and declare, That these United Colonies are, and of Right ought to be Free and Independent States; that they are Absolved from all Allegiance to the British Crown, and that all political connection between them and the State of Great Britain, is and ought to be totally dissolved; and that, as Free and Independent States, they have full Power to levy War, conclude Peace, contract Alliances, establish Commerce, and to do all other Acts and Things which Independent States may of right do. And for the support of this Declaration, with a firm reliance on the protection of divine Providence, we mutually pledge to each other our Lives, our Fortunes and our sacred Honor.

THE CONSTITUTION OF THE UNITED STATES OF AMERICA

We the People of the United States, in Order to form a more perfect Union, establish Justice, insure domestic Tranquility, provide for the common defence, promote the general Welfare, and secure the Blessings of Liberty to ourselves and our Posterity, do ordain and establish this Constitution for the United States of America.

Article I.

SECTION 1. All legislative Powers herein granted shall be vested in a Congress of the United States, which shall consist of a Senate and House of Representatives.

SECTION 2. The House of Representatives shall be composed of Members chosen every second Year by the People of the several States, and the Electors in each State shall have the Qualifications requisite for Electors of the most numerous Branch of the State Legislature.

No Person shall be a Representative who shall not have attained to the Age of twenty five Years, and been seven Years a Citizen of the United States, and who shall not, when elected, be an Inhabitant of that State in which he shall be chosen.

Representatives and direct Taxes[1] shall be apportioned among the several States which may be included within this Union, according to their respective Numbers, which shall be determined by adding to the whole Number of free Persons, including those bound to Service for a Term of Years, and excluding Indians not taxed, three fifths of all other Persons.[2]

The actual Enumeration shall be made within three Years after the first Meeting of the Congress of the United States, and within every subsequent Term of ten Years, in such Manner as they shall by Law direct. The Number of Representatives shall not exceed one for every thirty Thousand, but each State shall have at Least one Representative; and until such enumeration shall be made, the State of New Hampshire shall be entitled to chuse three; Massachusetts eight; Rhode Island and Providence Plantations one; Connecticut five; New York six; New Jersey four; Pennsylvania eight; Delaware one; Maryland six; Virginia ten; North Carolina five; South Carolina five; and Georgia three.

When vacancies happen in the Representation from any State, the Executive Authority thereof shall issue Writs of Election to fill such Vacancies.

The House of Representatives shall chuse their Speaker and other Officers; and shall have the sole Power of Impeachment.

SECTION 3. The Senate of the United States shall be composed of two Senators from each State, chosen by the Legislature thereof, for six Years; and each Senator shall have one Vote.[3]

Immediately after they shall be assembled in Consequence of the first Election, they shall be divided as equally as may be into three Classes. The Seats of the Senators of the first Class shall be vacated at the Expiration of the second Year, of the second Class at the Expiration of the fourth Year, and of the third Class at the Expiration of the sixth Year, so that one third may be chosen every second Year; and if Vacancies happen by Resignation, or otherwise, during the Recess of the Legislature of any State, the Executive thereof may make temporary Appointments until the next Meeting of the Legislature, which shall then fill such Vacancies.[4]

No Person shall be a Senator who shall not have attained to the Age of thirty Years, and been nine Years a Citizen of the United States, and who shall not, when elected, be an Inhabitant of that State for which he shall be chosen.

The Vice President of the United States shall be President of the Senate, but shall have no Vote, unless they be equally divided.

The Senate shall chuse their other Officers, and also a President pro tempore, in the Absence of the Vice President, or when he shall exercise the Office of President of the United States.

The Senate shall have the sole Power to try all Impeachments. When sitting for that Purpose, they shall be on Oath or Affirmation. When the President of the United States is tried, the Chief Justice shall preside: And no Person shall be convicted without the Concurrence of two thirds of the Members present.

Judgment in Cases of Impeachment shall not extend further than to removal from Office, and disqualification to hold and enjoy any Office of honor, Trust or Profit under the United States: but the Party convicted shall nevertheless be liable and subject to Indictment, Trial, Judgment and Punishment, according to Law.

SECTION 4. The Times, Places and Manner of holding Elections for Senators and Representatives, shall be prescribed in each State by the Legislature thereof, but the Congress may at any time by Law make or alter such Regulation, except as to the Places of chusing Senators.

The Congress shall assemble at least once in every Year, and such Meeting shall be on the first Monday in December, unless they shall by Law appoint a different Day.[5]

SECTION 5. Each House shall be the Judge of the Elections, Returns and Qualifications of its own Members, and a Majority

---

Text is from the engrossed copy in the National Archives. Original spelling, capitalization, and punctuation have been retained.
[1]Modified by the Sixteenth Amendment.
[2]Replaced by the Fourteenth Amendment.
[3]Superseded by the Seventeenth Amendment.
[4]Modified by the Seventeenth Amendment.
[5]Superseded by the Twentieth Amendment.

of each shall constitute a Quorum to do Business; but a smaller Number may adjourn from day to day, and may be authorized to compel the Attendance of absent Members, in such Manner, and under such Penalties as each House may provide.

Each House may determine the Rules of its Proceedings, punish its Members for disorderly Behaviour, and, with the Concurrence of two thirds, expel a Member.

Each House shall keep a Journal of its Proceedings, and from time to time publish the same, excepting such Parts as may in their Judgment require Secrecy; and the Yeas and Nays of the Members of either House on any question shall, at the Desire of one fifth of those Present, be entered on the Journal.

Neither House, during the Session of Congress, shall, without the Consent of the other, adjourn for more than three days, nor to any other Place than that in which the two Houses shall be sitting.

SECTION 6. The Senators and Representatives shall receive a Compensation for their Services, to be ascertained by Law, and paid out of the Treasury of the United States. They shall in all Cases, except Treason, Felony and Breach of the Peace, be privileged from Arrest during their Attendance at the Session of their respective Houses, and in going to and returning from the same; and for any Speech or Debate in either House, they shall not be questioned in any other Place.

No Senator or Representative shall, during the Time for which he was elected, be appointed to any civil Office under the Authority of the United States, which shall have been created, or the Emoluments whereof shall have been encreased during such time; and no Person holding any Office under the United States, shall be a Member of either House during his Continuance in Office.

SECTION 7. All Bills for raising Revenue shall originate in the House of Representatives; but the Senate may propose or concur with Amendments as on other Bills.

Every Bill which shall have passed the House of Representatives and the Senate shall, before it become a Law, be presented to the President of the United States; If he approve he shall sign it, but if not he shall return it, with his Objections to that House in which it shall have originated, who shall enter the Objections at large on their Journal, and proceed to reconsider it. If after such Reconsideration two thirds of that House shall agree to pass the Bill, it shall be sent, together with the Objections, to the other House, by which it shall likewise be reconsidered, and if approved by two thirds of that House, it shall become a Law. But in all such Cases the Votes of both Houses shall be determined by yeas and Nays, and the Names of the Persons voting for and against the Bill shall be entered on the Journal of each House respectively. If any Bill shall not be returned by the President within ten Days (Sundays excepted) after it shall have been presented to him, the Same shall be a Law, in like Manner as if he had signed it, unless the Congress by their Adjournment prevent its Return, in which Case it shall not be a Law.

Every Order, Resolution, or Vote to which the Concurrence of the Senate and House of Representatives may be necessary (except on a question of Adjournment) shall be presented to the President of the United States; and before the Same shall take Effect, shall be approved by him, or being disapproved by him shall be repassed by two thirds of the Senate and House of Representatives, according to the Rules and Limitations prescribed in the Case of a Bill.

SECTION 8. The Congress shall have power To lay and collect Taxes, Duties, Imposts and Excises, to pay the Debts and provide for the common Defence and general Welfare of the United States; but all Duties, Imposts and Excises shall be uniform throughout the United States; To borrow Money on the credit of the United States; To regulate Commerce with foreign Nations, and among the several States, and with the Indian Tribes; To establish an uniform Rule of Naturalization, and uniform Laws on the subject of Bankruptcies throughout the United States; To coin Money, regulate the Value thereof, and of foreign Coin, and fix the Standard of Weights and Measures; To provide for the Punishment of counterfeiting the Securities and current Coin of the United States; To establish Post Offices and post Roads; To promote the Progress of Science and useful Arts, by securing for limited Times to Authors and Inventors the exclusive Right to their respective Writings and Discoveries; To constitute Tribunals inferior to the supreme Court; To define and punish Piracies and Felonies committed on the high Seas, and Offences against the Law of Nations;

To declare War, grant Letters of Marque and Reprisal, and make Rules concerning Captures on Land and Water; To raise and support Armies, but no Appropriation of Money to that Use shall be for a longer Term than two Years; To provide and maintain a Navy; To make Rules for the Government and Regulation of the land and naval Forces; To provide for calling forth the Militia to execute the Laws of the Union, suppress Insurrections and repel Invasions; To provide for organizing, arming, and disciplining, the Militia, and for governing such Part of them as may be employed in the Service of the United States, reserving to the States respectively, the Appointment of the Officers, and the Authority of training the Militia according to the discipline prescribed by Congress; To exercise exclusive Legislation in all Cases whatsoever, over such District (not exceeding ten Miles square) as may, by Cession of particular States, and the Acceptance of Congress, become the Seat of the Government of the United States, and to exercise like Authority over all Places purchased by the Consent of the Legislature of the State in which the Same shall be, for the Erection of Forts, Magazines, Arsenals, dock-Yards, and other needful Buildings;—And To make all Laws which shall be necessary and proper for carrying into Execution the foregoing Powers, and all other Powers vested by this Constitution in the Government of the United States, or in any Department or Officer thereof.

SECTION 9. The Migration or Importation of such Persons as any of the States now existing shall think proper to admit, shall not be prohibited by the Congress prior to the Year one thousand eight hundred and eight, but a Tax or duty may be imposed on such Importation, not exceeding ten dollars for each Person.

The Privilege of the Writ of Habeas Corpus shall not be suspended, unless when in Cases of Rebellion or Invasion the public Safety may require it.

No Bill of Attainder or ex post facto Law shall be passed.

No Capitation, or other direct, Tax shall be laid, unless in Proportion to the Census or Enumeration herein before directed to be taken.

No Tax or Duty shall be laid on Articles exported from any State.

No Preference shall be given by any Regulation of Commerce or Revenue to the Ports of one State over those of another: nor shall Vessels bound to, or from, one State, be obliged to enter, clear, or pay Duties in another.

No Money shall be drawn from the Treasury, but in Consequence of Appropriations made by Law, and a regular Statement and Account of the Receipts and Expenditures of all public Money shall be published from time to time.

No Title of Nobility shall be granted by the United States: And no Person holding any Office of Profit or Trust under them, shall, without the Consent of the Congress, accept of any present, Emolument, Office, or Title, of any kind whatever, from any King, Prince, or foreign State.

SECTION 10. No State shall enter into any Treaty, Alliance, or Confederation; grant Letters of Marque and Reprisal; coin Money; emit Bills of Credit; make any Thing but gold and silver Coin a Tender in Payment of Debts; pass any Bill of Attainder, ex post facto Law, or Law impairing the Obligation of Contracts, or grant any Title of Nobility.

No State shall, without the Consent of the Congress, lay any Imposts or Duties on Imports or Exports, except what may be absolutely necessary for executing its inspection Laws: and the net Produce of all Duties and Imposts, laid by any State on Imports or Exports, shall be for the Use of the Treasury of the United States; and all such Laws shall be subject to the Revision and Controul of the Congress.

No State shall, without the Consent of Congress, lay any Duty of Tonnage, keep Troops, or Ships of War in time of Peace, enter into any Agreement or Compact with another State, or with a foreign Power, or engage in War, unless actually invaded, or in such imminent Danger as will not admit of delay.

Article II.

SECTION 1. The executive Power shall be vested in a President of the United States of America. He shall hold his Office during the Term of four Years, and, together with the Vice President, chosen for the same Term, be elected, as follows: Each State shall appoint, in such Manner as the Legislature thereof may direct, a Number of Electors, equal to the whole Number of Senators and Representatives to which the State may be entitled in the Congress: but no Senator or Representative, or Person holding an Office of Trust or Profit under the United States, shall be appointed an Elector.

The Electors shall meet in their respective States, and vote by Ballot for two Persons, of whom one at least shall not be an Inhabitant of the same State with themselves. And they shall make a List of all the Persons voted for, and of the Number of Votes for each; which List they shall sign and certify, and transmit sealed to the Seat of the Government of the United States, directed to the President of the Senate. The President of the Senate shall, in the Presence of the Senate and House of Representatives, open all the Certificates, and the Votes shall then be counted. The Person having the greatest Number of Votes shall be the President, if such Number be a Majority of the whole Number of Electors appointed; and if there be more than one who have such Majority, and have an equal Number of Votes, then the House of Representatives shall immediately chuse by Ballot one of them for President; and if no Person have a Majority, then from the five highest on the List the said House shall in like Manner chuse the President. But in chusing the President, the Votes shall be taken by States, the Representation from each State having one Vote; A quorum for this Purpose shall consist of a Member or Members from two thirds of the States, and a Majority of all the States shall be necessary to a Choice. In every Case, after the Choice of the President, the Person having the greatest Number of Votes of the Electors shall be the Vice President. But if there should remain two or more who have equal Votes, the Senate shall chuse from them by Ballot the Vice President.[6]

The Congress may determine the Time of chusing the Electors, and the Day on which they shall give their Votes; which Day shall be the same throughout the United States.

No Person except a natural born Citizen, or a Citizen of the United States, at the time of the Adoption of this Constitution, shall be eligible to the Office of President, neither shall any Person be eligible to that Office who shall not have attained to the Age of thirty five Years, and been fourteen Years a Resident within the United States.

In Case of the Removal of the President from Office, or of his Death, Resignation, or Inability to discharge the Powers and Duties of the said Office, the Same shall devolve on the Vice President, and the Congress may by Law provide for the Case of Removal, Death, Resignation or Inability, both of the President and Vice President, declaring what Officer shall then act as President, and such Officer shall act accordingly, until the Disability be removed, or a President shall be elected.[7]

The President shall, at stated Times, receive for his Services, a Compensation, which shall neither be encreased nor diminished during the Period for which he shall have been elected, and he shall not receive within that Period any other Emolument from the United States, or any of them.

Before he enter on the Execution of his Office, he shall take the following Oath or Affirmation:—"I do solemnly swear (or affirm) that I will faithfully execute the Office of President of the United States, and will to the best of my Ability, preserve, protect and defend the Constitution of the United States."

SECTION 2. The President shall be Commander in Chief of the Army and Navy of the United States, and of the Militia of the several States, when called into the actual Service of the United States; he may require the Opinion, in writing, of the principal Officer in each of the executive Departments, upon any Subject relating to the Duties of their respective Offices, and he shall have Power to grant Reprieves and Pardons for Offences against the United States, except in Cases of Impeachment.

He shall have Power, by and with the Advice and Consent of the Senate, to make Treaties, provided two thirds of the Senators present concur; and he shall nominate, and by and with the Advice and Consent of the Senate, shall appoint Ambassadors, other public Ministers and Consuls, Judges of the supreme Court, and all other Officers of the United States, whose Appointments are not herein otherwise provided for, and which shall be established by Law; but the Congress may by Law vest the Appointment of such inferior Officers, as they

---

[6]Superseded by the Twelfth Amendment.
[7]Modified by the Twenty-fifth Amendment.

think proper, in the President alone, in the Courts of Law, or in the Heads of Departments.

The President shall have Power to fill up all Vacancies that may happen during the Recess of the Senate, by granting Commissions which shall expire at the End of their next Session.

SECTION 3. He shall from time to time give the Congress Information of the State of the Union, and recommend to their Consideration such Measures as he shall judge necessary and expedient; he may, on extraordinary Occasions, convene both Houses, or either of them, and in Case of Disagreement between them, with Respect to the Time of Adjournment, he may adjourn them to such Time as he shall think proper; he shall receive Ambassadors and other public Ministers; he shall take Care that the Laws be faithfully executed, and shall Commission all the Officers of the United States.

SECTION 4. The President, Vice President and all civil Officers of the United States, shall be removed from Office on Impeachment for, and Conviction of, Treason, Bribery, or other high Crimes and Misdemeanors.

Article III.

SECTION 1. The judicial Power of the United States, shall be vested in one supreme Court, and in such inferior Courts as the Congress may from time to time ordain and establish.

The Judges, both of the supreme and inferior Courts, shall hold their Offices during good Behaviour, and shall, at stated Times, receive for their Services, a Compensation, which shall not be diminished during their Continuance in Office.

SECTION 2. The judicial Power shall extend to all Cases, in Law and Equity, arising under this Constitution, the Laws of the United States, and Treaties made, or which shall be made, under their Authority;—to all Cases affecting Ambassadors, other public Ministers and Consuls;—to all Cases of admiralty and maritime Jurisdiction;—to Controversies to which the United States shall be a Party;—to Controversies between two or more States;—between a State and Citizens of another State;[8]—between Citizens of different States,—between Citizens of the same State claiming Lands under Grants of different States, and between a State, or the Citizens thereof, and foreign States, Citizens or Subjects.

In all Cases affecting Ambassadors, other public Ministers and Consuls, and those in which a State shall be Party, the supreme Court shall have original Jurisdiction. In all the other Cases before mentioned, the supreme Court shall have appellate Jurisdiction, both as to Law and Fact, with such Exceptions, and under such Regulations as the Congress shall make.

The Trial of all Crimes, except in Cases of Impeachment, shall be by Jury; and such Trial shall be held in the State where the said Crimes shall have been committed; but when not committed within any State, the Trial shall be at such Place or Places as the Congress may by Law have directed.

SECTION 3. Treason against the United States, shall consist only in levying War against them, or in adhering to their Enemies, giving them Aid and Comfort. No Person shall be convicted of Treason unless on the Testimony of two Witnesses to the same overt Act, or on Confession in open Court.

The Congress shall have Power to declare the Punishment of Treason, but no Attainder of Treason shall work Corruption of Blood, or Forfeiture except during the Life of the Person attainted.

Article IV.

SECTION 1. Full Faith and Credit shall be given in each State to the public Acts, Records, and judicial Proceedings of every other State. And the Congress may by general Laws prescribe the Manner in which such Acts, Records and Proceedings shall be proved, and the Effect thereof.

SECTION 2. The Citizens of each State shall be entitled to all Privileges and Immunities of Citizens in the several States.

A Person charged in any State with Treason, Felony, or other Crime, who shall flee from Justice, and be found in another State, shall on Demand of the executive Authority of the State from which he fled, be delivered up, to be removed to the State having Jurisdiction of the Crime.

No Person held to Service or Labour in one State, under the Laws thereof, escaping into another, shall, in Consequence of any Law or Regulation therein, be discharged from such Service or Labour, but shall be delivered up on Claim of the Party to whom such Service or Labour may be due.

SECTION 3. New States may be admitted by the Congress into this Union; but no new State shall be formed or erected within the Jurisdiction of any other State, nor any State be formed by the Junction of two or more States, or Parts of States, without the Consent of the Legislatures of the States concerned as well as of the Congress.

The Congress shall have Power to dispose of and make all needful Rules and Regulations respecting the Territory or other Property belonging to the United States; and nothing in this Constitution shall be so construed as to Prejudice any Claims of the United States, or of any particular State.

SECTION 4. The United States shall guarantee to every State in this Union a Republican Form of Government, and shall protect each of them against Invasion; and on Application of the Legislature, or of the Executive (when the Legislature cannot be convened) against domestic Violence.

Article V.

The Congress, whenever two thirds of both Houses shall deem it necessary, shall propose Amendments to this Constitution, or, on the Application of the Legislatures of two thirds of the several States, shall call a Convention for proposing Amendments, which, in either Case, shall be valid to all Intents and Purposes, as Part of this Constitution, when ratified by the Legislatures of three fourths of the several States, or by Conventions in three fourths thereof, as the one or the other Mode of Ratification may be proposed by the Congress; Provided that no Amendment which may be made prior to the Year One thousand eight hundred and eight shall in any Manner affect the first and fourth Clauses in the Ninth Section of the first Article; and that no State, without its Consent, shall be deprived of its equal Suffrage in the Senate.

[8]Modified by the Eleventh Amendment.

Article VI.

All Debts contracted and Engagements entered into, before the Adoption of this Constitution, shall be as valid against the United States under this Constitution, as under the Confederation.

This Constitution, and the Laws of the United States which shall be made in Pursuance thereof; and all Treaties made, or which shall be made, under the Authority of the United States, shall be the supreme Law of the Land; and the Judges in every State shall be bound thereby, any Thing in the Constitution or Laws of any State to the Contrary notwithstanding.

The Senators and Representatives before mentioned, and the Members of the several State Legislatures, and all executive and judicial Officers, both of the United States and of the several States, shall be bound by Oath or Affirmation, to support this Constitution; but no religious Test shall ever be required as a Qualification to any Office or public Trust under the United States.

Article VII.

The Ratification of the Conventions of nine States, shall be sufficient for the Establishment of this Constitution between the States so ratifying the Same.

Done in Convention by the Unanimous Consent of the States present the Seventeenth Day of September in the Year of our Lord one thousand seven hundred and Eighty seven and of the Independence of the United States of America the Twelfth. In witness whereof We have hereunto subscribed our Names,

Articles in Addition to, and Amendment of, the Constitution of the United States of America, Proposed by Congress, and Ratified by the Legislatures of the Several States, Pursuant to the Fifth Article of the Original Constitution.

Amendment I[9]

Congress shall make no law respecting an establishment of religion, or prohibiting the free exercise thereof; or abridging the freedom of speech, or of the press; or the right of the people peaceably to assemble, and to petition the Government for a redress of grievances.

Amendment II

A well regulated Militia, being necessary to the security of a free State, the right of the people to keep and bear Arms shall not be infringed.

Amendment III

No Soldier shall, in time of peace, be quartered in any house, without the consent of the Owner, nor in time of war, but in a manner to be prescribed by law.

Amendment IV

The right of the people to be secure in their persons, houses, papers, and effects, against unreasonable searches and seizures, shall not be violated, and no Warrants shall issue, but upon probable cause, supported by Oath or affirmation, and particularly describing the place to be searched, and the persons or things to be seized.

Amendment V

No person shall be held to answer for a capital or otherwise infamous crime, unless on a presentment or indictment of a Grand Jury, except in cases arising in the land or naval forces, or in the Militia, when in actual service in time of War or public danger; nor shall any person be subject for the same offence to be twice put in jeopardy of life or limb; nor shall be compelled in any criminal case to be a witness against himself, nor be deprived of life, liberty, or property, without due process of law; nor shall private property be taken for public use, without just compensation.

Amendment VI

In all criminal prosecutions, the accused shall enjoy the right to a speedy and public trial, by an impartial jury of the State and district wherein the crime shall have been committed, which district shall have been previously ascertained by law, and to be informed of the nature and cause of the accusation; to be confronted with the witnesses against him; to have compulsory process for obtaining witnesses in his favor, and to have the Assistance of Counsel for his defence.

Amendment VII

In suits at common law, where the value in controversy shall exceed twenty dollars, the right of trial by jury shall be preserved, and no fact tried by a jury, shall be otherwise reexamined in any Court of the United States, than according to the rules of the common law.

Amendment VIII

Excessive bail shall not be required, nor excessive fines imposed, nor cruel and unusual punishments inflicted.

Amendment IX

The enumeration in the Constitution, of certain rights, shall not be construed to deny or disparage others retained by the people.

Amendment X

The powers not delegated to the United States by the Constitution; nor prohibited by it to the States, are reserved to the States respectively, or to the people.

Amendment XI[10]

The Judicial power of the United States shall not be construed to extend to any suit in law or equity, commenced or prosecuted against one of the United States by Citizens of another State, or by Citizens or Subjects of any Foreign State.

Amendment XII[11]

The Electors shall meet in their respective States and vote by ballot for President and Vice-President, one of whom, at least, shall not be an inhabitant of the same State with themselves; they shall name in their ballots the person voted for as President, and in distinct ballots the person voted for as Vice-President, and they shall make distinct lists of all persons voted for as President, and of all persons voted for as Vice-President, and

[9]The first ten amendments were passed by Congress September 25, 1789. They were ratified by three-fourths of the states December 15, 1791.
[10]Passed March 4, 1794. Ratified January 23, 1795.
[11]Passed December 9, 1803. Ratified June 15, 1804.

of the number of votes for each, which lists they shall sign and certify, and transmit sealed to the seat of the government of the United States, directed to the President of the Senate;—The President of the Senate shall, in the presence of the Senate and House of Representatives, open all the certificates and the votes shall then be counted;—The person having the greatest number of votes for President, shall be the President, if such number be a majority of the whole number of Electors appointed; and if no person have such majority, then from the persons having the highest numbers not exceeding three on the list of those voted for as President, the House of Representatives shall choose immediately, by ballot, the President.

But in choosing the President, the votes shall be taken by states, the representation from each state having one vote; a quorum for this purpose shall consist of a member or members from two-thirds of the states, and a majority of all the states shall be necessary to a choice. And if the House of Representatives shall not choose a President whenever the right of choice shall devolve upon them, before the fourth day of March next following, then the Vice-President shall act as President, as in the case of the death or other constitutional disability of the President.—The person having the greatest number of votes as Vice-President, shall be the Vice-President, if such number be a majority of the whole number of Electors appointed, and if no person have a majority, then from the two highest numbers on the list, the Senate shall choose the Vice-President; a quorum for the purpose shall consist of two-thirds of the whole number of Senators, and a majority of the whole number shall be necessary to a choice. But no person constitutionally ineligible to the office of President shall be eligible to that of Vice-President of the United States.

Amendment XIII[12]

SECTION 1. Neither slavery nor involuntary servitude, except as a punishment for crime whereof the party shall have been duly convicted, shall exist within the United States, or any place subject to their jurisdiction.

SECTION 2. Congress shall have power to enforce this article by appropriate legislation.

Amendment XIV[13]

SECTION 1. All persons born or naturalized in the United States, and subject to the jurisdiction thereof, are citizens of the United States and of the State wherein they reside. No State shall make or enforce any law which shall abridge the privileges or immunities of citizens of the United States; nor shall any State deprive any person of life, liberty, or property, without due process of law; nor deny to any person within its jurisdiction the equal protection of the laws.

SECTION 2. Representatives shall be apportioned among the several States according to their respective numbers, counting the whole number of persons in each State, excluding Indians not taxed. But when the right to vote at any election for the choice of electors for President and Vice-President of the United States, Representatives in Congress, the Executive and Judicial officers of a State, or the members of the Legislature thereof, is denied to any of the male inhabitants of such State, being twenty-one years of age, and citizens of the United States, or in any way abridged, except for participation in rebellion, or other crime, the basis of representation therein shall be reduced in the proportion which the number of such male citizens shall bear to the whole number of male citizens twenty-one years of age in such State.

SECTION 3. No person shall be a Senator or Representative in Congress, or elector of President and Vice-President, or hold any office, civil or military, under the United States, or under any State, who, having previously taken an oath, as a member of Congress, or as an officer of the United States, or as a member of any State legislature, or as an executive or judicial officer of any State, to support the Constitution of the United States, shall have engaged in insurrection or rebellion against the same, or given aid or comfort to the enemies thereof. But Congress may by a vote of two-thirds of each House, remove such disability.

SECTION 4. The validity of the public debt of the United States, authorized by law, including debts incurred for payment of pensions and bounties for services in suppressing insurrection or rebellion, shall not be questioned. But neither the United States nor any State shall assume or pay any debt or obligation incurred in aid of insurrection or rebellion against the United States, or any claim for the loss or emancipation of any slave; but all such debts, obligations, and claims shall be held illegal and void.

SECTION 5. The Congress shall have the power to enforce, by appropriate legislation, the provisions of this article.

Amendment XV[14]

SECTION 1. The right of citizens of the United States to vote shall not be denied or abridged by the United States or by any State on account of race, color, or previous conditions of servitude—

SECTION 2. The Congress shall have power to enforce this article by appropriate legislation.

Amendment XVI[15]

The Congress shall have power to lay and collect taxes on incomes, from whatever source derived, without apportionment among the several States, and without regard to any census or enumeration.

Amendment XVII[16]

The Senate of the United States shall be composed of two Senators from each State, elected by the people thereof, for six years; and each Senator shall have one vote. The electors in each State shall have the qualifications requisite for electors of the most numerous branch of the State legislatures.

---

[12]Passed January 31, 1865. Ratified December 6, 1865.
[13]Passed June 13, 1866. Ratified July 9, 1868.
[14]Passed February 26, 1869. Ratified February 2, 1870.
[15]Passed July 12, 1909. Ratified February 3, 1913.
[16]Passed May 13, 1912. Ratified April 8, 1913.

When vacancies happen in the representation of any State in the Senate, the executive authority of such State shall issue writs of election to fill such vacancies: Provided, That the legislature of any State may empower the executive thereof to make temporary appointments until the people fill the vacancies by election as the legislature may direct.

This amendment shall not be so construed as to affect the election or term of any Senator chosen before it becomes valid as part of the Constitution.

Amendment XVIII[17]

SECTION 1. After one year from the ratification of this article the manufacture, sale, or transportation of intoxicating liquors within, the importation thereof into, or the exportation thereof from the United States and all territory subject to the jurisdiction thereof for beverage purposes is hereby prohibited.

SECTION 2. The Congress and the several States shall have concurrent power to enforce this article by appropriate legislation.

SECTION 3. This article shall be inoperative unless it shall have been ratified as an amendment to the Constitution by the legislatures of the several States, as provided in the Constitution, within seven years from the date of the submission hereof to the States by the Congress.

Amendment XIX[18]

The right of citizens of the United States to vote shall not be denied or abridged by the United States or by any State on account of sex.

Congress shall have power to enforce this article by appropriate legislation.

Amendment XX[19]

SECTION 1. The terms of the President and Vice-President shall end at noon on the 20th day of January, and the terms of Senators and Representatives at noon on the 3d day of January, of the years in which such terms would have ended if this article had not been ratified; and the terms of their successors shall then begin.

SECTION 2. The Congress shall assemble at least once in every year, and such meeting shall begin at noon on the 3d day of January, unless they shall by law appoint a different day.

SECTION 3. If, at the time fixed for the beginning of the term of the President, the President elect shall have died, the Vice-President elect shall become President. If a President shall not have been chosen before the time fixed for the beginning of his term, or if the President elect shall have failed to qualify, then the Vice-President elect shall act as President until a President shall have qualified; and the Congress may by law provide for the case wherein neither a President elect nor a Vice-President elect shall have qualified, declaring who shall then act as President, or the manner in which one who is to act shall be selected, and such person shall act accordingly until a President or Vice-President shall have qualified.

SECTION 4. The Congress may by law provide for the case of the death of any of the persons from whom the House of Representatives may choose a President whenever the right of choice shall have devolved upon them, and for the case of the death of any of the persons from whom the Senate may choose a Vice-President whenever the right of choice shall have devolved upon them.

SECTION 5. Sections 1 and 2 shall take effect on the 15th day of October following the ratification of this article.

SECTION 6. This article shall be inoperative unless it shall have been ratified as an amendment to the Constitution by the legislatures of three-fourths of the several States within seven years from the date of its submission.

Amendment XXI[20]

SECTION 1. The eighteenth article of amendment to the Constitution of the United States is hereby repealed.

SECTION 2. The transportation or importation into any State, Territory, or possession of the United States for delivery or use therein of intoxicating liquors, in violation of the laws thereof, is hereby prohibited.

SECTION 3. This article shall be inoperative unless it shall have been ratified as an amendment to the Constitution by conventions in the several States, as provided in the Constitution, within seven years from the date of the submission hereof to the States by the Congress.

Amendment XXII[21]

No person shall be elected to the office of the President more than twice, and no person who has held the office of President, or acted as President, for more than two years of a term to which some other person was elected President shall be elected to the office of the President more than once.

But this Article shall not apply to any person holding the office of President when this Article was proposed by the Congress, and shall not prevent any person who may be holding the office of President, or acting as President, during the term within which this Article becomes operative from holding the office of President or acting as President during the remainder of such term.

Amendment XXIII[22]

SECTION 1. The District constituting the seat of Government of the United States shall appoint in such manner as the Congress may direct: A number of electors of President and Vice President equal to the whole number of Senators and Repre-

[17]Passed December 18, 1917. Ratified January 16, 1919.
[18]Passed June 4, 1919. Ratified August 18, 1920.
[19]Passed March 2, 1932. Ratified January 23, 1933.
[20]Passed February 20, 1933. Ratified December 5, 1933.
[21]Passed March 12, 1947. Ratified March 1, 1951.
[22]Passed June 16, 1960. Ratified April 3, 1961.

sentatives in Congress to which the District would be entitled if it were a State, but in no event more than the least populous State; they shall be in addition to those appointed by the States, but they shall be considered, for the purposes of the election of President and Vice President, to be electors appointed by the State; and they shall meet in the District and perform such duties as provided by the twelfth article of amendment.

SECTION 2. The Congress shall have power to enforce this article by appropriate legislation.

Amendment XXIV[23]

SECTION 1. The right of citizens of the United States to vote in any primary or other election for President or Vice President, or for Senator or Representative in Congress, shall not be denied or abridged by the United States or any State by reason of failure to pay any poll tax or other tax.

SECTION 2. The Congress shall have power to enforce this article by appropriate legislation.

Amendment XXV[24]

SECTION 1. In case of the removal of the President from office or of his death or resignation, the Vice President shall become President.

SECTION 2. Whenever there is a vacancy in the office of the Vice President, the President shall nominate a Vice President who shall take office upon confirmation by a majority vote of both Houses of Congress.

SECTION 3. Whenever the President transmits to the President pro tempore of the Senate and the Speaker of the House of Representatives his written declaration that he is unable to discharge the powers and duties of his office, and until he transmits them a written declaration to the contrary, such powers and duties shall be discharged by the Vice President as Acting President.

SECTION 4. Whenever the Vice President and a majority of either the principal officers of the executive department or of such other body as Congress may by law provide, transmit to the President pro tempore of the Senate and the Speaker of the House of Representatives their written declaration that the President is unable to discharge the powers and duties of his office, the Vice President shall immediately assume the powers and duties of the office of Acting President

Thereafter, when the President transmits to the President pro tempore of the Senate and the Speaker of the House of Representatives his written declaration that no inability exists, he shall resume the powers and duties of his office unless the Vice President and a majority of either the principal officers of the executive department or of such other body as Congress may by law provide, transmit within four days to the President pro tempore of the Senate and the Speaker of the House of Representatives their written declaration that the President is unable to discharge the powers and duties of his office. Thereupon Congress shall decide the issue, assembling within forty-eight hours for that purpose if not in session. If the Congress, within twenty-one days after receipt of the latter written declaration, or, if Congress is not in session, within twenty-one days after Congress is required to assemble, determines by two-thirds vote of both Houses that the President is unable to discharge the powers and duties of his office, the Vice President shall continue to discharge the same as Acting President; otherwise, the President shall resume the powers and duties of his office.

Amendment XXVI[25]

SECTION 1. The right of citizens of the United States, who are eighteen years of age or older, to vote shall not be denied or abridged by the United States or by any State on account of age.

SECTION 2. The Congress shall have power to enforce this article by appropriate legislation.

Amendment XXVII[26]

No law, varying the compensation for the service of the Senators and Representatives, shall take effect, until an election of Representatives shall have intervened.

[23]Passed August 27, 1962. Ratified January 23, 1964.
[24]Passed July 6, 1965. Ratified February 11, 1967.
[25]Passed March 23, 1971. Ratified July 5, 1971.
[26]Passed September 25, 1789. Ratified May 7, 1992.

1919 steel strike Walkout by 300,000 steelworkers in the Midwest demanding union recognition and an 8-hour day. It was defeated by employers and local and state police forces, who sometimes resorted to violence.

40 acres and a mule Largely unfulfilled hope of many former slaves that they would receive free land from the confiscated property of ex-Confederates.

9th and 10th U.S. Cavalry African-American army units that played pivotal roles in the Spanish-American war.

abolitionism Movement begun in the North about 1830 to abolish slavery immediately and without compensation to owners.

abolitionist A person who wanted to abolish slavery.

abrogating a treaty Process of abolishing a treaty so that it is no longer in effect.

affirmative action Program or policy that attempted to compensate for past injustice or discrimination to ensure more employment and educational opportunities.

affluence Abundance of material goods or wealth.

Agricultural Adjustment Administration (AAA) 1933 attempt to promote economic recovery by reducing supply of crops, dairy, and meat produced by American farmers.

Aguinaldo, Emilio Anticolonial leader who fought for independence of the Philippines first from Spain and then from the United States.

Alamo Battle between Texas revolutionaries and the Mexican army at the San Antonio mission called the *Alamo* on March 6, 1836, in which all 187 Texans were killed.

Albany Congress An intercolonial congress that met in Albany, New York, in June 1754. The delegates urged the Crown to assume direct control of Indian relations beyond the settled boundaries of the colonies, and they drafted a plan of confederation for the continental colonies. No colony ratified it, nor did the Crown or Parliament accept it.

Algonquians Indian peoples who spoke some dialect of the Algonquian language family.

alien Person from another country who is living in the United States.

American Anti-Slavery Society Organization created by northern abolitionists in 1833 that called for immediate, uncompensated emancipation of the slaves.

American Colonization Society Established by elite gentlemen of the middle and upper-south states in 1816, this organization encouraged voluntary emancipation of slaves, to be followed by their emigration to the West African colony of Liberia.

American System Program proposed by Henry Clay and others to foster national economic growth and interdependence among the geographical sections. It included a protective tariff, a national bank, and internal improvements.

Amerind The forerunner of the vast majority of Indian languages in the Americas.

amnesty General pardon granted to a large group of people.

anarchist Activist who called for the violent destruction of the capitalist system so that a new socialist order could be built.

Anasazi An advanced pre-Columbian cliff-dwelling culture that flourished for two centuries in what are now the states of Arizona, New Mexico, Utah, and Colorado before abandoning these sites in the late 13th century A.D.

Anderson, Marian Black opera singer who broke a color bar in 1939 when she sang to an interracial audience of 75,000 from the steps of the Lincoln Memorial.

Anglican A member of the legally established Church of England, or that church itself.

Anglos English-speaking people.

anxious bench Bench at or near the front of a religious revival meeting where the most likely converts were seated.

apartheid Legal system practiced in South Africa and based on elaborate rules of racial separation and subordination of blacks.

armistice A temporary stop in fighting. Often in effect before a final peace treaty is signed.

Article X of the Covenant Addendum to the Treaty of Versailles that empowered the League of Nations to undertake military actions against aggressor nations.

artisan A skilled laborer who works with his hands. In early America, artisans often owned their own shops and produced goods either for general sale or for special order.

Association Groups created by the First Continental Congress in local committees to enforce its trade sanctions against Britain. The creation of these groups was an important sign that Congress was beginning to act as a central government.

associationalism Herbert Hoover's approach to managing the economy. Firms and organizations in each economic sector would be asked to cooperate with each other in the pursuit of efficiency, profit, and the public good.

astrolabe A device that permitted accurate calculation of latitude or distances north and south.

Atlantic slave trade A European commerce that led to the enslavement of millions of people who were shipped from their African homelands to European colonies in the Americas.

attrition A type of warfare in which an effort is made to exhaust the manpower, supplies, and morale of the other side.

Auburn system Prison system designed to reform criminals and reduce expenses through the sale of items produced in workshops. Prisoners slept in solitary cells, marched in military formation to meals and workshops, and were forbidden to speak to one another at any time.

Australian ballot (secret ballot) Practice that required citizens to vote in private rather than in public and required the government (rather than political parties) to supervise the voting process.

Aztec The last pre-Columbian high culture in the Valley of Mexico. It was conquered by the Spaniards in 1519–1521.

baby boom Sudden increase in births in the years after World War II.

backcountry Term used in the 18th and early 19th centuries to refer to the western settlements and the supposed misfits who lived in them.

Bacon's Rebellion The most serious challenge to royal authority in the English mainland colonies prior to 1775. It erupted in Virginia in 1676 after the governor and Nathaniel Bacon, the principal rebel, could not agree on how best to wage war against frontier Indians.

balance of trade The relationship between imports and exports. The difference between exports and imports is the balance between the two. A healthy nation should export more than it imports. This is known as a favorable balance of trade.

bandeirantes Brazilian frontiersmen who traveled deep into South America to enslave Indians. The slaves then were worked to death on the sugar plantations.

banknotes Paper money, issued by banks, that circulated as currency.

barrios Spanish-speaking urban areas, usually separate districts in southwestern towns and cities.

bateau A light, flat-bottomed boat with narrow ends that was used in Canada and the northeastern part of the colonies.

Battle of Lexington The first military engagement of the Revolutionary War. It occurred on April 19, 1775, when British soldiers fired into a much smaller body of minutemen on Lexington green.

Battle of Little Big Horn A battle in eastern Montana Territory on the bluffs above Little Big Horn River on June 25, 1876.

Bay of Pigs Site of an ill-fated 1961 invasion of Cuba by a U.S.-trained force that attempted to overthrow the government of Fidel Castro.

Beatles Preeminent musical group associated with the "British invasion" in the 1960s.

belligerent Country actively engaged in a war.

Beringia A land bridge during the last ice age across the Bering Strait between Siberia and Alaska. It was once an area where plants, animals, and humans could live.

bicameral legislature A legislature with two houses or chambers.

Bill of Rights First ten amendments to the Constitution, which protect the rights of individuals from abuses by the federal government.

Black Codes Laws passed by southern states that restricted the rights and liberties of former slaves.

Black Power Mid-1960s movement that called for modifying integrationist goals in favor of gaining political and economic power for separate black-directed institutions and emphasized pride in African-American heritage.

Black Republicans Label coined by the Democratic Party to attack the Republican Party as believers in racial equality. The Democrats used this fear to convince many whites to remain loyal to them.

blacklist In the postwar years, a list of people who could no longer work in the entertainment industry because of alleged contacts with communists.

blitzkrieg A "lightning war"; a coordinated and massive military strike by German army and air forces.

block grants Part of Nixon's new economic plan in which a percentage of federal tax dollars would be returned to state and local governments to spend as they deemed fit.

blockade runner A ship designed to run through a blockade.

blockade The closing of a country's harbors by enemy ships to prevent trade and commerce, especially to prevent traffic in military supplies.

blockhouse A wooden fort with an overhanging second floor. The white settlers of Kentucky used blockhouses to defend themselves against Indians.

blood sports Sporting activities emphasizing bloodiness that were favored by working-class men of the cities. The most popular in the early 19th century were cockfighting, ratting, dogfights, and various types of violence between animals.

bonanza farms Huge wheat farms financed by eastern capital and cultivated with heavy machinery and hired labor.

Bonus Army Army veterans who marched on Washington, D.C., in 1932 to lobby for economic relief but who were rebuffed by Hoover.

Boone, Daniel A pioneer settler of Kentucky, Boone became the most famous American frontiersman of his generation.

border ruffians Term used to describe proslavery Missourians who streamed into Kansas in 1854, determined to vote as many times as necessary to install a proslavery government there.

Boston Massacre The colonial term for the confrontation between colonial protestors and British soldiers in front of the customs house on March 5, 1770. Five colonists were killed and six wounded.

Boston Tea Party In December 1773, Boston's Sons of Liberty threw 342 chests of East India Company tea into Boston harbor rather than allow them to be landed and pay the hated tea duty.

bounty jumpers Men who enlisted in the Union army to collect the bounties offered by some districts to fill military quotas; these men would enlist and then desert as soon as they got their money.

Boxers Chinese nationalist organization that instigated an uprising in 1900 to rid China of all foreign influence.

braceros Guest workers from Mexico allowed into the United States because of labor shortages from 1942 to 1964.

Brown v. Board of Education 1954 case in which the U.S. Supreme Court unanimously overruled the "separate but equal" doctrine and held that segregation in the public schools violated the principle of equal protection under the law.

"broad" wives Wives of slave men who lived on other plantations and were visited by their husbands during off hours.

Brown, John Prominent abolitionist who fought for the antislavery cause in Kansas (1856) and led a raid to seize the Harpers Ferry arsenal in 1859.

Bryan, William Jennings A two-term Democratic congressman from Nebraska who won the party's presidential nomination in 1896 after electrifying delegates with his "Cross of Gold" speech. Bryan was twice more nominated for president (1900 and 1908); he lost all three times.

Bull Moosers Followers of Theodore Roosevelt in the 1912 election.

bulldozing Using force to keep African Americans from voting.

Burr, Aaron Vice President under Thomas Jefferson who killed Alexander Hamilton in a duel and eventually hatched schemes to detach parts of the west from the United States.

Bush, George H. W. Republican President (1989–1993) who directed an international coalition against Iraq in the Persian Gulf War.

Bush, George W. Republican president (2001–) elected in the highly disputed 2000 contest decided by the Supreme Court.

bushwhackers Confederate guerrilla raiders especially active in Missouri. Jayhawkers were the Union version of the same type of people. Both groups did a tremendous amount of damage with raids, arson, ambush, and murder.

Butternuts Democrats from the southern river-oriented counties of the Northwest region whose name came from the yellow vegetable dye with which they colored their homespun clothing.

Cahokia The largest city created by Mississippian mound builders. Located in Illinois near modern St. Louis, it thrived from A.D. 900 to 1250 and then declined.

californios Spanish-speaking people whose families had resided in California for generations.

camp meeting Outdoor revival often lasting for days; a principal means of spreading evangelical Christianity in the United States.

Capra, Frank Popular 1930s filmmaker who celebrated the decency, honesty, and patriotism of ordinary Americans in such films as *Mr. Deeds Goes to Town* and *Mr. Smith Goes to Washington*.

caravel A new type of ocean-going vessel that could sail closer to a head wind than any other sailing ship and make speeds of from three to twelve knots per hour.
Carnegie, Andrew A Scottish immigrant who became the most efficient entrepreneur in the U.S. steel industry and earned a great fortune.
carpetbaggers Northerners who settled in the South during Reconstruction.
Carson, Rachel American marine biologist and author best known for *Silent Spring* (1962), a widely read book that questioned the use of chemical pesticides and helped stimulate the modern environmental movement.
Carter, Jimmy Democratic president (1977–1981) whose single term in office was marked by inflation, fuel shortages, and a hostage crisis.
cash and carry U.S. foreign policy prior to American entry into World War II that required belligerents to pay cash and carry products away in their own ships. This arrangement minimized risks to American exports, loans, and shipping.
Cavaliers Supporters of the Stuart family of Charles I during the civil wars.
changing system Elaborate system of neighborhood debts and bartering used primarily in the South and West where little cash money was available.
Chavez, Cesar Political activist, leader of the United Farm Workers of America, and the most influential Mexican American leader during the 1970s.
Cherokee War Between December 1759 and December 1761, the Cherokee Indians devastated the South Carolina backcountry. The British army intervened and in turn inflicted immense damage on the Cherokee.
Chicanismo Populistic pride in the Mexican-American heritage that emerged in the late 1960s. Chicano, once a term of derision, became a rallying cry among activists.
chinampas The highly productive gardens built on Lake Taxcoco by the Aztecs.
CIO The Committee and then Congress for Industrial Organization, founded in 1935 to organize the unskilled and semiskilled workers ignored by the AFL. The CIO reinvigorated the labor movement.
circuit court Court that meets at different places within a district.
circuit-riding preachers Methodist ministers who traveled from church to church, usually in rural areas.
Civil Rights Act of 1957 First civil rights act since Reconstruction, aimed at securing voting rights for African Americans in the South.
Civil Rights Act of 1964 Bipartisan measure that denied federal funding to segregated schools and barred discrimination by race and sex in employment, public accommodations, and labor unions.
Civil Rights Act of 1968 Measure that banned racial discrimination in housing and made interference with a person's civil rights a federal crime. It also stipulated that crossing state lines to incite a riot was a federal crime.
Clay, Henry Speaker of the House, senator from Kentucky, and National Republican presidential candidate who was the principal spokesman for the American System.
Clinton, Bill Democratic president (1993–2001) whose two-term presidency witnessed rapid economic growth but also a sexual scandal that fueled an impeachment effort, which he survived.
close-order assault Military tactic of attacking with little space between men. In the face of modern weapons used during the Civil War, such fighting produced a high casualty rate.
Clovis tip A superior spear point developed before 9000 B.C. It was in use nearly everywhere in North and South America and produced such an improvement in hunting ability that it contributed to the extinction of most large mammals.
Coercive (Intolerable) Acts Four statutes passed by Parliament in response to the Boston Tea Party, including one that closed the port of Boston until the tea was paid for, and another that overturned the Massachusetts Charter of 1691. The colonists called them the Intolerable Acts and included the Quebec Act under that label.
Cold War The political, military, cultural, and economic rivalry between the United States and the Soviet Union that developed after the Second World War and lasted until the disintegration of the Soviet State after 1989.
collective bargaining Negotiations between representatives of workers and employers on issues such as wages, hours, and working conditions.
Collier, John Activist head of the Bureau of Indian Affairs who improved U.S. policy toward Native Americans and guided the landmark Indian Reorganization Act through Congress.
colonial economy Economy based on the export of agricultural products and the import of manufactured goods; sometimes used to describe the dependence of the South on the North.
Columbus, Christopher The Genoese mariner who persuaded Queen Isabella of Spain to support his voyage of discovery across the Atlantic in 1492. Until his death in 1506, he believed he had reached East Asia. Instead he had discovered America.
Committee on Public Information U.S. Government agency established in 1917 to arouse support for the war and, later, to generate suspicion of war dissenters.
committees of correspondence Bodies formed on both the local and colonial levels that played an important role in exchanging ideas and information. They spread primarily anti-British material and were an important step in the first tentative unity of people in different colonies.
common law The heart of the English legal system was based on precedents and judicial decisions. Common-law courts offered due process through such devices as trial by jury, which usually consisted of local men.
common schools Tax-supported public schools built by state and local governments.
Communist Party Radical group that wanted America to follow the Soviet Union's path to socialism. The CP organized some of the country's poorest workers into unions and pushed the New Deal leftward, but was never popular enough to bid for power itself.
commutation fee $300 fee that could be paid by a man drafted into the Union army to exempt him from the current draft call.
compensated emancipation Idea that the federal government would offer compensation or money to states that voluntarily abolished slavery.
competence Understood in the early republic as the ability to live up to neighborhood economic standards while protecting the long-term independence of the household.
Compromise of 1850 Series of laws enacted in 1850 intended to settle all outstanding slavery issues.
Congressional Black Caucus (CBC) Congressional group formed in 1969 that focused on eliminating disparities between African Americans and white Americans.
congressional caucus In the early republic, the group of congressmen that traditionally chose the party's presidential candidates. By the 1820s, the American public distrusted the caucus as undemocratic because only one party contested for power. The caucus was replaced by the national nominating convention.
conquistadores The Spanish word for conquerors.
Conscience Whigs A group of antislavery members of the Whig Party.
Conservation Movement that called for managing the environment to ensure the careful and efficient use of the nation's natural resources.
consumer durable Consumer goods that were meant to last, such as washing machines and radios.
containment Label used to describe the global anticommunist national-security policies adopted by the United States to stop the expansion of communism during the late 1940s.
contraband of war Term used to describe slaves who came within the Union lines.
contras Military force in Nicaragua, trained and financed by the United States, that opposed the Nicaraguan socialist government led by the Sandinista Party.
convention In England, a meeting, usually of the houses of Parliament, to address an emergency, such as the flight of James II to France in 1688. The convention welcomed William and Mary, who then restored the traditional parliamentary system. In the United States by the 1780s, conventions had become the purest expression of the popular will, superior to the legislature, as in the convention that drafted the Massachusetts Constitution of 1780.
cooperatives Marketing groups established by such groups as the Farmers Alliance that eliminated "middlemen" and reduced prices to farmers. The idea also was tried by some labor groups and included other types of businesses such as factories.
Copperheads Term used by some Republicans to describe Peace Democrats to imply that they were traitors to the Union.
corrupt bargain Following the election of 1824, Andrew Jackson and his supporters alleged that, in a "corrupt bargain," Henry Clay sold his support during the House vote in the disputed election of 1824 of John Quincy Adams in exchange for appointment as Secretary of State.
Cortés, Hernán The Spanish conquistador who vanquished the Aztecs.
cotton Semitropical plant that produced white, fluffy fibers that could be made into textiles.
Coughlin, Father Charles The "radio priest" from the Midwest who alleged that the New Deal was being run by bankers. His growing anti-Semitism discredited him by 1939.
counterculture Anti-establishment movement that symbolized the youthful social upheaval of the 1960s. Ridiculing traditional attitudes toward such matters as clothing, hair styles, and sexuality, the counterculture urged a more open and less regimented approach to daily life.
coureur de bois A French phrase interpreted as "a roamer of the woods," referring to French colonists who participated in the fur trade with the Indians and lived part of the year with them.
court-packing plan 1937 attempt by Roosevelt to appoint one new Supreme Court justice for every sitting justice over the age of 70 and who had sat for at least 10 years. Roosevelt's purpose was to prevent conservative justices from dismantling the New Deal, but the plan died in Congress and inflamed opponents of the New Deal.
Covenant Chain of Peace An agreement negotiated by Governor Edmund Andros in 1677 that linked the colony of New York to the Iroquois Five Nations and was later expanded to include other colonies and Indian peoples.
covenant theology The belief that God made two personal covenants with humans: the covenant of works and the covenant of grace.
coverture A common-law doctrine under which the legal personality of the husband covered the wife, and he made all legally binding decisions.
Crazy Horse War chief of the Oglala Lakota (Sioux) Indians who forged an alliance with Cheyenne chiefs to resist white expansion into the Black Hills in 1874–1875; led the attack on Custer's 7th Cavalry at Little Big Horn.
Credit Mobilier Construction company for the Union Pacific Railroad that gave shares of stock to some congressmen in return for favors.
crisis conversion Understood in evangelical churches as a personal transformation that resulted from directly experiencing the Holy Spirit.
crop lien system System of credit used in the poor rural South whereby merchants in small country stores provided necessary goods on credit in return for a lien on the crop. As the price of crops fell, small farmers, black and white, drifted deeper into debt.
Cuban Missile Crisis (1962) Serious Cold War confrontation between the United States and the Soviet Union over the installation of Soviet missiles in Cuba.
Custer, George A. Civil War hero and postwar Indian fighter who was killed at Little Big Horn in 1876.
Davis, Jefferson Mississippi planter and prominent leader of the Southern Democrats in the 1850s, who later served as president of the Confederacy.
Dawes Plan 1924 U.S.-backed agreement to reduce German reparation payments by more than half. The plan also called on banks to invest $200 million in the German economy.
Debs, Eugene V. Leader of the Socialist Party who received almost a million votes in the election of 1912.
Declaration of Independence A document drafted primarily by Thomas Jefferson of Virginia; this document justified American independence to the world by affirming "that all men are created equal" and have a natural right to "life, liberty, and the pursuit of happiness." The longest section of the Declaration condemned George III as a tyrant.
deflation Decline in consumer prices or a rise in the purchasing power of money.
Deism Belief that God created the universe but did not intervene in its affairs.
Denmark Vesey Leader of a slave conspiracy in and around Charleston, South Carolina in 1822.
de-skilling Process in which the employment market produces jobs requiring fewer skill (and offering less income) than in the past.
détente An easing of tensions, particularly between the United States and the Soviet Union.
Dewey, John Philosopher who believed that American technological and industrial power could be made to serve the people and democracy.
direct election of senators Constitutional amendment that mandated the election of senators by the people rather than by selection by state legislatures.
dirty tricks Actions designed to destroy the reputation and effectiveness of political opponents of the Nixon administration.
disfranchisement Process of barring groups of adult citizens from voting.
dissenter Person who disagrees openly with the majority opinion.
Dix, Dorothea Boston reformer who traveled throughout the country campaigning for humane, state-supported asylums for the insane.
dollar diplomacy Diplomatic strategy formulated under President Taft that focused on expanding American investments abroad, especially in Latin America and East Asia.
domestic fiction Sentimental literature that centered on household and domestic themes that emphasized the toil and travails of women and children who overcame adversity through religious faith and strength of character.
Douglas, Stephen A. Senator from Illinois who emerged as a leading Democrat in 1850 and led efforts to enact the Compromise of 1850.
doves Opponents of military action, especially those who wanted quickly to end U.S. involvement in the Vietnam War.
dower rights The right of a widow to a portion of her deceased husband's estate (usually one third of the value of the estate). It was passed to their children upon her death.
dowry The cash or goods a woman received from her father when she married.
drawbacks Form of rebate offered to special customers by the railroads.

Dred Scott Missouri slave who sued for freedom on grounds of prolonged residence in a free state and free territory; in 1857, the Supreme Court found against his case, declaring the Missouri Compromise unconstitutional.
Du Bois, W. E. B. Leader of the NAACP, the editor of its newspaper, *The Crisis,* and an outspoken critic of Booker T. Washington and his accomodationist approach to race relations.
economy of scale Term used in both industry and agriculture to describe the economic advantages of concentrating capital, units of production, and output.
Eisenhower Doctrine Policy that stated that the United States would use armed force to respond to imminent or actual communist aggression in the Middle East.
Eisenhower, Dwight D. Supreme Commander of the Allied Forces in Europe, orchestrator of the Normandy Invasion, and President of the United States (1953–1961).
elect Those selected by God for salvation.
Electoral College The group that elects the president. Each state receives as many electors as it has congressmen and senators combined and can decide how to choose its electors. Every elector votes for two candidates, one of whom has to be from another state.
emancipation Refers to release from slavery or bondage. Gradual emancipation was introduced in Pennsylvania and provided for the eventual freeing of slaves born after a certain date when they reached age 28.
embargo Government order prohibiting the movement of merchant ships or goods in or out of its ports.
encomienda A system of labor introduced into the Western Hemisphere by the Spanish. It permitted the holder, or *encomendero*, to claim labor from Indians in a district for a stated period of time.
enfranchise To grant the right to vote.
Enlightenment The new learning in science and philosophy that took hold, at least in England, between 1660 and the American Revolution. Nearly all of its spokesmen were religious moderates who were more interested in science than religious doctrine and who favored broad religious toleration.
entail A legal device that required a landowner to keep his estate intact and pass it on to his heir.
enumerated commodities A group of colonial products that had to be shipped from the colony of origin to England or another English colony. The most important commodities were sugar and tobacco.
Environmental Protection Agency (EPA) Organization established in 1970 that brought under a single institutional umbrella the enforcement of laws intended to protect environmental quality.
environmentalism Movement with roots in earlier conservation, preservation, and public health movements that grew in power after 1970, when concern mounted over the disruption of ecological balances and critical habitats.
Equal Rights Amendment (ERA) Proposed amendment to the Constitution providing that equal rights could not be abridged on account of sex. It won congressional approval in 1972 but failed to gain ratification by the states.
Erie Canal Canal linking the Hudson River at Albany with the Great Lakes at Buffalo that helped to commercialize the farms of the Great Lakes watershed and to channel that commerce into New York City.
Espionage, Sabotage, and Sedition Acts Laws passed in 1917 and 1918 that gave the federal government sweeping powers to silence and even imprison dissenters.
established church The church in a European state or colony that was sustained by the government and supported by public taxes.
evangelical A style of Christian ministry that includes much zeal and enthusiasm. Evangelical ministers emphasized personal conversion and faith rather than religious ritual.
evangelicals Religious groups that generally placed an emphasis on conversion of non-Christians.
excise tax Internal tax on goods or services.
external taxes Taxes based on oceanic trade, such as port duties. Some colonists thought of them more as a means of regulating trade than as taxes for revenue.
factories A term used to describe small posts established for the early slave trade along the coast of Africa or on small offshore islands.
fall line A geographical landmark defined by the first waterfalls encountered when going up-river from the sea. These waterfalls prevented oceangoing ships from sailing further inland and thus made the fall line a significant early barrier. Land between the falls and the ocean was called the tidewater. Land above the falls but below the mountains was called the piedmont.
fascism Type of highly centralized government that used terror and violence to suppress opposition. Its rigid social and economic controls often incorporated strong nationalism and racism. Fascist governments were dominated by strong authority figures or dictators.
favorite son Candidate for president supported by delegates from his home state.
Federal Reserve Act Act that brought private banks and public authority together to regulate and strengthen the nation's financial system.
Federalists Supporters of the Constitution during the ratification process. Anti-Federalists resisted ratification.
feudal revival The reliance on old feudal charters for all of the profits that could be extracted from them. It took hold in several colonies in the mid-eighteenth century and caused serious problems between many landowners and tenants.
fiat money Paper money backed only by the promise of the government to accept it in payment of taxes. It originated in Massachusetts after a military emergency in 1690.
filibuster Congressional delaying tactic involving lengthy speeches that prevent legislation from being enacted.
filibustering A term used to describe several groups that invaded or attempted to invade various Latin American areas to attempt to add them to the slaveholding regions of the United States. The word originated from *filibustero,* meaning a freebooter or pirate.
fire-eaters Southerners who were eager, enthusiastic supporters of southern rights and later of secession.
First Continental Congress This intercolonial body met in Philadelphia in September and October 1774 to organize resistance against the Coercive Acts by defining American rights, petitioning the king, and appealing to the British and American people. It created the Association, local committees in each community to enforce nonimportation.
Five-Power Treaty 1922 treaty in which the United States, Britain, Japan, France, and Italy agreed to scrap more than 2 million tons of their warships.
flappers Rebellious middle-class young women who signaled their desire for independence and equality through style and personality rather than through politics.
flexible response Kennedy's approach to the Cold War that aimed to provide a wide variety of military and non-military methods to confront communist movements.
Ford, Gerald A GOP member of the House of Representatives, Gerald Ford became the first person to be appointed Vice President of the United States. When Richard Nixon resigned in 1974, Ford became President.
Fort Sumter Fort in Charleston's harbor occupied by United States troops after the secession of South Carolina.
Fourteen Points Plan laid out by Woodrow Wilson in January 1918 to give concrete form to his dream of a "peace without victory" and a new world order.
free silver Idea that the government would purchase all silver offered for sale and coin it into silver dollars at the preferred ratio between silver and gold of 16 to 1.
Freedmen's Bureau Federal agency created in 1865 to supervise newly freed people. It oversaw relations between whites and blacks in the South, issued food rations, and supervised labor contracts.
freedom riders Members of interracial groups who traveled the South on buses to test a series of federal court decisions declaring segregation on buses and in waiting rooms to be unconstitutional.
Freedom Summer Summer of 1964 when nearly a thousand white volunteers went to Mississippi to aid in voter registration and other civil rights projects.
free-labor ideology Belief that all work in a free society is honorable and that manual labor is degraded when it is equated with slavery or bondage.
Free-Soilers A term used to describe people who opposed the expansion of slavery into the territories. It came from the name of a small political party in the election of 1848.
French and Indian War Popular name for the struggle between Britain and France for the control of North America, 1754 to 1763, in which the British conquered New France. It merged into Europe's Seven Years' War (1756–1763) that pitted Britain and Prussia against France, Austria, and Russia.
Friedan, Betty Author of *The Feminine Mystique* (1963) and founder of the National Organization for Women (1966).
frontier An area on the advancing edge of American civilization.
fugitive slaves Runaway slaves who escaped to a free state.
Fulton, Robert Builder of the Clermont, the first practical steam-driven boat.
fundamentalists Religious groups that preached the necessity of fidelity to a strict moral code, individual commitment to Christ, and faith in the literal truth of the Bible.
funded national debt The state agreed to pay the interest due to its creditors before all other obligations.
Gabriel's rebellion Carefully planned but unsuccessful rebellion of slaves in Richmond and the surrounding area in 1800.
gang labor A system where planters organized their field slaves into gangs, supervised them closely, and kept them working in the fields all day. This type of labor was used on tobacco plantations.
Garvey, Marcus Jamaican-born black nationalist who attracted millions of African Americans in the early 1920s to a movement calling for black separatism and self-sufficiency.
gas and water socialists Term used to describe evolutionary socialists who focused their reform efforts on regulating municipal utilities in the public interest.
gentleman Term used to describe a person of means who performed no manual labor.
gentlemen's agreement (1907) Agreement by which the Japanese government promised to halt the immigration of its adult male laborers to the United States in return for President Theodore Roosevelt's pledge to end the discriminatory treatment of Japanese immigrant children in California's public schools.
GI Bill Officially called the Serviceman's Readjustment Act of 1944. It provided veterans with college and job-training assistance, preferential treatment in hiring, and subsidized home loans, and was later extended to Korean War veterans in 1952.
girdled trees Trees with a line cut around them so sap would not rise in the spring.
glasnost Russian term describing increased openness in Russian society under Mikhail Gorbachev.
Glorious Revolution The overthrow of King James II by Whigs and Tories, who invited William of Orange to England. William landed in November 1688, the army defected to him, James fled to France, and in early 1689 Parliament offered the throne to William and his wife Mary, a daughter of James. Contemporaries called the event "glorious" because almost no blood was shed in England.
gold bugs "Sound money" advocates who wanted to keep the United States on the international gold standard and believed the expanded coinage of silver was foolhardy.
Gompers, Samuel F. America's most famous trade unionist while serving as president of the AFL (1896–1924). He achieved his greatest success organizing skilled workers.
Good Neighbor Policy Roosevelt's foreign policy initiative that formally renounced the right of the United States to intervene in Latin American affairs, leading to improved relations between the United States and Latin American countries.
governor-general The French official responsible for military and diplomatic affairs and for appointment of all militia officers in a colony.
graduated income tax Tax based on income with rates that gradually rise as the level of income rises.
Grangers Members of the Patrons of Husbandry (a farmers' organization) and a contemptuous name for farmers used by ranchers in the West.
Grant, Ulysses S. General-in-chief of Union armies who led those armies to victory in the Civil War.
Great American Desert The treeless area in the plains most Americans considered unsuitable for settlement. It generally was passed over by settlers going to the Pacific Coast areas.
Great Awakening An immense religious revival that swept across the Protestant world in the 1730s and 1740s.
Great Depression Economic downturn triggered by the stock market crash in October 1929 and lasting until 1941.
Great Society Series of domestic initiatives announced in 1964 by President Lyndon Johnson to "end poverty and racial injustice." They included the Voting Rights Act of 1965; the establishment of the Department of Housing and Urban Development, Head Start, and job-training programs; Medicare and Medicaid expansion; and various community action programs.
Great White Fleet Naval ships sent on a 45,000-mile world tour by President Roosevelt (1907–1909) to showcase American military power.
Greeley, Horace Editor of the *New York Tribune*, one of the most influential newspapers in the country.
greenbacks Paper money issued by the federal government during the Civil War to help pay war expenses. They were called greenbacks because of their color.
Greene, Nathanael A general from Rhode Island whose superb strategy of irregular war reclaimed the Lower South for the American cause in 1780–1781.
Greenwich Village Community of radical artists and writers in lower Manhattan that provided a supportive environment for various kinds of radical ideals.
Grenville, George As head of the British government from 1763 to 1765, Grenville passed the Sugar Act, Quartering Act, Currency Act, and the Stamp Act, provoking the imperial crisis of 1765–1766.

Grimke, Sarah   Along with her sister Angelina, this elite South Carolina woman moved north and campaigned against slavery and for temperance and women's rights.

gross national product (GNP)   Total value of all goods and services produced during a specific period.

Gulf of Tonkin Resolution   Measure passed by Congress in August 1964 that provided authorization for an air war against North Vietnam after U.S. destroyers were allegedly attacked by North Vietnamese torpedoes. Johnson invoked it as authority for expanding the Vietnam War.

Gullah   A language spoken by newly imported African slaves. Originally, it was a simple second language for everyone who spoke it, but gradually evolved into modern black English.

habeas corpus   Right of an individual to obtain a legal document as protection against illegal imprisonment.

haciendas   Large, landed estates established by the Spanish.

Hale, Sarah Josepha   Editor of *Godey's Ladies Book* and an important arbiter of domesticity and taste for middle-class housewives.

Half-Way Covenant   The Puritan practice whereby parents who had been baptized but had not yet experienced conversion could bring their children before the church and have them baptized.

Hamilton, Alexander   Secretary of the Treasury under Washington who organized the finances of the new government and led the partisan fight against the Democratic Republicans.

Hard Money Democrats   Democrats who, in the 1830s and 1840s, wanted to eliminate paper money and regarded banks as centers of trickery and privilege.

Harlem Renaissance   1920s African-American literary and artistic awakening that sought to create works rooted in black culture instead of imitating white styles.

Harpers Ferry   Site of John Brown's 1859 raid on a U.S. armory and arsenal for the manufacture and storage of military rifles.

hawks   Supporters of intensified military efforts in the Vietnam War.

Haywood, William   Labor organizer known as "Big Bill" who led the radical union Industrial Workers of the World.

headright   A colonist received 50 acres of land for every person whose passage to America he financed, including himself. This system was introduced in Virginia.

heathen   A term used sometimes by Christians to refer to anyone who was not a Christian or a Jew.

herrenvolk democracy   Concept that emphasized the equality of all who belonged to the master race—not all mankind.

Hessians   A term used by Americans to describe the 17,000 mercenary troops hired by Britain from various German states, especially Hesse.

hidalgos   The minor nobility of Spain. Many possessed little wealth and were interested in improving their position through the overseas empire.

High Federalists   A term used to describe Alexander Hamilton and some of his less-moderate supporters. They wanted the naval war with France to continue and also wanted to severely limit the rights of an opposition party.

Highway Act of 1956   Act that appropriated $25 billion for the construction of more than 40,000 miles of interstate highways over a 10-year period.

hippies   People who identified with the 1960s counterculture. They were often depicted as embracing mind-altering drugs, communal living arrangements, and new forms of music.

Hiroshima   Japanese city destroyed by an atomic bomb on August 6, 1945.

Hiss, Alger   High-level State Department employee who was accused, in a controversial case, of being a communist and Soviet spy.

Hitler, Adolph   German fascist dictator whose aggressive policies touched off the Second World War.

HIV-AIDS   Acquired immune deficiency syndrome (AIDS) resulting from infection with the human immunodeficiency virus (HIV). It progressively impedes the body's ability to protect itself from disease.

Hmong   Ethnically distinct people who inhabited lands extending across the borders of the Indochinese countries of Vietnam, Cambodia, and Laos.

House of Burgesses   The assembly of early Virginia that settlers were allowed to elect. Members met with the governor and his council and enacted local laws. It first met in 1619.

House Un-American Activities Committee (HUAC)   Congressional committee (1938–1975) that zealously investigated suspected Nazi and Communist sympathizers.

household industry   Work such as converting raw materials into finished products done by women and children to provide additional household income.

Howe, William (General)   Howe commanded the British army in North America from 1776 to 1778. He won major victories in New York and northern New Jersey in 1776, but Washington regained control of New Jersey after his Trenton-Princeton campaign. Howe took Philadelphia in September 1777 but was recalled in disgrace after Britain's northern army surrendered at Saratoga.

Huguenots   French Protestants who followed the beliefs of John Calvin.

Hull House   First American settlement house established in Chicago in 1889 by Jane Addams and Ellen Gates Starr.

Human Genome Project   Program launched in 1985 to map all genetic material in the twenty-four human chromosomes. It sparked ongoing debate over potential consequences of genetic research and manipulation.

Hutchinson, Anne   A religious radical who attracted a large following in Massachusetts, especially in Boston. She warned that nearly all of the ministers were preaching a covenant of works instead of the covenant of grace. Convicted of the Antinomian heresy after claiming that she received direct messages from God, she and her most loyal followers were banished to Rhode Island in 1638.

hydraulic mining   Use of high-pressure streams of water to wash gold or other minerals from soil.

Immigration Act of 1924 (Johnson-Reed Act)   Limited immigration to the United States to 165,000 a year, shrank immigration from southern and eastern Europe to insignificance, and banned immigration from East and South Asia.

Immigration Act of 1965   Law eliminating the national-origins quota system for immigration and substituting preferences for people with certain skills or with relatives in the United States.

Immigration Restriction Act of 1917   Measure that denied any adult immigrant who failed a reading test entry into the United States, and banned immigration from the "Asiatic Barred Zone."

impeach   To charge government officeholders with misconduct in office.

impeachment   Act of charging a public official with misconduct in office.

imperialists   Those who wanted to expand their nation's world power through military prowess, economic strength, and control of foreign territory (often organized into colonies).

impressment   Removal of sailors from American ships by British naval officers.

Inca   The last and most extensive pre-Columbian empire in the Andes and along the Pacific coast of South America.

indentured servants   People who had their passage to America paid by a master or ship captain. They agreed to work for their master for a term of years in exchange for cost of passage, bed and board, and small freedom dues when their terms were up. The number of years served depended on the terms of the contract. Most early settlers in the English colonies outside of New England arrived as indentured servants.

Indian Removal Act (1830)   Legislation that offered the native peoples of the lower South the option of removal to federal lands west of the Mississippi. Those who did not take the offer were removed by force in 1838.

indigo   A blue dye obtained from plants that was used by the textile industry. The British government subsidized the commercial production of it in South Carolina.

information revolution   Acceleration of the speed and availability of information due to computer and satellite systems.

initiative   Reform that gave voters the right to propose and pass a law independently of their state legislature.

Inns of Court   England's law schools.

intendant   The officer who administered the system of justice in New France.

interchangeable parts   Industrial technique using machine tools to cut and shape a large number of similar parts that can be fitted together with other parts to make an entire item such as a gun.

internal improvements   Nineteenth-century term for transportation facilities such as roads, canals, and railroads.

internal taxes   Taxes that were imposed on land, on people, on retail items (such as excises), or on legal documents and newspapers (such as the Stamp Act). Most colonists thought that only their elective assemblies had the constitutional power to impose internal taxes.

Iran-*contra* affair   Reagan administration scandal in which the U.S. secretly sold arms to Iran, a country implicated in holding American hostages, and diverted the money to finance the attempt by the *contras* to overthrow the Sandinista government of Nicaragua. Both transactions violated acts of Congress, which had prohibited funding the *contras* and selling weapons to Iran.

Iroquois League   A confederation of five Indian nations centered around the Mohawk Valley who were very active in the fur trade. They first worked with the Dutch and then the English. They were especially successful in using adoption as a means of remaining strong.

irreconcilables   Group of fourteen midwestern and western senators who opposed the Treaty of Versailles.

irregular war   A type of war using men who were not part of a permanent or professional regular military force. It also can apply to guerilla-type warfare, usually against the civilian population.

itinerant preachers   Ministers who lacked their own parishes and who traveled from place to place.

Jackson State (incident)   Killing of two students on May 13, 1970, after an escalation in tensions between students at Jackson State University, a historically black institution, and National Guard troops in Mississippi.

Jackson, Andrew   President of the United States (1829–1837) who founded the Democratic Party, signed the Indian Removal Act, vetoed the Second Bank, and signed the Force Bill.

Jackson, Thomas J.   A native of Virginia, he emerged as one of the Confederacy's best generals in 1861–1862.

Jamestown   Founded in 1607, Jamestown became England's first permanent settlement in North America. It served as the capital of Virginia for most of the 17th century.

Japanese internment   Removal of first- and second-generation Japanese-Americans into secured camps, a 1942 action then justified as a security measure but since deemed unjustified by evidence.

Jim Crow laws   Laws passed by southern states mandating racial segregation in public facilities of all kinds.

Johnson, Lyndon B.   President (1963–1969) who undertook an ambitious Great Society program and a major military effort in Vietnam.

joint resolution   An act passed by both houses of Congress with a simple majority rather than the two-thirds majority in the Senate.

joint-stock company   A form of business organization that resembled a modern corporation. Individuals invested in the company through the purchase of shares. One major difference between then and today was that each stockholder had one vote regardless of how many shares he owned. The first permanent English colonies in North America were established by joint-stock companies.

journeyman   Wage-earning craftsman.

judicial review   Supreme Court's power to rule on the constitutionality of congressional acts.

Kansas-Nebraska Act   Law enacted in 1854 to organize the new territories of Kansas and Nebraska that effectively repealed the provision of the 1820 Missouri Compromise by leaving the question of slavery to the territories' settlers.

Kennan, George (Mr. X)   American diplomat and historian who recommended the policy of containment toward Soviet aggression in a famous article published under the pseudonym "X."

Kennedy, John F.   President from 1961 to 1963, noted for his youthful charm and vigor and his "New Frontier" vision for America.

Kent State (incident)   Killing of four students on May 4, 1970, by the National Guard at a Kent State University protest against the U.S. incursion into neutral Cambodia.

King George's War   Popular term in North America for the third of the four Anglo-French wars before the American Revolution (1744–1748). It is sometimes also applied to the War of Jenkins's Ear between Spain and Britain (1739–1748).

King, Martin Luther, Jr.   African-American clergyman who advocated nonviolent social change and shaped the civil rights movement of the 1950s and 1960s.

Know-Nothings   Adherents of nativist organizations and of the American party who wanted to restrict the political rights of immigrants.

Korean War   Conflict lasting from 1950 to 1953 between communist North Korea, aided by China, and South Korea, aided by United Nations forces consisting primarily of U.S. troops.

Ku Klux Klan   White terrorist organization in the South originally founded as a fraternal society in 1866. Reborn in 1915, it achieved popularity in the 1920s through its calls for Anglo-Saxon purity, Protestant supremacy, and the subordination of blacks, Catholics, and Jews.

La Raza Unida   Mexican American–based movement that scored some political successes in the Southwest in the late 1960s and early 1970s.

lame-duck administration   Period of time between and incumbent party's or officeholder's loss of an election and the succession to office of the winning party or candidate.

League of Women Voters   Successor to National American Woman Suffrage Association, it promoted women's role in politics and dedicated itself to educating voters.

Lee, Robert E.   U.S. army officer until his resignation to join the Confederacy as general-in-chief.

legal tender   Any type of money that the government requires everyone to accept at face value.

Lend-Lease Act   A 1941 act by which the United States "loaned" munitions to the Allies, hoping to avoid war by becoming an "arsenal" for the Allied cause.

levee   Earthen dike or mound, usually along the banks of rivers, used to prevent flooding.

Lewis and Clark   Explorers commissioned in 1804 by President Jefferson to survey the Louisiana Purchase.

liberal Protestants   Those who believed that religion had to be adapted to science and that the Bible was to be mined for its ethical values rather than for its literal meaning.

Liberty bonds   Thirty-year government bonds with an annual interest rate of 3½ percent sold to fund the war effort.

liberty tree   A term for the gallows on which enemies of the people deserved to be hanged. The best known was in Boston.

limited liability   Liability that protected directors and stockholders of corporations from corporate debts by separating those debts from personal liabilities.

Lincoln, Abraham   Illinois Whig who became the Republican Party's first successful presidential candidate in 1860 and led the Union during the Civil War.

Lincoln-Douglas Debates   Series of seven debates between Abraham Lincoln and Stephen Douglas in their contest for election to the U.S. Senate in 1858.

Lindbergh, Charles A.   First individual to fly solo across the Atlantic (1927) and the greatest celebrity of the 1920s.

lintheads   Term used by wealthier whites to describe poor whites who labored in southern cotton mills.

living room war   Phrase suggesting that television coverage had brought the Vietnam War into the living rooms of Americans and may have led many to question the war.

lockout   Act of closing down a business by the owners during a labor dispute.

Lodge, Henry Cabot   Republican Senator from Massachusetts who led the campaign to reject the Treaty of Versailles.

logistics   Military activity relating to such things as the transporting, supplying, and quartering of troops and their equipment.

long knives   The term Indians used to describe Virginians.

Long, Huey   Democratic senator and former governor of Louisiana who used the radio to attack the New Deal as too conservative. FDR regarded him as a major rival.

longhorn   Breed of cattle introduced into the Southwest by the Spanish that became the main breed of livestock on the cattle frontier.

Lost Generation   Term used by Gertrude Stein to describe U.S. writers and artists who fled to Paris in the 1920s after becoming disillusioned with America.

Louisiana Purchase   Land purchased from France in 1803 that doubled the size of the United States.

Lowell, Francis Cabot   Wealthy Bostonian who, with the help of the Boston Associates, built and operated integrated textile mills in eastern Massachusetts.

loyalist   People in the 13 colonies who remained loyal to Britain during the Revolution.

Ludlow massacre   Murder of 66 men, women, and children in April 1914 when company police of the Colorado Fuel and Iron Company fired randomly on striking United Mine Workers.

Luftwaffe   German air force.

Lusitania   British passenger ship sunk by a German U-boat on May 7, 1915, killing more than 1,000 men, women, and children.

MacArthur, Douglas   Supreme commander of Allied forces in the southwest Pacific during the Second World War; leader of the occupation forces in the reconstruction of Japan; and head of United Nations forces during the Korean War.

magistrate   An official who enforced the law. In colonial America, this person was usually a justice of the peace or a judge in a higher court.

Mahan, Alfred Thayer   Influential imperialist who advocated construction of a large navy as crucial to the successful pursuit of world power.

Malcolm X   Charismatic African American leader who criticized integration and urged the creation of separate black economic and cultural institutions. He became a hero to members of the Black Power movement.

mandamus   A legal writ ordering a person, usually a public official, to carry out a specific act. In Massachusetts in 1774, the new royal councilors were appointed by a writ of mandamus.

manifest destiny   The belief that the United States was destined to grow from the Atlantic to the Pacific and from the Arctic to the tropics. Providence supposedly intended for Americans to have this area for a great experiment in liberty.

manumission of slaves   The act of freeing a slave, done at the will of the owner.

Marbury v. Madison   1803 case involving the disputed appointment of a federal justice of the peace in which Chief Justice John Marshall expanded the Supreme Court's authority to review legislation.

maritime   Of, or relating to, the sea.

Marshall Plan   Plan of U.S. aid to Europe that aimed to contain communism by fostering postwar economic recovery. Proposed by Secretary of State George C. Marshall in 1947, it was known formally as the European Recovery Program.

Marshall, John   Chief Justice of the United States Supreme Court from 1801 to 1835. Appointed by Federalist President John Adams, Marshall's decisions tended to favor the federal government over the states and to clear legal blocks to private business.

martial law   Government by military force rather than by citizens.

mass production   High-speed and high-volume production.

Massachusetts Bay Company   A joint-stock company chartered by Charles I in 1629. It was controlled by Non-Separatists who took the charter with them to New England and, in effect, converted it into a written constitution for the colony.

massive retaliation   Assertion by the Eisenhower administration that the threat of U.S. atomic weaponry would hold Communist powers in check.

matrilineal   A society that determines inheritance and roles in life based on the female or maternal line.

Maya   A literate, highly urbanized Mesoamerican civilization that flourished for more than a thousand years before its sudden collapse in the ninth century A.D.

McCarthyism   Public accusations of disloyalty made with little or no regard to actual evidence. Named after Senator Joseph McCarthy, these accusations and the scandal and harm they caused came to symbolize the most virulent form of anticommunism.

McClellan, George B.   One of the most promising young officers in the U.S. army, he became the principal commander of Union armies in 1861–1862.

McKinley, William   A seven-term Republican congressman from Ohio whose signature issue was the protective tariff. He was the last Civil War veteran to be elected president.

Menéndez, Francisco   An escaped South Carolina slave who fought with the Yamasee Indians against the colony, fled to Florida, was reenslaved by the Spanish, became a militia captain, was freed again, and was put in charge of the free-black town of Mose near St. Augustine in the late 1730s, the first community of its kind in what is now the United States.

merger movement   Late-19th and early 20th-century effort to integrate different enterprises into single, giant corporations able to eliminate competition, achieve economic order, and boost profits.

Mesoamerica   An area embracing Central America and southern and central Mexico.

Metacom's War (King Philip's War)   A war that devastated much of southern New England in 1675–1676. It began as a conflict between Metacom's Wampanoags and Plymouth Colony but soon engulfed all of the New England colonies and most of the region's Indian nations.

Mexican repatriation   Secretary of Labor William Doak's plan to deport illegal Mexican aliens to Mexico. By 1935, over 500,000 Mexicans had left the United States.

microchips   Technological improvement that boosted the capability and reduced the size and cost of computer hardware.

middle class   Social group that developed in the early nineteenth century comprised of urban and country merchants, master craftsmen who had turned themselves into manufacturers, and market-oriented farmers—small-scale entrepreneurs who rose within market society in the early nineteenth century.

Middle Ground   The area of French and Indian cooperation west of Niagara and south of the Great Lakes. No one exercised sovereign power over this area, but the French used Indian rituals to negotiate treaties with their Algonquian trading partners, first against the Iroquois and later against the British.

midnight judges   Federal judicial officials appointed under the Judiciary Act of 1801, in the last days of John Adams's presidency.

militia   A community's armed force, made up primarily of ordinary male citizens rather than professional soldiers.

Millennium   The period at the end of history when Christ is expected to return and rule with his saints for a thousand years.

minstrel show   Popular form of theater among working men of the northern cities in which white men in blackface portrayed African Americans in song and dance.

missions   Outposts established by the Spanish along the northern frontier to aid in Christianizing the native peoples. They also were used to exploit their labor.

Missouri Compromise   Compromise that maintained sectional balance in Congress by admitting Missouri as a slave state and Maine as a free state and by drawing a line west from the 36° 30′ parallel separating future slave and free states.

modernists   Those who believed in science rather than religion and in moving toward equality for men and women and for whites and nonwhites.

Monroe Doctrine   Foreign policy doctrine proposed by Secretary of State John Quincy Adams in 1823 that denied the right of European powers to establish new colonies in the Americas while maintaining the United States' right to annex new territory.

Montgomery bus boycott   Political protest campaign mounted in 1955 to oppose the city's policy of racial segregation on its public transit system. The Supreme Court soon declared segregation on public transit unconstitutional.

morale   The general feeling of the people toward such events as a war. Good morale greatly enhances an ability to fight or sacrifice for a cause.

Mormons   Members of the Church of Jesus Christ of Latter-Day Saints, founded by Joseph Smith in 1830; the Book of Mormon is their Bible.

Mourning War   An Indian war often initiated by a widow or bereaved relative who insisted that her male relatives provide captives to repair the loss.

muckrakers   Investigative journalists who propelled Progressivism by exposing corruption, economic monopolies, and moral decay in American society.

napalm   Incendiary and toxic chemical contained in bombs used by the United States in Vietnam.

National American Women Suffrage Association   Organization established in 1890 to promote woman suffrage; stressed that women's special virtue made them indispensable to politics.

National Association for the Advancement of Colored People (NAACP)   Organization launched in 1910 to fight racial discrimination and prejudice and to promote civil rights for blacks.

National Recovery Administration (NRA)   1933 attempt to promote economic recovery by persuading private groups of industrialists to decrease production, limit hours of work per employee, and standardize minimum wages.

National Security Act (1947)   Reorganized the U.S. military forces within a new Department of Defense, and established the National Security Council and the Central Intelligence Agency.

National War Labor Board   U.S. government agency that brought together representatives of labor, industry, and the public to resolve labor disputes.

nativism   Hostility of native-born Americans toward immigrants.

naturalization   Process by which people born in a foreign country are granted full citizenship with all of its rights.

Navajo Signal Corp   Navajo Indians who conveyed military intelligence in their native language to preserve its secrecy.

naval stores   Items such as pitch, resin, and turpentine that were used to manufacture ships. Most of them were obtained from pine trees.

neoconservatives   Group of intellectuals, many of whom had been anticommunist Democrats during the 1950s and 1960s, who came to emphasize hard-line foreign policies and conservative social stances.

neo-Federalists   Nationalist Republicans who favored many Federalist economic programs such as protective tariffs and a national bank.

Neolithic   The period known also as the late Stone Age. Agriculture developed, and stone, rather than metal, tools were used.

Neutrality Acts of 1935 and 1936   Legislation that restricted loans, trade, and travel with belligerent nations in an attempt to avoid the entanglements that had brought the United States into the First World War.

neutrality   U.S. policy toward World War I from 1914 to 1917 that called for staying out of war but maintaining normal economic relations with both sides.

New Freedom   Wilson's reform program of 1912 that called for temporarily concentrating government power so as to dismantle the trusts and return America to 19th-century conditions of competitive capitalism.

New Lights   Term used to describe prorevival Congregationalists.

New Nationalism   Roosevelt's reform program between 1910 and 1912, which called for establishing a strong federal government to regulate corporations, stabilize the economy, protect the weak, and restore social harmony.

New Sides   Term used to describe evangelical Presbyterians.

New York's 369th Regiment   Black army unit recruited in Harlem that served under French command and was decorated with the *Croix de Guerre* for its valor.

nickelodeons Converted storefronts in working-class neighborhoods that showed early short silent films usually lasting 15 minutes, requiring little comprehension of English, and costing only a nickel to view.

Nixon, Richard President of the United States (1969–1974) during the final years of the Vietnam War. He resigned the presidency when he faced impeachment for the Watergate scandals.

nonimportation agreements Agreements not to import goods from Great Britain. They were designed to put pressure on the British economy and force the repeal of unpopular parliamentary acts.

Non-Separatists English Puritans who insisted that they were faithful members of the Church of England while demanding that it purge itself of its surviving Catholic rituals and vestments.

normal schools State colleges established for the training of teachers.

North American Free Trade Agreement (NAFTA) 1994 agreement that aimed to lower or eliminate barriers restricting the trade of goods and services between the United States, Canada, and Mexico.

North Atlantic Treaty Organization (NATO) Established by treaty in 1949 to provide for the collective defense of non-communist European and North American nations against possible aggression from the Soviet Union and to encourage political, economic, and social cooperation.

Northwest Ordinance This ordinance established the Northwest Territory between the Ohio River and the Great Lakes. Adopted by the Confederation Congress in 1787, it abolished slavery in the territory and provided that it be divided into 3 to 5 states that would eventually be admitted to the Union as full equals of the original 13.

NSC-68 National Security Council Document number 68 (1950) that provided the rationale and comprehensive strategic vision for U.S. policy during the Cold War.

nullification Beginning in the late 1820s, John C. Calhoun and others argued that the Union was a voluntary compact between sovereign states, that states were the ultimate judges of the constitutionality of federal law, that states could nullify federal laws within their borders, and that they had the right to secede from the Union.

Old Lights Antirevival Congregationalists.

Old Northwest The region west of Pennsylvania, north of the Ohio River, and east of the Mississippi River.

Old Sides Antirevival Presbyterians.

oligarchy A society dominated by a few persons or families.

Olmec The oldest pre-Columbian high culture to appear in what is now Mexico.

Onontio An Algonquian word that means "great mountain" and that was used by Indians of the Middle Ground to designate the governor of New France.

Open Door notes (1899–1900) Foreign policy tactic in which the United States asked European powers to respect China's independence and to open their spheres of influence to merchants from other nations.

Open Skies Eisenhower's proposal that U.S. and Soviet disarmament be verified by reconnaissance flights over each other's territory.

open-field agriculture A medieval system of land distribution used only in the New England colonies. Farmers owned scattered strips of land within a common field, and the town as a whole decided what crops to plant.

pacifist A person opposed to war or violence. The religious group most committed to pacifism is the Quakers.

Panama Canal An engineering marvel completed in 1914 across the new Central American nation of Panama. Connecting the Atlantic and Pacific Oceans, it shortened ship travel between New York and San Francisco by 8,000 miles.

parish A term used to describe an area served by one tax-supported church. The term was used primarily in regions settled by members of the Church of England.

Parks, Rosa African American seamstress in Montgomery, Alabama, who, after refusing to give up her bus seat to a white man, was arrested and fined. Her protest sparked a subsequent bus boycott that attracted national sympathy for the civil rights cause and put Martin Luther King, Jr., in the national spotlight.

parochial schools Schools associated with a church, usually Roman Catholic. The funding of these schools became a major political issue in the 1850s.

passive civil disobedience Nonviolent refusal to obey a law in an attempt to call attention to government policies considered unfair.

patronage The act of appointing people to government jobs or awarding them government contracts, often based on political favoritism rather than on abilities.

patronships Vast estates along the Hudson River that were established by the Dutch. They had difficulty attracting peasant labor, and most were not successful.

Peace of Paris The 1763 treaty that ended the war between Britain on the one side, and France and Spain on the other side. France surrendered New France to Britain. Spain ceded Florida to Britain, and France compensated its ally by ceding all of Louisiana to Spain.

peace without victory Woodrow Wilson's 1917 pledge to work for a peace settlement that did not favor one side over the other but ensured an equality among combatants.

Pearl Harbor Japan's December 7, 1941 attack on a U.S. base in Hawaii that brought the United States into the Second World War.

Penn, William A convert to the Society of Friends in the 1660s, Penn used his friendship with Charles II and James, Duke of York, to acquire a charter for Pennsylvania in 1681, and he then launched a major migration of Friends to the Delaware Valley.

people's capitalism An egalitarian capitalism in which all Americans could participate and enjoy the consumer goods that U.S. industry had made available.

per capita Term used to measure the wealth of a nation by dividing total income by population.

perestroika Russian term describing the economic liberalization that began in the late 1980s.

Perkins, Frances Secretary of Labor under Roosevelt and the first female Cabinet member.

Pershing, John J. Commander of the American Expeditionary Force that began landing in Europe in 1917 and that entered battle in the spring and summer of 1918.

personal liberty laws Laws enacted by nine northern states to prohibit the use of state law facilities such as jails or law officers in the recapture of fugitive slaves.

piedmont A term referring to the land above the fall line but below the Appalachian Mountains.

Pilgrims A pious, sentimental term used by later generations to describe the settlers who sailed on the Mayflower in 1620 and founded Plymouth Colony.

Pitt, William One of the most popular public officials in 18th-century Britain, he was best known as the minister who organized Britain's successful war effort against France in the French and Indian War.

placer mining Mining where minerals, especially gold, were found in glacial or alluvial deposits.

Platt Amendment Clause that the U.S. forced Cuba to insert into its constitution giving the U.S. broad control over Cuba's foreign and domestic policies.

plumbers Nixon's secret intelligence unit designed to stop information leaks to the media.

Plymouth Founded by Separatists in 1620, Plymouth was England's first permanent colony in New England.

political machines Organizations that controlled local political parties and municipal governments through bribery, election fraud, and support of urban vice while providing some municipal services to the urban poor.

politics of harmony A system in which the governor and the colonial assembly worked together through persuasion rather than through patronage or bullying.

politique A man who believed that the survival of the state took precedence over religious differences.

poll tax A tax based on people or population rather than property. It was usually a fixed amount per adult.

polygamy The act of having more than one wife.

Pontiac An Ottawa chief whose name has been attached to the great Indian uprising against the British in 1763–1764.

pools Technique used by railroads to divide up traffic and fix rates, thereby avoiding ruinous competition.

popular sovereignty The concept that settlers of each territory would decide for themselves whether to allow slavery.

postal campaign Abolitionist tactic to force the nation to confront the slavery question by flooding the mails, both North and South, with antislavery literature. Their hope was to raise controversy within an area that was the province of the federal government.

postmillennialism Belief (held mostly by middle-class evangelists) that Christ's Second Coming would occur when missionary conversion of the world brought about a thousand years of social perfection.

powwow Originally, a word used to identify tribal prophets or medicine men. Later it was used also to describe the ceremonies held by them.

praying Indians The Christian Indians of New England.

predestination A theory that states that God has decreed, even before he created the world, who will be saved and who will be damned.

Presbytery An intermediate level of organization in the Presbyterian church, above individual congregations but below the synod. One of its primary responsibilities was the ordination and placement of ministers.

presidios Military posts constructed by the Spanish to protect the settlers from hostile Indians. They also were used to keep non-Spanish settlers from the area.

Presley, Elvis Known as "the King" of Rock and Roll, he was the biggest pop star of the 1950s.

private fields Farms of up to five acres on which slaves working under the task system were permitted to produce items for their own use and sale in a nearby market.

privateers A privately owned ship that was authorized by a government to attack enemy ships during times of war. The owner of the ship got to claim a portion of whatever was captured. This practice damaged any enemy country that could not dramatically increase naval protection for its merchant ships.

Proclamation of 1763 It was issued by the Privy Council. Among other things, it tried to prevent the colonists from encroaching upon Indian lands by prohibiting settlement west of the Appalachian watershed unless the government first purchased those lands by treaty.

Progressive Party Political party formed by Theodore Roosevelt in 1912 when the Republicans refused to nominate him for president. The party adopted a sweeping reform program.

Prohibition Constitutional ban on the manufacture and sale of alcohol in the United States (1920–1933).

proprietary colony A colony owned by an individual(s) who had vast discretionary powers over the colony. Maryland was the first proprietary colony, but others were founded later.

protective tariff Tariff that increases the price of imported goods that compete with American products and thus protects American manufacturers from foreign competition.

Protestant Reformation A religious movement begun by Martin Luther in 1517 that led to the repudiation of the Roman Catholic Church in large parts of northern and central Europe.

provincial congress A type of convention elected by the colonists to organize resistance. They tended to be larger than the legal assemblies they displaced, and they played a major role in politicizing the countryside.

public Friends The men and women who spoke most frequently and effectively for the Society of Friends. They were as close as the Quakers came to having a clergy. They occupied special elevated seats in some meeting houses.

public virtue Meant, to the revolutionary generation, patriotism and the willingness of a free and independent people to subordinate their interests to the common good and even to die for their country.

Pueblo Revolt In the most successful Indian uprising in American history, the Pueblo people rose against the Spanish in 1680, killed most Spanish missionaries, devastated Spanish buildings, and forced the surviving Spaniards to retreat down the Rio Grande. The Pueblos maintained their autonomy for about a decade, but Spain reasserted control in the early 1690s.

Puritans An English religious group that followed the teachings of John Calvin. They wanted a fuller reformation of the Church of England and hoped to replace The Book of Common Prayer with sermons. They wanted to purify the Church of England of its surviving Catholic ceremonies and vestments.

Quakers A term of abuse used by opponents to describe members of the Society of Friends, who believed that God, in the form of the Inner Light, was present in all humans. Friends were pacifists who rejected oaths, sacraments, and all set forms of religious worship.

quasi-slavery Position that resembled slavery, such as that created by the Black Codes.

quitrent A relic of feudalism, a quitrent was a small required annual fee attached to a piece of land. It differed from other rents in that nonpayment did not lead to ejection from the land but to a suit for debt.

R&D Research and development.

racial profiling Law enforcement practice of using racial appearance to screen for potential wrongdoing.

railhead End of a railroad line, or the farthest point on the track.

railroad gauge Distance between the rails on which wheels of railroad cars fit.

"rainfall follows the plow" Erroneous belief that settlement and cultivation somehow changed the weather. It evolved due to heavier-than-normal precipitation during the 1870s and 1880s.

RAND Think tank developed by the U.S. military to conduct scientific research and development.

Reagan, Ronald Republican president (1981–1989) who steered domestic politics in a conservative direction and sponsored a huge military buildup.

real wages Relationship between wages and the consumer price index.

realism Form of thinking, writing, and art that prized detachment, objectivity, and skepticism.
rebates Practice by the railroads of giving certain big businesses reductions in freight rates or refunds.
recall Reform that gave voters the right to remove from office a public servant who had betrayed their trust.
Red Scare Widespread fear in 1919–1920 that radicals had coalesced to establish a communist government on American soil. In response, U.S. government and private citizens undertook a campaign to identify, silence, and, in some cases, imprison radicals.
redemptioners Servants with an indentured contract that allowed them to find masters after they arrived in the colonies. Many German immigrant families were redemptioners and thus were able to stay together while they served their terms.
redlining Refusal by banks and loan associations to grant loans for home buying and business expansion in neighborhoods that contained aging buildings, dense populations, and growing numbers of nonwhites.
referendum Procedure that allows the electorate to decide an issue through a direct vote.
Refugee Act of 1980 Law allowing refugees fleeing political persecution entry into United States.
religious bigotry Intolerance based on religious beliefs or practices.
religious right Christians who wedded their religious beliefs to a conservative political agenda and gained growing influence in Republican party politics after the late 1960s.
Republic of Texas Independent nation founded in 1836 when a revolution by residents in the Mexican province of Texas won their independence.
republics Independent Indian villages that were willing to trade with the British and remained outside the French system of Indian alliances.
Restoration era The period that began in 1660 when the Stuart dynasty under Charles II was restored to the throne of England. It ended with the overthrow of James II in 1688–1689.
restorationism Belief that all theological and institutional changes since the end of biblical times were man-made mistakes and that religious organizations must restore themselves to the purity and simplicity of the apostolic church.
restraint of trade Activity that prevented competition in the marketplace or free trade.
revival A series of emotional religious meetings that led to numerous public conversions.
revolving gun turret A low structure, often round, on a ship that moved horizontally and contained mounted guns.
rifling Process of cutting spiral grooves in a gun's barrel to impart a spin to the bullet. Perfected in the 1850s, it produced greater accuracy and longer range.
Robinson, Jackie African American whose addition to the Brooklyn Dodgers in 1947 began the lengthy process of integrating major league baseball.
rock 'n' roll Form of popular music that arose in the 1950s from a variety of musical styles, including rhythm and blues, country, and gospel. Its heavily accented beat attracted a large following among devotees of the emerging youth culture.
Rockefeller, John D. Founder of the Standard Oil Company whose aggressive practices drove many competitors out of business and made him one of the richest men in America.
Roe* v. *Wade Supreme Court decision in 1973 that ruled that a blanket prohibition against abortion violated a woman's right to privacy and prompted decades of political controversy.
rolling stock Locomotives, freight cars, and other types of wheeled equipment owned by railroads.
Roosevelt corollary 1904 corollary to the Monroe Doctrine, stating that the United States had the right to intervene in domestic affairs of hemispheric nations to quell disorder and forestall European intervention.
Roosevelt liberalism New reform movement that sought to regulate capitalism but not the morals or behavior of private citizens. This reform liberalism overcame divisions between southern agrarians and northeastern ethnics.
Roosevelt, Eleanor A politically engaged and effective First Lady, and an architect of American liberalism.
Roosevelt, Franklin D. President from 1933 to 1945 and the creator of the New Deal.
Rough Riders Much decorated volunteer cavalry unit organized by Theodore Roosevelt and Leonard Wood to fight in Cuba in 1898.
royal colony A colony controlled directly by the English monarch. The governor and council were appointed by the Crown.
Russo-Japanese War Territorial conflict between imperial Japan and Russia mediated by Theodore Roosevelt at Portsmouth, New Hampshire. The peace agreement gave Korea and other territories to Japan, ensured Russia's continuing control over Siberia, and protected China's territorial integrity.
Sacco and Vanzetti Case (1920) Controversial conviction of two Italian-born anarchists accused of armed robbery and murder.
sachem An Algonquian word that means "chief."
Safety-Fund Law New York state law that required banks to pool a fraction of their resources to protect both bankers and small stockholders in case of bank failures.
Salem witch trials About 150 people were accused of witchcraft in Massachusetts between March and September 1692. During the summer trials, 19 people were hanged and one was pressed to death after he refused to stand trial. All of those executed insisted they were innocent. Of the 50 who confessed, none was executed.
Saratoga A major turning point in the Revolutionary War. American forces prevented John Burgoyne's army from reaching Albany, cut off its retreat, and forced it to surrender in October 1777. This victory helped bring France into the war.
saturation bombing Intensive bombing designed to destroy everything in a target area.
scabs Strikebreakers who were willing to act as replacements for striking workers, thus undermining the effect of strikes as leverage against company owners.
scalawags Term used by southern Democrats to describe southern whites who worked with the Republicans.
scientific management Attempt to break down each factory job into its smallest components to increase efficiency, eliminate waste, and promote worker satisfaction.
secession The act of a state withdrawing from the Union. South Carolina was the first state to attempt to do this in 1860.
Second Continental Congress The intercolonial body that met in Philadelphia in May 1775 a few weeks after the Battles of Lexington and Concord. It organized the Continental Army, appointed George Washington commander-in-chief, and simultaneously pursued policies of military resistance and conciliation. When conciliation failed, it chose independence in July 1776 and in 1777 drafted the Articles of Confederation, which finally went into force in March 1781.
sedentary Societies that are rooted locally or are nonmigratory. Semisedentary societies are migratory for part of the year.
Seditious libel The common-law crime of openly criticizing a public official.
seigneurs The landed gentry who claimed most of the land between Quebec and Montreal. They were never as powerful as aristocrats in France.
Seneca Falls Convention (1848) First national convention of women's rights activists.
separation of powers The theory that a free government, especially in a republic, should have three independent branches capable of checking or balancing one another: the executive, the legislative (usually bicameral), and the judicial.
Separatists One of the most extreme English Protestant groups that were followers of John Calvin. They began to separate from the Church of England and form their own congregations.
September 11, 2001 Day on which U.S. airliners, hijacked by Al Qaeda operatives, were crashed into the World Trade Center and the Pentagon, killing around 3,000 people.
serfdom Early medieval Europe's predominant labor system, which tied peasants to their lords and the land. They were not slaves because they could not be sold from the land.
Seward, William H. Secretary of State under Abraham Lincoln and Andrew Jackson. He was best known for his purchase of Alaska from Russia.
share wages Payment of workers' wages with a share of the crop rather than with cash.
sharecropping Working land in return for a share of the crops produced instead of paying cash rent.
Shays's Rebellion An uprising of farmers in western Massachusetts in the winter of 1786–1787. They objected to high taxes and foreclosures for unpaid debts. Militia from eastern Massachusetts suppressed the rebels.
Sheppard-Towner Act Major social welfare program providing federal funds for prenatal and child health care, 1921–1929.
sickle cell A crescent- or sickle-shaped red blood cell sometimes found in African Americans. It helped protect them from malaria but exposed some children to the dangerous and painful condition of sickle cell anemia.
Sir Walter Raleigh An Elizabethan courtier who, in the 1580s, tried but failed to establish an English colony on Roanoke Island in what is now North Carolina.
sit-down strike Labor strike strategy in which workers occupied their factory but refused to do any work until the employer agreed to recognize the workers' union. This strategy succeeded against General Motors in 1937.
sit-in movement Activity that challenged legal segregation by demanding that blacks have the same access to public facilities as whites. These nonviolent demonstrations were staged at restaurants, bus and train stations, and other public places.
Sitting Bull Hunkapapa Lakota (Sioux) chief and holy man who led warriors against the U.S. Army in Montana Territory in 1876, culminating in battle of Little Big Horn.
slash and burn A system of agriculture in which trees were cut down, girdled, or in some way destroyed. The underbrush then was burned, and a crop was planted. Men created the farms, and women did the farming. The system eventually depleted the fertility of the soil, and the entire tribe would move to a new area after 10 or 20 years.
Smith, Alfred E. Irish American, Democratic governor of New York who became in 1928 the first Catholic ever nominated for the presidency by a major party.
Smith, John (Captain) A member of the Virginia Council; his strong leadership from 1607 to 1609 probably saved the colony from collapse.
Smith, Joseph Poor New York farm boy whose visions led him to translate the *Book of Mormon* in late 1820s. He became the founder and the prophet of the Church of Jesus Christ of Latter-day Saints (Mormons).
Social Darwinism Set of beliefs explaining human history as an ongoing evolutionary struggle between different groups of people for survival and supremacy that was used to justify inequalities between races, classes, and nations.
Social Security Act Centerpiece of the welfare state (1935) that instituted the first federal pension system and set up funds to take care of groups (such as the disabled and unmarried mothers with children) unable to support themselves.
socialism Political movement that called for the transfer of industry from private to public control, and the transfer of political power from elites to the laboring masses.
sodbuster Small farmer in parts of the West who adapted to the treeless plains and prairies, such as the construction of homes out of sod.
southern yeoman Farmer who owned relatively little land and few or no slaves.
sovereign power A term used to describe supreme or final power.
space shuttle Manned rocket that served as a space laboratory and could be flown back to the earth for reuse.
specie Also called "hard money" as against paper money. In colonial times, it usually meant silver, but it could also include gold coins.
spirituals Term later devised to describe the religious songs of slaves.
Spock, Dr. Benjamin Pediatrician who wrote *Baby and Child Care* (1946), the most widely used child-rearing book during the baby-boom generation.
spoils system System by which the victorious political party rewarded its supporters with government jobs.
Sputnik First Soviet satellite sent into orbit around the earth in 1957.
stagflation Condition of simultaneous economic stagnation and price inflation.
Stalin, Joseph Soviet communist dictator who worked with Allied leaders during Second World War.
Stamp Act Passed by the administration of George Grenville in 1765, the Stamp Act imposed duties on most legal documents in the colonies and on newspapers and other publications. Massive colonial resistance to the act created a major imperial crisis.
staple crop A crop grown for commercial sale. It usually was produced in a colonial area and was sold in Europe. The first staple crops were sugar and tobacco.
Starr, Kenneth Republican lawyer appointed as independent counsel to investigate possible wrongdoing by President Clinton.
States General The legislative assembly of the Netherlands.
stay laws A law that delays or postpones something. During the 1780s many states passed stay laws to delay the due date on debts because of the serious economic problems of the times.
Strategic Defense Initiative (SDI) Popularly termed "Star Wars," a proposal to develop technology for creation of a space-based defensive missile shield around the United States.
Student Nonviolent Coordinating Committee (SNCC) Interracial civil rights organization formed by young people involved in the sit-in movement that later adopted a direct-action approach to fighting segregation.
subtreasuries Plan to help farmers escape the ruinous interest rates of the crop lien system by storing their crops in federal warehouses until market prices were more favorable. Farmers could draw low-interest loans against the value of these crops.
subversive Systematic, deliberate attempt to overthrow or undermine a government or society by people working secretly within the country.
Sun Belt Southern rim of the United States running from Florida to California.
Sunday schools Schools that first appeared in the 1790s to teach working-class children to read and write but that by the 1820s and 1830s were becoming moral training grounds.

supply-side economics Economic theory that tax reductions targeted toward investors and businesses would stimulate production and eventually create jobs.
sweated Describes a type of worker, mostly women, who worked in her home producing items for subcontractors, usually in the clothing industry.
synod The governing body of the Presbyterian church. A synod was a meeting of Presbyterian ministers and prominent laymen to set policies for the whole church.
table a petition or bill Act of removing a petition or bill from consideration without debate by placing it at the end of the legislative agenda.
Taft, William Howard Roosevelt's successor as president (1909–1913) who tried but failed to mediate between reformers and conservatives in the Republican Party.
tariff A tax on imports.
task system A system of slave labor under which slaves had to complete specific assignments each day. After these assignments were finished, their time was their own. It was used primarily on rice plantations. Slaves often preferred this system over gang labor because it gave them more autonomy and free time.
Teapot Dome scandal Political scandal by which Secretary of Interior Albert Fall allowed oil tycoons access to government oil reserves in exchange for $400,000 in bribes.
Tecumseh Shawnee leader who assumed political and military leadership of the pan-Indian religious movement began by his brother Tenskwatawa.
tejanos Spanish-speaking settlers of Texas. The term comes from the Spanish word *Tejas* for Texas.
temperance Movement that supported abstaining from alcoholic beverages.
tenancy System under which farmers worked land that they did not own.
Tennessee Valley Authority (TVA) Ambitious and successful use of government resources and power to promote economic development throughout the Tennessee Valley.
Tenochtitlán The huge Aztec capital city destroyed by Cortés.
Tenskwatawa Brother of Tecumseh, whose religious vision of 1805 called for the unification of Indians west of the Appalachians and foretold the defeat and disappearance of the whites.
termination and relocation Policies designed to assimilate American Indians by terminating tribal status and relocating individuals off reservations.
Tet offensive Surprise National Liberation Front (NLF) attack during the lunar new year holiday in early 1968 that brought high casualties to the NLF but fuelled pessimism about the war's outcome in the United States.
The Man That Nobody Knows Bruce Barton's best-selling 1925 book depicting Jesus as a business executive.
think tank Group or agency organized to conduct intensive research or engage in problem solving, especially in developing new technology, military strategy, or social planning.
Third Reich New empire that Adolph Hitler promised the German people would bring glory and unity to the nation.
Third World Less economically developed areas of the world, primarily the Middle East, Asia, Latin America, and Africa.
Tierra del Fuego The region at the southern tip of South America.
tithe A portion of one's income that is owed to the church. In most places, it was one tenth.
toll roads Roads for which travelers were charged a fee for each use.
tories A term for Irish Catholic peasants who murdered Protestant landlords. It was used to describe the followers of Charles II and became one of the names of the two major political parties in England.
total war New kind of war requiring every combatant to devote virtually all his or her economic and political resources to the fight.
totalitarian movement Movement in which the individual is subordinated to the state and all areas of life are subjected to centralized, total control—usually by force.
Townshend Revenue Act Passed by Parliament in 1767, this act imposed import duties on tea, paper, glass, red and white lead, and painter's colors. It provoked the imperial crisis of 1767–1770. In 1770 Parliament repealed all of the duties except the one on tea.
traditionalists Those who believed that God's word transcended science and that America should continue to be guided by older hierarchies (men over women, whites over nonwhites, native-born over immigrants).
transcontinental railroad Railroad line that connected with other lines to provide continuous rail transportation from coast to coast.
treasury notes Paper money used by the Union to help finance the Civil War. One type of treasury note was known as a greenback because of its color.
Triangle Shirtwaist Company New York City site of a tragic 1911 industrial fire that killed 146 workers unable to find their way to safety.
Triple Alliance One set of combatants in World War I, consisting of Germany, Austria-Hungary, and Italy. When Italy left the alliance, this side became known as the Central Powers.
Triple Entente One set of combatants in World War I, consisting of Britain, France, and Russia. As the war went on, this side came to be known as the Allies or Allied Powers.
Truman, Harry S. Franklin Roosevelt's Vice President who became president when Roosevelt died on April 13, 1945.
trust Large corporations that controlled a substantial share of any given market.
Turner, Nat Baptist lay preacher whose religious visions encouraged him to lead a slave revolt in southern Virginia in 1831 in which 55 whites were killed—more than any other American slave revolt.
Turner's frontier thesis Theory developed by historian Frederick Jackson Turner, who argued that the frontier had been central to the shaping of American character and the success of the U.S. economy and democracy.
Twenty Negro Law Confederate conscription law that exempted from the draft one white man on every plantation owning 20 or more slaves. The law's purpose was to exempt overseers or owners who would ensure discipline over the slaves and keep up production but was regarded as discrimination by non-slaveholding families.
U-2 spy plane Aircraft specializing in high-altitude reconnaissance.
Ulster The northern province of Ireland that provided 70 percent of the Irish immigrants in the colonial period. Nearly all of them were Presbyterians whose fore-bears had moved to Ireland from Scotland in the previous century. They sometimes are called Scots-Irish today.
Uncle Tom's Cabin Published by Harriet Beecher Stowe in 1852, this sentimental novel told the story of the Christian slave Uncle Tom and became a best seller and the most powerful antislavery tract of the antebellum years.
underconsumptionism Theory that underconsumption, or a chronic weakness in consumer demand, had caused the depression. This theory guided the Second New Deal, leading to the passage of laws designed to stimulate consumer demand.
underground railroad A small group who helped slaves escape bondage in the South. It took on legendary status, and its role was much exaggerated.
UNESCO (United Nations Educational, Scientific, and Cultural Organization) UN organization intended to create peace and security through collaboration among member nations.
unicameral legislature A legislature with only one chamber or house.
Union Leagues Organizations that informed African-American voters of, and mobilized them to, support the Republican Party.
Unionists Southerners who remained loyal to the Union during the Civil War.
universal male suffrage System that allowed all adult males to vote without regard to property, religious, or race qualifications or limitations.
urban corridors Metropolitan strips of population running between older cities.
vestry A group of prominent men who managed the lay affairs of the local Anglican church, often including the choice of the minister, especially in Virginia.
vice-admiralty courts These royal courts handled the disposition of enemy ships captured in time of war, adjudicated routine maritime disputes between, for example, a ship's crew and its owner, and from time to time tried to decide cases involving parliamentary regulation of colonial commerce. This last category was the most controversial. These courts did not use juries.
Victorianism Moral code of conduct that advocated modesty, sexual restraint, and separate spheres of activity and influence for men and women.
Vietnam War Conflict lasting from 1946 to 1975, with direct U.S. military involvement from 1964 to 1973. Highly controversial, the war devastated the Vietnam countryside, spilled into all of Indochina, and ended in a victory for communist North Vietnam, which then united the country under its rule.
Vietnamization Policy whereby the South Vietnamese were to assume more of the military burdens of the war and allow the United States to withdraw combat troops.
virtual representation The English concept that Members of Parliament represented the entire empire, not just a local constituency and its voters. According to this theory, settlers were represented in Parliament in the same way that nonvoting subjects in Britain were represented. The colonists accepted virtual representation for nonvoting settlers within their colonies but denied that the term could describe their relationship with Parliament.
VJ Day August 15, 1945, day on which the war in the Pacific was won by the Allies.
Voting Rights Act of 1965 Law that provided new federal mechanisms to help guarantee African Americans the right to vote.
Wagner Act (NLRA) Named after its sponsor Senator Robert Wagner (D-NY), this 1935 act gave every worker the right to join a union and compelled employers to bargain with unions in good faith.
Walker, Madame C. J. Black entrepreneur who built a lucrative business from the hair and skin lotions she devised and sold to black customers throughout the country.
War Hawks Members of the Twelfth Congress, most of them young nationalists from southern and western areas, who promoted war with Britain.
War Industries Board U.S. government agency responsible for mobilizing American industry for war production.
war on terrorism Global effort, adopted after the attacks of September 11, 2001, by the United States and its allies to neutralize international groups deemed "terrorists," primarily radical Islamic groups such as Al Qaeda.
Washington, George A veteran of the French and Indian War, Washington was named commander in chief of the Continental Army by the Second Continental Congress in 1775 and won notable victories at Boston, Trenton, Princeton, and Yorktown, where Lord Cornwallis's army surrendered to him in 1781. His fellow delegates chose him to preside over the deliberations of the Philadelphia Convention in 1787, and after the federal Constitution was ratified, he was unanimously chosen the first president of the United States for two terms.
Watergate Business and residential complex in Washington, D.C., that came to stand for the political espionage and cover-ups directed by the Nixon administration. The complicated web of Watergate scandals brought about Nixon's resignation in 1974.
Western development Disproportionate amount of New Deal funds sent to Rocky Mountain and Pacific Coast areas to provide water and electricity for urban and agricultural development.
wheat blast A plant disease that affected wheat and first appeared in New England in the 1660s. There were no known remedies for the disease, and it gradually spread until wheat production in New England nearly ceased.
Wheatley, Phillis Eight-year-old Phillis Wheatley arrived in Boston from Africa in 1761 and was sold as a slave to wealthy John and Susannah Wheatley. Susannah taught her to read and write, and in 1767 she published her first poem in Boston. In 1773 she visited London to celebrate the publication there of a volume of her poetry, an event that made her a transatlantic sensation. On her return to Boston, the Wheatleys emancipated her.
Whigs The name of an obscure sect of Scottish religious extremists who favored the assassination of Charles and James of England. The term was used to denote one of the two leading political parties of late seventeenth-century England.
Whiskey Rebellion Revolt in Western Pennsylvania against the federal excise tax on whiskey.
whiskey ring Network of distillers and revenue agents that cheated the government out of millions of tax dollars.
Whitney, Eli The Connecticut-born tutor who invented the cotton gin.
wolfpacks German submarine groups that attacked enemy merchant ships or convoys.
Works Progress Administration Federal relief agency established in 1935 that disbursed billions to pay for infrastructural improvements and funded a vast program of public art.
Wounded Knee Site of a shootout between Indians and Army troops at the Pine Ridge Indian reservation in southwestern South Dakota.
XYZ Affair Incident that precipitated an undeclared war with France when three French officials (identified as X, Y, and Z) demanded that American emissaries pay a bribe before negotiating disputes between the two countries.
Yankee A Dutch word for New Englanders that originally meant something like "land pirate."
yankeephobia Popular term describing strong dislike of the United States, whose citizens were referred to as "yankees," in Latin America.
yellow dog contracts Written pledges by employees promising not to join a union while they were employed.
yellow journalism Newspaper stories embellished with sensational or titillating details when the true reports did not seem dramatic enough.
yeoman A farmer who owned his own farm.
"Young America" movement A group of young members of the Democratic Party who were interested in territorial expansion in the 1840s.
Yorktown The last major engagement of the Revolutionary War. Washington's army, two French armies, and a French fleet trapped Lord Cornwallis at Yorktown and forced his army to surrender in October 1781.
Zenger, John Peter Printer of the *New York Weekly Journal* who was acquitted in 1735 by a jury of the crime of seditious libel after his paper sharply criticized Governor William Cosby.
Zimmerman telegram Telegram from Germany's foreign secretary instructing the German minister in Mexico to ask that country's government to attack the United States in return for German assistance in regaining Mexico's "lost provinces" (Texas, New Mexico, and Arizona).
Zion A term used by the Mormons to describe their "promised land" where they could prosper and live without persecution.
Zionism Movement to establish a Jewish state in Palestine.
zoot suits Flamboyant outfits that featured oversized trousers; commonly worn by young Mexican-American men as a symbol of ethnic and cultural rebellion.

CREDITS